CONTACT WITH DRAMA

CONTACT
WITH DRAMA

David L. Hay

James F. Howell

CENTRAL MICHIGAN UNIVERSITY

SCIENCE RESEARCH ASSOCIATES, INC.
Chicago, Palo Alto, Toronto
Henley-on-Thames, Sydney, Paris

A Subsidiary of IBM

ISBN: 0-574-19020-1

"Relevance is the connection between knowledge and self."

—J. ROBERT BASHORE

CONTENTS

CHRONOLOGICAL
TABLE OF CONTENTS

ACKNOWLEDGMENTS

PHOTOGRAPHS

p. 67   HEDDA GABLER **(Hedda and Tesman)**
Courtesy of Bowling Green State University, Bowling Green, Ohio

p. 164   THE EFFECT OF GAMMA RAYS ON MAN-IN-THE-MOON MARI-GOLDS **(Tillie, Beatrice and Ruth)**
Courtesy of Alley Theatre, Houston, Texas, and actresses Varney Knapp, Chris Wilson, and Lynn Kevin. Photography by Marc St. Gil, Black Star

p. 199   ANTIGONE **(Creon and Antigone)**
Courtesy of the Asolo State Theater, Sarasota, Florida

p. 212   ANTIGONE **(Choragos and Creon)**
Courtesy of the Drama Production Office, University of California at Santa Barbara

p. 288   THE COUNTRY WIFE
Courtesy of Hilberry Theatre, Wayne State University, Detroit, Michigan

p. 301 and 258   THE COUNTRY WIFE **(Horner and Fidget; Pinchwife, Harcourt, and Dorilant)**
By permission of photographer Ken Howard, the Marin Shakespeare Festival, and actors Ron Mangravite', Warner Shook, Larry Hecht, Daniel Kern, and Tim Carryer. *The Country Wife* is one of four productions presented by the Marin Shakespeare Festival during its 1973 season at the Palace of Fine Arts in San Francisco.

p. 407   OTHELLO **(Iago and Othello)**
Courtesy of the Stratford Festival, Stratford, Ontario, Canada, and actors Douglas Rain and Nachum Buchman. Photography by Robert C. Ragsdale, Limited.

p. 493   SIX CHARACTERS IN SEARCH OF AN AUTHOR **(The Mother and The Father)**
Courtesy of Bowling Green State University, Bowling Green, Ohio

p. 511   SIX CHARACTERS IN SEARCH OF AN AUTHOR
Courtesy of the Educational Theatre Program of the New York University School of Education

pp. 535, 538, 544, and 549   AN OCCURRENCE AT OWL CREEK BRIDGE
From the film "An Occurrence at Owl Creek Bridge," courtesy of Contemporary
Films/McGraw-Hill Book Company. This film is available for inexpensive rental
or sale from Contemporary Films/McGraw-Hill, Princeton Rd., Hightstown,
N.J. 08520; 828 Custer Ave., Evanston, Ill. 60202; and 1714 Stockton St., San
Francisco, Ca. 94133.

TO THE STUDENT

The introductory comments throughout this text
are written to you,
not to our colleagues, your teacher, or the scholarly world.
They are intended to help you read, understand,
and above all enjoy, the plays that follow.
These comments are meant to be merely introductions,
not exhaustive statements.
This text will not teach you
everything you need to know about drama.
It will not give you the answers.
We have found that students' responses to plays
are frequently more exciting, more creative,
and certainly more honest and genuine
than answers or conclusions we might try to impose.
We feel that the value
of an introductory course in literature
lies in the process of arriving at your own interpretations
with the help of other students and your teacher.
We do not suggest that everyone should have
the same interpretation of a given work;
we hope they do not.
We do hope the introductions,
marginal comments, and questions
will suggest how you might go about
reading plays
and how you can evaluate
the validity and value of what you find.
The enjoyment is in the process.
We hope you will discover
the pleasure of experiencing drama.

PART ONE
INTRODUCTION

We believe that understanding literature is a way of understanding yourself. Drama, like all literature, can be experienced directly by you the reader or viewer. When you read or see a play, you become acquainted with the characters on the stage; you can identify with some of them and share their emotions, become involved in their actions and struggles, and ultimately learn about yourself through observing what happens to them and recognizing the human desires, problems, successes, and frustrations we all share. But accomplishing these things requires an understanding of the work. The greater our understanding, the more we can enjoy and respond to the play and come to understand ourselves.

The key to understanding and enjoying drama is paying attention to detail. Saying that someone knows more than most people about a particular subject usually means that he or she pays more attention to detail, to the subtle aspects of the subject. Enjoyment increases as we become more and more skilled at noticing and interpreting the details. Some people listen to music and hear only the melody; some hear melody and lyrics; some hear melody, lyrics, chord structure, and technique. In addition, some people even know the names and backgrounds of the musicians, have seen them in concert, and have followed their professional development. All these people derive pleasure from the music, but those who listen more carefully and hear the most details probably derive the greatest satisfaction from the work. The same is true of persons who have a special interest in football, art, nature, automobiles, or other people. The more details they perceive, the more rewarding their experience.

This principle holds true for drama. You may read a play and simply understand the plot, or you may understand the plot and feel sympathy for the main character. You derive some pleasure from this, but it is possible to gain even more. This book is intended to help you increase your enjoyment and pleasure in experiencing drama.

The approach used in this text is based on two assumptions: first, a good playwright has a reason for selecting each element he puts into his play, but he does not try to include every detail about a character or action or confrontation. Rather, he selects details that will help him achieve his purpose. In a good play nothing is accidental; therefore, we have the right to ask why each detail is included.

The second assumption is that the more skill you develop in noticing details and perceiving patterns or structures in those details, the better you will understand drama, and the more you will enjoy reading and seeing plays. This text does not attempt to teach you all there is to know about drama or make you a sophisticated literary critic. It does not provide the right answers or the correct interpretations of characters or scenes because there are no "right" answers. There are only different interpretations, and your interpretation of the play may be as valid as anyone else's. The purpose of this book is to help you read the plays independently, formulate opinions or conclusions about them based on your reading, and then determine the validity of your conclusions according to the details the playwright has given you. Ultimately, we hope you will come to enjoy plays and, from reading them, learn about yourself and your own life.

Drama is the playwright's medium for communicating his view of some aspect of the world. He does this artistically, including only what will help him convey his perceptions. His meaning is the view that he conveys, and we judge his work on the basis of how skillfully and truthfully he presents that view. His vision is his own, and he may perceive the world differently from other people. But the value of the art is in our ability to learn from, and thus enjoy, the experience.

Drama may vary in form and length. Not all plays are long; many brief plays contain all the elements needed to produce a single dramatic effect. The following play by John Millington Synge, an Irishman who wrote during the early 1900s, takes no more than half an hour to read, but it is rich in all the elements that comprise good drama. As you read the play, remember that reading drama requires more effort than viewing it. We must be alert to what the author tells us, both in stage directions and dialogue, in order to imagine how the action would appear on stage. When we see a play in production, we can respond immediately to what we see. But in reading a play we function, in a sense, as our own directors: we must interpret ambiguous words, create tone of voice, determine emphasis, and visualize the setting and the actors' movements within it. The author provides the basic elements needed to initiate this process, but we must contribute the refinements and subtleties.

Synge's play is presented in its entirety, uninterrupted by comments. Succeeding sections of the text will begin by examining a particular element and then will present an entire play in which this element is examined in context through brief marginal comments. We feel that what counts is the whole play and its achieved effect. Isolating particular elements serves only to increase our awareness of them, thus enabling us to appreciate the complete play more fully. After you have read *Riders to the Sea*, look over the comments that follow it.

RIDERS TO THE SEA

John Millington Synge

CHARACTERS

Maurya, an old woman
Bartley, her son
Cathleen, her daughter
Nora, a younger daughter
Men and **Women**

SCENE: An Island off the West of Ireland.

Cottage kitchen, with nets, oilskins, spinning-wheel, some new boards standing by the wall, etc. **Cathleen**, *a girl of about twenty, finishes kneading cake, and puts it down in the pot-oven by the fire; then wipes her hands, and begins to spin at the wheel.* **Nora**, *a young girl, puts her head in at the door.*

Nora (*in a low voice*): Where is she?
Cathleen: She's lying down, God help her, and maybe sleeping, if she's able.
  (**Nora** *comes in softly, and takes a bundle from under her shawl.*)
Cathleen (*spinning the wheel rapidly*): What is it you have?
Nora: The young priest is after bringing° them. It's a shirt and a plain stocking were got off a drowned man in Donegal.
  (**Cathleen** *stops her wheel with a sudden movement, and leans out to listen.*)
Nora: We're to find out if it's Michael's they are, some time herself° will be down looking by the sea.
Cathleen: How would they be Michael's, Nora? How would he go the length of that way to the far north?
Nora: The young priest says he's known the like of it. "If it's Michael's they are," says he, "you can tell herself he's got a clean burial by the grace of God, and if they're not his, let no one say a word about them, for she'll be getting her death," says he, "with crying and lamenting."
  (*The door which* **Nora** *half closed is blown open by a gust of wind.*)
Cathleen (*looking out anxiously*): Did you ask him would he stop Bartley going this day with the horses to the Galway fair?
Nora: "I won't stop him," says he, "but let you not be afraid. Herself does be saying prayers half through the night, and the Almighty God won't leave her destitute," says he, "with no son living."
Cathleen: Is the sea bad by the white rocks, Nora?
Nora: Middling bad, God help us. There's a great roaring in the west, and it's worse it'll be getting when the tide's turned to the wind. (*She goes over to the table with the bundle.*) Shall I open it now?
Cathleen: Maybe she'd wake up on us, and come in before we'd done. (*Coming to*

---

is . . . bringing has just brought   **herself** Maurya, the head of the household *the table.*) It's a long time we'll be, and the two of us crying.

Nora (*goes to the inner door and listens*): She's moving about on the bed. She'll be coming in a minute.

Cathleen: Give me the ladder, and I'll put them up in the turf-loft, the way° she won't know of them at all, and maybe when the tide turns she'll be going down to see would he be floating from the east.

(*They put the ladder against the gable of the chimney;* **Cathleen** *goes up a few steps and hides the bundle in the turf-loft.* **Maurya** *comes from the inner room.*)

Maurya (*looking up at* **Cathleen** *and speaking querulously*): Isn't it turf enough you have for this day and evening?

Cathleen: There's a cake baking at the fire for a short space (*throwing down the turf*), and Bartley will want it when the tide turns if he goes to Connemara.

(**Nora** *picks up the turf and puts it round the pot-oven.*)

Maurya (*sitting down on a stool at the fire*): He won't go this day with the wind rising from the south and west. He won't go this day, for the young priest will stop him surely.

Nora: He'll not stop him, mother, and I heard Eamon Simon and Stephen Pheety and Colum Shawn saying he would go.

Maurya: Where is he itself?

Nora: He went down to see would there be another boat sailing in the week, and I'm thinking it won't be long till he's here now, for the tide's turning at the green head, and the hooker's° tacking from the east.

Cathleen: I hear some one passing the big stones.

Nora (*looking out*): He's coming now, and he in a hurry.

Bartley (*comes in and looks around the room. Speaking sadly and quietly*): Where is the bit of new rope, Cathleen, was bought in Connemara?

Cathleen (*coming down*): Give it to him, Nora; it's on a nail by the white boards. I hung it up this morning, for the pig with the black feet was eating it.

Nora (*giving him a rope*): Is that it, Bartley?

Maurya: You'd do right to leave that rope, Bartley, hanging by the boards. (*Bartley takes the rope.*) It will be wanting in this place, I'm telling you, if Michael is washed up to-morrow morning, or the next morning, or any morning in the week, for it's a deep grave we'll make him by the grace of God.

Bartley (*beginning to work with the rope*): I've no halter the way I can ride down on the mare, and I must go now quickly. This is the one boat going for two weeks or beyond it, and the fair will be a good fair for horses I heard them saying below.

Maurya: It's a hard thing they'll be saying below if the body is washed up and there's no man in it° to make the coffin, and I after giving a big price for the finest white boards you'd find in Connemara.

(*She looks round at the boards.*)

Bartley: How would it be washed up, and we after looking° each day for nine days, and a strong wind blowing a while back from the west and south?

Maurya: If it isn't found itself,° that wind is raising the sea, and there was a star up against the moon, and it rising in the night. If it was a hundred horses, or a

---

the way so that
hooker a one-masted fishing vessel
it the house

we . . . looking when we have been looking
If it . . . itself even if it isn't found

thousand horses you had itself, what is the price of a thousand horses against a
son where there is one son only?

Bartley (*working at the halter, to* **Cathleen**): Let you go down each day, and see the
sheep aren't jumping in on the rye, and if the jobber comes you can sell the pig
with the black feet if there is a good price going.

Maurya: How would the like of her get a good price for a pig?

Bartley (*to* **Cathleen**): If the west wind holds with the last bit of the moon let you
and Nora get up weed° enough for another cock° for the kelp.° It's hard set
we'll be from this day with no one in it but one man to work.

Maurya: It's hard set we'll be surely the day you're drownd'd with the rest. What
way will I live and the girls with me, and I an old woman looking for the grave?
(**Bartley** *lays down the halter, takes off his old coat, and puts on a newer one of the same
flannel.*)

Bartley (*to* **Nora**): Is she coming to the pier?

Nora (*looking out*): She's passing the green head and letting fall her sails.

Bartley (*getting his purse and tobacco*): I'll have half an hour to go down, and you'll
see me coming again in two days, or in three days, or maybe in four days if the
wind is bad.

Maurya (*turning round to the fire, and putting her shawl over her head*): Isn't it a hard
and cruel man won't hear a word from an old woman, and she holding him from
the sea?

Cathleen: It's the life of a young man to be going on the sea, and who would listen
to an old woman with one thing and she saying it over?

Bartley (*taking the halter*): I must go now quickly. I'll ride down on the red mare,
and the gray pony'll run behind me. . . . The blessing of God on you.
(*He goes out.*)

Maurya (*crying out as he is in the door*): He's gone now, God spare us, and we'll not
see him again. He's gone now, and when the black night is falling I'll have no
son left me in the world.

Cathleen: Why wouldn't you give him your blessing and he looking round in the
door? Isn't it sorrow enough is on every one in this house without your sending
him out with an unlucky word behind him, and a hard word in his ear?

(**Maurya** *takes up the tongs and begins raking the fire aimlessly without looking round.*)

Nora (*turning towards her*): You're taking away the turf from the cake.

Cathleen (*crying out*): The Son of God forgive us, Nora, we're after forgetting his
bit of bread.

(*She comes over to the fire.*)

Nora: And it's destroyed° he'll be going till dark night, and he after eating nothing
since the sun went up.

Cathleen (*turning the cake out of the oven*): It's destroyed he'll be, surely. There's no
sense left on any person in a house where an old woman will be talking for ever.

(**Maurya** *sways herself on her stool.*)

Cathleen (*cutting off some of the bread and rolling it in a cloth; to* **Maurya**): Let you go
down now to the spring well and give him this and he passing. You'll see him

weed   seaweed
cock   conical rick
kelp   ashes of seaweed, from which iodine   is obtained
                                             destroyed   with hunger and fatigue

then and the dark word will be broken, and you can say "God speed you," the way he'll be easy in his mind.

Maurya (*taking the bread*): Will I be in it° as soon as himself?

Cathleen: If you go now quickly.

Maurya (*standing up unsteadily*): It's hard set I am to walk.

Cathleen (*looking at her anxiously*): Give her the stick, Nora, or maybe she'll slip on the big stones.

Nora: What stick?

Cathleen: The stick Michael brought from Connemara.

Maurya (*taking a stick* **Nora** *gives her*): In the big world the old people do be leaving things after them for their sons and children, but in this place it is the young men do be leaving things behind for them that do be old.

(*She goes out slowly.* **Nora** *goes over to the ladder.*)

Cathleen: Wait, Nora, maybe she'd turn back quickly. She's that sorry, God help her, you wouldn't know the thing she'd do.

Nora: Is she gone round by the bush?

Cathleen (*looking out*): She's gone now. Throw it down quickly, for the Lord knows when she'll be out of it again.

Nora (*getting the bundle from the loft*): The young priest said he'd be passing tomorrow, and we might go down and speak to him below if it's Michael's they are surely.

Cathleen (*taking the bundle*): Did he say what way they were found?

Nora (*coming down*): "There were two men," says he, "and they rowing round with poteen° before the cocks crowed, and the oar of one of them caught the body, and they passing the black cliffs of the north."

Cathleen (*trying to open the bundle*): Give me a knife, Nora, the string's perished with the salt water, and there's a black knot on it you wouldn't loosen in a week.

Nora (*giving her a knife*): I've heard tell it was a long way to Donegal.

Cathleen (*cutting the string*): It is surely. There was a man here a while ago—the man sold us that knife—and he said if you set off walking from the rocks beyond, it would be in seven days you'd be in Donegal.

Nora: And what time would a man take, and he floating?

(**Cathleen** *opens the bundle and takes out a bit of a stocking. They look at them eagerly.*)

Cathleen (*in a low voice*): The Lord spare us, Nora! isn't it a queer hard thing to say if it's his they are surely?

Nora: I'll get his shirt off the hook the way we can put the one flannel on the other. (*She looks through some clothes hanging in the corner.*) It's not with them, Cathleen, and where will it be?

Cathleen: I'm thinking Bartley put it on him in the morning, for his own shirt was heavy with the salt in it. (*Pointing to the corner.*) There's a bit of a sleeve was of the same stuff. Give me that and it will do.

(**Nora** *brings it to her and they compare the flannel.*)

Cathleen: It's the same stuff, Nora; but if it is itself aren't there great rolls of it in the shops of Galway, and isn't it many another man may have a shirt of it as well as Michael himself?

Nora (*who has taken up the stocking and counted the stitches, crying out*): It's Michael,

in it there   **poteen** moonshine whiskey

Cathleen, it's Michael; God spare his soul, and what will herself say when she hears this story, and Bartley on the sea?

Cathleen (*taking the stocking*): It's a plain stocking.

Nora: It's the second one of the third pair I knitted, and I put up three score stitches, and I dropped four of them.

Cathleen (*counts the stitches*): It's that number is in it. (*Crying out.*) Ah, Nora, isn't it a bitter thing to think of him floating that way to the far north, and no one to keen him but the black hags that do be flying on the sea?

Nora (*swinging herself half round, and throwing out her arms on the clothes*): And isn't it a pitiful thing when there is nothing left of a man who was a great rower and fisher, but a bit of an old shirt and a plain stocking?

Cathleen (*after an instant*): Tell me is herself coming, Nora? I hear a little sound on the path.

Nora (*looking out*): She is, Cathleen. She's coming up to the door.

Cathleen: Put these things away before she'll come in. Maybe it's easier she'll be after giving her blessing to Bartley, and we won't let on we've heard anything the time he's on the sea.

Nora (*helping **Cathleen** to close the bundle*): We'll put them here in the corner.

(*They put them into a hole in the chimney corner. **Cathleen** goes back to the spinning-wheel.*)

Nora: Will she see it was crying I was?

Cathleen: Keep your back to the door the way the light'll not be on you.

(***Nora** sits down at the chimney corner, with her back to the door. **Maurya** comes in very slowly, without looking at the girls, and goes over to her stool at the other side of the fire. The cloth with the bread is still in her hand. The girls look at each other, and **Nora** points to the bundle of bread.*)

Cathleen (*after spinning for a moment*): You didn't give him his bit of bread?

(***Maurya** begins to keen softly, without turning round.*)

Cathleen: Did you see him riding down?

(***Maurya** goes on keening.*)

Cathleen (*a little impatiently*): God forgive you; isn't it a better thing to raise your voice and tell what you seen, than to be making lamentation for a thing that's done? Did you see Bartley, I'm saying to you.

Maurya (*with a weak voice*): My heart's broken from this day.

Cathleen (*as before*): Did you see Bartley?

Maurya: I seen the fearfulest thing.

Cathleen (*leaves her wheel and looks out*): God forgive you; he's riding the mare now over the green head, and the gray pony behind him.

Maurya (*starts, so that her shawl falls back from her head and shows her white tossed hair. With a frightened voice*): The gray pony behind him. . . .

Cathleen (*coming to the fire*): What is it ails you, at all?

Maurya (*speaking very slowly*): I've seen the fearfulest thing any person has seen, since the day Bride Dara seen the dead man with the child in his arms.

Cathleen and Nora: Uah.

(*They crouch down in front of the old woman at the fire.*)

Nora: Tell us what it is you seen.

Maurya: I went down to the spring well, and I stood there saying a prayer to my-self. Then Bartley came along, and he riding on the red mare with the gray pony behind him. (*She puts up her hands, as if to hide something from her eyes.*) The Son of God spare us, Nora!

Cathleen: What is it you seen?

Maurya: I seen Michael himself.

Cathleen (*speaking softly*): You did not, mother. It wasn't Michael you seen, for his body is after being found in the far north, and he's got a clean burial by the grace of God.

Maurya (*a little defiantly*): I'm after seeing him this day, and he riding and galloping. Bartley came first on the red mare; and I tried to say "God speed you," but something choked the words in my throat. He went by quickly; and "the blessing of God on you," says he, and I could say nothing. I looked up then, and I crying, at the gray pony, and there was Michael upon it—with fine clothes on him, and new shoes on his feet.

Cathleen (*begins to keen*): It's destroyed we are from this day. It's destroyed, surely.

Nora: Didn't the young priest say the Almighty God won't leave her destitute with no son living?

Maurya (*in a low voice, but clearly*): It's little the like of him knows of the sea. . . . Bartley will be lost now, and let you call in Eamon and make me a good coffin out of the white boards, for I won't live after them. I've had a husband, and a husband's father, and six sons in this house—six fine men, though it was a hard birth I had with every one of them and they coming to the world—and some of them were found and some of them were not found, but they're gone now the lot of them. . . . There were Stephen, and Shawn, were lost in the great wind, and found after in the Bay of Gregory of the Golden Mouth, and carried up the two of them on one plank, and in by that door.

(*She pauses for a moment, the girls start as if they heard something through the door that is half open behind them.*)

Nora (*in a whisper*): Did you hear that, Cathleen? Did you hear a noise in the north-east?

Cathleen (*in a whisper*): There's some one after crying out by the seashore.

Maurya (*continues without hearing anything*): There was Sheamus and his father, and his own father again, were lost in a dark night, and not a stick or sign was seen of them when the sun went up. There was Patch after was drowned out of a curagh° that turned over. I was sitting here with Bartley, and he a baby, lying on my two knees, and I seen two women, and three women, and four women coming in, and they crossing themselves, and not saying a word. I looked out then, and there were men coming after them, and they holding a thing in the half of a red sail, and water dripping out of it—it was a dry day, Nora—and leaving a track to the door.

(*She pauses again with her hand stretched out towards the door. It opens softly and old women begin to come in, crossing themselves on the threshold, and kneeling down in front of the stage with their backs to the people, and the white waist-bands of the red petticoats they wear over their heads just seen from behind.*)

Maurya (*half in a dream, to* **Cathleen**): Is it Patch, or Michael, or what is it at all?

Cathleen: Michael is after being found in the far north, and when he is found there how could he be here in this place?

Maurya: There does be a power of young men floating round in the sea, and what

curagh a light, open boat

way would they know if it was Michael they had, or another man like him, for when a man is nine days in the sea, and the wind blowing, it's hard set his own mother would be to say what man was in it.

Cathleen: It's Michael, God spare him, for they're after sending us a bit of his clothes from the far north.

(*She reaches out and hands* **Maurya** *the clothes that belonged to Michael.* **Maurya** *stands up slowly, and takes them in her hands.* **Nora** *looks out.*)

Nora: They're carrying a thing among them and there's water dripping out of it and leaving a track by the big stones.

Cathleen (*in a whisper to the women who have come in*): Is it Bartley it is?

One of the Women: It is surely, God rest his soul.

(*Two younger women come in and pull out the table. Then men carry in the body of* **Bartley**, *laid on a plank, with a bit of a sail over it, and lay it on the table.*)

Cathleen (*to the women, as they are doing so*): What way was he drowned?

One of the Women: The gray pony knocked him over into the sea, and he was washed out where there is a great surf on the white rocks.

(**Maurya** *has gone over and knelt down at the head of the table. The women are keening softly and swaying themselves with a slow movement.* **Cathleen** *and* **Nora** *kneel at the other end of the table. The men kneel near the door.*)

Maurya (*raising her head and speaking as if she did not see the people around her*): They're all gone now, and there isn't anything more the sea can do to me. . . . I'll have no call now to be up crying and praying when the wind breaks from the south, and you can hear the surf is in the east, and the surf is in the west, making a great stir with the two noises, and they hitting one on the other. I'll have no call now to be going down and getting Holy Water in the dark nights after Samhain,° and I won't care what way the sea is when the other women will be keening. (*To* **Nora**.) Give me the Holy Water, Nora, there's a small cup still on the dresser.

(**Nora** *gives it to her.*)

Maurya (*drops Michael's clothes across* **Bartley's** *feet, and sprinkles the Holy Water over him*): It isn't that I haven't prayed for you, Bartley, to the Almighty God. It isn't that I haven't said prayers in the dark night till you wouldn't know what I'd be saying; but it's a great rest I'll have now, and it's time surely. It's a great rest I'll have now, and great sleeping in the long nights after Samhain, if it's only a bit of wet flour we do have to eat, and maybe a fish that would be stinking.

(*She kneels down again, crossing herself, and saying prayers under her breath.*)

Cathleen (*to an old man*): Maybe yourself and Eamon would make a coffin when the sun rises. We have fine white boards herself bought, God help her, thinking Michael would be found, and I have a new cake you can eat while you'll be working.

The Old Man (*looking at the boards*): Are there nails with them?

Cathleen: There are not, Colum; we didn't think of the nails.

Another Man: It's a great wonder she wouldn't think of the nails, and all the coffins she's seen made already.

Cathleen: It's getting old she is, and broken.

(**Maurya** *stands up again very slowly and spreads out the pieces of Michael's clothes beside the body, sprinkling them with the last of the Holy Water.*)

Nora (*in a whisper to* **Cathleen**): She's quiet now and easy; but the day Michael

Samhain All Souls' Day, November 1

was drowned you could hear her crying out from this to the spring well. It's fonder she was of Michael, and would any one have thought that?

Cathleen (*slowly and clearly*): An old woman will be soon tired with anything she will do, and isn't it nine days herself is after crying and keening, and making great sorrow in the house?

Maurya (*puts the empty cup mouth downwards on the table, and lays her hands together on* **Bartley's** *feet*): They're all together this time, and the end is come. May the Almighty God have mercy on Bartley's soul, and on Michael's soul, and on the souls of Sheamus and Patch, and Stephen and Shawn (*bending her head*); and may He have mercy on my soul, Nora, and on the soul of every one is left living in the world.

(*She pauses, and the keen rises a little more loudly from the women, then sinks away.*)

Maurya (*continuing*): Michael has a clean burial in the far north, by the grace of the Almighty God. Bartley will have a fine coffin out of the white boards, and a deep grave surely. What more can we want than that? No man at all can be living for ever, and we must be satisfied.

(*She kneels down again and the curtain falls slowly.*)

COMMENTARY

As mentioned earlier, succeeding sections of this text will present the basic elements of drama: setting, staging, language, character, structure, and irony. Before examining each of these in detail, let us see briefly how they function in the play you have just read.

Every play takes place at some time and in some place. In *Riders to the Sea* Synge identifies the place as "An Island off the West of Ireland" but leaves the time unspecified. Possibly he is suggesting that what occurs in the play cannot be limited to a specific time and could happen (with some alteration of physical detail) at any time in history. The entire play takes place in one room containing only the bare, practical necessities of existence; no object is mentioned that even hints of luxury. We learn early in the play that the inhabitants of the cottage are plain people who drudge their livelihood from the land and the sea. The land is sparse and rugged, only grudgingly yielding what hard work and sweat coax from it. The sea provides fish and seaweed, but with its winds it supplies the danger of death by shipwreck and drowning. In a sense, the cottage could represent man's attempt to protect himself, however futilely, from a stark and often dangerous environment.

The stage on which any play is presented is a kind of metaphor. Drama is a representation of some aspect of life—it is not life itself but stands for something the author wishes to say about human existence. For any drama to be significant, it must speak to each of us in some way: it must be universal. Thus the single room and the action that takes place in it represent a part of our lives—suffering, loss, and death. It is important then, given the setting of the play, that the physical staging be consistent with the author's metaphor. For example, early in the play Nora half-closes the door and it is blown open by the wind. Later Maurya leaves the door half-open, and through it we hear the first sounds that indicate Bartley is dead. Finally, Bartley's body, dripping sea water, is brought through the door. All these events seem to suggest that the cottage is not a sufficient bulwark against the elements or the sorrow of the world: the wind, the sea, and the grief-stricken laments penetrate with ease.

We have already noted the starkness of the room's contents—spinning wheel, turf loft, fireplace, rope, and coffin wood. All these objects continue and amplify the metaphor. Similarly, the physical actions of the characters serve the same purpose: Bartley's putting on his dead brother's coat, Cathleen's cutting the knot, the keening of the girls and women, the sprinkling of Holy Water.

The language of the play and the speeches of its characters reinforce what is accomplished by the setting and staging. The Aran dialect with its rural, Irish overtones reflects the simplicity of the island people. Much of the dialogue resembles proverbs, especially Maurya's lines: for example, "What is the price of a thousand horses against a son where there is one son only?" and later, "In the big world the old people do be leaving things after them for their sons and children, but in this place it is the young men do be leaving things behind for them that do be old." The proverbial tone of the language emphasizes the plainness of the people and suggests a kind of universality in what is said.

Synge also uses color to stress the rustic lives of the characters and the harshness of the island. A black knot holds together the package of Michael's clothes, and there are black feet on the pig who was eating the white rope. The coffin wood is white as are Maurya's hair and the rocks against which the surf crashes. Red is the color of Bartley's mare and the petticoats of the mourners. The pony is grey and so is the sea. All these are basic colors that reflect the elemental concerns of the play.

The most dominant character in the play is Maurya, and it is she on whom we the audience concentrate our attention. All the other characters revolve around her. Nora and Cathleen are more interested in her feelings than in their own—they control their grief by attending to practical tasks such as cooking and spinning. Their characters do not alter during the course of the play. Bartley exists only to fulfill his function as the last son to die. He doesn't protest against what necessity requires him to do for his family, nor does he react to his mother's pleas. The two men who each speak but one line at the end of the play concern themselves only with the practical business of building a coffin, commenting on Maurya's forgetting the nails. The keening women share Maurya's grief and serve to extend the feeling of loss beyond a particular mother grieving for her children. Although these characters do not especially engage us, their presence is necessary to provide information about Maurya and her tragic fate.

We learn about characters primarily from what they say, what they do, and what other characters say about them. From these sources we learn almost immediately that Maurya is griefstricken over the loss of her men, particularly Michael, and that she is certain that Bartley's trip to Galway Fair will mean his death. But early in the play we become aware that Maurya is more concerned about herself and her years of pain and tragedy than she is about the loss of her men individually. She is a mother, and her motherhood is based on the existence of sons, not daughters. The loss of her menfolk has enveloped her in unceasing anguish which has become almost unbearable. The thought of losing the last of her sons causes her harsh reactions as Bartley prepares to leave. She sees herself as a victim of the elements, especially the wind and the sea which have destroyed her family. However, after her vision of Michael on the grey pony, she can accept Bartley's death even before it is reported. Her reaction to this vision reflects a basic, heart-rending change in her outlook: The sea can do no more to her; she is freed from the prospect of further suffering. It is this freedom that is finally significant to her, not the loss of her last son. She has been deprived of everything that has meaning in her life and can lose no more. Her suffering ceases only when there is nothing left to suffer for.

The structure or plot of the play is not easily separable from the character of Maurya. Events do occur in the play—Bartley enters and leaves, Cathleen and Nora go about their duties, the islanders bring in and lament for Bartley's body—but all these actions are significant only as they apply to Maurya, just as the other characters gain their significance from her. The changes in Maurya's character and her reactions to the brutal life into which she has been thrust comprise the plot of the drama. She is first presented as a petulant old woman, protesting almost unreasonably against what her son feels he must do for the benefit of his family. She has suffered and sees nothing in the future but more suffering. But her vision of Michael, signifying the loss of Bartley, changes her attitude of protest and ineffective struggle to one of acceptance and resignation. The plot is charted from her original outlook through the actions of the play to her final position. The resolution of Maurya's conflict against the forces of nature is her eventual understanding of the necessity for enduring those forces.

At the end of the play, the gathering of the islanders and their ritualistic keening over the mother's loss universalize Maurya's grief. Her final statement transcends her specific situation and is applicable to all the inhabitants of the island and to all humanity: "No man at all can be living for ever, and we must be satisfied."

Although irony is a dominant element in this play, only a few types of irony are used. Dramatic irony generally occurs when the audience knows something important that another character does not know. Thus we know of Michael's death and the finding of his body before Maurya does, and, along with Cathleen and Nora, we know that she could not actually have seen him on the grey pony. But the natural and the supernatural are not sharply distinguished in this play, and what Maurya sees is perhaps more valid than what we know to be true. It is also ironic that the white wood bought for Michael's coffin is eventually used for Bartley, perhaps suggesting that death is arbitrary in its choice and cannot be channeled or limited by human acts. Perhaps a larger irony involves the world represented by the play. In such a world there can be no escape from suffering as long as we have something to lose; it is futile to struggle, as Maurya does in the beginning, against the power of nature both in its elements and in humanity. We can only accept what it brings us.

When combined, the elements we have discussed produce a unity which makes a dramatic statement about the condition of humanity. The play is more than a single element and greater than the sum of all its elements. The setting, stage properties, language, characterization, plot, and irony serve to complement, extend, amplify, and integrate with one another to produce a unified whole.

This process may be compared with the construction of a car or airplane: many different parts are combined to interact in a certain way so that the machine fulfills the designer's purpose. Synge has combined the various elements of drama to examine the loss and suffering that all humans must endure and to point out the existence of forces beyond our control that vitally affect our lives. He seems to suggest that struggling against these forces is ultimately futile but that we will continue to struggle as long as we have something worthwhile for which to struggle.

The play cannot, however, be reduced to these simple statements. To comprehend the full dramatic statement, we must experience the play; to perceive the depth and significance of the whole, we must be aware of the parts. With this knowledge we can approach the full enjoyment of drama, just as the music lover can experience full enjoyment of his music. Our examination of each individual element will begin with what we feel is the central concern of all drama—character.

PART TWO

CHARACTER

Throughout our lives most of us continually meet, relate to, and leave other people. We have developed certain rituals for this complex process, such as our ways of meeting and learning about each other—exchanging names and information about backgrounds, occupations, and interests. Often, getting to know someone means assessing how he or she relates to you, what you have in common, or how you differ.

There are always certain people whom we come to know more intimately than others, usually through common interests or shared experiences. We may feel sympathy or sorrow or love or happiness with these people and from the experience learn not only about them but about ourselves.

Rituals of separation are another important part of the process of relating to each other. In some cases we are parting only until the next day or the next week. In others, we may be moving away from people we have been close to and may never see again. Probably the most difficult kind of separation to deal with is death; this, too, becomes a part of our experience with others. For most of us the primary focus of our lives is our relations with other people.

It is therefore not surprising that when we read or see a play, our major interest is in the characters. We want to know who they are, what they are trying to do, and what is the significance of their experiences. Whether in a theater or in everyday life, we enjoy observing people who don't know we are watching, hoping that in an unguarded moment we will somehow learn the truth about a person through his candid actions, that we will see certain facets of his character that we haven't seen before. We are interested in the actions of a couple talking in the library; we enjoy seeing children play in the park. We watch people eating, drinking, talking, walking—even sleeping. This curiosity, both in our daily lives and in witnessing drama, is sparked by the desire to learn not only about these specific people, but about humanity in general, and especially about ourselves.

One such example of candid action from which we may learn about human experience occurred during a playoff game of the American Football Conference in 1971. The Miami Dolphins played the Kansas City Chiefs in a game that was to determine which team would play in the Super Bowl. It was a close game, but the Chiefs appeared to have a slight advantage. They had a chance to win when Jan Stenerud (perhaps the best placekicker in the league) attempted a thirty-two yard field goal with just thirty-five seconds left to play. It should have been an easy kick, but he missed, and Kansas City eventually lost the game 27 to 24 in sudden death overtime.

After Stenerud missed the kick, the camera—rather than cutting to a commercial or a shot of the teams lining up for the next play—remained focused on him; millions of people thus witnessed one man's reaction to personal failure. As the ball went wide of the goal post, Stenerud seemed to stare unbelievingly. His head dropped, eyes fixed on the ground, thoughts turned inward, probing for the reason for his failure. He walked slowly, slowly back to the bench. To him it must have seemed like a walk in hell—the rabid Miami fans screamed, whistled, clapped, and stamped their pleasure. He sat, head sagging, hands holding the sides of his helmet as if trying to shut out the noise—and the world. Completely absorbed, he contemplated his failure, oblivious to teammates who patted or touched him—they could not penetrate the shell of despair that had formed around Jan Stenerud.

Through witnessing such glimpses of people in their unguarded moments, we learn more about human nature, and perhaps more important, we may understand more about ourselves as we relate to those experiences. Perhaps you haven't missed a field goal in a playoff game, but you may have been rejected by that special person you would like to date, been denied membership in an important organization, dropped a tray in a crowded cafeteria, or frozen with fear when giving a speech. These failures may be unlike Stenerud's in degree but not in kind, for we all fail at some time or other. Such universal experiences are the substance of drama.

In the Stenerud incident, the camera showed us a dramatic situation, but once the camera was focused, the cameraman had no control over what happened. No one consciously chose the details of the scene. The cameraman or the director sensed that something significant might occur, but neither could cause or control it. Similarly, the playwright senses what is dramatic, but unlike the cameraman, he can control the scene he conveys. He does not simply report; he interprets. The playwright perceives the world in a particular way and then tries to express his vision to the audience. He creates situations, characters, and actions on stage that may parallel those occurring in daily life; he selects details and forms them into a structure that will express to others what he has perceived. The primary focus of the play, like the main focus of our lives, is on the characters.

All the other elements of drama combine to tell us about the characters and, by analogy, about ourselves. Later chapters of this text will provide greater detail showing how setting, plot, language, irony, and staging each add to our understanding of character. First, however, it seems appropriate to concentrate on the primary element, character.

As either reader or viewer, you learn about a character in several ways, one of which is physical appearance. As you are introduced to each character in the play, you form a general impression of his personality, social status, and perhaps even attitudes. The dramatist knows that, whether accurate or not, we tend to judge people by physical appearance. He uses this tendency to create immediate characterizations, especially of minor characters, through stereotypes. In costuming, for example, a character wearing a dark business suit, a half-size too small and frayed at the cuffs, creates quite a different impression from someone dressed in blue jeans, work shoes, and a grease-stained T-shirt with a pack of cigarettes rolled up in the sleeve. Even hand props associated with certain characters—a pocket watch, a fat cigar, or a walking stick—add to the characterization.

A playwright often is not satisfied, however, with creating simple stereotypes. A character who seems stereotyped in his appearance may be given greater depth and complexity through his actions or speech, thus emerging as an individual. A glamorous black revolutionary may lose his charm and become despicable when we see him pushing heroin to his young "brothers and sisters" in the ghetto. Similarly, a secretary who appears to be the stereotyped office sex symbol takes on greater dimensions as an individual when she is shown caring for her sick child or lecturing to college seniors about labor practices that discriminate against women.

Detailed physical features of the characters are also carefully selected by the playwright. He decides whether a character is young or old, tall or short, dark or fair, and may give him prominent features such as a scar, a large nose, a limp, or flaming red hair. Physical appearance, created through costuming, makeup, movement, and the like, is an essential tool used by the dramatist to convey specific information about each character. When he calls attention to certain details, he does so for a particular reason. On stage these details are created by the director and his staff—the costume designer, makeup artist, even the actors themselves—all taking their cues from the stage directions and dialogue. When specific directions are not given, these people must try to create physical images for the characters that seem appropriate to the text. The same clues and directions are available to you the reader as you create a character's physical appearance in your own imagination.

In addition to physical appearance, we can gain insight into characters through what they say. A person's opinions on certain issues, his attitudes toward himself and other characters, his biases, and his interests all may be expressed in his speeches. Keep in mind, however, that characters in a play, just as people in real life, are not always honest, wise, or accurate. A character's prejudices or weaknesses—dislike for people of a certain racial or regional group, fear of growing old, extreme jealousy, an inferiority complex—may distort his perception of those around him. A possessive husband who guards his wife jealously sees any man who even smiles at her as a threat to his marriage. If we listen only to him, we will probably never have an accurate impression of the other characters.

Certain distortions of a character's view of the world may result from his lack of knowledge in a particular subject. A successful general may be brilliant when discussing military tactics, but he may not demonstrate the same wisdom or insight when speaking about politics or educational reform. Besides these limitations, a character may choose to lie or tell only part of the truth, depending on the dramatic context, the topic of conversation, and the other characters present. The dramatist may sometimes have a character speak in *soliloquy*, expressing his thoughts aloud as he stands alone on stage; or when a character is part of the action in a scene, he may speak directly to the audience in an *aside*, commenting on the action or the other characters. In these instances the audience knows the character is speaking the truth—he has no reason to lie; however, at other times we must evaluate each character's statements according to what we know about him and his relationships with other characters.

Another source of information about a particular character is the dialogue of other characters. Keeping in mind that they might also be deceitful or ignorant or confused, we can nevertheless learn significant facts about a character's background or personality from what others say about him. Frequently you will find that in a play, as in everyday life, people hold widely differing opinions of a specific character. To some, a wealthy woman may seem proud and haughty, while others sense that she actually feels insecure and fears rejection. A politician may be considered by a group of teachers and students as a progressive supporter of education because he spoke to their university of the need for increased educational funds. This same politician, in the opinion of the conservatives in his home town, may be seen as their champion in the battle against costly, newfangled educational frills—because he expressed such views in talking with them. In using such varied opinions to gain insight into a character, we should consider who is speaking, how reliable he is, and in what context his statements are made.

Probably the most reliable means for learning about a character is observing his actions. A character may say that he will do many things, or others may predict his actions, but when we actually see what he does, we can then compare his actions with his words and better evaluate the strengths and weaknesses of his personality. As either viewers or readers, we are in the unique position of being able to observe a character in many situations with numerous other people and thereby judge him more reliably than the other characters can. In one scene a woman may seem to be deeply devoted to her husband; in another instance she may be plotting his death. A man may believe himself to be honest and noble, and yet we may see him behave toward other characters insensitively and deceitfully. We can observe the inconsistencies in someone's behavior, or see a character change his personality during the course of the play.

The dramatist provides the details needed to interpret the characters we see on stage; if he does not tell us about certain aspects—for example, a character's background or details of setting—then that information is not significant for his purpose, and the reader or audience need not concern themselves with it. Evaluating characters in a play is similar to judging people in everyday life—the more sensitive we become, the more accurate our judgments. And the more we learn about others, the better we come to know ourselves.

HEDDA GABLER

Henrik Ibsen

CHARACTERS

George Tesman
Hedda Tesman, his wife
Miss Juliana Tesman, his aunt
Mrs. Elvsted
Judge Brack
Eilert Lövborg
Berta, servant at the Tesmans'

The scene of the action is Tesman's villa, in the west end of Christiania.

ACT I

SCENE. *A spacious, handsome, and tastefully furnished drawing room, decorated in dark colors. In the back, a wide doorway with curtains drawn back, leading into a smaller room decorated in the same style as the drawing room. In the right-hand wall of the front room, a folding door leading out to the hall. In the opposite wall, on the left, a glass door, also with curtains drawn back. Through the panes can be seen part of a verandah outside, and trees covered with autumn foliage. An oval table, with a cover on it, and surrounded by chairs, stands well forward. In front, by the wall on the right, a wide stove of dark porcelain, a high-backed armchair, a cushioned footrest, and two footstools. A settee, with a small round table in front of it, fills the upper right-hand corner. In front, on the left, a little way from the wall, a sofa. Farther back than the glass door, a piano. On either side of the doorway at the back a whatnot with terra-cotta and majolica ornaments. Against the back wall of the inner room a sofa, with a table, and one or two chairs. Over the sofa hangs the portrait of a handsome elderly man in a General's uniform. Over the table a hanging lamp, with an opal glass shade. A number of bouquets are arranged about the drawing room, in vases and glasses. Others lie upon the tables. The floors in both rooms are covered with thick carpets. Morning light. The sun shines in through the glass door.*

    Miss Juliana Tesman, *with her bonnet on and carrying a parasol, comes in from the hall, followed by* **Berta**, *who carries a bouquet wrapped in paper.* **Miss Tesman** *is a comely and pleasant-looking lady of about sixty-five. She is nicely but simply dressed in a gray walking costume.* **Berta** *is a middle-aged woman of plain and rather countri-fied appearance.*

Miss Tesman (*stops close to the door, listens, and says softly*): Upon my word, I don't believe they are stirring yet!

Berta (*also softly*): I told you so, Miss. Remember how late the steamboat got in last night. And then, when they got home!—good Lord, what a lot the young mistress had to unpack before she could get to bed.

What does this tell us about Hedda?

Miss Tesman: Well, well—let them have their sleep out. But let us see that they get a good breath of the fresh morning air when they do appear. (*She goes to the glass door and throws it open.*)

Berta (*beside the table, at a loss what to do with the bouquet in her hand*): I declare there isn't a bit of room left. I think I'll put it down here, Miss. (*She places it on the piano.*)

Miss Tesman: So you've got a new mistress now, my dear Berta. Heaven knows it was a wrench to me to part with you.

Berta (*on the point of weeping*): And do you think it wasn't hard for me too, Miss? After all the blessed years I've been with you and Miss Rina.

Miss Tesman: We must make the best of it, Berta. There was nothing else to be done. George can't do without you, you see—he absolutely can't. He has had you to look after him ever since he was a little boy.

Berta: Ah, but, Miss Julia, I can't help thinking of Miss Rina lying helpless at home there, poor thing. And with only that new girl, too! She'll never learn to take proper care of an invalid.

Miss Tesman: Oh, I shall manage to train her. And of course, you know, I shall take most of it upon myself. You needn't be uneasy about my poor sister, my dear Berta.

Why afraid ? **Berta:** Well, but there's another thing, Miss. I'm so mortally afraid I shan't be able to suit the young mistress.

What kind of life **Miss Tesman:** Oh, well—just at first there may be one or two things——
is Hedda used **Berta:** Most like she'll be terrible grand in her ways.
to ?

Miss Tesman: Well, you can't wonder at that—General Gabler's daughter! Think of the sort of life she was accustomed to in her father's time. Don't you remember how we used to see her riding down the road along with the General? In that long black habit—and with feathers in her hat?

Berta: Yes, indeed—I remember well enough—! But good Lord, I should never have dreamt in those days that she and Master George would make a match of it.

Miss Tesman: Nor I. But, by-the-bye, Berta—while I think of it: in future you mustn't say Master George. You must say Dr. Tesman.

Berta: Yes, the young mistress spoke of that too—last night—the moment they set foot in the house. It is true, then, Miss?

Miss Tesman: Yes, indeed it is. Only think, Berta—some foreign university has made him a doctor—while he has been abroad, you understand. I hadn't heard a word about it, until he told me himself upon the pier.

Berta: Well, well, he's clever enough for anything, he is. But I didn't think he'd have gone in for doctoring people too.

Miss Tesman: No, no, it's not that sort of doctor he is. (*Nods significantly.*) But let me tell you, we may have to call him something still grander before long.

Berta: You don't say so! What can that be, Miss?

Miss Tesman (*smiling*): H'm—wouldn't you like to know! (*With emotion.*) Ah, dear, dear—if my poor brother could only look up from his grave now, and see what his little boy has grown into! (*Looks around.*) But bless me, Berta—why have you done this? Taken the chintz covers off all the furniture?

Berta: The mistress told me to. She can't abide covers on the chairs, she says.

Miss Tesman: Are they going to make this their everyday sitting room then?

Berta: Yes, that's what I understood—from the mistress. Master George—the doctor—he said nothing.

(**George Tesman** *comes from the right into the inner room, humming to himself, and carrying an unstrapped empty portmanteau. He is a middle-sized, young-looking man of thirty-three, rather stout, with a round, open, cheerful face, fair hair and beard. He wears spectacles, and is somewhat carelessly dressed in comfortable indoor clothes.*)

Miss Tesman: Good morning, good morning, George.

Tesman (*in the doorway between the rooms*): Aunt Julia! Dear Aunt Julia! (*Goes up to her and shakes hands warmly.*) Come all this way—so early! Eh?

Miss Tesman: Why of course I had to come and see how you were getting on.

Tesman: In spite of your having had no proper night's rest?

Miss Tesman: Oh, that makes no difference to me.

Tesman: Well, I suppose you got home all right from the pier? Eh?

Miss Tesman: Yes, quite safely, thank goodness. Judge Brack was good enough to see me right to my door.

Tesman: We were so sorry we couldn't give you a seat in the carriage. But you saw what a pile of boxes Hedda had to bring with her.

Miss Tesman: Yes, she had certainly plenty of boxes.

Berta (*to* **Tesman**): Shall I go in and see if there's anything I can do for the mistress?

Tesman: No, thank you, Berta—you needn't. She said she would ring if she wanted anything.

Berta (*going towards the right*): Very well.

Tesman: But look here—take this portmanteau with you.

Berta (*taking it*): I'll put it in the attic. (*She goes out by the hall door.*)

Tesman: Fancy, Aunty—I had the whole of that portmanteau chock full of copies of documents. You wouldn't believe how much I have picked up from all the archives I have been examining—curious old details that no one has had any idea of——

Miss Tesman: Yes, you don't seem to have wasted your time on your wedding trip, George.

Tesman: No, that I haven't. But do take off your bonnet, Auntie. Look here! Let me untie the strings—eh?

Miss Tesman (*while he does so*): Well, well—this is just as if you were still at home with us.

Tesman (*with the bonnet in his hand, looks at it from all sides*): Why, what a gorgeous bonnet you've been investing in!

Miss Tesman: I bought it on Hedda's account.

Tesman: On Hedda's account? Eh?

Miss Tesman: Yes, so that Hedda needn't be ashamed of me if we happened to go out together. *Does she too fear Hedda?*

Tesman (*patting her cheek*): You always think of everything, Aunt Julia. (*Lays the bonnet on a chair beside the table.*) And now, look here—suppose we sit comfortably on the sofa and have a little chat, till Hedda comes.

(*They seat themselves. She places her parasol in the corner of the sofa.*)

Miss Tesman (*takes both his hands and looks at him*): What a delight it is to have you again, as large as life, before my very eyes, George! My George—my poor brother's own boy!

Tesman: And it's a delight for me, too, to see you again, Aunt Julia! You, who have been father and mother in one to me.

Miss Tesman: Oh, yes, I know you will always keep a place in your heart for your old aunts.

Tesman: And what about Aunt Rina? No improvement—eh!

Miss Tesman: Oh, no—we can scarcely look for any improvement in her case, poor thing. There she lies, helpless, as she has lain for all these years. But heaven grant I may not lose her yet awhile! For if I did, I don't know what I should make of my life, George—especially now that I haven't you to look after any more.

Tesman (*patting her back*): There, there, there——!

Miss Tesman (*suddenly changing her tone*): And to think that here you are a married man, George!—And that you should be the one to carry off Hedda Gabler, the beautiful Hedda Gabler! Only think of it—she, that was so beset with admirers!

Proud as punch **Tesman** (*hums a little and smiles complacently*): Yes, I fancy I have several good friends about town who would like to stand in my shoes—eh?

Miss Tesman: And then this fine long wedding tour you have had! More than five—nearly six months——

Tesman: Well, for me it has been a sort of tour of research as well. I have had to do so much grubbing among old records—and to read no end of books too, Auntie.

Miss Tesman: Oh, yes, I suppose so. (*More confidentially, and lowering her voice a little.*) But listen now, George—have you nothing—nothing special to tell me?

Tesman: As to our journey?

Miss Tesman: Yes.

Tesman: No, I don't know of anything except what I have told you in my letters. I had a doctor's degree conferred on me—but that I told you yesterday.

Miss Tesman: Yes, yes, you did. But what I mean is—haven't you any—any—expectations——?

Tesman: Expectations?

Miss Tesman: Why, you know, George—I'm your old auntie!

Tesman: Why, of course I have expectations.

Miss Tesman: Ah!

Tesman: I have every expectation of being a professor one of these days.

Miss Tesman: Oh, yes, a professor——

Tesman: Indeed, I may say I am certain of it. But my dear Auntie—you know all about that already!

Miss Tesman (*laughing to herself*): Yes, of course I do. You are quite right there. (*Changing the subject.*) But we were talking about your journey. It must have cost a great deal of money, George?

Tesman: Well, you see—my handsome traveling scholarship went a good way.

Miss Tesman: But I can't understand how you can have made it go far enough for two.

Tesman: No, that's not so easy to understand—eh?

Miss Tesman: And especially traveling with a lady—they tell me that makes it ever so much more expensive.

Tesman: Yes, of course—it makes it a little more expensive. But Hedda had to *Hedda's need for* have this trip, Auntie! She really had to. Nothing else would have done. *expensive things*

Miss Tesman: No, no, I suppose not. A wedding tour seems to be quite indispensable nowadays. But tell me now—have you gone thoroughly over the house yet?

Tesman: Yes, you may be sure I have. I have been afoot ever since daylight.

Miss Tesman: And what do you think of it all?

Tesman: I'm delighted! Quite delighted! Only I can't think what we are to do with the two empty rooms between this inner parlor and Hedda's bedroom.

Miss Tesman (*laughing*): Oh, my dear George, I dare say you may find some use for them—in the course of time.

Tesman: Why of course you are quite right, Aunt Julia! You mean as my library increases—eh?

Miss Tesman: Yes, quite so, my dear boy. It was your library I was thinking of.

Tesman: I am specially pleased on Hedda's account. Often and often, before we were engaged, she said that she would never care to live anywhere but in Secretary Falk's villa.

Miss Tesman: Yes, it was lucky that this very house should come into the market, just after you had started.

Tesman: Yes, Aunt Julia, the luck was on our side, wasn't it—eh?

Miss Tesman: But the expense, my dear George! You will find it very expensive, all this.

Tesman (*looks at her, a little cast down*): Yes, I suppose I shall, Aunt!

Miss Tesman: Oh, frightfully!

Tesman: How much do you think? In round numbers?—Eh?

Miss Tesman: Oh, I can't even guess until all the accounts come in.

Tesman: Well, fortunately, Judge Brack has secured the most favorable terms *Why write to* for me—so he said in a letter to Hedda. *Hedda of business matters?*

Miss Tesman: Yes, don't be uneasy, my dear boy. Besides, I have given security for the furniture and all the carpets.

Tesman: Security? You? My dear Aunt Julia—what sort of security could you give?

Miss Tesman: I have given a mortgage on our annuity.

Tesman (*jumps up*): What! On your—and Aunt Rina's annuity!

Miss Tesman: Yes, I knew of no other plan, you see.

Tesman (*placing himself before her*): Have you gone out of your senses, Auntie! Your annuity—it's all that you and Aunt Rina have to live upon.

Miss Tesman: Well, well, don't get so excited about it. It's only a matter of form you know—Judge Brack assured me of that. It was he that was kind enough to arrange the whole affair for me. A mere matter of form, he said.

Tesman: Yes, that may be all very well. But nevertheless——

Miss Tesman: You will have your own salary to depend upon now. And, good heavens, even if we did have to pay up a little——! To eke things out a bit at the start——! Why, it would be nothing but a pleasure to us.

Tesman: Oh, Auntie—will you never be tired of making sacrifices for me!

Miss Tesman (*rises and lays her hands on his shoulders*): Have I had any other *Julia as we now* happiness in this world except to smooth your way for you, my dear boy? *know her.* You, who have had neither father nor mother to depend on. And now we have reached the goal, George! Things have looked black enough for us, sometimes; but, thank heaven, now you have nothing to fear.

Tesman: Yes, it is really marvelous how everything has turned out for the best.

Miss Tesman: And the people who opposed you—who wanted to bar the way for you—now you have them at your feet. They have fallen, George. Your most dangerous rival—his fall was the worst. And now he has to lie on the bed he has made for himself—poor misguided creature.

Tesman: Have you heard anything of Eilert? Since I went away, I mean.

Miss Tesman: Only that he is said to have published a new book.

Tesman: What! Eilert Lövborg! Recently—eh?

Miss Tesman: Yes, so they say. Heaven knows whether it can be worth anything! Ah, when your new book appears—that will be another story, George! What is it to be about?

Tesman: It will deal with the domestic industries of Brabant during the Middle Ages.

Miss Tesman: Fancy—to be able to write on such a subject as that.

Tesman: However, it may be some time before the book is ready. I have all these collections to arrange first, you see.

Miss Tesman: Yes, collecting and arranging—no one can beat you at that. There you are my poor brother's own son.

Tesman: I am looking forward eagerly to setting to work at it; especially now that I have my own delightful home to work in.

Miss Tesman: And, most of all, now that you have got the wife of your heart, my dear George.

Tesman (*embracing her*): Oh, yes, yes, Aunt Julia. Hedda—she is the best part of all! (*Looks towards the doorway.*) I believe I hear her coming—eh?

(**Hedda** *enters from the left through the inner room. She is a woman of nine-and-twenty. Her face and figure show refinement and distinction. Her complexion is pale and opaque. Her steel-gray eyes express a cold, unruffled repose. Her hair is of an agreeable medium brown, but not particularly abundant. She is dressed in a tasteful, somewhat loose-fitting morning gown.*)

What does this description lead us to expect? Why comment on her hair? Her steel-gray eyes?

Miss Tesman (*going to meet* **Hedda**): Good morning, my dear Hedda! Good morning, and a hearty welcome.

Hedda (*holds out her hand*): Good morning, dear Miss Tesman! So early a call! That is kind of you.

Miss Tesman (*with some embarrassment*): Well—has the bride slept well in her new home?

Hedda: Oh yes, thanks. Passably.

Tesman (*laughing*): Passably! Come, that's good, Hedda! You were sleeping like a stone when I got up.

Hedda: Fortunately. Of course one has always to accustom one's self to new surroundings, Miss Tesman—little by little. (*Looking towards the left.*) Oh—there the servant has gone and opened the verandah door, and let in a whole flood of sunshine.

She does not like harsh light. Why?

Miss Tesman (*going towards the door*): Well, then, we will shut it.

Hedda: No, no, not that! Tesman, please draw the curtains. That will give a softer light.

Tesman (*at the door*): All right—all right. There now, Hedda, now you have both shade and fresh air.

Hedda: Yes, fresh air we certainly must have, with all these stacks of flowers —— But—won't you sit down, Miss Tesman?

Miss Tesman: No, thank you. Now that I have seen that everything is all right here—thank heaven! I must be getting home again. My sister is lying longing for me, poor thing.

Tesman: Give her my very best love, Auntie; and say I shall look in and see her later in the day.

Miss Tesman: Yes, yes, I'll be sure to tell her. But by-the-bye, George—(*feeling in her dress pocket*)—I have almost forgotten—I have something for you here.

Tesman: What is it, Auntie? Eh?

Miss Tesman (*produces a flat parcel wrapped in newspaper and hands it to him*): Look here, my dear boy.

Tesman (*opening the parcel*): Well, I declare! Have you really saved them for me, Aunt Julia! Hedda! isn't this touching—eh?

Hedda (*beside the whatnot on the right*): Well, what is it?

Tesman: My old morning shoes! My slippers.

Hedda: Indeed. I remember you often spoke of them while we were abroad.

Tesman: Yes, I missed them terribly. (*Goes up to her.*) Now you shall see them, Hedda!

Hedda (*going towards the stove*): Thanks, I really don't care about it.

Tesman (*following her*): Only think—ill as she was, Aunt Rina embroidered these for me. Oh, you can't think how many associations cling to them.

Hedda (*at the table*): Scarcely for me.

Miss Tesman: Of course not for Hedda, George.

Tesman: Well, but now that she belongs to the family, I thought——

Hedda (*interrupting*): We shall never get on with this servant, Tesman.

Miss Tesman: Not get on with Berta?

Tesman: Why, dear, what puts that in your head? Eh?

Hedda (*pointing*): Look there! She has left her old bonnet lying about on a chair.

Tesman (*in consternation, drops the slippers on the floor*): Why, Hedda——

Hedda: Just fancy, if any one should come in and see it.

Tesman: But Hedda—that's Aunt Julia's bonnet.

Hedda: Is it!

Miss Tesman (*taking up the bonnet*): Yes, indeed it's mine. And what's more, it's not old, Madame Hedda.

Hedda: I really did not look closely at it, Miss Tesman.

Miss Tesman (*trying on the bonnet*): Let me tell you it's the first time I have worn it—the very first time.

Tesman: And a very nice bonnet it is too—quite a beauty!

Miss Tesman: Oh, it's no such great thing, George. (*Looks around her.*) My parasol——? Ah, here. (*Takes it.*) For this is mine too—(*mutters*)—not Berta's.

Tesman: A new bonnet and a new parasol! Only think, Hedda!

Hedda: Very handsome indeed.

Tesman: Yes, isn't it? But Auntie, take a good look at Hedda before you go! See how handsome she is!

Miss Tesman: Oh, my dear boy, there's nothing new in that. Hedda was always lovely. (*She nods and goes towards the right.*)

Tesman (*following*): Yes, but have you noticed what splendid condition she is in? How she has filled out on the journey?

Hedda (*crossing the room*): Oh, do be quiet——!

Miss Tesman (*who has stopped and turned*): Filled out?

Tesman: Of course you don't notice it so much now that she has that dress on. But I, who can see——

Is Hedda pregnant? **Hedda** (*at the glass door, impatiently*): Oh, you can't see anything.

Tesman: It must be the mountain air in the Tyrol——

Hedda (*curtly, interrupting*): I am exactly as I was when I started.

Tesman: So you insist; but I'm quite certain you are not. Don't you agree with me, Auntie?

Miss Tesman (*who has been gazing at her with folded hands*): Hedda is lovely—lovely—lovely. (*Goes up to her, takes her head between both hands, draws it downwards, and kisses her hair*). God bless and preserve Hedda Tesman—for George's sake.

Hedda (*gently freeing herself*): Oh! Let me go.

Miss Tesman (*in quiet emotion*): I shall not let a day pass without coming to see you.

Tesman: No you won't, will you, Auntie? Eh?

Miss Tesman: Good-by—good-by!

(*She goes out by the hall door.* **Tesman** *accompanies her. The door remains half open.* **Tesman** *can be heard repeating his message to Aunt Rina and his thanks for the slippers.*

Compare these actions with her initial description.   (*In the meantime,* **Hedda** *walks about the room raising her arms and clenching her hands as if in desperation. Then she flings back the curtains from the glass door, and stands there looking out.*

(*Presently* **Tesman** *returns and closes the door behind him.*)

Tesman (*picks up the slippers from the floor*): What are you looking at, Hedda?

Hedda (*once more calm and mistress of herself*): I am only looking at the leaves. They are so yellow—so withered.

Tesman (*wraps up the slippers and lays them on the table*): Well you see, we are well into September now.

How old is Hedda? **Hedda** (*again restless*): Yes, to think of it! Already in—in September.

Tesman: Don't you think Aunt Julia's manner was strange, dear? Almost solemn? Can you imagine what was the matter with her? Eh?

Hedda: I scarcely know her, you see. Is she often like that?

Tesman: No, not as she was today.

Hedda (*leaving the glass door*): Do you think she was annoyed about the bonnet?

Tesman: Oh, scarcely at all. Perhaps a little, just at the moment——

Hedda: But what an idea, to pitch her bonnet about in the drawing room! No one does that sort of thing.

Tesman: Well you may be sure Aunt Julia won't do it again.

Hedda: In any case, I shall manage to make my peace with her.

Tesman: Yes, my dear, good Hedda, if you only would.

Hedda: When you call this afternoon, you might invite her to spend the evening here.

Tesman: Yes, that I will. And there's one thing more you could do that would delight her heart.

Hedda: What is it?

Tesman: If you could only prevail on yourself to say *du*° to her. For my sake, Hedda? Eh?

Hedda: No, no, Tesman—you really mustn't ask that of me. I have told you so already. I shall try to call her "Aunt"; and you must be satisfied with that.

Tesman: Well, well. Only I think now that you belong to the family, you——

Hedda: H'm—I can't in the least see why——

(*She goes up towards the middle doorway.*)

Tesman (*after a pause*): Is there anything the matter with you, Hedda? Eh?

Hedda: I'm only looking at my old piano. It doesn't go at all well with all the other things.

Tesman: The first time I draw my salary, we'll see about exchanging it.

Hedda: No, no—no exchanging. I don't want to part with it. Suppose we put it there in the inner room, and then get another here in its place. When it's convenient, I mean.

Considering their finances, what does this reveal about Hedda?

Tesman (*a little taken aback*): Yes—of course we could do that.

Hedda (*takes up the bouquet from the piano*): These flowers were not here last night when we arrived.

Tesman: Aunt Julia must have brought them for you.

Hedda (*examining the bouquet*): A visiting card. (*Takes it out and reads.*) "Shall return later in the day." Can you guess whose card it is?

Tesman: No. Whose? Eh?

Hedda: The name is "Mrs. Elvsted."

Tesman: Is it really? Sheriff Elvsted's wife? Miss Rysing that was.

Hedda: Exactly. The girl with the irritating hair, that she was always showing off. An old flame of yours, I've been told.

Tesman (*laughing*): Oh, that didn't last long; and it was before I knew you, Hedda. But fancy her being in town!

Hedda: It's odd that she should call upon us. I have scarcely seen her since we left school.

Tesman: I haven't seen her either for—heaven knows how long. I wonder how she can endure to live in such an out-of-the-way hole—eh?

Hedda (*after a moment's thought says suddenly*): Tell me, Tesman—isn't it somewhere near there that he—that—Eilert Lövborg is living?

Tesman: Yes, he is somewhere in that part of the country.

(**Berta** *enters by the hall door.*)

Berta: That lady, ma'am, that brought some flowers a little while ago, is here again. (*Pointing.*) The flowers you have in your hand, ma'am.

Hedda: Ah, is she? Well, please show her in.

(**Berta** *opens the door for* **Mrs. Elvsted**, *and goes out herself.* **Mrs. Elvsted** *is a woman of fragile figure, with pretty, soft features. Her eyes are light blue, large, round, and somewhat prominent, with a startled, inquiring expression. Her hair is remarkably light, almost flaxen, and unusually abundant and wavy. She is a couple of years younger than* **Hedda**. *She wears a dark visiting dress, tasteful, but not quite in the latest fashion.*)

Why call attention to the women's hair?

Hedda (*receives her warmly*): How do you do, my dear Mrs. Elvsted? It's delightful to see you again.

---

du thou, the familiar form of the pronoun *you*.

Mrs. Elvsted (*nervously, struggling for self-control*): Yes, it's a very long time since we met.

Tesman (*gives her his hand*): And we too—eh?

Hedda: Thanks for your lovely flowers——

Mrs. Elvsted: Oh, not at all—— I would have come straight here yesterday afternoon; but I heard that you were away——

Tesman: Have you just come to town? Eh?

Mrs. Elvsted: I arrived yesterday, about midday. Oh, I was quite in despair when I heard that you were not at home.

Hedda: In despair! How so?

Tesman: Why, my dear Mrs. Rysing—I mean Mrs. Elvsted——

Hedda: I hope that you are not in any trouble?

Mrs. Elvsted: Yes, I am. And I don't know another living creature here that I can turn to.

Hedda (*laying the bouquet on the table*): Come—let us sit here on the sofa——

Mrs. Elvsted: Oh, I am too restless to sit down.

Compare her reception to Julia's.

Hedda: Oh no, you're not. Come here. (*She draws* **Mrs. Elvsted** *down upon the sofa and sits at her side.*)

Tesman: Well? What is it, Mrs. Elvsted?

Hedda: Has anything particular happened to you at home?

Mrs. Elvsted: Yes—and no. Oh—I am so anxious you should not misunderstand me——

Hedda: Then your best plan is to tell us the whole story, Mrs. Elvsted.

Tesman: I suppose that's what you have come for—eh?

Mrs. Elvsted: Yes, yes—of course it is. Well then, I must tell you—if you don't already know—that Eilert Lövborg is in town, too.

Hedda: Lövborg——!

Tesman: What! Has Eilert Lövborg come back? Fancy that, Hedda!

Hedda: Well, well—I hear it.

Mrs. Elvsted: He has been here a week already. Just fancy—a whole week! In this terrible town, alone! With so many temptations on all sides.

Hedda: But my dear Mrs. Elvsted—how does he concern you so much?

Mrs. Elvsted (*looks at her with a startled air, and says rapidly*): He was the children's tutor.

Hedda: Your children's?

Mrs. Elvsted: My husband's. I have none.

Hedda: Your step-children's, then?

Mrs. Elvsted: Yes.

Tesman (*somewhat hesitatingly*): Then was he—I don't know how to express it—was he—regular enough in his habits to be fit for the post? Eh?

Mrs. Elvsted: For the last two years his conduct has been irreproachable.

Notice how often George uses this phrase.

Tesman: Has it indeed? Fancy that, Hedda!

Hedda: I hear it.

Mrs. Elvsted: Perfectly irreproachable, I assure you! In every respect. But all the same—now that I know he is here—in this great town—and with a large sum of money in his hands—I can't help being in mortal fear for him.

Tesman: Why did he not remain where he was? With you and your husband? Eh?

Mrs. Elvsted: After his book was published he was too restless and unsettled to remain with us.

Tesman: Yes, by-the-bye, Aunt Julia told me he had published a new book.

Mrs. Elvsted: Yes, a big book, dealing with the march of civilization—in broad outline, as it were. It came out about a fortnight ago. And since it has sold so well, and been so much read—and made such a sensation——

Tesman: Has it indeed? It must be something he has had lying by since his better days.

Mrs. Elvsted: Long ago, you mean?

Tesman: Yes.

Mrs. Elvsted: No, he has written it all since he has been with us—within the last year.

Tesman: Isn't that good news. Hedda? Think of that.

Mrs. Elvsted: Ah, yes, if only it would last!

Hedda: Have you seen him here in town?

Mrs. Elvsted: No, not yet. I have had the greatest difficulty in finding out his address. But this morning I discovered it at last.

Hedda (*looks searchingly at her*): Do you know, it seems to me a little odd of your husband—h'm——

Mrs. Elvsted (*starting nervously*): Of my husband! What?

Hedda: That he should send you to town on such an errand—that he does not come himself and look after his friend.

Mrs. Elvsted: Oh no, no—my husband has no time. And besides, I—I had some shopping to do.

Hedda (*with a slight smile*): Ah, that is a different matter.

Mrs. Elvsted (*rising quickly and uneasily*): And now I beg and implore you, Mr. Tesman—receive Eilert Lövborg kindly if he comes to you! And that he is sure to do. You see you were such great friends in the old days. And then you are interested in the same studies—the same branch of science—so far as I can understand.

Tesman: We used to be, at any rate.

Mrs. Elvsted: That is why I beg so earnestly that you—you too—will keep a sharp eye upon him. Oh, you will promise me that, Mr. Tesman—won't you?

Tesman: With the greatest of pleasure, Mrs. Rysing——

Hedda: Elvsted.

Tesman: I assure you I shall do all I possibly can for Eilert. You may rely upon me.

Mrs. Elvsted: Oh, how very, very kind of you! (*Presses his hands.*) Thanks, thanks, thanks! (*Frightened.*) You see, my husband is very fond of him!

Hedda (*rising*): You ought to write to him, Tesman. Perhaps he may not care to come to you of his own accord.

Tesman: Well, perhaps it would be the right thing to do, Hedda? Eh?

Hedda: And the sooner the better. Why not at once?

Mrs. Elvsted (*imploringly*): Oh, if you only would!

Tesman: I'll write this moment. Have you his address. Mrs.—Mrs. Elvsted.

Mrs. Elvsted: Yes. (*Takes a slip of paper from her pocket, and hands it to him.*) Here it is.

Tesman: Good, good. Then I'll go in——(*Looks about him.*) By-the-bye—my slippers? Oh, here. (*Takes the packet, and is about to go.*)

Hedda: Be sure you write him a cordial, friendly letter. And a good long one too.

Tesman: Yes, I will.

Mrs. Elvsted: But please, please don't say a word to show that I have suggested it.

Tesman: No, how could you think I would? Eh? (*He goes out to the right, through the inner room.*)

Hedda (*goes up to* **Mrs. Elvsted**, *smiles, and says in a low voice*): There. We have killed two birds with one stone.

Mrs. Elvsted: What do you mean?

Hedda: Could you not see that I wanted him to go?

Mrs. Elvsted: Yes, to write the letter——

Hedda: And that I might speak to you alone.

Mrs. Elvsted (*confused*): About the same thing?

Hedda: Precisely.

Mrs. Elvsted (*apprehensively*): But there is nothing more, Mrs. Tesman! Absolutely nothing!

What does this action suggest about control?

Hedda: Oh, yes, but there is. There is a great deal more—I can see that. Sit here—and we'll have a cosy, confidential chat. (*She forces* **Mrs. Elvsted** *to sit in the easy chair beside the stove, and seats herself on one of the footstools.*)

Mrs. Elvsted (*anxiously, looking at her watch*): But, my dear Mrs. Tesman—I was really on the point of going.

Hedda: Oh, you can't be in such a hurry. Well? Now tell me something about your life at home.

Mrs. Elvsted: Oh, that is just what I care least to speak about.

Fear again— Berta, Julia, Thea

Hedda: But to me, dear——? Why, weren't we schoolfellows?

Mrs. Elvsted: Yes, but you were in the class above me. Oh, how dreadfully afraid of you I was then!

Hedda: Afraid of me?

Mrs. Elvsted: Yes, dreadfully. For when we met on the stairs you used always to pull my hair.

Hedda: Did I, really?

A violent Hedda

Mrs. Elvsted: Yes, and once you said you would burn it off my head.

Hedda: Oh, that was all nonsense, of course.

Mrs. Elvsted: Yes, but I was so silly in those days. And since then, too—we have drifted so far—far apart from each other. Our circles have been so entirely different.

Hedda: Well then, we must try to drift together again. Now listen! At school we said *du* to each other; and we called each other by our Christian names——

Mrs. Elvsted: No, I am sure you must be mistaken.

Hedda: No, not at all! I can remember quite distinctly. So now we are going to renew our old friendship. (*Draws the footstool closer to* **Mrs. Elvsted**.) There now! (*Kisses her cheek.*) You must say *du* to me and call me Hedda.

Good friends? What is Hedda after?

Mrs. Elvsted (*presses and pats her hands*): Oh, how good and kind you are! I am not used to such kindness.

Hedda: There, there, there! And I shall say *du* to you, as in the old days, and call you my dear Thora.

Mrs. Elvsted: My name is Thea.

Hedda: Why, of course! I meant Thea. (*Looks at her compassionately.*) So you are not accustomed to goodness and kindness, Thea? Not in your own home?

Mrs. Elvsted: Oh, if I only had a home! But I haven't any; I have never had a home.

Hedda (*looks at her for a moment*): I almost suspected as much.

Mrs. Elvsted (*gazing helplessly before her*): Yes—yes—yes.

Hedda: I don't quite remember—was it not as housekeeper that you first went to Mr. Elvsted's?

Mrs. Elvsted: I really went as governess. But his wife—his late wife—was an invalid—and rarely left her room. So I had to look after the housekeeping as well.

Hedda: And then—at last—you became mistress of the house.

Mrs. Elvsted (*sadly*): Yes, I did.

Hedda: Let me see—about how long ago was that?

Mrs. Elvsted: My marriage?

Hedda: Yes.

Mrs. Elvsted: Five years ago.

Hedda: To be sure; it must be that.

Mrs. Elvsted: Oh, those five years——! Or at all events the last two or three of them! Oh, if you° could only imagine——

Hedda (*giving her a little slap on the hand*): De? Fie, Thea!

Mrs. Elvsted: Yes, yes, I will try—— Well if—you could only imagine and understand——

Hedda (*lightly*): Eilert Lövborg has been in your neighborhood about three years, hasn't he?

Mrs. Elvsted (*looks at her doubtfully*): Eilert Lövborg? Yes—he has.

Hedda: Had you known him before, in town here?

Mrs. Elvsted: Scarcely at all. I mean—I knew him by name of course.

Hedda: But you saw a good deal of him in the country?

Mrs. Elvsted: Yes, he came to us every day. You see, he gave the children lessons; for in the long run I couldn't manage it all myself.

Hedda: No, that's clear. And your husband——? I suppose he is often away from home?

Mrs. Elvsted: Yes. Being Sheriff, you know, he has to travel about a good deal in his district.

Hedda (*leaning against the arm of the chair*): Thea—my poor, sweet Thea—now you must tell me everything—exactly as it stands.

Mrs. Elvsted: Well then, you must question me.

Hedda: What sort of a man is your husband, Thea? I mean—you know—in everyday life. Is he kind to you?

Mrs. Elvsted (*evasively*): I am sure he means well in everything.

Hedda: I should think he must be altogether too old for you. There is at least twenty years' difference between you, is there not?

Mrs. Elvsted (*irritably*): Yes, that is true, too. Everything about him is repellent to me! We have not a thought in common. We have no single point of sympathy—he and I.

Hedda: But is he not fond of you all the same? In his own way?

Mrs. Elvsted here uses the formal pronoun *De*, whereupon Hedda rebukes her.
In her next speech Mrs. Elvsted says *du*.

Mrs. Elvsted: Oh, I really don't know. I think he regards me simply as a useful property. And then it doesn't cost much to keep me. I am not expensive.

Hedda: That is stupid of you.

Mrs. Elvsted (*shakes her head*): It cannot be otherwise—not with him. I don't think he really cares for any one but himself—and perhaps a little for the children.

Hedda: And for Eilert Lövborg, Thea.

Mrs. Elvsted (*looking at her*): For Eilert Lövborg? What puts that into your head?

Hedda: Well, my dear—I should say, when he sends you after him all the way to town—— (*Smiling almost imperceptibly.*) And besides, you said so yourself, to Tesman.

Mrs. Elvsted (*with a little nervous twitch*): Did I? Yes, I suppose I did. (*Vehemently, but not loudly.*) No—I may just as well make a clean breast of it at once! For it must all come out in any case.

Hedda: Why, my dear Thea——?

Mrs. Elvsted: Well, to make a long story short: My husband did not know that I was coming.

Hedda: What! Your husband didn't know it!

Mrs. Elvsted: No, of course not. For that matter, he was away from home himself—he was traveling. Oh, I could bear it no longer, Hedda! I couldn't indeed—so utterly alone as I should have been in future.

Hedda: Well? And then?

Mrs. Elvsted: So I put together some of my things—what I needed most—as quietly as possible. And then I left the house.

Hedda: Without a word?

Mrs. Elvsted: Yes—and took the train straight to town.

Hedda: Why, my dear, good Thea—to think of you daring to do it!

Mrs. Elvsted (*rises and moves about the room*): What else could I possibly do?

Hedda: But what do you think your husband will say when you go home again?

Mrs. Elvsted (*at the table, looks at her*): Back to him.

Hedda: Of course.

Mrs. Elvsted: I shall never go back to him again.

Hedda (*rising and going towards her*): Then you have left your home—for good and all?

Mrs. Elvsted: Yes. There was nothing else to be done.

Hedda: But then—to take flight so openly.

Mrs. Elvsted: Oh, it's impossible to keep things of that sort secret.

Hedda: But what do you think people will say of you, Thea?

Mrs. Elvsted: They may say what they like for aught *I* care. (*Seats herself wearily and sadly on the sofa.*) I have done nothing but what I had to do.

Hedda (*after a short silence*): And what are your plans now? What do you think of doing?

Hedda manipulates Thea to learn the truth.

Mrs. Elvsted: I don't know yet. I only know this, that I must live here, where Eilert Lövborg is—if I am to live at all.

Hedda (*takes a chair from the table, seats herself beside her, and strokes her hands*): My dear Thea—how did this—this friendship—between you and Eilert Lövborg come about?

Mrs. Elvsted: Oh, it grew up gradually. I gained a sort of influence over him.

Hedda: Indeed?

Mrs. Elvsted: He gave up his old habits. Not because I asked him to, for I never dared do that. But of course he saw how repulsive they were to me; and so he dropped them.

Hedda (*concealing an involuntary smile of scorn*): Then you have reclaimed him— as the saying goes—my little Thea.

Mrs. Elvsted: So he says himself, at any rate. And he, on his side, has made a real human being of me—taught me to think, and to understand so many things.

Hedda: Did he give you lessons too, then?

Mrs. Elvsted: No, not exactly lessons. But he talked to me—talked about such an infinity of things. And then came the lovely, happy time when I began to share in his work—when he allowed me to help him!

Hedda: Oh, he did, did he?

Mrs. Elvsted: Yes! He never wrote anything without my assistance.

Hedda: You were two good comrades, in fact?

Mrs. Elvsted (*eagerly*): Comrades! Yes, fancy, Hedda—that is the very word he used! Oh, I ought to feel perfectly happy; and yet I cannot; for I don't know how long it will last.

Hedda: Are you no surer of him than that?

Mrs. Elvsted (*gloomily*): A woman's shadow stands between Eilert Lövborg and me.

Hedda (*looks at her anxiously*): Who can that be?

Mrs. Elvsted: I don't know. Some one he knew in his—in his past. Some one he has never been able wholly to forget.

Hedda: What has he told you—about this?

Mrs. Elvsted: He has only once—quite vaguely—alluded to it.

Hedda: Well! And what did he say?

Mrs. Elvsted: He said that when they parted, she threatened to shoot him with a pistol.

Hedda (*with cold composure*): Oh, nonsense! No one does that sort of thing here.

Mrs. Elvsted: No. And that is why I think it must have been that redhaired singing woman whom he once——

Hedda: Yes, very likely.

Mrs. Elvsted: For I remember they used to say of her that she carried loaded firearms.

Hedda: Oh—then of course it must have been she.

Mrs. Elvsted (*wringing her hands*): And now just fancy, Hedda—I hear that this singing woman—that she is in town again! Oh, I don't know what to do——

Hedda (*glancing towards the inner room*): Hush! Here comes Tesman. (*Rises and whispers.*) Thea—all this must remain between you and me.

Mrs. Elvsted (*springing up*): Oh, yes, yes! for heaven's sake——!

(**George Tesman**, *with a letter in his hand, comes from the right through the inner room.*)

Tesman: There now—the epistle is finished.

Hedda: That's right. And now Mrs. Elvsted is just going. Wait a moment— I'll go with you to the garden gate.

Tesman: Do you think Berta could post the letter, Hedda dear?

Hedda (*takes it*): I will tell her to.

(**Berta** *enters from the hall.*)

Berta: Judge Brack wishes to know if Mrs. Tesman will receive him.

Hedda: Yes, ask Judge Brack to come in. And look here—put this letter in the post.

Berta (*taking the letter*): Yes, ma'am.

(*She opens the door for* **Judge Brack** *and goes out herself.* **Brack** *is a man of forty-five; thickset, but well built and elastic in his movements. His face is roundish with an aristocratic profile. His hair is short, still almost black, and carefully dressed. His eyes are lively and sparkling. His eyebrows thick. His moustaches are also thick, with short-cut ends. He wears a well-cut walking suit, a little too youthful for his age. He uses an eyeglass, which he now and then lets drop.*)

Ibsen stresses face, hair, eyes, dress. Compare Hedda, Thea, Brack.

Judge Brack (*with his hat in his hand, bowing*): May one venture to call so early in the day?

Hedda: Of course one may.

Tesman (*presses his hand*): You are welcome at any time. (*Introducing him.*) Judge Brack—Miss Rysing——

Hedda: Oh——!

Brack (*bowing*): Ah—delighted——

Hedda (*looks at him and laughs*): It's nice to have a look at you by daylight, Judge!

Brack: Do you find me—altered?

Hedda: A little younger, I think.

Brack: Thank you so much.

Tesman: But what do you think of Hedda—eh? Doesn't she look flourishing? She has actually——

Hedda: Oh, do leave me alone. You haven't thanked Judge Brack for all the trouble he has taken——

Brack: Oh, nonsense—it was a pleasure to me——

Hedda: Yes, you are a friend indeed. But here stands Thea all impatience to be off—so *au revoir*, Judge. I shall be back again presently. (*Mutual salutations.* **Mrs. Elvsted** *and* **Hedda** *go out by the hall door.*)

Brack: Well, is your wife tolerably satisfied——

Tesman: Yes, we can't thank you sufficiently. Of course she talks of a little rearrangement here and there; and one or two things are still wanting. We shall have to buy some additional trifles.

Brack: Indeed!

Tesman: But we won't trouble about these things. Hedda says she herself will look after what is wanting.——Shan't we sit down? Eh?

Brack: Thanks, for a moment. (*Seats himself beside the table.*) There is something I wanted to speak to you about, my dear Tesman.

Tesman: Indeed? Ah, I understand! (*Seating himself.*) I suppose it's the serious part of the frolic that is coming now. Eh?

Brack: Oh, the money question is not so very pressing; though, for that matter, I wish we had gone a little more economically to work.

Tesman: But that would never have done, you know! Think of Hedda, my dear fellow! You, who know her so well—— I couldn't possibly ask her to put up with a shabby style of living!

Brack: No, no—that is just the difficulty.

Tesman: And then—fortunately—it can't be long before I receive my appointment.

Brack: Well, you see—such things are often apt to hang fire for a time.

Tesman: Have you heard anything definite? Eh?

Brack: Nothing exactly definite—— (*Interrupting himself.*) But, by-the-bye—I have one piece of news for you.

Tesman: Well?

Brack: Your old friend, Eilert Lövborg, has returned to town.

Tesman: I know that already.

Brack: Indeed! How did you learn it?

Tesman: From that lady who went out with Hedda.

Brack: Really? What was her name? I didn't quite catch it.

Tesman: Mrs. Elvsted.

Brack: Aha—Sheriff Elvsted's wife? Of course—he has been living up in their regions.

Tesman: And fancy—I'm delighted to hear that he is quite a reformed character!

Brack: So they say.

Tesman: And then he has published a new book—eh?

Brack: Yes, indeed he has.

Tesman: And I hear it has made some sensation!

Brack: Quite an unusual sensation.

Tesman: Fancy—isn't that good news! A man of such extraordinary talents—— I felt so grieved to think that he had gone irretrievably to ruin.

Brack: That was what everybody thought.

Tesman: But I cannot imagine what he will take to now! How in the world will he be able to make his living? Eh?

(*During the last words,* **Hedda** *has entered by the hall door.*)

Hedda (*to* **Brack**, *laughing with a touch of scorn*): Tesman is forever worrying about how people are to make their living.

Tesman: Well, you see, dear—we were talking about poor Eilert Lövborg.

Hedda (*glancing at him rapidly*): Oh, indeed? (*Seats herself in the arm-chair beside the stove and asks indifferently.*) What is the matter with him?

What do these actions indicate?

Tesman: Well—no doubt he has run through all his property long ago; and he can scarcely write a new book every year—eh? So I really can't see what is to become of him.

Brack: Perhaps I can give you some information on that point.

Tesman: Indeed!

Brack: You must remember that his relations have a good deal of influence.

Tesman: Oh, his relations, unfortunately, have entirely washed their hands of him.

Brack: At one time they called him the hope of the family.

Tesman: At one time, yes! But he has put an end to all that.

Hedda: Who knows? (*With a slight smile.*) I hear they have reclaimed him up at Sheriff Elvsted's——

Brack: And then this book that he has published——

Tesman: Well, well, I hope to goodness they may find something for him to do. I have just written to him. I asked him to come and see us this evening, Hedda dear.

Brack: But, my dear fellow, you are booked for my bachelors' party this evening. You promised on the pier last night.

Hedda: Had you forgotten, Tesman?

Tesman: Yes, I had utterly forgotten.

Brack: But it doesn't matter, for you may be sure he won't come.

Tesman: What makes you think that? Eh?

Brack (*with a little hesitation, rising and resting his hands on the back of his chair*): My dear Tesman—and you too, Mrs. Tesman—I think I ought not to keep you in the dark about something that—that——

Tesman: That concerns Eilert——?

Brack: Both you and him.

Tesman: Well, my dear Judge, out with it.

Brack: You must be prepared to find your appointment deferred longer than you desired or expected.

Tesman (*jumping up uneasily*): Is there some hitch about it? Eh?

Brack: The nomination may perhaps be made conditional on the result of a competition——

Tesman: Competition! Think of that, Hedda!

Hedda (*leans farther back in the chair*): Aha—aha!

Tesman: But who can my competitior be? Surely not——?

Brack: Yes, precisely—Eilert Lövborg.

Tesman (*clasping his hands*): No, no—it's quite inconceivable! Quite impossible! Eh?

Brack: H'm—that is what it may come to, all the same.

Tesman: Well but, Judge Brack—it would show the most incredible lack of consideration for me. (*Gesticulates with his arms.*) For—just think—I'm a married man. We have been married on the strength of these prospects, Hedda and I; and run deep into debt; and borrowed money from Aunt Julia too. Good heavens, they had as good as promised me the appointment. Eh?

Brack: Well, well, well—no doubt you will get it in the end; only after a contest.

Hedda (*immovable in her armchair*): Fancy, Tesman, there will be a sort of sporting interest in that.

Tesman: Why, my dearest Hedda, how can you be so indifferent about it?

Wifely concern? Hedda (*as before*): I am not at all indifferent. I am most eager to see who wins.

Brack: In any case, Mrs. Tesman, it is best that you should know how matters stand. I mean—before you set about the little purchases I hear you are threatening.

Hedda: This can make no difference.

Brack: Indeed! Then I have no more to say. Good-by! (*To* Tesman.) I shall look in on my way back from my afternoon walk, and take you home with me.

Tesman: Oh yes, yes—your news has quite upset me.

Hedda (*reclining, holds out her hand*): Good-by, Judge; and be sure you call in the afternoon.

Brack: Many thanks. Good-by, good-by!

Tesman (*accompanying him to the door*): Good-by, my dear Judge! You must really excuse me—— (Judge Brack *goes out by the hall door.*)

Tesman (*crosses the room*): Oh, Hedda—one should never rush into adventures. Eh?

Hedda (*looks at him, smiling*): Do you do that?

Tesman: Yes, dear—there is no denying—it was adventurous to go and marry and set up house upon mere expectations.

Hedda: Perhaps you are right there.

Tesman: Well—at all events, we have our delightful home, Hedda! Fancy, the home we both dreamed of—the home we were in love with, I may almost say. Eh?

Hedda (*rising slowly and wearily*): It was part of our compact that we were to go into society—to keep open house.

Tesman: Yes, if you only knew how I had been looking forward to it! Fancy— to see you as hostess—in a select circle? Eh? Well, well, well—for the present we shall have to get on without society, Hedda—only to invite Aunt Julia now and then. Oh, I intended you to lead such an utterly different life, dear——!

Hedda: Of course I cannot have my man in livery just yet.

Tesman: Oh no, unfortunately. It would be out of the question for us to keep a footman, you know.

Hedda: And the saddle horse I was to have had——

Tesman (*aghast*): The saddle horse!

Hedda: ——I suppose I must not think of that now.

Tesman: Good heavens, no!—that's as clear as daylight.

How would she say this line?

Hedda (*goes up the room*): Well, I shall have one thing at least to kill time with in the meanwhile.

Tesman (*beaming*): Oh, thank heaven for that! What is it, Hedda? Eh?

Hedda (*in the middle doorway, looks at him with covert scorn*): My pistols, George.

Tesman (*in alarm*): Your pistols!

Where was another reference to pistols?

Hedda (*with cold eyes*): General Gabler's pistols. (*She goes out through the inner room, to the left.*)

Tesman (*rushes up to the middle doorway and calls after her*): No, for heaven's sake, Hedda darling—don't touch those dangerous things! For my sake, Hedda! Eh?

ACT II

SCENE: *The room at the* **Tesmans'** *as in the first Act, except that the piano has been removed, and an elegant little writing table with bookshelves put in its place. A smaller table stands near the sofa at the left. Most of the bouquets have been taken away.* **Mrs. Elvsted's** *bouquet is upon the large table in front. It is afternoon.*

Hedda, dressed to receive callers, is alone in the room. She stands by the open glass door, loading a revolver. The fellow to it lies in an open pistol case on the writing table.

Hedda (*looks down the garden, and calls*): So you are here again, Judge!

Brack (*is heard calling from a distance*): As you see, Mrs. Tesman!

Hedda (*raises the pistol and points*): Now I'll shoot you, Judge Brack!

Brack (*calling unseen*): No, no, no! Don't stand aiming at me!

Hedda: This is what comes of sneaking in by the back way.° (*She fires.*)

Brack (*nearer*): Are you out of your senses——!

Hedda: Dear me—did I happen to hit you?

Bagveje means both "back ways" and "underhand courses."

Brack (*still outside*): I wish you would let these pranks alone!

Hedda: Come in then, Judge.

(**Judge Brack**, *dressed as though for a men's party, enters by the glass door. He carries a light overcoat over his arm.*)

Brack: What the deuce—haven't you tired of that sport, yet? What are you shooting at?

Hedda: Oh, I am only firing in the air.

Brack (*gently takes the pistol out of her hand*): Allow me, madam! (*Looks at it.*) Ah—I know this pistol well! (*Looks around.*) Where is the case? Ah, here it is. (*Lays the pistol in it, and shuts it.*) Now we won't play at that game any more today.

Hedda: Then what in heaven's name would you have me do with myself?

Brack: Have you had no visitors?

Hedda (*closing the glass door*): Not one. I suppose all our set are still out of town.

Brack: And is Tesman not at home either?

Hedda (*at the writing table, putting the pistol case in a drawer which she shuts*): No. He rushed off to his aunt's directly after lunch; he didn't expect you so early.

Brack: H'm—how stupid of me not to have thought of that!

Hedda (*turning her head to look at him*): Why stupid?

Brack: Because if I had thought of it I should have come a little—earlier.

Hedda (*crossing the room*): Then you would have found no one to receive you; for I have been in my room changing my dress ever since lunch.

Brack: And is there no sort of little chink that we could hold a parley through?

Hedda: You have forgotten to arrange one.

Brack: That was another piece of stupidity.

Hedda: Well, we must just settle down here—and wait. Tesman is not likely to be back for some time yet.

Brack: Never mind; I shall not be impatient.

(**Hedda** *seats herself in the corner of the sofa.* **Brack** *lays his overcoat over the back of the nearest chair, and sits down, but keeps his hat in his hand. A short silence. They look at each other.*)

Hedda: Well?

Brack (*in the same tone*): Well?

Hedda: I spoke first.

Brack (*bending a little forward*): Come, let us have a cosy little chat, Mrs. Hedda.

Hedda (*leaning further back in the sofa*): Does it not seem like a whole eternity since our last talk? Of course I don't count those few words yesterday evening and this morning.

Brack: You mean since our last confidential talk? Our last tête-à-tête?

Hedda: Well, yes—since you put it so.

Brack: Not a day has passed but I have wished that you were home again.

Hedda: And I have done nothing but wish the same thing.

Brack: You? Really, Mrs. Hedda? And I thought you had been enjoying your tour so much!

Hedda: Oh, yes, you may be sure of that!

Brack: But Tesman's letters spoke of nothing but happiness.

Hedda: Oh, Tesman! You see, he thinks nothing so delightful as grubbing in libraries and making copies of old parchments, or whatever you call them.

Brack (*with a spice of malice*): Well, that is his vocation in life—or part of it at any rate.

Hedda: Yes, of course; and no doubt when it's your vocation—— But *I!* Oh, my dear Mr. Brack, how mortally bored I have been.

Brack (*sympathetically*): Do you really say so? In downright earnest?

Hedda: Yes, you can surely understand it——! To go for six whole months without meeting a soul that knew anything of our circle, or could talk about the things we are interested in.

Brack: Yes, yes—I too should feel that a deprivation.

Hedda: And then, what I found most intolerable of all——

Brack: Well?

Hedda: ——was being everlastingly in the company of—one and the same person——

Brack (*with a nod of assent*): Morning, noon, and night, yes—at all possible times and seasons.

Hedda: I said "everlastingly."

Brack: Just so. But I should have thought, with our excellent Tesman, one could——

Hedda: Tesman is—a specialist, my dear Judge.

Brack: Undeniably.

Hedda: And specialists are not at all amusing to travel with. Not in the long run at any rate.

Brack: Not even—the specialist one happens to love?

Hedda: Faugh—don't use that sickening word!

Brack (*taken aback*): What do you say, Mrs. Hedda?

Hedda (*half laughing, half irritated*): You should just try it! To hear of nothing but the history of civilization, morning, noon, and night——

Brack: Everlastingly.

Hedda: Yes, yes, yes! And then all this about the domestic industry of the middle ages——! That's the most disgusting part of it!

Brack (*looks searchingly at her*): But tell me—in that case, how am I to understand your——? H'm——

Hedda: My accepting George Tesman, you mean?

Brack: Well, let us put it so.

Hedda: Good heavens, do you see anything so wonderful in that?

Brack: Yes and no—Mrs. Hedda.

Hedda: I had positively danced myself tired, my dear Judge. My day was done—— (*With a slight shudder.*) Oh no—I won't say that; nor think it either!

What does this show about her feelings?

Brack: You have assuredly no reason to.

Hedda: Oh, reasons—— (*Watching him closely.*) George Tesman—after all, you must admit that he is correctness itself.

She is 29; it is September; the leaves are yellow.

Brack: His correctness and respectability are beyond all question.

Hedda: And I don't see anything absolutely ridiculous about him. Do you?

Brack: Ridiculous? N—no—I shouldn't exactly say so——

Hedda: Well—and his powers of research, at all events, are untiring. I see no reason why he should not one day come to the front, after all.

Brack (*looks at her hesitatingly*): I thought that you, like every one else, expected him to attain the highest distinction.

Hedda (*with an expression of fatigue*): Yes, so I did.—And then, since he was bent, at all hazards, on being allowed to provide for me—I really don't know why I should not have accepted his offer?

Brack: No—if you look at it in that light——

Hedda: It was more than my other adorers were prepared to do for me, my dear Judge.

Brack (*laughing*): Well, I can't answer for all the rest; but as for myself, you know quite well that I have always entertained a—a certain respect for the marriage tie—for marriage as an institution, Mrs. Hedda.

Hedda (*jestingly*): Oh, I assure you I have never cherished any hopes with respect to you.

Brack: All I require is a pleasant and intimate interior, where I can make myself useful in every way, and am free to come and go as—as a trusted friend——

Hedda: Of the master of the house, do you mean?

Brack (*bowing*): Frankly—of the mistress first of all; but of course of the master, too, in the second place. Such a triangular friendship—if I may call it so—is really a great convenience for all parties, let me tell you.

Hedda: Yes, I have many a time longed for some one to make a third on our travels. Oh—those railway-carriage tête-à-têtes——!

Brack: Fortunately your wedding journey is over now.

Hedda (*shaking her head*): Not by a long—long way. I have only arrived at a station on the line.

Brack: Well, then the passengers jump out and move about a little, Mrs. Hedda.

Hedda: I never jump out.

Brack: Really?

Hedda: No—because there is always some one standing by to——

Brack (*laughing*): To look at your ankles, do you mean?

Hedda: Precisely.

Brack: Well but, dear me——

Hedda (*with a gesture of repulsion*): I won't have it. I would rather keep my seat where I happen to be—and continue the tête-à-tête.

Brack: But suppose a third person were to jump in and join the couple.

Hedda: Ah—that is quite another matter!

Brack: A trusted, sympathetic friend——

Hedda: ——with a fund of conversation on all sorts of lively topics——

Brack: ——and not the least bit of a specialist!

Hedda (*with an audible sigh*): Yes, that would be a relief indeed.

Brack (*hears the front door open, and glances in that direction*): The triangle is completed.

Hedda (*half aloud*): And on goes the train.

(**George Tesman**, *in a gray walking suit, with a soft felt hat, enters from the hall. He has a number of unbound books under his arm and in his pockets.*)

Tesman (*goes up to the table beside the corner setee*): Ouf—what a load for a warm day—all these books. (*Lays them on the table.*) I'm positively perspiring, Hedda. Hallo—are you there already, my dear Judge? Eh? Berta didn't tell me.

Brack (*rising*): I came in through the garden.

Hedda: What books have you got there?

Tesman (*stands looking them through*): Some new books on my special subjects —quite indispensable to me.

Hedda: Your special subjects?

Key passage: Hedda won't leave her safe compartment but permits others to enter. What does she fear?

Brack: Yes, books on his special subjects, Mrs. Tesman. (**Brack** *and* **Hedda** *exchange a confidential smile.*)

Hedda: Do you need still more books on your special subjects?

Tesman: Yes, my dear Hedda, one can never have too many of them. Of course one must keep up with all that is written and published.

Hedda: Yes, I suppose one must.

Tesman (*searching among his books*): And look here—I have got hold of Eilert Lövborg's new book too. (*Offering it to her.*) Perhaps you would like to glance through it, Hedda? Eh?

Hedda: No, thank you. Or rather—afterwards perhaps.

Tesman: I looked into it a little on the way home.

Brack: Well, what do you think of it—as a specialist?

Tesman: I think it shows quite remarkable soundness of judgment. He never wrote like that before. (*Putting the books together.*) Now I shall take all these into my study. I'm longing to cut the leaves——! And then I must change my clothes. (*To* **Brack**.) I suppose we needn't start just yet? Eh?

Brack: Oh, dear no—there is not the slightest hurry.

Tesman: Well then, I will take my time. (*Is going with his books, but stops in the doorway and turns.*) By-the-bye, Hedda—Aunt Julia is not coming this evening.

Hedda: Not coming? Is it that affair of the bonnet that keeps her away?

Tesman: Oh, not at all. How could you think such a thing of Aunt Julia? Just fancy——! The fact is, Aunt Rina is very ill.

Hedda: She always is.

Tesman: Yes, but today she is much worse than usual, poor dear.

Hedda: Oh, then it's only natural that her sister should remain with her. I must bear my disappointment.

Tesman: And you can't imagine, dear, how delighted Aunt Julia seemed to be—because you had come home looking so flourishing!

Hedda (*half aloud, rising*): Oh, those everlasting aunts!

Tesman: What?

Hedda (*going to the glass door*): Nothing.

Tesman: Oh, all right. (*He goes through the inner room, out to the right.*)

Brack: What bonnet were you talking about?

Hedda: Oh, it was a little episode with Miss Tesman this morning. She had laid down her bonnet on the chair there—(*Looks at him and smiles.*)—and I pretended to think it was the servant's.

Brack (*shaking his head*): Now my dear Mrs. Hedda, how could you do such a thing? To that excellent old lady, too!

Hedda (*nervously crossing the room*): Well, you see—these impulses come over me all of a sudden; and I cannot resist them. (*Throws herself down in the easy chair by the stove.*) Oh, I don't know how to explain it.

Brack (*behind the easy chair*): You are not really happy—that is at the bottom of it.

Hedda (*looking straight before her*): I know of no reason why I should be—happy. Perhaps you can give me one?

Brack: Well—amongst other things, because you have got exactly the home you had set your heart on.

Hedda (*looks up at him and laughs*): Do you too believe in that legend?

Brack: Is there nothing in it, then?

Hedda: Oh, yes, there is something in it.

Brack: Well?

Hedda: There is this in it, that I made use of Tesman to see me home from evening parties last summer——

Brack: I, unfortunately, had to go quite a different way.

Hedda: That's true. I know you were going a different way last summer.

Brack (*laughing*): Oh fie, Mrs. Hedda! Well, then—you and Tesman——?

Hedda: Well, we happened to pass here one evening; Tesman, poor fellow, was writhing in the agony of having to find conversation; so I took pity on the learned man——

Brack (*smiles doubtfully*): You took pity? H'm——

Hedda: Yes, I really did. And so—to help him out of his torment—I happened to say, in pure thoughtlessness, that I should like to live in this villa.

Brack: No more than that?

Hedda: Not that evening.

Brack: But afterwards?

Hedda: Yes, my thoughtlessness had consequences, my dear Judge.

Brack: Unfortunately that too often happens, Mrs. Hedda.

Hedda: Thanks! So you see it was this enthusiasm for Secretary Falk's villa that first constituted a bond of sympathy between George Tesman and me. From that came our engagement and our marriage, and our wedding journey, and all the rest of it. Well, well, my dear Judge—as you make your bed so you must lie, I could almost say.

Brack: This is exquisite! And you really cared not a rap about it all the time.

Hedda: No, heaven knows I didn't.

Brack: But now? Now that we have made it so homelike for you?

Hedda: Uh—the rooms all seem to smell of lavender and dried rose leaves. —But perhaps it's Aunt Julia that has brought that scent with her.

Brack (*laughing*): No, I think it must be a legacy from the late Mrs. Secretary Falk.

Hedda: Yes, there is an odor of mortality about it. It reminds me of a bouquet —the day after the ball. (*Clasps her hands behind her head, leans back in her chair and looks at him.*) Oh, my dear Judge—you cannot imagine how horribly I shall bore myself here.

Brack: Why should not you, too, find some sort of vocation in life, Mrs. Hedda?

Hedda: A vocation—that should attract me?

Brack: If possible, of course.

Hedda: Heaven knows what sort of a vocation that could be. I often wonder whether——(*Breaking off.*) But that would never do either.

Brack: Who can tell? Let me hear what it is.

What do her boredom and her ideas for relieving it reveal about her?

Hedda: Whether I might not get Tesman to go into politics, I mean.

Brack (*laughing*): Tesman? No, really now, political life is not the thing for him—not at all in his line.

Hedda: No, I daresay not. But if I could get him into it all the same?

Brack: Why—what satisfaction could you find in that? If he is not fitted for that sort of thing, why should you want to drive him into it?

Hedda: Because I am bored, I tell you! (*After a pause.*) So you think it quite out of the question that Tesman should ever get into the ministry?

Brack: H'm—you see, my dear Mrs. Hedda—to get into the ministry, he would have to be a tolerably rich man.

Hedda (*rising impatiently*): Yes, there we have it! It is this genteel poverty I have managed to drop into——! (*Crosses the room.*) That is what makes life so pitiable! So utterly ludicrous! For that's what it is.

Brack: Now *I* should say the fault lay elsewhere.

Hedda: Where, then?

Brack: You have never gone through any really stimulating experience.

Hedda: Anything serious, you mean?

Brack: Yes, you may call it so. But now you may perhaps have one in store.

Hedda (*tossing her head*): Oh, you're thinking of the annoyances about this wretched professorship! But that must be Tesman's own affair. I assure you I shall not waste a thought upon it.

Brack: No, no, I daresay not. But suppose now that what people call—in elegant language—a solemn responsibility were to come upon you? (*Smiling.*) A new responsibility, Mrs. Hedda?

Hedda (*angrily*): Be quiet! Nothing of that sort will ever happen!

Brack (*warily*): We will speak of this again a year hence—at the very outside.

Hedda (*curtly*): I have no turn for anything of the sort, Judge Brack. No responsibilities for me! *How does she feel about motherhood?*

Brack: Are you so unlike the generality of women as to have no turn for duties which——?

Hedda (*beside the glass door*): Oh, be quiet, I tell you! I often think there is only one thing in the world I have any turn for.

Brack (*drawing near to her*): And what is that, if I may ask?

Hedda (*stands looking out*): Boring myself to death. Now you know it. (*Turns, looks towards the inner room, and laughs.*) Yes, as I thought! Here comes the Professor.

Brack (*softly, in a tone of warning*): Come, come, come, Mrs. Hedda!

(**George Tesman**, *dressed for the party, with his gloves and hat in his hand, enters from the right through the inner room.*)

Tesman: Hedda, has no message come from Eilert Lövborg? Eh?

Hedda: No.

Tesman: Then you'll see he'll be here presently.

Brack: Do you really think he will come?

Tesman: Yes, I am almost sure of it. For what you were telling us this morning must have been a mere floating rumor.

Brack: You think so?

Tesman: At any rate, Aunt Julia said she did not believe for a moment that he would ever stand in my way again. Fancy that!

Brack: Well then, that's all right.

Tesman (*placing his hat and gloves on a chair on the right*): Yes, but you must really let me wait for him as long as possible.

Brack: We have plenty of time yet. None of my guests will arrive before seven or half-past.

Tesman: Then meanwhile we can keep Hedda company, and see what happens. Eh?

Hedda (*placing* **Brack's** *hat and overcoat upon the corner settee*): And at the worst Mr. Lövborg can remain here with me.

Brack (*offering to take his things*): Oh, allow me, Mrs. Tesman! What do you mean by "At the worst"?

Hedda: If he won't go with you and Tesman.

Tesman (*looks dubiously at her*): But, Hedda dear—do you think it would quite do for him to remain with you? Eh? Remember, Aunt Julia can't come.

Hedda: No, but Mrs. Elvsted is coming. We three can have a cup of tea together.

Tesman: Oh, yes, that will be all right.

Brack (*smiling*): And that would perhaps be the safest plan for him.

Hedda: Why so?

Brack: Well, you know, Mrs. Tesman, how you used to gird at my little bachelor parties. You declared they were adapted only for men of the strictest principles.

Hedda: But no doubt Mr. Lövborg's principles are strict enough now. A converted sinner——(**Berta** *appears at the hall door.*)

Berta: There's a gentleman asking if you are at home, ma'am——

Hedda: Well, show him in.

Tesman (*softly*): I'm sure it is he! Fancy that!

(**Eilert Lövborg** *enters from the hall. He is slim and lean; of the same age as* **Tesman**, *but looks older and somewhat worn-out. His hair and beard are of a blackish brown, his face long and pale, but with patches of color on the cheekbones. He is dressed in a well-cut black visiting suit, quite new. He has dark gloves and a silk hat. He stops near the door, and makes a rapid bow, seeming somewhat embarrassed.*)

Tesman (*goes up to him and shakes him warmly by the hand*): Well, my dear Eilert—so at last we meet again!

Lövborg (*speaks in a subdued voice*): Thanks for your letter, Tesman. (*Approaching* **Hedda**.) Will you too shake hands with me, Mrs. Tesman?

Hedda (*taking his hand*): I am glad to see you, Mr. Lövborg. (*With a motion of her hand.*) I don't know whether you two gentlemen——?

Lövborg (*bowing slightly*): Judge Brack, I think.

Brack (*doing likewise*): Oh, yes, in the old days——

Tesman (*to* **Lövborg**, *with his hands on his shoulders*): And now you must make yourself entirely at home, Eilert! Mustn't he, Hedda? For I hear you are going to settle in town again? Eh?

Lövborg: Yes, I am.

Tesman: Quite right, quite right. Let me tell you, I have got hold of your new book; but I haven't had time to read it yet.

Lövborg: You may spare yourself the trouble.

Tesman: Why so?

Lövborg: Because there is very little in it.

Tesman: Just fancy—how can you say so?

Brack: But it has been very much praised, I hear.

Lövborg: That was what I wanted; so I put nothing into the book but what every one would agree with.

Brack: Very wise of you.

Tesman: Well but, my dear Eilert——!

Lövborg: For now I mean to win myself a position again—to make a fresh start.

Tesman (*a little embarrassed*): Ah, that is what you wish to do? Eh?

Lövborg (*smiling, lays down his hat, and draws a packet, wrapped in paper, from his coat pocket*): But when this one appears, George Tesman, you will have to read it. For this is the real book—the book I have put my true self into.

Tesman: Indeed? And what is it?

Lövborg: It is the continuation.

Tesman: The continuation? Of what?

Lövborg: Of the book.

Tesman: Of the new book?

Lövborg: Of course.

Tesman: Why, my dear Eilert—does it not come down to our own days?

Lövborg: Yes, it does; and this one deals with the future.

Tesman: With the future! But, good heavens, we know nothing of the future.

Lövborg: No; but there is a thing or two to be said about it all the same. (*Opens the packet.*) Look here——

George writes about the past; Eilert the future. Significance ?

Tesman: Why, that's not your handwriting.

Lövborg: I dictated it. (*Turning over the pages.*) It falls into two sections. The first deals with the civilizing forces of the future. And here is the second—(*running through the pages towards the end*)—forecasting the probable line of development.

Tesman: How odd now! I should never have thought of writing anything of that sort.

Hedda (*at the glass door, drumming on the pane*): H'm—I daresay not.

Lövborg (*replacing the manuscript in its paper and laying the packet on the table*): I brought it, thinking I might read you a little of it this evening.

Tesman: That was very good of you, Eilert. But this evening——? (*Looking at* **Brack.**) I don't quite see how we can manage it——

Lövborg: Well then, some other time. There is no hurry.

Brack: I must tell you, Mr. Lövborg—there is a little gathering at my house this evening—mainly in honor of Tesman, you know——

Lövborg (*looking for his hat*): Oh—then I won't detain you——

Brack: No, but listen—will you not do me the favor of joining us?

Lövborg (*curtly and decidedly*): No, I can't—thank you very much.

Brack: Oh, nonsense—do! We shall be quite a select little circle. And I assure you we shall have a "lively time," as Mrs. Hed—as Mrs. Tesman says.

Lövborg: I have no doubt of it. But nevertheless——

Brack: And then you might bring your manuscript with you, and read it to Tesman at my house. I could give you a room to yourselves.

Tesman: Yes, think of that, Eilert,—why shouldn't you? Eh?

Hedda (*interposing*): But, Tesman, if Mr. Lövborg would really rather not! I am sure Mr. Lövborg is much more inclined to remain here and have supper with me.

Lövborg (*looking at her*): With you, Mrs. Tesman?

Hedda: And with Mrs. Elvsted.

Lövborg: Ah—— (*Lightly.*) I saw her for a moment this morning.

Hedda: Did you? Well, she is coming this evening. So you see you are almost bound to remain, Mr. Lövborg, or she will have no one to see her home.

Lövborg: That's true. Many thanks, Mrs. Tesman—in that case I will remain.

Hedda: Then I have one or two orders to give the servant——

(*She goes to the hall door and rings.* **Berta** *enters.* **Hedda** *talks to her in a whisper, and points toward the inner room.* **Berta** *nods and goes out again.*)

Tesman (*at the same time, to* **Lövborg**): Tell me, Eilert—is it this new subject— the future—that you are going to lecture about?

Lövborg: Yes.

Tesman: They told me at the bookseller's, that you are going to deliver a course of lectures this autumn.

Lövborg: That is my intention. I hope you won't take it ill, Tesman.

Tesman: Oh no, not in the least! But——?

Lövborg: I can quite understand that it must be de disagreeable to you.

Tesman (*cast down*): Oh, I can't expect you, out of consideration for me, to——

Lövborg: But I shall wait till you have received your appointment.

Tesman: Will you wait? Yes, but—yes, but—are you not going to compete with me? Eh?

Lövborg: No; it is only the moral victory I care for.

Tesman: Why, bless me—then Aunt Julia was right after all! Oh yes—I knew it! Hedda! Just fancy—Eilert Lövborg is not going to stand in our way!

Hedda (*curtly*): Our way? Pray leave me out of the question.

(*She goes up towards the inner room, where* **Berta** *is placing a tray with decanters and glasses on the table.* **Hedda** *nods approval, and comes forward again.* **Berta** *goes out.*)

Tesman (*at the same time*): And you, Judge Brack—what do you say to this? Eh?

Brack: Well, I say that a moral victory—h'm—may be all very fine——

Tesman: Yes, certainly. But all the same——

Hedda (*looking at* **Tesman** *with a cold smile*): You stand there looking as if you were thunderstruck——

Tesman: Yes—so I am—I almost think——

Brack: Don't you see, Mrs. Tesman, a thunderstorm has just passed over?

Hedda (*pointing towards the inner room*): Will you not take a glass of cold punch, gentlemen?

Brack (*looking at his watch*): A stirrup cup? Yes, it wouldn't come amiss.

Tesman: A capital idea, Hedda! Just the thing? Now that the weight has been taken off my mind——

Hedda: Will you not join them, Mr. Lövborg?

Lövborg (*with a gesture of refusal*): No, thank you. Nothing for me.

Brack: Why, bless me—cold punch is surely not poison.

Lövborg: Perhaps not for every one.

Hedda: I will keep Mr. Lövborg company in the meantime.

Tesman: Yes, yes, Hedda dear, do.

(*He and* **Brack** *go into the inner room, seat themselves, drink punch, smoke cigarettes, and carry on a lively conversation during what follows.* **Eilert Lövborg** *remains beside the stove.* **Hedda** *goes to the writing table.*)

Hedda (*raising her voice a little*): Do you care to look at some photographs, Mr. Lövborg? You know Tesman and I made a tour in the Tyrol on our way home?

(*She takes up an album, and places it on the table beside the sofa, in the further corner of which she seats herself.* **Eilert Lövborg** *approaches, stops, and looks at her. Then he takes a chair and seats himself at her left, with his back towards the inner room.*)

Hedda (*opening the album*): Do you see this range of mountains, Mr. Lövborg? It's the Ortler group. Tesman has written the name underneath. Here it is: "The Ortler group near Meran."

Lövborg (*who has never taken his eyes off her, says softly and slowly*): Hedda—Gabler!

Hedda (*glancing hastily at him*): Ah! Hush!

Lövborg (*repeats softly*): Hedda Gabler!

Hedda (*looking at the album*): That was my name in the old days—when we two knew each other.

Lövborg: And I must teach myself never to say Hedda Gabler again—never, as long as I live.

Hedda (*still turning over the pages*): Yes, you must. And I think you ought to practice in time. The sooner the better, I should say.

Lövborg (*in a tone of indignation*): Hedda Gabler married? And married to—George Tesman!

Hedda: Yes—so the world goes.

Lövborg: Oh, Hedda, Hedda—how could you° throw yourself away!

Hedda (*looks sharply at him*): What? I can't allow this!

Lövborg: What do you mean? (**Tesman** *comes into the room and goes toward the sofa.*)

Hedda (*hears him coming and says in an indifferent tone*): And this is a view from the Val d'Ampezzo, Mr. Lövborg. Just look at these peaks! (*Looks affectionately up at* **Tesman**.) What's the name of these curious peaks, dear?

Tesman: Let me see? Oh, those are the Dolomites.

Hedda: Yes, that's it! Those are the Dolomites, Mr. Lövborg.

Tesman: Hedda dear, I only wanted to ask whether I shouldn't bring you a little punch after all? For yourself at any rate—eh?

Hedda: Yes, do, please; and perhaps a few biscuits.

Tesman: No cigarettes?

Hedda: No.

Tesman: Very well.

(*He goes into the inner room and out to the right.* **Brack** *sits in the inner room, and keeps an eye from time to time on* **Hedda** *and* **Lövborg**.)

Lövborg (*softly, as before*): Answer me, Hedda—how could you go and do this?

Hedda (*apparently absorbed in the album*): If you continue to say *du* to me I won't talk to you.

Lövborg: May I say *du* when we are alone?

Hedda: No. You may think it; but you mustn't say it.

Lövborg: Ah, I understand. It is an offense against George Tesman, whom you°—love.

Hedda (*glances at him and smiles*): Love? What an idea!

Lövborg: You don't love him then!

Hedda: But I won't hear of any sort of unfaithfulness! Remember that.

Lövborg: Hedda—answer me one thing——

[margin note] We begin to understand their relationship. Is she now Hedda Gabler or Hedda Tesman?

you He uses the familiar *du*.

you From this point onward Lövborg uses the formal *De*.

Hedda: Hush! (**Tesman** *enters with a small tray from the inner room.*)

Tesman: Here you are! Isn't this tempting? (*He puts the tray on the table.*)

Hedda: Why do you bring it yourself?

Tesman (*filling the glasses*): Because I think it's such fun to wait upon you, Hedda.

Hedda: But you have poured out two glasses. Mr. Lövborg said he wouldn't have any——

Tesman: No, but Mrs. Elvsted will soon be here, won't she?

Hedda: Yes, by-the-bye—Mrs. Elvsted——

Tesman: Had you forgotten her? Eh?

Hedda: We were so absorbed in these photographs. (*Shows him a picture.*) Do you remember this little village?

Tesman: Oh, it's that one just below the Brenner Pass. It was there we passed the night——

Hedda: ——and met that lively party of tourists.

Tesman: Yes, that was the place. Fancy—if we could only have had you with us, Eilert! Eh? (*He returns to the inner room and sits beside* **Brack**.)

Lövborg: Answer me this one thing, Hedda——

Hedda: Well?

Lövborg: Was there no love in your friendship for me either? Not a spark—not a tinge of love in it?

Hedda: I wonder if there was? To me it seems as though we were two good comrades—two thoroughly intimate friends. (*Smilingly.*) You especially were frankness itself.

Lövborg: It was you that made me so.

Hedda: As I look back upon it all, I think there was really something beautiful, something fascinating—something daring—in—in that secret intimacy—that comradeship which no living creature so much as dreamed of.

Lövborg: Yes, yes, Hedda! Was there not? When I used to come to your father's in the afternoon—and the General sat over at the window reading his papers—with his back towards us——

Hedda: And we two on the corner sofa——

Lövborg: Always with the same illustrated paper before us——

Hedda: For want of an album, yes.

Lövborg: Yes, Hedda, and when I made my confessions to you—told you about myself, things that at that time no one else knew! There I would sit and tell you of my escapades—my days and nights of devilment. Oh, Hedda—what was the power in you that forced me to confess these things?

Hedda: Do you think it was any power in me?

Lövborg: How else can I explain it? And all those—those roundabout questions you used to put to me——

Hedda: Which you understood so particularly well——

Lövborg: How could you sit and question me like that? Question me quite frankly——

Is she manipulating Eilert as she did Thea?

Hedda: In roundabout terms, please observe.

Lövborg: Yes, but frankly nevertheless. Cross-question me about—all that sort of thing?

Hedda: And how could you answer, Mr. Lövborg?

Lövborg: Yes, that is just what I can't understand—in looking back upon it.

But tell me now, Hedda—was there not love at the bottom of our friendship? On your side, did you not feel as though you might purge my stains away if I made you my confessor? Was it not so?

Hedda: No, not quite.

Lövborg: What was your motive, then?

Hedda: Do you think it quite incomprehensible that a young girl—when it can be done—without any one knowing——

Lövborg: Well?

Hedda: ——should be glad to have a peep, now and then, into a world which——

Lövborg: Which——?

Hedda: ——which she is forbidden to know anything about?

Lövborg: So that was it?

Hedda: Partly. Partly—I almost think.

Lövborg: Comradeship in the thirst for life. But why should not that, at any rate, have continued?

Hedda: The fault was yours.

Lövborg: It was you that broke with me.

Hedda: Yes, when our friendship threatened to develop into something more serious. Shame upon you, Eilert Lövborg! How could you think of wronging your—your frank comrade?

Lövborg (*clenching his hands*): Oh, why did you not carry out your threat? Why did you not shoot me down?

Hedda: Because I have such a dread of scandal.

Lövborg: Yes, Hedda, you are a coward at heart.

Hedda: A terrible coward. (*Changing her tone.*) But it was a lucky thing for you. And now you have found ample consolation at the Elvsteds'.

Lövborg: I know what Thea has confided to you.

Hedda: And perhaps you have confided to her something about us?

Lövborg: Not a word. She is too stupid to understand anything of that sort.

Hedda: Stupid?

Lövborg: She is stupid about matters of that sort.

Hedda: And I am cowardly. (*Bends over towards him, without looking him in the face, and says more softly.*) But now I will confide something to you.

Lövborg (*eagerly*): Well?

Hedda: The fact that I dared not shoot you down——

Lövborg: Yes!

Hedda: ——that was not my most arrant cowardice—that evening.

Lövborg (*looks at her a moment, understands, and whispers passionately*): Oh, Hedda! Hedda Gabler! Now I begin to see a hidden reason beneath our comradeship! You° and I——! After all, then, it was your craving for life——

Hedda (*softly, with a sharp glance*): Take care! Believe nothing of the sort! (*Twilight has begun to fall. The hall door is opened from without by* **Berta**.)

Hedda (*closes the album with a bang and calls smilingly*): Ah, at last! My darling Thea, come along!

Cowardly, perhaps, in many ways. Why did she marry George?

In his speech he once more says *du*. Hedda addresses him throughout as *De*.

(**Mrs. Elvsted** *enters from the hall. She is in evening dress. The door is closed behind her.*)

Hedda (*on the sofa, stretches out her arms towards her*): My sweet Thea—you can't think how I have been longing for you!

(**Mrs. Elvsted**, *in passing, exchanges slight salutations with the gentlemen in the inner room, then goes up to the table and gives* **Hedda** *her hands.* **Eilert Lövborg** *has risen. He and* **Mrs. Elvsted** *greet each other with a silent nod.*)

Mrs. Elvsted: Ought I to go in and talk to your husband for a moment?

Hedda: Oh, not at all. Leave those two alone. They will soon be going.

Mrs. Elvsted: Are they going out?

Hedda: Yes, to a supper party.

Mrs. Elvsted (*quickly, to* **Lövborg**): Not you?

Lövborg: No.

Hedda: Mr. Lövborg remains with us.

Mrs. Elvsted (*takes a chair and is about to seat herself at his side*): Oh, how nice it is here!

Hedda: No, thank you, my little Thea! Not there! You'll be good enough to come over here to me. I will sit between you.

Mrs. Elvsted: Yes, just as you please.

(*She goes round the table and seats herself on the sofa on* **Hedda's** *right.* **Lövborg** *reseats himself on his chair.*)

Lövborg (*after a short pause, to* **Hedda**): Is not she lovely to look at?

Hedda (*lightly stroking her hair*): Only to look at?

Lövborg: Yes. For we two—she and I—we are two real comrades. We have absolute faith in each other; so we can sit and talk with perfect frankness——

Hedda: Not round about, Mr. Lövborg?

Lövborg: Well——

Mrs. Elvsted (*softly clinging close to* **Hedda**): Oh, how happy I am, Hedda; for, only think, he says I have inspired him too.

Hedda (*looks at her with a smile*): Ah! Does he say that, dear?

Notice play on words: coward, brave, courage

Lövborg: And then she is so brave, Mrs. Tesman!

Mrs. Elvsted: Good heavens—am I brave?

Lövborg: Exceedingly—where your comrade is concerned.

Hedda: Ah, yes—courage! If one only had that!

Lövborg: What then? What do you mean?

Hedda: Then life would perhaps be liveable, after all. (*With a sudden change of tone.*) But now, my dearest Thea, you really must have a glass of cold punch.

Mrs. Elvsted: No, thanks—I never take anything of that kind.

Hedda: Well then, you, Mr. Lövborg.

Lövborg: Nor I, thank you.

Who controls Eilert?

Mrs. Elvsted: No, he doesn't either.

Hedda (*looks fixedly at him*): But if I say you shall?

Lövborg: It would be no use.

Hedda (*laughing*): Then I, poor creature, have no sort of power over you?

Lövborg: Not in that respect.

Hedda: But seriously, I think you ought to—for your own sake.

Mrs. Elvsted: Why, Hedda——!

Lövborg: How so?

Hedda: Or rather on account of other people.

Lövborg: Indeed?

Hedda: Otherwise people might be apt to suspect that—in your heart of hearts—you did not feel quite secure—quite confident of yourself.

Mrs. Elvsted (*softly*): Oh please, Hedda——

Lövborg: People may suspect what they like—for the present.

Mrs. Elvsted (*joyfully*): Yes, let them!

Hedda: I saw it plainly in Judge Brack's face a moment ago.

Lövborg: What did you see?

Hedda: His contemptuous smile, when you dared not go with them into the inner room.

Lövborg: Dared not? Of course I preferred to stop here and talk to you.

Mrs. Elvsted: What could be more natural,, Hedda?

Hedda: But the Judge could not guess that. And I saw, too, the way he smiled and glanced at Tesman when you dared not accept his invitation to this wretched little supper party of his.

Lövborg: Dared not! Do you say I dared not?

Hedda: *I* don't say so. But that was how Judge Brack understood it.

Lövborg: Well, let him.

Hedda: Then you are not going with them?

Lövborg: I will stay here with you and Thea.

Mrs. Elvsted: Yes, Hedda—how can you doubt that?

Hedda (*smiles and nods approvingly to* **Lövborg**): Firm as a rock! Faithful to your principles, now and forever! Ah, that is how a man should be! (*Turns to* **Mrs. Elvsted** *and caresses her.*) Well now, what did I tell you, when you came to us this morning in such a state of distraction ——

Lövborg (*surprised*): Distraction!

Mrs. Elvsted (*terrified*): Hedda—oh Hedda——!

Hedda: You can see for yourself; you haven't the slightest reason to be in such mortal terror—— (*Interrupting herself.*) There! Now we can all three enjoy ourselves! *Why has she betrayed Thea?*

Lövborg (*who has given a start*): Ah—what is all this, Mrs. Tesman?

Mrs. Elvsted: Oh my God, Hedda! What are you saying? What are you doing?

Hedda: Don't get excited! That horrid Judge Brack is sitting watching you.

Lövborg: So she was in mortal terror! On my account!

Mrs. Elvsted (*softly and piteously*): Oh, Hedda—now you have ruined everything!

Lövborg (*looks fixedly at her for a moment. His face is distorted*): So that was my comrade's frank confidence in me?

Mrs. Elvsted (*imploringly*): Oh, my dearest friend—only let me tell you——

Lövborg (*takes one of the glasses of punch, raises it to his lips, and says in a low, husky voice*): Your health, Thea! *Hedda has won.*

(*He empties the glass, puts it down, and takes the second.*)

Mrs. Elvsted (*softly*): Oh, Hedda, Hedda—how could you do this?

Hedda: *I* do it? *I?* Are you crazy?

Lövborg: Here's to your health too, Mrs. Tesman. Thanks for the truth. Hurrah for the truth!

(*He empties the glass and is about to refill it.*)

Hedda (*lays her hand on his arm*): Come, come—no more for the present. Remember you are going out to supper.

Mrs. Elvsted: No, no, no!

Hedda: Hush! They are sitting watching you.

Lövborg (*putting down the glass*): Now, Thea—tell me the truth——

Mrs. Elvsted: Yes.

Lövborg: Did your husband know that you had come after me?

Mrs. Elvsted (*wringing her hands*): Oh, Hedda—do you hear what he is asking?

Lövborg: Was it arranged between you and him that you were to come to town and look after me? Perhaps it was the Sheriff himself that urged you to come? Aha, my dear—no doubt he wanted my help in his office! Or was it at the card table that he missed me?

Mrs. Elvsted (*softly, in agony*): Oh, Lövborg, Lövborg——!

Lövborg (*seizes a glass and is on the point of filling it*): Here's a glass for the old Sheriff too!

Hedda (*preventing him*): No more just now. Remember you have to read your manuscript to Tesman.

Lövborg (*calmly, putting down the glass*): It was stupid of me all this, Thea—to take it in this way, I mean. Don't be angry with me, my dear, dear comrade. You shall see—both you and the others—that if I was fallen once—now I have risen again! Thanks to you. Thea.

Mrs. Elvsted (*radiant with joy*): Oh, heaven be praised——!

(**Brack** *has in the meantime looked at his watch. He and* **Tesman** *rise and come into the drawing room.*)

Brack (*takes his hat and overcoat*): Well, Mrs. Tesman, our time has come.

Hedda: I suppose it has.

Lövborg (*rising*): Mine too, Judge Brack.

Mrs. Elvsted (*softly and imploringly*): Oh, Lövborg, don't do it!

When was she **Hedda** (*pinching her arm*): They can hear you!
violent before? **Mrs. Elvsted** (*with a suppressed shriek*): Ow!

Lövborg (*to* **Brack**): You were good enough to invite me.

Brack: Well, are you coming after all?

Lövborg: Yes, many thanks.

Brack: I'm delighted——

Lövborg (*to* **Tesman**, *putting the parcel of MS. in his pocket*): I should like to show you one or two things before I send it to the printer's.

Tesman: Fancy—that will be delightful. But, Hedda dear, how is Mrs. Elvsted to get home? Eh?

Hedda: Oh, that can be managed somehow.

Lövborg (*looking towards the ladies.*): Mrs. Elvsted? Of course, I'll come again and fetch her. (*Approaching.*) At ten or thereabouts, Mrs. Tesman? Will that do?

Hedda: Certainly. That will do capitally.

Tesman: Well, then, that's all right. But you must not expect me so early, Hedda.

Hedda: Oh, you may stop as long—as long as ever you please.

Mrs. Elvsted (*trying to conceal her anxiety*): Well then, Mr. Lövborg—I shall remain here until you come.

Lövborg (*with his hat in his hand*): Pray do, Mrs. Elvsted.

Brack: And now off goes the excursion train, gentlemen! I hope we shall have a lively time, as a certain fair lady puts it.

Hedda: Ah, if only the fair lady could be present unseen——!

Brack: Why unseen?

Hedda: In order to hear a little of your liveliness at first hand, Judge Brack.

Brack (*laughing*): I should not advise the fair lady to try it.

Tesman (*also laughing*): Come, you're a nice one, Hedda! Fancy that!

Brack: Well, good-by, ladies.

Lövborg (*bowing*): About ten o'clock, then.

(**Brack**, **Lövborg**, *and* **Tesman** *go out by the hall door. At the same time* **Berta** *enters from the inner room with a lighted lamp, which she places on the dining room table; she goes out by the way she came.*)

Mrs. Elvsted (*who has risen and is wandering restlessly about the room*): Hedda— Hedda—what will come of all this?

Hedda: At ten o'clock—he will be here. I can see him already—with vine leaves in his hair—flushed and fearless——

Mrs. Elvsted: Oh, I hope he may.

Hedda: And then, you see—then he will have regained control over himself. Then he will be a free man for all his days.

Mrs. Elvsted: Oh God!—if he would only come as you see him now!

Hedda: He will come as I see him—so, and not otherwise! (*Rises and approaches* **Thea**). You may doubt him as long as you please; I believe in him. And now we will try——

Mrs. Elvsted: You have some hidden motive in this, Hedda!

Hedda: Yes, I have. I want for once in my life to have power to mold a human destiny. *Hedda's motivation as she knows it*

Mrs. Elvsted: Have you not the power?

Hedda: I have not—and have never had it.

Mrs. Elvsted: Not your husband's?

Hedda: Do you think that is worth the trouble? Oh, if you could only understand how poor I am. And fate has made you so rich! (*Clasps her passionately in her arms.*) I think I must burn your hair off, after all.

Mrs. Elvsted: Let me go! Let me go! I am afraid of you, Hedda!

Berta (*in the middle doorway*): Tea is laid in the dining room, ma'am.

Hedda: Very well. We are coming.

Mrs. Elvsted: No, no, no! I would rather go home alone! At once!

Hedda: Nonsense! First you shall have a cup of tea, you little stupid. And then—at ten o'clock—Eilert Lövborg will be here—with vine leaves in his hair. (*She drags* **Mrs. Elvsted** *almost by force towards the middle doorway.*)

ACT III

SCENE.   *The room at the* **Tesmans'**. *The curtains are drawn over the middle doorway, and also over the glass door. The lamp, half turned down, and with a shade over it, is burning on the table. In the stove, the door of which stands open, there has been a fire, which is now nearly burnt out.*

  Mrs. Elvsted, *wrapped in a large shawl, and with her feet upon a footrest, sits close to the stove, sunk back in the armchair.* Hedda, *fully dressed, lies sleeping upon the sofa, with a sofa blanket over her.*

Mrs. Elvsted (*after a pause, suddenly sits up in her chair, and listens eagerly. Then she sinks back again wearily, moaning to herself*): Not yet!—Oh God—oh God—not yet!

(**Berta** *slips in by the hall door. She has a letter in her hand.*)

Mrs. Elvsted (*turns and whispers eagerly*): Well—has any one come?

Berta (*softly*): Yes, a girl has brought this letter.

Mrs. Elvsted (*quickly, holding out her hand*): A letter! Give it to me!

Berta: No, it's for Dr. Tesman, ma'am.

Mrs. Elvsted: Oh, indeed.

Berta: It was Miss Tesman's servant that brought it. I'll lay it here on the table.

Mrs. Elvsted: Yes, do.

Berta (*laying down the letter*): I think I had better put out the lamp. It's smoking.

Mrs. Elvsted: Yes, put it out. It must soon be daylight now.

Berta (*putting out the lamp*): It is daylight already, ma'am.

Mrs. Elvsted: Yes, broad day! And no one come back yet——!

Berta: Lord bless you, ma'am! I guessed how it would be.

Mrs. Elvsted: You guessed?

Berta: Yes, when I saw that a certain person had come back to town—and that he went off with them. For we've heard enough about that gentleman before now.

Mrs. Elvsted: Don't speak so loud. You will waken Mrs. Tesman.

Berta (*looks towards the sofa and sighs*): No, no—let her sleep, poor thing. Shan't I put some wood on the fire?

Mrs. Elvsted: Thanks, not for me.

Berta: Oh, very well. (*She goes softly out by the hall door.*)

Hedda (*is awakened by the shutting of the door, and looks up*): What's that——?

Mrs. Elvsted: It was only the servant——

Hedda (*looking about her*): Oh, we're here——! Yes, now I remember. (*Sits erect upon the sofa, stretches herself, and rubs her eyes.*) What o'clock is it, Thea?

Mrs. Elvsted (*looks at her watch*): It's past seven.

Hedda: When did Tesman come home?

Mrs. Elvsted: He has not come.

Hedda: Not come home yet?

Mrs. Elvsted (*rising*): No one has come.

Hedda: Think of our watching and waiting here till four in the morning——

Mrs. Elvsted (*wringing her hands*): And how I watched and waited for him!

Hedda (*yawns, and says with her hand before her mouth*): Well, well—we might have spared ourselves the trouble.

Mrs. Elvsted: Did you get a little sleep?

Hedda: Oh yes; I believe I have slept pretty well. Have you not?

Mrs. Elvsted: Not for a moment. I couldn't, Hedda—not to save my life.

Hedda (*rises and goes towards her*): There, there, there! There's nothing to be so alarmed about. I understand quite well what has happened.

Mrs. Elvsted: Well, what do you think? Won't you tell me?

Hedda: Why, of course it has been a very late affair at Judge Brack's——

Mrs. Elvsted: Yes, yes, that is clear enough. But all the same——

Hedda: And then, you see, Tesman hasn't cared to come home and ring us up in the middle of the night. (*Laughing.*) Perhaps he wasn't inclined to show himself either—immediately after a jollification.

Mrs. Elvsted: But in that case—where can he have gone?

Hedda: Of course he has gone to his aunts' and slept there. They have his old room ready for him.

Mrs. Elvsted: No, he can't be with them; for a letter has just come for him from Miss Tesman. There it lies.

Hedda: Indeed? (*Looks at the address.*) Why yes, it's addressed in Aunt Julia's own hand. Well then, he has remained at Judge Brack's. And as for Eilert Lövborg—he is sitting, with vine leaves in his hair, reading his manuscript.

Mrs. Elvsted: Oh Hedda, you are just saying things you don't believe a bit.

Hedda: You really are a little blockhead, Thea.

Mrs. Elvsted: Oh yes, I suppose I am.

Hedda: And how mortally tired you look.

Mrs. Elvsted: Yes, I am mortally tired.

Hedda: Well then, you must do as I tell you. You must go into my room and lie down for a little while.

Mrs. Elvsted: Oh no, no—I shouldn't be able to sleep.

Hedda: I am sure you would.

Mrs. Elvsted: Well, but your husband is certain to come soon now; and then I want to know at once——

Hedda: I shall take care to let you know when he comes.

Mrs. Elvsted: Do you promise me, Hedda?

Hedda: Yes, rely upon me. Just you go in and have a sleep in the meantime.

Mrs. Elvsted: Thanks; then I'll try to. (*She goes off through the inner room.*)

(**Hedda** *goes up to the glass door and draws back the curtains. The broad daylight streams into the room. Then she takes a little hand glass from the writing table, looks at herself in it, and arranges her hair. Next she goes to the hall door and presses the bell button.*)

(**Berta** *presently appears at the hall door.*)

Berta: Did you want anything, ma'am?

Hedda: Yes; you must put some more wood in the stove. I am shivering.

Berta: Bless me—I'll make up the fire at once. (*She rakes the embers together and lays a piece of wood upon them; then stops and listens.*) That was a ring at the front door, ma'am.

Hedda: Then go to the door. I will look after the fire.

Berta: It'll soon burn up. (*She goes out by the hall door.*)

(**Hedda** *kneels on the footrest and lays some more pieces of wood in the stove.*)

(*After a short pause,* **George Tesman** *enters from the hall. He looks tired and rather serious. He steals on tiptoe towards the middle doorway and is about to slip through the curtains.*)

Hedda (*at the stove, without looking up*): Good morning.

Tesman (*turns*): Hedda! (*Approaching her.*) Good heavens—are you up so early? Eh?

Hedda: Yes, I am up very early this morning.

Tesman: And I never doubted you were still sound asleep! Fancy that, Hedda!

Hedda: Don't speak so loud. Mrs. Elvsted is resting in my room.

Tesman: Has Mrs. Elvsted been here all night?

Hedda: Yes, since no one came to fetch her.

Tesman: Ah, to be sure.

Hedda (*closes the door of the stove and rises*): Well, did you enjoy yourself at Judge Brack's?

Tesman: Have you been anxious about me? Eh?

Hedda: No, I should never think of being anxious. But I asked if you had enjoyed yourself.

Tesman: Oh yes—for once in a way. Especially the beginning of the evening; for then Eilert read me part of his book. We arrived more than an hour too early—fancy that! And Brack had all sorts of arrangements to make—so Eilert read to me.

Hedda (*seating herself by the table on the right*): Well? Tell me, then——

Tesman (*sitting on a footstool near the stove*): Oh Hedda, you can't conceive what a book that is going to be! I believe it is one of the most remarkable things that have ever been written. Fancy that!

Hedda: Yes, yes; I don't care about that——

Tesman: I must make a confession to you, Hedda. When he had finished reading—a horrid feeling came over me.

Hedda: A horrid feeling?

Tesman: I felt jealous of Eilert for having had it in him to write such a book. Only think, Hedda!

Hedda: Yes, yes, I am thinking!

Tesman: And then how pitiful to think that he—with all his gifts—should be irreclaimable after all.

Hedda: I suppose you mean that he has more courage than the rest?

Tesman: No, not at all—I mean that he is incapable of taking his pleasures in moderation.

Hedda: And what came of it all—in the end?

Tesman: Well, to tell the truth, I think it might be best described as an orgy, Hedda.

Hedda: Had he vine leaves in his hair?

Tesman: Vine leaves? No, I saw nothing of the sort. But he made a long, rambling speech in honor of the woman who had inspired him in his work— that was the phrase he used.

Hedda: Did he name her?

Tesman: No, he didn't; but I can't help thinking he meant Mrs. Elvsted. You may be sure he did.

Hedda: Well—where did you part from him?

Tesman: On the way to town. We broke up—the last of us at any rate—all together; and Brack came with us to get a breath of fresh air. And then, you see, we agreed to take Eilert home; for he had had far more than was good for him.

Hedda: I daresay.

Tesman: But now comes the strange part of it, Hedda; or, I should rather say, the melancholy part of it. I declare I am almost ashamed—on Eilert's account —to tell you——

Hedda: Oh, go on——

Tesman: Well, as we were getting near town, you see, I happened to drop a little behind the others. Only for a minute or two—fancy that!

Hedda: Yes, yes, yes, but——?

Tesman: And then, as I hurried after them—what do you think I found by the wayside? Eh?

Hedda: Oh, how should I know!

Tesman: You mustn't speak of it to a soul, Hedda! Do you hear! Promise me, for Eilert's sake. (*Draws a parcel, wrapped in paper, from his coat pocket*). Fancy, dear—I found this.

Hedda: Is not that the parcel he had with him yesterday?

Tesman: Yes, it is the whole of his precious, irreplaceable manuscript! And he had gone and lost it, and knew nothing about it. Only fancy, Hedda! So deplorably——

Hedda: But why did you not give him back the parcel at once?

Tesman: I didn't dare to—in the state he was then in——

Hedda: Did you not tell any of the others that you had found it?

Tesman: Oh, far from it! You can surely understand that, for Eilert's sake, I wouldn't do that.

Hedda: So no one knows that Eilert Lövborg's manuscript in in your possession?

Tesman: No. And no one must know it.

Hedda: Then what did you say to him afterwards?

Tesman: I didn't talk to him again at all; for when we got in among the streets, he and two or three of the others gave us the slip and disappeared. Fancy that!

Hedda: Indeed! They must have taken him home then.

Tesman: Yes, so it would appear. And Brack, too, left us.

Hedda: And what have you been doing with yourself since?

Tesman: Well, I and some of the others went home with one of the party, a jolly fellow, and took our morning coffee with him; or perhaps I should rather call it our night coffee—eh? But now, when I have rested a little, and given Eilert, poor fellow, time to have his sleep out, I must take this back to him.

Hedda (*holds out her hand for the packet*): No—don't give it to him! Not in such a hurry, I mean. Let me read it first.

Tesman: No, my dearest Hedda, I mustn't, I really mustn't.

Hedda: You must not?

Tesman: No—for you can imagine what a state of despair he will be in when he awakens and misses the manuscript. He has no copy of it, you must know! He told me so.

Hedda (*looking searchingly at him*): Can such a thing not be reproduced? Written over again?

Tesman: No, I don't think that would be possible. For the inspiration, you see——

Hedda: Yes, yes—I suppose it depends on that. (*Lightly.*) But, by-the-bye—here is a letter for you.

Tesman: Fancy——!

Hedda (*handing it to him*): It came early this morning.

Tesman: It's from Aunt Julia! What can it be? (*He lays the packet on the other footstool, opens the letter, runs his eye through it, and jumps up.*) Oh, Hedda—she says that poor Aunt Rina is dying!

Hedda: Well, we were prepared for that.

Tesman: And that if I want to see her again, I must make haste. I'll run in to them at once.

Hedda (*suppressing a smile*): Will you run?

Tesman: Oh, dearest Hedda—if you could only make up your mind to come with me! Just think!

She refuses to see reality. Compare her view of Eilert with vine leaves in his hair.

Hedda (*rises and says wearily, repelling the idea*): No, no, don't ask me. I will not look upon sickness and death. I loathe all sorts of ugliness.

Tesman: Well, well, then——! (*Bustling around.*) My hat—my overcoat——? Oh, in the hall—I do hope I mayn't come too late, Hedda! Eh?

Hedda: Oh, if you run——

(**Berta** *appears at the hall door.*)

Berta: Judge Brack is at the door, and wishes to know if he may come in.

Tesman: At this time! No, I can't possibly see him.

Hedda: But I can. (*To* **Berta**.) Ask Judge Brack to come in. (**Berta** *goes out.*)

Hedda (*quickly whispering*): The parcel, Tesman! (*She snatches it up from the stool.*)

Tesman: Yes, give it to me!

Hedda: No, no, I will keep it till you come back.

(*She goes to the writing table and places it in the bookcase.* **Tesman** *stands in a flurry of haste, and cannot get his gloves on.*)

(**Judge Brack** *enters from the hall.*)

Hedda (*nodding to him*): You are an early bird, I must say.

Brack: Yes, don't you think so? (*To* **Tesman**.) Are you on the move, too?

Tesman: Yes, I must rush off to my aunts'. Fancy—the invalid one is lying at death's door, poor creature.

Brack: Dear me, is she indeed? Then on no account let me detain you. At such a critical moment——

Tesman: Yes, I must really rush——Good-by! Good-by! (*He hastens out by the hall door.*)

Hedda (*approaching*): You seem to have made a particularly lively night of it at your rooms, Judge Brack.

Brack: I assure you I have not had my clothes off, Mrs. Hedda.

Hedda: Not you, either?

Brack: No, as you may see. But what has Tesman been telling you of the night's adventures?

Hedda: Oh, some tiresome story. Only that they went and had coffee somewhere or other.

Brack: I have heard about that coffee-party already. Eilert Lövborg was not with them, I fancy?

Hedda: No, they had taken him home before that.

Brack: Tesman, too?

Hedda: No, but some of the others, he said.

Brack (*smiling*): George Tesman is really an ingenuous creature, Mrs. Hedda.

Hedda: Yes, heaven knows he is. Then is there something behind all this?

Brack: Yes, perhaps there may be.

Hedda: Well then, sit down, my dear Judge, and tell your story in comfort.

(*She seats herself to the left of the table.* **Brack** *sits near her, at the long side of the table.*)

Hedda: Now then?

Brack: I had special reasons for keeping track of my guests—or rather of some of my guests—last night.

Hedda: Of Eilert Lövborg among the rest, perhaps?

Brack: Frankly, yes.

Hedda: Now you make me really curious——

Brack: Do you know where he and one or two of the others finished the night, Mrs. Hedda?

Hedda: If it is not quite unmentionable, tell me.

Brack: Oh no, it's not at all unmentionable. Well, they put in an appearance at a particularly animated soirée.

Hedda: Of the lively kind?

Brack: Of the very liveliest——

Hedda: Tell me more of this, Judge Brack——

Brack: Lövborg, as well as the others, had been invited in advance. I knew all about it. But he had declined the invitation; for now, as you know, he has become a new man.

Hedda: Up at the Elvsteds', yes. But he went after all, then?

Brack: Well, you see, Mrs. Hedda—unhappily the spirit moved him at my rooms last evening——

Hedda: Yes, I hear he found inspiration.

Brack: Pretty violent inspiration. Well, I fancy that altered his purpose; for we men folk are unfortunately not always so firm in our principles as we ought to be.

Hedda: Oh, I am sure you are an exception, Judge Brack. But as to Lövborg——?

Brack: To make a long story short—he landed at last in Mademoiselle Diana's rooms.

Hedda: Mademoiselle Diana's?

Brack: It was Mademoiselle Diana that was giving the soirée, to a select circle of her admirers and her lady friends.

Hedda: Is she a red-haired woman?

Brack: Precisely.

Hedda: A sort of a—singer?

Brack: Oh yes—in her leisure moments. And moreover a mighty huntress—of men—Mrs. Hedda. You have no doubt heard of her. Eilert Lövborg was one of her most enthusiastic protectors—in the days of his glory.

Hedda: And how did all this end?

Brack: Far from amicably, it appears. After a most tender meeting, they seem to have come to blows——

Hedda: Lövborg and she?

Brack: Yes. He accused her or her friends of having robbed him. He declared that his pocketbook had disappeared—and other things as well. In short, he seems to have made a furious disturbance.

Hedda: And what came of it all?

Brack: It came to a general scrimmage, in which the ladies as well as the gentlemen took part. Fortunately the police at last appeared on the scene.

Hedda: The police too?

Brack: Yes. I fancy it will prove a costly frolic for Eilert Lövborg, crazy being that he is.

Hedda: How so?

Brack: He seems to have made a violent resistance—to have hit one of the constables on the head and torn the coat off his back. So they had to march him off to the police station with the rest.

Hedda: How have you learnt all this?

Brack: From the police themselves.

Hedda (*gazing straight before her*): So that is what happened. Then he had no vine leaves in his hair.

Brack: Vine leaves, Mrs. Hedda?

Hedda (*changing her tone*): But tell me now, Judge—what is your real reason for tracking out Eilert Lövborg's movements so carefully?

Brack: In the first place, it could not be entirely indifferent to me if it should appear in the police court that he came straight from my house.

Hedda: Will the matter come into court, then?

Brack: Of course. However, I should scarcely have troubled so much about that. But I thought that, as a friend of the family, it was my duty to supply you and Tesman with a full account of his nocturnal exploits.

Hedda: Why so, Judge Brack?

Brack: Why, because I have a shrewd suspicion that he intends to use you as a sort of blind.

Hedda: Oh, how can you think such a thing!

Brack: Good heavens, Mrs. Hedda—we have eyes in our head. Mark my words! This Mrs. Elvsted will be in no hurry to leave town again.

Hedda: Well, even if there should be anything between them, I suppose there are plenty of other places where they could meet.

Brack: Not a single home. Henceforth, as before, every respectable house will be closed against Eilert Lövborg.

Hedda: And so ought mine to be, you mean?

Brack: Yes. I confess it would be more than painful to me if this personage were to be made free of your house. How superfluous, how intrusive, he would be, if he were to force his way into——

Hedda: ——into the triangle?

Brack: Precisely. It would simply mean that I should find myself homeless.

Hedda (*looks at him with a smile*): So you want to be the one cock in the basket—that is your aim.

Brack (*nods slowly and lowers his voice*): Yes, that is my aim. And for that I will fight—with every weapon I can command.

Hedda (*her smile vanishing*): I see you are a dangerous person—when it comes to the point.

Brack: Do you think so?

How does she feel about control? **Hedda:** I am beginning to think so. And I am exceedingly glad to think—that you have no sort of hold over me.

Brack (*laughing equivocally*): Well, well, Mrs. Hedda—perhaps you are right there. If I had, who knows what I might be capable of?

Hedda: Come, come now, Judge Brack. That sounds almost like a threat.

Brack (*rising*): Oh, not at all! The triangle, you know, ought, if possible, to be spontaneously constructed.

Hedda: There I agree with you.

Brack: Well, now I have said all I had to say; and I had better be getting back to town. Good-by, Mrs. Hedda. (*He goes towards the glass door.*)

Hedda (*rising*): Are you going through the garden?

Brack: Yes, it's a short cut for me.

Hedda: And then it is the back way, too.

Brack: Quite so. I have no objection to back ways. They may be piquant enough at times.

Hedda: When there is ball practice going on, you mean?

Brack (*in the doorway, laughing to her*): Oh, people don't shoot their tame poultry, I fancy.

Hedda (*also laughing*): Oh no, when there is only one cock in the basket——

(*They exchange laughing nods of farewell. He goes. She closes the door behind him.*

(**Hedda,** *who has become quite serious, stands for a moment looking out. Presently she goes and peeps through the curtain over the middle doorway. Then she goes to the writing table, takes* **Lövborg's** *packet out of the bookcase, and is on the point of looking through its contents.* **Berta** *is heard speaking loudly in the hall.* **Hedda** *turns and listens. Then she hastily locks up the packet in the drawer, and lays the key on the inkstand.*

(**Eilert Lövborg**, *with his great coat on and his hat in his hand, tears open the hall door. He looks somewhat confused and irritated.*)

Lövborg (*looking towards the hall*): And I tell you I must and will come in! There! (*He closes the door, turns and sees* **Hedda**, *at once regains his self-control, and bows.*)

Hedda (*at the writing table*): Well, Mr. Lövborg, this is rather a late hour to call for Thea.

Lövborg: You mean rather an early hour to call on you. Pray pardon me.

Hedda: How do you know that she is still here?

Lövborg: They told me at her lodgings that she had been out all night.

Hedda (*going to the oval table*): Did you notice anything about the people of the house when they said that?

Lövborg (*looks inquiringly at her*): Notice anything about them?

Hedda: I mean, did they seem to think it odd?

Lövborg (*suddenly understanding*): Oh yes, of course! I am dragging her down with me! However, I didn't notice anything.—I suppose Tesman is not up yet?

Hedda: No—I think not—— *Why does she lie?*

Lövborg: When did he come home?

Hedda: Very late.

Lövborg: Did he tell you anything?

Hedda: Yes, I gathered that you had had an exceedingly jolly evening at Judge Brack's.

Lövborg: Nothing more?

Hedda: I don't think so. However, I was so dreadfully sleepy——

(**Mrs. Elvsted** *enters through the curtains of the middle doorway.*)

Mrs. Elvsted (*going towards him*): Ah, Lövborg! At last——!

Lövborg: Yes, at last. And too late!

Mrs. Elvsted (*looks anxiously at him*): What is too late?

Lövborg: Everything is too late now. It is all over with me.

Mrs. Elvsted: Oh no, no—don't say that!

Lövborg: You will say the same when you hear——

Mrs. Elvsted: I won't hear anything!

Hedda: Perhaps you would prefer to talk to her alone! If so, I will leave you.

Lövborg: No, stay—you too. I beg you to stay.

Mrs. Elvsted: Yes, but I won't hear anything, I tell you.

Lövborg: It is not last night's adventures that I want to talk about.

Mrs. Elvsted: What is it then——?

Lövborg: I want to say that now our ways must part.

Mrs. Elvsted: Part!

Hedda (*involuntarily*): I knew it!

Lövborg: You can be of no more service to me, Thea.

Mrs. Elvsted: How can you stand there and say that! No more service to you! Am I not to help you now, as before? Are we not to go on working together?

Lövborg: Henceforward I shall do no work.

Mrs. Elvsted (*despairingly*): Then what am I to do with my life?

Lövborg: You must try to live your life as if you had never known me.

Mrs. Elvsted: But you know I cannot do that!

Lövborg: Try if you cannot, Thea. You must go home again——

Mrs. Elvsted (*in vehement protest*): Never in this world! Where you are, there will I be also! I will not let myself be driven away like this! I will remain here! I will be with you when the book appears.

Hedda (*half aloud, in suspense*): Ah yes—the book!

Lövborg (*looks at her*): My book and Thea's; for that is what it is.

Mrs. Elvsted: Yes, I feel that it is. And that is why I have a right to be with you when it appears! I will see with my own eyes how respect and honor pour in upon you afresh. And the happiness—the happiness—oh, I must share it with you!

Lövborg: Thea—our book will never appear.

Hedda: Ah!

Mrs. Elvsted: Never appear!

Lövborg: Can never appear.

Mrs. Elvsted (*in agonized foreboding*): Lövborg—what have you done with the manuscript?

Hedda (*looks anxiously at him*): Yes, the manuscript——?

Mrs. Elvsted: Where is it?

Lövborg: Oh Thea—don't ask me about it!

Mrs. Elvsted: Yes, yes, I will know. I demand to be told at once.

Lövborg: The manuscript—Well then—I have torn the manuscript into a thousand pieces.

Mrs. Elvsted (*shrieks*): Oh no, no——!

Hedda (*involuntarily*): But that's not——

Lövborg (*looks at her*): Not true, you think?

Why does she conceal the manuscript? **Hedda** (*collecting herself*): Oh well, of course—since you say so. But it sounded so improbable——

Lövborg: It is true, all the same.

Mrs. Elvsted (*wringing her hands*): Oh God—oh God, Hedda—torn his own work to pieces!

Lövborg: I have torn my own life to pieces. So why should I not tear my life-work too——?

Mrs. Elvsted: And you did this last night?

Lövborg: Yes, I tell you! Tore it into a thousand pieces and scattered them on the fiord—far out. There there is cool sea water at any rate—let them drift upon it—drift with the current and the wind. And then presently they will sink—deeper and deeper—as I shall, Thea.

Mrs. Elvsted: Do you know, Lövborg, that what you have done with the book —I shall think of it to my dying day as though you had killed a little child.

Lövborg: Yes, you are right. It is a sort of child murder.

Mrs. Elvsted: How could you, then——! Did not the child belong to me too?

Hedda (*almost inaudibly*): Ah, the child——

Mrs. Elvsted (*breathing heavily*): It is all over then. Well, well, now I will go, Hedda.

Hedda: But you are not going away from town?

Mrs. Elvsted: Oh, I don't know what I shall do. I see nothing but darkness before me. (*She goes out by the hall door.*)

Hedda (*stands waiting for a moment*): So you are not going to see her home, Mr. Lövborg?

Lövborg: I? Through the streets? Would you have people see her walking with me?

Hedda: Of course I don't know what else may have happened last night. But is it so utterly irretrievable?

Lövborg: It will not end with last night—I know that perfectly well. And the thing is that now I have no taste for that sort of life either. I won't begin it anew. She has broken my courage and my power of braving life out.

Hedda (*looking straight before her*): So that pretty little fool has had her fingers in a man's destiny. (*Looks at him.*) But all the same, how could you treat her so heartlessly?

She did what Hedda has never been able to do.

Lövborg: Oh, don't say that it was heartless!

Hedda: To go and destroy what has filled her whole soul for months and years! You do not call that heartless!

Lövborg: To you I can tell the truth, Hedda.

Hedda: The truth?

Lövborg: First promise me—give me your word—that what I now confide to you Thea shall never know.

Hedda: I give you my word.

Lövborg: Good. Then let me tell you that what I said just now was untrue.

Hedda: About the manuscript?

Lövborg: Yes. I have not torn it to pieces—nor thrown it into the fiord.

Hedda: No, n—But—where is it then!

Lövborg: I have destroyed it none the less—utterly destroyed it, Hedda!

Hedda: I don't understand.

Lövborg: Thea said that what I had done seemed to her like a child murder.

Hedda: Yes, so she said.

Lövborg: But to kill his child—that is not the worst thing a father can do to it.

Hedda: Not the worst?

Lövborg: No. I wanted to spare Thea from hearing the worst.

Hedda: Then what is the worst?

Lövborg: Suppose now, Hedda, that a man—in the small hours of the morning—came home to his child's mother after a night of riot and debauchery, and said: "Listen—I have been here and there—in this place and in that. And I have taken our child with me—to this place and to that. And I have lost the child—utterly lost it. The devil knows into what hands it may have fallen—who may have had their clutches on it."

Hedda: Well—but when all is said and done, you know—that was only a book—

Lövborg: Thea's pure soul was in that book.

Hedda: Yes, so I understand.

Lövborg: And you can understand, too, that for her and me together no future is possible.

Hedda: What path do you mean to take then?

"To mold a human destiny"

Lövborg: None. I will only try to make an end of it all—the sooner the better.

Hedda (*a step nearer to him*): Eilert Lövborg—listen to me. Will you not try to—to do it beautifully?

Lövborg: Beautifully? (*Smiling.*) With vine leaves in my hair, as you used to dream in the old days——?

Hedda: No, no. I have lost my faith in the vine leaves. But beautifully, nevertheless! For once in a way!—Good-by! You must go now—and do not come here any more.

Lövborg: Good-by, Mrs. Tesman. And give George Tesman my love. (*He is on the point of going.*)

Hedda: No, wait! I must give you a memento to take with you.

(*She goes to the writing table and opens the drawer and the pistol case; then returns to* **Lövborg** *with one of the pistols.*)

Lövborg: Good-by, Hedda Gabler. (*He goes out by the hall door.*)

Hedda (*nodding slowly*): Do you recognize it? It was aimed at you once.

Lövborg: You should have used it then.

Hedda: Take it—and do you use it now.

Lövborg (*puts the pistol in his breast pocket*): Thanks!

Hedda: And beautifully, Eilert Lövborg. Promise me that!

Lövborg: Good-by, Hedda Gabler. (*He goes out by the hall door.*)

(**Hedda** *listens for a moment at the door. Then she goes up to the writing table, takes out the packet of manuscript, peeps under the cover, draws a few of the sheets half out, and looks at them. Next she goes over and seats herself in the armchair beside the stove, with the packet in her lap. Presently she opens the stove door, and then the packet.*)

Violence, power, pregnancy, envy, death. Do it beautifully.

Hedda (*throws one of the quires into the fire and whispers to herself*): Now I am burning your child, Thea!—Burning it, curlylocks! (*Throwing one or two more quires into the stove.*) Your child and Eilert Lövborg's. (*Throws the rest in.*) I am burning—I am burning your child.

ACT IV

SCENE.   *The same rooms at the* **Tesmans'**. *It is evening. The drawing room is in darkness. The back room is lighted by the hanging lamp over the table. The curtains over the glass door are drawn close.*

What details suggest Hedda is nervous and uneasy?

Hedda, *dressed in black, walks to and fro in the dark room. Then she goes into the back room and disappears, for a moment to the left. She is heard to strike a few chords on the piano. Presently she comes in sight again, and returns to the drawing room.*

Berta *enters from the right, through the inner room, with a lighted lamp, which she places on the table in front of the corner settee in the drawing room. Her eyes are red with weeping, and she has black ribbons in her cap. She goes quietly and circumspectly out to the right.*

Hedda, *goes up to the glass door, lifts the curtain a little aside, and looks out into the darkness.*

Shortly afterwards, **Miss Tesman**, *in mourning, with a bonnet and veil on, comes in from the hall.* **Hedda** *goes towards her and holds out her hand.*

Miss Tesman: Yes, Hedda, here I am, in mourning and forlorn; for now my poor sister has at last found peace.

Hedda: I have heard the news already, as you see. Tesman sent me a card.

Miss Tesman: Yes, he promised me he would. But nevertheless I thought that to Hedda—here in the house of life—I ought myself to bring the tidings of death.

Hedda: That was very kind of you.

Miss Tesman: Ah, Rina ought not to have left us just now. This is not the time for Hedda's house to be a house of mourning.

Hedda (*changing the subject*): She died quite peacefully, did she not, Miss Tesman?

Miss Tesman: Oh, her end was so calm, so beautiful. And then she had the unspeakable happiness of seeing George once more—and bidding him good-by. Has he come home yet?

Hedda: No. He wrote that he might be detained. But won't you sit down?

Miss Tesman: No thank you, my dear, dear Hedda. I should like to, but I have so much to do. I must prepare my dear one for her rest as well as I can. She shall go to her grave looking her best.

Hedda: Can I not help you in any way?

Miss Tesman: Oh, you must not think of it! Hedda Tesman must have no hand in such mournful work. Nor let her thoughts dwell on it either—not at this time.

Hedda: One is not always mistress of one's thoughts——

Miss Tesman (*continuing*): Ah yes, it is the way of the world. At home we shall be sewing a shroud; and here there will soon be sewing too, I suppose—but of another sort, thank God!

(**George Tesman** *enters by the hall door.*)

Hedda: Ah, you have come at last!

Tesman: You here, Aunt Julia? With Hedda? Fancy that!

Miss Tesman: I was just going, my dear boy. Well, have you done all you promised?

Tesman: No; I'm really afraid I have forgotten half of it. I must come to you again tomorrow. Today my brain is all in a whirl. I can't keep my thoughts together.

Miss Tesman: Why, my dear George, you mustn't take it in this way.

Tesman: Mustn't——? How do you mean?

Miss Tesman: Even in your sorrow you must rejoice, as I do—rejoice that she is at rest.

Tesman: Oh yes, yes—you are thinking of Aunt Rina.

Hedda: You will feel lonely now, Miss Tesman.

Miss Tesman: Just at first, yes. But that will not last very long, I hope. I daresay I shall soon find an occupant for poor Rina's little room.

Tesman: Indeed? Who do you think will take it? Eh?

Miss Tesman: Oh, there's always some poor invalid or other in want of nursing, unfortunately.

Hedda: Would you really take such a burden upon you again?

Miss Tesman: A burden! Heaven forgive you, child—it has been no burden to me.

Hedda: But suppose you had a total stranger on your hands——

Is this true of Hedda ?

Miss Tesman: Oh, one soon makes friends with sick folk; and it's such an absolute necessity for me to have some one to live for. Well, heaven be praised, there may soon be something in this house, too, to keep an old aunt busy.

Hedda: Oh, don't trouble about anything here.

Tesman: Yes, just fancy what a nice time we three might have together, if——?

Hedda: If——?

Tesman (*uneasily*): Oh, nothing. It will all come right. Let us hope so—eh?

Miss Tesman: Well, well, I daresay you two want to talk to each other. (*Smiling.*) And perhaps Hedda may have something to tell you too, George. Good-by! I must go home to Rina. (*Turning at the door.*) How strange it is to think that now Rina is with me and with my poor brother as well!

Tesman: Yes, fancy that, Aunt Julia! Eh?

(**Miss Tesman** *goes out by the hall door.*)

Hedda (*follows* **Tesman** *coldly and searchingly with her eyes*): I almost believe your Aunt Rina's death affects you more than it does your Aunt Julia.

Tesman: Oh, it's not that alone. It's Eilert I am so terribly uneasy about.

Hedda (*quickly*): Is there anything new about him?

Tesman: I looked in at his rooms this afternoon, intending to tell him the manuscript was in safe keeping.

Hedda: Well, did you not find him?

Tesman: No. He wasn't at home. But afterwards I met Mrs. Elvsted, and she told me that he had been here early this morning.

Hedda: Yes, directly after you had gone.

Tesman: And he said that he had torn his manuscript to pieces—eh?

Hedda: Yes, so he declared.

Tesman: Why, good heavens, he must have been completely out of his mind! And I suppose you thought it best not to give it back to him, Hedda?

Hedda: No, he did not get it.

Tesman: But of course you told him that we had it?

Hedda: No. (*Quickly.*) Did you tell Mrs. Elvsted?

Tesman: No, I thought I had better not. But you ought to have told him. Fancy, if, in desperation, he should go and do himself some injury! Let me have the manuscript, Hedda! I will take it to him at once. Where is it?

Hedda (*cold and immovable, leaning on the armchair*): I have not got it.

Tesman: Have not got it? What in the world do you mean?

Hedda: I have burnt it—every line of it.

Tesman (*with a violent movement of terror*): Burnt! Burnt Eilert's manuscript!

Hedda: Don't scream so. The servant might hear you.

Tesman: Burnt! Why, good God——! No, no, no! It's impossible!

Hedda: It is so, nevertheless.

Tesman: Do you know what you have done, Hedda? It's unlawful appropriation of lost property. Fancy that! Just ask Judge Brack, and he'll tell you what it is.

Hedda: I advise you not to speak of it—either to Judge Brack, or to any one else.

Tesman: But how could you do anything so unheard-of? What put it into your head? What possessed you? Answer me that—eh?

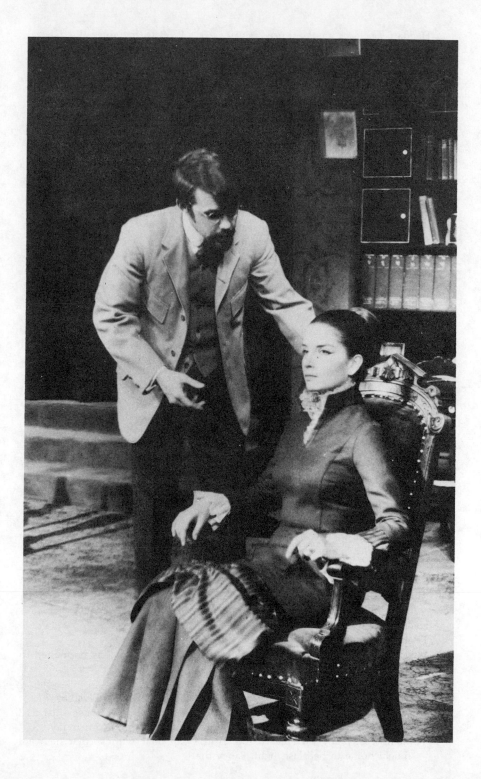

Hedda (*suppressing an almost imperceptible smile*): I did it for your sake, George.

Tesman: For my sake!

Hedda: This morning, when you told me about what he had read to you——

Tesman: Yes, yes—what then?

Hedda: You acknowledged that you envied him his work.

Tesman: Oh, of course I didn't mean that literally.

Hedda: No matter—I could not bear the idea that any one should throw you into the shade.

Tesman (*in an outburst of mingled doubt and joy*): Hedda! Oh, is this true? But—but—I never knew you to show your love like that before. Fancy that!

Hedda: Well, I may as well tell you that—just at this time——(*Impatiently, breaking off.*) No, no; you can ask Aunt Julia. She will tell you, fast enough.

Tesman: Oh, I almost think I understand you, Hedda! (*Clasps his hands together.*) Great heavens! do you really mean it! Eh?

Hedda: Don't shout so. The servant might hear.

Tesman (*laughing in irrepressible glee*): The servant! Why, how absurd you are, Hedda. It's only my old Berta! Why, I'll tell Berta myself.

Hedda (*clenching her hands together in desperation*): Oh, it is killing me—it is killing me, all this!

Tesman: What is, Hedda? Eh?

Hedda (*coldly, controlling herself*): All this—absurdity—George.

Tesman: Absurdity! Do you see anything absurd in my being overjoyed at the news! But after all perhaps I had better not say anything to Berta.

Hedda: Oh—why not that too?

Tesman: No, no, not yet! But I must certainly tell Aunt Julia. And then that you have begun to call me George too! Fancy that! Oh, Aunt Julia will be so happy—so happy.

Hedda: When she hears that I have burnt Eilert Lövborg's manuscript—for your sake?

Tesman: No, by-the-bye—that affair of the manuscript—of course nobody must know about that. But that you love me so much, Hedda—Aunt Julia must really share my joy in that! I wonder, now, whether this sort of thing is usual in young wives? Eh?

Hedda: I think you had better ask Aunt Julia that question too.

Tesman: I will indeed, some time or other. (*Looks uneasy and downcast again.*) And yet the manuscript—the manuscript! Good God! It is terrible to think what will become of poor Eilert now.

(**Mrs. Elvsted**, *dressed as in the first Act, with hat and cloak, enters by the hall door.*)

Mrs. Elvsted (*greets them hurriedly, and says in evident agitation*): Oh, dear Hedda, forgive my coming again.

Hedda: What is the matter with you, Thea?

Tesman: Something about Eilert Lövborg again—eh?

Mrs. Elvsted: Yes! I am dreadfully afraid some misfortune has happened to him.

Hedda (*seizes her arm*): Ah, do you think so?

Tesman: Why, good Lord—what makes you think that, Mrs. Elvsted?

Mrs. Elvsted: I heard them talking of him at my boarding house—just as I came in. Oh, the most incredible rumors are afloat about him today.

Tesman: Yes, fancy, so I heard too! And I can bear witness that he went straight home to bed last night. Fancy that!

Hedda: Well, what did they say at the boarding house?

Mrs. Elvsted: Oh, I couldn't make out anything clearly. Either they knew nothing definite, or else—— They stopped talking when they saw me; and I did not dare to ask.

Tesman (*moving about uneasily*): We must hope—we must hope that you misunderstood them, Mrs. Elvsted.

Mrs. Elvsted: No, no; I am sure it was of him they were talking. And I heard something about the hospital or——

Tesman: The hospital?

Hedda: No—surely that cannot be!

Mrs. Elvsted: Oh, I was in such mortal terror! I went to his lodgings and asked for him there.

Hedda: You could make up your mind to that, Thea!

Mrs. Elvsted: What else could I do? I really could bear the suspense no longer.

Tesman: But you didn't find him either—eh?

Mrs. Elvsted: No. And the people knew nothing about him. He hadn't been home since yesterday afternoon, they said.

Tesman: Yesterday! Fancy, how could they say that?

Mrs. Elvsted: Oh, I am sure something terrible must have happened to him.

Tesman: Hedda dear—how would it be if I were to go and make inquiries——?

Hedda: No, no—don't you mix yourself up in this affair.

(**Judge Brack**, *with his hat in his hand, enters by the hall door, which* **Berta** *opens, and closes behind him. He looks grave and bows in silence.*)

Tesman: Oh, is that you, my dear Judge? Eh?

Brack: Yes. It was imperative I should see you this evening.

Tesman: I can see you have heard the news about Aunt Rina.

Brack: Yes, that among other things.

Tesman: Isn't it sad—eh?

Brack: Well, my dear Tesman, that depends on how you look at it.

Tesman (*looks doubtfully at him*): Has anything else happened?

Brack: Yes.

Hedda (*in suspense*): Anything sad, Judge Brack?

Brack: That, too, depends on how you look at it, Mrs. Tesman.

Mrs. Elvsted (*unable to restrain her anxiety*): Oh! it is something about Eilert Lövborg!

Brack (*with a glance at her*): What makes you think that, Madam? Perhaps you have already heard something——?

Mrs. Elvsted (*in confusion*): No, nothing at all, but——

Tesman: Oh, for heaven's sake, tell us!

Brack (*shrugging his shoulders*): Well, I regret to say Eilert Lövborg has been taken to the hospital. He is lying at the point of death.

Mrs. Elvsted (*shrieks*): Oh God! Oh God——

Tesman: To the hospital! And at the point of death.

Hedda (*involuntarily*): So soon then——

Mrs. Elvsted (*wailing*): And we parted in anger, Hedda!

Hedda (*whispers*): Thea—Thea—be careful!

Mrs. Elvsted (*not heeding her*): I must go to him! I must see him alive!

Brack: It is useless, Madam. No one will be admitted.

Mrs. Elvsted: Oh, at least tell me what has happened to him? What is it?

Tesman: You don't mean to say that he has himself—— Eh?

How would she say this line?

Her wish is fulfilled. **Hedda:** Yes, I am sure he has.

Tesman: Hedda, how can you——?

Brack (*keeping his eyes fixed upon her*): Unfortunately you have guessed quite correctly, Mrs. Tesman.

Mrs. Elvsted: Oh, how horrible!

Tesman: Himself, then! Fancy that!

Hedda: Shot himself!

Brack: Rightly guessed again, Mrs. Tesman.

Mrs. Elvsted (*with an effort at self-control*): When did it happen, Mr. Brack?

Brack: This afternoon—between three and four.

Tesman: But, good Lord, where did he do it? Eh?

Brack (*with some hesitation*): Where? Well—I suppose at his lodgings.

Mrs. Elvsted: No, that cannot be; for I was there between six and seven.

Brack: Well, then, somewhere else. I don't know exactly. I only know that he was found——. He had shot himself—in the breast!

Mrs. Elvsted: Oh, how terrible! That he should die like that!

Hedda (*to Brack*): Was it in the breast?

Brack: Yes—as I told you.

Hedda: Not in the temple?

Brack: In the breast, Mrs. Tesman.

Hedda: Well, well—the breast is a good place, too.

Brack: How do you mean, Mrs. Tesman?

Hedda (*evasively*): Oh, nothing—nothing.

Tesman: And the wound is dangerous, you say—eh?

Brack: Absolutely mortal. The end has probably come by this time.

Mrs. Elvsted: Yes, yes, I feel it. The end! The end! Oh, Hedda——!

Tesman: But tell me, how have you learnt all this?

Brack (*curtly*): Through one of the police. A man I had some business with.

Hedda (*in a clear voice*): At least a deed worth doing!

Tesman (*terrified*): Good heavens, Hedda! what are you saying?

Hedda: I say there is beauty in this.

Brack: H'm, Mrs. Tesman——

Tesman: Beauty! Fancy that!

Mrs. Elvsted: Oh, Hedda, how can you talk of beauty in such an act!

She thinks she's responsible for Eilert's beautiful suicide. **Hedda:** Eilert Lövborg has himself made up his account with life. He has had the courage to do—the one right thing.

Mrs. Elvsted: No, you must never think that was how it happened! It must have been in delirium that he did it.

Tesman: In despair!

Hedda: That he did not. I am certain of that.

Mrs. Elvsted: Yes, yes! In delirium! Just as when he tore up our manuscript.

Brack (*starting*): The manuscript? Has he torn that up?

Mrs. Elvsted: Yes, last night.

Tesman (*whispers softly*): Oh, Hedda, we shall never get over this.

Brack: H'm, very extraordinary.

Tesman (*moving about the room*): To think of Eilert going out of the world in this way! And not leaving behind him the book that would have immortalized his name——

Mrs. Elvsted: Oh, if only it could be put together again!

Tesman: Yes, if it only could! I don't know what I would not give——

Mrs. Elvsted: Perhaps it can, Mr. Tesman.

Tesman: What do you mean?

Mrs. Elvsted (*searches in the pocket of her dress*): Look here. I have kept all the loose notes he used to dictate from.

Hedda (*a step forward*): Ah——!

Tesman: You have kept them, Mrs. Elvsted! Eh?

Mrs. Elvsted: Yes I have them here. I put them in my pocket when I left home. Here they still are——

Tesman: Oh, do let me see them!

Mrs. Elvsted (*hands him a bundle of papers*): But they are in such disorder—all mixed up.

Tesman: Fancy, if we could make something out of them, after all! Perhaps if we two put our heads together——

Mrs. Elvsted: Oh, yes, at least let us try——

Tesman: We will manage it! We must! I will dedicate my life to this task.

Hedda: You, George? Your life?

Tesman: Yes, or rather all the time I can spare. My own collections must wait in the meantime. Hedda—you understand, eh? I owe this to Eilert's memory.

Hedda: Perhaps.

Tesman: And so, my dear Mrs. Elvsted, we will give our whole minds to it. There is no use in brooding over what can't be undone—eh? We must try to control our grief as much as possible, and——

Mrs. Elvsted: Yes, yes, Mr. Tesman, I will do the best I can.

Tesman: Well then, come here. I can't rest until we have looked through the notes. Where shall we sit? Here? No, in there, in the back room. Excuse me, my dear Judge. Come with me, Mrs. Elvsted.

Mrs. Elvsted: Oh, if only it were possible!

(**Tesman** and **Mrs. Elvsted** *go into the back room. She takes off her hat and cloak. They both sit at the table under the hanging lamp, and are soon deep in an eager examination of the papers.* **Hedda** *crosses to the stove and sits in the armchair. Presently* **Brack** *goes up to her.*)

Hedda (*in a low voice*): Oh, what a sense of freedom it gives one, this act of Eilert Lövborg's.

She no longer needs to control.

Brack: Freedom, Mrs. Hedda? Well, of course, it is a release for him——

Hedda: I mean for me. It gives me a sense of freedom to know that a deed of deliberate courage is still possible in this world—a deed of spontaneous beauty.

Brack (*smiling*): H'm—my dear Mrs. Hedda——

Hedda: Oh, I know what you are going to say. For you are a kind of a specialist too, like—you know!

Brack (*looking hard at her*): Eilert Lövborg was more to you than perhaps you are willing to admit to yourself. Am I wrong?

Hedda: I don't answer such questions. I only know Eilert Lövborg has had the courage to live his life after his own fashion. And then—the last great act, with its beauty! Ah! that he should have the will and the strength to turn away from the banquet of life—so early.

Brack: I am sorry, Mrs. Hedda—but I fear I must dispel an amiable illusion.

Hedda: Illusion?

Brack: Which could not have lasted long in any case.

Hedda: What do you mean?

Brack: Eilert Lövborg did not shoot himself voluntarily.

Hedda: Not voluntarily?

Brack: No. The thing did not happen exactly as I told it.

Hedda (*in suspense*): Have you concealed something? What is it?

Brack: For poor Mrs. Elvsted's sake I idealized the facts a little.

Hedda: What are the facts?

Brack: First, that he is already dead.

Hedda: At the hospital?

Brack: Yes—without regaining consciousness.

Hedda: What more have you concealed?

Brack: This—the event did not happen at his lodgings.

Hedda: Oh, that can make no difference.

Brack: Perhaps it may. For I must tell you—Eilert Lövborg was found shot in—in Mademoiselle Diana's boudoir.

Hedda (*makes a motion as if to rise, but sinks back again*): That is impossible, Judge Brack! He cannot have been there again today.

Brack: He was there this afternoon. He went there, he said, to demand the return of something which they had taken from him. Talked wildly about a lost child——

Hedda: Ah—so that was why——

Brack: I thought probably he meant his manuscript; but now I hear he destroyed that himself. So I suppose it must have been his pocketbook.

Hedda: Yes, no doubt. And there—there he was found?

Brack: Yes, there. With a pistol in his breast-pocket, discharged. The ball had lodged in a vital part.

Hedda: In the breast—yes.

Brack: No—in the bowels.

It wasn't beautiful; she failed to control; she must look at ugliness.

Hedda (*looks up at him with an expression of loathing*): That too! Oh what curse is it that makes everything I touch turn ludicrous and mean?

Brack: There is one point more, Mrs. Hedda—another disagreeable feature in the affair.

Hedda: And what is that?

Brack: The pistol he carried——

Hedda (*breathless*): Well? What of it?

Brack: He must have stolen it.

Hedda (*leaps up*): Stolen it! That is not true! He did not steal it!

Brack: No other explanation is possible. He must have stolen it—— Hush! (**Tesman** and **Mrs. Elvsted** *have risen from the table in the back room, and come into the drawing room.*)

Tesman (*with the papers in both his hands*): Hedda dear, it is almost impossible to see under that lamp. Think of that!

Hedda: Yes, I am thinking.

Tesman: Would you mind our sitting at your writing table—eh?

Hedda: If you like. (*Quickly.*) No, wait! Let me clear it first!

Tesman: Oh, you needn't trouble, Hedda. There is plenty of room.

Hedda: No, no; let me clear it, I say! I will take these things in and put them on the piano. There! (*She has drawn out an object, covered with sheet music, from* *under the bookcase, places several other pieces of music upon it, and carries the whole into the inner room to the left.* **Tesman** *lays the scraps of paper on the writing table, and moves the lamp there from the corner table.* **Hedda** *returns.*)

Hedda (*behind* **Mrs. Elvsted's** *chair, gently ruffling her hair*): Well, my sweet Thea, how goes it with Eilert Lövborg's monument?

Mrs. Elvsted (*looks dispiritedly up at her*): Oh, it will be terribly hard to put in order.

Tesman: We must manage it. I am determined. And arranging other people's papers is just the work for me.

(**Hedda** *goes over to the stove, and seats herself on one of the footstools.* **Brack** *stands over her, leaning on the armchair.*)

Hedda (*whispers*): What did you say about the pistol?

Brack (*softly*): That he must have stolen it.

Hedda: Why stolen it?

Brack: Because every other explanation ought to be impossible, Mrs. Hedda.

Hedda: Indeed?

Brack (*glances at her*): Of course Eilert Lövborg was here this morning. Was he not?

Hedda: Yes.

Brack: Were you alone with him?

Hedda: Part of the time.

Brack: Did you not leave the room whilst he was here?

Hedda: No.

Brack: Try to recollect. Were you not out of the room a moment?

Hedda: Yes, perhaps just a moment—out in the hall.

Brack: And where was your pistol case during that time?

Hedda: I had it locked up in——

Brack: Well, Mrs. Hedda?

Hedda: The case stood there on the writing table.

Brack: Have you looked since, to see whether both the pistols are there?

Hedda: No.

Brack: Well, you need not. I saw the pistol found in Lövborg's pocket, and I knew it at once as the one I had seen yesterday—and before, too.

Hedda: Have you it with you?

Brack: No; the police have it.

Hedda: What will the police do with it?

Brack: Search till they find the owner.

Hedda: Do you think they will succeed?

Brack (*bends over her and whispers*): No, Hedda Gabler—not so long as I say nothing.

Hedda (*looks frightened at him*): And if you do not say nothing—what then?

Brack (*shrugs his shoulders*): There is always the possibility that the pistol was stolen.

Hedda (*firmly*): Death rather than that.

Brack (*smiling*): People say such things—but they don't do them.

Hedda (*without replying*): And supposing the pistol was stolen, and the owner is discovered? What then?

Brack: Well, Hedda—then comes the scandal.

Hedda: The scandal!

Brack: Yes, the scandal—of which you are mortally afraid. You will, of course, be brought before the court—both you and Mademoiselle Diana. She will have to explain how the thing happened—whether it was an accidental shot or murder. Did the pistol go off as he was trying to take it out of his pocket, to threaten her with? Or did she tear the pistol out of his hand, shoot him, and push it back into his pocket? That would be quite like her; for she is an able-bodied young person, this same Mademoiselle Diana.

Hedda: But *I* have nothing to do with all this repulsive business.

Brack: No. But you will have to answer the question: Why did you give Eilert Lövborg the pistol? And what conclusions will people draw from the fact that you did give it to him?

Hedda (*lets her head sink*): That is true. I did not think of that.

Brack: Well, fortunately, there is no danger, so long as I say nothing.

She could not control Eilert; her greatest fear will now be realized.

Hedda (*looks up at him*): So I am in your power, Judge Brack. You have me at your beck and call, from this time forward.

Brack (*whispers softly*): Dearest Hedda—believe me—I shall not abuse my advantage.

Hedda: I am in your power none the less. Subject to your will and your demands. A slave, a slave then! (*Rises impetuously.*) No, I cannot endure the thought of that! Never!

Brack (*looks half-mockingly at her*): People generally get used to the inevitable.

Hedda (*returns his look*): Yes, perhaps. (*She crosses to the writing table. Suppressing an involuntary smile, she imitates* **Tesman's** *intonations.*) Well? Are you getting on, George? Eh?

Tesman: Heaven knows, dear. In any case it will be the work of months.

Hedda (*as before*): Fancy that! (*Passes her hands softly through* **Mrs. Elvsted's** *hair.*) Doesn't it seem strange to you, Thea? Here are you sitting with Tesman—just as you used to sit with Eilert Lövborg?

Mrs. Elvsted: Ah, if I could only inspire your husband in the same way.

Hedda: Oh, that will come too—in time.

Tesman: Yes, do you know, Hedda—I really think I begin to feel something of the sort. But won't you go and sit with Brack again?

She has no one to influence but herself.

Hedda: Is there nothing I can do to help you two?

Tesman: No, nothing in the world. (*Turning his head.*) I trust to you to keep Hedda company, my dear Brack.

Brack (*with a glance at* **Hedda**): With the very greatest of pleasure.

Hedda: Thanks. But I am tired this evening. I will go in and lie down a little on the sofa.

Tesman: Yes, do dear—eh?

(**Hedda** *goes into the back room and draws the curtains. A short pause. Suddenly she is heard playing a wild dance on the piano.*)

Mrs. Elvsted (*starts from her chair*): Oh—what is that?

Tesman (*runs to the doorway*): Why, my dearest Hedda—don't play dance music tonight! Just think of Aunt Rina! And of Eilert too!

Hedda (*puts her head out between the curtains*): And of Aunt Julia. And of all the rest of them. After this, I will be quiet. (*Closes the curtains again.*)

Tesman (*at the writing table*): It's not good for her to see us at this distressing work. I'll tell you what, Mrs. Elvsted, you shall take the empty room at Aunt

Julia's, and then I will come over in the evenings, and we can sit and work there—eh?

Hedda (*in the inner room*): I hear what you are saying, Tesman. But how am *I* to get through the evenings out here?

Tesman (*turning over the papers*): Oh, I daresay Judge Brack will be so kind as to look in now and then, even though I am out.

Brack (*in the armchair, calls out gaily*): Every blessed evening, with all the pleasure in life, Mrs. Tesman! We shall get on capitally together, we two!

Hedda (*speaking loud and clear*): Yes, don't you flatter yourself we will, Judge Brack? Now that you are the one cock in the basket——

(*A shot is heard within.* **Tesman**, **Mrs. Elvsted**, *and* **Brack** *leap to their feet.*)

Tesman: Oh, now she is playing with those pistols again.

(*He throws back the curtains and runs in, followed by* **Mrs. Elvsted.** **Hedda** *lies stretched on the sofa, lifeless. Confusion and cries.* **Berta** *enters in alarm from the right.*)

Tesman (*shrieks to* **Brack**): Shot herself! Shot herself in the temple! Fancy that!

Brack (*half-fainting in the armchair*): Good God!—people don't do such things.

Courage or cowardice? Has she won or lost?

DEATH OF A SALESMAN

Arthur Miller

CHARACTERS

Willy Loman	Howard Wagner
Linda	Jenny
Biff	Stanley
Happy	Miss Forsythe
Bernard	Letta
The Woman	Charley
Uncle Ben	

THE PLACE.   Willy Loman's house and yard and various places he visits in the New York and Boston of today.

Throughout the play, in the stage directions, left and right mean stage left and stage right.

ACT I

A melody is heard, played upon a flute. It is small and fine, telling of grass and trees and the horizon. The curtain rises.

Before us is the Salesman's house. We are aware of towering, angular shapes behind it, surrounding it on all sides. Only the blue light of the sky falls upon the house and forestage; the surrounding area shows an angry glow of orange. As more light appears, we see a solid vault of apartment houses around the small, fragile-seeming home. An air of the dream clings to the place, a dream rising out of reality. The kitchen at center seems actual enough, for there is a kitchen table with three chairs, and a refrigerator. But no other fixtures are seen. At the back of the kitchen there is a draped entrance, which leads to the living-room. To the right of the kitchen, on a level raised two feet, is a bedroom furnished only with a brass bedstead and a straight chair. On a shelf over the bed a silver athletic trophy stands. A window opens onto the apartment house at the side.

Behind the kitchen, on a level raised six and a half feet, is the boys' bedroom, at present barely visible. Two beds are dimly seen, and at the back of the room a dormer window. (This bedroom is above the unseen living-room.) At the left a stairway curves up to it from the kitchen.

*The entire setting is wholly or, in some places, partially transparent. The roof-line of the house is one-dimensional; under and over it we see the apartment buildings. Before the house lies an apron, curving beyond the forestage into the orchestra. This forward area serves as the back yard as well as the locale of all **Willy's** imaginings and of his city scenes.*

Whenever the action is in the present the actors observe the imaginary wall-lines, entering the house only through its door at the left. But in the scenes of the past these boundaries are broken, and characters enter or leave a room by stepping "through" a wall onto the forestage.

From the right, **Willy Loman***, the Salesman, enters, carrying two large sample cases. The flute plays on. He hears but is not aware of it. He is past sixty years of age, dressed quietly. Even as he crosses the stage to the doorway of the house, his exhaustion is apparent. He unlocks the door, comes into the kitchen, and thankfully lets his burden down, feeling the soreness of his palms. A word-sigh escapes his lips—it might be "Oh, boy, oh, boy." He closes the door, then carries his cases out into the living-room, through the draped kitchen doorway.*

Linda*, his wife, has stirred in her bed at the right. She gets out and puts on a robe, listening. Most often jovial, she has developed an iron repression of her exceptions to* **Willy's** *behavior—she more than loves him, she admires him, as though his mercurial nature, his temper, his massive dreams and little cruelties, served her only as sharp reminders of the turbulent longings within him, longings which she shares but lacks the temperament to utter and follow to their end.*

Linda (*hearing* **Willy** *outside the bedroom, calls with some trepidation*): Willy!

Willy: It's all right. I came back.

Linda: Why? What happened? (*Slight pause*) Did something happen, Willy?

Willy: No, nothing happened.

Linda: You didn't smash the car, did you?

Willy (*with casual irritation*): I said nothing happened. Didn't you hear me?

Linda: Don't you feel well?

Willy: I'm tired to the death. (*The flute has faded away. He sits on the bed beside her, a little numb.*) I couldn't make it. I just couldn't make it, Linda.

Linda (*very carefully, delicately*): Where were you all day? You look terrible.

Willy: I got as far as a little above Yonkers. I stopped for a cup of coffee. Maybe it was the coffee.

Linda: What?

Willy (*after a pause*): I suddenly couldn't drive any more. The car kept going off onto the shoulder, y'know?

Linda (*helpfully*): Oh. Maybe it was the steering again. I don't think Angelo knows the Studebaker.

Willy: No, it's me, it's me. Suddenly I realize I'm goin' sixty miles an hour and I don't remember the last five minutes. I'm—I can't seem to—keep my mind to it.

Linda: Maybe it's your glasses. You never went for your new glasses.

Willy: No, I see everything. I came back ten miles an hour. It took me nearly four hours from Yonkers.

Linda (*resigned*): Well, you'll just have to take a rest, Willy, you can't continue this way.

Willy: I just got back from Florida.

Linda: But you didn't rest your mind. Your mind is overactive, and the mind is what counts, dear.

Willy: I'll start out in the morning. Maybe I'll feel better in the morning. (*She is taking off his shoes.*) These goddam arch supports are killing me.

Linda: Take an aspirin. Should I get you an aspirin? It'll soothe you.

Willy (*with wonder*): I was driving along, you understand? And I was fine. I was even observing the scenery. You can imagine, me looking at scenery, on the road every week of my life. But it's so beautiful up there, Linda, the trees are so thick, and the sun is warm. I opened the windshield and just let the warm air bathe over me. And then all of a sudden I'm goin' off the road! I'm tellin' ya, I absolutely forgot I was driving. If I'd've gone the other way over the white line I might've killed somebody. So I went on again—and five minutes later I'm dreamin' again, and I nearly—(*He presses two fingers against his eyes.*) I have such thoughts, I have such strange thoughts.

Linda: Willy, dear. Talk to them again. There's no reason why you can't work in New York.

Willy: They don't need me in New York. I'm the New England man. I'm vital in New England.

Linda: But you're sixty years old. They can't expect you to keep traveling every week.

Willy: I'll have to send a wire to Portland. I'm supposed to see Brown and Morrison tomorrow morning at ten o'clock to show the line. Goddammit, I could sell them! (*He starts putting on his jacket.*)

Linda (*taking the jacket from him*): Why don't you go down to the place tomorrow and tell Howard you've simply got to work in New York? You're too accommodating, dear.

Willy: If old man Wagner was alive I'd a been in charge of New York now! That man was a prince, he was a masterful man. But that boy of his, that Howard, he don't appreciate. When I went north the first time, the Wagner Company didn't know where New England was!

Linda: Why don't you tell those things to Howard, dear?

Willy (*encouraged*): I will, I definitely will. Is there any cheese?

Linda: I'll make you a sandwich.

Willy: No, go to sleep. I'll take some milk. I'll be up right away. The boys in?

Linda: They're sleeping. Happy took Biff on a date tonight.

Willy (*interested*): That so?

Linda: It was so nice to see them shaving together, one behind the other, in the bathroom. And going out together. You notice? The whole house smells of shaving lotion.

Willy: Figure it out. Work a lifetime to pay off a house. You finally own it, and there's nobody to live in it.

Linda: Well, dear, life is a casting off. It's always that way.

Willy: No, no, some people—some people accomplish something. Did Biff say anything after I went this morning?

Linda: You shouldn't have criticized him, Willy, especially after he just got off the train. You mustn't lose your temper with him.

Willy: When the hell did I lose my temper? I simply asked him if he was making any money. Is that a criticism?

Linda: But, dear, how could he make any money?

Willy (*worried and angered*): There's such an undercurrent in him. He became a moody man. Did he apologize when I left this morning?

Linda: He was crestfallen, Willy. You know how he admires you. I think if he finds himself, then you'll both be happier and not fight any more.

Willy: How can he find himself on a farm? Is that a life? A farmhand? In the beginning, when he was young, I thought, well, a young man, it's good for him to tramp around, take a lot of different jobs. But it's more than ten years now and he has yet to make thirty-five dollars a week!

Linda: He's finding himself, Willy.

Willy: Not finding yourself at the age of thirty-four is a disgrace!

Linda: Shh!

Willy: The trouble is he's lazy, goddammit!

Linda: Willy, please!

Willy: Biff is a lazy bum!

Linda: They're sleeping. Get something to eat. Go on down.

Willy: Why did he come home? I would like to know what brought him home.

Linda: I don't know. I think he's still lost, Willy. I think he's very lost.

Willy: Biff Loman is lost. In the greatest country in the world a young man with such—personal attractiveness, gets lost. And such a hard worker. There's one thing about Biff—he's not lazy.

Linda: Never.

Willy (*with pity and resolve*): I'll see him in the morning; I'll have a nice talk with him. I'll get him a job selling. He could be big in no time. My God! Remember how they used to follow him around in high school? When he smiled at one of them their faces lit up. When he walked down the street . . . (*He loses himself in reminiscences.*)

Linda (*trying to bring him out of it*): Willy, dear, I got a new kind of American-type cheese today. It's whipped.

Willy: Why do you get American when I like Swiss?

Linda: I just thought you'd like a change——

Willy: I don't want a change! I want Swiss cheese. Why am I always being contradicted?

Linda (*with a covering laugh*): I thought it would be a surprise.

Willy: Why don't you open a window in here, for God's sake?

Linda (*with infinite patience*): They're all open, dear.

Willy: The way they boxed us in here. Bricks and windows, windows and bricks.

Linda: We should've bought the land next door.

Willy: The street is lined with cars. There's not a breath of fresh air in the neighborhood. The grass don't grow any more, you can't raise a carrot in the back yard. They should've had a law against apartment houses. Remember those two beautiful elm trees out there? When I and Biff hung the swing between them?

Linda: Yeah, like being a million miles from the city.

Willy: They should've arrested the builder for cutting those down. They massacred the neighborhood. (*Lost*) More and more I think of those days, Linda. This time of the year it was lilac and wisteria. And then the peonies would come out, and the daffodils. What fragrance in this room!

Linda: Well, after all, people had to move somewhere.

Willy: No, there's more people now.

Linda: I don't think there's more people. I think——

Willy: There's more people! That's what's ruining this country! Population is getting out of control. The competition is maddening! Smell the stink from that apartment house! And another one on the other side . . . How can they whip cheese?

(*On **Willy's** last line, Biff and Happy raise themselves up in their beds, listening.*)

Linda: Go down, try it. And be quiet.

Willy (*turning to **Linda***, *guiltily*): You're not worried about me, are you, sweetheart?

Biff: What's the matter?

Happy: Listen!

Linda: You've got too much on the ball to worry about.

Willy: You're my foundation and my support, Linda.

Linda: Just try to relax, dear. You make mountains out of molehills.

Willy: I won't fight with him any more. If he wants to go back to Texas, let him go.

Linda: He'll find his way.

Willy: Sure. Certain men just don't get started till later in life. Like Thomas Edison, I think. Or B. F. Goodrich. One of them was deaf. (*He starts for the bedroom doorway.*) I'll put my money on Biff.

Linda: And Willy—if it's warm Sunday we'll drive in the country. And we'll open the windshield, and take lunch.

Willy: No, the windshields don't open on the new cars.

Linda: But you opened it today.

Willy: Me? I didn't. (*He stops.*) Now isn't that peculiar! Isn't that a remarkable—— (*He breaks off in amazement and fright as the flute is heard distantly.*)

Linda: What, darling?

Willy: That is the most remarkable thing.

Linda: What, dear?

Willy: I was thinking of the Chevvy. (*Slight pause*) Nineteen twenty-eight . . . when I had that red Chevvy—(*Breaks off*) That's funny? I coulda sworn I was driving that Chevvy today.

Linda: Well, that's nothing. Something must've reminded you.

Willy: Remarkable. Ts. Remember those days? The way Biff used to simonize that car? The dealer refused to believe there was eighty thousand miles on it. (*He shakes his head.*) Heh! (*To* **Linda**) Close your eyes, I'll be right up. (*He walks out of the bedroom.*)

Happy (*to* **Biff**): Jesus, maybe he smashed up the car again!

Linda (*calling after* **Willy**): Be careful on the stairs, dear! The cheese is on the middle shelf! (*She turns, goes over to the bed, takes his jacket, and goes out of the bedroom.*)

(*Light has risen on the boys' room. Unseen,* **Willy** *is heard talking to himself, "Eighty thousand miles," and a little laugh.* **Biff** *gets out of bed, comes downstage a bit, and stands attentively.* **Biff** *is two years older than his brother* **Happy,** *well built, but in these days bears a worn air and seems less self-assured. He has succeeded less, and his dreams are stronger and less acceptable than* **Happy's.** **Happy** *is tall, powerfully made. Sexuality is like a visible color on him, or a scent that many women have discovered. He, like his brother, is lost, but in a different way, for he has never allowed himself to turn his face toward defeat and is thus more confused and hard-skinned, although seemingly more content.*)

Happy (*getting out of bed*): He's going to get his license taken away if he keeps that up. I'm getting nervous about him, y'know, Biff?

Biff: His eyes are going.

Happy: No, I've driven with him. He sees all right. He just doesn't keep his mind on it. I drove into the city with him last week. He stops at a green light and then it turns red and he goes. (*He laughs.*)

Biff: Maybe he's color-blind.

Happy: Pop? Why he's got the finest eye for color in the business. You know that.

Biff (*sitting down on his bed*): I'm going to sleep.

Happy: You're not still sour on Dad, are you, Biff?

Biff: He's all right, I guess.

Willy (*underneath them, in the living-room*): Yes, sir, eighty thousand miles—eighty-two thousand!

Biff: You smoking?

Happy (*holding out a pack of cigarettes*): Want one?

Biff (*taking a cigarette*): I can never sleep when I smell it.

Willy: What a simonizing job, heh!

Happy (*with deep sentiment*): Funny, Biff, y'know? Us sleeping in here again? The old beds. (*He pats his bed affectionately.*) All the talk that went across those two beds, huh? Our whole lives.

Biff: Yeah. Lotta dreams and plans.

Happy (*with a deep and masculine laugh*): About five hundred women would like to know what was said in this room.

(*They share a soft laugh.*)

Biff: Remember that big Betsy something—what the hell was her name—over on Bushwick Avenue?

Happy (*combing his hair*): With the collie dog!

Biff: That's the one. I got you in there, remember?

Happy: Yeah, that was my first time—I think. Boy, there was a pig! (*They laugh, almost crudely.*) You taught me everything I know about women. Don't forget that.

Biff: I bet you forgot how bashful you used to be. Especially with girls.

Happy: Oh, I still am, Biff.

Biff: Oh, go on.

Happy: I just control it, that's all. I think I got less bashful and you got more so. What happened, Biff? Where's the old humor, the old confidence? (*He shakes* **Biff's** *knee.* **Biff** *gets up and moves restlessly about the room.*) What's the matter?

Biff: Why does Dad mock me all the time?

Happy: He's not mocking you, he——

Biff: Everything I say there's a twist of mockery on his face. I can't get near him.

Happy: He just wants you to make good, that's all. I wanted to talk to you about Dad for a long time, Biff. Something's—happening to him. He—talks to himself.

Biff: I noticed that this morning. But he always mumbled.

Happy: But not so noticeable. It got so embarrassing I sent him to Florida. And you know something? Most of the time he's talking to you.

Biff: What's he say about me?

Happy: I can't make it out.

Biff: What's he say about me?

Happy: I think the fact that you're not settled, that you're still kind of up in the the air . . .

Biff: There's one or two other things depressing him, Happy.

Happy: What do you mean?

Biff: Never mind. Just don't lay it all to me.

Happy: But I think if you just got started—I mean—is there any future for you out there?

Biff: I tell ya, Hap, I don't know what the future is. I don't know—what I'm supposed to want.

Happy: What do you mean?

Biff: Well, I spent six or seven years after high school trying to work myself up. Shipping clerk, salesman, business of one kind or another. And it's a measly manner of existence. To get on that subway on the hot mornings in summer. To devote your whole life to keeping stock, or making phone calls, or selling or buying. To suffer fifty weeks of the year for the sake of a two-week vacation, when all you really desire is to be outdoors, with your shirt off. And always to have to get ahead of the next fella. And still—that's how you build a future.

Happy: Well, you really enjoy it on a farm? Are you content out there?

Biff (*with rising agitation*): Hap, I've had twenty or thirty different kinds of jobs since I left home before the war, and it always turns out the same. I just realized it lately. In Nebraska when I herded cattle, and the Dakotas, and Arizona, and now in Texas. It's why I came home now, I guess, because I realized it. This farm I work on, it's spring there now, see? And they've got about fifteen new colts. There's nothing more inspiring or—beautiful than the sight of a mare and a new colt. And it's cool there now, see? Texas is cool now, and it's spring. And whenever spring comes to where I am, I suddenly get the feeling, my God, I'm not gettin' anywhere! What the hell am I doing, playing around with horses, twenty-eight dollars a week! I'm thirty-four years old, I oughta be makin' my future. That's when I come running home. And now, I get here, and I don't know what to do with myself. (*After a pause*) I've always made a point of not wasting my life, and everytime I come back here I know that all I've done is to waste my life.

Happy: You're a poet, you know that, Biff? You're a—you're an idealist!

Biff: No, I'm mixed up very bad. Maybe I oughta get married. Maybe I oughta get stuck into something. Maybe that's my trouble. I'm like a boy. I'm not married, I'm not in business, I just—I'm like a boy. Are you content, Hap? You're a success, aren't you? Are you content?

Happy: Hell, no!

Biff: Why? You're making money, aren't you?

Happy (*moving about with energy, expressiveness*): All I can do now is wait for the merchandise manager to die. And suppose I get to be merchandise manager? He's a good friend of mine, and he just built a terrific estate on Long Island. And he lived there about two months and sold it, and now he's building another one. He can't enjoy it once it's finished. And I know that's just what I would do. I don't know what the hell I'm workin' for. Sometimes I sit in my apartment—all alone. And I think of the rent I'm paying. And it's crazy. But then, it's what I always wanted. My own apartment, a car, and plenty of women. And still, goddammit, I'm lonely.

Biff (*with enthusiasm*): Listen, why don't you come out West with me?

Happy: You and I, heh?

Biff: Sure, maybe we could buy a ranch. Raise cattle, use our muscles. Men built like we are should be working out in the open.

Happy (*avidly*): The Loman Brothers, heh?

Biff (*with vast affection*): Sure, we'd be known all over the counties!

Happy (*enthralled*): That's what I dream about, Biff. Sometimes I want to just rip my clothes off in the middle of the store and outbox that goddam merchandise manager. I mean I can outbox, outrun, and outlift anybody in that store, and I have to take orders from those common, petty sons-of-bitches till I can't stand it any more.

Biff: I'm tellin' you, kid, if you were with me I'd be happy out there.

Happy (*enthused*): See, Biff, everybody around me is so false that I'm constantly lowering my ideals . . .

Biff: Baby, together we'd stand up for one another, we'd have someone to trust.

Happy: If I were around you——

Biff: Hap, the trouble is we weren't brought up to grub for money. I don't know how to do it.

Happy: Neither can I!

Biff: Then let's go!

Happy: The only thing is—what can you make out there?

Biff: But look at your friend. Builds an estate and then hasn't the peace of mind to live in it.

Happy: Yeah, but when he walks into the store the waves part in front of him. That's fifty-two thousand dollars a year coming through the revolving door, and I got more in my pinky finger than he's got in his head.

Biff: Yeah, but you just said——

Happy: I gotta show some of those pompous, self-important executives over there that Hap Loman can make the grade. I want to walk into the store the way he walks in. Then I'll go with you, Biff. We'll be together yet, I swear. But take those two we had tonight. Now weren't they gorgeous creatures?

Biff: Yeah, yeah, most gorgeous I've had in years.

Happy: I get that any time I want, Biff. Whenever I feel disgusted. The only trouble is, it gets like bowling or something. I just keep knockin' them over and it doesn't mean anything. You still run around a lot?

Biff: Naa. I'd like to find a girl—steady, somebody with substance.

Happy: That's what I long for.

Biff: Go on! You'd never come home.

Happy: I would! Somebody with character, with resistance! Like Mom, y'know? You're gonna call me a bastard when I tell you this. That girl Charlotte I was with tonight is engaged to be married in five weeks. (*He tries on his new hat.*)

Biff: No kiddin'!

Happy: Sure, the guy's in line for the vice-presidency of the store. I don't know what gets into me, maybe I just have an overdeveloped sense of competition or something, but I went and ruined her, and furthermore I can't get rid of her. And he's the third executive I've done that to. Isn't that a crummy characteristic? And to top it all, I go to their weddings! (*Indignantly, but laughing*) Like I'm not supposed to take bribes. Manufacturers offer me a hundred-dollar bill now and then to throw an order their way. You know how honest I am, but it's like this girl, see. I hate myself for it. Because I don't want the girl, and, still, I take it and—I love it!

Biff: Let's go to sleep.

Happy: I guess we didn't settle anything, heh?

Biff: I just got one idea that I think I'm going to try.

Happy: What's that?

Biff: Remember Bill Oliver?

Happy: Sure, Oliver is very big now. You want to work for him again?

Biff: No, but when I quit he said something to me. He put his arm on my shoulder, and he said, "Biff, if you ever need anything, come to me."

Happy: I remember that. That sounds good.

Biff: I think I'll go to see him. If I could get ten thousand or even seven or eight thousand dollars I could buy a beautiful ranch.

Happy: I bet he'd back you. 'Cause he thought highly of you, Biff. I mean, they all do. You're well liked, Biff. That's why I say to come back here, and we both have the apartment. And I'm tellin' you, Biff, any babe you want . . .

Biff: No, with a ranch I could do the work I like and still be something. I just wonder though. I wonder if Oliver still thinks I stole that carton of basketballs.

Happy: Oh, he probably forgot that long ago. It's almost ten years. You're too sensitive. Anyway, he didn't really fire you.

Biff: Well, I think he was going to. I think that's why I quit. I was never sure whether he knew or not. I know he thought the world of me, though. I was the only one he'd let lock up the place.

Willy (*below*): You gonna wash the engine, Biff?

Happy: Shh!

(**Biff** looks at **Happy**, who is gazing down, listening. **Willy** is mumbling in the parlor.)

Happy: You hear that?

(*They listen.* **Willy** laughs warmly.)

Biff (*growing angry*): Doesn't he know Mom can hear that?

Willy: Don't get your sweater dirty, Biff!

(*A look of pain crosses* **Biff's** face.)

Happy: Isn't that terrible? Don't leave again, will you? You'll find a job here. You gotta stick around. I don't know what to do about him, it's getting embarrassing.

Willy: What a simonizing job!

Biff: Mom's hearing that!

Willy: No kiddin', Biff, you got a date? Wonderful!

Happy: Go on to sleep. But talk to him in the morning, will you?

Biff (*reluctantly getting into bed*): With her in the house. Brother!

Happy (*getting into bed*): I wish you'd have a good talk with him.

(*The light on their room begins to fade.*)

Biff (*to himself in bed*): That selfish, stupid . . .

Happy: Sh . . . Sleep, Biff.

(*Their light is out. Well before they have finished speaking,* **Willy's** *form is dimly seen below in the darkened kitchen. He opens the refrigerator, searches in there, and takes out a bottle of milk. The apartment houses are fading out, and the entire house and surroundings become covered with leaves. Music insinuates itself as the leaves appear.*)

Willy: Just wanna be careful with those girls, Biff, that's all. Don't make any promises. No promises of any kind. Because a girl, y'know, they always believe what you tell 'em, and you're very young, Biff, you're too young to be talking seriously to girls.

(*Light rises on the kitchen.* **Willy**, *talking, shuts the refrigerator door and comes downstage to the kitchen table. He pours milk into a glass. He is totally immersed in himself, smiling faintly.*)

Willy: Too young entirely, Biff. You want to watch your schooling first. Then when you're all set, there'll be plenty of girls for a boy like you. (*He smiles broadly at a kitchen chair.*) That so? The girls pay for you? (*He laughs.*) Boy, you must really be makin' a hit.

(**Willy** is gradually addressing—physically—a point offstage, speaking through the wall of the kitchen, and his voice has been rising in volume to that of a normal conversation.)

Willy: I been wondering why you polish the car so careful. Ha! Don't leave the hubcaps, boys. Get the chamois to the hubcaps. Happy, use newspaper on the windows, it's the easiest thing. Show him how to do it, Biff! You see, Happy? Pad it up, use it like a pad. That's it, that's it, good work. You're doin' all right, Hap. (*He pauses, then nods in approbation for a few seconds, then looks upward.*) Biff, first thing we gotta do when we get time is clip that big branch over the house.

Afraid it's gonna fall in a storm and hit the roof. Tell you what. We get a rope and sling her around, and then we climb up there with a couple of saws and take her down. Soon as you finish the car, boys, I wanna see ya. I got a surprise for you, boys.

Biff (*offstage*): Whatta ya got, Dad?

Willy: No, you finish first. Never leave a job till you're finished—remember that. (*Looking toward the "big trees"*) Biff, up in Albany I saw a beautiful hammock. I think I'll buy it next trip, and we'll hang it right between those two elms. Wouldn't that be something? Just swingin' there under those branches. Boy, that would be . . .

(*Young* **Biff** *and Young* **Happy** *appear from the direction* **Willy** *was addressing.* **Happy** *carries rags and a pail of water.* **Biff**, *wearing a sweater with a block "S," carries a football.*)

Biff (*pointing in the direction of the car offstage*): How's that, Pop, professional?

Willy: Terrific. Terrific job, boys. Good work, Biff.

Happy: Where's the surprise, Pop?

Willy: In the back seat of the car.

Happy: Boy! (*He runs off.*)

Biff: What is it, Dad? Tell me, what'd you buy?

Willy (*laughing, cuffs him*): Never mind, something I want you to have.

Biff (*turns and starts off*): What is it, Hap?

Happy (*offstage*): It's a punching bag!

Biff: Oh, Pop!

Willy: It's got Gene Tunney's signature on it!

(**Happy** *runs onstage with a punching bag.*)

Biff: Gee, how'd you know we wanted a punching bag?

Willy: Well, it's the finest thing for the timing.

Happy (*lies down on his back and pedals with his feet*): I'm losing weight, you notice, Pop?

Willy (*to* **Happy**): Jumping rope is good too.

Biff: Did you see the new football I got?

Willy (*examining the ball*): Where'd you get a new ball?

Biff: The coach told me to practice my passing.

Willy: That so? And he gave you the ball, heh?

Biff: Well, I borrowed it from the locker room. (*He laughs confidentially.*)

Willy (*laughing with him at the theft*): I want you to return that.

Happy: I told you he wouldn't like it!

Biff (*angrily*): Well, I'm bringing it back!

Willy (*stopping the incipient argument, to* **Happy**): Sure, he's gotta practice with a regulation ball, doesn't he? (*To* **Biff**) Coach'll probably congratulate you on your initiative!

Biff: Oh, he keeps congratulating my initiative all the time, Pop.

Willy: That's because he likes you. If somebody else took that ball there'd be an uproar. So what's the report, boys, what's the report?

Biff: Where'd you go this time, Dad? Gee, we were lonesome for you.

Willy (*pleased, puts an arm around each boy and they come down to the apron*): Lonesome, heh?

Biff: Missed you every minute.

Willy: Don't say? Tell you a secret, boys. Don't breathe it to a soul. Someday I'll have my own business, and I'll never have to leave home any more.

Happy: Like Uncle Charley, heh?

Willy: Bigger than Uncle Charley! Because Charley is not—liked. He's liked, but he's not—well liked.

Biff: Where'd you go this time, Dad?

Willy: Well, I got on the road, and I went north to Providence. Met the Mayor.

Biff: The Mayor of Providence!

Willy: He was sitting in the hotel lobby.

Biff: What'd he say?

Willy: He said, "Morning!" And I said, "You got a fine city here, Mayor." And then he had coffee with me. And then I went to Waterbury. Waterbury is a fine city. Big clock city, the famous Waterbury clock. Sold a nice bill there. And then Boston—Boston is the cradle of the Revolution. A fine city. And a couple of other towns in Mass., and on to Portland and Bangor and straight home!

Biff: Gee, I'd love to go with you sometime, Dad.

Willy: Soon as summer comes.

Happy: Promise?

Willy: You and Hap and I, and I'll show you all the towns. America is full of beautiful towns and fine, upstanding people. And they know me, boys, they know me up and down New England. The finest people. And when I bring you fellas up, there'll be open sesame for all of us, 'cause one thing, boys: I can park my car in any street in New England, and the cops protect it like their own. This summer, heh?

Biff *and* **Happy** (*together*): Yeah! You bet!

Willy: We'll take our bathing suits.

Happy: We'll carry your bags, Pop!

Willy: Oh, won't that be something! Me comin' into the Boston stores with you boys carryin' my bags. What a sensation!

(**Biff** *is prancing around, practicing passing the ball.*)

Willy: You nervous, Biff, about the game?

Biff: Not if you're gonna be there.

Willy: What do they say about you in school, now that they made you captain?

Happy: There's a crowd of girls behind him everytime the classes change.

Biff (*taking* **Willy's** *hand*): This Saturday, Pop, this Saturday—just for you, I'm going to break through for a touchdown.

Happy: You're supposed to pass.

Biff: I'm takin' one play for Pop. You watch me, Pop, and when I take off my helmet, that means I'm breakin' out. Then you watch me crash through that line!

Willy (*kisses* **Biff**): Oh, wait'll I tell this in Boston!

(**Bernard** *enters in knickers. He is younger than* **Biff**, *earnest and loyal, a worried boy.*)

Bernard: Biff, where are you? You're supposed to study with me today.

Willy: Hey, looka Bernard. What're you lookin' so anemic about, Bernard?

Bernard: He's gotta study, Uncle Willy. He's got Regents next week.

Happy (*tauntingly, spinning* **Bernard** *around*): Let's box, Bernard!

Bernard: Biff! (*He gets away from* **Happy**.) Listen, Biff, I heard Mr. Birnbaum say that if you don't start studyin' math he's gonna flunk you, and you won't graduate. I heard him!

Willy: You better study with him, Biff. Go ahead now.

Bernard: I heard him!

Biff: Oh, Pop, you didn't see my sneakers! (*He holds up a foot for* **Willy** *to look at.*)

Willy: Hey, that's a beautiful job of printing!

Bernard (*wiping his glasses*): Just because he printed University of Virginia on his sneakers doesn't mean they've got to graduate him. Uncle Willy!

Willy (*angrily*): What're you talking about? With scholarships to three universities they're gonna flunk him?

Bernard: But I heard Mr. Birnbaum say——

Willy: Don't be a pest, Bernard! (*To his boys*) What an anemic!

Bernard: Okay, I'm waiting for you in my house, Biff.

(**Bernard** *goes off. The Lomans laugh.*)

Willy: Bernard is not well liked, is he?

Biff: He's liked, but he's not well liked.

Happy: That's right, Pop.

Willy: That's just what I mean. Bernard can get the best marks in school, y'understand, but when he gets out in the business world, y'understand, you are going to be five times ahead of him. That's why I thank Almighty God you're both built like Adonises. Because the man who makes an appearance in the business world, the man who creates personal interest, is the man who gets ahead. Be liked and you will never want. You take me, for instance. I never have to wait in line to see a buyer. "Willy Loman is here!" That's all they have to know, and I go right through.

Biff: Did you knock them dead, Pop?

Willy: Knocked 'em cold in Providence, slaughtered 'em in Boston.

Happy (*on his back, pedaling again*): I'm losing weight, you notice, Pop?

(**Linda** *enters, as of old, a ribbon in her hair, carrying a basket of washing.*)

Linda (*with youthful energy*): Hello, dear!

Willy: Sweetheart!

Linda: How'd the Chevvy run?

Willy: Chevrolet, Linda, is the greatest car ever built. (*To the boys*) Since when do you let your mother carry wash up the stairs?

Biff: Grab hold there, boy!

Happy: Where to, Mom?

Linda: Hang them up on the line. And you better go down to your friends, Biff. The cellar is full of boys. They don't know what to do with themselves.

Biff: Ah, when Pop comes home they can wait!

Willy (*laughs appreciatively*): You better go down and tell them what to do, Biff.

Biff: I think I'll have them sweep out the furnace room.

Willy: Good work, Biff.

Biff (*goes through wall-line of kitchen to doorway at back and calls down*): Fellas! Everybody sweep out the furnace room! I'll be right down!

Voices: All right! Okay, Biff.

Biff: George and Sam and Frank, come out back! We're hangin' up the wash! Come on Hap, on the double! (*He and* **Happy** *carry out the basket.*)

Linda: The way they obey him!

Willy: Well, that's training, the training. I'm tellin' you, I was sellin' thousands and thousands, but I had to come home.

Linda: Oh, the whole block'll be at that game. Did you sell anything?

Willy: I did five hundred gross in Providence and seven hundred gross in Boston.

Linda: No! Wait a minute, I've got a pencil. (*She pulls pencil and paper out of her apron pocket.*) That makes your commission . . . Two hundred—my God! Two hundred and twelve dollars!

Willy: Well, I didn't figure it yet, but . . .

Linda: How much did you do?

Willy: Well, I—I did—about a hundred and eighty gross in Providence. Well, no—it came to—roughly two hundred gross on the whole trip.

Linda (*without hesitation*): Two hundred gross. That's . . . (*She figures.*)

Willy: The trouble was that three of the stores were half closed for inventory in Boston. Otherwise I woulda broke records.

Linda: Well, it makes seventy dollars and some pennies. That's very good.

Willy: What do we owe?

Linda: Well, on the first there's sixteen dollars on the refrigerator——

Willy: Why sixteen?

Linda: Well, the fan belt broke, so it was a dollar eighty.

Willy: But it's brand new.

Linda: Well, the man said that's the way it is. Till they work themselves in, y'know. (*They move through the wall-line into the kitchen.*)

Willy: I hope we didn't get stuck on that machine.

Linda: They got the biggest ads of any of them!

Willy: I know, it's a fine machine. What else?

Linda: Well, there's nine-sixty for the washing machine. And for the vacuum cleaner there's three and a half due on the fifteenth. Then the roof, you got twenty-one dollars remaining.

Willy: It don't leak, does it?

Linda: No, they did a wonderful job. Then you owe Frank for the carburetor.

Willy: I'm not going to pay that man! That goddam Chevrolet, they ought to prohibit the manufacture of that car!

Linda: Well, you owe him three and a half. And odds and ends, comes to around a hundred and twenty dollars by the fifteenth.

Willy: A hundred and twenty dollars! My God, if business don't pick up I don't know what I'm gonna do!

Linda: Well, next week you'll do better.

Willy: Oh, I'll knock 'em dead next week. I'll go to Hartford. I'm very well liked in Hartford. You know, the trouble is, Linda, people don't seem to take to me. (*They move onto the forestage.*)

Linda: Oh, don't be foolish.

Willy: I know it when I walk in. They seem to laugh at me.

Linda: Why? Why would they laugh at you? Don't talk that way, Willy. (**Willy** *moves to the edge of the stage.* **Linda** *goes into the kitchen and starts to darn stockings.*)

Willy: I don't know the reason for it, but they just pass me by. I'm not noticed.

Linda: But you're doing wonderful, dear. You're making seventy to a hundred dollars a week.

Willy: But I gotta be at it ten, twelve hours a day. Other men—I don't know—they do it easier. I don't know why—I can't stop myself—I talk too much. A man oughta come in with a few words. One thing about Charley. He's a man of few words, and they respect him.

Linda: You don't talk too much, you're just lively.

Willy (*smiling*): Well, I figure, what the hell, life is short, a couple of jokes. (*To himself*) I joke too much! (*The smile goes.*)

Linda: Why? You're——

Willy: I'm fat. I'm very—foolish to look at, Linda. I didn't tell you, but Christmas time I happened to be calling on F. H. Stewarts, and a salesman I know, as I was going in to see the buyer I heard him say something about—walrus. And I—I cracked him right across the face. I won't take that. I simply will not take that. But they do laugh at me. I know that.

Linda: Darling . . .

Willy: I gotta overcome it. I know I gotta overcome it. I'm not dressing to advantage, maybe.

Linda: Willy, darling, you're the handsomest man in the world——

Willy: Oh, no, Linda.

Linda: To me you are. (*Slight pause*) The handsomest.

(*From the darkness is heard the laughter of a woman.* **Willy** *doesn't turn to it, but it continues through* **Linda's** *lines.*)

Linda: And the boys, Willy. Few men are idolized by their children the way you are.

(*Music is heard as behind a scrim, to the left of the house,* **The Woman**, *dimly seen, is dressing.*)

Willy (*with great feeling*): You're the best there is, Linda, you're a pal, you know that? On the road—on the road I want to grab you sometimes and just kiss the life outa you.

(*The laughter is loud now, and he moves into a brightening area at the left, where* **The Woman** *has come from behind the scrim and is standing, putting on her hat, looking into a "mirror" and laughing.*)

Willy: 'Cause I get so lonely—especially when business is bad and there's nobody to talk to. I get the feeling that I'll never sell anything again, that I won't make a living for you, or a business, a business for the boys. (*He talks through* **The Woman's** *subsiding laughter;* **The Woman** *primps at the "mirror."*) There's so much I want to make for——

The Woman: Me? You didn't make me, Willy. I picked you.

Willy (*pleaded*): You picked me?

The Woman (*who is quite proper-looking,* **Willy's** *age*): I did. I've been sitting at that desk watching all the salesmen go by, day in, day out. But you've got such a sense of humor, and we do have such a good time together, don't we?

Willy: Sure, sure. (*He takes her in his arms.*) Why do you have to go now?

The Woman: It's two o'clock . . .

Willy: No, come on in! (*He pulls her.*)

The Woman: . . . my sisters'll be scandalized. When'll you be back?

Willy: Oh, two weeks about. Will you come up again?

The Woman: Sure thing. You do make me laugh. It's good for me. (*She squeezes his arm, kisses him.*) And I think you're a wonderful man.

Willy: You picked me, heh?

The Woman: Sure. Because you're so sweet. And such a kidder.

Willy: Well, I'll see you next time I'm in Boston.

The Woman: I'll put you right through to the buyers.

Willy (*slapping her bottom*): Right. Well, bottoms up!

The Woman (*slaps him gently and laughs*): You just kill me, Willy. (*He suddenly grabs* *her and kisses her roughly.*) You kill me. And thanks for the stockings. I love a lot of stockings. Well, good night.

Willy: Good night. And keep your pores open!

The Woman: Oh, Willy!

(**The Woman** *bursts out laughing, and* **Linda's** *laughter blends in.* **The Woman** *disappears into the dark. Now the area at the kitchen table brightens.* **Linda** *is sitting where she was at the kitchen table, but now is mending a pair of her silk stockings.*)

Linda: You are, Willy. The handsomest man. You've got no reason to feel that——

Willy (*coming out of* **The Woman's** *dimming area and going over to* **Linda**): I'll make it all up to you, Linda, I'll—

Linda: There's nothing to make up, dear. You're doing fine, better than——

Willy (*noticing her mending*): What's that?

Linda: Just mending my stockings. They're so expensive——

Willy (*angrily, taking them from her*): I won't have you mending stockings in this house! Now throw them out!

(**Linda** *puts the stockings in her pocket.*)

Bernard (*entering on the run*): Where is he? If he doesn't study!

Willy (*moving to the forestage, with great agitation*): You'll give him the answers!

Bernard: I do, but I can't on a Regents! That's a state exam! They're liable to arrest me!

Willy: Where is he? I'll whip him, I'll whip him!

Linda: And he'd better give back that football, Willy, it's not nice.

Willy: Biff! Where is he? Why is he taking everything?

Linda: He's too rough with the girls, Willy. All the mothers are afraid of him!

Willy: I'll whip him!

Bernard: He's driving the car without a license!

(**The Woman's** *laugh is heard.*)

Willy: Shut up!

Linda: All the mothers——

Willy: Shut up!

Bernard (*backing quietly away and out*): Mr. Birnbaum says he's stuck up.

Willy: Get outa here!

Bernard: If he doesn't buckle down he'll flunk math! (*He goes off.*)

Linda: He's right, Willy, you've gotta——

Willy (*exploding at her*): There's nothing the matter with him! You want him to be a worm like Bernard? He's got spirit, personality . . .

(*As he speaks,* **Linda**, *almost in tears, exits into the living-room.* **Willy** *is alone in the kitchen, wilting and staring. The leaves are gone. It is night again, and the apartment houses look down from behind.*)

Willy: Loaded with it. Loaded! What is he stealing? He's giving it back, isn't he? Why is he stealing? What did I tell him? I never in my life told him anything but decent things.

(**Happy** *in pajamas has come down the stairs;* **Willy** *suddenly becomes aware of* **Happy's** *presence.*)

Happy: Let's go now, come on.

Willy (*sitting down at the kitchen table*): Huh! Why did she have to wax the floors herself? Everytime she waxes the floors she keels over. She knows that!

Happy: Shh! Take it easy. What brought you back tonight?

Willy: I got an awful scare. Nearly hit a kid in Yonkers. God! Why didn't I go to Alaska with my brother Ben that time! Ben! That man was a genius, that man was success incarnate! What a mistake! He begged me to go.

Happy: Well, there's no use in——

Willy: You guys! There was a man started with the clothes on his back and ended up with diamond mines!

Happy: Boy, someday I'd like to know how he did it.

Willy: What's the mystery? The man knew what he wanted and went out and got it! Walked into a jungle, and comes out, the age of twenty-one, and he's rich! The world is an oyster, but you don't crack it open on a mattress.

Happy: Pop, I told you I'm gonna retire you for life.

Willy: You'll retire me for life on seventy goddam dollars a week? And your women and your car and your apartment, and you'll retire me for life! Christ's sake, I couldn't get past Yonkers today! Where are you guys, where are you? The woods are burning! I can't drive a car!

(**Charley** *has appeared in the doorway. He is a large man, slow of speech, laconic, immovable. In all he says, despite what he says, there is pity, and, now, trepidation. He has a robe over pajamas, slippers on his feet. He enters the kitchen.*)

Charley: Everything all right?

Happy: Yeah, Charley, everything's . . .

Willy: What's the matter?

Charley: I heard some noise. I thought something happened. Can't we do something about the walls? You sneeze in here, and in my house hats blow off.

Happy: Let's go to bed, Dad. Come on.

(**Charley** *signals to* **Happy** *to go.*)

Willy: You go ahead, I'm not tired at the moment.

Happy (*to* **Willy**): Take it easy, huh? (*He exits.*)

Willy: What're you doin' up?

Charley (*sitting down at the kitchen table opposite* **Willy**): Couldn't sleep good. I had a heartburn.

Willy: Well, you don't know how to eat.

Charley: I eat with my mouth.

Willy: No, you're ignorant. You gotta know about vitamins and things like that.

Charley: Come on, let's shoot. Tire you out a little.

Willy (*hesitantly*): All right. You got cards?

Charley (*taking a deck from his pocket*): Yeah, I got them. Someplace. What is it with those vitamins?

Willy (*dealing*): They build up your bones. Chemistry.

Charley: Yeah, but there's no bones in a heartburn.

Willy: What are you talkin' about? Do you know the first thing about it?

Charley: Don't get insulted.

Willy: Don't talk about something you don't know anything about.

(*They are playing. Pause.*)

Charley: What're you doin' home?

Willy: A little trouble with the car.

Charley: Oh. (*Pause*) I'd like to take a trip to California.

Willy: Don't say.

Charley: You want a job?

Willy: I got a job, I told you that. (*After a slight pause*) What the hell are you offering me a job for?

Charley: Don't get insulted.

Willy: Don't insult me.

Charley: I don't see no sense in it. You don't have to go on this way.

Willy: I got a good job. (*Slight pause*) What do you keep comin' in here for?

Charley: You want me to go?

Willy (*after a pause, withering*): I can't understand it. He's going back to Texas again. What the hell is that?

Charley: Let him go.

Willy: I got nothin' to give him, Charley, I'm clean, I'm clean.

Charley: He won't starve. None a them starve. Forget about him.

Willy: Then what have I got to remember?

Charley: You take it too hard. To hell with it. When a deposit bottle is broken you don't get your nickel back.

Willy: That's easy enough for you to say.

Charley: That ain't easy for me to say.

Willy: Did you see the ceiling I put up in the living-room?

Charley: Yeah, that's a piece of work. To put up a ceiling is a mystery to me. How do you do it?

Willy: What's the difference?

Charley: Well, talk about it.

Willy: You gonna put up a ceiling?

Charley: How could I put up a ceiling?

Willy: Then what the hell are you bothering me for?

Charley: You're insulted again.

Willy: A man who can't handle tools is not a man. You're disgusting.

Charley: Don't call me disgusting, Willy.

(**Uncle Ben**, *carrying a valise and an umbrella, enters the forestage from around the right corner of the house. He is a stolid man, in his sixties, with a mustache and an authoritative air. He is utterly certain of his destiny, and there is an aura of far places about him. He enters exactly as* **Willy** *speaks.*)

Willy: I'm getting awfully tired, Ben.

(**Ben's** *music is heard.* **Ben** *looks around at everything.*)

Charley: Good, keep playing; you'll sleep better. Did you call me Ben?

(**Ben** *looks at his watch.*)

Willy: That's funny. For a second there you reminded me of my brother Ben.

Ben: I only have a few minutes.

(*He strolls, inspecting the place.* **Willy** *and* **Charley** *continue playing.*)

Charley: You never heard from him again, heh? Since that time?

Willy: Didn't Linda tell you? Couple of weeks ago we got a letter from his wife in Africa. He died.

Charley: That so.

Ben (*chuckling*): So this is Brooklyn, eh?

Charley: Maybe you're in for some of his money.

Willy: Naa, he had seven sons. There's just one opportunity I had with that man . . .

Ben: I must make a train, William. There are several properties I'm looking at in Alaska.

Willy: Sure, sure! If I'd gone with him to Alaska that time, everything would've been totally different.

Charley: Go on, you'd froze to death up there.

Willy: What're you talking about?

Ben: Opportunity is tremendous in Alaska, William. Surprised you're not up there.

Willy: Sure, tremendous.

Charley: Heh?

Willy: There was the only man I ever met who knew the answers.

Charley: Who?

Ben: How are you all?

Willy (*taking a pot, smiling*): Fine, fine.

Charley: Pretty sharp tonight.

Ben: Is Mother living with you?

Willy: No, she died a long time ago.

Charley: Who?

Ben: That's too bad. Fine specimen of a lady, Mother.

Willy (*to* **Charley**): Heh?

Ben: I'd hoped to see the old girl.

Charley: Who died?

Ben: Heard anything from Father, have you?

Willy (*unnerved*): What do you mean, who died?

Charley (*taking a pot*): What're you talkin' about?

Ben (*looking at his watch*): William, it's half-past eight!

Willy (*as though to dispel his confusion he angrily stops* **Charley's** hand): That's my build!

Charley: I put the ace——

Willy: If you don't know how to play the game I'm not gonna throw my money away on you!

Charley (*rising*): It was my ace, for God's sake!

Willy: I'm through, I'm through!

Ben: When did Mother die?

Willy: Long ago. Since the beginning you never knew how to play cards.

Charley (*picks up the cards and goes to the door*): All right! Next time I'll bring a deck with five aces.

Willy: I don't play that kind of game!

Charley (*turning to him*): You ought to be ashamed of yourself!

Willy: Yeah?

Charley: Yeah! (*He goes out.*)

Willy (*slamming the door after him*): Ignoramus!

Ben (*as* **Willy** *comes toward him through the wall-line of the kitchen*): So you're William.

Willy (*shaking* **Ben's** *hand*): Ben! I've been waiting for you so long! What's the answer? How did you do it?

Ben: Oh, there's a story in that.

(**Linda** *enters the forestage, as of old, carrying the wash basket.*)

Linda: Is this Ben?

Ben (*gallantly*): How do you do, my dear.

Linda: Where've you been all these years? Willy's always wondered why you——

Willy (*pulling* **Ben** *away from her impatiently*): Where is Dad? Didn't you follow him? How did you get started?

Ben: Well, I don't know how much you remember.

Willy: Well, I was just a baby, of course, only three or four years old——

Ben: Three years and eleven months.

Willy: What a memory, Ben!

Ben: I have many enterprises, William, and I have never kept books.

Willy: I remember I was sitting under the wagon in—was it Nebraska?

Ben: It was South Dakota, and I gave you a bunch of wild flowers.

Willy: I remember you walking away down some open road.

Ben (*laughing*): I was going to find Father in Alaska.

Willy: Where is he?

Ben: At that age I had a very faulty view of geography, William. I discovered after a few days that I was heading due south, so instead of Alaska, I ended up in Africa.

Linda: Africa!

Willy: The Gold Coast!

Ben: Principally diamond mines.

Linda: Diamond mines!

Ben: Yes, my dear. But I've only a few minutes——

Willy: No! Boys! Boys! (**Young Biff** *and* **Happy** *appear.*) Listen to this. This is your Uncle Ben, a great man! Tell my boys, Ben!

Ben: Why, boys, when I was seventeen I walked into the jungle, and when I was twenty-one I walked out. (*He laughs.*) And by God I was rich.

Willy (*to the boys*): You see what I been talking about? The greatest things can happen!

Ben (*glancing at his watch*): I have an appointment in Ketchikan Tuesday week.

Willy: No, Ben! Please tell about Dad. I want my boys to hear. I want them to know the kind of stock they spring from. All I remember is a man with a big beard, and I was in Mamma's lap, sitting around a fire, and some kind of high music.

Ben: His flute. He played the flute.

Willy: Sure, the flute, that's right!

(*New music is heard, a high, rollicking tune.*)

Ben: Father was a very great and a very wild-hearted man. We would start in Boston, and he'd toss the whole family into the wagon, and then he'd drive the team right across the country; through Ohio, and Indiana, Michigan, Illinois, and all the Western states. And we'd stop in the towns and sell the flutes that he'd made on the way. Great inventor, Father. With one gadget he made more in a week than a man like you could make in a lifetime.

Willy: That's just the way I'm bringing them up, Ben—rugged, well-liked, all-around.

Ben: Yeah? (*To* **Biff**) Hit that, boy—hard as you can. (*He pounds his stomach.*)

Biff: Oh, no, sir!

Ben (*taking boxing stance*): Come on, get to me! (*He laughs.*)

Willy: Go to it, Biff! Go ahead, show him!

Biff: Okay! (*He cocks his fists and starts in.*)

Linda (*to* **Willy**): Why must he fight, dear?

Ben (*sparring with* **Biff**): Good boy! Good boy!

Willy: How's that, Ben, heh?

Happy: Give him the left, Biff!

Linda: Why are you fighting?

Ben: Good boy! (*Suddenly comes in, trips* **Biff**, *and stands over him, the point of his umbrella poised over* **Biff's** *eye.*)

Linda: Look out, Biff!

Biff: Gee!

Ben (*patting* **Biff's** *knee*): Never fight fair with a stranger, boy. You'll never get out of the jungle that way. (*Taking* **Linda's** *hand and bowing*) It was an honor and a pleasure to meet you, Linda.

Linda (*withdrawing her hand coldly, frightened*): Have a nice—trip.

Ben (*to* **Willy**): And good luck with your—what do you do?

Willy: Selling.

Ben: Yes. Well . . . (*He raises his hand in farewell to all.*)

Willy: No, Ben, I don't want you to think . . . (*He takes* **Ben's** *arm to show him.*) It's Brooklyn, I know, but we hunt too.

Ben: Really, now.

Willy: Oh, sure, there's snakes and rabbits and—that's why I moved out here. Why, Biff can fell any one of these trees in no time! Boys! Go right over to where they're building the apartment house and get some sand. We're gonna rebuild the entire front stoop right now! Watch this, Ben!

Biff: Yes, sir! On the double, Hap!

Happy (*as he and* **Biff** *run off*): I lost weight, Pop, you notice?

(**Charley** *enters in knickers, even before the boys are gone.*)

Charley: Listen, if they steal any more from that building the watchman'll put the cops on them!

Linda (*to* **Willy**): Don't let Biff . . .

(**Ben** *laughs lustily.*)

Willy: You shoulda seen the lumber they brought home last week. At least a dozen six-by-tens worth all kinds a money.

Charley: Listen, if that watchman——

Willy: I gave them hell, understand. But I got a couple of fearless characters there.

Charley: Willy, the jails are full of fearless characters.

Ben (*clapping* **Willy** *on the back, with a laugh at* **Charley**): And the stock exchange, friend!

Willy (*joining in* **Ben's** *laughter*): Where are the rest of your pants?

Charley: My wife bought them.

Willy: Now all you need is a golf club and you can go upstairs and go to sleep. (*To* **Ben**) Great athlete! Between him and his son Bernard they can't hammer a nail!

Bernard (*rushing in*): The watchman's chasing Biff!

Willy (*angrily*): Shut up! He's not stealing anything!

Linda (*alarmed, hurrying off left*): Where is he? Biff, dear! (*She exits.*)

Willy (*moving toward the left, away from* **Ben**): There's nothing wrong. What's the matter with you?

Ben: Nervy boy. Good!

Willy (*laughing*): Oh, nerves of iron, that Biff!

Charley: Don't know what it is. My New England man comes back and he's bleedin', they murdered him up there.

Willy: It's contacts, Charley, I got important contacts!

Charley (*sarcastically*): Glad to hear it, Willy. Come in later, we'll shoot a little casino. I'll take some of your Portland money. (*He laughs at* **Willy** *and exits.*)

Willy (*turning to* **Ben**): Business is bad, it's murderous. But not for me, of course.

Ben: I'll stop by on my way back to Africa.

Willy (*longingly*): Can't you stay a few days? You're just what I need, Ben, because

I—I have a fine position here, but I—well, Dad left when I was such a baby and I never had a chance to talk to him and I still feel—kind of temporary about myself.

Ben: I'll be late for my train.

(*They are at opposite ends of the stage.*)

Willy: Ben, my boys—can't we talk? They'd go into the jaws of hell for me, but I—

Ben: William, you're being first-rate with your boys. Outstanding, manly chaps!

Willy (*hanging on to his words*): Oh, Ben, that's good to hear! Because sometimes I'm afraid that I'm not teaching them the right kind of—Ben, how should I teach them?

Ben (*giving great weight to each word, and with a certain vicious audacity*): William, when I walked into the jungle, I was seventeen. When I walked out I was twenty-one. And, by God, I was rich! (*He goes off into darkness around the right corner of the house.*)

Willy: . . . was rich! That's just the spirit I want to imbue them with! To walk into a jungle! I was right! I was right! I was right!

(**Ben** *is gone, but* **Willy** *is still speaking to him as* **Linda**, *in nightgown and robe, enters the kitchen, glances around for* **Willy**, *then goes to the door of the house, looks out and sees him. Comes down to his left. He looks at her.*)

Linda: Willy, dear? Willy?

Willy: I was right!

Linda: Did you have some cheese? (*He can't answer.*) It's very late, darling. Come to bed, heh?

Willy (*looking straight up*): Gotta break your neck to see a star in this yard.

Linda: You coming in?

Willy: Whatever happened to that diamond watch fob? Remember? When Ben came from Africa that time? Didn't he give me a watch fob with a diamond in it?

Linda: You pawned it, dear. Twelve, thirteen years ago. For Biff's radio correspondence course.

Willy: Gee, that was a beautiful thing. I'll take a walk.

Linda: But you're in your slippers.

Willy (*starting to go around the house at the left*): I was right! I was! (*Half to* **Linda**, *as he goes, shaking his head*) What a man! There was a man worth talking to. I was right!

Linda (*calling after* **Willy**): But in your slippers, Willy!

(**Willy** *is almost gone when* **Biff**, *in his pajamas, comes down the stairs and enters the kitchen.*)

Biff: What is he doing out there?

Linda: Sh!

Biff: God Almighty, Mom, how long has he been doing this?

Linda: Don't, he'll hear you.

Biff: What the hell is the matter with him?

Linda: It'll pass by morning.

Biff: Shouldn't we do anything?

Linda: Oh, my dear, you should do a lot of things, but there's nothing to do, so go to sleep.

(**Happy** *comes down the stairs and sits on the steps.*)

Happy: I never heard him so loud, Mom.

Linda: Well, come around more often; you'll hear him. (*She sits down at the table and mends the lining of* **Willy's** *jacket.*)

Biff: Why didn't you ever write me about this, Mom?

Linda: How would I write to you? For over three months you had no address.

Biff: I was on the move. But you know I thought of you all the time. You know that, don't you, pal?

Linda: I know, dear, I know. But he likes to have a letter. Just to know that there's still a possibility for better things.

Biff: He's not like this all the time, is he?

Linda: It's when you come he's always the worst.

Biff: When I come home?

Linda: When you write you're coming, he's all smiles, and talks about the future, and—he's just wonderful. And then the closer you seem to come, the more shaky he gets, and then, by the time you get here, he's arguing, and he seems angry at you. I think it's just that maybe he can't bring himself to—to open up to you. Why are you so hateful to each other? Why is that?

Biff (*evasively*): I'm not hateful, Mom.

Linda: But you no sooner come in the door than you're fighting!

Biff: I don't know why. I mean to change. I'm tryin', Mom, you understand?

Linda: Are you home to stay now?

Biff: I don't know. I want to look around, see what's doin'.

Linda: Biff, you can't look around all your life, can you?

Biff: I just can't take hold, Mom. I can't take hold of some kind of a life.

Linda: Biff, a man is not a bird, to come and go with the springtime.

Biff: Your hair . . . (*He touches her hair.*) Your hair got so gray.

Linda: Oh, it's been gray since you were in high school. I just stopped dyeing it, that's all.

Biff: Dye it again, will ya? I don't want my pal looking old. (*He smiles.*)

Linda: You're such a boy! You think you can go away for a year and . . . You've got to get it into your head now that one day you'll knock on this door and there'll be strange people here——

Biff: What are you talking about? You're not even sixty, Mom.

Linda: But what about your father?

Biff (*lamely*): Well, I meant him too.

Happy: He admires Pop.

Linda: Biff, dear, if you don't have any feeling for him, then you can't have any feeling for me.

Biff: Sure I can, Mom.

Linda: No. You can't just come to see me, because I love him. (*With a threat, but only a threat, of tears*) He's the dearest man in the world to me, and I won't have anyone making him feel unwanted and low and blue. You've got to make up your mind now, darling, there's no leeway any more. Either he's your father and you pay him that respect, or else you're not to come here. I know he's not easy to get along with—nobody knows that better than me—but . . .

Willy (*from the left, with a laugh*): Hey, hey, Biffo!

Biff (*starting to go out after* **Willy**): What the hell is the matter with him? (**Happy** *stops him.*)

Linda: Don't—don't go near him!

Biff: Stop making excuses for him! He always, always wiped the floor with you. Never had an ounce of respect for you.

Happy: He's always had respect for——

do you know about it?

st don't call him crazy!

character—Charley wouldn't do this. Not in his own house—

at vomit from his mind.

never had to cope with what he's got to.

worse off than Willy Loman. Believe me, I've seen them.

nake Charley your father, Biff. You can't do that, can you? I don't say he's a great man. Willy Loman never made a lot of money. His name was never in the paper. He's not the finest character that ever lived. But he's a human being, and a terrible thing is happening to him. So attention must be paid. He's not to be allowed to fall into his grave like an old dog. Attention, attention must be finally paid to such a person. You called him crazy——

Biff: I didn't mean——

Linda: No, a lot of people think he's lost his—balance. But you don't have to be very smart to know what his trouble is. The man is exhausted.

Happy: Sure!

Linda: A small man can be just as exhausted as a great man. He works for a company thirty-six years this March, opens up unheard-of territories to their trademark, and now in his old age they take his salary away.

Happy (*indignantly*): I didn't know that, Mom.

Linda: You never asked, my dear! Now that you get your spending money someplace else you don't trouble your mind with him.

Happy: But I gave you money last——

Linda: Christmas time, fifty dollars! To fix the hot water it cost ninety-seven fifty! For five weeks he's been on straight commission, like a beginner, an unknown!

Biff: Those ungrateful bastards!

Linda: Are they any worse than his sons? When he brought them business, when he was young, they were glad to see him. But now his old friends, the old buyers that loved him so and always found some order to hand him in a pinch—they're all dead, retired. He used to be able to make six, seven calls a day in Boston. Now he takes his valises out of the car and puts them back and takes them out again and he's exhausted. Instead of walking he talks now. He drives seven hundred miles, and when he gets there no one knows him any more, no one welcomes him. And what goes through a man's mind, driving seven hundred miles home without having earned a cent? Why shouldn't he talk to himself? Why? When he has to go to Charley and borrow fifty dollars a week and pretend to me that it's his pay? How long can that go on? How long? You see what I'm sitting here and waiting for? And you tell me he has no character? The man who never worked a day but for your benefit? When does he get the medal for that? Is this his reward—to turn around at the age of sixty-three and find his sons, who he loved better than his life, one a philandering bum——

Happy: Mom!

Linda: That's all you are, my baby! (*To* **Biff**) And you! What happened to the love you had for him? You were such pals! How you used to talk to him on the phone every night! How lonely he was till he could come home to you!

Biff: All right, Mom. I'll live here in my room, and I'll get a job. I'll keep away from him, that's all.

Linda: No, Biff. You can't stay here and fight all the time.

Biff: He threw me out of this house, remember that.

Linda: Why did he do that? I never knew why.

Biff: Because I know he's a fake and he doesn't like anybody around who knows!

Linda: Why a fake? In what way? What do you mean?

Biff: Just don't lay it all at my feet. It's between me and him—that's all I have to say. I'll chip in from now on. He'll settle for half my pay check. He'll be all right. I'm going to bed. (*He starts for the stairs.*)

Linda: He won't be all right.

Biff (*turning on the stairs, furiously*): I hate this city and I'll stay here. Now what do you want?

Linda: He's dying, Biff.

(**Happy** *turns quickly to her, shocked.*)

Biff (*after a pause*): Why is he dying?

Linda: He's been trying to kill himself.

Biff (*with great horror*): How?

Linda: I live from day to day.

Biff: What're you talking about?

Linda: Remember I wrote you that he smashed up the car again? In February?

Biff: Well?

Linda: The insurance inspector came. He said that they have evidence. That all these accidents in the last year—weren't—weren't—accidents.

Happy: How can they tell that? That's a lie.

Linda: It seems there's a woman . . . (*She takes a breath as*)

Biff (*sharply but contained*): What woman?

Linda (*simultaneously*): . . . and this woman . . .

Linda: What?

Biff: Nothing. Go ahead.

Linda: What did you say?

Biff: Nothing. I just said what woman?

Happy: What about her?

Linda: Well, it seems she was walking down the road and saw his car. She says that he wasn't driving fast at all, and that he didn't skid. She says he came to that little bridge, and then deliberately smashed into the railing, and it was only the shallowness of the water that saved him.

Biff: Oh, no, he probably just fell asleep again.

Linda: I don't think he fell asleep.

Biff: Why not?

Linda: Last month . . . (*With great difficulty*) Oh, boys, it's so hard to say a thing like this! He's just a big stupid man to you, but I tell you there's more good in him than in many other people. (*She chokes, wipes her eyes.*) I was looking for a fuse. The lights blew out, and I went down the cellar. And behind the fuse box—it happened to fall out—was a length of rubber pipe—just short.

Happy: No kidding?

Linda: There's a little attachment on the end of it. I knew right away. And sure enough, on the bottom of the water heater there's a new little nipple on the gas pipe.

Happy (*angrily*): That—jerk.

Biff: Did you have it taken off?

Linda: I'm—I'm ashamed to. How can I mention it to him? Every day I go down and take away that little rubber pipe. But, when he comes home, I put it back where it was. How can I insult him that way? I don't know what to do. I live from day to day, boys. I tell you, I know every thought in his mind. It sounds so old-fashioned and silly, but I tell you he put his whole life into you and you've turned your backs on him. (*She is bent over in the chair, weeping, her face in her hands.*) Biff, I swear to God! Biff, his life is in your hands!

Happy (*to* **Biff**): How do you like that damned fool!

Biff (*kissing her*): All right, pal, all right. It's all settled now. I've been remiss. I know that, Mom. But now I'll stay, and I swear to you, I'll apply myself. (*Kneeling in front of her, in a fever of self-reproach*) It's just—you see, Mom, I don't fit in business. Not that I won't try. I'll try, and I'll make good.

Happy: Sure you will. The trouble with you in business was you never tried to please people.

Biff: I know, I—

Happy: Like when you worked for Harrison's. Bob Harrison said you were tops, and then you go and do some damn fool thing like whistling whole songs in the elevator like a comedian.

Biff (*against* **Happy**): So what? I like to whistle sometimes.

Happy: You don't raise a guy to a responsible job who whistles in the elevator!

Linda: Well, don't argue about it now.

Happy: Like when you'd go off and swim in the middle of the day instead of taking the line around.

Biff (*his resentment rising*): Well, don't you run off? You take off sometimes, don't you? On a nice summer day?

Happy: Yeah, but I cover myself!

Linda: Boys!

Happy: If I'm going to take a fade the boss can call any number where I'm supposed to be and they'll swear to him that I just left. I'll tell you something that I hate to say, Biff, but in the business world some of them think you're crazy.

Biff (*angered*): Screw the business world!

Happy: All right, screw it! Great, but cover yourself!

Linda: Hap, Hap!

Biff: I don't care what they think! They've laughed at Dad for years, and you know why? Because we don't belong in this nuthouse of a city! We should be mixing cement on some open plain, or—or carpenters. A carpenter is allowed to whistle! (**Willy** *walks in from the entrance of the house, at left.*)

Willy: Even your grandfather was better than a carpenter. (*Pause. They watch him.*) You never grew up. Bernard does not whistle in the elevator, I assure you.

Biff (*as though to laugh* **Willy** *out of it*): Yeah, but you do, Pop.

Willy: I never in my life whistled in an elevator! And who in the business world thinks I'm crazy?

Biff: I didn't mean it like that, Pop. Now don't make a whole thing out of it, will ya?

Willy: Go back to the West! Be a carpenter, a cowboy, enjoy yourself!

Linda: Willy, he was just saying—

Willy: I heard what he said!

Happy (*trying to quiet* **Willy**): Hey, Pop, come on now . . .

Willy (*continuing over* **Happy's** *line*): They laugh at me, heh? Go to Filene's, go to the Hub, go to Slattery's, Boston. Call out the name Willy Loman and see what happens! Big shot!

Biff: All right, Pop.

Willy: Big!

Biff: All right!

Willy: Why do you always insult me?

Biff: I didn't say a word. (*To* **Linda**) Did I say a word?

Linda: He didn't say anything, Willy.

Willy (*going to the doorway of the living-room*): All right, good night, good night.

Linda: Willy, dear, he just decided . . .

Willy (*to* **Biff**): If you get tired hanging around tomorrow, paint the ceiling I put up in the living-room.

Biff: I'm leaving early tomorrow.

Happy: He's going to see Bill Oliver, Pop.

Willy (*interestedly*): Oliver? For what?

Biff (*with reserve, but trying, trying*): He always said he'd stake me. I'd like to go into business, so maybe I can take him up on it.

Linda: Isn't that wonderful?

Willy: Don't interrupt. What's wonderful about it? There's fifty men in the City of New York who'd stake him. (*To* **Biff**) Sporting goods?

Biff: I guess so. I know something about it and——

Willy: He knows something about it! You know sporting goods better than Spalding, for God's sake! How much is he giving you?

Biff: I don't know, I didn't even see him yet, but——

Willy: Then what're you talkin' about?

Biff (*getting angry*): Well, all I said was I'm gonna see him, that's all!

Willy (*turning away*): Ah, you're counting your chickens again.

Biff (*starting left for the stairs*): Oh, Jesus, I'm going to sleep!

Willy (*calling after him*): Don't curse in this house!

Biff (*turning*): Since when did you get so clean?

Happy (*trying to stop them*): Wait a . . .

Willy: Don't use that language to me! I won't have it!

Happy (*grabbing* **Biff**, *shouts*): Wait a minute! I got an idea. I got a feasible idea. Come here, Biff, let's talk this over now, let's talk some sense here. When I was down in Florida last time, I thought of a great idea to sell sporting goods. It just came back to me. You and I, Biff—we have a line, the Loman Line. We train a couple of weeks, and put on a couple of exhibitions, see?

Willy: That's an idea!

Happy: Wait! We form two basketball teams, see? Two water-polo teams. We play each other. It's a million dollars' worth of publicity. Two brothers, see? The Loman Brothers. Displays in the Royal Palms—all the hotels. And banners over the ring and the basketball court: "Loman Brothers." Baby, we could sell sporting goods!

Willy: That is a one-million-dollar idea!

Linda: Marvelous!

Biff: I'm in great shape as far as that's concerned.

Happy: And the beauty of it is, Biff, it wouldn't be like a business. We'd be out playin' ball again . . .

Biff (*enthused*): Yeah, that's . . .

Willy: Million-dollar . . .

Happy: And you wouldn't get fed up with it, Biff. It'd be the family again. There'd be the old honor, and comradeship, and if you wanted to go off for a swim or somethin'—well, you'd do it! Without some smart cooky gettin' up ahead of you!

Willy: Lick the world! You guys together could absolutely lick the civilized world.

Biff: I'll see Oliver tomorrow. Hap, if we could work that out . . .

Linda: Maybe things are beginning to——

Willy (*wildly enthused, to* **Linda**): Stop interrupting! (*To* **Biff**) But don't wear a sports jacket and slacks when you see Oliver.

Biff: No, I'll——

Willy: A business suit, and talk as little as possible, and don't crack any jokes.

Biff: He did like me. Always liked me.

Linda: He loved you!

Willy (*to* **Linda**): Will you stop! (*To* **Biff**) Walk in very serious. You are not applying for a boy's job. Money is to pass. Be quiet, fine, and serious. Everybody likes a kidder, but nobody lends him money.

Happy: I'll try to get some myself, Biff. I'm sure I can.

Willy: I see great things for you kids, I think your troubles are over. But remember, start big and you'll end big. Ask for fifteen. How much you gonna ask for?

Biff: Gee, I don't know——

Willy: And don't say "Gee." "Gee" is a boy's word. A man walking in for fifteen thousand dollars does not say "Gee!"

Biff: Ten, I think, would be top though.

Willy: Don't be so modest. You always started too low. Walk in with a big laugh. Don't look worried. Start off with a couple of your good stories to lighten things up. It's not what you say, it's how you say it—because personality always wins the day.

Linda: Oliver always thought the highest of him——

Willy: Will you let me talk?

Biff: Don't yell at her, Pop, will ya?

Willy (*angrily*): I was talking, wasn't I?

Biff: I don't like you yelling at her all the time, and I'm tellin' you, that's all.

Willy: What're you, takin' over this house?

Linda: Willy——

Willy (*turning on her*): Don't take his side all the time, goddammit!

Biff (*furiously*): Stop yelling at her!

Willy (*suddenly pulling on his cheek, beaten down, guilt ridden*): Give my best to Bill Oliver—he may remember me. (*He exits through the living-room doorway.*)

Linda (*her voice subdued*): What'd you have to start that for? (**Biff** *turns away.*) You see how sweet he was as soon as you talked hopefully? (*She goes over to* **Biff**.) Come up and say good night to him. Don't let him go to bed that way.

Happy: Come on, Biff, let's buck him up.

Linda: Please, dear. Just say good night. It takes so little to make him happy. Come. (*She goes through the living-room doorway, calling upstairs from within the living-room.*) Your pajamas are hanging in the bathroom, Willy!

Happy (*looking toward where* **Linda** *went out*): What a woman! They broke the mold when they made her. You know that, Biff?

Biff: He's off salary. My God, working on commission!

Happy: Well, let's face it: he's no hot-shot selling man. Except that sometimes, you have to admit, he's a sweet personality.

Biff (*deciding*): Lend me ten bucks, will ya? I want to buy some new ties.

Happy: I'll take you to a place I know. Beautiful stuff. Wear one of my striped shirts tomorrow.

Biff: She got gray. Mom got awful old. Gee, I'm gonna go in to Oliver tomorrow and knock him for a——

Happy: Come on up. Tell that to Dad. Let's give him a whirl. Come on.

Biff (*steamed up*): You know, with ten thousand bucks, boy!

Happy (*as they go into the living-room*): That's the talk, Biff, that's the first time I've heard the old confidence out of you! (*From within the living-room, fading off*) You're gonna live with me, kid, and any babe you want just say the word . . . (*The last lines are hardly heard. They are mounting the stairs to their parents' bedroom.*)

Linda (*entering her bedroom and addressing* **Willy**, *who is in the bathroom. She is straightening the bed for him*): Can you do anything about the shower? It drips.

Willy (*from the bedroom*): All of a sudden everything falls to pieces! Goddam plumbing, oughta be sued, those people. I hardly finished putting it in and the thing . . . (*His words rumble off.*)

Linda: I'm just wondering if Oliver will remember him. You think he might?

Willy (*coming out of the bathroom in his pajamas*): Remember him? What's the matter with you, you crazy? If he'd've stayed with Oliver he'd be on top by now! Wait'll Oliver gets a look at him. You don't know the average caliber any more. The average young man today—(*he is getting into bed*)—is got a caliber of zero. Greatest thing in the world for him was to bum around.

(**Biff** *and* **Happy** *enter the bedroom. Slight pause.*)

Willy (*stops short, looking at* **Biff**): Glad to hear it, boy.

Happy: He wanted to say good night to you, sport.

Willy (*to* **Biff**): Yeah. Knock him dead, boy. What'd you want to tell me?

Biff: Just take it easy, Pop. Good night. (*He turns to go.*)

Willy (*unable to resist*): And if anything falls off the desk while you're talking to him—like a package or something—don't you pick it up. They have office boys for that.

Linda: I'll make a big breakfast——

Willy: Will you let me finish? (*To* **Biff**) Tell him you were in the business in the West. Not farm work.

Biff: All right, Dad.

Linda: I think everything——

Willy (*going right through her speech*): And don't undersell yourself. No less than fifteen thousand dollars.

Biff (*unable to bear him*): Okay. Good night, Mom. (*He starts moving.*)

Willy: Because you got a greatness in you, Biff, remember that. You got all kinds of greatness . . .

(*He lies back, exhausted.* **Biff** *walks out.*)

Linda (*calling after* **Biff**): Sleep well, darling!

Happy: I'm gonna get married, Mom. I wanted to tell you.

Linda: Go to sleep, dear.

Happy (*going*): I just wanted to tell you.

Willy: Keep up the good work. (**Happy** *exits.*) God . . . remember that Ebbets Field game? The championship of the city?

Linda: Just rest. Should I sing to you?

Willy: Yeah. Sing to me. (**Linda** *hums a soft lullaby.*) When that team came out— he was the tallest, remember?

Linda: Oh, yes. And in gold.

(**Biff** *enters the darkened kitchen, takes a cigarette, and leaves the house. He comes downstage into a golden pool of light. He smokes, staring at the night.*)

Willy: Like a young god. Hercules—something like that. And the sun, the sun all around him. Remember how he waved to me? Right up from the field, with the representatives of three colleges standing by? And the buyers I brought, and the cheers when he came out—Loman, Loman, Loman! God Almighty, he'll be great yet. A star like that, magnificent, can never really fade away!

(*The light on* **Willy** *is fading. The gas heater begins to glow through the kitchen wall, near the stairs, a blue flame beneath red coils.*)

Linda (*timidly*): Willy dear, what has he got against you?

Willy: I'm so tired. Don't talk any more.

(**Biff** *slowly returns to the kitchen. He stops, stares toward the heater.*)

Linda: Will you ask Howard to let you work in New York?

Willy: First thing in the morning. Everything'll be all right.

(**Biff** *reaches behind the heater and draws out a length of rubber tubing. He is horrified and turns his head toward* **Willy's** *room, still dimly lit, from which the strains of* **Linda's** *desperate but monotonous humming rise.*)

Willy (*staring through the window into the moonlight*): Gee, look at the moon moving between the buildings!

(**Biff** *wraps the tubing around his hand and quickly goes up the stairs.*)

ACT II

Music is heard, gay and bright. The curtain rises as the music fades away. **Willy**, in shirt sleeves, is sitting at the kitchen table, sipping coffee, his hat in his lap. **Linda** is filling his cup when she can.

Willy: Wonderful coffee. Meal in itself.

Linda: Can I make you some eggs?

Willy: No. Take a breath.

Linda: You look so rested, dear.

Willy: I slept like a dead one. First time in months. Imagine, sleeping till ten on a Tuesday morning. Boys left nice and early, heh?

Linda: They were out of here by eight o'clock.

Willy: Good work!

Linda: It was so thrilling to see them leaving together. I can't get over the shaving lotion in this house!

Willy (*smiling*): Mmm——

Linda: Biff was very changed this morning. His whole attitude seemed to be hopeful. He couldn't wait to get downtown to see Oliver.

Willy: He's heading for a change. There's no question, there simply are certain men that take longer to get—solidified. How did he dress?

Linda: His blue suit. He's so handsome in that suit. He could be a—anything in that suit!

(**Willy** *gets up from the table.* **Linda** *holds his jacket for him.*)

Willy: There's no question, no question at all. Gee, on the way home tonight I'd like to buy some seeds.

Linda (*laughing*): That'd be wonderful. But not enough sun gets back there. Nothing'll grow any more.

Willy: You wait, kid, before it's all over we're gonna get a little place out in the country, and I'll raise some vegetables, a couple of chickens . . .

Linda: You'll do it yet, dear.

(**Willy** *walks out of his jacket.* **Linda** *follows him.*)

Willy: And they'll get married, and come for a weekend. I'd build a little guest house. 'Cause I got so many fine tools, all I'd need would be a little lumber and some peace of mind.

Linda (*joyfully*): I sewed the lining . . .

Willy: I would build two guest houses, so they'd both come. Did he decide how much he's going to ask Oliver for?

Linda (*getting him into the jacket*): He didn't mention it, but I imagine ten or fifteen thousand. You going to talk to Howard today?

Willy: Yeah. I'll put it to him straight and simple. He'll just have to take me off the road.

Linda: And, Willy, don't forget to ask for a little advance, because we've got the insurance premium. It's the grace period now.

Willy: That's a hundred . . .?

Linda: A hundred and eight, sixty-eight. Because we're a little short again.

Willy: Why are we short?

Linda: Well, you had the motor job on the car . . .

Willy: That goddam Studebaker!

Linda: And you got one more payment on the refrigerator . . .

Willy: But it just broke again!

Linda: Well, it's old, dear.

Willy: I told you we should've bought a well-advertised machine. Charley bought a General Electric and it's twenty years old and it's still good, that son-of-a-bitch.

Linda: But, Willy——

Willy: Whoever heard of a Hastings refrigerator? Once in my life I would like to own something outright before it's broken! I'm always in a race with the junkyard! I just finished paying for the car and it's on its last legs. The refrigerator consumes belts like a goddam maniac. They time those things. They time them so when you finally paid for them, they're used up.

Linda (*buttoning up his jacket as he unbuttons it*): All told, about two hundred dollars would carry us, dear. But that includes the last payment on the mortgage. After this payment, Willy, the house belongs to us.

Willy: It's twenty-five years!

Linda: Biff was nine years old when we bought it.

Willy: Well, that's a great thing. To weather a twenty-five year mortgage is——

Linda: It's an accomplishment.

Willy: All the cement, the lumber, the reconstruction I put in this house! There ain't a crack to be found in it any more.

Linda: Well, it served its purpose.

Willy: What purpose? Some stranger'll come along, move in, and that's that. If only Biff would take this house, and raise a family . . . (*He starts to go.*) Good-by, I'm late.

Linda (*suddenly remembering*): Oh, I forgot! You're supposed to meet them for dinner.

Willy: Me?

Linda: At Frank's Chop House on Forty-eighth near Sixth Avenue.

Willy: Is that so! How about you?

Linda: No, just the three of you. They're gonna blow you to a big meal!

Willy: Don't say! Who thought of that?

Linda: Biff came to me this morning, Willy, and he said, "Tell Dad, we want to blow him to a big meal." Be there six o'clock. You and your two boys are going to have dinner.

Willy: Gee whiz! That's really somethin'. I'm gonna knock Howard for a loop, kid. I'll get an advance, and I'll come home with a New York job. Goddammit, now I'm gonna do it!

Linda: Oh, that's the spirit, Willy!

Willy: I will never get behind a wheel the rest of my life!

Linda: It's changing, Willy, I can feel it changing!

Willy: Beyond a question. G'by, I'm late. (*He starts to go again.*)

Linda (*calling after him as she runs to the kitchen table for a handkerchief*): You got your glasses?

Willy (*feels for them, then comes back in*): Yeah, yeah, got my glasses.

Linda (*giving him the handkerchief*): And a handkerchief.

Willy: Yeah, handkerchief.

Linda: And your saccharine?

Willy: Yeah, my saccharine.

Linda: Be careful on the subway stairs.

(*She kisses him, and a silk stocking is seen hanging from her hand.* **Willy** *notices it.*)

Willy: Will you stop mending stockings? At least while I'm in the house. It gets me nervous. I can't tell you. Please.

(**Linda** *hides the stocking in her hand as she follows* **Willy** *across the forestage in front of the house.*)

Linda: Remember, Frank's Chop House.

Willy (*passing the apron*): Maybe beets would grow out there.

Linda (*laughing*): But you tried so many times.

Willy: Yeah. Well, don't work hard today. (*He disappears around the right corner of the house.*)

Linda: Be careful!

(*As* **Willy** *vanishes,* **Linda** *waves to him. Suddenly the phone rings. She runs across the stage and into the kitchen and lifts it.*)

Linda: Hello? Oh, Biff! I'm so glad you called, I just . . . Yes, sure, I just told him. Yes, he'll be there for dinner at six o'clock, I didn't forget. Listen, I was just dying to tell you. You know that little rubber pipe I told you about? That he connected to the gas heater? I finally decided to go down the cellar this morning and take it away and destroy it. But it's gone! Imagine? He took it away himself, it isn't there! (*She listens.*) When? Oh, then you took it. Oh—nothing, it's just that I'd hoped he'd taken it away himself. Oh, I'm not worried, darling, because this morning he left in such high spirits, it was like the old days! I'm not afraid any more. Did Mr. Oliver see you? . . . Well, you wait there then. And make a nice impression on him, darling. Just don't perspire too much before you see him. And have a nice time with Dad. He may have big news too! . . . That's right, a New York job. And be sweet to him tonight, dear. Be loving to him. Because he's only a little boat looking for a harbor. (*She is trembling with sorrow and joy.*) Oh, that's wonderful, Biff, you'll save his life. Thanks, darling. Just put your arm around him when he comes into the restaurant. Give him a smile. That's the boy . . . Good-by, dear . . . You got your comb? . . . That's fine. Good-by, Biff dear.

(*In the middle of her speech,* **Howard Wagner**, *thirty-six, wheels on a small typewriter table on which is a wire-recording machine and proceeds to plug it in. This on the left fore-stage. Light slowly fades on* **Linda** *as it rises on* **Howard**. **Howard** *is intent on threading the machine and only glances over his shoulder as* **Willy** *appears.*)

Willy: Pst! Pst!

Howard: Hello, Willy, come in.

Willy: Like to have a little talk with you, Howard.

Howard: Sorry to keep you waiting. I'll be with you in a minute.

Willy: What's that, Howard?

Howard: Didn't you ever see one of these? Wire recorder.

Willy: Oh. Can we talk a minute?

Howard: Records things. Just got delivery yesterday. Been driving me crazy, the most terrific machine I ever saw in my life. I was up all night with it.

Willy: What do you do with it?

Howard: I bought it for dictation, but you can do anything with it. Listen to this. I had it home last night. Listen to what I picked up. The first one is my daughter. Get this. (*He flicks the switch and "Roll Out the Barrel" is heard being whistled.*) Listen to that kid whistle.

Willy: That is lifelike, isn't it?

Howard: Seven years old. Get that tone.

Willy: Ts, ts. Like to ask a little favor if you . . .

(*The whistling breaks off, and the voice of* **Howard's** *daughter is heard.*)

His Daughter: "Now you, Daddy."

Howard: She's crazy for me! (*Again the same song is whistled.*) That's me! Ha! (*He winks.*)

Willy: You're very good!

(*The whistling breaks off again. The machine runs silent for a moment.*)

Howard: Sh! Get this now, this is my son.

His Son: "The capital of Alabama is Montgomery; the capital of Arizona is Phoenix; the capital of Arkansas is Little Rock; the capital of California is Sacramento . . ." (*and on, and on*).

Howard (*holding up five fingers*): Five years old, Willy!

Willy: He'll make an announcer some day!

His Son (*continuing*): "The capital . . ."

Howard: Get that—alphabetical order! (*The machine breaks off suddenly.*) Wait a minute. The maid kicked the plug out.

Willy: It certainly is a——

Howard: Sh, for God's sake!

His Son: "It's nine o'clock, Bulova watch time. So I have to go to sleep."

Willy: That really is——

Howard: Wait a minute! The next is my wife.

(*They wait.*)

Howard's Voice: "Go on, say something." (*Pause*) "Well, you gonna talk?"

His Wife: "I can't think of anything."

Howard's Voice: "Well, talk—it's turning."

His Wife (*shyly, beaten*): "Hello." (*Silence*) "Oh, Howard, I can't talk into this . . ."

Howard (*snapping the machine off*): That was my wife.

Willy: That is a wonderful machine. Can we——

Howard: I tell you, Willy, I'm gonna take my camera, and my bandsaw, and all my hobbies, and out they go. This is the most fascinating relaxation I ever found.

Willy: I think I'll get one myself.

Howard: Sure, they're only a hundred and a half. You can't do without it. Supposing you wanna hear Jack Benny, see? But you can't be at home at that hour. So you tell the maid to turn the radio on when Jack Benny comes on, and this automatically goes on with the radio . . .

Willy: And when you come home you . . .

Howard: You can come home twelve o'clock, one o'clock, any time you like, and you get yourself a Coke and sit yourself down, throw the switch, and there's Jack Benny's program in the middle of the night!

Willy: I'm definitely going to get one. Because lots of time I'm on the road, and I think to myself, what I must be missing on the radio!

Howard: Don't you have a radio in the car?

Willy: Well, yeah, but who ever thinks of turning it on?

Howard: Say, aren't you supposed to be in Boston?

Willy: That's what I want to talk to you about, Howard. You got a minute? (*He draws a chair in from the wing.*)

Howard: What happened? What're you doing here?

Willy: Well . . .

Howard: You didn't crack up again, did you?

Willy: Oh, no. No . . .

Howard: Geez, you had me worried there for a minute. What's the trouble?

Willy: Well, tell you the truth, Howard. I've come to the decision that I'd rather not travel any more.

Howard: Not travel! Well, what'll you do?

Willy: Remember, Christmas time, when you had the party here? You said you'd try to think of some spot for me here in town.

Howard: With us?

Willy: Well, sure.

Howard: Oh, yeah, yeah. I remember. Well, I couldn't think of anything for you, Willy.

Willy: I tell ya, Howard. The kids are all grown up, y'know. I don't need much any more. If I could take home—well, sixty-five dollars a week, I could swing it.

Howard: Yeah, but Willy, see I——

Willy: I tell ya why, Howard. Speaking frankly and between the two of us, y'know —I'm just a little tired.

Howard: Oh, I could understand that, Willy. But you're a road man, Willy, and we do a road business. We've only got a half-dozen salesmen on the floor here.

Willy: God knows, Howard, I never asked a favor of any man. But I was with the firm when your father used to carry you in here in his arms.

Howard: I know that, Willy, but——

Willy: Your father came to me the day you were born and asked me what I thought of the name of Howard, may he rest in peace.

Howard: I appreciate that, Willy, but there just is no spot here for you. If I had a spot I'd slam you right in, but I just don't have a single solitary spot.

(*He looks for his lighter.* **Willy** *has picked it up and gives it to him. Pause.*)

Willy (*with increasing anger*): Howard, all I need to set my table is fifty dollars a week.

Howard: But where am I going to put you, kid?

Willy: Look, it isn't a question of whether I can sell merchandise, is it?

Howard: No, but it's a business, kid, and everybody gotta pull his own weight.

Willy (*desperately*): Just let me tell you a story, Howard——

Howard: 'Cause you gotta admit, business is business.

Willy (*angrily*): Business is definitely business, but just listen for a minute. You don't understand this. When I was a boy—eighteen, nineteen—I was already on the road. And there was a question in my mind as to whether selling had a future for me. Because in those days I had a yearning to go to Alaska. See, there were three gold strikes in one month in Alaska, and I felt like going out. Just for the ride, you might say.

Howard (*barely interested*): Don't say.

Willy: Oh, yeah, my father lived many years in Alaska. He was an adventurous man. We've got quite a little streak of self-reliance in our family. I thought I'd go out with my older brother and try to locate him, and maybe settle in the North with the old man. And I was almost decided to go, when I met a salesman in the Parker House. His name was Dave Singleman. And he was eighty-four years old, and he'd drummed merchandise in thirty-one states. And old Dave, he'd go up to his room, y'understand, put on his green velvet slippers—I'll never forget—and pick up his phone and call the buyers, and without ever leaving his room, at the age of eighty-four, he made his living. And when I saw that, I realized that selling was the greatest career a man could want. 'Cause what could be more satisfying than to be able to go, at the age of eighty-four, into twenty or thirty different cities, and pick up a phone, and be remembered and loved and helped by so many different people? Do you know? When he died—and by the way he died the death of a salesman, in his green velvet slippers in the smoker of the New York, New Haven and Hartford, going into Boston—when he died, hundreds of salesmen and buyers were at his funeral. Things were sad on a lotta trains for months after that. (*He stands up.* **Howard** *has not looked at him.*) In those days there was personality in it, Howard. There was respect, and comradeship, and gratitude in it. Today, it's all cut and dried, and there's no chance for bringing friendship to bear—or personality. You see what I mean? They don't know me any more.

Howard (*moving away, to the right*): That's just the thing, Willy.

Willy: If I had forty dollars a week—that's all I'd need. Forty dollars, Howard.

Howard: Kid, I can't take blood from a stone, I——

Willy (*desperation is on him now*): Howard, the year Al Smith was nominated, your father came to me and——

Howard (*starting to go off*): I've got to see some people, kid.

Willy (*stopping him*): I'm talking about your father! There were promises made across this desk! You mustn't tell me you've got people to see—I put thirty-four years into this firm, Howard, and now I can't pay my insurance! You can't eat the orange and throw the peel away—a man is not a piece of fruit! (*After a pause*) Now pay attention. Your father—in 1928 I had a big year. I averaged a hundred and seventy dollars a week in commissions.

Howard (*impatiently*): Now, Willy, you never averaged——

Willy (banging his hand on the desk): I averaged a hundred and seventy dollars a week in the year of 1928! And your father came to me—or rather, I was in the office here—it was right over this desk—and he put his hand on my shoulder—

Howard (*getting up*): You'll have to excuse me, Willy, I gotta see some people. Pull yourself together. (*Going out*) I'll be back in a little while.

(*On* **Howard's** *exit, the light on his chair grows very bright and strange.*)

Willy: Pull myself together! What the hell did I say to him? My God, I was yelling at him! How could I! (**Willy** *breaks off, staring at the light, which occupies the chair, animating it. He approaches this chair, standing across the desk from it.*) Frank, Frank, don't you remember what you told me that time? How you put your hand on my shoulder, and Frank . . . (*He leans on the desk and as he speaks the dead man's name he accidentally switches on the recorder, and instantly*)

Howard's Son: ". . . of New York is Albany. The capital of Ohio is Cincinnati, the capital of Rhode Island is . . ." (*The recitation continues.*)

Willy (*leaping away with fright, shouting*): Ha! Howard! Howard! Howard!

Howard (*rushing in*): What happened?

Willy (*pointing at the machine, which continues nasally, childishly, with the capital cities*): Shut it off! Shut it off!

Howard (*pulling the plug out*): Look, Willy . . .

Willy (*pressing his hands to his eyes*): I gotta get myself some coffee. I'll get some coffee . . .

(**Willy** *starts to walk out.* **Howard** *stops him.*)

Howard (*rolling up the cord*): Willy, look . . .

Willy: I'll go to Boston.

Howard: Willy, you can't go to Boston for us.

Willy: Why can't I go?

Howard: I don't want you to represent us. I've been meaning to tell you for a long time now.

Willy: Howard, are you firing me?

Howard: I think you need a good long rest, Willy.

Willy: Howard——

Howard: And when you feel better, come back, and we'll see if we can work something out.

Willy: But I gotta earn money, Howard. I'm in no position to——

Howard: Where are your sons? Why don't your sons give you a hand?

Willy: They're working on a very big deal.

Howard: This is no time for false pride, Willy. You go to your sons and you tell them that you're tired. You've got two great boys, haven't you?

Willy: Oh, no question, no question, but in the meantime . . .

Howard: Then that's that, heh?

Willy: All right, I'll go to Boston tomorrow.

Howard: No, no.

Willy: I can't throw myself on my sons. I'm not a cripple!

Howard: Look, kid, I'm busy this morning.

Willy (*grasping* **Howard's** *arm*): Howard, you've got to let me go to Boston!

Howard (*hard, keeping himself under control*): I've got a line of people to see this morning. Sit down, take five minutes, and pull yourself together, and then go home, will ya? I need the office, Willy. (*He starts to go, turns, remembering the recorder, starts to push off the table holding the recorder.*) Oh, yeah. Whenever you can this week, stop by and drop off the samples. You'll feel better, Willy, and then come back and we'll talk. Pull yourself together, kid, there's people outside. (**Howard** *exits, pushing the table off left.* **Willy** *stares into space, exhausted. Now the music is heard—***Ben's** *music—first distantly, then closer, closer. As* **Willy** *speaks,* **Ben** *enters from the right. He carries valise and umbrella.*)

Willy: Oh, Ben, how did you do it? What is the answer? Did you wind up the Alaska deal already?

Ben: Doesn't take much time if you know what you're doing. Just a short business trip. Boarding ship in an hour. Wanted to say good-by.

Willy: Ben, I've got to talk to you.

Ben (*glancing at his watch*): Haven't the time, William.

Willy (*crossing the apron to* **Ben**): Ben, nothing's working out. I don't know what to do.

Ben: Now, look here, William. I've bought timberland in Alaska and I need a man to look after things for me.

Willy: God, timberland! Me and my boys in those grand outdoors!

Ben: You've a new continent at your doorstep, William. Get out of these cities, they're full of talk and time payments and courts of law. Screw on your fists and you can fight for a fortune up there.

Willy: Yes, yes! Linda, Linda!

(**Linda** *enters as of old, with the wash.*)

Linda: Oh, you're back?

Ben: I haven't much time.

Willy: No, wait! Linda, he's got a proposition for me in Alaska.

Linda: But you've got—(*To* **Ben**) He's got a beautiful job here.

Willy: But in Alaska, kid, I could——

Linda: You're doing well enough, Willy!

Ben (*to* **Linda**): Enough for what, my dear?

Linda (*frightened of* **Ben** *and angry at him*): Don't say those things to him! Enough to be happy right here, right now. (*To* **Willy**, *while* **Ben** *laughs*) Why must everybody conquer the world? You're well liked, and the boys love you, and someday —(*to* **Ben**)—why, old man Wagner told him just the other day that if he keeps it up he'll be a member of the firm, didn't he Willy?

Willy: Sure, sure. I am building something with this firm, Ben, and if a man is building something he must be on the right track, mustn't he?

Ben: What are you building? Lay your hand on it. Where is it?

Willy (*hesitantly*): That's true, Linda, there's nothing.

Linda: Why? (*To* **Ben**) There's a man eighty-four years old——

Willy: That's right, Ben, that's right. When I look at that man I say, what is there to worry about?

Ben: Bah!

Willy: It's true, Ben. All he has to do is go into any city, pick up the phone, and he's making his living and you know why?

Ben (*picking up his valise*): I've got to go.

Willy (*holding* **Ben** *back*): Look at this boy!

(**Biff**, *in his high school sweater, enters carrying suitcase.* **Happy** *carries* **Biff's** *shoulder guards, gold helmet, and football pants.*)

Willy: Without a penny to his name, three great universities are begging for him, and from there the sky's the limit, because it's not what you do, Ben. It's who you know and the smile on your face! It's contacts, Ben, contacts! The whole wealth of Alaska passes over the lunch table at the Commodore Hotel, and that's the wonder, the wonder of this country, that a man can end with diamonds here on the basis of being liked! (*He turns to* **Biff**) And that's why when you get on that field today, it's important. Because thousands of people will be rooting for you and loving you. (*To* **Ben**, *who has again begun to leave*) And Ben! when he walks into a business office his name will sound out like a bell and all the doors will open to him! I've seen it, Ben, I've seen it a thousand times! You can't feel it with your hand like timber, but it's there!

Ben: Good-by, William.

Willy: Ben, am I right? Don't you think I'm right? I value your advice.

Ben: There's a new continent at your doorstep, William. You could walk out rich. Rich! (*He is gone.*)

Willy: We'll do it here, Ben! You hear me? We're gonna do it here!

(*Young* **Bernard** *rushes in. The gay music of the boys is heard.*)

Bernard: Oh, gee, I was afraid you left already!

Willy: Why? What time is it?

Bernard: It's half-past one!

Willy: Well, come on, everybody! Ebbets Field next stop! Where's the pennants? (*He rushes through the wall-line of the kitchen and out into the living-room.*)

Linda (*to* **Biff**): Did you pack fresh underwear?

Biff (*who has been limbering up*): I want to go!

Bernard: Biff, I'm carrying your helmet, ain't I?

Happy: No, I'm carrying the helmet.

Bernard: Oh, Biff, you promised me.

Happy: I'm carrying the helmet.

Bernard: How am I going to get in the locker room?

Linda: Let him carry the shoulder guards. (*She puts her coat and hat on in the kitchen.*)

Bernard: Can I, Biff? 'Cause I told everybody I'm going to be in the locker room.

Happy: In Ebbets Field it's the clubhouse.

Bernard: I meant the clubhouse, Biff!

Happy: Biff!

Biff (*grandly, after a slight pause*): Let him carry the shoulder guards.

Happy (*as he gives* **Bernard** *the shoulder guards*): Stay close to us now.

(**Willy** *rushes in with the pennants.*)

Willy (*handing them out*): Everybody wave when Biff comes out on the field. (**Happy** *and* **Bernard** *run off.*) You set now, boy?

(*The music has died away.*)

Biff: Ready to go, Pop. Every muscle is ready.

Willy (*at the edge of the apron*): You realize what this means?

Biff: That's right, Pop.

Willy (*feeling* **Biff's** *muscles*): You're comin' home this afternoon captain of the All-Scholastic Championship Team of the City of New York.

Biff: I got it, Pop. And remember, pal, when I take off my helmet, that touchdown is for you.

Willy: Let's go! (*He is starting out, with his arm around* **Biff**, *when* **Charley** *enters, as of old, in knickers.*) I got no room for you, Charley.

Charley: Room? For what?

Willy: In the car.

Charley: You goin' for a ride? I wanted to shoot some casino.

Willy (*furiously*): Casino! (*Incredulously*) Don't you realize what today is?

Linda: Oh, he knows, Willy. He's just kidding you.

Willy: That's nothing to kid about!

Charley: No, Linda, what's goin' on?

Linda: He's playing in Ebbets Field.

Charley: Baseball in this weather?

Willy: Don't talk to him. Come on, come on! (*He is pushing them out.*)

Charley: Wait a minute, didn't you hear the news?

Willy: What?

Charley: Don't you listen to the radio? Ebbets Field just blew up.

Willy: You go to hell! (**Charley** *laughs. Pushing them out*) Come on, come on! We're late.

Charley (*as they go*): Knock a homer, Biff, knock a homer!

Willy (*the last to leave, turning to* **Charley**): I don't think that was funny, Charley. This is the greatest day of his life.

Charley: Willy, when are you going to grow up?

Willy: Yeah, heh? When this game is over, Charley, you'll be laughing out of the other side of your face. They'll be calling him another Red Grange. Twenty-five thousand a year.

Charley (*kidding*): Is that so?

Willy: Yeah, that's so.

Charley: Well, then, I'm sorry, Willy. But tell me something.

Willy: What?

Charley: Who is Red Grange?

Willy: Put up your hands. Goddam you, put up your hands!

(**Charley**, *chuckling, shakes his head and walks away, around the left corner of the stage.* **Willy** *follows him. The music rises to a mocking frenzy.*)

Willy: Who the hell do you think you are, better than everybody else? You don't know everything, you big, ignorant, stupid . . . Put up your hands!

(*Light rises, on the right side of the forestage, on a small table in the reception room of* **Charley's** *office. Traffic sounds are heard.* **Bernard**, *now mature, sits whistling to himself. A pair of tennis rackets and an overnight bag are on the floor beside him.*)

Willy (*offstage*): What are you walking away for? Don't walk away! If you're going to say something say it to my face! I know you laugh at me behind my back. You'll laugh out of the other side of your goddam face after this game. Touch-down! Touchdown! Eighty thousand people! Touchdown! Right between the goal posts.

(**Bernard** *is a quiet, earnest, but self-assured young man.* **Willy's** *voice is coming from right upstage now.* **Bernard** *lowers his feet off the table and listens.* **Jenny**, *his father's secretary, enters.*)

Jenny (*distressed*): Say, Bernard, will you go out in the hall?

Bernard: What is that noise? Who is it?

Jenny: Mr. Loman. He just got off the elevator.

Bernard (*getting up*): Who's he arguing with?

Jenny: Nobody. There's nobody with him. I can't deal with him any more, and your father gets all upset everytime he comes. I've got a lot of typing to do, and your father's waiting to sign it. Will you see him?

Willy (*entering*): Touchdown! Touch—(*He sees* **Jenny**.) Jenny, Jenny, good to see you. How're ya? Workin'? Or still honest?

Jenny: Fine. How've you been feeling?

Willy: Not much any more, Jenny. Ha, Ha! (*He is surprised to see the rackets.*)

Bernard: Hello, Uncle Willy.

Willy (*almost shocked*): Bernard! Well, look who's here! (*He comes quickly, guiltily, to* **Bernard** *and warmly shakes his hand.*)

Bernard: How are you? Good to see you.

Willy: What are you doing here?

Bernard: Oh, just stopped by to see Pop. Get off my feet till my train leaves. I'm going to Washington in a few minutes.

Willy: Is he in?

Bernard: Yes, he's in his office with the accountant. Sit down.

Willy (*sitting down*): What're you going to do in Washington?

Bernard: Oh, just a case I've got there, Willy.

Willy: That so? (*Indicating the rackets*) You going to play tennis there?

Bernard: I'm staying with a friend who's got a court.

Willy: Don't say. His own tennis court. Must be fine people, I bet.

Bernard: They are, very nice. Dad tells me Biff's in town.

Willy (*with a big smile*): Yeah, Biff's in. Working on a very big deal, Bernard.

Bernard: What's Biff doing?

Willy: Well, he's been doing very big things in the West. But he decided to establish himself here. Very big. We're having dinner. Did I hear your wife had a boy?

Bernard: That's right. Our second.

Willy: Two boys! What do you know!

Bernard: What kind of a deal has Biff got?

Willy: Well, Bill Oliver—very big sporting goods man—he wants Biff very badly. Called him in from the West. Long distance, carte blanche, special deliveries. Your friends have their own private tennis court?

Bernard: You still with the old firm, Willy?

Willy (*after a pause*): I'm—I'm overjoyed to see how you made the grade, Bernard, overjoyed. It's an encouraging thing to see a young man really—really—Looks very good for Biff—very—(*He breaks off, then*) Bernard—(*He is so full of emotion, he breaks off again.*)

Bernard: What is it, Willy?

Willy (*small and alone*): What—what's the secret?

Bernard: What secret?

Willy: How—how did you? Why didn't he ever catch on?

Bernard: I wouldn't know that, Willy.

Willy (*confidentially, desperately*): You were his friend, his boyhood friend. There's something I don't understand about it. His life ended after that Ebbets Field game. From the age of seventeen nothing good ever happened to him.

Bernard: He never trained himself for anything.

Willy: But he did, he did. After high school he took so many correspondence courses. Radio mechanics; television; God knows what, and never made the slightest mark.

Bernard (*taking off his glasses*): Willy, do you want to talk candidly?

Willy (*rising, faces* **Bernard**): I regard you as a very brilliant man, Bernard. I value your advice.

Bernard: Oh, the hell with the advice, Willy. I couldn't advise you. There's just one thing I've always wanted to ask you. When he was supposed to graduate, and the math teacher flunked him——

Willy: Oh, that son-of-a-bitch ruined his life.

Bernard: Yeah, but, Willy, all he had to do was go to summer school and make up that subject.

Willy: That's right, that's right.

Bernard: Did you tell him not to go to summer school?

Willy: Me? I begged him to go. I ordered him to go!

Bernard: Then why wouldn't he go?

Willy: Why? Why! Bernard, that question has been trailing me like a ghost for the past fifteen years. He flunked the subject, and laid down and died like a hammer hit him!

Bernard: Take it easy, kid.

Willy: Let me talk to you—I got nobody to talk to. Bernard, Bernard, was it my fault? Y'see? It keeps going around in my mind, maybe I did something to him. I got nothing to give him.

Bernard: Don't take it so hard.

Willy: Why did he lay down? What is the story there? You were his friend!

Bernard: Willy, I remember, it was June, and our grades came out. And he'd flunked math.

Willy: That son-of-a-bitch!

Bernard: No, it wasn't right then. Biff just got very angry, I remember, and he was ready to enroll in summer school.

Willy (*surprised*): He was?

Bernard: He wasn't beaten by it at all. But then, Willy, he disappeared from the block for almost a month. And I got the idea that he'd gone up to New England to see you. Did he have a talk with you then?

(**Willy** *stares in silence.*)

Bernard: Willy?

Willy (*with a strong edge of resentment in his voice*): Yeah, he came to Boston. What about it?

Bernard: Well, just that when he came back—I'll never forget this, it always mystifies me. Because I thought so well of Biff, even though he'd always taken advantage of me. I loved him, Willy, y'know? And he came back after that month and took his sneakers—remember those sneakers with "University of Virginia" printed on them? He was so proud of those, wore them every day. And he took them down in the cellar, and burned them up in the furnace. We had a fist fight. It lasted at least half an hour. Just the two of us, punching each other down the cellar, and crying right through it. I've often thought of how strange it was that I knew he'd given up his life. What happened in Boston, Willy?

(**Willy** *looks at him as at an intruder.*)

Bernard: I just bring it up because you asked me.

Willy (*angrily*): Nothing. What do you mean, "What happened?" What's that got to do with anything?

Bernard: Well, don't get sore.

Willy: What are you trying to do, blame it on me? If a boy lays down is that my fault?

Bernard: Now, Willy, don't get——

Willy: Well, don't—don't talk to me that way! What does that mean, "What happened?"

(**Charley** *enters. He is in his vest, and he carries a bottle of bourbon.*)

Charley: Hey, you're going to miss that train. (*He waves the bottle.*)

Bernard: Yeah, I'm going. (*He takes the bottle.*) Thanks, Pop. (*He picks up his rackets and bag.*) Good-by, Willy, and don't worry about it. You know, "If at first you don't succeed . . ."

Willy: Yes, I believe in that.

Bernard: But sometimes, Willy, it's better for a man just to walk away.

Willy: Walk away?

Bernard: That's right.

Willy: But if you can't walk away?

Bernard (*after a slight pause*): I guess that's when it's tough. (*Extending his hand*) Good-by, Willy.

Willy (*shaking **Bernard's** hand*): Good-by, boy.

Charley (*an arm on **Bernard's** shoulder*): How do you like this kid? Gonna argue a case in front of the Supreme Court.

Bernard (*protesting*): Pop!

Willy (*genuinely shocked, pained, and happy*): No! The Supreme Court!

Bernard: I gotta run. 'By, Dad!

Charley: Knock 'em dead, Bernard!

(**Bernard** *goes off.*)

Willy (*as **Charley** takes out his wallet*): The Supreme Court! And he didn't even mention it!

Charley (*counting out money on the desk*): He don't have to—he's gonna do it.

Willy: And you never told him what to do, did you? You never took any interest in him.

Charley: My salvation is that I never took any interest in anything. There's some money—fifty dollars. I got an accountant inside.

Willy: Charley, look . . . (*With difficulty*) I got my insurance to pay. If you can manage it—I need a hundred and ten dollars.

(**Charley** *doesn't reply for a moment; merely stops moving.*)

Willy: I'd draw it from my bank but Linda would know, and I . . .

Charley: Sit down, Willy.

Willy (*moving toward the chair*): I'm keeping an account of everything, remember. I'll pay every penny back. (*He sits.*)

Charley: Now listen to me, Willy.

Willy: I want you to know I appreciate . . .

Charley (*sitting down on the table*): Willy, what're you doin'? What the hell is goin' on in your head?

Willy: Why? I'm simply . . .

Charley: I offered you a job. You can make fifty dollars a week. And I won't send you on the road.

Willy: I've got a job.

Charley: Without pay? What kind of a job is a job without pay? (*He rises.*) Now, look, kid, enough is enough. I'm no genius but I know when I'm being insulted.

Willy: Insulted!

Charley: Why don't you want to work for me?

Willy: What's the matter with you? I've got a job.

Charley: Then what're you walkin' in here every week for?

Willy (*getting up*): Well, if you don't want me to walk in here——

Charley: I am offering you a job.

Willy: I don't want your goddam job!

Charley: When the hell are you going to grow up?

Willy (*furiously*): You big ignoramus, if you say that to me again I'll rap you one! I don't care how big you are! (*He's ready to fight.*)

(*Pause.*)

Charley (*kindly, going to him*): How much do you need, Willy?

Willy: Charley, I'm strapped. I'm strapped. I don't know what to do. I was just fired.

Charley: Howard fired you?

Willy: That snotnose. Imagine that? I named him. I named him Howard.

Charley: Willy, when're you gonna realize that them things don't mean anything? You named him Howard, but you can't sell that. The only thing you got in this world is what you can sell. And the funny thing is that you're a salesman, and you don't know that.

Willy: I've always tried to think otherwise, I guess. I always felt that if a man was impressive, and well liked, that nothing——

Charley: Why must everybody like you? Who liked J. P. Morgan? Was he impressive? In a Turkish bath he'd look like a butcher. But with his pockets on he was very well liked. Now listen, Willy, I know you don't like me, and nobody can say I'm in love with you, but I'll give you a job because—just for the hell of it, put it that way. Now what do you say?

Willy: I—I just can't work for you, Charley.

Charley: What're you, jealous of me?

Willy: I can't work for you, that's all, don't ask me why.

Charley (*angered, takes out more bills*): You been jealous of me all your life, you damned fool! Here, pay your insurance. (*He puts the money in **Willy's** hand.*)

Willy: I'm keeping strict accounts.

Charley: I've got some work to do. Take care of yourself. And pay your insurance.

Willy (*moving to the right*): Funny, y'know? After all the highways, and the trains, and the appointments, and the years, you end up worth more dead than alive.

Charley: Willy, nobody's worth nothin' dead. (*After a slight pause*) Did you hear what I said? (**Willy** *stands still, dreaming.*) Willy!

Willy: Apologize to Bernard for me when you see him. I didn't mean to argue with him. He's a fine boy. They're all fine boys, and they'll end up big—all of them. Someday they'll all play tennis together. Wish me luck, Charley. He saw Bill Oliver today.

Charley: Good luck.

Willy (*on the verge of tears*): Charley, you're the only friend I got. Isn't that a remarkable thing? (*He goes out.*)

Charley: Jesus!

(**Charley** *stares after him a moment and follows. All light blacks out. Suddenly raucous music is heard, and a red glow rises behind the screen at right.* **Stanley**, *a young waiter, appears, carrying a table, followed by* **Happy**, *who is carrying two chairs.*)

Stanley (*putting the table down*): That's all right, Mr. Loman, I can handle it myself. (*He turns and takes the chairs from* **Happy** *and places them at the table.*)

Happy (*glancing around*): Oh, this is better.

Stanley: Sure, in the front there you're in the middle of all kinds a noise. Whenever you got a party, Mr. Loman, you just tell me and I'll put you back here. Y'know, there's a lotta people they don't like it private, because when they go out they like to see a lotta action around them because they're sick and tired to stay in the house by theirself. But I know you, you ain't from Hackensack. You know what I mean?

Happy (*sitting down*): So how's it coming, Stanley?

Stanley: Ah, it's a dog's life. I only wish during the war they'd a took me in the Army. I coulda been dead by now.

Happy: My brother's back, Stanley.

Stanley: Oh, he come back, heh? From the Far West.

Happy: Yeah, big cattle man, my brother, so treat him right. And my father's coming too.

Stanley: Oh, your father too!

Happy: You got a couple of nice lobsters?

Stanley: Hundred per cent, big.

Happy: I want them with the claws.

Stanley: Don't worry, I don't give you no mice. (**Happy** *laughs.*) How about some wine? It'll put a head on the meal.

Happy: No. You remember, Stanley, that recipe I brought you from overseas? With the champagne in it?

Stanley: Oh, yeah, sure. I still got it tacked up yet in the kitchen. But that'll have to cost a buck apiece anyways.

Happy: That's all right.

Stanley: What'd you, hit a number or somethin'?

Happy: No, it's a little celebration. My brother is—I think he pulled off a big deal today. I think we're going into business together.

Stanley: Great! That's the best for you. Because a family business, you know what I mean?—that's the best.

Happy: That's what I think.

Stanley: 'Cause what's the difference? Somebody steals? It's in the family. Know what I mean? (*Sotto voce*) Like this bartender here. The boss is goin' crazy what kinda leak he's got in the cash register. You put it in but it don't come out.

Happy (*raising his head*): Sh!

Stanley: What?

Happy: You notice I wasn't lookin' right or left, was I?

Stanley: No.

Happy: And my eyes are closed.

Stanley: So what's the——?

Happy: Strudel's comin'.

Stanley (*catching on, looks around*): Ah, no, there's no——

(*He breaks off as a furred, lavishly dressed girl enters and sits at the next table. Both follow her with their eyes.*)

Stanley: Geez, how'd ya know?

Happy: I got radar or something. (*Staring directly at her profile*) Oooooooo . . . Stanley.

Stanley: I think that's for you, Mr. Loman.

Happy: Look at that mouth. Oh, God. And the binoculars.

Stanley: Geez, you got a life, Mr. Loman.

Happy: Wait on her.

Stanley (*going to the* **Girl's** *table*): Would you like a menu, ma'am?

Girl: I'm expecting someone, but I'd like a——

Happy: Why don't you bring her—excuse me, miss, do you mind? I sell champagne, and I'd like you to try my brand. Bring her a champagne, Stanley.

Girl: That's awfully nice of you.

Happy: Don't mention it. It's all company money. (*He laughs.*)

Girl: That's a charming product to be selling, isn't it?

Happy: Oh, gets to be like everything else. Selling is selling, y'know.

Girl: I suppose.

Happy: You don't happen to sell, do you?

Girl: No, I don't sell.

Happy: Would you object to a compliment from a stranger? You ought to be on a magazine cover.

Girl (*looking at him a little archly*): I have been.

(**Stanley** *comes in with a glass of champagne.*)

Happy: What'd I say before, Stanley? You see? She's a cover girl.

Stanley: Oh, I could see, I could see.

Happy (*to the* **Girl**): What magazine?

Girl: Oh, a lot of them. (*She takes the drink.*) Thank you.

Happy: You know what they say in France, don't you? "Champagne is the drink of the complexion"—Hya, Biff!

(**Biff** *has entered and sits with* **Happy**.)

Biff: Hello, kid. Sorry I'm late.

Happy: I just got here. Uh, Miss——?

Girl: Forsythe.

Happy: Miss Forsythe, this is my brother.

Biff: Is Dad here?

Happy: His name is Biff. You might've heard of him. Great football player.

Girl: Really? What team?

Happy: Are you familiar with football?

Girl: No, I'm afraid I'm not.

Happy: Biff is quarterback with the New York Giants.

Girl: Well, that is nice, isn't it? (*She drinks.*)

Happy: Good health.

Girl: I'm happy to meet you.

Happy: That's my name. Hap. It's really Harold, but at West Point they called me Happy.

Girl (*now really impressed*): Oh, I see. How do you do? (*She turns her profile.*)

Biff: Isn't Dad coming?

Happy: You want her?

Biff: Oh, I could never make that.

Happy: I remember the time that idea would never come into your head. Where's the old confidence. Biff?

Biff: I just saw Oliver——

Happy: Wait a minute. I've got to see that old confidence again. Do you want her? She's on call.

Biff: Oh, no. (*He turns to look at the* **Girl**.)

Happy: I'm telling you. Watch this. (*Turning to the* **Girl**) Honey? (*She turns to him.*) Are you busy?

Girl: Well, I am . . . but I could make a phone call.

Happy: Do that, will you, honey? And see if you can get a friend. We'll be here for a while. Biff is one of the greatest football players in the country.

Girl (*standing up*): Well, I'm certainly happy to meet you.

Happy: Come back soon.

Girl: I'll try.

Happy: Don't try, honey, try hard.

(*The* **Girl** *exits.* **Stanley** *follows, shaking his head in bewildered admiration.*)

Happy: Isn't that a shame now? A beautiful girl like that? That's why I can't get married. There's not a good woman in a thousand. New York is loaded with them, kid!

Biff: Hap, look——

Happy: I told you she was on call!

Biff (*strangely unnerved*): Cut it out, will ya? I want to say something to you.

Happy: Did you see Oliver?

Biff: I saw him all right. Now look, I want to tell Dad a couple of things and I want you to help me.

Happy: What? Is he going to back you?

Biff: Are you crazy? You're out of your goddam head, you know that?

Happy: Why? What happened?

Biff (*breathlessly*): I did a terrible thing today, Hap. It's been the strangest day I ever went through. I'm all numb, I swear.

Happy: You mean he wouldn't see you?

Biff: Well, I waited six hours for him, see? All day. Kept sending my name in. Even tried to date his secretary so she'd get me to him, but no soap.

Happy: Because you're not showin' the old confidence, Biff. He remembered you, didn't he?

Biff (*stopping* **Happy** *with a gesture*): Finally, about five o'clock, he comes out. Didn't remember who I was or anything. I felt like such an idiot, Hap.

Happy: Did you tell him my Florida idea?

Biff: He walked away. I saw him for one minute. I got so mad I could've torn the walls down! How the hell did I ever get the idea I was a salesman there? I even believed myself that I'd been a salesman for him! And then he gave me one look and—I realized what a ridiculous lie my whole life has been! We've been talking in dream for fifteen years. I was a shipping clerk.

Happy: What'd you do?

Biff (*with great tension and wonder*): Well, he left, see. And the secretary went out. I was all alone in the waiting-room. I don't know what came over me, Hap. The next thing I know I'm in his office—paneled walls, everything. I can't explain it. I—Hap, I took his fountain pen.

Happy: Geez, did he catch you?

Biff: I ran out. I ran down all eleven flights. I ran and ran and ran.

Happy: That was an awful dumb—what'd you do that for?

Biff (*agonized*): I don't know, I just—wanted to take something, I don't know. You gotta help me, Hap, I'm gonna tell Pop.

Happy: You crazy? What for?

Biff: Hap, he's got to understand that I'm not the man somebody lends that kind of money to. He thinks I've been spiting him all these years and it's eating him up.

Happy: That's just it. You tell him something nice.

Biff: I can't.

Happy: Say you got a lunch date with Oliver tomorrow.

Biff: So what do I do tomorrow?

Happy: You leave the house tomorrow and come back at night and say Oliver is thinking it over. And he thinks it over for a couple of weeks, and gradually it fades away and nobody's the worse.

Biff: But it'll go on forever!

Happy: Dad is never so happy as when he's looking forward to something!
(**Willy** *enters.*)

Happy: Hello, scout!

Willy: Gee, I haven't been here in years!

(**Stanley** *has followed* **Willy** *in and sets a chair for him.* **Stanley** *starts off but* **Happy** *stops him.*)

Happy: Stanley!

(**Stanley** *stands by, waiting for an order.*)

Biff (*going to* **Willy** *with guilt, as to an invalid*): Sit down, Pop. You want a drink?

Willy: Sure, I don't mind.

Biff: N-no. (*To* **Stanley**) Scotch all around. Make it doubles.

Stanley: Doubles, right. (*He goes.*)

Willy: You had a couple already, didn't you?

Biff: Just a couple, yeah.

Willy: Well, what happened, boy? (*Nodding affirmatively, with a smile*) Everything go all right?

Biff (*takes a breath, then reaches out and grasps* **Willy's** *hand*): Pal . . . (*He is smiling bravely, and* **Willy** *is smiling too.*) I had an experience today.

Happy: Terrific, Pop.

Willy: That so? What happened?

Biff (*high, slightly alcoholic, above the earth*): I'm going to tell you everything from first to last. It's been a strange day. (*Silence. He looks around, composes himself as best he can, but his breath keeps breaking the rhythm of his voice.*) I had to wait quite a while for him, and——

Willy: Oliver?

Biff: Yeah, Oliver. All day, as a matter of cold fact. And a lot of—instances—facts, Pop, facts about my life came back to me. Who was it, Pop? Who ever said I was a salesman with Oliver?

Willy: Well, you were.

Biff: No, Dad, I was a shipping clerk.

Willy: But you were practically——

Biff (*with determination*): Dad, I don't know who said it first, but I was never a salesman for Bill Oliver.

Willy: What're you talking about?

Biff: Let's hold on to the facts tonight, Pop. We're not going to get anywhere bullin' around. I was a shipping clerk.

Willy (*angrily*): All right, now listen to me——

Biff: Why don't you let me finish?

Willy: I'm not interested in stories about the past or any crap of that kind because the woods are burning, boys, you understand? There's a big blaze going on all around. I was fired today.

Biff (*shocked*): How could you be?

Willy: I was fired, and I'm looking for a little good news to tell your mother, because the woman has waited and the woman has suffered. The gist of it is that I haven't got a story left in my head, Biff. So don't give me a lecture about facts and aspects. I am not interested. Now what've you got to say to me?

(**Stanley** *enters with three drinks. They wait until he leaves.*)

Willy: Did you see Oliver?

Biff: Jesus, Dad!

Willy: You mean you didn't go up there?

Happy: Sure he went up there.

Biff: I did. I—saw him. How could they fire you?

Willy (*on the edge of his chair*): What kind of a welcome did he give you?

Biff: He won't even let you work on commission?

Willy: I'm out! (*Driving*) So tell me, he gave you a warm welcome?

Happy: Sure, Pop, sure!

Biff (*driven*): Well it was kind of——

Willy: I was wondering if he'd remember you. (*To* **Happy**) Imagine, man doesn't see him for ten, twelve years and gives him that kind of a welcome!

Happy: Damn right!

Biff (*trying to return to the offensive*): Pop look——

Willy: You know why he remembered you, don't you? Because you impressed him in those days.

Biff: Let's talk quietly and get this down to the facts, huh?

Willy (*as though* **Biff** *had been interrupting*): Well, what happened? It's great news, Biff. Did he take you into his office or'd you talk in the waiting-room?

Biff: Well, he came in, see, and——

Willy (*with a big smile*): What'd he say? Betcha he threw his arm around you.

Biff: Well, he kinda——

Willy: He's a fine man. (*To* **Happy**) Very hard man to see, y'know.

Happy (*agreeing*): Oh, I know.

Willy (*to* **Biff**): Is that where you had the drinks?

Biff: Yeah, he gave me a couple of—no, no!

Happy (*cutting in*): He told him my Florida idea.

Willy: Don't interrupt. (*To* **Biff**) How'd he react to the Florida idea?

Biff: Dad, will you give me a minute to explain?

Willy: I've been waiting for you to explain since I sat down here! What happened? He took you into his office and what?

Biff: Well—I talked. And—and he listened, see.

Willy: Famous for the way he listens, y'know. What was his answer?

Biff: His answer was—(*He breaks off, suddenly angry.*) Dad, you're not letting me tell you what I want to tell you!

Willy (*accusing, angered*): You didn't see him, did you?

Biff: I did see him!

Willy: What'd you insult him or something? You insulted him, didn't you?

Biff: Listen, will you let me out of it, will you just let me out of it!

Happy: What the hell!

Willy: Tell me what happened!

Biff (*to* **Happy**): I can't talk to him!

(*A single trumpet note jars the ear. The light of green leaves stains the house, which holds the air of night and a dream.* **Young Bernard** *enters and knocks on the door of the house.*)

Young Bernard (*frantically*): Mrs. Loman, Mrs. Loman!

Happy: Tell him what happened!

Biff (*to* **Happy**): Shut up and leave me alone!

Willy: No, no! You had to go and flunk math!

Biff: What math? What're you talking about?

Young Bernard: Mrs. Loman, Mrs. Loman!

(**Linda** *appears in the house, as of old.*)

Willy (*wildly*): Math, math, math!

Biff: Take it easy, Pop!

Young Bernard: Mrs. Loman!

Willy (*furiously*): If you hadn't flunked you'd've been set by now!

Biff: Now, look, I'm gonna tell you what happened, and you're going to listen to me.

Young Bernard: Mrs. Loman!

Biff: I waited six hours—

Happy: What the hell are you saying?

Biff: I kept sending in my name but he wouldn't see me. So finally he . . . (*He continues unheard as light fades low on the restaurant.*)

Young Bernard: Biff flunked math!

Linda: No!

Young Bernard: Birnbaum flunked him! They won't graduate him!

Linda: But they have to. He's gotta go to the university. Where is he? Biff! Biff!

Young Bernard: No, he left. He went to Grand Central.

Linda: Grand—You mean he went to Boston!

Young Bernard: Is Uncle Willy in Boston?

Linda: Oh, maybe Willy can talk to the teacher. Oh, the poor, poor boy!
(*Light on house area snaps out.*)

Biff (*at the table, now audible, holding up a gold fountain pen*): . . . so I'm washed up with Oliver, you understand? Are you listening to me?

Willy (*at a loss*): Yeah, sure. If you hadn't flunked——

Biff: Flunked what? What're you talking about?

Willy: Don't blame everything on me! I didn't flunk math—you did! What pen!

Happy: That was awful dumb, Biff, a pen like that is worth——

Willy (*seeing the pen for the first time*): You took Oliver's pen?

Biff (*weakening*): Dad, I just explained it to you.

Willy: You stole Bill Oliver's fountain pen!

Biff: I didn't exactly steal it! That's just what I've been explaining to you!

Happy: He had it in his hand and just then Oliver walked in, so he got nervous and stuck it in his pocket!

Willy: My God, Biff!

Biff: I never intended to do it, Dad!

Operator's Voice: Standish Arms, good evening!

Willy (*shouting*): I'm not in my room!

Biff (*frightened*): Dad, what's the matter? (*He and* **Happy** *stand up.*)

Operator: Ringing Mr. Loman for you!

Willy: I'm not there, stop it!

Biff (*horrified, gets down on one knee before* **Willy**): Dad, I'll make good, I'll make good. (**Willy** *tries to get to his feet.* **Biff** *holds him down.*) Sit down now.

Willy: No, you're no good, you're no good for anything.

Biff: I am, Dad, I'll find something else, you understand? Now don't worry about anything. (*He holds up* **Willy's** *face.*) Talk to me, Dad.

Operator: Mr. Loman does not answer. Shall I page him?

Willy (*attempting to stand, as though to rush and silence the* **Operator**): No, no, no!

Happy: He'll strike something, Pop.

Willy: No, no . . .

Biff (*desperately, standing over* **Willy**): Pop, listen! Listen to me! I'm telling you something good. Oliver talked to his partner about the Florida idea. You listening? He—he talked to his partner, and he came to me . . . I'm going to be all right, you hear? Dad, listen to me, he said it was just a question of the amount!

Willy: Then you . . . got it?

Happy: He's gonna be terrific, Pop!

Willy (*trying to stand*): Then you got it, haven't you? You got it! You got it!

Biff (*agonized, holds* **Willy** *down*): No, no. Look, Pop. I'm supposed to have lunch with them tomorrow. I'm just telling you this so you'll know that I can still make an impression, Pop. And I'll make good somewhere, but I can't go tomorrow, see?

Willy: Why not? You simply——

Biff: But the pen, Pop!

Willy: You give it to him and tell him it was an oversight!

Biff: I can't say that——

Willy: You were doing a crossword puzzle and accidentally used his pen!

Biff: Listen, kid, I took those balls years ago, now I walk in with his fountain pen? That clinches it, don't you see? I can't face him like that! I'll try elsewhere.

Page's Voice: Paging Mr. Loman!

Willy: Don't you want to be anything?

Biff: Pop, how can I go back?

Willy: You don't want to be anything, is that what's behind it?

Biff (*now angry at* **Willy** *for not crediting his sympathy*): Don't take it that way! You think it was easy walking into that office after what I'd done to him? A team of horses couldn't have dragged me back to Bill Oliver!

Willy: Then why'd you go?

Biff: Why did I go? Why did I go! Look at you! Look at what's become of you! (*Off left,* **The Woman** *laughs.*)

Willy: Biff, you're going to go to that lunch tomorrow, or——

Biff: I can't go. I've got no appointment!

Happy: Biff, for . . . !

Willy: Are you spiting me?

Biff: Don't take it that way! Goddammit!

Willy (*strikes* **Biff** *and falters away from the table*): You rotten little louse! Are you spiting me?

The Woman: Someone's at the door, Willy!

Biff: I'm no good, can't you see what I am?

Happy (*separating them*): Hey, you're in a restaurant! Now cut it out, both of you! (**The Girls** *enter.*) Hello, girls, sit down. (**The Woman** *laughs, off left.*)

Miss Forsythe: I guess we might as well. This is Letta.

The Woman: Willy, are you going to wake up?

Biff (*ignoring* **Willy**): How're ya, miss, sit down. What do you drink?

Miss Forsythe: Letta might not be able to stay long.

Letta: I gotta get up very early tomorrow. I got jury duty. I'm so excited! Were you fellows ever on a jury?

Biff: No, but I been in front of them! (**The Girls** *laugh.*) This is my father.

Letta: Isn't he cute? Sit down with us, Pop.

Happy: Sit him down, Biff!

Biff (*going to him*): Come on, slugger, drink us under the table. To hell with it! Come on, sit down, pal.

(*On* **Biff's** *last insistence,* **Willy** *is about to sit.*)

The Woman (*now urgently*): Willy, are you going to answer the door!

(**The Woman's** *call pulls* **Willy** *back. He starts right, befuddled.*)

Biff: Hey, where are you going?

Willy: Open the door.

Biff: The door?

Willy: The washroom . . . the door . . . where's the door?

Biff (*leading* **Willy** *to the left*): Just go straight down.

(**Willy** *moves left.*)

The Woman: Willy, Willy, are you going to get up, get up, get up, get up?

(**Willy** *exits left.*)

Letta: I think it's sweet you bring your daddy along.

Miss Forsythe: Oh, he isn't really your father!

Biff (*at left, turning to her resentfully*): Miss Forsythe, you've just seen a prince walk by. A fine, troubled prince. A hard-working, unappreciated prince. A pal, you understand? A good companion. Always for his boys.

Letta: That's so sweet.

Happy: Well, girls, what's the program? We're wasting time. Come on, Biff. Gather round. Where would you like to go?

Biff: Why don't you do something for him?

Happy: Me!

Biff: Don't you give a damn for him, Hap?

Happy: What're you talking about? I'm the one who——

Biff: I sense it, you don't give a good goddam about him. (*He takes the rolled-up hose from his pocket and puts it on the table in front of* **Happy**.) Look what I found in the cellar, for Christ's sake. How can you bear to let it go on?

Happy: Me? Who goes away? Who runs off and——

Biff: Yeah, but he doesn't mean anything to you. You could help him—I can't! Don't you understand what I'm talking about? He's going to kill himself, don't you know that?

Happy: Don't I know it! Me!

Biff: Hap, help him! Jesus . . . help him . . . Help me, help me, I can't bear to look at his face! (*Ready to weep, he hurries out, up right.*)

Happy (*starting after him*): Where are you going?

Miss Forsythe: What's he so mad about?

Happy: Come on, girls, we'll catch up with him.

Miss Forsythe (*as* **Happy** *pushes her out*): Say, I don't like that temper of his!

Happy: He's just a little overstrung, he'll be all right!

Willy (*off left, as* **The Woman** *laughs*): Don't answer! Don't answer!

Letta: Don't you want to tell your father——

Happy: No, that's not my father. He's just a guy. Come on, we'll catch Biff, and, honey, we're going to paint this town! Stanley, where's the check! Hey, Stanley! (*They exit.* **Stanley** *looks toward left.*)

Stanley (*calling to* **Happy** *indignantly*): Mr. Loman! Mr. Loman!

(**Stanley** *picks up a chair and follows them off. Knocking is heard off left.* **The Woman** *enters, laughing.* **Willy** *follows her. She is in a black slip; he is buttoning his shirt. Raw, sensuous music accompanies their speech.*)

Willy: Will you stop laughing? Will you stop?

The Woman: Aren't you going to answer the door? He'll wake the whole hotel.

Willy: I'm not expecting anybody.

The Woman: Whyn't you have another drink, honey, and stop being so damn self-centered?

Willy: I'm so lonely.

The Woman: You know you ruined me, Willy? From now on, whenever you come
to the office, I'll see that you go right through to the buyers. No waiting at my
desk any more, Willy. You ruined me.

Willy: That's nice of you to say that.

The Woman: Gee, you are self-centered! Why so sad? You are the saddest, self-
centeredest soul I ever did see-saw. (*She laughs. He kisses her.*) Come on inside,
drummer boy. It's silly to be dressing in the middle of the night. (*As knocking is
heard*) Aren't you going to answer the door?

Willy: They're knocking on the wrong door.

The Woman: But I felt the knocking. And he heard us talking in here. Maybe the
hotel's on fire!

Willy (*his terror rising*): It's a mistake.

The Woman: Then tell him to go away!

Willy: There's nobody there.

The Woman: It's getting on my nerves, Willy. There's somebody standing out
there and it's getting on my nerves!

Willy (*pushing her away from him*): All right, stay in the bathroom here, and don't
come out. I think there's a law in Massachusetts about it, so don't come out.
It may be that new room clerk. He looked very mean. So don't come out. It's a
mistake, there's no fire.

(*The knocking is heard again. He takes a few steps away from her, and she vanishes into
the wing. The light follows him, and now he is facing* **Young Biff,** *who carries a suitcase.*
Biff *steps toward him. The music is gone.*)

Biff: Why didn't you answer?

Willy: Biff! What are you doing in Boston?

Biff: Why didn't you answer? I've been knocking for five minutes, I called you on
the phone——

Willy: I just heard you. I was in the bathroom and had the door shut. Did anything happen home?

Biff: Dad—I let you down.

Willy: What do you mean?

Biff: Dad . . .

Willy: Biffo, what's this about? (*Putting his arm around* **Biff**) Come on, let's go downstairs and get you a malted.

Biff: Dad, I flunked math.

Willy: Not for the term?

Biff: The term. I haven't got enough credits to graduate.

Willy: You mean to say Bernard wouldn't give you the answers?

Biff: He did, he tried, but I only got a sixty-one.

Willy: And they wouldn't give you four points.

Biff: Birnbaum refused absolutely. I begged him, Pop, but he won't give me those
points. You gotta talk to him before they close the school. Because if he saw the
kind of man you are, and you just talked to him in your way, I'm sure he'd come
through for me. The class came right before practice, see, and I didn't go enough.
Would you talk to him? He'd like you, Pop. You know the way you could talk.

Willy: You're on. We'll drive right back.

Biff: Oh, Dad, good work! I'm sure he'll change it for you!

Willy: Go downstairs and tell the clerk I'm checkin' out. Go right down.

Biff: Yes, sir! See, the reason he hates me, Pop—one day he was late for class so I got up at the blackboard and imitated him. I crossed my eyes and talked with a lithp.

Willy (*laughing*): You did? The kids like it?

Biff: They nearly died laughing!

Willy: Yeah? What'd you do?

Biff: The thquare root of thixthy twee is . . . (**Willy** *bursts out laughing;* **Biff** *joins him.*) And in the middle of it he walked in!

(**Willy** *laughs and* **The Woman** *joins in offstage.*)

Willy (*without hesitation*): Hurry downstairs and——

Biff: Somebody in there?

Willy: No, that was next door.

(**The Woman** *laughs offstage.*)

Biff: Somebody got in your bathroom!

Willy: No, it's the next room, there's a party——

The Woman (*enters, laughing. She lisps this*): Can I come in? There's something in the bathtub, Willy, and it's moving!

(**Willy** *looks at* **Biff,** *who is staring open-mouthed and horrified at* **The Woman.**)

Willy: Ah—you better go back to your room. They must be finished painting by now. They're painting her room so I let her take a shower here. Go back, go back . . . (*He pushes her.*)

The Woman (*resisting*): But I've got to get dressed, Willy, I can't——

Willy: Get out of here! Go back, go back . . . (*Suddenly striving for the ordinary*) This is Miss Francis, Biff, she's a buyer. They're painting her room. Go back, Miss Francis, go back . . .

The Woman: But my clothes, I can't go out naked in the hall!

Willy (*pushing her offstage*): Get outa here! Go back, go back!

(**Biff** *slowly sits down on his suitcase as the argument continues offstage.*)

The Woman: Where's my stockings? You promised me stockings, Willy!

Willy: I have no stockings here!

The Woman: You had two boxes of size nine sheers for me, and I want them!

Willy: Here, for God's sake, will you get outa here!

The Woman (*enters holding a box of stockings*): I just hope there's nobody in the hall. That's all I hope. (*To* **Biff**) Are you football or baseball?

Biff: Football.

The Woman (*angry, humiliated*): That's me too. G'night. (*She snatches her clothes from* **Willy** *and walks out.*)

Willy (*after a pause*): Well, better get going. I want to get to the school first thing in the morning. Get my suits out of the closet. I'll get my valise. (**Biff** *doesn't move.*) What's the matter? (**Biff** *remains motionless, tears falling.*) She's a buyer. Buys for J. H. Simmons. She lives down the hall—they're painting. You don't imagine— (*He breaks off. After a pause*) Now listen, pal, she's just a buyer. She sees merchandise in her room and they have to keep it looking just so . . . (*Pause. Assuming command*) All right, get my suits. (**Biff** *doesn't move.*) Now stop crying and do as I say. I gave you an order. Biff, I gave you an order! Is that what you do when I give you an order? How dare you cry! (*Putting his arm around* **Biff**) Now look, Biff, when you grow up you'll understand about these things. You mustn't—you mustn't overemphasize a thing like this. I'll see Birnbaum first thing in the morning.

Biff: Never mind.

Willy (*getting down beside* **Biff**): Never mind! He's going to give you those points. I'll see to it.

Biff: He wouldn't listen to you.

Willy: He certainly will listen to me. You need those points for the U. of Virginia.

Biff: I'm not going there.

Willy: Heh? If I can't get him to change that mark you'll make it up in summer school. You've got all summer to——

Biff (*his weeping breaking from him*): Dad . . .

Willy (*infected by it*): Oh, my boy . . .

Biff: Dad . . .

Willy: She's nothing to me, Biff. I was lonely, I was terribly lonely.

Biff: You—you gave her Mama's stockings! (*His tears break through and he rises to go.*)

Willy (*grabbing for* **Biff**): I gave you an order!

Biff: Don't touch me, you—liar!

Willy: Apologize for that!

Biff: You fake! You phony little fake! You fake! (*Overcome, he turns quickly and weeping fully goes out with his suitcase.* **Willy** *is left on the floor on his knees.*)

Willy: I gave you an order! Biff, come back here or I'll beat you! Come back here! I'll whip you!

(**Stanley** *comes quickly in from the right and stands in front of* **Willy**.)

Willy (*shouts at* **Stanley**): I gave you an order . . .

Stanley: Hey, let's pick it up, pick it up, Mr. Loman. (*He helps* **Willy** *to his feet.*) Your boys left with the chippies. They said they'll see you home.

(*A second waiter watches some distance away.*)

Willy: But we were supposed to have dinner together.

(*Music is heard,* **Willy's** *theme.*)

Stanley: Can you make it?

Willy: I'll—sure, I can make it. (*Suddenly concerned about his clothes*) Do I—I look all right?

Stanley: Sure, you look all right. (*He flicks a speck off* **Willy's** *lapel.*)

Willy: Here—here's a dollar.

Stanley: Oh, your son paid me. It's all right.

Willy (*putting it in* **Stanley's** *hand*): No, take it. You're a good boy.

Stanley: Oh, no, you don't have to . . .

Willy: Here's some more, I don't need it any more. (*After a slight pause*) Tell me— is there a seed store in the neighborhood?

Stanley: Seeds? You mean like to plant?

(*As* **Willy** *turns,* **Stanley** *slips the money back into his jacket pocket.*)

Willy: Yes. Carrots, peas . . .

Stanley: Well, there's hardware stores on Sixth Avenue, but it may be too late now.

Willy (*anxiously*): Oh, I'd better hurry. I've got to get some seeds. (*He starts off to the right.*) I've got to get some seeds, right away. Nothing's planted. I don't have a thing in the ground.

(**Willy** *hurries out as the light goes down.* **Stanley** *moves over to the right after him, watches him off. The other waiter has been staring at* **Willy**.)

Stanley (*to the waiter*): Well, whatta you looking at?

(*The waiter picks up the chairs and moves off right.* **Stanley** *takes the table and follows him. The light fades on this area. There is a long pause, the sound of the flute coming over.*

The light gradually rises on the kitchen, which is empty. **Happy** *appears at the door of the house, followed by* **Biff**. **Happy** *is carrying a large bunch of long-stemmed roses. He enters the kitchen, looks around for* **Linda**. *Not seeing her, he turns to* **Biff**, *who is just outside the house door, and makes a gesture with his hands, indicating "Not here, I guess." He looks into the living-room and freezes. Inside,* **Linda**, *unseen, is seated,* **Willy's** *coat on her lap. She rises ominously and quietly and moves toward* **Happy**, *who backs up into the kitchen, afraid.)*

Happy: Hey, what're you doing up? (**Linda** *says nothing but moves toward him implacably.*) Where's Pop? (*He keeps backing to the right, and now* **Linda** *is in full view in the doorway to the living-room.*) Is he sleeping?

Linda: Where were you?

Happy (*trying to laugh it off*): We met two girls, Mom, very fine types. Here, we brought you some flowers. (*Offering them to her*) Put them in your room, Ma. (*She knocks them to the floor at* **Biff's** *feet. He has now come inside and closed the door behind him. She stares at* **Biff**, *silent.*)

Happy: Now what'd you do that for? Mom, I want you to have some flowers——

Linda (*cutting* **Happy** *off, violently to* **Biff**): Don't you care whether he lives or dies?

Happy (*going to the stairs*): Come upstairs, Biff.

Biff (*with a flare of disgust, to* **Happy**): Go away from me! (*To* **Linda**) What do you mean, lives or dies? Nobody's dying around here, pal.

Linda: Get out of my sight! Get out of here!

Biff: I wanna see the boss.

Linda: You're not going near him!

Biff: Where is he? (*He moves into the living-room and* **Linda** *follows.*)

Linda (*shouting after* **Biff**): You invite him for dinner. He looks forward to it all day—(**Biff** *appears in his parents' bedroom, looks around, and exits*)—and then you desert him there. There's no stranger you'd do that to!

Happy: Why? He had a swell time with us. Listen, when I—(**Linda** *comes back into the kitchen*)—desert him I hope I don't outlive the day!

Linda: Get out of here!

Happy: Now look, Mom . . .

Linda: Did you have to go to women tonight? You and your lousy rotten whores! (**Biff** *re-enters the kitchen.*)

Happy: Mom, all we did was follow Biff around trying to cheer him up! (*To* **Biff**) Boy, what a night you gave me!

Linda: Get out of here, both of you, and don't come back! I don't want you tormenting him any more. Go on now, get your things together! (*To* **Biff**) You can sleep in his apartment. (*She starts to pick up the flowers and stops herself.*) Pick up this stuff, I'm not your maid any more. Pick it up, you bum, you!

(**Happy** *turns his back to her in refusal.* **Biff** *slowly moves over and gets down on his knees, picking up the flowers.*)

Linda: You're a pair of animals! Not one, not another living soul would have had the cruelty to walk out on that man in a restaurant!

Biff (*not looking at her*): Is that what he said?

Linda: He didn't have to say anything. He was so humiliated he nearly limped when he came in.

Happy: But, Mom, he had a great time with us——

Biff (*cutting him off violently*): Shut up!

(*Without another word,* **Happy** *goes upstairs.*)

Linda: You! You didn't even go in to see if he was all right!

Biff (*still on the floor in front of* **Linda**, *the flowers in his hand; with self-loathing*): No. Didn't. Didn't do a damned thing. How do you like that, heh? Left him babbling in a toilet.

Linda: You louse. You . . .

Biff: Now you hit it on the nose! (*He gets up, throws the flowers in the wastebasket.*) The scum of the earth, and you're looking at him!

Linda: Get out of here!

Biff: I gotta talk to the boss, Mom. Where is he?

Linda: You're not going near him. Get out of this house!

Biff (*with absolute assurance, determination*): No. We're gonna have an abrupt conversation, him and me.

Linda: You're not talking to him!

(*Hammering is heard from outside the house, off right.* **Biff** *turns toward the noise.*)

Linda (*suddenly pleading*): Will you please leave him alone?

Biff: What's he doing out there?

Linda: He's planting the garden!

Biff (*quietly*): Now? Oh, my God!

(**Biff** *moves outside,* **Linda** *following. The light dies down on them and comes up on the center of the apron as* **Willy** *walks into it. He is carrying a flashlight, a hoe, and a handful of seed packets. He raps the top of the hoe sharply to fix it firmly, and then moves to the left, measuring off the distance with his foot. He holds the flashlight to look at the seed packets, reading off the instructions. He is in the blue of the night.*)

Willy: Carrots . . . quarter-inch apart. Rows . . . one-foot rows. (*He measures it off.*) One foot. (*He puts down a package and measures off.*) Beets. (*He puts down another package and measures again.*) Lettuce. (*He reads the package, puts it down.*) One foot—(*He breaks off as* **Ben** *appears at the right and moves slowly down to him.*) What a proposition, ts, ts. Terrific, terrific. 'Cause she's suffered, Ben, the woman has suffered. You understand me? A man can't go out the way he came in. Ben, a man has got to add up to something. You can't, you can't—(**Ben** *moves toward him as though to interrupt.*) You gotta consider, now. Don't answer so quick. Remember, it's a guaranteed twenty-thousand-dollar proposition. Now look, Ben, I want you to go through the ins and outs of this thing with me. I've got nobody to talk to, Ben, and the woman has suffered, you hear me?

Ben (*standing still, considering*): What's the proposition?

Willy: It's twenty thousand dollars on the barrelhead. Guaranteed, gilt-edged, you understand?

Ben: You don't want to make a fool of yourself. They might not honor the policy.

Willy: How can they dare refuse? Didn't I work like a coolie to meet every premium on the nose? And now they don't pay off? Impossible!

Ben: It's called a cowardly thing, William.

Willy: Why? Does it take more guts to stand here the rest of my life ringing up a zero?

Ben (*yielding*): That's a point, William. (*He moves, thinking, turns.*) And twenty thousand—that *is* something one can feel with the hand, it is there.

Willy (*now assured, with rising power*): Oh, Ben, that's the whole beauty of it! I see it like a diamond, shining in the dark, hard and rough, that I pick up and touch in my hand. Not like—like an appointment! This would not be another damned-fool appointment, Ben, and it changes all the aspects. Because he thinks I'm nothing, see, and so he spites me. But the funeral—(*Straightening up*) Ben, that funeral will be massive! They'll come from Maine, Massachusetts, Vermont, New Hampshire! All the old-timers with the strange license plates—that boy will be thunderstruck, Ben, because he never realized—I am known! Rhode Island, New York, New Jersey—I am known, Ben, and he'll see it with his eyes once and for all. He'll see what I am, Ben! He's in for a shock, that boy!

Ben (*coming down to the edge of the garden*): He'll call you a coward.

Willy (*suddenly fearful*): No, that would be terrible.

Ben: Yes. And a damned fool.

Willy: No, no, he mustn't, I won't have that! (*He is broken and desperate.*)

Ben: He'll hate you, William.

(*The gay music of the boys is heard.*)

Willy: Oh, Ben, how do we get back to all the great times? Used to be so full of light, and comradeship, the sleigh-riding in winter and the ruddiness on his cheeks. And always some kind of good news coming up, always something nice coming up ahead. And never even let me carry the valises in the house, and simonizing, simonizing that little red car! Why, why can't I give him something and not have him hate me?

Ben: Let me think about it. (*He glances at his watch.*) I still have a little time. Remarkable proposition, but you've got to be sure you're not making a fool of yourself. (**Ben** *drifts off upstage and goes out of sight.* **Biff** *comes down from the left.*)

Willy (*suddenly conscious of* **Biff**, *turns and looks up at him, then begins picking up the packages of seeds in confusion*): Where the hell is that seed? (*Indignantly*) You can't see nothing out here! They boxed in the whole goddam neighborhood!

Biff: There are people all around here. Don't you realize that?

Willy: I'm busy. Don't bother me.

Biff (*taking the hoe from* **Willy**): I'm saying good-by to you, Pop. (**Willy** *looks at him, silent, unable to move.*) I'm not coming back any more.

Willy: You're not going to see Oliver tomorrow?

Biff: I've got no appointment, Dad.

Willy: He put his arms around you, and you've got no appointment?

Biff: Pop, get this now, will you? Every time I've left it's been a fight that sent me out of here. Today I realized something about myself and I tried to explain it to you and I—I think I'm just not smart enough to make any sense out of it for you. To hell with whose fault it is or anything like that. (*He takes* **Willy's** *arm.*) Let's just wrap it up, heh? Come on in, we'll tell Mom. (*He gently tries to pull* **Willy** *to left.*)

Willy (*frozen, immobile, with guilt in his voice*): No, I don't want to see her.

Biff: Come on! (*He pulls again, and* **Willy** *tries to pull away.*)

Willy (*highly nervous*): No, no, I don't want to see her.

Biff (*tries to look into* **Willy's** *face, as if to find the answer there*): Why don't you want to see her?

Willy (*more harshly now*): Don't bother me, will you?

Biff: What do you mean, you don't want to see her? You don't want them calling you yellow do you? This isn't your fault; it's me, I'm a bum. Now come inside! (**Willy** *strains to get away.*) Did you hear what I said to you?

(**Willy** *pulls away and quickly goes by himself into the house.* **Biff** *follows.*)

Linda (*to* **Willy**): Did you plant, dear?

Biff (*at the door, to* **Linda**): All right, we had it out. I'm going and I'm not writing any more.

Linda (*going to* **Willy** *in the kitchen*): I think that's the best way, dear. 'Cause there's no use drawing it out, you'll just never get along.

(**Willy** *doesn't respond.*)

Biff: People ask where I am and what I'm doing, you don't know, and you don't care. That way it'll be off your mind and you can start brightening up again. All right? That clears it, doesn't it? (**Willy** *is silent, and* **Biff** *goes to him.*) You gonna wish me luck, scout? (*He extends his hand.*) What do you say?

Linda: Shake his hand, Willy.

Willy (*turning to her, seething with hurt*): There's no necessity to mention the pen at all, y'know.

Biff (*gently*): I've got no appointment, Dad.

Willy (*erupting fiercely*): He put his arm around . . . ?

Biff: Dad, you're never going to see what I am, so what's the use of arguing? If I strike oil I'll send you a check. Meantime forget I'm alive.

Willy (*to* **Linda**): Spite, see?

Biff: Shake hands, Dad.

Willy: Not my hand.

Biff: I was hoping not to go this way.

Willy: Well, this is the way you're going. Good-by.

(**Biff** *looks at him a moment, then turns sharply and goes to the stairs.*)

Willy (*stops him with*): May you rot in hell if you leave this house!

Biff (*turning*): Exactly what is it that you want from me?

Willy: I want you to know, on the train, in the mountains, in the valleys, wherever you go, that you cut down your life for spite!

Biff: No, no.

Willy: Spite, spite, is the word of your undoing! And when you're down and out, remember what did it. When you're rotting somewhere beside the railroad tracks, remember, and don't you dare blame it on me!

Biff: I'm not blaming it on you!

Willy: I won't take the rap for this, you hear?

(**Happy** *comes down the stairs and stands on the bottom step, watching.*)

Biff: That's just what I'm telling you!

Willy (*sinking into a chair at the table, with full accusation*): You're trying to put a knife in me—don't think I don't know what you're doing!

Biff: All right, phony! Then let's lay it on the line. (*He whips the rubber tube out of his pocket and puts it on the table.*)

Happy: You crazy——

Linda: Biff! (*She moves to grab the hose, but* **Biff** *holds it down with his hand.*)

Biff: Leave it there! Don't move it!

Willy (*not looking at it*): What is that?

Biff: You know goddam well what that is.

Willy (*caged, wanting to escape*): I never saw that.

Biff: You saw it. The mice didn't bring it into the cellar! What is this supposed to do, make a hero out of you? This supposed to make me sorry for you?

Willy: Never heard of it.

Biff: There'll be no pity for you, you hear it? No pity!

Willy (*to* **Linda**): You hear the spite!

Biff: No, you're going to hear the truth—what you are and what I am!

Linda: Stop it!

Willy: Spite!

Happy (*coming down toward* **Biff**): You cut it now!

Biff (*to* **Happy**): The man don't know who we are! The man is gonna know! (*To* **Willy**) We never told the truth for ten minutes in this house!

Happy: We always told the truth!

Biff (*turning on him*): You big blow, are you the assistant buyer? You're one of the two assistants to the assistant, aren't you?

Happy: Well, I'm practically——

Biff: You're practically full of it! We all are! And I'm through with it. (*To* **Willy**) Now hear this, Willy, this is me.

Willy: I know you!

Biff: You know why I had no address for three months? I stole a suit in Kansas City and I was in jail. (*To* **Linda**, *who is sobbing*) Stop crying. I'm through with it. (**Linda** *turns away from them, her hands covering her face.*)

Willy: I suppose that's my fault!

Biff: I stole myself out of every good job since high school!

Willy: And whose fault is that?

Biff: And I never got anywhere because you blew me so full of hot air I could never stand taking orders from anybody! That's whose fault it is!

Willy: I hear that!

Linda: Don't, Biff!

Biff: It's goddam time you heard that! I had to be boss big shot in two weeks, and I'm through with it!

Willy: Then hang yourself! For spite, hang yourself!

Biff: No! Nobody's hanging himself, Willy! I ran down eleven flights with a pen in my hand today. And suddenly I stopped, you hear me? And in the middle of that office building, do you hear this? I stopped in the middle of that building and I saw—the sky. I saw the things that I love in this world. The work and the food and time to sit and smoke. And I looked at the pen and said to myself, what the hell am I grabbing this for? Why am I trying to become what I don't want to be? What am I doing in an office, making a contemptuous, begging fool of myself, when all I want is out there, waiting for me the minute I say I know who I am! Why can't I say that, Willy?

(*He tries to make* **Willy** *face him, but* **Willy** *pulls away and moves to the left.*)

Willy (*with hatred, threateningly*): The door of your life is wide open!

Biff: Pop! I'm a dime a dozen, and so are you!

Willy (*turning on him now in an uncontrolled outburst*): I am not a dime a dozen! I am Willy Loman, and you are Biff Loman!

(**Biff** *starts for* **Willy**, *but is blocked by* **Happy**. *In his fury,* **Biff** *seems on the verge of attacking his father.*)

Biff: I am not a leader of men, Willy, and neither are you. You were never anything but a hard-working drummer who landed in the ash can like all the rest of them! I'm one dollar an hour, Willy! I tried seven states and couldn't raise it. A buck an hour! Do you gather my meaning? I'm not bringing home any prizes any more, and you're going to stop waiting for me to bring them home!

Willy (*directly to* **Biff**): You vengeful, spiteful mutt!

(**Biff** *breaks from* **Happy. Willy**, *in fright, starts up the stairs.* **Biff** *grabs him.*)

Biff (*at the peak of his fury*): Pop, I'm nothing! I'm nothing, Pop. Can't you under-stand that? There's no spite in it any more. I'm just what I am, that's all.

(**Biff's** *fury has spent itself, and he breaks down, sobbing, holding on to* **Willy**, *who dumbly fumbles for* **Biff's** *face.*)

Willy (*astonished*): What're you doing? What're you doing? (*To* **Linda**) Why is he crying?

Biff (*crying, broken*): Will you let me go, for Christ's sake? Will you take that phony dream and burn it before something happens? (*Struggling to contain himself, he pulls away and moves to the stairs.*) I'll go in the morning. Put him—put him to bed. (*Exhausted*, **Biff** *moves up the stairs to his room.*)

Willy (*after a long pause, astonished, elevated*): Isn't that—isn't that remarkable? Biff—he likes me!

Linda: He loves you, Willy!

Happy (*deeply moved*): Always did, Pop.

Willy: Oh, Biff! (*Staring wildly*) He cried! Cried to me. (*He is choking with his love, and now cries out his promise.*) That boy—that boy is going to be magnificent!

(**Ben** *appears in the light just outside the kitchen.*)

Ben: Yes, outstanding, with twenty thousand behind him.

Linda (*sensing the racing of his mind, fearfully, carefully*): Now come to bed, Willy. It's all settled now.

Willy (*finding it difficult not to rush out of the house*): Yes, we'll sleep. Come on. Go to sleep, Hap.

Ben: And it does take a great kind of a man to crack the jungle.

(*In accents of dread*, **Ben's** *idyllic music starts up.*)

Happy (*his arm around* **Linda**): I'm getting married, Pop, don't forget it. I'm chang-ing everything. I'm gonna run that department before the year is up. You'll see, Mom. (*He kisses her.*)

Ben: The jungle is dark but full of diamonds, Willy.

(**Willy** *turns, moves, listening to* **Ben.**)

Linda: Be good. You're both good boys, just act that way, that's all.

Happy: 'Night, Pop. (*He goes upstairs.*)

Linda (*to* **Willy**): Come, dear.

Ben (*with greater force*): One must go in to fetch a diamond out.

Willy (*to* **Linda**, *as he moves slowly along the edge of the kitchen, toward the door*): I just want to get settled down, Linda. Let me sit alone for a little.

Linda (*almost uttering her fear*): I want you upstairs.

Willy (*taking her in his arms*): In a few minutes, Linda. I couldn't sleep right now. Go on, you look awful tired. (*He kisses her.*)

Ben: Not like an appointment at all. A diamond is rough and hard to the touch.

Willy: Go on now. I'll be right up.

Linda: I think this is the only way, Willy.

Willy: Sure, it's the best thing.

Ben: Best thing!

Willy: The only way. Everything is gonna be—go on, kid, get to bed. You look so tired.

Linda: Come right up.

Willy: Two minutes.

(**Linda** *goes into the living-room, then reappears in her bedroom.* **Willy** *moves just outside the kitchen door.*)

Willy: Loves me. (*Wonderingly*) Always loved me. Isn't that a remarkable thing? Ben, he'll worship me for it!

Ben (*with promise*): It's dark there, but full of diamonds.

Willy: Can you imagine that magnificence with twenty thousand dollars in his pocket?

Linda (*calling from her room*): Willy! Come up!

Willy (*calling into the kitchen*): Yes! Yes. Coming! It's very smart, you realize that, don't you, sweetheart? Even Ben sees it. I gotta go, baby. 'By! 'By! (*Going over to* **Ben**, *almost dancing*) Imagine? When the mail comes he'll be ahead of Bernard again!

Ben: A perfect proposition all around.

Willy: Did you see how he cried to me? Oh, if I could kiss him, Ben!

Ben: Time, William, time!

Willy: Oh, Ben, I always knew one way or another we were gonna make it, Biff and I!

Ben (*looking at his watch*): The boat. We'll be late. (*He moves slowly off into the darkness.*)

Willy (*elegiacally, turning to the house*): Now when you kick off, and when you hit, hit low and hit hard, because it's important, boy. (*He swings around and faces the audience.*) There's all kinds of important people in the stands, and the first thing you know . . . (*Suddenly realizing he is alone*) Ben! Ben, where do I . . . ? (*He makes a sudden movement of search.*) Ben, how do I . . . ?

Linda (*calling*): Willy, you coming up?

Willy (*uttering a gasp of fear, whirling about as if to quiet her*): Sh! (*He turns around as if to find his way; sounds, faces, voices, seem to be swarming in upon him and he flicks at them, crying*) Sh! Sh! (*Suddenly music, faint and high, stops him. It rises in intensity, almost to an unbearable scream. He goes up and down on his toes, and rushes off around the house.*) Shhh!

Linda: Willy?

(*There is no answer.* **Linda** *waits.* **Biff** *gets up off his bed. He is still in his clothes.* **Happy** *sits up.* **Biff** *stands listening.*)

Linda (*with real fear*): Willy, answer me! Willy!

(*There is the sound of a car starting and moving away at full speed.*)

Linda: No!

Biff (*rushing down the stairs*): Pop!

(*As the car speeds off, the music crashes down in a frenzy of sound, which becomes the soft pulsation of a single cello string.* **Biff** *slowly returns to his bedroom. He and* **Happy** *gravely don their jackets.* **Linda** *slowly walks out of her room. The music has developed into a dead march. The leaves of day are appearing over everything.* **Charley** *and* **Bernard**, *somberly dressed, appear and knock on the kitchen door.* **Biff** *and* **Happy** *slowly descend the stairs to the kitchen as* **Charley** *and* **Bernard** *enter. All stop a moment when* **Linda**, *in clothes of mourning, bearing a little bunch of roses, comes through the draped doorway into the kitchen. She goes to* **Charley** *and takes his arm. Now all move toward the audience, through the wall-line of the kitchen. At the limit of the apron,* **Linda** *lays down the flowers, kneels, and sits back on her heels. All stare down at the grave.*)

REQUIEM

Charley: It's getting dark, Linda.

(**Linda** *doesn't react. She stares at the grave.*)

Biff: How about it, Mom? Better get some rest, heh? They'll be closing the gate soon.

(**Linda** *makes no move. Pause.*)

Happy (*deeply angered*): He had no right to do that. There was no necessity for it. We would've helped him.

Charley (*grunting*): Hmmm.

Biff: Come along, Mom.

Linda: Why didn't anybody come?

Charley: It was a very nice funeral.

Linda: But where are all the people he knew? Maybe they blame him.

Charley: Naa. It's a rough world, Linda. They wouldn't blame him.

Linda: I can't understand it. At this time especially. First time in thirty-five years we were just about free and clear. He only needed a little salary. He was even finished with the dentist.

Charley: No man only needs a little salary.

Linda: I can't understand it.

Biff: There were a lot of nice days. When he'd come home from a trip; or on Sundays, making the stoop; finishing the cellar; putting on the new porch; when he built the extra bathroom; and put up the garage. You know something, Charley, there's more of him in that front stoop than in all the sales he ever made.

Charley: Yeah. He was a happy man with a batch of cement.

Linda: He was so wonderful with his hands.

Biff: He had the wrong dreams. All, all, wrong.

Happy (*almost ready to fight* **Biff**): Don't say that!

Biff: He never knew who he was.

Charley (*stopping* **Happy's** *movement and reply. To* **Biff**): Nobody dast blame this man. You don't understand: Willy was a salesman. And for a salesman, there is no rock bottom to the life. He don't put a bolt to a nut, he don't tell you the law or give you medicine. He's a man way out there in the blue, riding on a smile and a shoestring. And when they start not smiling back—that's an earthquake. And then you get yourself a couple of spots on your hat, and you're finished. Nobody dast blame this man. A salesman is got to dream, boy. It comes with the territory.

Biff: Charley, the man didn't know who he was.

Happy (*infuriated*): Don't say that!

Biff: Why don't you come with me, Happy?

Happy: I'm not licked that easily. I'm staying right in this city, and I'm gonna beat this racket! (*He looks at* **Biff**, *his chin set.*) The Loman Brothers!

Biff: I know who I am, kid.

Happy: All right, boy. I'm gonna show you and everybody else that Willy Loman did not die in vain. He had a good dream. It's the only dream you can have—to come out number-one man. He fought it out here, and this is where I'm gonna win it for him.

Biff (*with a hopeless glance at* **Happy**, *bends toward his mother*): Let's go, Mom.

Linda: I'll be with you in a minute. Go on, Charley. (*He hesitates.*) I want to, just for a minute. I never had a chance to say good-by.

(**Charley** *moves away, followed by* **Happy**. **Biff** *remains a slight distance up and left of* **Linda**. *She sits there, summoning herself. The flute begins, not far away, playing behind her speech.*)

Linda: Forgive me, dear. I can't cry. I don't know what it is, but I can't cry. I don't understand it. Why did you ever do that? Help me, Willy, I can't cry. It seems to me that you're just on another trip. I keep expecting you. Willy, dear, I can't cry. Why did you do it? I search and search and I search, and I can't understand it, Willy. I made the last payment on the house today. Today, dear. And there'll be nobody home. (*A sob rises in her throat.*) We're free and clear. (*Sobbing more fully, released*) We're free. (**Biff** *comes slowly toward her.*) We're free . . . We're free . . .

(**Biff** *lifts her to her feet and moves out up right with her in his arms.* **Linda** *sobs quietly.* **Bernard** *and* **Charley** *come together and follow them, followed by* **Happy**. *Only the music of the flute is left on the darkening stage as over the house the hard towers of the apartment buildings rise into sharp focus, and the curtain falls.*)

PART THREE
SETTING

All characters and dramatic action exist and occur within some particular time and place. In our daily lives we recognize the importance of the relationship between ourselves and our physical surroundings. People have favorite places where they can be quiet and relaxed or where they can talk loudly and laugh. Every weekend many people try to "get away from it all." For most people that phrase seems to mean changing their physical surroundings to help foster changes in their mental attitudes and feelings. If they live in the city, they go to the country—to nature, to lakes and mountains. If they live in the suburbs, they retreat to cabins and campers, or head for the seashore.

Thousands more travel from one country to another, changing their surroundings, their attitudes and feelings, and their life styles. Those who can't afford to travel may change their lives by altering the pictures, plants, furniture, walls, windows, books, records, smells, and tastes they live with day by day.

Because physical surroundings have a tremendous effect on personality and attitude, we tend to stereotype people according to their place of origin. For example, we expect a person from Brooklyn to have different attitudes and traits from someone from Biloxi, Mississippi, or an Irishman to differ from an Italian.

The dramatist recognizes this important relationship between his characters and their place in time and physical surroundings. He has the freedom to set his play in any time and place that suit his purpose; the selections he does make are therefore significant.

People in real life have no control over the time in which they live. They may try to alter certain aspects of the period by furnishing their homes in particular ways or by ignoring much of what goes on around them, but they cannot actually change the period in which they are born. A playwright has no such limitations in writing his play. He may set it two hundred years ago, ten years ago, fifty years in the future, or at no specific time, and hence for all time. A good playwright does not make such choices frivolously, because the period in which he sets his play carries with it all the attitudes, customs, and moral views of the times and must affect the play itself. If the setting is 1920, the characters cannot know about television or World War II. If it is Greece in 400 B.C., we can expect the characters to be well acquainted with gods and goddesses and to believe the earth is the center of the universe.

It is impossible, of course, to separate place from time. New York in 1925 is different from Paris in 1925; Harlem is different from Park Avenue; a factory is different from a bar; and the playwright selects the place of his play as carefully as he does the time. When he chooses a specific aspect of setting, he eliminates all the other possibilities, recognizing the ideas, attitudes, and values that go with that choice. In London in 1300 most people believed the world was flat; in Florence in the fifteenth century the Renaissance of learning and art was at its peak; in Berlin in 1940, many people accepted concentration camps and the concept of a master race. Facts like these and hundreds more are automatically true of each time and place a playwright may choose. As readers or viewers we must be aware of his choices and attempt to determine their significance. The dramatist conveys a great deal of information about his characters through his selection of the world in which he places them, whether it is real or fictitious. To fully understand these characters, we need to be conscious of details such as historical period, geographical location, climate, and any dominant or unusual physical characteristics of the locale. Is it excessively cold or hot? Is it civilized and secure, like a small town in Ohio, or is it an island threatened by the sea, or a tiny village dominated by high mountains? Is the location wealthy or poor? Is it a single bare room, lonely and desolate, or an office on a noisy downtown street, tense and crowded?

The playwright calls your attention to these details by several means. The most obvious clue is his choice of physical objects to be placed on stage to emphasize certain aspects of the setting. Heavy, ornate furniture, cages of animals, a large stove in the middle of the room, fishnets on the wall, a view of tall office buildings out the window—all such items may draw your attention to certain characteristics of the time and place of the play.

Certain aspects of setting may be emphasized verbally through dialogue. Characters talking to one another may casually convey a number of significant facts about the setting. They may discuss certain objects on the stage or make frequent references to features of the surrounding area, such as the colors of the landscape, the beasts that inhabit the region, or the sounds of the night. Such aspects of the setting have been carefully selected by the playwright; when he draws your attention to these details, he does so for a particular reason. If nothing is said about the weather or the building next door or the time of day or year, those details are not important; but if such references *are* made, then we need to ask why.

Setting is important in a play because of its effect on character. Just as your own setting, or surroundings, reveal a great deal about you, the setting of a play helps to explain or emphasize certain aspects of a character's motivation or personality. A character may be similar to the setting in which he lives, gaining a part of his identity from it. For example, a man may become old and gnarled, fixed and useless, like the dead trees that surround his house.

On the other hand, a character may be unlike his setting and in conflict with it. A young, vibrant woman living in her aunt's dark, gloomy, Victorian house might have such a conflict; indeed, the focus of the whole play might be the struggle between the woman and her environment. If the setting changes within the play, this may cause or reflect changes within the characters. If the woman moves out of her aunt's house to an apartment in the city, her character may change accordingly, forcing us to reevaluate her personality.

Sometimes physical surroundings may even take on the function of a character in the play. The sea that continues to pound the rocky coast after all the people in the play have died may be seen as such an enduring force that it becomes a character in its own right. An attic that contains a family's stored and forgotten articles may become that family when contrasted with strangers or younger relatives.

All these examples illustrate the close relationship that exists between people and their surroundings. The playwright uses this relationship to help create certain desired effects. He usually simplifies the relationship by selecting certain details to emphasize and ignoring others—but he is writing a play, not creating real life. We the audience must pay attention to the details he has chosen and ask what effects he is trying to create with the setting in which he has placed his characters.

THE EFFECT OF GAMMA RAYS ON MAN-IN-THE-MOON MARIGOLDS

Paul Zindel

Setting
Character
symbol

CHARACTERS

Tillie, The Girl

"In front of my eyes, one part of the world was becoming another. Atoms exploding . . . atom after atom breaking down into something new . . . It would go on for millions of years . . ."

Beatrice, The Mother

"This long street, with all the doors of the houses shut and everything crowded next to each other . . . And then I start getting afraid that the vegetables are going to spoil . . . and that nobody's going to buy anything . . ."

Ruth, The Other Daughter *much like Beatrice; thinks of herself*

"Well, they say I came out of my room . . . and I started down the stairs, step by step . . . and I heard the choking and banging on the bed . . ."

Nanny

Janice Vickery

THE SETTING: *A room of wood which was once a vegetable store—and a point of debarkation for a horse-drawn wagon to bring its wares to a small town.*

*But the store is gone, and a widow of confusion has placed her touch on everything. A door to **Nanny's** room leads off from this main room, and in front of the door hang faded curtains which allow ventilation in the summer. There is a hallway and a telephone. A heavy wood staircase leads to a landing with a balustrade, two doors, and a short hall. **Beatrice** sleeps in one room; **Tillie** and **Ruth** share the other.*

Objects which respectable people usually hide in closets are scattered about the main room: newspapers, magazines, dishes; empty bottles; clothes; suitcases; last week's sheets. Such carelessness is the type which is so perfected it must have evolved from hereditary processes; but in all fairness to the occupants, it can be pointed out that after twilight, when shadows and weak bulbs work their magic, the room becomes interesting.

The playwright provides many details of setting. What overall impression do they create?

On a table near the front left of the room is a small wire cage designed to hold a rabbit. Near this are several school books, notebook papers, and other weapons of high school children. A kitchen area, boasting a hot plate, has been carved near the bottom of the staircase, and the window, which was formerly the front of the vegetable store, is now mostly covered with old newspapers so that passers-by cannot see in. A bit of the clear glass remains at the top—but drab, lifeless drapes line the sides of the window.

ACT I

The lights go down slowly as music creeps in—a theme for lost children, the near misbegotten.

From the blackness **Tillie's Voice** *speaks against the music.*

Tillie's Voice: He told me to look at my hand, for a part of it came from a star that exploded too long ago to imagine. This part of me was formed from a tongue of fire that screamed through the heavens until there was our sun. And this part of me—this tiny part of me—was on the sun when it itself exploded and whirled in a great storm until the planets came to be.

(Lights start in.)

And this small part of me was then a whisper of the earth. When there was life, perhaps this part of me got lost in a fern that was crushed and covered until it was coal. And then it was a diamond millions of years later—it must have been a diamond as beautiful as the star from which it had first come.

Tillie *(taking over from recorded voice)*: Or perhaps this part of me became lost in a terrible beast, or became part of a huge bird that flew above the primeval swamps.

And he said this thing was so small—this part of me was so small it couldn't be seen—but it was there from the beginning of the world.

And he called this bit of me an atom. And when he wrote the word, I fell in love with it.

Atom.

Atom.

What a beautiful word.

(The phone rings.)

Beatrice *(off stage)*: Will you get that please?

(The phone rings again before **Beatrice** *appears in her bathrobe from the kitchen.)*

No help! Never any help!

(She answers the phone.)

Hello? Yes it is. Who is this? . . . I hope there hasn't been any trouble at school . . . Oh, she's always been like that. She hardly says a word around here, either. I always say some people were born to speak and others born to listen . . .

You know I've been meaning to call you to thank you for that lovely rabbit you gave Matilda. She and I just adore it and it's gotten so big . . .

Well, it certainly was thoughtful. Mr. Goodman, I don't mean to change the subject but aren't you that delightful young man Tillie said hello to a couple of months back at the A & P? You were by the lobster tank and I was near the frozen foods? That delightful and handsome young man? . . . Why, I would very much indeed use the expression *handsome*. Yes, and . . .

Well, I encourage her at every opportunity at home. Did she say I didn't? Both my daughters have their own desks and I put 75-watt bulbs right near them . . . Yes . . . Yes . . . I think those tests are very much overrated, anyway, Mr. Goodman . . . Well, believe me she's nothing like that around this house . . .

Now I don't want you to think I don't appreciate what you're trying to do, Mr. Goodman, but I'm afraid it's simply useless. I've tried just everything,

Tillie sees beauty within herself. Compare to her physical surroundings

Part of setting. Why emphasize 75-watt bulb?

but she isn't a pretty girl—I mean, let's be frank about it—she's going to have her problems. Are you married, Mr. Goodman? Oh, that's too bad. I don't know what's the matter with women today letting a handsome young man like you get away . . .

Well, some days she just doesn't feel like going to school. You just said how bright she is, and I'm really afraid to put too much of a strain on her after what happened to her sister. You know, too much strain is the worst thing in this modern world, Mr. Goodman, and I can't afford to have another convulsive on my hands, now can I? But don't you worry about Matilda. There will be some place for her in this world. And, like I said, some were born to speak and others just to listen . . . and do call again, Mr. Goodman. It's been a true pleasure speaking with you. Goodbye.

Ruth is a convulsive. Relate her condition to appearance of room.

(**Beatrice** *hangs up the phone and advances into the main room. The lights come up.*) Matilda, that wasn't very nice of you to tell them I was forcibly detaining you from school. Why, the way that Mr. Goodman spoke, he must think I'm running a concentration camp. Do you have any idea how embarrassing it is to be accused of running a concentration camp for your own children?

Well, it isn't embarrassing at all.

That school of yours is forty years behind the times anyway, and believe me you learn more around here than that ugly Mr. Goodman can teach you! You know, I really feel sorry for him. I never saw a man with a more effeminate face in my life. When I saw you talking to him by the lobster tank I said to myself, "Good Lord, for a science teacher my poor girl has got herself a Hebrew hermaphrodite." Of course, he's not as bad as Miss Hanley. The idea of letting her teach girl's gym is staggering.

And you have to place me in the embarrassing position of giving them a reason to call me at eight-thirty in the morning, no less.

Tillie: I didn't say anything.

Beatrice: What do you tell them when they want to know why you stay home once in a while?

Tillie: I tell them I'm sick.

Beatrice: Oh, you're sick all right, the exact nature of the illness not fully realized, but you're sick all right. Any daughter that would turn her mother in as the administrator of a concentration camp has got to be suffering from something very peculiar.

Tillie: Can I go in today, Mother?

Beatrice: You'll go in, all right.

Tillie: Mr. Goodman said he was going to do an experiment——

Beatrice: Why, he looks like the kind that would do his experimenting after sundown.

Tillie: On radioactivity——

Beatrice: On radioactivity? That's all that high school needs!

Tillie: He's going to bring in the cloud chamber——

Beatrice: Why, what an outstanding event. If you had warned me yesterday I would've gotten all dressed to kill and gone with you today. I love seeing cloud chambers being brought in.

Tillie: You can actually see——

Beatrice: You're giving me a headache.

Tillie: Please?

Beatrice: No, my dear, the fortress of knowledge is not going to be blessed with your presence today. I have a good number of exciting duties for you to take care of, not the least of which is rabbit droppings.

What does this detail add to impression of setting?

Tillie: Oh, Mother, please . . . I'll do it after school.

Beatrice: If we wait a minute longer this house is going to ferment. I found rabbit droppings in my bedroom even.

Tillie: I could do it after Mr. Goodman's class. I'll say I'm ill and ask for a sick pass.

Beatrice: Do you want me to chloroform that thing right this minute?

Tillie: No!

Beatrice: Then shut up.

(**Ruth** *comes to the top of the stairs. She is dressed for school, and though her clothes are simple she gives the impression of being slightly strange. Her hair isn't quite combed, her sweater doesn't quite fit, etc.*)

Ruth: Do you have Devil's Kiss down there?

Beatrice: It's in the bathroom cabinet.

(**Ruth** *comes downstairs and goes to the bathroom door, located under the stairs. She flings it open and rummages in the cabinet.*)

Have you ever seen a place so messy it almost drove you crazy?

Ruth: There's so much junk in here it's driving me crazy.

Beatrice: Maybe it's in my purse . . . If you don't hurry up you'll be late for school.

Ruth: Well, I couldn't very well go in without Devil's Kiss, now could I?

Beatrice: Doesn't anyone go to school these days without that all over their lips?

Ruth (*finding the lipstick*): Nobody I know, except Tillie, that is. And if she had a little lipstick on I'll bet they wouldn't have laughed at her so much yesterday.

Beatrice: Why were they laughing?

Ruth: The assembly. Didn't she tell you about the assembly?

Beatrice: Ruth, you didn't tell me she was in an assembly.

Ruth: Well, I just thought of it right now. How could I tell you anything until I think of it—did you ever stop to consider that? Some crummy science assembly.

Beatrice (*to* **Tillie**): What is she talking about?

Ruth: I thought she'd tell the whole world. Imagine, right in front of the assembly, with everybody laughing at her.

Beatrice: Will you be quiet, Ruth? *Why were they laughing at you?*

Tillie: I don't know.

Ruth: You don't know? My heavens, she was a sight. She had that old jumper on—the faded one with that low collar—and a raggy slip that showed all over and her hair looked like she was struck by lightning.

Beatrice: You're exaggerating . . .

Ruth: She was cranking this model of something——

Tillie: The atom.

Ruth: This model of the atom . . . you know, it had this crank and a long tower so that when you turned it these little colored balls went spinning around like crazy. And there was Tillie, cranking away, looking weird as a coot . . . that old jumper with the raggy slip and the lightning hair . . . cranking away while some boy with glasses was reading this stupid speech . . . and everybody burst into laughter until the teachers yelled at them.

And all day long, the kids kept coming up to me saying, "Is that really your sister? How can you bear it?" And you know, Chris Burns says to me—"*She* looks like the one that went to the looney doctors." I could have kissed him there and then.

Beatrice (*taking a backscratcher*): Matilda, if you can't get yourself dressed properly before going to school you're never going to go again. I don't like the idea of everybody laughing at you, because when they laugh at you they're laughing at me. And I don't want you cranking any more . . . atoms.

Ruth (*putting the lipstick back in* **Beatrice's** *bag*): You're almost out of Devil's Kiss.

Beatrice: If you didn't put so much on it would last longer.

Ruth: Who was that calling?

Beatrice: Matilda turned me in to the Gestapo.

Ruth: Can I earn a cigarette this morning?

Beatrice: Why not?

(**Beatrice** *offers her the backscratcher along with a cigarette.*)

Ruth: Was it Mr. Goodman?

Beatrice: Who?

Ruth (*lighting the cigarette*): The call this morning. Was it Mr. Goodman?

Beatrice: Yes.

Ruth (*using the backscratcher on* **Beatrice**, *who squirms with ecstasy*): I figured it would be.

Beatrice: A little higher, please.

Ruth: There?

Beatrice: Yes, there . . . Why did you figure it would be Mr. Goodman?

Ruth: Well, he called me out of sewing class yesterday—I remember because my blouse wasn't all buttoned—and he wanted to know why Tillie's out of school so much.

Beatrice: Lower. A little lower . . . And what did you tell him?

Ruth: I wish you'd go back to Kools. I liked Kools better.

Tillie (*gravely concerned*): What did you tell him?

Ruth: I told him you were ill, and he wanted to know what kind, so I told him you had leprosy.

Tillie: You didn't!

Ruth: You should have seen his face. He was so cute. And I told him you had ringworm and gangrene.

Beatrice: What did he say?

Ruth: And I told him you had what Mother's last patient had . . . whatchamacallit?

Beatrice: Psoriasis?

Ruth: Yeah. Something like that.

Tillie: Tell me you didn't, Ruth!

Ruth: O.K. I didn't . . . But I really did.

Beatrice: He knew you were joking.

Ruth: And then I told him to go look up the *history* and then he'd find out. Whenever they go look up the history then they don't bother me anymore 'cause they think I'm crazy.

Beatrice: Ruth——

Ruth: And I told him the disease you had was fatal and that there wasn't much hope for you.

Part of Tillie's other world. Is Ruth's view reliable?

What is Ruth's world like?

Beatrice: What kind of *history* is it?

Ruth: Just a little folder with the story of our lives in it, that's all.

Beatrice: How did you ever see it?

Ruth: I read the whole thing last term when Miss Hanley dragged me into the record room because I didn't want to climb the ropes in gym and I told her my skull was growing.

Beatrice: A little *lower*, please.

Ruth: Lower! Higher! I wish you'd make up your mind. If you'd switch back to Kools it might be worth it, but ugh! these are awful. You know, I really did think my skull was growing. Either that or a tumor. So she dragged me out of gym class, and she thought I couldn't read upside down while she was sitting opposite me with the history. But I could.

Beatrice: What does it say?

Part of setting **Ruth:** Oh, it says you're divorced and that I went crazy . . . and my father took a heart attack at Star Lake . . . and now you're a widow——

Beatrice (*referring to the backscratching*): That's it! Hold it right there! Aaah!

Ruth: And it says that I exaggerate and tell stories and that I'm afraid of death and have nightmares . . . and all that stuff.

Beatrice: And what else does it say?

Ruth: I can't remember everything you know. Remember this, remember that . . . remember this, that . . .

(*Go to dark. Music in.*)

Tillie's Voice: Today I saw it. Behind the glass a white cloud began to form. He placed a small piece of metal in the center of the chamber and we waited until I saw the first one—a trace of smoke that came from nowhere and then disappeared. And then another . . . and another, until I knew it was coming *Tillie's dream* from the metal. They looked like water-sprays from a park fountain, and *world of the future* they went on and on for as long as I watched.

And he told me the fountain of smoke would come forth for a long time, and if I had wanted to, I could have stayed there all my life and it would never have ended—that fountain, so close I could have touched it. In front of my eyes, one part of the world was becoming another. Atoms exploding, flinging off tiny bullets that caused the fountain, atom after atom breaking down into something new. And no one could stop the fountain. It would go on for millions of years—on and on, this fountain from eternity.

What does Tillie's (*By the end of this speech, the lights are in to show* **Tillie** *preparing boxes of dirt in* *close association* *which to plant seeds. The rabbit is in the cage near her, and* **Beatrice** *is reading a* *with the rabbit* *newspaper on the other side of the room. She is sipping coffee from a huge coffee cup.*) *and the flowers* *reveal ?* **Beatrice:** I thought we had everything, but leave it to you to think of the one thing we're missing . . .

(*She reads from the newspaper.*)

Twenty-two acres in Prince's Bay. Small pond. $6,000 . . . That's cheap. I'd take a look at it if I had any money . . .

What kind of seeds are they?

Tillie: Marigolds. *They've been exposed to cobalt-60.*

Beatrice: If there's one thing I've always wanted, it's been a living room planted with marigolds that have been exposed to cobalt-60. While you're at it, why don't you throw in a tomato patch in the bathroom?

Tillie: Just let me keep them here for a week or so until they get started and then I'll transplant them to the backyard.

Beatrice (*reading again*): Four-family house. Six and a half and six and a half over five and five. Eight garages. I could really do something with that. A nursing home . . .

Don't think I'm not kicking myself that I didn't finish that real estate course. I should have finished beauty school, too . . .

What has she finished? Look around the room.

God, what I could do with eight garages . . .

(*There is a sound from beyond the curtained doorway.* **Beatrice** *gestures in that direction.*)

You know, I'm thinking of getting rid of *that* and making this place into something.

Tillie: Yes.

Beatrice: I've been thinking about a tea shop. Have you noticed there aren't many of them around anymore?

Tillie: Yes.

Beatrice: And this is just the type of neighborhood where a good tea shop could make a go of it. We'd have a good cheesecake. You've got to have a good cheesecake.

(*She calculates.*)

Eight times ten—well, eight times eight, if they're falling down—that's sixty-four dollars a month from the garages alone . . . I swear money makes money.

(*There is a rustling at the curtains. Two thin and wrinkled hands push the curtains apart slowly and then the ancient face of* **Nanny** *appears. She negotiates her way through the curtains. She is utterly wrinkled and dried, perhaps a century old. Time has left her with a whisper of a smile—a smile from a soul half-departed. If one looked closely, great cataracts could be seen on each eye, and it is certain that all that can pierce her soundless prison are mere shadows from the outside world. She pervades the room with age.*

Does Nanny fit in or contrast with the room?

Nanny *supports herself by a four-legged tubular frame which she pushes along in front of her with a shuffling motion that reminds one of a ticking clock. Inch by inch she advances into the room.* **Tillie** *and* **Beatrice** *continue speaking, knowing that it will be minutes before she is close enough to know they are there.*)

Beatrice: What is cobalt-60?

Tillie: It's something that causes . . . changes in seeds. Oh, Mother—he set the cloud chamber up just for me and he told me about radioactivity and half-life and he got the seeds for me.

Beatrice (*her attention still on the newspaper*): What does half-life mean?

(**Nanny** *is well into the room as* **Tillie** *replies.*)

Tillie (*reciting from memory*): The half-life of Polonium-210 is one hundred and forty days.

The half-life of Radium-226 is one thousand five hundred and ninety years.

The half-life of Uranium-238 is four and one-half billion years.

Beatrice (*putting away her newspaper*): Do you know you're giving me a head-ache? (*Then, in a loud, horribly saccharine voice, she speaks to* **Nanny** *as if she were addressing a deaf year-old child.*) LOOK WHO'S THERE! IT'S NANNY! NANNY CAME ALL THE WAY OUT HERE BY HERSELF!

I'm going to need a cigarette for this.

NANNY! YOU COME SIT DOWN AND WE'LL BE RIGHT WITH HER!

You know, sometimes I've got to laugh. I've got *this* on my hands and all you're worried about is planting marigolds.

I'VE GOT HOTSY WATER FOR YOU, NANNY. WOULD YOU LIKE SOME HOTSY WATER AND HONEY?

(**Nanny** *has seated herself at a table, smiling but oblivious to her environment.*)

I've never seen it to fail. Every time I decide to have a cup of coffee I see that face at the curtains. I wonder what she'd do . . .

(*She holds pot of boiling water.*) . . . if I just poured this right over her head. I'll bet she wouldn't even notice it.

NANNY'S GOING TO GET JUST WHAT SHE NEEDS!

(*She fills a cup for her and places a honey jar near her.*)

You know if someone told me when I was young that I'd end up feeding honey to a zombie, I'd tell them they were crazy.

SOMETHING WRONG, NANNY? OH DID I FORGET NANNY'S SPOON? MERCY! MERCY! I FORGOT NANNY'S SPOON!

(*She gets a spoon and stands behind* **Nanny**.)

I'll give you a spoon, Nanny, I'll give you a spoon.

(*She makes a motion behind* **Nanny's** *back as if she's going to smack her on the head with the spoon.*)

Matilda! Watch me give Nanny her spoon.

A SPOON FOR NANNY!

(*It manages to be slightly funny and* **Tillie** *yields to a laugh, along with her mother.*)

Fifty dollars a week. Fifty dollars. I look at you, Nanny, and I wonder if it's worth it. I think I'd be better off driving a cab.

TAKE HONEY, NANNY. HONEY WITH HOTSY WATER!

You should have seen her daughter bring her here last week . . . I could have used you that day . . . She came in pretending she was Miss Career Woman of the Year. She said she was in real estate and *such a busy little woman,* such a busy little woman—she just couldn't give all the love and care and affection her little momsy needed anymore . . .

(*Then, with a great smile, she speaks right into* **Nanny's** *uncomprehending face.*)

Nanny's quite a little cross to bear, now aren't you, Nanny dear? But you're a little better than Mr. Mayo was—with the tumor on his brain—or Miss Marion Minto with her cancer, or Mr. Brougham . . . what was his first name?

Tillie: Alexander.

Beatrice: Mr. Alexander Brougham with the worms in his legs.

WHY, NANNY'S QUITE SOME LITTLE GIRL, AREN'T YOU, NANNY? A GIRL DRINKING HER HOTSY AND HONEY! . . .

Cobalt-60. Ha! You take me for a fool, don't you?

Tillie: No, Mother.

Beatrice: Science, science, science! Don't they teach our misfits anything anymore? Anything decent and meaningful and sensitive? Do you know what I'd be now if it wasn't for this mud pool I got sucked into? I'd probably be a dancer. Miss Betty Frank, The Best Dancer of the Class of 19 . . . something. One minute I'm the best dancer in school—smart as a whip—the head of the whole crowd! And the next minute . . .

One mistake. That's how it starts. Marry the wrong man and before you know it he's got you tied down with two stones around your neck for the rest of your life.

When I was in that lousy high school I was one of the most respected kids you ever saw.

I used to wonder why people always said, "Why, just yesterday . . . why, just yesterday . . . why, just yesterday."

Before I know what happened I lost my dancing legs and got varicose legs. Beautiful varicose legs. Do you know, everything I ever thought I'd be has exploded!

The debris is all around her.

NANNY, YOU HURRY UP WITH THAT HONEY!

Exploded! You know, I almost forgot about everything I was supposed to be . . .

NANNY'S ALMOST FINISHED. ISN'T THAT WONDERFUL?

She's almost finished, all right.

NANNY'S DAUGHTER IS COMING TO SEE YOU SOON. WILL THAT MAKE NANNY HAPPY?

The day Miss Career Woman of the Year comes to visit again I think I'll drop dead. Nobody's too busy for anything they want to do, don't you tell me. What kind of an idiot do people take me for?

NANNY, YOU'RE SPILLING YOUR HOTSY! JESUS CHRIST!

You know, I ought to kick you right out and open that tea shop tomorrow.

Oh, it's coming. I can feel it. And the first thing I'll do is get rid of that rabbit.

Tillie (*hardly listening*): Yes, Mother.

Beatrice: You think I'm kidding?

Tillie: No, I don't.

Beatrice: You bet I'm not!

(*She rummages through some drawers in a chest.*)

I was going to do this a month ago.

(*She holds up a small bottle.*)

Here it is. Here's a new word for you.

(*She reads.*)

Trichloro . . . methane. Do you know what this is, Matilda? Well, it's chloroform!

(*She puts the bottle away.*)

I'm saving it for that Angora manure machine of yours. Speaking of manure machines, IS NANNY READY TO GO MAKE DUTY?

(*She starts helping* **Nanny** *out of the chair and props her up with the tubular frame.*)

NANNY IS ALWAYS READY FOR DUTY, AREN'T YOU NANNY? BE-CAUSE NANNY'S A GOODY-GOODY GIRL AND GOODY-GOODY GIRLS ALWAYS GET GOODY-GOODY THINGS. GOD LOOKS OUT FOR GOODY-GOODY GIRLS AND GIVES THEM HOTSY AND HONEY —RIGHT, NANNY?

(**Beatrice** *sits down in the hall and watches* **Nanny** *make her way toward the bathroom. There is a pause as the woman's shuffling continues.*

The lights go low on **Tillie, Nanny** *becomes a silhouette, and the light remains on* **Beatrice.** *She starts to read the paper again, but the shuffling gets on her nerves and she flings the paper down.*)

Half-life! If you want to know what a half-life is, just ask me. You're looking at the original half-life!

I got stuck with one daughter with half a mind; another one who's half a

Beatrice's view
of her world

test tube; half a husband—a house full of rabbit crap—and half a corpse!
That's what I call a half-life, Matilda! Me and cobalt-60! Two of the biggest
half-*lifes* you ever saw!

(*The set goes to dark. After a few seconds, the sound of someone dialing a phone can
be heard. As the spot comes up on her, we see* **Beatrice** *holding the phone and struggling
to get a cigarette.*)

Beatrice (*on the phone*): Hello—Mr. Goodman, please . . . How would I know
if he's got a class? . . . Hello, Mr. Goodman? Are you Mr. Goodman? . . .
Oh, I beg your pardon, Miss Torgersen . . . Yes, I'll wait.

(*She lights her cigarette.*)

Couldn't you find him, Miss Torgersen? . . . Oh! Excuse me, Mr. Goodman.
How are you? . . . I'll bet you'll never guess who this is—it's Mrs. Hunsdorfer—remember the frozen foods?

(*She laughs.*)

You know, Ruth told me she's your new secretary and I certainly think that's
a delight. You were paying so much attention to Matilda that I'll bet Ruth
just got jealous. She does things like that, you know. I hope she works hard
for you, although I can't imagine what kind of work Ruth could be doing in
that great big science office. She's a terrible snoop . . .

(*She takes a puff.*)

Your attendance? Isn't that charming. And the *cut* cards! Imagine. You trust
her with . . . why, I didn't know she could type *at all* . . . imagine. Well
. . . I'll . . . Of course, *too* much work isn't good for anyone, either. No
wonder she's failing everything. I mean, I never knew a girl who failed everything regardless of what they were suffering from. I suppose I should say
recovering from . . .

Well, it's about the seeds you gave Matilda . . . Well, she's had them in
the house for a week now and they're starting to grow. Now, she told me they
had been subjected to radioactivity, and I hear such terrible things about
radioactivity that I automatically associated radioactivity with sterility, and it
positively horrifies me to have those seeds right here in my living room.
Couldn't she just grow plain marigolds like everyone else?

(*She takes a puff.*)

Oh . . .

(*Another big puff, forming a mushroom cloud.*)

It does sound like an interesting project, but . . .

(*The biggest puff yet.*)

No, I must admit that at this very moment I don't know what a *mutation*
is . . .

(*She laughs uncomfortably.*)

Mr. Goodman . . . Mr. Goodman! I don't want you to think I'm not interested, but please spare me definitions over the phone. I'll go to the library
next week and pick me out some little book on science and then I'll know all
about mutations . . . No, you didn't insult me, but I just want you to know
that I'm not *stupid* . . .

I just thought prevention was better than a tragedy, Mr. Goodman. I mean,
Matilda has enough problems to worry about without *sterility* . . .

Well, I was just concerned, but you've put my poor mother's heart at ease.
You know, really, our schools need more exciting young men like you, I
really mean that. Really, Oh I do. Goodbye, Mr. Goodman.

(*By the end of her talk on the phone, her face is left in a spotlight, and then the stage goes black. The music theme comes in, in a minor key, softly at first, but accentuated by increasingly loud pulses which transmute into thunder crashes.*

There is a scream heard from upstairs and we see the set in night shadows.

Tillie *tears open her bedroom door and rushes into* **Beatrice's** *room.* **Ruth** *screams again.*)

Tillie: Mother! She's going to have one!

(**Ruth** *appears on the landing and releases another scream which breaks off into gasps. She starts down the stairs and stops halfway to scream again. There is another tremendous thunder crash as* **Beatrice** *comes out of her room, puts on the hall light, and catches the hysterical girl on the stairs.*)

Beatrice (*shouting*): Stop it! Stop it, Ruth!

Tillie (*at the top of the stairs*): She's going!

Beatrice: Ruth! Stop it!

Tillie: She's going to go!

Beatrice (*yelling at* **Tillie**): Shut up and get back in your room!

(**Ruth** *screams.*)

You're not going to let yourself go, do you hear me, Ruth? You're not going to go!

Ruth: He's after me!

(*She screams, lightning and thunder crash follow.*)

Beatrice: You were dreaming, do you hear me? Nobody's after you! Nobody!

Tillie: I saw her eyes start to go back——

Beatrice (*to* **Tillie**): Get back in your room!

(*She helps* **Ruth** *down the rest of the stairs.*)

There, now, nobody's after you. Nice and easy. Breathe deeply . . . Did the big bad man come after my little girl?

(*She sits* **Ruth** *down and then puts both hands up to her own face and pulls her features into a comic mask.* **Ruth** *begins to laugh at her.*)

That big bad bogey man?

(*They both laugh heartily.*)

Now that wasn't so bad, was it?

Ruth: It was the dream, with Mr. Mayo again.

Beatrice: Oh. Well, we'll just get a you a little hot milk and——

(*A tremendous thunder crash throws the set into shadows.*)

Why, the electricity's gone off. Do you remember what happened to those candles?

Ruth: What candles?

Beatrice: The little white ones from my birthday cake last year.

Ruth: Tillie melted then down for school a long time ago.

Beatrice (*searching through drawers*): She had no right doing that.

Ruth: She asked you. She used them to attach a paper straw to a milk bottle with a balloon over it, and it was supposed to tell if it was going to rain.

Beatrice (*finding a flashlight*): There! It works. I don't want her wasting anything of mine unless she's positive I won't need it. You always need candles.

(*She steers* **Ruth** *toward the couch as lightning flashes.*)

Why, Ruth—your skin just turned ice cold!

(*She rummages through one of the boxes and grabs a blanket.*)

This will warm you up . . . What's the matter?

Ruth: The flashlight——

Why emphasize the storm?

Beatrice: What's wrong with it?

Ruth: It's the same one I used to check on Mr. Mayo with.

Beatrice: So it is. We don't need it.

Ruth: No, let me keep it.

(*Starting to laugh.*)

Do you want to know how they have it in the history?

Beatrice: No, I don't.

Ruth: Well, they say I came out of my room . . .

(*She flashes the light on her room.*)

. . . And I started down the stairs, step by step . . . and I heard the choking and banging on the bed, and . . .

Beatrice: I'm going back to bed.

Ruth: No!

Beatrice: Well, talk about something nice, then.

Ruth: Oh, Mama, tell me about the wagon.

Beatrice: You change so fast I can't keep up with you.

Ruth: Mama, *please* . . . the story about the wagon.

Beatrice: I don't know anything about telling stories. Get those great big smart teachers of yours to do that sort of stuff.

Ruth: Tell me about the horses again, and how you stole the wagon.

Beatrice: Don't get me started on that.

Ruth: Mama, *please* . . .

Beatrice (*taking out a pack of cigarettes*): Do you want a cigarette?

Ruth (*taking one*): Leave out the part where they shoot the horses, though.

(*They both light up.*)

Beatrice: Honey, you know the whole story——

Ruth: "Apples! Pears! Cu . . . cumbers!"

Compare her precision about the past with her carelessness of the present.

Beatrice: No, It's "Apples! Pears! Cucum . . . bers!"

(*They say it together.*)

"Apples! Pears! Cucum . . . bers!"

(*And they laugh.*)

Ruth: How did you get the wagon out without him seeing you?

Beatrice: That was easy. Every time he got home for the day he'd make us both some sandwiches—my mama had been dead for years—and he'd take a nap on the old sofa that used to be . . . there!

(*She points to a corner of the room.*)

And while he was sleeping I got the horses hitched up and went riding around the block waving to everyone.

Ruth: Oh, Mama, you didn't!

Beatrice: Of course I did. I had more nerve than a bear when I was a kid. Let me tell you it takes nerve to sit up on that wagon every day yelling "Apples! . . .

(*Both together.*)

Pears! Cucum . . . bers!"

(*They laugh again.*)

Ruth: Did he find out you took the wagon?

Beatrice: Did he find out? He came running down the street after me and started spanking me right on top of the wagon—not hard—but it was so embarrassing—and I had one of those penny marshmallow ships in the back pocket of my overalls, and it got all squished. And you better believe I never did it again . . .

You would have loved him, Ruth, and gone out with him on the wagon . . . all over Stapleton yelling as loud as you wanted.

Ruth: "Apples! Pears! *Cu* . . . cumbers!"

Beatrice: No!

Ruth: "*Cucum* . . . bers!"

Beatrice: My father made up for all the other men in this whole world, Ruth. If only you two could have met. He'd only be about seventy now, do you realize that? And I'll bet he'd still be selling vegetables around town. All that fun—and then I don't think I ever knew what really hit me.

Ruth: Don't tell about——

Beatrice: Don't worry about the horses.

Ruth: What hit you?

Beatrice: Well it was just me and Papa . . . and your father hanging around. And then Papa got sick . . . and I drove with him up to the sanatorium. And then I came home and there were the horses——

Ruth: Mother!

Beatrice: And I had the horses . . . taken care of. And then Papa got terribly sick and he begged me to marry so that he'd be sure I'd be taken care of. (*She laughs.*)

If he knew how I was taken care of he'd turn over in his grave.

And *nightmares*! Do you want to know the nightmare I used to have?

I never had nightmares over the fights with your father, or the divorce, or his thrombosis—he deserved it—I never had nightmares over any of that.

Let me tell you abut my nightmare that used to come back and back:

Well, I'm on Papa's wagon, but it's newer and shinier, and it's being pulled by beautiful white horses, not dirty workhorses—these are like circus horses with long manes and tinsel—and the wagon is blue, shiny blue. And it's full—filled with yellow apples and grapes and green squash.

You're going to laugh when you hear this. I'm wearing a lovely gown with jewels all over it, and my hair is piled up on top of my head with a long feather in it, and the bells are ringing. *Compare Beatrice's dream world to Tillie's.*

Huge bells swinging on a gold braid strung across the back of the wagon, and they're going DONG, DONG . . . DONG, DONG. And I'm yelling "APPLES! PEARS! CUCUM . . . BERS!"

Ruth: That doesn't sound like a nightmare to me.

Beatrice: And then I turn down our street and all the noise stops. This long street, with all the doors of the houses shut and everything crowded next to each other, and there's not a soul around. And then I start getting afraid that the vegetables are going to spoil . . . and that nobody's going to buy anything, and I feel as though I shouldn't be on the wagon, and I keep trying to call out.

But there isn't a sound. Not a single sound. Then I turn my head and look at the house across the street. I see an upstairs window, and a pair of hands pull the curtains slowly apart. I see the face of my father and my heart stands still . . . *Her dream still ends this way.*

Ruth: . . . take the light out of my eyes.

(*A long pause.*)

Ruth: Is Nanny going to die here?

Beatrice: No.

Ruth: How can you be sure?

Beatrice: I can tell.

Ruth: Are you crying?

Beatrice: What's left for me, Ruth?

Ruth: What, Mama?

(*The stage goes slowly to dark as the drizzling rain becomes louder and then disappears.*

When the lights come up again **Nanny** *is seated at the kitchen table with a bottle of beer and a glass in front of her.* **Tillie** *comes in the front door with a box of large marigold plants and sets them down where they'll be inconspicuous. She gets the rabbit out of its cage, sits down near* **Nanny** *and gives her a little wave.* **Beatrice** *suddenly appears at the top of the stairs and drops a stack of newspapers with a loud thud. She goes back into her room and lets fly another armful of junk.*)

Tillie: What are you doing?

Beatrice: A little housecleaning, and you're going to help. You can start by getting rid of that rabbit or I'll suffocate the bastard.

(*She takes a drink from a glass of whiskey.*)

You don't think I will, do you? You wait and see. Where's Ruth? She's probably running around the schoolyard in her brassiere.

(*She comes downstairs.*)

Tillie: Mother, they want me to do something at school.

Beatrice: NANNY! DID YOU HEAR THAT? THEY WANT HER TO DO SOMETHING AT SCHOOL! ISN'T THAT MOMENTOUS, NANNY? Well I want you to do something around here. Like get rid of that bunny. I'm being generous! I'll let you give it away. Far away. Give it to Mr. Goodman. I'd chloroform the thing myself, but that crazy sister of yours would throw convulsions for fifty years . . . and I hate a house that vibrates. And get rid of those sterile marigolds. They stink!

HI, NANNY—HOW ARE YOU, HONEY? HOW WOULD YOU LIKE TO GO ON A LONG TRIP?

You see, everybody, I spent today taking stock of my life and I've come up with zero. I added up all the separate departments and the total reads zero . . .

zero zero zero zero zero zero zero

zero zero zero zero zero

zero zero zero

zero zero

zero

. . . And do you know how you pronounce that, with all your grammatical schoolin' and foolin'? You pronounce it, o,o,o,o,O,O,O,O,O,O! o,o,o,o,O,O, O,O,O,O,O!

Right, Nanny? RIGHT, NANNY?

So, by the end of the week, you get rid of that cottontail compost heap and we'll get you a job down at the five-and-ten-cent store. And if you don't do so well with the public, we'll fix you up with some kind of machine. Wouldn't that be nice?

(**Ruth** *enters at a gallop, throwing her books down and babbling a mile a minute.*)

Ruth (*enthusiastically*): Can you believe it? I didn't, until Chris Burns came up and told me about it in Geography, and then Mr. Goodman told me himself during the eighth period in the office when I was eavesdropping. Aren't you so happy you could bust? Tillie? I'm so proud I can't believe it, Mama. Everybody was talking about it and nobody . . . well, it was the first time they all came up screaming about her and I said, "Yes, she's my sister!" I said it, "She's my sister! My sister! My *sister*!" Give me a cigarette.

Beatrice: Get your hands off my personal property.

Ruth: I'll scratch your back later.

Beatrice: I don't want you to touch me!

Ruth: Did he call yet? My God, I can't believe it, I just can't!

Beatrice: Did who call yet?

Ruth: I'm not supposed to tell you, as Mr. Goodman's private secretary, but you're going to get a call from school.

Beatrice (*to* **Tillie**): What is she talking about?

Tillie: I was in the Science Fair at school.

Ruth: Didn't she tell you yet? Oh, Tillie, how could you? She's fantastic, Mama! She's a finalist in the Science Fair. There were only five of them out of hundreds and hundreds. She won with all those plants over there. They're freaks! Isn't that a scream? Dr. Berg picked her himself. The principal! And I heard Mr. Goodman say she was going to be another Madam Pasteur and he never saw a girl do anything like that before and . . . so I told everybody, "Yes, she's my sister!" Tillie, "You're my sister!" I said. And Mr. Goodman called the Advance and they're coming to take your picture. Oh, Mama, isn't it crazy? And nobody laughed at her, Mama. She beat out practically everybody and nobody laughed at her. "She's my sister," I said. "She's my sister!"

(*The telephone rings.*)

That must be him! Mama, answer it—I'm afraid.

(*Ring.*)

Answer it before he hangs up!

(*Ring.*)

Mama! He's gonna hang up!

(**Ruth** *grabs the phone.*)

Hello? . . . Yes . . .

(*Aside to* **Beatrice**)

It's him! . . . Just a minute, please . . .

(*Covering the mouthpiece.*)

He wants to talk to you.

Beatrice: Who?

Ruth: The *principal*!

Beatrice: Hang up.

Ruth: I told him you were here! Mama!

(**Beatrice** *gets up and shuffles slowly to the phone.*)

Beatrice (*finally, into the phone*): Yes? . . . I know who you are, Dr. Berg . . . I see . . . Couldn't you get someone else? There's an awfully lot of work that has to be done around here, because she's not as careful with her home duties as she is with man-in-the-moon marigolds . . .

Me? What would you want with me up on the stage? . . . The other mothers can do as they please . . . I would have thought you had enough in your *history* without . . . I'll think about it . . . Goodbye, Dr. Berg . . .

(*Pause, then screaming.*)

I SAID I'D THINK ABOUT IT!

(*She hangs up the phone, turns her face slowly to* **Ruth**, *then to* **Tillie**, *who has her face hidden in shame in the rabbit's fur.*)

Ruth: What did he say?

Why is Beatrice afraid to leave the house and go to the school ? Compare hers and Ruth's reactions to the news.

Beatrice (*flinging her glass on the floor*): How could you do this to me? HOW COULD YOU LET THAT MAN CALL OUR HOME!

I have no clothes, do you hear me? I'd look just like you up on the stage, ugly little you!

DO YOU WANT THEM TO LAUGH AT US? LAUGH AT THE TWO OF US?

Ruth (*disbelievingly*): Mother . . . aren't you proud of her? Mother . . . it's an *honor*.

(**Tillie** *breaks into tears and moves away from* **Beatrice**. *It seems as though she is crushed, but then she halts and turns to face her mother.*)

Tillie (*through tears*): But . . . nobody laughed at me.

(**Beatrice's** *face begins to soften as she glimpses what she's done to* **Tillie**.)

Beatrice: Oh, my God . . .

(**Tillie** *starts toward her.* **Beatrice** *opens her arms to receive her as music starts in and lights fade. A chord of finality punctuates the end of Act I.*)

ACT II

(*About two weeks later.*

The room looks somewhat cheery and there is excitement in the air. It is early evening and preparations are being made for **Tillie** to take her project to the final judging of the Science Fair.

Compare costumes in this scene. What do they reveal ?

Tillie has been dressed by her mother in clothes which are clean but too girlish for her awkwardness. Her hair has been curled, she sports a large bow, and her dress is a starched flair.

Ruth has dressed herself up as well. She has put on too much makeup, and her lipstick has been extended beyond the natural line of her lips. She almost appears to be sinister.

Visual clue: Is this play about the past, present, and future ?

A large three-panel screen stands on one of the tables. THE EFFECT OF GAMMA RAYS ON MAN-IN-THE-MOON MARIGOLDS is printed in large letters running across the top of the three panels. Below this on each panel there is a subtopic: THE PAST; THE PRESENT; THE FUTURE. Additional charts and data appear below the titles.)

Ruth: The only competition you have to worry about is Janice Vickery. They say she caught it near Princess Bay Boulevard and it was still alive when she took the skin off it.

Tillie (*taking some plants from* **Ruth**): Let me do that, please, Ruth.

Ruth: I'm sorry I touched them, really.

Tillie: Why don't you feed Peter?

Ruth: Because I don't feel like feeding him . . . Now I feel like feeding him. (*She gets some lettuce from a bag.*)

I heard that it screamed for three minutes after she put it in because the water wasn't boiling yet. How much talent does it take to boil the skin off a cat and then stick the bones together again? That's what I want to know. Ugh.

I had a dream about that, too. I figure she did it in less than a day and she ends up as one of the top five winners . . . and you spend months growing atomic flowers.

Tillie: Don't you think you should finish getting ready?

Ruth: Finish? This is it!

Tillie: Are you going to wear that sweater?

Ruth: Look, don't worry about me. I'm not getting up on any stage, and if I did I wouldn't be caught dead with a horrible bow like that.

Tillie: Mother put it——

Ruth: They're going to laugh you off the stage again like when you cranked that atom in assembly . . . I didn't mean that . . . The one they're going to laugh at is Mama.

Tillie: What?

Ruth: I said the one they're going to laugh at is Mama . . . Oh, let me take that bow off.

Tillie: It's all right.

Ruth: Look, just sit still. I don't want everybody making fun of you.

Tillie: What made you say that about Mama?

Ruth: Oh, I heard them talking in the Science Office yesterday. Mr. Goodman and Miss Hanley. She's getting $12.63 to chaperon the thing tonight.

Tillie: What were they saying?

Ruth: Miss Hanley was telling Mr. Goodman about Mama . . . when she found out you were one of the five winners. And he wanted to know if there was something wrong with Mama because she sounded crazy over the phone. And Miss Hanley said she *was* crazy and she always has been crazy and she can't wait to see what she looks like after all these years. Miss Hanley said her nickname used to be *Betty the Loon.*

Compare with Beatrice's description of her past.

Tillie (*as* **Ruth** *combs her hair*): Ruth, you're hurting me.

Ruth: She was just like you and everybody thought she was a big weirdo. There! You look much better!

(*She goes back to the rabbit.*)

Peter, if anybody stuck you in a pot of boiling water I'd kill them, do you know that? . . .

(*Then to* **Tillie**.)

What do they call boiling the skin off a cat? I call it murder, that's what I call it. They say it was hit by a car and Janice just scooped it up and before you could say *bingo* it was screaming in a pot of boiling water . . .

Do you know what they're all waiting to see? Mama's feathers! That's what Miss Hanley said. She said Mama blabs as though she was the Queen of England and just as proper as can be, and that her idea of getting dressed up is to put on all the feathers in the world and go as a bird. Always trying to get somewhere, like a great big bird.

Tillie: Don't tell Mama, please. It doesn't matter.

Ruth: I was up there watching her getting dressed and sure enough, she's got the feathers out.

Tillie: You didn't tell her what Miss Hanley said?

Ruth: Are you kidding? I just told her I didn't like the feathers and I didn't think she should wear any. But I'll bet she doesn't listen to me.

Tillie: It doesn't matter.

Ruth: It doesn't matter? Do you think I want to be laughed right out of the school tonight, with Chris Burns there, and all? Laughed right out of the school, with your electric hair and her feathers on that stage, and Miss Hanley splitting her sides?

Tillie: Promise me you won't say anything.

Ruth: On one condition.

Tillie: What?

Ruth: Give Peter to me.

Tillie (*ignoring her*): The taxi will be here any minute and I won't have all this stuff ready. Did you see my speech?

Ruth: I mean it. Give Peter to me.

Tillie: He belongs to all of us.

Ruth: For me. All for me. What do you care? He doesn't mean anything to you anymore, now that you've got all those crazy plants.

Tillie: Will you stop?

Ruth: If you don't give him to me I'm going to tell Mama that everybody's waiting to laugh at her.

Tillie: Where are those typewritten cards?

Ruth: I MEAN IT! Give him to me!

Tillie: Does he mean that much to you?

Ruth: Yes!

Tillie: All right.

Ruth (*after a burst of private laughter*): Betty the Loon . . .

(*She laughs again.*)

That's what they used to call her, you know. Betty the Loon!

Tillie: I don't think that's very nice.

Ruth: First they had Betty the Loon, and now they've got Tillie the Loon . . .

(*To rabbit.*)

You don't have to worry about me turning you in for any old plants . . .
How much does a taxi cost from here to the school?

Tillie: Not much.

Ruth: I wish she'd give me the money it costs for a taxi—and for all that cardboard and paint and flowerpots and stuff. The only time she ever made a fuss over me was when she drove me nuts.

Tillie: Tell her to hurry, please.

Ruth: By the way, I went over to see Janice Vickery's pot, that she did you know what in, and I started telling her and her mother about the worms in Mr. Alexander Brougham's legs, and I got thrown out because it was too near dinner time. That Mrs. Vickery kills me. She can't stand worms in somebody else's legs but she lets her daughter cook a cat.

Tillie (*calling upstairs*): Mother! The taxi will be here any minute.

(**Beatrice** *comes to the top of the stairs. Her costume is strange, but not that strange, by any means. She is even a little attractive tonight, and though her words say she is greatly annoyed with having to attend the night's function, her tone and direction show she is very, very proud.*)

Beatrice: You're lucky I'm coming, without all this rushing me.

Tillie: Mama, you look beautiful.

Beatrice: Don't put it on too thick. I said I'd go and I guess there's no way to get out of it. Do you mind telling me how I'm supposed to get up on the stage? Do they call my name or what? And where are you going to be? If you ask me, they should've sent all the parents a mimeographed sheet of instructions. If this is supposed to be such a great event, why don't they do it right?

Tillie: You just sit on the stage with the other parents before it begins.

Beatrice: How long is this thing going to last? And remember, I don't care even if you do win the whole damn thing, I'm not making any speech. I can hold my own anywhere, but I hated that school when I went there and I hate it now . . . and the only thing I'd have to say is, what a pack of stupid teachers and vicious children they have. Imagine someone tearing the skin off a cat. *Doesn't she try to kill or suffocate?*

Ruth: She didn't tear it. She boiled it off.

Beatrice: You just told me upstairs that girl tore the skin off with an orange knife and . . . do you know, sometimes you exasperate me?

(To **Tillie***.)*

If you've got all the plants in this box, I can manage the folding thing. Do you know I've got a headache from doing those titles? And you probably don't even like them.

Tillie: I like them very much.

Beatrice: Look, if you don't want me to go tonight, I don't have to. You're about as enthusiastic as a dummy about this whole thing.

Tillie: I'm sorry.

Beatrice: And I refuse to let you get nervous. Put that bow back in your hair.

Ruth: I took it out.

Beatrice: What did you do that for?

Ruth *(taking the rabbit in her arms)*: Because it made her look crazy.

Beatrice: How would you know what's crazy or not? If that sweater of yours was any tighter it'd cut off the circulation in your chest.

(Fussing over **Tillie***.)*

The bow looks very nice in your hair. There's nothing wrong with looking proper, Matilda, and if you don't have enough money to look expensive and perfect, people like you for *trying* to look nice. You know, one day maybe you will be pretty. You'll have some nice features, when that hair revives and you do some tricks with makeup. I hope you didn't crowd the plants too close together. Did you find your speech?

Tillie: Yes, Mother.

Beatrice: You know, Matilda, I was wondering about something. Do you think you're really going to win? I mean, not that you won't be the best, but there's so much politics in school. Don't laugh, but if there's anyone who's an expert on that, it's me, and someday I'm going to write a book and blast that school to pieces. If you're just a little bit different in this world, they try to kill you off. *society has killed off Beatrice*

Ruth *(putting on her coat)*: Tillie gave Peter to me.

Beatrice: Oh? Then you inherited the rabbit droppings I found upstairs. What are you doing with your coat on?

Ruth: I'm going out to wait for the taxi.

Beatrice: Oh, no you're not. You start right in on the rabbit droppings. Or you won't get another cigarette even if you scratch my back with an orange knife.

Ruth: I'm going down to the school with you.

Beatrice: Oh, no you're not! You're going to keep company with that corpse in there. If she wakes up and starts gagging just slip her a shot of whiskey.

(The taxi horn blows outside.)

Quick! Grab the plants, Matilda—I'll get the big thing.

Ruth: I want to go! I promised Chris Burns I'd meet him.

Beatrice: Can't you understand English?

Ruth: I've got to go!

Beatrice: Shut up!

Ruth (*almost berserk*): I don't care. I'M GOING ANYWAY!

Beatrice (*shoving* **Ruth** *hard*): WHAT DID YOU SAY!

Tillie: Mother!

(*After a pause, the horn blows again.*)

Beatrice: Hurry up with that box, Matilda, and tell him to stop blowing the horn. HURRY UP!

(**Tillie** *reluctantly exits with the box of plants.*)

I don't know where you ever got the idea you were going tonight. Did you think nobody was going to hold down the fort?

Now you know how I felt all those years you and everybody else was running out whenever they felt like it—because there was always me to watch over the fifty-dollar-a-week corpse. If there's one thing I demand it's respect I don't ask for anything from you but respect.

Ruth (*pathetically*): Why are you ashamed of me?

Beatrice: I've been seen with a lot worse than you. I don't even know why I'm going tonight, do you know that? Do you think I give one goddam about the whole thing? . . .

(*She starts to fold the large three-panel screen with the titles: THE PAST, THE PRESENT, and THE FUTURE.*)

Do you want to know why I'm going? Do you really want to know why this once somebody else has to stick with that dried prune for a few minutes? Because this is the first time in my life I've ever felt just a little bit proud over something. Isn't that silly? Somewhere in the back of this turtle-sized brain of mine I feel just a little *proud*! Jesus Christ! And you begrudge me even that, you little bastard.

(*The taxi horn blows impatiently.*)

Ruth (*in a hard voice*): Hurry up. They're waiting for you . . . They're *all* waiting for you.

Why emphasize this detail?

Beatrice (*carrying the folded screen so that THE PAST is faced out in bold black letters*): I hope the paint is dry . . . Who's waiting for me?

Ruth: Everybody . . . including Miss Hanley. She's been telling all the teachers . . . about you . . . and they're all waiting.

Beatrice: You're such a little liar, Ruth, do you know that? When you can't have what you want, you try to ruin it for everybody else.

(*She starts to the door.*)

What memories would this awaken for Beatrice? Can she escape her past?

Ruth: Goodnight, *Betty the Loon.*

(**Beatrice** *stops as if she's been stabbed.*

The taxi horn blows several times as **Beatrice** *puts down the folding screen.*)

Beatrice (*helplessly*): Take this thing.

Ruth: What for?

Beatrice: Go with Matilda.

Ruth: I don't want to go now.

Beatrice (*blasting*): GET OUT OF HERE!

Ruth (*after a long pause*): Now Tillie's going to blame it on me that you're not going—and take the rabbit back.

(*The taxi beeps again, as* **Ruth** *puts her coat on.*)

I can't help it what people call you.

(*She picks up the screen.*)

I'll tell Tillie you'll be down later, all right? . . .

    Don't answer me. What do I care!

(**Ruth** *exits.*

    Beatrice *breaks into tears that shudder her body, and the lights go down slowly on her pathetic form. Music in.*

    *Suddenly a bolt of light strikes an area in the right stage—***Janice Vickery** *is standing in the spotlight holding the skeleton of a cat mounted on a small platform. Her face and voice are smug.*)

Janice: *The Past:* I got the cat from the A.S.P.C.A. immediately after it had been killed by a high-altitude pressure system. That explains why some of the rib bones are missing, because that method sucks the air out of the animal's lungs and ruptures all cavities. They say it prevents cruelty to animals but I think it's horrible.

(*She laughs.*)

Then I boiled the cat in a sodium hydroxide solution until most of the skin pulled right off, but I had to scrape some of the grizzle off the joints with a knife. You have no idea how difficult it is to get right down to the bones.

(*A little gong sounds.*)

I have to go on to the *The Present*, now—but I did want to tell you how long it took me to put the thing together. I mean, as it is now, it's extremely useful for students of anatomy, even with the missing rib bones, and it can be used to show basic anatomical aspects of many, many animals that are in the same family as felines. I suppose that's about the only present uses I can think for it, but it is nice to remember as an accomplishment, and it looks good on college applications to show you did something else in school besides dating.

(*She laughs, and a second gong sounds.*)

The Future: The only future plans I have for Tabby—my little brother asked the A.S.P.C.A. what its name was when he went to pick it up and they said it was called Tabby, but I think they were kidding him——

(*She laughs again.*)

I mean as far as future plans, I'm going to donate it to the science department, of course, and next year, if there's another Science Fair perhaps I'll do the same thing with a dog.

(*A third gong sounds.*)

Thank you very much for your attention, and I hope I win!

(**Janice** *and her spotlight disappear as suddenly as they had arrived, and music returns as the lights come up slowly on* **Beatrice**.

    She has obviously been drinking and is going through a phone book. Finding her number, she goes to the phone and dials.)

Beatrice (*into the phone*): I want to talk to the principal, please . . .

    Well, you'll have to get him down off the stage . . .

    It's none of your goddam business who I am! . . .

Oh, I see . . . Yes. I have a message for him and Mr. Goodman, and you, too . . . And this is for Miss Hanley, too . . .

Tell them Mrs. Hunsdorfer called to thank them for making her wish she was dead . . . Would you give them that message, please? . . . Thank you very much.

She alters physical surroundings. Does it indicate a change in her character or in her life?

(*She hangs up the phone, pauses, then surveys the room. Her attention fixes on the store window covered with newspapers. The phone rings several times but she ignores it. She goes to the window and proceeds to rip the paper from it. That finished, she turns and surveys the room again. She goes to the kitchen table and rearranges its position. She spies a card table with school supplies and hurls them on the floor. Next, she goes to a bureau and rummages through drawers, finding tablecloths and napkins. She throws cloths on two or three tables and is heading toward the kitchen table when the phone rings again. The ringing triggers off something else she wants to do. She empties a cup filled with scraps of paper and finds a telephone number. She lifts the receiver off the ringing phone and hangs up immediately. She lifts the receiver again, checks to make sure there's a dial tone, and then dials the number on the scrap of paper.*)

Beatrice (*into the phone*): Hello. This is Mrs. Hunsdorfer . . . I'm sorry if I frightened you, I wouldn't want you to think Nanny had deceased or anything like that—I can imagine how terrible you'd feel if anything like that ever happened . . . Terrible tragedy that would be, Miss Career Woman of the Year . . .

Yes, I'll tell you why I'm calling. I want her out of here by tomorrow. I told you when you rolled her in here I was going to try her out for a while and if I didn't like her she was to get the hell out. Well I don't like her, so get her the hell out . . .

It's like this. I don't like the way she cheats at solitaire. Is that a good enough reason? . . . Fine. And if she's not out of here by noon I'll send her collect in an ambulance, you son of a bitch!

(*She slams down the phone and bursts into laughter. The laughter subsides somewhat as she pours herself another drink. She takes the drink to a chair and as she sits down her foot accidentally hits the rabbit cage. She gives the cage a little kick and then an idea strikes. She gets up and finds a large blue towel which she flings over her shoulder. She gets the bottle of chloroform and approaches the cage. Having reached a decision she picks up the cage and takes it upstairs.*

Music in and lights fade.

From the darkness a beam of light falls on **Tillie** *in the same way* **Janice Vickery** *had been presented.*)

Tillie (*deathly afraid, and referring to her cards*): The Past: The seeds were exposed to various degrees . . . of gamma rays from radiation sources in Oak Ridge . . .

Mr. Goodman helped me pay for the seeds . . . their growth was plotted against . . . time.

(*She loses her voice for a moment and then the first gong sounds.*)

The Present: The seeds which received little radiation have grown to plants which are normal in appearance. The seeds which received moderate radiation gave rise to mutations such as double blooms, giant stems, and variegated leaves. The seeds closest to the gamma source were killed or yielded dwarf plants.

(*The second gong rings.*)

The Future: After radiation is better understood, a day will come when the power from exploding atoms will change the whole world we know. *(With inspiration.)* Some of the mutations will be good ones—wonderful things beyond our dreams—and I believe, I believe this with all my heart, THE DAY WILL COME WHEN MANKIND WILL THANK GOD FOR THE STRANGE AND BEAUTIFUL ENERGY FROM THE ATOM.

(Part of her last speech is reverberated electronically. Deep pulses of music are added as the light focuses on **Tillie's** *face.*

Suddenly there is silence, except for **Ruth** *picking up* **Tillie's** *last words.*

The lights come up on the main set, and the room is empty.

Ruth *bursts in the front door. She is carrying the three-panel card and a shopping bag of plants, both of which she drops on the floor.)*

Ruth: MAMA! MAMA! She won! Mama! Where are you? She won!

(She runs back to the front door and yells to **Tillie.***)*

Hurry up! Hurry! Oh, my God, I can't believe it!

(Then yelling upstairs.)

Mama! Come on down! Hurry!

*(**Tillie** comes in the front door, carrying the rest of her plants, and the large trophy.*

Ruth *takes the trophy.)*

(She starts upstairs.)

Mama! Wait till you see this!

*(**Beatrice** appears at the top of the stairs. She has been drinking a great deal, and clings fast to a bunch of old cheap curtains and other material.)*

Mama! She won . . .

*(**Beatrice** continues mechanically on down the stairs.)*

Didn't you hear me? Tillie won the whole thing! . . . Mama? . . . What's the matter with you? What did you rip the paper off the windows for?

*(**Beatrice** commences tacking up one of the curtains.)*

Tillie: Mama? Are you going to open a . . . shop?

Ruth: What's the matter? Can't you even answer?

Beatrice *(to* **Tillie***):* Hand me some of those tacks.

Ruth *(screaming):* I SAID SHE WON! ARE YOU DEAF?

Beatrice: Ruth, if you don't shut up I'm going to have you put away.

Ruth: They ought to put *you* away. BETTY THE LOON!

(There is a long pause.)

Beatrice: The rabbit is in your room. I want you to bury it in the morning.

Ruth: If you did anything . . . I'LL KILL YOU!

(She runs upstairs.)

Tillie: Mother, you didn't kill it, did you?

Beatrice: Nanny goes tomorrow. First thing tomorrow.

(There is a cry from upstairs.)

Tillie: Ruth? Are you all right?

Beatrice: I don't know what it's going to be. Maybe a tea shop. Maybe not.

*(**Ruth** appears in the doorway of her room. She is holding the dead rabbit on the blue towel. As she reaches the top of the stairs she begins to moan deeply.)*

After school you're going to have regular hours. You'll work in the kitchen, you'll learn how to cook, and you're going to earn your keep, just like in any other business.

Is Tillie's world already changing? Compare the speeches of the two contestants.

(**Tillie** *starts slowly up the stairs toward* **Ruth**.)

Tillie (*with great fear*): Mama . . . I think she's *going to go.*

(**Ruth** *commences to tremble.* **Tillie** *speaks softly to her.*)

Don't go . . . don't go . . .

(**Ruth's** *eyes roll in her head, and the trembling of her body becomes pronounced throbbing. She drops the rabbit with the towel covering it.*)

Help me! Mama! Help me!

Beatrice: Snap out of it, do you hear me? RUTH, DON'T LET YOURSELF GO!

(*To* **Tillie**.)

Help me get her downstairs!

(*By the time the trio reaches the bottom of the stairs,* **Ruth** *is consumed by a violent convulsion.* **Beatrice** *holds her down and pushes* **Tillie** *out of the way.*)

Beatrice (*screaming*): Get the wooden spoon!

(**Tillie** *responds as* **Beatrice** *gets* **Ruth** *onto a sofa. The convulsion runs its course of a full minute, then finally subsides.* **Tillie** *gets a blanket and covers* **Ruth**.)

Tillie: Shall I call the doctor?

(*There is a long pause.*)

Shall I call the doctor?

Beatrice: No. She'll be all right.

Tillie: I think we should call him.

Beatrice: I DIDN'T ASK YOU WHAT YOU THOUGHT! . . . We're going to need every penny to get this place open.

(**Beatrice** *spreads a tablecloth on one of the tables and places a pile of old cloth napkins on it. She sits down and lights a cigarette.*)

Tillie (*picking up the rabbit on the stairs*): I'd better bury him in the backyard.

(*She starts out.*)

Beatrice: Don't bury the towel.

(**Tillie** *stops, sobs audibly, then gets control.*)

Tillie: I'll do it in the morning.

(*She gently lays the rabbit near the door. She tucks* **Ruth** *in on the couch and sits a few minutes by her sleeping sister.*

Music starts in softly as **Beatrice** *continues folding napkins with her back to the others.*

There is the sound of someone at the curtained doorway, and **Nanny** *commences negotiating herself into the room. Slowly she advances with the frame—unaware, desiccated, in some other land.*)

Beatrice (*weakly*): Matilda?

Tillie: Yes, Mama?

Beatrice: I hate the world. Do you know that, Matilda?

Tillie: Yes, Mama.

Beatrice: I hate the world.

(*The lights have started down, the music makes its presence known, and a spot clings to* **Tillie**. *She moves to the staircase and the rest of the set goes to black during the following speech. As she starts up the stairs her recorded voice takes over as in the opening of the play.*)

Tillie's Voice: *The Conclusion:* My experiment has shown some of the strange effects radiation can produce . . . and how dangerous it can be if not handled correctly.

Where is her world? Can she change it?

This play stresses change. Compare changes in physical set to those within characters.

see her beauty and significance

Mr. Goodman said I should tell in this conclusion what my future plans are and how this experiment has helped me make them.

For one thing, the effect of gamma rays on man-in-the-moon marigolds has made me curious about the sun and the stars, for the universe itself must be like a world of great atoms—and I want to know more about it.

But most important, I suppose, my experiment has made me feel important —every atom in me, in everybody, has come from the sun—from places beyond our dreams. The atoms of our hands, the atoms of our hearts . . . (*All sound out.*

Tillie *speaks the rest live—hopeful, glowing.*)

Atom.

Atom.

What a beautiful word.

Reread initial description of set. How do these details relate to your understanding of the play?

THE END

THE EMPEROR JONES

Eugene O'Neill

CHARACTERS

Brutus Jones, Emperor

Henry Smithers, A Cockney Trader

An Old Native Woman

Lem, A Native Chief

Soldiers, Adherents of Lem

The Little Formless Fears

Jeff

The Negro Convicts

The Prison Guard

The Planters

The Auctioneer

The Slaves

The Congo Witch-Doctor

The Crocodile God

The action of the play takes place on an island in the West Indies as yet not self-determined by white Marines. The form of native government is, for the time being, an empire.

SCENE I

Scene. The audience chamber in the palace of the Emperor—a spacious, high-ceilinged room with bare, white-washed walls. The floor is of white tiles. In the rear, to the left of center, a wide archway giving out on a portico with white pillars. The palace is evidently situated on high ground for beyond the portico nothing can be seen but a vista of distant hills, their summits crowned with thick groves of palm trees. In the right wall, center, a smaller arched doorway leading to the living quarters of the palace. The room is bare of furniture with the exception of one huge chair made of uncut wood which stands at center, its back to rear. This is very apparently the Emperor's throne. It is painted a dazzling, eye-smiting scarlet. There is a brilliant orange cushion on the seat and another smaller one is placed on the floor to serve as a footstool. Strips of matting, dyed scarlet, lead from the foot of the throne to the two entrances.

It is late afternoon but the sunlight still blazes yellowly beyond the portico and there is an oppressive burden of exhausting heat in the air.

*As the curtain rises, a native Negro woman sneaks in cautiously from the entrance on the right. She is very old, dressed in cheap calico, bare-footed, a red bandana handkerchief covering all but a few stray wisps of white hair. A bundle bound in colored cloth is carried over her shoulder on the end of a stick. She hesitates beside the doorway, peering back as if in extreme dread of being discovered. Then she begins to glide noiselessly, a step at a time, toward the doorway in the rear. At this moment, **Smithers** appears beneath the portico.*

Smithers is a tall, stoop-shouldered man about forty. His bald head, perched on a long neck with an enormous Adam's apple, looks like an egg. The tropics have tanned his naturally pasty face with its small, sharp features to a sickly yellow, and native rum has painted his pointed nose to a startling red. His little, washy-blue eyes are red-rimmed and dart about him like a ferret's. His expression is one of unscrupulous meanness, cowardly and dangerous. He is dressed in a worn riding suit of dirty white drill, puttees, spurs, and wears a white cork helmet. A cartridge belt with an automatic revolver is around his waist. He carries a riding whip in his hand. He sees the woman and stops to watch her suspiciously. Then, making up his mind, he steps quickly on tiptoe into the room. The woman, looking back over her shoulder continually, does not see him until it is too late. When she does **Smithers** *springs forward and grabs her firmly by the shoulder. She struggles to get away, fiercely but silently.*

Smithers (*tightening his grasp—roughly*): Easy! None o' that, me birdie. You can't wriggle out now. I got me 'ooks on yer.

Woman (*seeing the uselessness of struggling, gives way to frantic terror, and sinks to the ground, embracing his knees supplicatingly*): No tell him! No tell him, Mister!

Smithers (*with great curiosity*): Tell'im? (*Then scornfully.*) Oh, you mean 'is bloomin' Majesty. What's the game, any 'ow? What are you sneakin' away for? Been stealin' a bit, I s'pose. (*He taps her bundle with his riding whip significantly.*)

Woman (*shaking her head vehemently*): No, me no steal.

Smithers: Bloody liar! But tell me what's up. There's somethin' funny goin' on. I smelled it in the air first thing I got up this mornin'. You blacks are up to some devilment. This palace of 'is is like a bleedin' tomb. Where's all the 'ands?

(*The woman keeps sullenly silent.* **Smithers** *raises his whip threateningly.*)

Ow, yer won't, won't yer? I'll show yer what's what.

Woman (*coweringly*): I tell, Mister. You no hit. They go—all go. (*She makes a sweeping gesture toward the hills in the distance.*)

Smithers: Run away—to the 'ills?

Woman: Yes, Mister. Him Emperor—Great Father. (*She touches her forehead to the floor with a quick mechanical jerk.*) Him sleep after eat. Then they go—all go. Me old woman. Me left only. Now me go too.

Smithers (*his astonishment giving way to an immense, mean satisfaction*): Ow! So that's the ticket! Well, I know bloody well wot's in the air—when they runs orf to the 'ills. The tom-tom 'll be thumping out there bloomin' soon. (*With extreme vindictiveness.*) And I'm bloody glad of it, for one! Serve 'im right! Puttin' on airs, the stinkin' nigger! 'Is Majesty! Gawd blimey! I only 'opes I'm there when they takes 'im out to shoot 'im. (*Suddenly*) 'E's still 'ere all right, ain't e?

Woman: Yes. Him sleep.

Smithers: 'E's bound to find out soon as 'e wakes up. 'E's cunnin' enough to know when 'is time's come.

(*He goes to the doorway on right and whistles shrilly with his fingers in his mouth. The old woman springs to her feet and runs out of the doorway, rear.* **Smithers** *goes after her, reaching for his revolver.*)

Stop or I'll shoot! (*Then stopping—indifferently.*) Pop orf then, if yer like, yer black cow. (*He stands in the doorway, looking after her.*)

(**Jones** *enters from the right. He is a tall, powerfully-built, full-blooded Negro of middle age. His features are typically negroid, yet there is something decidedly distinctive about his face—an underlying strength of will, a hardy, self-reliant confidence in himself that inspires respect. His eyes are alive with a keen, cunning intelligence. In manner he is shrewd, suspicious, evasive. He wears a light blue uniform coat, sprayed with brass buttons, heavy gold chevrons on his shoulders, gold braid on the collar, cuffs, etc. His pants are bright red with a light blue stripe down the side. Patent-leather laced boots with brass spurs, and a belt with a long-barreled, pearl-handled revolver in a holster complete his make up. Yet there is something not altogether ridiculous about his grandeur. He has a way of carrying it off.*)

Jones (*not seeing anyone—greatly irritated and blinking sleepily—shouts*): Who dare whistle dat way in my palace? Who dare wake up de Emperor? I'll git de hide fravled off some o' you niggers sho'!

Smithers (*showing himself—in a manner half-afraid and half-defiant*): It was me whistled to yer. (*As* **Jones** *frowns angrily.*) I got news for yer.

Jones (*putting on his suavest manner, which fails to cover up his contempt for the white man*): Oh, it's you, Mister Smithers. (*He sits down on his throne with easy dignity.*) What news you got to tell me?

Smithers (*coming close to enjoy his discomfiture*): Don't yer notice nothin' funny today?

Jones (*coldly*): Funny? No. I ain't perceived nothin' of de kind!

Smithers: Then yer ain't so foxy as I thought yer was. Where's all your court? (*Sarcastically.*) The Generals and the Cabinet Ministers and all?

Jones (*imperturbably*): Where dey mostly runs de minute I closes my eyes—drinkin' rum and talkin' big down in de town. (*Sarcastically.*) How come you don't know dat? Ain't you sousin' with 'em most every day?

Smithers (*stung but pretending indifference—with a wink*): That's part of the day's work. I got ter—ain't I—in my business?

Jones (*contemptuously*): Yo' business!

Smithers (*imprudently enraged*): Gawd blimey, you was glad enough for me ter take yer in on it when you landed her first. You didn' 'ave no 'igh and mighty airs in them days!

Jones (*his hand going to his revolver like a flash—menacingly*): Talk polite, white man! Talk polite, you heah me! I'm boss heah now, is you fergettin'? (*The Cockney seems about to challenge this last statement with the facts but something in the other's eyes holds and cows him.*)

Smithers (*in a cowardly whine*): No 'arm meant, old top.

Jones (*condescendingly*): I accepts yo' apology. (*Lets his hand fall from his revolver.*) No use'n you rakin' up ole times. What I was den is one thing. What I is now 's another. You didn't let me in on yo' crooked work out o' no kind feelin's dat time. I done de dirty work fo' you—and most o' de brain work, too, fo' dat matter—and I was wu'th money to you, dat's de reason.

Smithers: Well blimey, I give yer a start, didn't I—when no one else would. I wasn't afraid to 'ire yer like the rest was—'count of the story about your breakin' jail back in the States.

Jones: No, you didn't have no s'cuse to look down on me fo' dat. You been in jail you'self more'n once.

Smithers (*furiously*): It's a lie! (*Then trying to pass it off by an attempt at scorn.*) Garn! Who told yer that fairy tale?

Jones: Dey's some tings I ain't got to be tole. I kin see 'em in folk's eyes. (*Then after a pause—meditatively.*) Yes, you sho' give me a start. And it didn't take long from dat time to git dese fool, woods' niggers right where I wanted dem. (*With pride.*) From stowaway to Emperor in two years! Dat's goin' some!

Smithers (*with curiosity*): And I bet you got yer pile o' money 'id safe some place.

Jones (*with satisfaction*): I sho' has! And it's in a foreign bank where no pusson don't ever git it out but me no matter what come. You didn't s'pose I was holdin' down dis Emperor job for de glory in it, did you? Sho'! De fuss and glory part of it, dat's only to turn de heads o' de low-flung, bush niggers dat's here. Dey wants de big circus show for deir money. I gives it to 'em an' I gits de money. (*With a grin.*) De long green, dat's me every time! (*Then rebukingly.*) But you ain't got no kick agin me, Smithers. I'se paid you back all you done for me many times. Ain't I pertected you and winked at all de crooked tradin' you been doin' right out in de broad day? Sho' I has—and me makin' laws to stop it at de same time! (*He chuckles.*)

Smithers (*grinning*): But, meanin' no 'arm, you been grabbin' right and left yourself, ain't yer? Look at the taxes you've put on 'em! Blimey! You've squeezed 'em dry!

Jones (*chuckling*): No, dey ain't *all* dry yet. I'se still heah, ain't I?

Smithers (*smiling at his secret thought*): They're dry right now, you'll find out. (*Changing the subject abruptly.*) And as for me breakin' laws, you've broke 'em all yerself just as fast as yer made 'em.

Jones: Ain't I de Emperor? De laws don't go for him. (*Judicially.*) You heah what I tells you, Smithers. Dere's little stealin' like you does, and dere's big stealin' like I does. For de little stealin' dey gits you in jail soon or late. For de big stealin' dey makes you Emperor and puts you in de Hall o' Fame when you croaks. (*Reminiscently.*) If dey's one thing I learns in ten years on de Pullman ca's listenin' to de white quality talk, it's dat same fact. And when I gits a chance to use it I winds up Emperor in two years.

Smithers (*unable to repress the genuine admiration of the small fry for the large*): Yes, yer turned the bleedin' trick, all right. Blimey, I never seen a bloke 'as 'ad the bloomin' luck you 'as.

Jones (*severely*): Luck? What you mean—luck?

Smithers: I suppose you'll say as that swank about the silver bullet ain't luck—and that was what first got the fool blacks on yer side the time of the revolution, wasn't it?

Jones (*with a laugh*): Oh, dat silver bullet! Sho' was luck! But I makes dat luck, you heah? I loads de dice! Yessuh! When dat murderin' nigger ole Lem hired to kill me takes aim ten feet away and his gun misses fire and I shoots him dead, what you heah me say?

Smithers: You said yer'd got a charm so's no lead bullet'd kill yer. You was so strong only a silver bullet could kill yer, you told 'em. Blimey, wasn't that swank fer yer—and plain, fat-'eaded luck?

Jones (*proudly*): I got brains and I uses 'em quick. Dat ain't luck.

Smithers: Yer know they wasn't 'ardly liable to get no silver bullets. And it was luck 'e didn't 'it you that time.

Jones (*laughing*): And dere all dem fool, bush niggers was kneelin' down and bumpin' deir heads on de ground like I was a miracle out o' de Bible. Oh Lawd, from dat time on I has dem all eatin' out of my hand. I cracks de whip and dey jumps through.

Smithers (*with a sniff*): Yankee bluff done it.

Jones: Ain't a man's talkin' big what makes him big—long as he makes folks believe it? Sho', I talks large when I ain't got nothin' to back it up, but I ain't talkin' wild just de same. I knows I kin fool 'em—I *knows* it—and dat's backin' enough fo' my game. And ain't I got to learn deir lingo and teach some of dem English befo' I kin talk to 'em? Ain't dat wuk? You ain't never learned ary word er it, Smithers, in de ten years you been heah, dough yo' knows it's money in yo' pocket tradin' wid 'em if you does. But you'se too shiftless to take de trouble.

Smithers (*flushing*): Never mind about me. What's this I've 'eard about yer really 'avin' a silver bullet moulded for yourself?

Jones: It's playin' out my bluff. I has de silver bullet moulded and I tells 'em when de time comes I kills myself wid it. I tells 'em dat's 'cause I'm de on'y man in de world big enuff to git me. No use'n deir tryin'. And dey falls down and bumps deir heads. (*He laughs.*) I does dat so's I kin take a walk in peace without no jealous nigger gunnin' at me from behind de trees.

Smithers (*astonished*): Then you 'ad it made—'onest?

Jones: Sho' did. Heah she be. (*He takes out his revolver, breaks it, and takes the silver bullet out of one chamber.*) Five lead an' dis silver baby at de last. Don't she shine pretty? (*He holds it in his hand, looking at it admiringly, as if strangely fascinated.*)

Smithers: Let me see. (*Reaches out his hand for it.*)

Jones (*harshly*): Keep yo' hands whar dey b'long, white man. (*He replaces it in the chamber and puts the revolver back on his hip.*)

Smithers (*snarling*): Gawd blimey! Think I'm a bleedin' thief, you would.

Jones: No, 'tain't dat. I knows you'se scared to steal from me. On'y I ain't 'lowin' nary body to touch dis baby. She's my rabbit's foot.

Smithers (*sneering*): A bloomin' charm, wot? (*Venomously.*) Well, you'll need all the bloody charms you 'as before long, s' 'elp me!

Jones (*judicially*): Oh, I'se good for six months yit 'fore dey gits sick o' my game. Den, when I sees trouble comin', I makes my getaway.

Smithers: Ho! You got it all planned, ain't yer?

Jones: I ain't no fool. I knows dis Emperor's time is sho't. Dat why I make hay when de sun shine. Was you thinkin' I'se aimin' to hold down dis job for life? No, suh! What good is gittin' money if you stays back in dis raggedy country? I wants action when I spends. And when I sees dese niggers gittin' up deir nerve to tu'n me out, and I'se got all de money in sight, I resigns on de spot and beats it quick.

Smithers: Where to?

Jones: None o' yo' business.

Smithers: Not back to the bloody States, I'll lay my oath.

Jones (*suspiciously*): Why don't I? (*Then with an easy laugh.*) You mean 'count of dat story 'bout me breakin' from jail back dere? Dat's all talk.

Smithers (*skeptically*): Ho, yes!

Jones (*sharply*): You ain't 'sinuatin' I'se a liar, is you?

Smithers (*hastily*): No, Gawd strike me! I was only thinkin' o' the bloody lies you told the blacks 'ere about killin' white men in the States.

Jones (*angered*): How come dey're lies?

Smithers: You'd 'ave been in jail if you 'ad, wouldn't yer then? (*With venom.*) And from what I've 'eard, it ain't 'ealthy for a black to kill a white man in the States. They burns 'em in oil, don't they?

Jones (*with cool deadliness*): You mean lynchin' 'd scare me? Well, I tells you, Smithers, maybe I does kill one white man back dere. Maybe I does. And maybe I kills another right heah 'fore long if he don't look out.

Smithers (*trying to force a laugh*): I was on'y spoofin' yer. Can't yer take a joke? And you was just sayin' you'd never been in jail.

Jones (*in the same tone—slightly boastful*): Maybe I goes to jail dere for gettin' in an argument wid razors ovah a crap game. Maybe I gits twenty years when dat colored man die. Maybe I gits in 'nother argument wid de prison guard was overseer ovah us when we're wukin' de roads. Maybe he hits me wid a whip and I splits his head wid a shovel and runs away and files de chain off my leg and gits away safe. Maybe I does all dat an' maybe I don't. It's a story I tells you so's you knows I'se de kind of man dat if you evah repeats one word of it, I ends yo' stealin' on dis yearth mighty damn quick!

Smithers (*terrified*): Think I'd peach on yer? Not me! Ain't I always been yer friend?

Jones (*suddenly relaxing*): Sho' you has—and you better be.

Smithers (*recovering his composure—and with it his malice*): And just to show yer I'm yer friend, I'll tell yer that bit o' news I was goin' to.

Jones: Go ahead! Shoot de piece. Must be bad news from de happy way you look.

Smithers (*warningly*): Maybe it's gettin' time for you to resign—with that bloomin' silver bullet, wot? (*He finishes with a mocking grin.*)

Jones (*puzzled*): What's dat you say? Talk plain.

Smithers: Ain't noticed any of the guards or servants about the place today, I 'aven't.

Jones (*carelessly*): Dey're all out in de garden sleepin' under de trees. When I sleeps, dey sneaks a sleep, too, and I pretends I never suspicions it. All I got to do is to ring de bell and dey come flyin', makin' a bluff dey was wukin' all de time.

Smithers (*in the same mocking tone*): Ring the bell now an' you'll bloody well see what I means.

Jones (*startled to alertness, but preserving the same careless tone*): Sho' I rings. (*He reaches below the throne and pulls out a big, common dinner bell which is painted the same vivid scarlet as the throne. He rings this vigorously—then stops to listen. Then he goes to both doors, rings again, and looks out.*)

Smithers (*watching him with malicious satisfaction, after a pause—mockingly*): The bloody ship is sinkin' an' the bleedin' rats 'as slung their 'ooks.

Jones (*in a sudden fit of anger flings the bell clattering into a corner*): Low-flung, woods' niggers! (*Then catching* **Smithers'** *eye on him, he controls himself and suddenly bursts into a low chuckling laugh.*) Reckon I overplays my hand dis once! A man can't take de pot on a bob-tailed flush all de time. Was I sayin' I'd sit in six months mo'? Well I'se changed my mind den. I cashes in and resigns de job of Emperor right dis minute.

Smithers (*with real admiration*): Blimey, but you're a cool bird, and no mistake.

Jones: No use'n fussin'. When I knows de game's up I kisses it good-bye widout no long waits. Dey've all run off to de hills, ain't dey?

Smithers: Yes—every bleedin' man jack of 'em.

Jones: Den de revolution is at de post. And de Emperor better git his feet smokin' up de trail. (*He starts for the door in rear.*)

Smithers: Goin' out to look for your 'orse? Yer won't find any. They steals the 'orses first thing. Mine was gone when I went for 'im this mornin'. That's wot first give me a suspicion of wot was up.

Jones (*alarmed for a second, scratches his head, then philosophically*): Well, den I hoofs it. Feet, do yo' duty! (*He pulls out a gold watch and looks at it.*) Three-thuty. Sundown's at six-thuty or dereabouts. (*Puts his watch back—with cool confidence.*) I got plenty o' time to make it easy.

Smithers: Don't be so bloomin' sure of it. They'll be after you 'ot and 'eavy. Ole Lem is at the bottom o' this business an' 'e 'ates you like 'ell. 'E'd rather do for you than eat 'is dinner, 'e would!

Jones (*scornfully*): Dat fool no-count nigger! Does you think I'se scared o' him? I stands him on his thick head more'n once befo' dis, and I does it again if he comes in my way . . . (*Fiercely.*) And dis time I leave him a dead nigger fo' sho'!

Smithers: You'll 'ave to cut through the big forest—an' these blacks 'ere can sniff and follow a trail in the dark like 'ounds. You'd 'ave to 'ustle to get through that forest in twelve hours even if you knew all the bloomin' trails like a native.

Jones (*with indignant scorn*): Look-a-heah, white man! Does you think I'se a natural bo'n fool? Give me credit fo' havin' some sense, fo' Lawd's sake! Don't you s'pose I'se looked ahead and made sho' of all de chances? I'se gone out in dat big forest, pretendin' to hunt, so many times dat I knows it high an' low like a book. I could go through on dem trails wid my eyes shut. (*With great contempt.*) Think dese ign'rent bush niggers dat ain't got brains enuff to know deir own names even can catch Brutus Jones? Huh, I s'pects not! Not on yo' life! Why, man, de white men went after me wid bloodhounds where I come from an' I jes' laughs at 'em. It's a shame to fool dese black trash around heah, dey're so easy. You watch me, man! I'll make dem look sick, I will. I'll be 'cross de plain to de edge of de forest by time dark comes. Once in de woods in de night, dey got a swell chance o' findin' dis baby! Dawn tomorrow I'll be out at de oder side and on de coast whar dat French gunboat is stayin'. She picks me up, take me to Martinique when she go dar, and dere I is safe wid a mighty big bankroll in my jeans. It's easy as rollin' off a log.

Smithers (*maliciously*): But s'posin' somethin' 'appens wrong an' they do nab yer?

Jones (*decisively*): Dey don't—dat's de answer.

Smithers: But, just for argyment's sake—what'd you do?

Jones (*frowning*): I'se got five lead bullets in dis gun good enuff fo' common bush niggers—and after dat I got de silver bullet left to cheat 'em out o' gittin' me.

Smithers (*jeeringly*): Ho, I was fergettin' that silver bullet. You'll bump yourself orf in style, won't yer? Blimey!

Jones (*gloomily*): You kin bet yo' whole roll on one thing, white man. Dis baby plays out his string to de end and when he quits, he quits wid a bang de way he ought. Silver bullet ain't none too good for him when he go, dat's a fac'! (*Then shaking off his nervousness—with a confident laugh.*) Sho'! What is I talkin' about? Ain't come to dat yit and I never will—not wid trash niggers like dese yere. (*Boastfully.*) Silver bullet bring me luck anyway. I kin outguess, outrun, outfight, an' outplay de whole lot o' dem all ovah de board any time o' de day er night! You watch me!

(*From the distant hills comes the faint, steady thump of a tom-tom, low and vibrating. It starts at a rate exactly corresponding to normal pulse beat—72 to the minute—and continues at a gradually accelerating rate from this point uninterruptedly to the very end of the play.*

Jones starts at the sound. A strange look of apprehension creeps into his face for a moment as he listens. Then he asks, with an attempt to regain his most casual manner.): What's dat drum beatin' fo'?

Smithers (*with a mean grin*): For you. That means the bleedin' ceremony 'as started. I've 'eard it before and I knows.

Jones: Cer'mony? What cer'mony?

Smithers: The blacks is 'oldin' a bloody meetin', 'avin' a war dance, gettin' their courage worked up b'fore they starts after you.

Jones: Let dem! Dey'll sho' need it!

Smithers: And they're there 'oldin' their 'eathen religious service—makin' no end of devil spells and charms to 'elp 'em against your silver bullet.

(*He guffaws loudly.*) Blimey, but they're balmy as 'ell!

Jones (*a tiny bit awed and shaken in spite of himself*): Huh! Takes more'n dat to scare dis chicken!

Smithers (*scenting the other's feeling—maliciously*): Ternight when it's pitch black in the forest, they'll 'ave their pet devils and ghosts 'oundin' after you. You'll find yer bloody 'air 'll be standin' on end before termorrow mornin'. (*Seriously.*) It's a bleedin' queer place, that stinkin' forest, even in daylight. Yer don't know what might 'appen in there, it's that rotten still. Always sends the cold shivers down my back minute I gets in it.

Jones (*with a contemptuous sniff*): I ain't no chicken-liver like you is. Trees an' me, we'se friends, and dar's a full moon comin' bring me light. And let dem po' niggers make all de fool spells dey'se a min' to. Does yo' s'pect I'se silly enuff to b'lieve in ghosts an' ha'nts an' all dat ole woman's talk? G'long, white man! You ain't talkin' to me. (*With a chuckle.*) Doesn't you know dey's got to do wid a man was member in good standin' o' de Baptist Church? Sho' I was dat when I was porter on de Pullmans, befo' I gits into my little trouble. Let dem try deir heathen tricks. De Baptist Church done pertect me and land dem all in hell. (*Then with more confident satisfaction.*) And I'se got little silver bullet o' my own, don't forgit.

Smithers: Ho! You 'aven't give much 'eed to your Baptist Church since you been down 'ere. I've 'eard myself you 'ad turned yer coat an' was takin' up with their blarsted witch-doctors, or whatever the 'ell yer calls the swine.

Jones (*vehemently*): I pretends to! Sho' I pretends! Dat's part o' my game from de fust. If I finds out dem niggers believes dat black is white, den I yells it out louder 'n deir loudest. It don't git me nothin' to do missionary work for de Baptist Church. I'se after de coin, an' I lays my Jesus on de shelf for de time bein'. (*Stops abruptly to look at his watch—alertly.*) But I ain't got de time to waste no more fool talk wid you. I'se gwine away from heah dis secon'. (*He reaches in under the throne and pulls out an expensive Panama hat with a bright multi-colored band and sets it jauntily on his head.*) So long, white man! (*With a grin.*) See you in jail sometime, maybe!

Smithers: Not me, you won't. Well, I wouldn't be in yer bloody boots for no bloomin' money, but 'ere's wishin' yer luck just the same.

Jones (*contemptuously*): Yo're de frightenedest man evah I see! I tells you I'se safe's 'f I was in New York City. It takes dem niggers from now to dark to git up de nerve to start somethin'. By dat time, I'se got a head start dey never kotch up wid.

Smithers (*maliciously*): Give my regards to any ghosts yer meets up with.

Jones (*grinning*): If dat ghost got money, I'll tell him never ha'nt you less'n he wants to lose it.

Smithers (*flattered*): Garn! (*Then curiously.*) Ain't yer takin' no luggage with yer?

Jones: I travels light when I wants to move fast. And I got tinned grub buried on de edge o' de forest. (*Boastfully.*) Now say dat I don't look ahead an' use my brains! (*With a wide, liberal gesture.*) I will all dat's left in de palace to you—and you better grab all you kin sneak away wid befo' dey gits here.

Smithers (*gratefully*): Righto—and thanks ter yer. (*As **Jones** walks toward the door in rear—cautioningly.*) Say! Look 'ere, you ain't goin' out that way, are yer?

Jones: Does you think I'd slink out de back door like a common nigger? I'se Emperor yit, ain't I? And de Emperor Jones leaves de way he comes, and dat black trash don't dare stop him—not yit, leastways. (*He stops for a moment in the doorway, listening to the far-off but insistent beat of the tom-tom.*) Listen to dat roll-call, will you? Must be mighty big drum carry dat far. (*Then with a laugh.*) Well, if dey ain't no whole brass band to see me off, I sho' got de drum part of it. So long, white man. (*He put his hands in his pockets and with studied carelessness, whistling a tune, he saunters out of the doorway and off to the left.*)

Smithers (*looks after him with a puzzled admiration*): 'E's got 'is bloomin' nerve with 'im, s'elp me! (*Then angrily.*) Ho—the bleedin' nigger—puttin' on 'is bloody airs! I 'opes they nabs 'im an' gives 'im what's what! (*Then putting business before the pleasure of this thought, looking around him with cupidity.*) A bloke ought to find a 'ole lot in this palace that'd go for a bit of cash. Let's take a look, 'Arry, me lad. (*He starts for the doorway on right as*

THE CURTAIN FALLS

SCENE II

Scene. Nightfall. The end of the plain where the Great Forest begins. The foreground is sandy, level ground dotted by a few stones and clumps of stunted bushes covering close against the earth to escape the buffeting of the trade wind. In the rear the forest is a wall of darkness dividing the world. Only when the eye becomes accustomed to the gloom can the outlines of separate trunks of the nearest trees be made out, enormous pillars of deeper blackness. A somber monotone of wind lost in the leaves moans in the air. Yet this sound serves but to intensify the impression of the forest's relentless immobility, to form a background throwing into relief its brooding, implacable silence.

Jones enters from the left, walking rapidly. He stops as he nears the edge of the forest, looks around him quickly, peering into the dark as if searching for some familiar landmark. Then, apparently, satisfied that he is where he ought to be, he throws himself on the ground, dog-tired.

Well, heah I is. In de nick o' time, too! Little mo' an' it'd be blacker'n de ace of spades heahabouts. (*He pulls a bandana handkerchief from his hip pocket and mops off his perspiring face.*) Sho'! Gimme air! I'se tuckered out sho' nuff. Dat soft Emperor job ain't no trainin' fo' a long hike ovah dat plain in de brilin' sun. (*Then with a chuckle.*) Cheah up, nigger, de worst is yet to come. (*He lifts his head and stares at the forest. His chuckle peters out abruptly. In a tone of awe.*) My goodness, look at dem woods, will you? Dat no-count Smithers said dey'd be black an' he sho' called de turn. (*Turning away from them quickly and looking down at his feet, he snatches at a chance to change the subject—solicitously.*) Feet, you is holdin' up yo' end fine an' I sutinly hopes you ain't blisterin' none. It's time you git a rest. (*He takes off his shoes, his eyes studiously avoiding the forest. He feels of the soles of his feet gingerly.*) You is still in de pink—on'y a little mite feverish. Cool yo'selfs. Remember you done got a long journey yit befo' you. (*He sits in a weary attitude, listening to the rhythmic beating of the tom-tom. He grumbles in a loud tone to cover up a growing uneasiness.*) Bush niggers! Wonder dey wouldn' get sick o' beatin' dat drum. Sound louder, seem like. I wonder if dey's startin' after me? (*He scrambles to his feet, looking back across the plain.*) Couldn't see dem now, nohow, if dey was hundred feet away. (*Then shaking himself like a wet dog to get rid of these depressing thoughts.*) Sho', dey's miles an' miles behind. What you gittin' fidgety about? (*But he sits down and begins to lace up his shoes in great haste, all the time muttering reassuringly.*) You know what? Yo' belly is empty, dat's what's de matter wid you. Come time to eat! Wid nothin' but wind on yo' stumach, o' course you feels jiggedy. Well, we eats right heah an' now soon's I gits dese pesky shoes laced up! (*He finishes lacing up his shoes.*) Dere! Now le's see. (*Gets on his hands and knees and searches the ground around him with his eyes.*) White stone, white stone, where is you? (*He sees the first white stone and crawls to it—with satisfaction.*) Heah you is! I knowed dis was de right place. Box of grub, come to me. (*He turns over the stone and feels in under it—in a tone of dismay.*) Ain't heah! Gorry, is I in de right place or isn't I? Dere's 'nother stone. Guess dat's it. (*He scrambles to the next stone and turns it over.*) Ain't heah, neither! Grub, whar is you? Ain't heah. Gorry, has I got to go hungry into dem woods—all de night? (*While he is talking he scrambles from one stone to another, turning them over in frantic haste. Finally, he jumps to his feet excitedly.*) Is I lost de place? Must have! But how dat happen when I was followin' de trail across de plain in broad daylight? (*Almost plaintively.*) I'se hungry, I is! I gotta git my feed. Whar's my strength gonna come from if I doesn't? Gorry, I gotta find dat grub high an' low somehow! Why it come dark so quick like dat? Can't see nothin'. (*He scratches a match on his trousers and peers about him. The rate of the beat of the far-off tom-tom increases perceptibly as he does so. He mutters in a bewildered voice.*) How come all dese white stones come heah when I only remembers one? (*Suddenly, with a frightened gasp, he flings the match on the ground and stamps on it.*) Nigger, is you gone crazy mad? Is you lightin' matches to show dem whar you is? Fo' Lawd's sake, use yo' haid. Gorry, I'se got to be careful! (*He stares at the plain behind him apprehensively, his hand on his revolver.*) But how come all dese white stones? And whar's dat tin box o' grub I had all wrapped up in oil cloth?

(*While his back is turned, the* **Little Formless Fears** *creep out from the deeper blackness of the forest. They are black, shapeless, only their glittering little eyes can be seen. If they have any describable form at all it is that of a grubworm about the size of a creeping child. They move noiselessly, but with deliberate, painful effort, striving to raise themselves on end, failing and sinking prone again.* **Jones** *turns about to face the forest. He stares up at the tops of the trees, seeking vainly to discover his whereabouts by their conformation.*)

Can't tell nothin' from dem trees! Gorry, nothin' 'round heah look like I evah seed it befo'. I'se done lost de place sho' 'nuff! (*With mournful foreboding.*) It's mighty queer! It's mighty queer! (*With sudden forced defiance—in an angry tone.*) Woods, is you tryin' to put somethin' ovah on me?

(*From the formless creatures on the ground in front of him comes a tiny gale of low mocking laughter like a rustling of leaves. They squirm upward toward him in twisted attitudes.* **Jones** *looks down, leaps backward with a yell of terror, yanking out his revolver as he does so—in a quavering voice.*)

What's dat? Who's dar? What is you? Git away from me befo' I shoots you up! You don't? . . .

(*He fires. There is a flash, a loud report, then silence broken only by the far-off, quickened throb of the tom-tom. The formless creatures have scurried back into the forest.* **Jones** *remains fixed in his position, listening intently. The sound of the shot, the reassuring feel of the revolver in his hand, have somewhat restored his shaken nerve. He addresses himself with renewed confidence.*)

Dey're gone. Dat shot fix 'em. Dey was only little animals—little wild pigs, I reckon. Dey've maybe rooted out yo' grub an' eat it. Sho', you fool nigger, what you think dey is—ha'nts? (*Excitedly.*) Gorry, you give de game away when you fire dat shot. Dem niggers heah dat fo' su'tin! Time you beat it in de woods widout no long waits. (*He starts for the forest—hesitates before the plunge—then urging himself in with manful resolution.*) Git in, nigger! What you skeered at? Ain't nothin' dere but de trees! Git in! (*He plunges boldly into the forest.*)

SCENE III

Scene. Nine o'clock. In the forest. The moon has just risen. Its beams, drifting through the canopy of leaves, make a barely perceptible, suffused, eerie glow. A dense low wall of under-brush and creepers is in the nearer foreground, fencing in a small triangular clearing. Beyond this is the massed blackness of the forest like an encompassing barrier. A path is dimly dis-cerned leading down to the clearing from left, rear, and winding away from it again toward the right. As the scene opens nothing can be distinctly made out. Except for the beating of the tom-tom, which is a trifle louder and quicker than in the previous scene, there is silence, broken every few seconds by a queer, clicking sound. Then gradually the figure of the Negro, **Jeff***, can be discerned crouching on his haunches at the rear of the triangle. He is middle-aged, thin, brown in color, is dressed in a Pullman porter's uniform, cap, etc. He is throwing a pair of dice on the ground before him, picking them up, shaking them, casting them out with the regular, rigid, mechanical movements of an automaton. The heavy, plodding foot-steps of someone approaching along the trail from the left are heard and* **Jones'** *voice, pitched in a slightly higher key and strained in a cheering effort to overcome its own tremors.*

De moon's rizen. Does you heah dat, nigger? You gits more light from dis out. No mo' buttin' yo' fool head agin' de trunks an' scratchin' de hide off yo' legs in de bushes. Now you sees whar yo'se gwine. So cheer up! From now on you has a snap. (*He steps just to the rear of the triangular clearing and mops off his face on his sleeve. He has lost his Panama hat. His face is scratched, his brilliant uniform shows several large rents.*) What time's it gittin' to be, I wonder? I dassent light no match to find out. Phoo'. It's wa'm an' dat's a fac'! (*Wearily.*) How long I been makin' tracks in dese woods? Must be hours an' hours. Seems like fo'evah! Yit can't be, when de moon's jes' riz. Dis am a long night fo' yo', yo' Majesty! (*With a mournful chuckle.*) Majesty! Der ain't much majesty 'bout dis baby now. (*With attempted cheerfulness.*) Never min'. It's all part o' de game. Dis night come to an end like everything else. And when you gits dar safe and has dat bankroll in yo' hands you laughs at all dis. (*He starts to whistle but checks himself abruptly.*) What yo' whistlin' for, you po' dope! Want all de worl' to heah you? (*He stops talking to listen.*) Heah dat ole drum! Sho' gits nearer from de sound. Dey're packin' it along wid 'em. Time fo' me to move. (*He takes a step forward, then stops—worriedly.*) What's dat odder queer clickety sound I heah? Dere it is! Sound close! Sound like—sound like—Fo' God sake, sound like some nigger was shootin' crap! (*Frightenedly.*) I better beat it quick when I gits dem notions. (*He walks quickly into the clear space—then stands transfixed as he sees* **Jeff**—*in a terrified gasp.*) Who dar? Who dat? Is dat you, Jeff? (*Starting toward the other, forgetful for a moment of his surroundings and really believing it is a living man that he sees—in a tone of happy relief.*) Jeff! I'se sho' mightly glad to see you! Dey tol' me you done died from dat razor cut I gives you. (*Stopping suddenly, bewilderedly.*) But how you come to be heah, nigger? (*He stares fascinatedly at the other who continues his mechanical play with the dice.* **Jones'** *eyes begin to roll wildly. He stutters.*) Ain't you gwine—look up—can't you speak to me? Is you—is you—a ha'nt? (*He jerks out his revolver in a frenzy of terrified rage.*) Nigger, I kills you dead once. Has I got to kill you again? You take it den. (*He fires. When the smoke clears away* **Jeff** *has disappeared.* **Jones** *stands trembling—then with a certain reassurance.*) He's gone, anyway. Ha'nt or no ha'nt, dat shot fix him. (*The beat of the far-off tom-tom is perceptibly louder and more rapid.* **Jones** *becomes conscious of it—with a start, looking back over his shoulder.*) Dey's gittin' near! Dey's comin' fast! And heah I is shootin' shots to let 'em know jes' whar I is. Oh, Gorry, I'se got to run. (*Forgetting the path he plunges wildly into the underbrush in the rear and disappears in the shadow.*)

SCENE IV

Scene. Eleven o'clock. In the forest. A wide dirt road runs diagonally from right, front, to left, rear. Rising sheer on both sides the forest walls it in. The moon is now up. Under its light the road glimmers ghastly and unreal. It is as if the forest had stood aside momentarily to let the road pass through and accomplish its veiled purpose. This done, the forest will fold in upon itself again and the road will be no more. Jones *stumbles in from the forest on the right. His uniform is ragged and torn. He looks about him with numbed surprise when he sees the road, his eyes blinking in the bright moonlight. He flops down exhaustedly and pants heavily for a while. Then with sudden anger.*

I'm meltin' wid heat! Runnin' an' runnin' an' runnin'! Damn dis heah coat! Like a strait-jacket! (*He tears off his coat and flings it away from him, revealing himself stripped to the waist.*) Dere! Dat's better! Now I kin breathe! (*Looking down at his feet, the spurs catch his eye.*) And to hell wid dese high-fangled spurs. Dey're what's been a-trippin' me up an' breakin' my neck. (*He unstraps them and flings them away disgustedly.*) Dere! I gits rid o' dem frippety Emperor trappin's an' I travels lighter. Lawd! I'se tired! (*After a pause, listening to the insistent beat of the tom-tom in the distance.*) I must 'a put some distance between myself an' dem—runnin' like dat—and yit—dat damn drum sound jes' de same—nearer, even. Well, I guess I a'most holds my lead anyhow. Dey won't never catch up. (*With a sigh.*) If on'y my fool legs stands up. Oh, I'se sorry I evah went in for dis. Dat Emperor job is sho' hard to shake. (*He looks around him suspiciously.*) How'd dis road evah git heah? Good level road, too. I never remembers seein' it befo'. (*Shaking his head apprehensively.*) Dese woods is sho' full o' de queerest things at night. (*With a sudden terror.*) Lawd God, don't let me see no more o' dem ha'nts! Dey gits my goat! (*Then trying to talk himself into confidence.*) Ha'nts! You fool nigger, dey ain't no such things! Don't de Baptist parson tell you dat many time? Is you civilized, or is you like dese ign'rent black niggers heah? Sho'! Dat was all in yo' own head. Wasn't nothin' dere. Wasn't no Jeff! Know what? You jus' get seein' dem things 'cause yo' belly's empty and you's sick wid hunger inside. Hunger 'fects yo' head and yo' eyes. Any fool know dat. (*Then pleading fervently.*) But bless God, I don't come across no more o' dem, whatever dey is! (*Then cautiously.*) Rest! Don't talk! Rest! You needs it. Den you gits on yo' way again. (*Looking at the moon.*) Night's half gone a'most. You hits de coast in de mawning! Den you'se all safe.

(*From the right forward a small gang of Negroes enter. They are dressed in striped convict suits, their heads are shaven, one leg drags limpingly, shackled to a heavy ball and chain. Some carry picks, the others shovels. They are followed by a white man dressed in the uniform of a prison guard. A Winchester rifle is slung across his shoulders and he carries a heavy whip. At a signal from the* Guard *they stop on the road opposite where* Jones *is sitting.* Jones, *who has been staring up at the sky, unmindful of their noiseless approach, suddenly looks down and sees them. His eyes pop out, he tries to get to his feet and fly, but sinks back, too numbed by fright to move. His voice catches in a choking prayer.*)
Lawd Jesus!

(*The* Prison Guard *cracks his whip—noiselessly—and at that signal all the convicts start to work on the road. They swing their picks, they shovel, but not a sound comes from their labor. Their movements, like those of* Jeff *in the preceding scene, are those of automatons,—rigid, slow, and mechanical. The* Prison Guard *points sternly at* Jones *with his whip, motions him to take his place among the other shovelers.* Jones *gets to his feet in a hypnotized stupor. He mumbles subserviently.*)

Yes, suh! Yes, suh! I'se comin'.

(*As he shuffles, dragging one foot, over to his place, he curses under his breath with rage and hatred.*)

God damn yo' soul, I gits even wid you yit, sometime.

(*As if there were a shovel in his hands he goes through weary, mechanical gestures of digging up dirt, and throwing it to the roadside. Suddenly the* **Guard** *approaches him angrily, threateningly. He raises his whip and lashes* **Jones** *viciously across the shoulders with it.* **Jones** *winces with pain and cowers abjectly. The* **Guard** *turns his back on him and walks away contemptuously. Instantly* **Jones** *straightens up. With arms upraised as if his shovel were a club in his hands he springs murderously at the unsuspecting* **Guard**. *In the act of crashing down his shovel on the white man's skull,* **Jones** *suddenly becomes aware that his hands are empty. He cries despairingly.*)

Whar's my shovel? Gimme my shovel till I splits his damn head! (*Appealing to his fellow convicts.*) Gimme a shovel, one o' you, fo' God's sake!

(*They stand fixed in motionless attitudes, their eyes on the ground. The* **Guard** *seems to wait expectantly, his back turned to the attacker.* **Jones** *bellows with baffled, terrified rage, tugging frantically at his revolver.*)

I kills you, you white debil, if it's de last thing I evah does! Ghost or debil, I kill you again!

(*He frees the revolver and fires point blank at the* **Guard's** *back. Instantly the walls of the forest close in from both sides, the road and the figures of the convict gang are blotted out in an enshrouding darkness. The only sounds are a crashing in the underbrush as* **Jones** *leaps away in mad flight and the throbbing of the tom-tom, still far distant, but increased in volume of sound and rapidity of beat.*)

SCENE V

Scene. One o'clock. A large circular clearing, enclosed by the serried ranks of gigantic trunks of tall trees whose tops are lost to view. In the center is a big dead stump worn by time into a curious resemblance to an auction block. The moon floods the clearing with a clear light. **Jones** *forces his way in through the forest on the left. He looks wildly about the clearing with hunted, fearful glances. His pants are in tatters, his shoes cut and misshapen, flapping about his feet. He slinks cautiously to the stump in the center and sits down in a tense position, ready for instant flight. Then he holds his head in his hands and rocks back and forth, moaning to himself miserably.*

Oh Lawd, Lawd! Oh Lawd, Lawd! (*Suddenly he throws himself on his knees and raises his clasped hands to the sky—in a voice of agonized pleading.*) Lawd Jesus, heah my prayer! I'se a po' sinner, a po' sinner! I knows I done wrong, I knows it! When I cotches Jeff cheatin' wid loaded dice my anger overcomes me and I kills him dead! Lawd, I done wrong! When dat guard hits me wid de whip, my anger overcomes me, and I kills him dead. Lawd, I done wrong! And down heah whar dese fool bush niggers raises me up to the seat o' de mighty, I steals all I could grab. Lawd, I done wrong! I knows it! I'se sorry! Forgive me, Lawd! Forgive dis po' sinner! (*Then beseeching terrifiedly.*) And keep dem away, Lawd! Keep dem away from me! And stop dat drum soundin' in my ears! Dat begin to sound ha'nted, too. (*He gets to his feet, evidently slightly reassured by his prayer—with attempted confidence.*) De Lawd'll preserve me from dem ha'nts after dis. (*Sits down on the stump again.*) I ain't skeered o' real men. Let dem come. But dem odders . . . (*He shudders—then looks down at his feet, working his toes inside the shoes—with a groan.*) Oh, my po' feet! Dem shoes ain't no use no more 'ceptin' to hurt. I'se better off widout dem. (*He unlaces them and pulls them off—holds the wrecks of the shoes in his hands and regards them mournfully.*) You was real, A-one patin' leather, too. Look at you now. Emperor, you'se gittin' mighty low!

(*He sits dejectedly and remains with bowed shoulders, staring down at the shoes in his hands as if reluctant to throw them away. While his attention is thus occupied, a crowd of figures silently enter the clearing from all sides. All are dressed in Southern costumes of the period of the fifties of the last century. There are middle-aged men who are evidently well-to-do planters. There is one spruce, authoritative individual—the Auctioneer. There is a crowd of curious spectators, chiefly young belles and dandies who have come to the slave-market for diversion. All exchange courtly greetings in dumb show and chat silently together. There is something stiff, rigid, unreal, marionettish about their movements. They group themselves about the stump. Finally a batch of slaves are led in from the left by an attendant —three men of different ages, two women, one with a baby in her arms, nursing. They are placed to the left of the stump, beside Jones.*

The white planters look them over appraisingly as if they were cattle, and exchange judgments on each. The dandies point with their fingers and make witty remarks. The belles titter bewitchingly. All this in silence save for the ominous throb of the tom-tom. The Auctioneer holds up his hand, taking his place at the stump. The group strain forward attentively. He touches Jones on the shoulder peremptorily, motioning for him to stand on the stump—the auction block.

Jones looks up, sees the figures on all sides, looks wildly for some opening to escape, sees none, screams and leaps madly to the top of the stump to get as far away from them as possible. He stands there, cowering, paralyzed with horror. The Auctioneer begins his silent spiel. He points to Jones, appeals to the planters to see for themselves. Here is a good field hand, sound in wind and limb as they can see. Very strong still in spite of his being middle-aged. Look at that back. Look at those shoulders. Look at the muscles in his arms and his sturdy legs. Capable of any amount of hard labor. Moreover, of a good disposition, intelligent and tractable. Will any gentleman start the bidding? The Planters raise their fingers, make their bids. They are apparently all eager to possess Jones. The bidding is lively, the crowd interested. While this has been going on, Jones has been seized by the courage of desperation. He dares to look down and around him. Over his face abject terror gives way to mystification, to gradual realization—stutteringly.)

What you all doin', white folks? What's all dis? What you all lookin' at me fo'? What you doin' wid me, anyhow? (*Suddenly convulsed with raging hatred and fear.*) Is dis a auction? Is you sellin' me like dey uster befo' de war? (*Jerking out his revolver just as the Auctioneer knocks him down to one of the planters—glaring from him to the purchaser.*) And *you* sells me? And *you* buys me? I shows you I'se a free nigger, damn yo' souls!

(*He fires at the Auctioneer and at the Planter with such rapidity that the two shots are almost simultaneous. As if this were a signal the walls of the forest fold in. Only blackness remains and silence broken by Jones as he rushes off, crying with fear—and by the quickened, ever louder beat of the tom-tom.*)

SCENE VI

Scene. Three o'clock. A cleared space in the forest. The limbs of the trees meet over it forming a low ceiling about five feet from the ground. The interlocked ropes of creepers reaching upward to entwine the tree trunks give an arched appearance to the sides. The space thus

*enclosed is like the dark, noisome hold of some ancient vessel. The moonlight is almost com-
pletely shut out and only a vague, wan light filters through. There is the noise of someone
approaching from the left, stumbling and crawling through the undergrowth.* Jones' *voice
is heard between chattering moans.*

Oh, Lawd, what I gwine do now? Ain't got no bullet left on'y de silver one. If
mo' o' dem ha'nts come after me, how I gwine skeer dem away? Oh, Lawd, on'y de
silver one left—an' I gotta save dat fo' luck. If I shoots dat one I'm a goner sho'!
Lawd, it's black heah! Whar's de moon? Oh, Lawd, don't dis night evah come to
an end? (*By the sounds, he is feeling his way cautiously forward.*) Dere! Dis feels like a
clear space. I gotta lie down an' rest. I don't care if dem niggers does cotch me.
I gotta rest.

(*He is well forward now where his figure can be dimly made out. His pants have been so
torn away that what is left of them is no better than a breech cloth. He flings himself full
length, face downward on the ground, panting with exhaustion. Gradually it seems to grow
lighter in the enclosed space and two rows of seated figures can be seen behind* Jones. *They
are sitting in crumpled, despairing attitudes, hunched, facing one another with their backs
touching the forest walls as if they were shackled to them. All are Negroes, naked save for
loin cloths. At first they are silent and motionless. Then they begin to sway slowly forward
toward each other and back again in unison, as if they were laxly letting themselves follow
the long roll of a ship at sea. At the same time, a low, melancholy murmur rises among them,
increasing gradually by rhythmic degrees which seem to be directed and controlled by the
throb of the tom-tom in the distance, to a long, tremulous wail of despair that reaches a
certain pitch, unbearably acute, then falls by slow gradations of tone into silence and is taken
up again.* Jones *starts, looks up, sees the figures, and throws himself down again to shut
out the sight. A shudder of terror shakes his whole body as the wail rises up about him
again. But the next time, his voice, as if under some uncanny compulsion, starts with the
others. As their chorus lifts he rises to a sitting posture similar to the others, swaying back
and forth. His voice reaches the highest pitch of sorrow, of desolation. The light fades out,
the other voices cease, and only darkness is left.* Jones *can be heard scrambling to his feet
and running off, his voice sinking down the scale and receding as he moves farther and
farther away in the forest. The tom-tom beats louder, quicker, with a more insistent trium-
phant pulsation.*)

SCENE VII

*Scene. Five o'clock. The foot of a gigantic tree by the edge of a great river. A rough structure
of boulders, like an altar, is by the tree. The raised river bank is in the nearer background.
Beyond this the surface of the river spreads out, brilliant and unruffled in the moonlight,
blotted out and merged into a veil of bluish mist in the distance.* Jones' *voice is heard from
the left rising and falling in the long, despairing wail of the chained slaves, to the rhythmic
beat of the tom-tom. As his voice sinks into silence, he enters the open space. The expression
of his face is fixed and stony, his eyes have an obsessed glare, he moves with a strange de-
liberation like a sleepwalker or one in a trance. He looks around at the tree, the rough stone
altar, the moonlit surface of the river beyond, and passes his hand over his head with a
vague gesture of puzzled bewilderment. Then, as if in obedience to some obscure impulse,
he sinks into a kneeling, devotional posture before the altar. Then he seems to come to himself
partly, to have an uncertain realization of what he is doing, for he straightens up and stares
about him horrifiedly—in an incoherent mumble.*

What—what is I doin'? What is—dis place? Seems like—seems like I know dat tree—an' dem stones—an' de river. I remember—seems like I been heah befo'. (*Tremblingly.*) Oh, Gorry, I'se skeered in dis place! I'se skeered! Oh, Lawd, pertect dis sinner!

(*Crawling away from the altar, he cowers close to the ground, his face hidden, his shoulders heaving with sobs of hysterical fright. From behind the trunk of the tree, as if he had sprung out of it, the figure of the* **Congo Witch-Doctor** *appears. He is wizened and old, naked except for the fur of some small animal tied about his waist, its bushy tail hanging down in front. His body is stained all over a bright red. Antelope horns are on each side of his head, branching upward. In one hand he carries a bone rattle, in the other a charm stick with a bunch of white cockatoo feathers tied to the end. A great number of glass beads and bone ornaments are about his neck, ears, wrists, and ankles. He struts noiselessly with a queer prancing step to a position in the clear ground between* **Jones** *and the altar. Then with a preliminary, summoning stamp of his foot on the earth, he begins to dance and to chant. As if in response to his summons the beating of the tom-tom grows to a fierce, exultant boom whose throbs seem to fill the air with vibrating rhythm.* **Jones** *looks up, starts to spring to his feet, reaches a half-kneeling, half-squatting position and remains rigidly fixed there, paralyzed with awed fascination by this new apparition. The* **Witch-Doctor** *sways, stamping with his foot, his bone rattle clicking the time. His voice rises and falls in a weird, monotonous croon, without articulate word divisions. Gradually his dance becomes clearly one of a narrative in pantomime, his croon is an incantation, a charm to allay the fierceness of some implacable deity demanding sacrifice. He flees, he is pursued by devils, he hides, he flees again. For wilder and wilder becomes his flight, nearer and nearer draws the pursuing evil, more and more the spirit of terror gains possession of him. His croon, rising to intensity, is punctuated by shrill cries.* **Jones** *has become completely hypnotized. His voice joins in the incantation, in the cries, he beats time with his hands and sways his body to and fro from the waist. The whole spirit and meaning of the dance has entered into him, has become his spirit. Finally the theme of the pantomime halts on a howl of despair, and is taken up again in a note of savage hope. There is a salvation. The forces of evil demand sacrifice. They must be appeased. The* **Witch-Doctor** *points with his wand to the sacred tree, to the river beyond, to the altar, and finally to* **Jones** *with a ferocious command.* **Jones** *seems to sense the meaning of this. It is he who must offer himself for sacrifice. He beats his forehead abjectly to the ground, moaning hysterically.*)

Mercy, Oh Lawd! Mercy! Mercy on dis po' sinner.

(*The* **Witch-Doctor** *springs to the river bank. He stretches out his arms and calls to some god within its depths. Then he starts backward slowly, his arms remaining out. A huge head of a crocodile appears over the bank and its eyes, glittering greenly, fasten upon* **Jones**. *He stares into them fascinatedly. The* **Witch-Doctor** *prances up to him, touches him with his wand, motions with hideous command toward the waiting monster.* **Jones** *squirms on his belly nearer and nearer, moaning continually.*)

Mercy, Lawd! Mercy!

(*The crocodile heaves more of his enormous bulk onto the land.* **Jones** *squirms toward him. The* **Witch-Doctor's** *voice shrills out in furious exultation, the tom-tom beats madly.* **Jones** *cries out in a fierce, exhausted spasm of anguished pleading.*)

Lawd, save me! Lawd Jesus, heah my prayer!

(*Immediately, in answer to his prayer, comes the thought of the one bullet left him. He snatches at his hip, shouting defiantly.*)

De silver bullet! You don't git me yit!

(*He fires at the green eyes in front of him. The head of the crocodile sinks back behind the river bank, the* **Witch-Doctor** *springs behind the sacred tree and disappears.* **Jones** *lies with his face to the ground, his arms outstretched, whimpering with fear as the throb of the tom-tom fills the silence about him with a somber pulsation, a baffled but revengeful power.*)

SCENE VIII

Scene. Dawn. Same as Scene II, the dividing line of forest and plain. The nearest tree trunks are dimly revealed but the forest behind them is still a mass of glooming shadows. The tom-tom seems on the very spot, so loud and continuously vibrating are its beats. **Lem** *enters from the left, followed by a small squad of his soldiers, and by the Cockney trader,* **Smithers**. **Lem** *is a heavy-set, ape-faced old savage of the extreme African type, dressed only in a loin cloth. A revolver and cartridge belt are about his waist. His soldiers are in different degrees of rag-concealed nakedness. All wear broad palm-leaf hats. Each one carries a rifle.* **Smithers** *is the same as in Scene I. One of the soldiers, evidently a tracker, is peering about keenly on the ground. He grunts and points to the spot where* **Jones** *entered the forest.* **Lem** *and* **Smithers** *come to look.*

Smithers (*after a glance, turns away in disgust*): That's where 'e went in right enough. Much good it'll do yer. 'E's miles orf by this an' safe to the Coast, damn 'is 'ide! I tole yer yer'd lose 'im, didn't I?—wastin' the 'ole bloomin' night beatin' yer bloody drum and castin' yer silly spells! Gawd blimey, wot a pack!

Lem (*gutturally*): We cotch him. You see. (*He makes a motion to his soldiers who squat down on their haunches in a semicircle.*)

Smithers (*exasperatedly*): Well, ain't yer goin' in an' 'unt 'im in the woods? What the 'ell's the good of waitin'?

Lem (*imperturbably—squatting down himself*): We cotch him.

Smithers (*turning away from him contemptuously*): Aw! Garn! 'E's a better man than the lot o' you put together. I 'ates the sight o' 'im but I'll say that for 'im.
(*A sound of snapping twigs comes from the forest. The soldiers jump to their feet, cocking their rifles alertly.* **Lem** *remains sitting with an imperturbable expression, but listening intently. The sound from the woods is repeated.* **Lem** *makes a quick signal with his hand. His followers creep quickly but noiselessly into the forest, scattering so that each enters at a different spot.*)

Smithers (*in the silence that follows—in a contemptuous whisper*): You ain't thinkin' that would be 'im, I 'ope?

Lem (*calmly*): We cotch him.

Smithers: Blarsted fat 'eads! (*Then after a second's thought—wonderingly.*) Still an' all, it might 'appen. If 'e lost 'is bloody way in these stinkin' woods 'e'd likely turn in a circle without 'is knowin' it. They all does.

Lem (*peremptorily*): Sssh!
(*The reports of several rifles sound from the forest, followed a second later by savage, exultant yells. The beating of the tom-tom abruptly ceases.* **Lem** *looks up at the white man with a grin of satisfaction.*)
We cotch him. Him dead.

Smithers (*with a snarl*): 'Ow d'yer know it's 'im an' 'ow d'yer know 'e's dead?

Lem: My mens dey got 'um silver bullets. Dey kill him shore.

Smithers (*astonished*): They got silver bullets?

Lem: Lead bullet no kill him. He got um strong charm. I cook um money, make um silver bullet, make um strong charm, too.

Smithers (*light breaking upon him*): So that's wot you was up to all night, wot? You was scared to put after 'im till you'd moulded silver bullets, eh?

Lem (*simply stating a fact*): Yes. Him got strong charm. Lead no good.

Smithers (*slapping his thigh and guffawing*): Haw-haw! If yer don't beat all 'ell! (*Then recovering himself—scornfully.*) I'll bet yer it ain't 'im they shot at all, yer bleedin' looney!

Lem (*calmly*): Dey come bring him now.

(*The soldiers come out of the forest, carrying* **Jones'** *limp body. There is a little reddish-purple hole under his left breast. He is dead. They carry him to* **Lem**, *who examines his body with great satisfaction.* **Smithers** *leans over his shoulder—in a tone of frightened awe.*) Well, they did for yer right enough, Jonsey me lad! Dead as a 'erring! (*Mockingly.*) Where's yer 'igh an' mighty airs now, yer bloomin' Majesty? (*Then with a grin.*) Silver bullets! Gawd blimey, but yer died in the 'eighth o' style, any'ow! (**Lem** *makes a motion to the soldiers to carry the body out left.* **Smithers** *speaks to him sneeringly.*)

Smithers: And I s'pose you think it's yer bleedin' charms and yer silly beatin' the drum that made 'im run in a circle when 'e'd lost 'imself, don't yer?

(*But* **Lem** *makes no reply, does not seem to hear the question, walks out left after his men.* **Smithers** *looks after him with contemptuous scorn.*)

Stupid as 'ogs, the lot of 'em! Blarsted niggers!

CURTAIN FALLS

PART FOUR
STRUCTURE

We all have conflicts of various kinds in our lives. Some are minor: you want to sleep but your roommates are having a party; you plan to play golf but it is raining; you really want to study for a test, but everyone is going drinking, and tonight is the last night the band is playing. Other conflicts are major: you love her, but she doesn't want to be tied down to one person; you want to learn a trade, but your parents insist that you go to college; you know you are better qualified for the job than she, but she is hired.

Conflict is the basis of drama. If characters are the major focus of attention in a play, their actions are how we best come to know them. The playwright puts his characters into a situation, gives them motives, supplies their goals, sets them in conflict, allows them to act and the conflict to develop, and eventually resolves the conflict in some way. The accumulation and combination of all these actions make up the plot of the play.

Plot shows us what characters do and what happens to them as a result of their actions. In well-written drama, the events that occur are believable, given their dramatic context, and they exist in a causal relationship to each other—each event proceeds logically and necessarily from those which precede it. And the driving mechanism of the plot—the force which propels it—is conflict.

The playwright begins by placing his characters in a particular situation. Since all plays begin in the middle of the action, the playwright usually supplies background information, or *exposition*, that will help us understand who the characters are and what they are trying to do. All the necessary background may be provided early in the play, or we may come to know more and more about it as the play develops. We will never know everything that has happened before the play begins. The playwright could never tell us everything that has influenced even one character, nor does he need to. He selects only those details that are important to our understanding of his play; therefore, the details that he does include about background are significant.

Through exposition, we also learn what a character is trying to achieve and the reasons for his actions—in other words, his goals and motives. The action of the play, or plot, really begins with these.

Each character in the play tries to achieve something; each has a goal. For minor characters such as servants or messengers, the goals may be trivial within the framework of the play. For the major characters the goals are likely to be more complex and more significant. Motivations for goals usually become apparent early in the play. They may be influenced or determined by events that have occurred before the play begins, or they may arise out of the action of the play itself. The range of possible motives or combinations of motives that may appear in a play is almost infinite. Motives may be defined abstractly, such as greed or power or desire for freedom, or they may be identified more concretely: the desire to climb a mountain in order to win five-thousand dollars, to coach a football team and have a feeling of control over the players, or to desert the army to escape regimentation and confinement. As these motives become defined in dialogue and action, the plot develops through the movement of the characters toward their goals.

As the play progresses, the motives of different characters may come into conflict. For example, a wife might want to establish meaningful relationships with other men, but her husband's need for security prompts him to try to prevent her; or two men are each driven to become vice president of their firm and may try to destroy each other in order to succeed.

A character's motives may also conflict with his environment. A number of young Americans found themselves in opposition to society's demand that they participate in the Vietnam war. Many were motivated by the feeling that the war was immoral and chose to leave the country rather than contradict their beliefs. A farmer might be forced to sell his farm and take a factory job in the city. But the noisy monotony of his work and the city atmosphere may conflict with his desire for a quiet life close to the land.

Several motives within a single character may sometimes conflict with each other. For instance, a person in love with his or her best friend's fiancé may be torn between the ties of friendship and feelings for the fiancé. Or, someone finds a wallet containing $121.00—and the owner's name and address. Greed and honesty must conflict with each other before a resolution can occur.

All such conflicts or combinations of them may be present within a single play or a single character. As is true in most human experience, conflicts in drama are often complex and difficult to resolve. They spring from numerous causes that are hard to explain and may produce actions that seem erratic or unusual to someone who doesn't understand their origin. But as in life, all action is motivated by something. Though we may not always be sure of or agree on the causes, the result is often much more rewarding if we make an effort to understand, rather than simply dismissing something or someone as "weird" or different from ourselves. Often when we try to understand another's motivations, we may discover something about our own.

As the play progresses and we have more contact with characters, their motives may become clearer. We may see them in various situations that make their purpose more apparent. For example, early in the play a character may seem to be a helpful adviser, someone to whom other characters go to discuss their problems and ask for help. Later in the play this character may use the information he has collected for his own gain. We can then understand more clearly his motives for appearing so helpful earlier.

A character may, however, change his motives during the course of a play, or they may become less clear and more complex. Because of events that occur, he may expand, diminish, or completely alter his goals. For instance, a character may initially submerge himself in his job, trying to get ahead, trying to achieve wealth and power. However, his involvement with work takes him away from his family, which begins to disintegrate. He is faced with the conflict of family versus job. He may decide to deemphasize the job and devote his time to preserving his family. As a result, his primary motivation will have shifted, and we will have gained a deeper insight into his character.

The above example points up an essential aspect of the relationship of character and conflict. As conflicts arise, the character is faced with a choice or a series of choices. He must decide what to do: fight, remain passive, choose one thing or another. His choices might establish a pattern: a character might consistently select alternatives that progressively alienate him from his family, his associates, his society, his world; or his selections might reveal a shift in values, motives, and goals, as in the previous example. Each choice a character makes when confronted with a conflict is significant and provides further insight into that character.

Our interest in the plot is usually centered on a certain major character or group of characters. A playwright may choose to focus attention on one or several major conflicts in one play. A single play could include the conflicts of a daughter trying to establish her freedom and individuality in an oppressive, restrictive family and of her father wrestling with the decision to accept or refuse a contract for weapons manufacturing when he is violently opposed to war.

In addition to the central focus, the dramatist may present minor conflicts which comment on the major action. A group of executives confront the prospect of wife-swapping, while at the same time one of their daughters must decide whether or not to live with her boyfriend. Both must make choices, deal with peer pressure, and set their morality against the possible choices.

The conflict faced by one character may be parallel to that of another, yet the two may act in opposite ways. Two students who intensely dislike their respective roommates are given an opportunity to change at the semester. One does so because she is seriously depressed in that room and her studies are suffering. The other declines, realizing that her roommate needs someone to cling to and talk to, and thus she sacrifices her own well-being for the possible good of another. One character's actions serve as a comment on the other's. Groups of characters, scenes, and even entire plots may be parallel so that one group, scene, or plot may inform us about another in the play.

Often the very arrangement of scenes within a play gives us insight into its meaning. The playwright selects the entire sequence of scenes with specific effects in mind. One might immediately follow another to comment on the preceding action: a typical, contented suburban family entertaining their friends at a backyard barbeque may be placed next to the scene of a widow with three emaciated children, trying to convince the authorities that she is entitled to food stamps. Serious and light scenes might alternate so that the serious scene is undercut or made ridiculous by the lighter one: following a scene in which a general talks to his staff about the glory, heroism, and honor of a military career, we see a group of enlisted men drunkenly dancing in the Trevi fountain in the middle of Rome. One scene might foreshadow actions that will occur later, or scenes might move progressively from humorous to serious. Scenes following one another in a logical, causal pattern could reflect an ordered view of the world. Or scenes superficially unrelated to the others may seem to be haphazardly inserted, suggesting that the world is chaotic and arbitrary. There are many possible patterns; as you read or see drama take particular notice of the playwright's design of these structural elements.

Ultimately, however, we are interested in how characters try to resolve their conflicts and in what happens to them in the process. This process usually results in a resolution of the conflicts presented. The play moves from exposition through conflict to resolution.

exposition ⟶ **conflict** ⟶ **resolution**

A character may achieve his goal or fail. He may achieve his goal but lose something significant or become changed in so doing. He may begin as a sympathetic character who is seeking something beneficial to himself and those around him. By the end of the play he may have achieved the desired goal, but what he has experienced has so altered him that we no longer feel sympathy for him or identify with him. A man may work through his labor union to improve working conditions and wages for his fellow workers, but in the process he may become so obsessed with power and control that these become the ends toward which he works. Even though he may have accomplished his original goals, the audience, seeing his grasp of power, may well lose sympathy for him.

Generally at the end of a play the audience feels a sense of completion or finality to the action. Something has been decided. If the major conflicts are not resolved, there is at least the realization that they are eternal conflicts which will never be settled. For example, a major character dies at the end of a play, still raging at the social forces that have oppressed him. Although his death is a kind of resolution for him, we understand that people will always be in conflict with society.

From the resolution of the conflict an audience generally derives some sort of meaning from the play, if such meaning exists. The meaning is not a moral or a one-line statement about what the playwright meant or what his message was. Such a statement oversimplifies the artistic creation; if a play conveys its meaning as economically and as succinctly as the playwright felt possible, it would be presumptuous to try to reduce his work to one or two statements. It may be possible to isolate one particular subject or theme within a play—such as love, revenge, or identity—but neither the theme nor the subject is the meaning of the play. The meaning is the experience of the play itself. We meet characters, see their conflicts, watch them interact, and observe what happens to them. That is the structure, or plot, of the play, and out of plot comes the revelation of human experience. In the truth of that human experience, as it relates to each of us, lies meaning.

ANTIGONE

Sophocles

PERSONS REPRESENTED

Antigone	Haimon
Ismene	Teiresias
Eurydice	A Sentry
Creon	A Messenger
Chorus	

SCENE. Before the palace of **Creon**, King of Thebes. A central double door, and two lateral doors. A platform extends the length of the façade, and from this platform three steps lead down into the "orchestra," or chorus-ground.
TIME. Dawn of the day after the repulse of the Argive army from the assault on Thebes.

PROLOGUE

(**Antigone** and **Ismene** enter from the central door of the Palace.)
Antigone: Ismene, dear sister,
  You would think that we had already suffered enough
  For the curse on Oedipus: *Original audience*
  I cannot imagine any grief   *knew the story*
  That you and I have not gone through. And now——
  Have they told you of the new decree of our King Creon?
Ismene: I have heard nothing: I know
  That two sisters lost two brothers, a double death
  In a single hour; and I know that the Argive army
  Fled in the night; but beyond this, nothing.
Antigone: I thought so. And that is why I wanted you   *knows her sister*
  To come out here with me. There is something we must do.
Ismene: Why do you speak so strangely?
Antigone: Listen, Ismene:
  Creon buried our brother Eteocles
  With military honors, gave him a soldier's funeral,   *both equal; should be*
  And it was right that he should; but Polyneices,   *treated as such*
  Who fought as bravely and died as miserably,——   *Exposition*
  They say that Creon has sworn
  No one shall bury him, no one mourn for him,
  But his body must lie in the fields, a sweet treasure
  For carrion birds to find as they search for food.
  That is what they say, and our good Creon is coming here
  To announce it publicly; and the penalty——
  Stoning to death in the public square!

There it is,
And now you can prove what you are:
A true sister, or a traitor to your family.

Ismene: Antigone, you are mad! What could I possibly do?

Antigone: You must decide whether you will help me or not.

Ismene: I do not understand you. Help you in what?

Antigone: Ismene, I am going to bury him. Will you come?

Ismene: Bury him! You have just said the new law forbids it.

Antigone: He is my brother. And he is your brother, too.

Ismene: But think of the danger! Think what Creon will do!

Antigone: Creon is not strong enough to stand in my way.

Ismene: Ah sister!
Oedipus died, everyone hating him
For what his own search brought to light, his eyes
Ripped out by his own hand; and Iocaste died,
His mother and wife at once: she twisted the cords
That strangled her life; and our two brothers died,
Each killed by the other's sword. And we are left:
But oh, Antigone,
Think how much more terrible than these
Our own death would be if we should go against Creon
And do what he has forbidden! We are only women,
We cannot fight with men, Antigone!
The law is strong, we must give in to the law
In this thing, and in worse. I beg the Dead
To forgive me, but I am helpless. I must yield
To those in authority. And I think it is dangerous business
To be always meddling.

Antigone: If that is what you think,
I should not want you, even if you asked to come.
You have made your choice, you can be what you want to be.
But I will bury him; and if I must die,
I say that this crime is holy: I shall lie down
With him in death, and I shall be as dear
To him as he is to me.

                    It is the dead,
Not the living, who make the longest demands:
We die for ever . . .

                    You may do as you like,
Since apparently the laws of the gods mean nothing to you.

Ismene: They mean a great deal to me; but I have no strength
To break laws that were made for the public good.

Antigone: That must be your excuse, I suppose. But as for me,
I will bury the brother I love.

Ismene: Antigone,
I am so afraid for you!

Antigone: You need not be:
You have yourself to consider, after all.

Ismene: But no one must hear of this, you must tell no one!
I will keep it a secret, I promise!

Antigone: Oh tell it! Tell everyone!
  Think how they'll hate you when it all comes out
  If they learn that you knew about it all the time!
Ismene: So fiery! You should be cold with fear.
Antigone: Perhaps. But I am doing only what I must.
Ismene: But can you do it? I say that you cannot.
Antigone: Very well: when my strength gives out, I shall do no more.
Ismene: Impossible things should not be tried at all. *—afraid to take a chance*
Antigone: Go away, Ismene:
  I shall be hating you soon, and the dead will too,
  For your words are hateful. Leave me my foolish plan: *makes decision*
  I am not afraid of the danger; if it means death, *knowing what will*
  It will not be the worst of deaths—death without honor. *happen*
Ismene: Go then, if you feel that you must.
  You are unwise, *understatement*
  But a loyal friend indeed to those who love you.
  (*Exit into the Palace.* **Antigone** *goes off, L. Enter the* **Chorus.**)

PARODOS

Chorus: Now the long blade of the sun, lying   [STROPHE 1]
  Level east to west, touches with glory
  Thebes of the Seven Gates. Open, unlidded
  Eye of golden day! O marching light
  Across the eddy and rush of Dirce's stream,
  Striking the white shields of the enemy
  Thrown headlong backward from the blaze of morning!
Choragos: Polyneices their commander
  Roused them with windy phrases,
  He the wild eagle screaming
  Insults above our land,
  His wings their shields of snow,
  His crest their marshalled helms.

Chorus: Against our seven gates in a yawning ring   [ANTISTROPHE 1]
  The famished spears came onward in the night;
  But before his jaws were sated with our blood,
  Or pinefire took the garland of our towers.
  He was thrown back; and as he turned, great Thebes——
  No tender victim for his noisy power——
  Rose like a dragon behind him, shouting war.
Choragos: For God hates utterly
  The bray of bragging tongues;
  And when he beheld their smiling,
  Their swagger of golden helms,
  The frown of his thunder blasted
  Their first man from our walls.

Chorus: We heard his shout of triumph high in the air   [STROPHE 2]
  Turn to a scream; far out in a flaming arc

He fell with his windy torch, and the earth struck him.
And others storming in fury no less than his
Found shock of death in the dusty joy of battle.

Exposition. How does Choragos describe the battle?

Choragos: Seven captains at seven gates
Yielded their clanging arms to the god
That bends the battle-line and breaks it.
These two only, brothers in blood,
Face to face in matchless rage,
Mirroring each the other's death,
Clashed in long combat.

Chorus: But now in the beautiful morning of victory   [ANTISTROPHE 2]
Let Thebes of the many chariots sing for joy!
With hearts for dancing we'll take leave of war;
Our temples shall be sweet with hymns of praise,
And the long night shall echo with our chorus.

SCENE I

Choragos: But now at last our new King is coming:
Creon of Thebes, Menoikeus' son.
In this auspicious dawn of his reign

Why are these questions asked? Why placed here?

What are the new complexities
That shifting Fate has woven for him?
What is his counsel? Why has he summoned
The old men to hear him?
(*Enter* **Creon** *from the Palace, C. He addresses the* **Chorus** *from the top step.*)

Creon: Gentlemen: I have the honor to inform you that our Ship of State, which recent storms have threatened to destroy, has come safely to harbor at last, guided by the merciful wisdom of Heaven. I have summoned you here this morning because I know that I can depend upon you: your devotion to King Laïos was absolute; you never hesitated in your duty to our late ruler Oedipus; and when Oedipus died, your loyalty was transferred to his children. Unfortunately, as you know, his two sons, the princes Eteocles and Polyneices, have killed each other in battle; and I, as the next in blood, have succeeded to the full power of the throne.

I am aware, of course, that no Ruler can expect complete loyalty from his subjects until he has been tested in office. Nevertheless, I say to you at the very outset that I have nothing but contempt for the kind of Governor who is afraid, for whatever reason, to follow the course that he knows is best for the State; and as for the man who sets private friendship above the public welfare,—I have no use for him, either. I call God to witness that if I saw my country headed for ruin, I should not be afraid to speak out plainly; and I need hardly remind you that I would never have any dealings with an enemy of the people. No one values friendship more highly than I; but we must remember that friends made at the risk of wrecking our Ship are not real friends at all.

These are my principles, at any rate, and that is why I have made the following decision concerning the sons of Oedipus: Eteocles, who died as a man should die, fighting for his country, is to be buried with full military honors, with all the ceremony that is usual when the greatest heroes die; but his brother Polyneices, who broke his exile to come back with fire and sword against his native city and the shrines of his fathers' gods, whose one idea was to spill the blood of his blood and sell his own people into slavery— Polyneices, I say, is to have no burial: no man is to touch him or say the least prayer for him; he shall lie on the plain, unburied; and the birds and the scavenging dogs can do with him whatever they like.

According to Creon, what motivated his decision?

This is my command, and you can see the wisdom behind it. As long as I am King, no traitor is going to be honored with the loyal man. But whoever shows by word and deed that he is on the side of the State,—he shall have my respect while he is living, and my reverence when he is dead.

Choragos: If that is your will, Creon son of Menoikeus,
You have the right to enforce it: we are yours.
Creon: That is my will. Take care that you do your part.
Choragos: We are old men: let the younger ones carry it out.
Creon: I do not mean that: the sentries have been appointed.
Choragos: Then what is it that you would have us do?
Creon: You will give no support to whoever breaks this law.
Choragos: Only a crazy man is in love with death!
Creon: And death it is; yet money talks, and the wisest — *often brings up bribery*
Have sometimes been known to count a few coins too many.
(*Enter* **Sentry** *from L.*)
Sentry: I'll not say that I'm out of breath from running, King, because every time I stopped to think about what I have to tell you, I felt like going back. And all the time a voice kept saying, "You fool, don't you know you're walking straight into trouble?"; and then another voice: "Yes, but if you let somebody else get the news to Creon first, it will be even worse than that for you!" But good sense won out, at least I hope it was good sense, and here I am with a story that makes no sense at all; but I'll tell it anyhow, because, as they say, what's going to happen's going to happen, and——

Notice rhythm of play: Sentry is comic, following scene of intense action. What effect on audience?

Creon: Come to the point. What have you to say?
Sentry: I did not do it. I did not see who did it. You must not punish me for what someone else has done.
Creon: A comprehensive defense! More effective, perhaps,
If I knew its purpose. Come: what is it?
Sentry: A dreadful thing . . . I don't know how to put it——
Creon: Out with it!
Sentry: Well, then;
The dead man——
                Polyneices——
(*Pause. The* **Sentry** *is overcome, fumbles for words.* **Creon** *waits impassively.*)
                out there——
                        Someone,——
New dust on the slimy flesh!
(*Pause. No sign from* **Creon**.)
Someone has given it burial that way, and
Gone . . .

Conflict: His authority has been challenged.

(*Long pause.* **Creon** *finally speaks with deadly control.*)
Creon: And the man who dared do this?
Sentry: I swear I
Do not know! You must believe me!
                                        Listen:
The ground was dry, not a sign of digging, no,
Not a wheeltrack in the dust, no trace of anyone.
It was when they relieved us this morning: and one of them,
The corporal, pointed to it.
                              There it was,
The strangest——
            Look:
The body, just mounded over with light dust: you see?
Not buried really, but as if they'd covered it
Just enough for the ghost's peace. And no sign
Of dogs or any wild animal that had been there.

Like Ismene, what is their first concern? Compare with Antigone's position.

And then what a scene there was! Every man of us
Accusing the other: we all proved the other man did it,
We all had proof that we could not have done it.
We were ready to take hot iron in our hands,
Walk through fire, swear by all the gods,
IT WAS NOT I!
I DO NOT KNOW WHO IT WAS, BUT IT WAS NOT I!
(**Creon's** *rage has been mounting steadily, but the* **Sentry** *is too intent upon his story to notice it.*)
And then, when this came to nothing, someone said
A thing that silenced us and made us stare
Down at the ground: you had to be told the news,
And one of us had to do it! We threw the dice,
And the bad luck fell to me. So here I am,
No happier to be here than you are to have me:
Nobody likes the man who brings bad news.
Choragos: I have been wondering, King: can it be that the gods have done this?
Creon (*furiously*): Stop!
Must you doddering wrecks
Go out of your heads entirely? "The gods!"
Intolerable!
The gods favor this corpse? Why? How had he served them?
Tried to loot their temples, burn their images,
Yes, and the whole State, and its laws with it!
Is it your senile opinion that the gods love to honor bad men?
A pious thought!——
                    No, from the very beginning
There have been those who have whispered together, — *paranoid*
Stiff-necked anarchists, putting their heads together,
Scheming against me in alleys. These are the men,
And they have bribed my own guard to do this thing.
(*Sententiously.*)
Money!

There's nothing in the world so demoralizing as money.
Down go your cities,
Homes gone, men gone, honest hearts corrupted,
Crookedness of all kinds, and all for money!
(*To* **Sentry**.)   But you——!
I swear by God and by the throne of God,
The man who has done this thing shall pay for it!
Find that man, bring him here to me, or your death
Will be the least of your problems: I'll string you up
Alive, and there will be certain ways to make you
Discover your employer before you die;
And the process may teach you a lesson you seem to have missed:
The dearest profit is sometimes all too dear:
That depends on the source. Do you understand me?
A fortune won is often misfortune.

Sentry: King, may I speak?
Creon: Your very voice distresses me.
Sentry: Are you sure that it is my voice, and not your conscience?
Creon: By God, he wants to analyze me now!
Sentry: It is not what I say, but what has been done, that hurts you.
Creon: You talk too much.
Sentry: Maybe; but I've done nothing.
Creon: Sold your soul for some silver: that's all you've done.
Sentry: How dreadful it is when the right judge judges wrong!
Creon: Your figures of speech
May entertain you now; but unless you bring me the man,
You will get little profit from them in the end.
(*Exit* **Creon** *into the Palace.*)

Sentry: "Bring me the man"—!
I'd like nothing better than bringing him the man!
But bring him or not, you have seen the last of me here.
At any rate, I am safe!
(*Exit* **Sentry**.)

What do you now know about background? What conflicts were introduced? Who sides with whom?

ODE I

Chorus: Numberless are the world's wonders, but none   [STROPHE 1]
More wonderful than man; the stormgray sea
Yields to his prows, the huge crests bear him high;
Earth, holy and inexhaustible, is graven
With shining furrows where his plows have gone
Year after year, the timeless labor of stallions.

The lightboned birds and beasts that cling to cover,   [ANTISTROPHE 1]
The lithe fish lighting their reaches of dim water,
All are taken, tamed in the net of his mind;
The lion on the hull, the wild horse windy maned,
Resign to him; and his blunt yoke has broken
The sultry shoulders of the mountain bull.

Words also, and thought as rapid as air, [STROPHE 2]
He fashions to his good use; statecraft is his,
And his the skill that deflects the arrows of snow,
The spears of winter rain: from every wind
He has made himself secure—from all but one
In the late wind of death he cannot stand.

O clear intelligence, force beyond all measure! [ANTISTROPHE 2]
O fate of man, working both good and evil!
When the laws are kept, how proudly his city stands!

Stance of the When the laws are broken, what of his city then?
Chorus at this Never may the anárchic man find rest at my hearth,
point? Never be it said that my thoughts are his thoughts.

SCENE II

(*Re-enter* **Sentry** *leading* **Antigone**.)
Choragos: What does this mean? Surely this captive woman
Is the Princess, Antigone. Why should she be taken?
Sentry: Here is the one who did it! We caught her
In the very act of burying him.—Where is Creon?
Choragos: Just coming from the house.
(*Enter* **Creon**, C.)
Creon: What has happened?
Why have you come back so soon?
Sentry (*expansively*):   O King,
A man should never be too sure of anything: I would have sworn
That you'd not see me here again: your anger
Frightened me so, and the things you threatened me with;
But how could I tell then
That I'd be able to solve the case so soon?

No dice-throwing this time: I was only too glad to come!

Here is this woman. She is the guilty one:
We found her trying to bury him.
Take her, then; question her; judge her as you will.
I am through with the whole thing now, and glád óf it.

How does this **Creon:** But this is Antigone! Why have you brought her here?
news complicate **Sentry:** She was burying him, I tell you!
Creon's position? **Creon** (*severely*):   Is this the truth?
Sentry: I saw her with my own eyes. Can I say more?
Creon: The details: come, tell me quickly!
Sentry: It was like this:
After those terrible threats of yours, King,
We went back and brushed the dust away from his body.
The flesh was soft by now, and stinking,
So we sat on a hill to windward and kept guard.
No napping this time! We kept each other awake.

But nothing happened until the white round sun
Whirled in the center of the round sky over us:
Then, suddenly,
A storm of dust roared up from the earth, and the sky
Went out, the plain vanished with all its trees
In the stinging dark. We closed our eyes and endured it.
The whirlwind lasted a long time, but it passed;
And then we looked, and there was Antigone!
I have seen
A mother bird come back to a stripped nest, heard
Her crying bitterly a broken note or two
For the young ones stolen. Just so, when this girl
Found the bare corpse, and all her love's work wasted,
She wept, and cried on heaven to damn the hands
That had done this thing.
                  And then she brought more dust
And sprinkled wine three times for her brother's ghost.

We ran and took her at once. She was not afraid,
Not even when we charged her with what she had done.
She denied nothing.
              And this was a comfort to me,
And some uneasiness: for it is a good thing
To escape from death, but it is no great pleasure
To bring death to a friend.
                 Yet I always say
There is nothing so comfortable as your own safe skin!

Is it always good?
For Antigone?

Creon (*slowly, dangerously*): And you, Antigone,
You with your head hanging,—do you confess this thing?
Antigone: I do. I deny nothing.
Creon (*to* **Sentry**):   You may go.   (*Exit* **Sentry.**)
(*To* **Antigone**) Tell me, tell me briefly:
Had you heard my proclamation touching this matter?
Antigone: It was public. Could I help hearing it?
Creon: And yet you dared defy the law.
Antigone: I dared.
It was not God's proclamation. That final Justice
That rules the world below makes no such laws.
Your edict, King, was strong,
But all your strength is weakness itself against
The immortal unrecorded laws of God.

Antigone and God
vs. Creon and the
state

They are not merely now: they were, and shall be,
Operative for ever, beyond man utterly.
I knew I must die, even without your decree:
I am only mortal. And if I must die
Now, before it is my time to die,
Surely this is no hardship: can anyone
Living, as I live, with evil all about me,
Think Death less than a friend? This death of mine

Is of no importance; but if I had left my brother
Living in death unburied, I should have suffered.
Now I do not.

            You smile at me. Ah Creon,
Think me a fool, if you like; but it may well be
That a fool convicts me of folly.

Choragos: Like father, like daughter: both headstrong, deaf to reason!
She has never learned to yield.

Creon: She has much to learn.
The inflexible heart breaks first, the toughest iron
Cracks first, and the wildest horses bend their necks
At the pull of the smallest curb.

                Pride? In a slave?
This girl is guilty of a double insolence,
Breaking the given laws and boasting of it.
Who is the man here,
She or I, if this crime goes unpunished?
Sister's child, or more than sister's child,
Or closer yet in blood—she and her sister
Win bitter death for this!

(*To* **Servants**.)   Go, some of you,
Arrest Ismene. I accuse her equally.
Bring her: you will find her sniffling in the house there.

Her mind's a traitor: crimes kept in the dark
Cry for light, and the guardian brain shudders;
But how much worse than this
Is brazen boasting of barefaced anarchy!

Antigone: Creon, what more do you want than my death?

Creon: Nothing.
That gives me everything.

Antigone: Then I beg you: kill me.
Thus talking is a great weariness: your words
Are distasteful to me, and I am sure that mine
Seem so to you. And yet they should not seem so:
I should have praise and honor for what I have done.
All these men here would praise me
Were their lips not frozen shut with fear of you.

(*Bitterly*.)
Ah the good fortune of kings,
Licensed to say and do whatever they please!

Creon: You are alone here in that opinion.

Antigone: No, they are with me. But they keep their tongues in leash.

Creon: Maybe. But you are guilty, and they are not.

Antigone: There is no guilt in reverence for the dead.

Creon: But Eteocles—was he not your brother too?

Antigone: My brother too.

Creon: And you insult his memory?

Antigone (*softly*): The dead man would not say that I insult it.

[margin note: Is Creon angry at the attitude or the act ?]

[margin note: True ? Compare with Chorus at end of Ode I.]

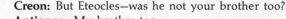

[margin note: pride]

7 deadly
sins
1 Pride
2 Anger
3 Averous
4 glutny
5 lechery
6 envy
7. sloth

Creon: He would: for you honor a traitor as much as him.

Antigone: His own brother, traitor or not, and equal in blood.

Creon: He made war on his country. Eteocles defended it.

Antigone: Nevertheless, there are honors due all the dead.

Creon: But not the same for the wicked as for the just.

Antigone: Ah Creon, Creon,

   Which of us can say what the gods hold wicked?

Creon: An enemy is an enemy, even dead.

How does this relate to conflict?

Antigone: It is my nature to join in love, not hate.

Creon (*finally losing patience*): Go join them, then; if you must have your love,

   Find it in hell!

Choragos: But see, Ismene comes:

   (*Enter* **Ismene**, *guarded.*)

   Those tears are sisterly, the cloud

   That shadows her eyes rains down gentle sorrow.

Creon: You too, Ismene,

   Snake in my ordered house, sucking my blood

   Stealthily—and all the time I never knew

   That these two sisters were aiming at my throne!

                                             Ismene,

   Do you confess your share in this crime, or deny it?

   Answer me.

Why does Ismene say this? What conflict does she feel?

Ismene: Yes, if she will let me say so. I am guilty.

Antigone (*coldly*): No, Ismene. You have no right to say so.

   You would not help me, and I will not have you help me.

Ismene: But now I know what you meant; and I am here

   To join you, to take my share of punishment.

Antigone: The dead man and the gods who rule the dead

   Know whose act this was. Words are not friends.

Ismene: Do you refuse me, Antigone? I want to die with you:

   I too have a duty that I must discharge to the dead.

How is Antigone's motivation becoming more complex?

Antigone: You shall not lessen my death by sharing it.

Ismene: What do I care for life when you are dead?

Antigone: Ask Creon. You're always hanging on his opinions.

Ismene: You are laughing at me. Why, Antigone?

Antigone: It's a joyless laughter, Ismene.

Ismene: But can I do nothing?

Antigone: Yes. Save yourself. I shall not envy you.

   There are those who will praise you; I shall have honor, too.

Ismene: But we are equally guilty!

Antigone: No more, Ismene.

   You are alive, but I belong to Death.

Creon (*to the* **Chorus**): Gentlemen, I beg you to observe these girls:

   One has just now lost her mind; the other,

   It seems, has never had a mind at all.

Ismene: Grief teaches the steadiest minds to waver, King.

Creon: Yours certainly did, when you assumed guilt with the guilty!

Ismene: But how could I go on living without her?

Creon: You are.
   She is already dead.
Ismene: But your own son's bride!
Creon: There are places enough for him to push his plow.
   I want no wicked women for my sons!
Ismene: O dearest Haimon, how your father wrongs you!
Creon: I've had enough of your childish talk of marriage!
Choragos: Do you really intend to steal this girl from your son?
Creon: No; Death will do that for me.
Choragos: Then she must die?
Creon (*ironically*): You dazzle me.
                 —But enough of this talk!
   (*To* **Guards**.)
   You, there, take them away and guard them well;
   For they are but women, and even brave men run
   When they see Death coming.
   (*Exeunt* **Ismene**, **Antigone**, *and* **Guards**.)

How does this complicate Creon's conflict?

What does Creon sense?

ODE II

                                                    [STROPHE 1]
Chorus: Fortunate is the man who has never tasted God's vengeance!
   Where once the anger of heaven has struck, that house is shaken
   For ever: damnation rises behind each child
   Like a wave cresting out of the black northeast,
   When the long darkness under sea roars up
   And bursts drumming death upon the windwhipped sand.

I have seen this gathering sorrow from time long past   [ANTISTROPHE 1]
   Loom upon Oedipus' children: generation from generation
   Takes the compulsive rage of the enemy god.
   So lately this last flower of Oedipus' line
   Drank the sunlight! but now a passionate word
   And a handful of dust have closed up all its beauty.

          What mortal arrogance   [STROPHE 2]
          Transcends the wrath of Zeus?
   Sleep cannot lull him, nor the effortless long months
   Of the timeless gods: but he is young for ever,
   And his house is the shining day of high Olympos.
          All that is and shall be,
          And all the past, is his.
   No pride on earth is free of the curse of heaven.

Is Creon also proud?

          The straying dreams of men   [ANTISTROPHE 2]
          May bring them ghosts of joy:
   But as they drowse, the waking embers burn them;
   Or they walk with fíxed éyes, as blind men walk.
   But the ancient wisdom speaks for our own time:

Foreshadowing?

Fate works most for woe
With Folly's fairest show
Man's little pleasure is the spring of sorrow.

SCENE III

Choragos: But here is Haimon, King, the last of all your sons.
Is it grief for Antigone that brings him here,
And bitterness at being robbed of his bride?
(*Enter* **Haimon**.)
Creon: We shall soon see, and no need of diviners.
—Son,

You have heard my final judgment on that girl:
Have you come here hating me, or have you come
With deference and with love, whatever I do?

Parallel with
Ismene's and
Sentry's position?

Haimon: I am your son, father. You are my guide.
You make things clear for me, and I obey you.
No marriage means more to me than your continuing wisdom.
Creon: Good. That is the way to behave: subordinate
Everything else, my son, to your father's will.

Is this what every
ruler prays for?

This is what a man prays for, that he may get
Sons attentive and dutiful in his house,
Each one hating his father's enemies,
Honoring his father's friends. But if his sons
Fail him, if they turn out unprofitably,
What has he fathered but trouble for himself
And amusement for the malicious?
So you are right
Not to lose your head over this woman.
Your pleasure with her would soon grow cold, Haimon,
And then you'd have a hellcat in bed and elsewhere.
Let her find her husband in Hell!
Of all the people in this city, only she
Has had contempt for my law and broken it.
Do you want me to show myself weak before the people?
Or to break my sworn word? No, and I will not.
The woman dies.
I suppose she'll plead "family ties." Well, let her.
If I permit my own family to rebel,
How shall I earn the world's obedience?
Show me the man who keeps his house in hand,
He's fit for public authority.
I'll have no dealings
With law-breakers, critics of the government:
Whoever is chosen to govern should be obeyed——
Must be obeyed, in all things, great and small,
Just and unjust! O Haimon,
The man who knows how to obey, and that man only,
Knows how to give commands when the time comes.

You can depend on him, no matter how fast
The spears come: he's a good soldier, he'll stick it out.
Anarchy, anarchy! Show me a greater evil!
This is why cities tumble and the great houses rain down,
This is what scatters armies!

No, no: good lives are made so by discipline.
We keep the laws then, and the lawmakers,
And no woman shall seduce us. If we must lose,
Let's lose to a man, at least! Is a woman stronger than we?

Choragos: Unless time has rusted my wits,
What you say, King, is said with point and dignity.

Haimon (*boysihly earnest*): Father:
Reason is God's crowning gift to man, and you are right
To warn me against losing mine. I cannot say——
I hope that I shall never want to say!—that you
Have reasoned badly. Yet there are other men
Who can reason, too; and their opinions might be helpful.
You are not in a position to know everything
That people say or do, or what they feel:
Your temper terrifies them—everyone
Will tell you only what you like to hear.
But I, at any rate, can listen; and I have heard them
Muttering and whispering in the dark about this girl.
They say no woman has ever, so unreasonably,
Died so shameful a death for a generous act:
"She covered her brother's body. Is this indecent?
She kept him from dogs and vultures. Is this a crime?
Death?—She should have all the honor that we can give her!"

This is the way they talk out there in the city.

You must believe me:
Nothing is closer to me than your happiness.
What could be closer? Must not any son
Value his father's fortune as his father does his?
I beg you, do not be unchangeable:
Do not believe that you alone can be right.
The man who thinks that,
The man who maintains that only he has the power
To reason correctly, the gift to speak, the soul——
A man like that, when you know him, turns out empty.

It is not reason never to yield to reason!
In flood time you can see how some trees bend,
And because they bend, even their twigs are safe,
While stubborn trees are torn up, roots and all
And the same thing happens in sailing:
Make your sheet fast, never slacken,—and over you go,
Head over heels and under: and there's your voyage.
Forget you are angry! Let yourself be moved!
I know I am young; but please let me say this:

Chorus seems to take clear stand, but Antigone and now Haimon suggest its ambivalence. Whom should we believe?

The ideal condition
Would be, I admit, that men should be right by instinct;
But since we are all too likely to go astray,
The reasonable thing is to learn from those who can teach.

Choragos: You will do well to listen to him, King,
If what he says is sensible. And you, Haimon,
Must listen to your father.—Both speak well.

Creon: You consider it right for a man of my years and experience
To go to school to a boy? *(I'm older; I know best)*

Haimon: It is not right
If I am wrong. But if I am young, and right,
What does my age matter?

Creon: You think it right to stand up for an anarchist?

Haimon: Not at all. I pay no respect to criminals.

Creon: Then she is not a criminal?

Haimon: The City would deny it, to a man.

What is effect of Creon's rigid position? **Creon:** And the City proposes to teach me how to rule?

Haimon: Ah. Who is it that's talking like a boy now?

Creon: My voice is the one voice giving orders in this City!

Haimon: It is no City if it takes orders from one voice.

Creon: The State is the King!

Haimon: Yes, if the State is a desert.

(*Pause.*)

Creon: This boy, it seems, has sold out to a woman.

Haimon: If you are a woman: my concern is only for you.

Creon: So? Your "concern"! In a public brawl with your father!

Haimon: How about you, in a public brawl with justice?

Creon: With justice, when all that I do is within my rights?

The conflict clearly stated **Haimon:** You have no right to trample on God's right.

Creon (*completely out of control*): Fool, adolescent fool! Taken in by
a woman!

Haimon: You'll never see me taken in by anything vile.

Creon: Every word you say is for her!

Haimon (*quietly, darkly*):   And for you.
And for me. And for the gods under the earth.

Creon: You'll never marry her while she lives.

Haimon: Then she must die.—But her death will cause another. *threatens to kill himself.*

Creon: Another?
Have you lost your senses? Is this an open threat?

Haimon: There is no threat in speaking to emptiness.

Creon: I swear you'll regret this superior tone of yours!
You are the empty one!

Compare with Haimon's opening lines. **Haimon:**   If you were not my father,
I'd say you were perverse.

Creon: You girlstruck fool, don't play at words with me!

Haimon: I am sorry. You prefer silence.

Creon: Now, by God—!
I swear, by all the gods in heaven above us,
You'll watch it, I swear you shall!

(*To the* **Servants**.)   Bring her out!
Bring the woman out! Let her die before his eyes!
Here, this instant, with her bridegroom beside her!

Haimon: Not here, no; she will not die here, King.
And you will never see my face again.
Go on raving as long as you've a friend to endure you.
(*Exit* **Haimon**.)

Choragos: Gone, gone.
Creon, a young man in a rage is dangerous!

Creon: Let him do, or dream to do, more than a man can.
He shall not save these girls from death.

Choragos: These girls?
You have sentenced them both?

Creon: No, you are right.
I will not kill the one whose hands are clean.

Choragos: But Antigone?

Creon (*somberly*):   I will carry her far away
Out there in the wilderness, and lock her
Living in a vault of stone. She shall have food,
As the custom is, to absolve the State of her death.
And there let her pray to the gods of hell:
They are her only gods:
Perhaps they will show her an escape from death,
Or she may learn,
            though late,
That piety shown the dead is pity in vain.
(*Exit* **Creon**.)

> Compare Haimon's attempts to persuade Creon with Antigone's.

ODE III

Chorus: Love, unconquerable   [STROPHE]
Waster of rich men, keeper
Of warm lights and all-night vigil
In the soft face of a girl:
Sea-wanderer, forest-visitor!
Even the pure Immortals cannot escape you,
And mortal man, in his one day's dusk,
Trembles before your glory.

Surely you swerve upon ruin   [ANTISTROPHE]
The just man's consenting heart,
As here you have made bright anger   *Creon*
Strike between father and son——
And none has conquered but Love!
A girl's glánce wórking the will of heaven:
Pleasure to her alone who mocks us,
Merciless Aphrodite.

> Why is this ode placed here? How does it relate to scenes III and IV?

Goddess of Love

pride, law, love,

SCENE IV

(As **Antigone** enters guarded.)

Choragos: But I can no longer stand in awe of this,
Nor, seeing what I see, keep back my tears.
Here is Antigone, passing to that chamber
Where all find sleep at last.

Antigone: Look upon me, friends, and pity me   [STROPHE 1]
Turning back at the night's edge to say
Good-by to the sun that shines for me no longer;
Now sleepy Death
Summons me down to Acheron, that cold shore:
There is no bridesong there, nor any music.

Relate diagram on page 187 to changing position of Chorus.

Chorus: Yet not unpraised, not without a kind of honor,
You walk at last into the underworld;
Untouched by sickness, broken by no sword.
What woman has ever found your way to death?

life cut off before she is able to be wed; Acheron a river making outline of hell

Antigone: How often I have heard the story of Niobe,   [ANTISTROPHE 1]
Tantalos' wretched daughter, how the stone
Clung fast about her, ivy-close: and they say
The rain falls endlessly
And sifting soft snow; her tears are never done.
I feel the loneliness of her death in mine.

greek mythology

Chorus: But she was born of heaven, and you
Are woman, woman-born. If her death is yours,
A mortal woman's, is this not for you
Glory in our world and in the world beyond?

Antigone: You laugh at me. Ah, friends, friends,   [STROPHE 2]
Can you not wait until I am dead? O Thebes,
O men many-charioted, in love with Fortune,
Dear springs of Dirce, sacred Theban grove,
Be witnesses for me, denied all pity,

Does this clarify her motives?

Unjustly judged! and think a word of love
For her whose path turns
Under dark earth, where there are no more tears.

Chorus: You have passed beyond human daring and come at last
Into a place of stone where Justice sits.
I cannot tell
What shape of your father's guilt appears in this.

Antigone: You have touched it at last: that bridal bed   [ANTISTROPHE 2]
Unspeakable, horror of son and mother mingling:
Their crime, infection of all our family!
O Oedipus, father and brother!
Your marriage strikes from the grave to murder mine.
I have been a stranger here in my own land:

All my life
The blasphemy of my birth has followed me.
Chorus: Reverence is a virtue, but strength
Lives in established law: that must prevail.
You have made your choice,
Your death is the doing of your conscious hand.

Has she made a free choice or is she a victim of fate ?

Antigone: Then let me go, since all your words are bitter,   [EPODE]
And the very light of the sun is cold to me.
Lead me to my vigil, where I must have
Neither love nor lamentation; no song, but silence.
(**Creon** *interrupts impatiently.*)

Creon: If dirges and planned lamentations could put off death,
Men would be singing for ever.
(*To the* **Servants**.)   Take her, go!
You know your orders: take her to the vault
And leave her alone there. And if she lives or dies,
That's her affair, not ours: our hands are clean.
Antigone: O tomb, vaulted bride-bed in eternal rock,
Soon I shall be with my own again
Where Persephone welcomes the thin ghosts underground:
And I shall see my father again, and you, mother,
And dearest Polyneices—
                    dearest indeed
To me, since it was my hand
That washed him clean and poured the ritual wine:
And my reward is death before my time!

And yet, as men's hearts know, I have done no wrong,
I have not sinned before God. Or if I have,
I shall know the truth in death. But if the guilt
Lies upon Creon who judged me, then, I pray,
May his punishment equal my own.
Choragos: O passionate heart,
Unyielding, tormented still by the same winds!
Creon: Her guards shall have good cause to regret their delaying.
Antigone: Ah! That voice is like the voice of death!
Creon: I can give you no reason to think you are mistaken.
Antigone: Thebes, and you my fathers' gods,
And rulers of Thebes, you see me now, the last
Unhappy daughter of a line of kings,
Your kings, led away to death. You will remember
What things I suffer, and at what men's hands.
Because I would not transgress the laws of heaven.
(*To the* **Guards**, *simply.*)

Come: let us wait no longer.
(*Exit* **Antigone**, *L., guarded.*)

ODE IV

Why is ode placed here? How related to what precedes? What does it suggest will follow?

Chorus: All Danae's beauty was locked away   [STROPHE 1]
In a brazen cell where the sunlight could not come:
A small room, still as any grave, enclosed her.
Yet she was a princess too,
And Zeus in a rain of gold poured love upon her.
O child, child,
No power in wealth or war
Or tough sea-blackened ships
Can prevail against untiring Destiny!

And Dryas' son also, that furious king.   [ANTISTROPHE 1]
Bore the god's prisoning anger for his pride:
Sealed up by Dionysos in deaf stone,
His madness died among echoes.
So at the last he learned what dreadful power
His tongue had mocked:
For he had profaned the revels,
And fired the wrath of the nine
Implacable Sisters that love the sound of the flute.

And old men tell a half-remembered tale   [STROPHE 2]
Of horror done where a dark ledge splits the sea
And a double surf beats on the gráy shóres:
How a king's new woman, sick
With hatred for the queen he had imprisoned,
Ripped out his two sons' eyes with her bloody hands
While grinning Ares watched the shuttle plunge
Four times: four blind wounds crying for revenge,

Crying, tears and blood mingled.—Piteously born,   [ANTISTROPHE 2]
Those sons whose mother was of heavenly birth!
Her father was the god of the North Wind
And she was cradled by gales,
She raced with young colts on the glittering hills
And walked untrammeled in the open light:
But in her marriage deathless Fate found means
To build a tomb like yours for all her joy.

SCENE V

(*Enter blind* **Teiresias,** *led by a* **Boy.** *The opening speeches of* **Teiresias** *should be in singsong contrast to the realistic lines of* **Creon.**)

Teiresias: This is the way the blind man comes, Princes, Princes,
    Lock-step, two heads lit by the eyes of one.
Creon: What new thing have you to tell us old Teiresias?
Teiresias: I have much to tell you: listen to the prophet, Creon.
Creon: I am not aware that I have ever failed to listen.

Teiresias: Then you have done wisely, King, and ruled well.
Creon: I admit my debt to you. But what have you to say?
Teiresias: This, Creon: you stand once more on the edge of fate.
Creon: What do you mean? Your words are a kind of dread.
Teiresias: Listen, Creon:
    I was sitting in my chair of augury, at the place
    Where the birds gather about me. They were all a-chatter,
    As is their habit, when suddenly I heard
    A strange note in their jangling, a scream, a
    Whirring fury; I knew that they were fighting,
    Tearing each other, dying
    In a whirlwind of wings clashing. And I was afraid.
    I began the rites of burnt-offering at the altar,
    But Hephaistos failed me: instead of bright flame,
    There was only the sputtering slime of the fat thigh-flesh
    Melting: the entrails dissolved in gray smoke,
    The bare bone burst from the welter. And no blaze!

    This was a sign from heaven. My boy described it,
    Seeing for me as I see for others.

    I tell you, Creon, you yourself have brought
    This new calamity upon us. Our hearths and altars
    Are stained with the corruption of dogs and carrion birds
    That glut themselves on the corpse of Oedipus' son.
    The gods are deaf when we pray to them, their fire
    Recoils from our offering, their birds of omen
    Have no cry of comfort, for they are gorged
    With the thick blood of the dead.
                O my son,
    These are no trifles! Think: all men make mistakes,
    But a good man yields when he knows his course is wrong,
    And repairs the evil. The only crime is pride.

    Give in to the dead man, then: do not fight with a corpse——
    What glory is it to kill a man who is dead?
    Think, I beg you:
    It is for your own good that I speak as I do.
    You should be able to yield for your own good.

What force does Teiresias represent in the conflict ?

Creon: It seems that prophets have made me their especial province.
    All my life long
    I have been a kind of butt for the dull arrows
    Of doddering fortune-tellers!
                No, Teiresias:
    If your birds—if the great eagles of God himself
    Should carry him stinking bit by bit to heaven,
    I would not yield. I am not afraid of pollution:
    No man can defile the gods.
                Do what you will,

Go into business, make money, speculate
In India gold or that synthetic gold from Sardis,
Get rich otherwise than by my consent to bury him.
Teiresias, it is a sorry thing when a wise man
Sells his wisdom, lets out his words for hire!

Creon rejects
Teiresias. How
does this limit
him ?

Teiresias: Ah Creon! Is there no man left in the world——
Creon: To do what?—come, let's have the aphorism!
Teiresias: No man who knows that wisdom outweighs any wealth?
Creon: As surely as bribes are baser than any baseness.
Teiresias: You are sick, Creon! You are deathly sick!
Creon: As you say: it is not my place to challenge a prophet.
Teiresias: Yet you have said my prophecy is for sale.
Creon: The generation of prophets has always loved gold.
Teiresias: The generation of kings has always loved brass.
Creon: You forget yourself! You are speaking to your King.
Teiresias: I know it. You are a king because of me.
Creon: You have a certain skill; but you have sold out.
Teiresias: King, you will drive me to words that ——
Creon: Say them, say them!
Only remember: I will not pay you for them.
Teiresias: No, you will find them too costly.
Creon: No doubt. Speak:
Whatever you say, you will not change my will.
Teiresias: Then take this, and take it to heart!
The time is not far off when you shall pay back
Corpse for corpse, flesh of your own flesh.
You have thrust the child of this world into living night,
You have kept from the gods below the child that is theirs:
The one in a grave before her death, the other,
Dead, denied the grave. This is your crime:
And the Furies and the dark gods of Hell   .
Are swift with terrible punishment for you.

Do you want to buy me now, Creon?
                              Not many days,
And your house will be full of men and women weeping,
And curses will be hurled at you from far
Cities grieving for sons unburied, left to rot
Before the walls of Thebes.

These are my arrows, Creon: they are all for you,

(*To* **Boy**.)
But come, child: lead me home.
Let him waste his fine anger upon younger men.
Maybe he will learn at last
To control a wiser tongue in a better head.
(*Exit* **Teiresias**.)
Choragos: The old man has gone, King, but his words
Remain to plague us. I am old, too,
But I cannot remember that he was ever false.

Creon: That is true. . . . It troubles me.
  Oh it is hard to give in! but it is worse
  To risk everything for stubborn pride.
Choragos: Creon: take my advice.
Creon: What shall I do?
Choragos: Go quickly: free Antigone from her vault
  And build a tomb for the body of Polyneices.
Creon: You would have me do this?
Choragos: Creon, yes!
  And it must be done at once: God moves
  Swiftly to cancel the folly of stubborn men.
Creon: It is hard to deny the heart! But I
  Will do it: I will not fight with destiny.
Choragos: You must go yourself, you cannot leave it to others.
Creon: I will go.
        —Bring axes, servants:
  Come with me to the tomb. I buried her, I
  Will set her free.
            Oh quickly!
  My mind misgives—
  The laws of the gods are mighty, and a man must serve them
  To the last day of his life!
(*Exit* **Creon**.)

What conflict does Creon recognize?

PAEAN

Choragos: God of many names
Chorus: O Iacchos
                son
  of Kadmeian Sémele
            O born of the Thunder!
  Guardian of the West
            Regent
  of Eleusis' plain
           O Prince of maenad Thebes
  and the Dragon Field by rippling Ismenos:

[STROPHE 1]

Song reinforces Creon's recognition of the power of the gods and fate.

Choragos: God of many names
Chorus: the flame of torches
  flares on our hills
           the nymphs of Iacchos
  dance at the spring of Castalia:
  from the vine-close mountain
              come ah come in ivy:
  Evohé evohé! sings through the streets of Thebes

[ANTISTROPHE 1]

Choragos: God of many names
Chorus: Iacchos of Thebes
  heavenly Child
           of Sémele bride of the Thunderer!

[STROPHE 2]

The shadow of plague is upon us:

come

with clement feet

oh come from Parnasos

down the long slopes

across the lamenting water

Chor"agos: Io Fire! Chorister of the throbbing stars!   [ANTISTROPHE 2]
O purest among the voices of the night!
Thou son of God, blaze for us!
Chorus: Come with choric rapture of circling Maenads
Who cry *Io Iacche!*

God of many names!

EXODOS

(*Enter* **Messenger**, *L.*)
Messenger: Men of the line of Kadmos, you who live
Near Amphion's citadel.

I cannot say
Of any condition of human life "This is fixed,
This is clearly good, or bad." Fate raises up,
And Fate casts down the happy and unhappy alike:
No man can foretell his Fate.

Take the case of Creon: *Summarizes plot*
Creon was happy once, as I count happiness:
Victorious in battle, sole governor of the land,
Fortunate father of children nobly born.
And now it has all gone from him! Who can say
That a man is still alive when his life's joy fails?
He is a walking dead man. Grant him rich,
Let him live like a king in his great house:
If his pleasure is gone, I should not give
So much as the shadow of smoke for all he owns.
Choragos: Your words hint at sorrow: what is your news for us?
Messenger: They are dead. The living are guilty of their death.
Choragos: Who is guilty? Who is dead? Speak!
Messenger: Haimon.
Haimon is dead; and the hand that killed him
Is his own hand.
Choragos: His father's? or his own?
Messenger: His own, driven and mad by the murder his father had done.
Choragos: Teiresias, how clearly you saw it all!
Messenger: This is my news: you must draw what conclusions you can from
it.
Choragos: But look: Eurydice, our Queen:
Has she overheard us?

(*Enter* **Eurydice** *from the Palace, C.*)
Eurydice: I have heard something, friends:
As I was unlocking the gate of Pallas' shrine,

For I needed her help today, I heard a voice
Telling of some new sorrow. And I fainted
There at the temple with all my maidens about me.
But speak again: whatever it is, I can bear it:
Grief and I are no strangers.

Messenger: Dearest Lady,
I will tell you plainly all that I have seen.
I shall not try to comfort you: what is the use,
Since comfort could lie only in what is not true?
The truth is always best.

                                   I went with Creon
To the outer plain where Polyneices was lying,
No friend to pity him, his body shredded by dogs.
We made our prayers in that place to Hecate
And Pluto, that they would be merciful. And we bathed
The corpse with holy water, and we brought
Fresh-broken branches to burn what was left of it,
And upon the urn we heaped up a towering barrow
Of the earth of his own land.

                                   When we were done, we ran
To the vault where Antigone lay on her couch of stone.
One of the servants had gone ahead,
And while he was yet far off he heard a voice
Grieving within the chamber, and he came back
And told Creon. And as the King went closer,
The air was full of wailing, the words lost,
And he begged us to make all haste. "Am I a prophet?"
He said, weeping, "And must I walk this road,
The saddest of all that I have gone before?
My son's voice calls me on. Oh quickly, quickly!
Look through the crevice there, and tell me
If it is Haimon, or some deception of the gods!"
We obeyed; and in the cavern's farthest corner
We saw her lying:

Resolution is set in motion; Creon is powerless to halt it.

She had made a noose of her fine linen veil
And hanged herself. Haimon lay beside her,
His arms about her waist, lamenting her,
His love lost under ground, crying out
That his father had stolen her away from him.
When Creon saw him the tears rushed to his eyes
And he called to him: "What have you done, child? Speak to me.
What are you thinking that makes your eyes so strange?
O my son, my son, I come to you on my knees!"
But Haimon spat in his face. He said not a word,
Staring——
                                   And suddenly drew his sword
And lunged. Creon shrank back, the blade missed; and the boy,
Desperate against himself, drove it half its length
Into his own side, and fell. And as he died

He gathered Antigone close in his arms again,
Choking, his blood bright red on her white cheek.
And now he lies dead with the dead, and she is his
At last, his bride in the houses of the dead.
(*Exit* **Eurydice** *into the Palace.*)

What was Haimon's conflict?

Choragos: She has left us without a word. What can this mean?
Messenger: It troubles me, too; yet she knows what is best,
Her grief is too great for public lamentation,
And doubtless she has gone to her chamber to weep
For her dead son, leading her maidens in his dirge.
Choragos: It may be so: but I fear this deep silence.
(*Pause.*)
Messenger: I will see what she is doing. I will go in.
(*Exit* **Messenger** *into the Palace. Enter* **Creon** *with attendants, bearing* **Haimon's** *body.*)
Choragos: But here is the King himself: oh look at him,
Bearing his own damnation in his arms.
Creon: Nothing you say can touch me any more.
My own blind heart has brought me
From darkness to final darkness. Here you see
The father murdering, the murdered son——
And all my civic wisdom!

Light/dark and blind/seeing images picked up from beginning of scenes IV and V.

Haimon my son, so young, so young to die,
I was the fool, not you; and you died for me.
Choragos: That is the truth; but you were late in learning it.
Creon: This truth is hard to bear. Surely a god
Has crushed me beneath the hugest weight of heaven.
And driven me headlong a barbaric way
To trample out the thing I held most dear.

The pains that men will take to come to pain!
(*Enter* **Messenger** *from the Palace.*)
Messenger: The burden you carry in your hands is heavy,
But it is not all: you will find more in your house.
Creon: What burden worse than this shall I find there?
Messenger: The Queen is dead.
Creon: O port of death, deaf world,
Is there no pity for me? And you, Angel of evil,
I was dead, and your words are death again.
Is it true, boy? Can it be true?
Is my wife dead? Has death bred death?
Messenger: You can see for yourself.
(*The doors are opened, and the body of* **Eurydice** *is disclosed within.*)
Creon: Oh pity!
All true, all true, and more than I can bear!
O my wife, my son!
Messenger: She stood before the altar, and her heart
Welcomed the knife her own hand guided.
And a great cry burst from her lips for Megareus dead,

And for Haimon dead, her sons; and her last breath
Was a curse for their father, the murderer of her sons,
And she fell, and the dark flowed in through her closing eyes.
Creon: O God, I am sick with fear.
Are there no swords here? Has no one a blow for me?
Messenger: Her curse is upon you for the deaths of both.
Creon: It is right that it should be. I alone am guilty.
I know it, and I say it. Lead me in,
Quickly, friends.
I have neither life nor substance. Lead me in.
Choragos: You are right, if there can be right in so much wrong.
The briefest way is best in a world of sorrow.

Final resolution: death for all major characters. What has Creon learned?

Creon: Let it come.
Let death come quickly, and be kind to me.
I would not ever see the sun again.
Choragos: All that will come when it will; but we, meanwhile,
Have much to do. Leave the future to itself.
Creon: All my heart was in that prayer!
Choragos: Then do not pray any more: the sky is deaf.
Creon: Lead me away. I have been rash and foolish.
I have killed my son and my wife.
I look for comfort; my comfort lies here dead.

State vs. God, pride vs. fate— Creon experienced these conflicts. Was he alone responsible for outcome?

Whatever my hands have touched has come to nothing.
Fate has brought all my pride to a thought of dust.
(*As* **Creon** *is being led into the house, the* **Choragos** *advances and
speaks directly to the audience.*)
Choragos: There is no happiness where there is no wisdom;
No wisdom but in submission to the gods.
Big words are always punished,
And proud men in old age learn to be wise.

IACCHOS OF THEBES . . .
The shadow of plague is upon us:
                                            come
with clement feet
                        oh come from Parnassos
down the long slopes
                        across the lamenting water

SLEUTH

Anthony Shaffer

SCENE. Andrew Wyke's country home at Wiltshire, England

ACT I. A summer evening

ACT II. Two days later

ACT I

The living room of Andrew Wyke's Norman Manor House in Wiltshire, England. It is stone flagged, and a tall window runs the height of the back wall. It is divided laterally by a minstrels gallery which, in turn, is approached by a winding staircase. A wardrobe, stage left, and a grandfather clock, and bureau stage right stand on the gallery. Upstage right is the hallway leading to the unseen front door. Upstage left a corridor leads into another part of the house. Standing in this corridor is a large basket hamper. Games of all kinds adorn the room, ranging in complexity from chess, draughts and checkers, to early dice and card games and even earlier blocking games like Senat ant Nine Men Morris. Sitting by the window, under the gallery, is a life-sized figure of a Laughing Sailor.

A summer evening.

Andrew Wyke is sitting at his desk, typing. He is a strongly built, tall, fleshy man of fifty-seven, gone slightly to seed. His fair hair carries on it the suspicion that chemical aid has been invoked to keep the grey at bay. His face, sourly amused and shadowed with evaded self-knowledge, is beginning to reflect the absence of constant, arduous employment. He wears a smoking jacket and black tie.

The clock strikes eight o'clock. Andrew turns to look at clock, finishes typing, takes the page from the typewriter and begins to read.

Andrew: "Since you appear to know so much, Lord Merridew, sir," said the Inspector humbly, "I wonder if you could explain just how the murderer managed to leave the body of his victim in the middle of the tennis court, and effect his escape without leaving any tracks behind him in the red dust. Frankly, sir, we in the Police Force are just plain baffled. There seems no way he could have done it, short of black magic." St. John Lord Merridew, the great detective, rose majestically, his huge Father Christmas face glowing with mischievous delight. Slowly he brushed the crumbs of seedy cake from the folds of his pendulous waistcoat. "The police may be baffled, Inspector," he boomed, "but Merridew is not. It's all a question of a little research and a little ratiocination. Thirty years ago, the murderer, Doctor Grayson, was a distinguished member of the Ballets Russes, dancing under the name of Oleg Graysinski. The years may have altered his appearance, but his old skill had not deserted him. He carried the body out to the center of the tennis court, walking on his points along the white tape which divides the service boxes. From there he threw it five feet into the court, towards the base line, where it was found, and then, with a neatly executed fouetté, faced about and returned the way he had come, thus leaving no traces. There, Inspector, that is Merridew's solution."

(*He picks up his drink*)

Splendid! Absolutely splendid! Merridew loses none of his cunning, I'm glad to say. He's as neat *and* as gaudy as ever he was.

(*The doorbell rings.* **Andrew** *finishes his drink slowly, then exits to hallway*)

Andrew: (*Offstage in hall*) Oh hullo. Good evening, Milo Tindle, is it?

Milo: (*Offstage in hall*) Yes. Mr. Wyke?

Andrew: Yes. Do come in, won't you?

Milo: Thank you.

(*The front door is heard to close.* **Andrew** *walks back into the room, followed by* **Milo Tindle.** *He is about thirty-five, slim, dark-haired and of medium height. He has a sharp, sallow face alive with a faintly Mediterranean wariness. Everything about him is neat, from his exactly parted hair to the squared-off white handkerchief in the breast pocket of his blue mohair suit*)

Andrew: Let me take your coat. (*He hangs coat on coat rack*) Did you find the entrance to the lane all right?

Milo: Yes. (*He walks about surveying room*)

Andrew: Well done. Most people go straight past it. It's very nice of you to come.

Milo: Not at all. I found your note when I got down from London this afternoon.

Andrew: Oh good. I pushed it through your letter box.

Milo: Er . . . What's this? (*He indicates the figure of the Laughing Sailor*)

Andrew: Oh that's Jolly Jack Tar the Jovial Sailor. He and I have a very good relationship. I make the jokes and he laughs at them. (*He moves the sailor's head manually*) You see, ha-ha-ha! Now let me get you a drink. (*He crosses to drinks table*) What will you have? Scotch, gin, vodka?

Milo: Scotch.

Andrew: How do you like it? Soda, water, ice?

Milo: Just ice. And what's this?

(**Milo** *has crossed to a table on which there is a large game*)

Andrew: Oh, that's a game.

Milo: A child's game. (*He picks up one of the pieces*)

Andrew: It's anything but childish, I can assure you. I've been studying it for months, and I'm still only a novice. It's called Senat, played by the ancient Egyptians. It's an early blocking game, not unlike our own Nine Men Morris. Would you mind putting that back where you found it? It's taken me a long time to get it there. How are you settling in at Laundry Cottage?

Milo: Very well.

Andrew: Using it for weekends, that sort of thing?

Milo: Yes, that's the sort of thing.

Andrew: It's a charming little place. Well, cheers.

Milo: Cheers.

Andrew: Now do come and sit down. Forgive me if I just tidy up a bit. I've just reached the denouement of my new book, "The Body on the Tennis Court." Tell me, would you agree that the detective story is the normal recreation of noble minds?

Milo: Who said that?

Andrew: Oh, I'm quoting Philip Guedalla. A biographer of the thirties. The golden age when every cabinet minister had a thriller by his bedside, and all the detectives were titled. Before your time, I expect.

Milo: Perhaps it would have been truer to say that noble minds were the normal recreation of detective story writers.

Andrew: Yes. Good point. You know, even in these days I still set my own work among the gentry. And a great number of people enjoy it, in spite of the Welfare State.

Milo: I'm surprised they haven't done any of your stuff on television.

Andrew: Oh, God forbid.

Milo: Well, they're always doing crime stories.

Andrew: What—you mean those ghastly things where the police race around in cars and call all the suspects chummy?

Milo: Yes. That's the kind of thing.

Andrew: Oh no. That's not my line of country at all. That is detective fact, not detective fiction.

Milo: And of course as such is of much less interest to noble minds.

Andrew: Yes, yes, you've put it in a nutshell, my dear Milo, if I may so address you?

Milo: Of course.

Andrew: Thank you, we need to be friendly. Now do sit down and let me get you another drink. I'm one up on you already. (**Milo** *starts to sit in chair below staircase.* **Andrew** *moves to drinks table*) I understand you want to marry my wife. (*A pause.* **Milo** *is disconcerted by the directness of the question*) You'll forgive me raising the matter, but as Marguerite is away for a few days, she's up in the North you know, visiting some relatives.

Milo: Is she?

Andrew: Yes, so I thought it an appropriate time for a little chat.

Milo: Yes.

Andrew: Well, is it true?

Milo: Well . . . Well, yes, with your permission of course.

Andrew: Oh, yes, of course. (*He crosses to* **Milo** *with his drink*) Zere, put zat behind your necktie.

Milo: Cheers.

Andrew: Prost. (*He stands in front of fireplace*) Yes, I'm glad to see you're not like so many young men these days, seem to think they can do anything they like without asking anyone's permission.

Milo: Certainly not.

Andrew: Good. I'm pleased to hear it. I know you won't object then if I ask you a few questions about your parents and so on.

Milo: My mother was born in Hereford, a farmer's daughter. My father is an Italian who came to this country in the thirties.

Andrew: Jewish?

Milo: Half, on his mother's side, that for the Fascists was the important side. The male, they felt, didn't transmit the disease so virulently.

Andrew: (*Tut-tutting*) Dreadful business, dreadful.

Milo: Of course I'm not at all religious myself. I'm an agnostic.

Andrew: (*Crosses to center of room*) My dear boy, you don't have to explain to me. We're all liberals here. I have no prejudice against Jews, or even half-Jews. Why some of my best friends are half-Jews . . . Mind you, I hope you have no objections to any children that you and my wife may have being brought up Church of England?

Milo: None whatsoever if that's what Marguerite wants.

Andrew: You haven't discussed it yet?

Milo: Not yet, it doesn't seem to have cropped up.

Andrew: Well, I suppose in some ways that's rather a relief. But if you take my advice, you'll opt for the Established Church. It's so much simpler. A couple of hours on Christmas Eve and Good Friday and you've seen the whole thing off nicely. And if you throw in Remembrance Sunday, they give you the Good Christian medal with oak leaf cluster.

Milo: It's the same with a lot of Jews. My father used to say, "Most people only talk to their really old friends two or three times a year. Why should God be angry if He gets the same treatment?"

Andrew: (*Insincerely*) Very amusing. Your father? Was his name Tindle? It doesn't sound very Italian.

Milo: His name was Tindolini. But if you had a name like that in England in those days, you had to make a-da-nice cream. He was a watchmaker and so he changed it.

Andrew: Was he a successful man?

Milo: No. His business failed. He went back to Italy. I send him money from time to time and go and visit him and get a little sun or skiing, depending, of course, on the season.

Andrew: Ah!

Milo: It's not that I'm disloyal to Britain, you understand. It's just that the Scottish Highlands and Brighton don't offer the same attractions.

Andrew: And you? What do you do?

Milo: I'm in the travel business. I have my own agency in Dulwich.

Andrew: Tindle's Travels, eh? I see, and where do you live?

Milo: I live above the office.

Andrew: In Dulwich?

Milo: Yes, I rent the whole house. It's really most convenient, and . . . and it's most attractive, too. It's Georgian.

Andrew: H'm, I'm sure it's perfectly delightful, but I doubt whether an eighteenth-century architectural gem in Dulwich whispers quite the same magic to Marguerite as it does to you.

Milo: She adores old houses. She can't wait to live there.

Andrew: I understood she was already living there—at least for a couple of nights a week. I'm not mistaken, am I? (**Milo** *shrugs in embarrassment*) And surely your motive in renting the cottage down here was to increase the incidence of this hebdomadal coupling?

Milo: I came to be near the woman I love. It is a great pain for us to be apart. You wouldn't understand.

Andrew: Possibly. But I understand Marguerite well enough to know that she does not adore old houses. She's lived here quite a time, and between them the rising damp and the deathwatch beetle have put the boot into her good and proper. She's only got to see a mullioned window and it brings her out in lumps.

Milo: (*Hotly*) Perhaps it wasn't the house so much as the person she had to share it with.

Andrew: Now, now. I thought you were well brought up. Surely you know it's very rude to make personal remarks.

Milo: I'm sorry. You were disparaging my lover.

Andrew: On the contrary, I was reminiscing about my wife.

Milo: It comes to the same thing.

Andrew: Things mostly do, you know. I'll wager that within a year, it's *you* who will be doing the disparaging, and *I* who will be doing the rhapsodizing, having quite forgotten how intolerably tiresome, vain, spendthrift, self-indulgent and generally bloody crafty she really is.

Milo: If you don't love Marguerite, you don't have to abuse her.

Andrew: Never speak ill of the deadly, eh?

Milo: Now look here . . .

Andrew: If I choose to say that my wife converses like a child of six, cooks like a Brightlingsea landlady, and makes love like a coelacanth, I shall.

Milo: That's just about enough . . .

Andrew: And I certainly don't need her lover's permission to do so either. In fact, the only thing I need to know from you is, can you afford to take her off my hands?

Milo: Afford to . . .

Andrew: Afford to support her in the style to which she wasn't accustomed before she met me, but now is.

Milo: (*Gestures around the room*) She won't need all this when we're married. It'll be a different life—a life of love and simplicity. Now go ahead—sneer at that. It's almost a national sport in this country—sneering at love.

Andrew: I don't have to sneer at it. I simply don't believe you. For Marguerite, love is the fawning of a willing lap dog, and simplicity a square cut ten-carat diamond from Van Cleef and Arpels.

(**Milo** *rises to his feet, and moves to drinks table to put down glass*)

Milo: I don't know what I'm doing here. With a little effort I'm sure you could find a much more appreciative audience.

Andrew: Oh now, Milo. You disappoint me. Rising to your feet like that and *bridling*.

Milo: (*Abashed*) I wasn't bridling. I was protesting.

Andrew: It looked like a good old-fashioned Hedy Lamarr bridle to me.

Milo: (*Turning to* **Andrew**) Who?

Andrew: Oh, very good! Very good! Why don't you just sit down and we'll talk about something that matters desperately to both of us.

Milo: Marguerite?

Andrew: Money! Have you got any?

Milo: Well I'm not a millionaire, but I've got the lease on the house and some capital equipment, and the turnover in the business this year has been growing every month. By this time next year I . . .

Andrew: This year, next year, sometime never. What you're saying in fact is that at present you're skint.

Milo: I'll survive.

Andrew: I'm sure you will, but survival is not the point. Presumably when you're married to Marguerite you'll want a fast car, a little place in the sun, and a couple of mistresses.

Milo: Why "presumably"? Just because you need those things.

Andrew: Certainly I do. And so does every right-thinking, insecure, deceitful man. The point is how to get them. (*He moves to drinks table*)

Milo: I'm sure you do all right. (*He crosses to fireplace*)

Andrew: Me? Oh NO. Just this fading mansion, the slowest Bentley in Wiltshire, and only one mistress, I'm afraid.

Milo: Tēa? The Finnish lady who runs the sauna bath at Swindon.

Andrew: Oh, so you know about her, do you?

Milo: Marguerite and I have no secrets from each other.

Andrew: Not even mine, it seems. (*Mock mystical*) Tēa is a Karelian Goddess. Her mother was Ilma, supreme divinity of the air; her father was Jumala, the great Creator. Her golden hair smells of pine, and her cobalt eyes are the secret forest pools of Finlandia.

Milo: I hear she's a scrubbed blonde with all the sex appeal of chilled Lysol.

Andrew: (*With dignity*) There are those who believe that cleanliness is next to sexiness. And if I were you, I wouldn't pay much attention to what Marguerite says. You can take it from me that Tēa's an engaging little trollop, and she suits me mightily. Mind you, she takes a bit of keeping up with; it's a good thing I'm pretty much of an Olympic sexual athlete.

Milo: I suppose these days you're concentrating on the sprints rather than the long distance stuff.

Andrew: Not so, dear boy. (*He sits*) I'm in the pink of condition. I could copulate for England at any distance.

Milo: Well, they do say in Olympic circles, that the point is to take part, rather than to win, so I suppose there's hope for us all. Are you going to marry her?

Andrew: Marry a goddess? I wouldn't presume. I might get turned into a birch tree for my audacity. Oh, no, I simply want to live with her.

Milo: So what's stopping you?

Andrew: Basically the firm of Prurient and Pry Ltd., whom you and Marguerite have seen fit to employ. Don't look so innocent. Those nicotine-stained private detectives who've been camping outside Tēa's flat for the last week.

Milo: (*Crossing to center of room*) So you spotted them?

Andrew: A Bantu with glaucoma couldn't have missed them. No one can read the *Evening News* for four hours in a Messerschmitt bubble car, and expect to remain undetected.

Milo: Sorry about that. It was Marguerite's idea.

Andrew: Who else's? Who paid?

Milo: I did.

Andrew: I wonder you could afford it.

Milo: It was an insurance policy against you changing your mind about divorcing Marguerite.

Andrew: My dear boy, let us have no misunderstanding. I've nothing against you marrying Marguerite. There's nothing I want more than to see you two tucked up together. But it's got to be a fixture. I want to be rid of her for life, not just a two-week Tindle Tour, economy class. No, you listen to me. You don't know her like I do. You think you do, but you don't. The real truth of the matter is that if you fail her, by which I mean canceling the account at Harrods, or shortchanging her on winter in Jamaica, she'll be back to me in a jiffy, mewing for support—and guilty wife or no, she may be entitled to get it.

Milo: Don't be so bloody pathetic. Winter in Jamaica? I'm not going to take her for winter in Jamaica. You're worrying unnecessarily. Once Marguerite is married to me she'll never think of returning to you. Never. And don't worry about my being able to look after her either.

Andrew: I see. You mean that as soon as you and she are married, Marguerite will joyously substitute plain water in the bath for her customary asses milk?

Milo: So she's used to luxury. Whose fault is that?

Andrew: It's not a fault if you can afford it. But can you? Knowing you to be hard up has she shown any sign of mending her ways in these last idyllic three months? Come on now, let's get down to the good guts of the matter. When did she last turn down Bolinger for the blandishments of Babycham? Or reject crêpes suzette in favor of roly-poly? No, no, I'm not joking, how much has this brief liaison cost you so far? Five hundred pounds? eight hundred, a thousand? And that father of yours in Italy, when did you last send him any money? You see why I'm concerned. I tell you. She'll ruin you. To coin a phrase, in two years you'll be a used gourd. And what's more, a used gourd with a sizable overdraft.

Milo: We've often talked about money. I've told her we spend too much.

Andrew: And she takes no notice?

Milo: (*Low*) None.

Andrew: A silvery laugh? A coquettish turn of the head?

Milo: Something like that.

Andrew: Exactly. Well, it's to solve this little problem that I have invited you here tonight. This, as they say, is where the plot thickens.

Milo: Ah!

Andrew: I'll get you another drink. (*He crosses to drinks table. In "Listen with Mother" style:*) Are you sitting comfortably? Then I'll begin. Once upon a time there was an Englishman called Andrew Wyke who, in common with most of his countrymen, was virtually castrated by taxation. To avoid total emasculation, his accountants advised him, just before the last devaluation, to put a considerable part of his money, some 135,000 pounds, into jewelry. His wife, of course, was delighted.

Milo: You made her a present of it?

Andrew: Absolutely not. It's still mine, as well she knows. But we felt she might as well wear it, as bank it. After all, it's fully insured.

Milo: I see what you mean by the plot thickening. It usually does when insurance is mentioned.

Andrew: I'm glad you follow me so readily. I want you to steal that jewelry.

Milo: (*Astounded*) What?

Andrew: Tonight, for choice. Marguerite is out of the house. It's an admirable opportunity.

Milo: You must be joking.

Andrew: You would know it if I were.

Milo: (*Playing for time*) But . . . But what about the servants?

Andrew: I've sent Mr. and Mrs. Hawkins to the seaside for a forty-eight-hour paddle. They won't be back till Sunday night. So, the house is empty.

Milo: I see.

Andrew: What do you say?

Milo: It sounds criminal.

Andrew: Of course it's criminal. All good money-making schemes in England have *got* to be these days. The jewelry, when it's not in the bank, lives in the safe under the stairs. It's there now. All you have to do is steal them, and sell them abroad and live happily ever after with Marguerite. All I have to do is to claim the insurance money and live happily ever after with Têa. (*Pause*) Well, in my case perhaps, not ever after, but at least until I get fed up with a cuisine based on the elk.

Milo: Is that what you asked me over to hear? A scummy little plot to defraud the insurance company?

Andrew: I'm sorry you find the plot scummy. I thought it was nicely clear and simple.

Milo: Nicely obvious and clearly unworkable. Supposing I do as you say and take the jewels. If I sell them under my own name, I'll be picked up just as soon as you report their loss. If I sell them to a fence, always supposing I could find one, I'd get a fraction of their value.

Andrew: Not with the fences I know.

Milo: (*Derisory*) What fences would you know?

Andrew: I know some of the finest fences in Europe. Prudent yet prodigal. I met them some years ago while researching "The Deadly Affair of the Druce Diamond."

Milo: Never read it.

Andrew: Pity, it was an absolute fizzer—sold a hundred-thousand copies. Anyway on your behalf I have already contacted a certain gentleman in Amsterdam. He will treat you very well; you won't get full value of the jewels but you will get two-thirds, say ninety-thousand pounds, and you'll get it in cash.

Milo: Why should this man be so generous?

Andrew: Because he will have what fences never have—title to the jewels. I will see to it that in addition to the jewels, you also steal the receipts I got for them. All you have to do is hand them over together. Now what does my insurance company discover when it swings into action, antennae pulsing with suspicion? It discovers that someone impersonating Andrew Wyke sold the jewels for ninety-thousand pounds cash. They've still got to pay me. Hard cheese. Think it over. Take your time. There's no hurry.

(*A pause.* **Milo** *considers the proposition.* **Andrew** *walks away from* **Milo***, humming lightly to himself. He stops by a roll-a-penny wall game and plays it to a successful conclusion.* **Milo** *paces up and down, indecisive. He suddenly turns and faces* **Andrew**)

Milo: Look, I know this sounds stupid, but . . . but well, have you had any experience—I mean, have you ever actually committed a crime before?

Andrew: Only in the mind's eye, so to speak. For the purpose of my books. St. John Lord Merridew would have a pretty lean time of it if I didn't give him any crime to solve.

Milo: Who?

Andrew: My detective, St. John Lord Merridew. Known to millions all over the civilized world. "An ambulatory tun of port with the face of Father Christmas." That's how I describe him. "A classical scholar with a taste for good pipes and bad puns, but with a nose for smelling out evil, superior to anything in the force."

Milo: Oh, yes, the police are always stupid in your kind of story, aren't they? They never solve anything. Only an amateur sleuth ever knows what's happening. But that is detective fiction. This is fact.

Andrew: I am aware of the difference, Milo. I also know that insurance investigators are sharp as razors, and that's why, as Queen Victoria said to Lord Melbourne on the occasion of her coronation, everything's got to be done kosher and according to cocker.

Milo: I'm just saying there's a difference between writing and real life, that's all. And there's another thing. How do I know this thing isn't one big frame-up?

Andrew: Frame-up?

Milo: Yes. That you really hate my association with your wife, and would give five years of Olympian sexual athleticism to see me in jail. Once I'm clear of the house, an anonymous phone call to the police . . . .

Andrew: And be stuck with Marguerite for another bickering eternity? Bodystockings on the breakfast tray, false eyelashes in the washbasin, the bottles, the lo-tions, the unguents, the oils, the tribal record player and that ceaseless vapid yak. Oh yes, I could shop you to the police, nothing easier, but whatever for. Still, it's for you to evaluate, old boy.

Milo: Well, I . . . I, er . . .

Andrew: If you don't trust me . . .

Milo: Oh, I trust you, but . . .

Andrew: It's a very simple proposition. You have an expensive woman and no money. It seems to me if you want to keep Marguerite, there is only one thing you can do—you must steal those jewels.

Milo: Why don't *you* steal them and simply hand them over to me?

Andrew: I should have thought that was obvious. The burglary has to look real. The house has actually to be broken into.

Milo: Well, why don't *you* break into it?

Andrew: (*Brooklyn accent*) Hey, Milo baby, will you do me a favor. Leave this to me, huh? You know what I mean? Crime is my specialty. I've got such a great plan and I've got it all worked out to the last detail. You're the star, I'm just the producer.

Milo: Ninety-thousand pounds?

Andrew: Ninety-thousand pounds tax free. In cash. It would take a lot of Tindle Tours to make that kind of money.

Milo: All right, I'll do it. Where shall I break in? (*He rushes for the stairs*)

Andrew: Hold your horses. Now the first thing you've got to do is disguise yourself.

Milo: What on earth for?

Andrew: Supposing someone saw you climbing in?

Milo: Who? You're not overlooked.

Andrew: Who knows? A dallying couple. A passing sheep rapist. And, dear boy, remember the clues we're to leave for the police and the insurance company. We don't want your footsteps in the flower beds, or your coat button snagged on the window sill. Oh no, you must be disguised.

Milo: All right, what do you suggest?

Andrew: (*He crosses to corridor and brings back a large hamper*) As Marguerite has assuredly told you, in younger days we were always dressing up in this house. What with amateur dramatics and masquerades and costume balls, there was virtually no end to the concealment of identity.

Milo: She's never mentioned it.

Andrew: No . . .? (*A touch wistful*) Well, it was all some years ago. (*Briskly*) Anyway, let's see what we've got. (*He opens basket and holds up the pieces of the burglar suit, one by one*) Item. A face mask, a flat cap, a striped jersey and bag marked Loot.

Milo: I thought the idea was that I was *not* to be taken as a burglar.

Andrew: Fashions have changed, you know.

Milo: Not quickly enough. It's asking for trouble.

(**Andrew** *puts the costume back and brings out a Ku Klux Klan outfit*)

Andrew: Ku Klux Klan invade country home. Fiery cross, flames on Salisbury plain. Police baffled.

Milo: Isn't it a trifle conspicuous for Wiltshire?

Andrew: Yes, you may be right! (*He holds up a monk's costume*) Here is one of my favorites. How about Brother Lightfingers?

Milo: Oh, for God's sake . . . (*He shakes his head decisively*)

Andrew: Oh, come on. Let's make this a Gothic folly. (*Edgar Lustgarten voice*) Perhaps we shall never know the identity of the cowled figure seen haunting the grounds of the Manor House on the night of the terrible murder. Even today, some locals claim to hear the agonized screams of the victim echoing around the chimney pots.

Milo: Murder? Anguished screams of the victim? What are you talking about? It's a simple robbery we're staging here, that's all.

(*An uneasy pause*)

Andrew: (*Normal voice*) Quite right, Milo. I was carried away for a moment. I'm not sure I wasn't going to add a crucified countess entombed in her bedroom, guarded by a man-eating sparrow hawk.

Milo: Look here, Andrew, you probably think this is one huge joke. But it's my freedom you're playing with.

Andrew: I'm merely trying to bring a little romance into modern crime, and incidentally into your life.

Milo: Marguerite will bring all the romance into my life I need, thank you all the same.

Andrew: Marguerite romantic? Marguerite couldn't have got Johann Strauss to waltz.

Milo: Look, Andrew, these are great costumes, but haven't you just got an old pair of wellies, a raincoat, and a sock that I can pull over my head?

Andrew: Old pair of wellies and a sock? How dreary! That's the whole trouble with crime today. No imagination. I mean, you tell me, does your heart beat any faster when you hear that a truck load of cigarettes has been knocked off in the Walworth Road?

Milo: Not particularly.

Andrew: Well of course not. Or that a ninety-three-year-old night watchman has had his silly interfering old skull split open with a lead pipe?

Milo: Of course not.

Andrew: Well, then, what's the matter with you? Where's your spunk? Let's give our crime the true sparkle of the thirties, a little amateur aristocratic quirkiness. Think of all that wonderful material. There's the ice dagger, the poison that leaves no trace, the Regie cigarette stubbed in the ash tray, charred violet notepaper in the grate, Dusenberg tire marks in the driveway, the gramophone record simulating conversation, the clutching hand from behind the arras, sinister Orientals, twin brothers from Australia—"Hi there, cobber, hi there, blue"—where were you on the night of the thirteenth? I swear I didn't do it, Inspector, I'm innocent I tell you, innocent . . .

Milo: God, you've gone off like a firecracker!

Andrew: And why not? We're on the brink of a great crime. Don't you feel the need to give your old archenemy Inspector Plodder of the Yard a run for his money? And you're the star, you're the who-what-dun-it!

Milo: Well what about this? (*He holds up courtier's costume*)

Andrew: Ah! Monsieur Beaucaire. He's very good. Lots of beauty spots and wig powder to let fall all over the place. Or what about this? Little Bo Peep?

(**Andrew** *sings Little Bo Peep and dances about holding up the costume*)

Milo: No.

Andrew: Why not?

Milo: I haven't got the figure for it.

Andrew: Are you quite sure? An indifferent figure shouldn't materially affect the execution of this crime.

Milo: Quite sure.

Andrew: Well, you are choosy, aren't you? There's not a great deal left. (*He pulls out a clown's costume. Large pantaloons, waiter's dicky, tail coat*) We'll have to settle for "Joey."

Milo: Wow!

Andrew: Can't you see it all, the tinsel, the glitter, the lights, the liberty horses, the roar of the crowd, and Milo all the kiddies love you.

Milo: (*Happily*) All right! It seems the costume most appropriate to this scheme.

Andrew: Well, give me your coat. I'll hang it up for you. We don't want the police to find any fibers of this beautiful suit. (**Milo** *takes off his jacket and gives it to* **Andrew**) Oh, and the shirt and trousers too.

Milo: What?

Andrew: Oh, yes, you know how clever they are in those laboratories of theirs. That's it. Don't be shy. Into your smalls. Oh, I know a well-brought-up boy when I see one. Folds his pants at night.

(**Milo** *gives him his carefully folded trousers.* **Andrew** *runs up the stairs, and with a sudden violent gesture, roughly throws the suit into the wardrobe, while* **Milo** *takes off his shirt and tie and shoes*)

Milo: Shirt and shoes. (**Milo** *holds up his shirt, shoes and tie*)

Andrew: Very good, sir. The Quick Clean Valet Service always at your disposal, sir. (*He pushes them into the wardrobe, then watches* **Milo** *changing with great satisfaction. Softly*) Give a clown your finger and he'll take your hand.

Milo: What was that?

Andrew: Just an old English proverb I was thinking of.

(**Milo** *sings to himself "On With The Motley" and ends it with "Ninety-thousand pounds tax free, in cash" as he dresses*)

Milo: Ecco, Milo!

Andrew: Bravissimo! Now all you need are the boots.

(**Milo** *pulls a huge pair of boots from the basket*)

Milo: Hey, I could go skiing on these when I go to Italy.

Andrew:
"The clown is such a happy chap,
His nose is painted red,
His trousers baggy as can be,
A topper on his head.
He jumps around the circus ring,
And juggles for his bread,
Then comes the day he tries a trick,
And drops down . . ."
Come on do us a trick.

Milo: What sort of trick?

Andrew: Oh, I don't know. Trip up—fall on your arse.

Milo: Certainly not, I don't think that's a very good idea.

Andrew: Well, what about a bit of juggling then.

(**Andrew** *takes two oranges from the drinks table and throws them to* **Milo**. *He then produces an umbrella from the basket and throws it to* **Milo** *who opens it and runs about the room and finally trips up on his boots*)

Milo: Christ!

Andrew: Sorry, dear boy. But you know the rule of the circus. If at first you don't succeed . . .

Milo: Give up. Can we get on with this charade, please!

Andrew: Of course. Yours to command. (*He opens swag bag*) Here are the tools of your trade. One glass cutter to break in with; a piece of putty for holding on to the cut piece of glass so it doesn't clatter onto the floor and awake the ravenous Doberman pinscher you suspect lurks inside; and a stethoscope.

Milo: A stethoscope?

Andrew: Safe breakers for the use of. The theory is you tried to pick the lock by listening to the tumblers, failed, and then employed gelignite.

Milo: (*Alarmed*) Gelignite?

Andrew: Yes. Leave that to me. Now how about some bizarre touch—say a signed photograph of Grock left impaled on a splinter of glass.

Milo: A signed photograph of Grock. (*Angry*) Why don't you take a full page ad in *The Times* and tell them what we're doing.

Andrew: I was only trying to lighten Inspector Plodder's day for him . . . If you don't like the idea . . .

Milo: (*Earnestly*) There's no such animal as Inspector Plodder outside of books. It'll be Inspector Early Bird, or Superintendent No Stone Unturned. You can bet your bottom dollar on that and I can't walk in this costume. These boots are ridiculous. (*He stumbles and starts to take them off*)

Andrew: Keep them on. Can't you see it all. Wiltshire paralyzed. The West Country in a ferment. Where will Big Boot strike next?

Milo: But . . .

Andrew: (*Reasonably*) All these boots will tell the police is that a true professional realized the flower beds would carry footprints, and decided to disguise his own perhaps a trifle eccentrically. Now are you ready? Got everything? Glass cutter? Putty?

Andrew: ⎫
Milo: ⎭ The mask!

(**Andrew** *takes top hat and mask from basket.* **Milo** *puts them on*)

Andrew: Good. Now go through that door, round the house and across the lawn. To your right you will discover a shed. In it is a ladder. Bring the ladder back and stand it against the house so you can break in at the gallery.

Milo: Will you come out and hold it steady?

Andrew: Certainly not. I don't want *my* footprints in the flowerbeds.

Milo: I'm not very good at heights.

Andrew: Improvise. Place one foot above the other. It's called climbing.

Milo: OK.

Andrew: Good luck.

(**Milo** *bows and goes through the hall door.* **Andrew** *takes a length of flex and black box with gelignite, black tape and detonator from desk drawer. After a few minutes* **Milo** *appears at window*)

Andrew: For Christ's sake can't you keep those bloody boots off my Busy Lizzies. (**Milo** *disappears and presently reappears with the ladder which he places against the window and starts to climb.* **Andrew** *sits with his back to the window and reacts to the noises he hears. As he attaches the detonator to the flex he speaks in an old woman's voice*) Puss, Puss, Puss, do you hear a noise, Puss! Was that a step on the stairs. No, it was just the wind. You know, Puss, I sometimes think there's a curse on this house. But you shouldn't pay any attention to me. I'm just a silly old woman who is afraid of her own shadow. (*Noise of glass cutter scoring window*) What was that, Puss? Someone's prowling in the grounds. We're all going to be murdered in our beds. No, no, the front door's locked, and the window's too high, no one can get into our snug little home.

(**Milo** *drops pane of glass*)

Andrew: (*Exasperated*) What *are* you doing now?

Milo: I dropped the glass. (**Andrew** *groans theatrically. After a further struggle,* **Milo** *succeeds in climbing in through the window, onto the gallery*) Whew! What do I do with the putty? (*He indicates the putty*)

Andrew: Stick it on the wall.

Milo: I can lose this at any rate. (*He puts mask on bureau*) Now for the safe!

Andrew: No. Not straight away. You're not meant to know where they are. Search around. Go into the bedroom. Disturb a few things. Throw some clothes on the floor—Marguerite's for choice . . . That's it.

(**Milo** *goes into the bedroom and returns with a pile of women's clothes which he puts neatly on the floor*)

Andrew: (*Rushes up to gallery*) Don't pack 'em. Ravage 'em. Don't you know how burglars leave a place? (*He takes a flying kick at the pile of his wife's clothes—sending them flying all over the room*) Now try the wardrobe. Rumple the contents a little. Actually that's enough. Those shirts were made for me by Baget and Grub, chemise makers to monarchs.

Milo: (*Throws the shirts out with relish*) Got to be thorough. It would be suspicious if the burglar played favorites.

(**Andrew's** *socks and underwear follow, cascading out all over the gallery*)

Andrew: Oh, it's a martyrdom. (*Shouting*) Will you stop that, Milo, and rifle that bureau immediately.

(*Reluctantly* **Milo** *crosses to the bureau and tries a drawer*)

Milo: It's locked.

Andrew: Of course it's bloody locked! Use your jimmy on it.

Milo: I haven't got a jimmy. You didn't give me one.

Andrew: (*Exasperated*) Well, we'd better go and find one, hadn't we? (They tramp downstairs) Honestly, Milo, you are the soppiest night interloper I've ever met. I can't think what Marguerite sees in you.

Milo: The sympathy and kindness of a kindred spirit, actually.

Andrew: It's like a Bengali tiger lying down with a bush baby.

Milo: I know we're a damn sight happier than you are with your ice maiden.

Andrew: You probably take it more seriously, that's all.

Milo: You have to be serious if you want to be in love.

Andrew: You have to be serious about crime if you want to afford to be in love. Now get cracking on that bureau.

(**Milo** *climbs the stairs. He starts work on the bureau with the jimmy. After a pause the drawer yields and he opens it*)

Milo: There is a set of false teeth. They look like a man's.

Andrew: (*Furious*) Put them back at once.

Milo: Sorry. Your spares?

Andrew: (*Pause*) Come down at once. (Milo comes down the stairs and crosses to Andrew who has plugged the flex into a light switch) Keep your feet off the flex.

Right, stand by for count down five—four—three—two—one. Contact!
(*Noise of explosion and puff of smoke from safe*)

Milo: There she blows. Ah! It's hot.

Andrew: You've got gloves on! Get in there! (**Milo** *rummages in the safe and finds a large jewel box. He examines it carefully, occasionally shaking it gently*) What the hell are you shaking it for? It's a jewel box, not a maraca.

Milo: I thought it might have some secret catch on it. It's locked, you see.

Andrew: Well, smash it open. Jesus! You've all the killer instinct of a twenty-year-old Sealyham.

(**Milo** *attacks the box with his jimmy*)

Milo: It's such a pretty box—it seems such a waste. (*The box opens to reveal its precious contents.* **Milo** *stands entranced, letting the jewels flash and sparkle through his fingers*) Dear God!

Andrew: Ah! Moses looks upon the promised land.

Milo: (*Sits at base of stairs*) They're very beautiful. Look at this ruby necklace.

Andrew: That we got on our honeymoon.

Milo: It's fantastic.

Andrew: I never cared for it myself. I always thought it made Marguerite look like a blood sacrifice.

Milo: I'd like my father to be here now. Poor blighter, he had no idea what it was all about . . . sitting there every night, hunched up over those watches like a little old gnome, squinting his eyesight away, and for what—to give me an education at a second-rate prep school. I suppose he thought he had to do it—that he owed it to me and the brave new Anglo-Saxon world he'd adopted. Poor old bugger.

Andrew: Here, put them in your pocket for a start. I'll get you the receipts in a moment. Now! This is the fun bit. It's the moment when the householder, his attention attracted by the noise of the explosion, surprises his burglar. In the ensuing struggle, the house is sacked.

Milo: Why is it necessary for you to surprise me at all?

Andrew: Because if I've seen you at close quarters, I can always describe you to the police . . .

(**Milo** *reacts as if hit*)

Milo: Now look here . . .

Andrew: . . . wrongly. (**Inspector's** *voice*) Did you manage to get a good look at the intruder's face, sir? (*Normal voice*) Yes, Inspector, I did. It may just have been a trick of the light, but his face didn't look wholly human. If you can imagine a kind of prognathic stoat, fringed about with lilac-colored hair, and seemingly covered with a sort of boot polish . . .

Milo: (*Patiently*) I understand. How much sacking do you want done?

Andrew: A decent bit, I think, a few chairs on their backs, some china ornaments put to the sword. You know—convincing but not Carthaginian. (**Milo** *carefully turns a chair over and leans a small table against the sofa. He takes a china ornament and stands it upright on the floor.* **Andrew** *watches impatiently*) Surely you don't call that convincing? (**Andrew** *throws over another table, spills the contents of a drawer, and turns books out of his bookcase*) That's better. Let the encyclopedias fly like autumn leaves. (**Milo** *throws papers in the air*) We'll let my assistant sort that lot out. You know I never liked Saltglaze. (*He drops a china ornament to the floor where it breaks*) I can't think why Marguerite is devoted to it. (*The two men survey the room*) It still doesn't look right. Come on. Let's see what accident does to artifice.

(**Andrew** *seizes* **Milo** *and wrestles him round the room, overturning things as they go.* **Milo**, *apart from being the shorter, is much hampered by his big boots and floppy clown's clothing, so that* **Andrew** *is able to pummel him severely*)

Milo: You're bigger than I am. It's not fair.

Andrew: Nonsense. You're the underdog, aren't you? You've got the support of the crowd.

Milo: A good big'un will always lick a good little'un.

Andrew: The bigger they are the harder they fall.

(**Milo** *receives a particularly hard blow*)

Milo: Here, steady on, old man!

Andrew: They never come back. (*He pushes* **Milo** *over the fender into the fireplace*)

Milo: Christ! That hurt!

(**Andrew** *helps him up*)

Andrew: Come on, back into the ring. Don't despair. This fight is fixed. It's about now that I take a dive. This is where you lay me out cold.

Milo: What? For real?

Andrew: Naturally. When the police come I must be able to show them a real bump. (**Milo** *smiles weakly*) I thought you'd like this bit.

Milo: (*Tentatively moving towards a lamp*) What shall I use?

Andrew: Not my opaline if you don't mind.

Milo: (*Picks up the brass poker*) This is it. The poker, the original blunt instrument. (*He beats logs viciously*)

Andrew: (*Eyes the poker apprehensively*) Steady on, Milo. Don't get carried away.

Milo: Well, I'm doing my best.

Andrew: We are not talking about a murder weapon. We are discussing an object from which I receive, in the classic formula, a glancing blow which renders me temporarily unconscious.

Milo: Such as?

Andrew: Well I don't know exactly. Why don't you use your imagination? Ask yourself what those fathers of the scientific detective story—R. Austin Freeman or Arthur B. Reeve—would have come up with.

Milo: Huh?

Andrew: You know—"The Red Thumb Mark," 1907. "The Silent Bullet," 1912. (**Milo** *still looks blank*) Oh, do try . . . I know, perhaps we could think of a device which will raise a lump but not damage the cranium.

Milo: (*Trapped into joining in*) How about a bee sting projected into the scalp with a blowpipe?

Andrew: Do you have such sting, pipe or bee?

Milo: Well . . . no.

Andrew: No. Still seven out of ten for trying. I know, you can always tie me up and gag me and leave me to be found by the cleaning woman. (*Charlady's voice*): Lawks, Mr. Wyke, what are doing all trussed up like a turkey cock? (*He mimes being tied up and gagged and trying to get the Charlady to untie him*) Mmmmmm mmmmmmm . . . Mmmmmmmmmmmm . . . Mmmmmmmmmmmm . . . (*Charlady's voice*): Trying out something for one of them creepy books of yours, are you, sir? Well, don't mind me. I won't disturb you. I'll just get on with the dusting.

Milo: (*Patiently*) If I don't knock you out, how do I manage to tie you up?

Andrew: (*Normal voice*) That's a very good question. I know. You could hold a gun on me.

Milo: We professional burglars don't like firearms much.

Andrew: But, as you're a rank amateur, you can conquer your scruples. (*He produces a gun from the desk drawer*) Here. How about this? Don't you think its wicked-looking blue barrel is just the thing.

Milo: Is it loaded?

Andrew: Naturally. What use would it be otherwise? Perhaps it should go off in the struggle.

Milo: Why?

Andrew: It would add credence to my story of your holding a gun on me. Hearing a noise and fearing burglars, I took my revolver and went to investigate. You attacked me. In the struggle it went off, blowing to smithereens several priceless heirlooms. Being an old fraidy cat householder, I allowed brutish you to take possession of it. You then held it on me while you tied me up. Right?

Milo: I suppose so.

Andrew: Uninventive but believable. Now then, what to sacrifice? What do you say to the demolition of that gaudy Swansea puzzle jug? The gloriously witty idea is that when you tip it up the liquid pours out of a hole in the back, and not through the spout.

Milo: A bit obvious, really.

Andrew: Exactly! Obvious and ugly. Let us expose its shortcomings. (*He draws a bead on it, then lowers the gun*) On the other hand, the crème brulé coloring lends it an attractive solidity I should miss. Now how about that giant Staffordshire mug with the inscription on it? What does it say?

Milo: (*Moves a little toward it and reads aloud*) "In the real cabinet of friendship everyone helped his neighbor and said to his brother, be of good cheer."

Andrew: Proletarian pomposity! (*He suddenly raises his gun and fires, shattering the jug.* **Milo** *turns in surprise, as he realizes the bullet must have passed reasonably close to his head*) You might have said good shot.

Milo: Good shot.

Andrew: (*Insouciant*) It's nothing. (*He looks around him. His eye falls on a china figurine poised on the banister rail above him. He takes aim*) Down with all imperialistic, deviationist, reactionary Dresden shepherdesses. (*He shoots and the Dresden shepherdess flies into pieces*)

Milo: Bravo!

Andrew: What fun this is! Did you ever know Charlie Begby?

Milo: I don't think so.

Andrew: Terribly funny fellow. I once saw him bag three brace of duck with one shot. The only trouble was they were china ducks on his auntie's drawing room wall. I said, "Oh Charlie, you can't do that, it's the closed season." (*He presses button on desk and the sailor laughs*) I told you he always laughs at my jokes. (**Milo** *laughs.* **Andrew's** *mood changes abruptly*) It's not really all that funny. There's an open season on some creatures all the year round. (*He turns the gun on* **Milo**) Seducers and wife stealers for example.

Milo: (*Nervous*) Only in Italian opera, surely.

Andrew: (*Hard*) You should know. It's your country of origin, is it not?

Milo: No. I was actually born here in England.

Andrew: Were you now. Dear old cradle-of-the-parliamentary-system-who-screws-my-wife-merits-a-large-pink-gin-England?

Milo: Sense-of-humor-fair-trial-England, I mean.

Andrew: That's the way a foreigner talks. In private he thinks, filthy wet country, ugly red cold men who don't know how to treat women.

Milo: What's brought all this on? What are you doing with that gun?

Andrew: Pretty obviously pointing it at you.

Milo: For God's sake, why?

Andrew: (*Slowly, Italian accent*) Because I'm going to kill you.

Milo: You're going to . . . (*Laughs nervously*) Oh Jesus! I suppose this is some sort of game.

Andrew: Yes. We've been playing it all evening. It's called "You're going to die and no-one will suspect murder."

(*A pause.* **Milo** *considers his position*)

Milo: You mean all this steal-my-wife's-jewels stuff was just a . . .

Andrew: Of course! I invited you here to set up the circumstances of your own death. The break in, the disguise, the jewels in your pocket, the householder aroused, the gun going off in the struggle and then the final fatal shot. I might even get a commendation from the police, for "having a go."

Milo: For God's sake, Andrew, knock it off!

Andrew: Can you find a flaw in it?

Milo: (*Beginning to feel desperate*) Marguerite! They'll trace the connection between me and Marguerite. They'll know that's why you did it.

Andrew: I am quite entitled to tackle a man wearing a mask, plundering my house in the middle of the night. How was I expected to know who you were. Oh no, the law will have every sympathy with me. Property has always been more highly regarded than people in England. Even Marguerite will assume you were just an adventurer who only loved her for her jewels—a petty sneak thief who found larceny less burdensome than marriage. You really are a dead duck, aren't you? Not a moral or romantic attitude left.

Milo: I believe you *are* serious.

Andrew: I'm not afraid of killing you, if that's what you mean.

Milo: You've got to be. Mortally afraid for your soul.

Andrew: I didn't think the Jews believed in hell.

Milo: We believe in not playing games with life.

Andrew: Ha! Wit in the face of adversity. You've learnt something from the English. All right, here's another thing. A sporting chance. Why don't you make a run for it?

Milo: And give you the chance to shoot me down in cold blood?

Andrew: Hot blood, you mean. I'm going to shoot you down in cold blood anyway.

(**Milo** *tries to run but falls over his boots*)

Milo: Look, stop pointing that gun at me . . . I hate guns . . . please . . . this is sick.

Andrew: You should be flattered by the honor I'm doing you—to take your life light-heartedly—to make your death the center piece of an arranged bit of fun. To put it another way, your demise will recreate a noble mind.

Milo: This is where I came in.

Andrew: And where you go out, I'm afraid. The only question to be decided is where the police shall find you. Sprawled over the desk like countless colonels in countless studies? Or propped up in the log basket like a rag doll? Which do you think? Early Agatha Christie or middle S. S. Van Dine?

Milo: For Christ's sake, Andrew, this is not a detective story, this is real life. You are talking of doing a real murder. Of killing a real man—don't you understand?

Andrew: Perhaps I shouldn't do it with a gun at all. Perhaps I should shove the ham knife into you, and leave you face down in the middle of the room—(*Melo-dramatic voice*)—your blood staining the flagstones a deep carmine.

Milo: (*Shudders*) Oh God!

Andrew: Or best of all, how about a real 1930's murder weapon—the mashie niblick. I've got one in my golf bag. (*He fetches the golf club from the hall.* **Milo** *dives for the telephone but is too late*) You would be discovered in the fireplace, I think, in a fair old mess. (*Dramatic voice*) The body lay on its back, its limbs grotesquely splayed like a broken puppet. The whole head has been pulped as if by some superhuman force. "My God," breathed the Inspector, blanching. "Thompson, you'd better get a tarpaulin . . . Excuse me, sir, but was all this violence strictly necessary?" "I'm sorry, Inspector. It was when I saw him handling my wife's nightdresses. I must have completely lost control of myself." (**Andrew** *throws down the golf club*) No. I think the scene the police find is simply this. After the fight you flee up the stairs, back to your ladder. I catch you on the landing and in the renewed struggle I shoot you. Nothing succeeds like simplicity, don't you agree, Milo? Now then, some of my own fingerprints on my own revolver. (*He takes his glove off and holds the gun in his naked hand*) On your feet, up! (**Andrew** *forces* **Milo** *to mount the stairs by shoving the gun in his back.* **Milo** *gives a sudden spasmodic shudder*) Did you know that Charles I put on two shirts the morning of his execution? "If I tremble with cold," he said, "my enemies will say it was from fear; I will not expose myself to such reproaches." You must also attempt dignity as you mount the steps to the scaffold.

(**Milo** *demurs and sinks to his knees near the top step*)

Milo: (*Terrified and pleading*) But why, Andrew? Why?

Andrew: Don't snivel. You can't think it'll gain you mercy.

Milo: I must know why!

Andrew: I'm amazed you have to ask. But since you do, it's perfectly simple. I hate you. I hate your smarmy, good-looking Latin face and your easy manner. I'll bet you're easy in a ski lodge, and easy on a yacht, and easy on a beach. I'll bet you a pound to a penny that you wear a gold charm round your neck, and that your chest is hairy and in summer matted with sun oil. I hate you because you are a mock humble, jeweled, shot cufflinked sponger, world is my oyster-er, a seducer of silly women, and a king among marshmallow snakes. I hate you because you are a culling spick. A wop—a not one-of-me. Come, little man, did you really believe I would give up my wife and jewels to you? That I would make myself *that* ridiculous.

Milo: Why not? You're not in love with her.

Andrew: She's mine whether I love her or not. I found her, I've kept her. I am familiar with her. And once, she was in love with me.

Milo: And now she's in love with me, and the dog in the manger won't let go. (*He tries to attack him*) The mad dog in the manger who should be put down for everyone's sake.

Andrew: (*Deadly*) And you are a young man, dressed as a clown about to be murdered. Put the mask on, Milo. (*A pause*)

Milo: No, please.

(**Andrew** *reaches up and lifts the clown mask off the banister where* **Milo** *had previously hung it*)

Andrew: Put it on! (**Milo** *takes the mask and fumbles it onto his face*) Excellent. Farewell, Punchinello!

(**Andrew** *lifts the pistol to* **Milo's** *head.* **Milo** *is shaking with fear*)

Milo: (*High falsetto*) Please . . .

(**Andrew** *slowly pulls the trigger.* **Milo** *falls backwards down the stairs and lies still.* **Andrew** *walks past him, pausing to peer closely to see whether there is any sign of life. He lifts the lolling head and lets it thump back, carelessly, onto the stairs. Satisfied that he has done his work well, he straightens up, and smiles to himself*)

Andrew: Game and set, I believe.

SLOW CURTAIN

ACT TWO

Two days later.

The curtain rises to the sound of the slow movement of Beethoven's Seventh Symphony which is playing on a record player. **Andrew** *enters from kitchen with a tray containing a large pot of caviare, toast, wedge of lemon, a bottle of champagne and glass. He puts tray on desk and stands conducting the music. The movement comes to an end.* **Andrew** *crosses to record player and turns over the record. He returns to desk and starts to eat. The telephone rings.*

Andrew: Hullo . . . Yes, Hawkins, where are you? What? Well you should have checked the times of the trains . . . I've had to get my own supper for the third time running . . . Yes, yes, I daresay, but you know how helpless I am without you and Mrs. H. Man cannot live by baked beans alone, you know . . . All right . . . All right, tomorrow morning. But the first thing, mind you.

(**Andrew** *continues for some minutes. The front doorbell rings. After a slight pause* **Andrew** *goes to answer it*)

Doppler: (*Offstage, in hall*) Good evening, sir.

Andrew: (*Offstage*) Evening.

Doppler: Mr. Wyke.

Andrew: Yes.

Doppler: My name is Inspector Doppler, sir. Detective Inspector Doppler. Of the Wiltshire County Constabulary. I'm sorry to be calling so late. May I have a few words with you on a very important matter?

(**Andrew** *enters, followed by* **Inspector Doppler**, *a heavily built, tallish man of about fifty. His hair is balding, and he wears cheap, round spectacles on his fleshy nose, above a greying moustache. His clothes—dark rumpled suit, under a half-open light-colored mackintosh—occasion no surprise, nor does his porkpie hat*)

Andrew: The Wiltshire County Constabulary you say? (*Turning off music*) Come in. Always pleased to see the police.

Doppler: Can't say the same about everyone, sir. Most people seem to have what you might call an allergy to us.

Andrew: Would you join me in a brandy, Inspector? Or are you going to tell me you don't drink on duty?

Doppler: Oh, no, sir. I always drink on duty. I can't afford to in my own time. (*He sits down*)

Andrew: (*Handing the* **Inspector** *a brandy*) Well, what can I do for you, Inspector?

Doppler: I'm investigating a disappearance, sir.

Andrew: Disappearance?

Doppler: Yes, sir. Of a Mr. Milo Tindle. Do you know him, sir?

Andrew: Yes, that's the chap who's taken Laundry Cottage.

Doppler: He walked out of his cottage on Friday night and hasn't been seen since.

Andrew: Great Scott!

Doppler: Do you know this gentleman well, sir?

Andrew: Vaguely. He came to the house once or twice. How can I help you?

Doppler: When did you last see Mr. Tindle, sir?

Andrew: Oh, months ago. I can't exactly remember. As I told you, he wasn't a close friend; rather more an acquaintance.

Doppler: Really, sir? That doesn't quite accord with our information. In fact, he told Jack Benn, the licensee of the White Lion, he was coming to see you, two nights ago.

Andrew: Barmen are notorious opponents of exactitude, Inspector. Vinous gossip is their stock in trade. In particular, I've always found that Jack Benn's observations need constant correction.

Doppler: Really, sir? I was wondering if you could correct something else for me.

Andrew: What's that?

Doppler: The impression gained by a man who happened to be passing your house two nights ago, that a fierce struggle was taking place in here.

Andrew: Does it look like it?

Doppler: And that shots were fired?

Andrew: (*Uncertainly*) Shots?

Doppler: Three, our man thinks.

Andrew: A car backfiring?

Doppler: No, sir. These were shots. From a gun. Our man is positive.

Andrew: May I ask why you took two days to call round and ask me about all this?

Doppler: Well, sir, things take longer to check out than you think. We like to be certain of our facts before troubling a gentleman like yourself.

Andrew: Facts? What facts?

Doppler: After our informant reported the incident, we did a spot of checking in the village, and as I say, Mr. Benn was very helpful.

Andrew: There's an upright citizen, then.

Doppler: Quite so, sir.

Andrew: If there were more like him . . .

Doppler: He told us that Mr. Tindle popped into the pub Friday evening for a quick one, and said he was just on his way up to you. Well, what with him being a newcomer to these parts and all, we thought we'd better have a word with him, and see if he could throw any light on the subject. But as I previously indicated, he seems to have disappeared, sir.

Andrew: But what's that got to do with me?

Doppler: He wasn't at his cottage all of Saturday, nor all today. We must have called half a dozen times.

Andrew: By Jove, Merridew would have been proud of you. Now Inspector, if that's all you have to say . . .

Doppler: When we stepped inside Mr. Tindle's cottage to make sure he'd come to no harm, we found this note, sir. (*Reading*) "Urgent we talk. Come Friday night eight o'clock. Wyke." May I ask whether this is your handwriting, sir?

(**Doppler** *shows him the note.* **Andrew** *tries to retain it, but* **Doppler** *takes it back*)

Andrew: (*Trapped*) Yes. It's mine all right.

Doppler: So Mr. Tindle *was* here?

Andrew: Yes. The Potman spoke sooth.

Doppler: Perhaps you wouldn't mind answering my original question now, sir.

Andrew: Which one?

Doppler: Was there a struggle here two nights ago?

Andrew: In a manner of speaking, yes. It was a game we were playing.

Doppler: A game? What kind of game?

Andrew: It's rather difficult to explain. It's called Burglary.

Doppler: Please don't joke, sir.

Andrew: Isn't it about time you told me I don't know the seriousness of my own position?

Doppler: A man comes here, there is a fight. Shots are heard. He disappears. What would you make of that if you were me?

Andrew: An open and shut case. But things are not always what they seem, Inspector. In "The Case of the Drowned Dummy" my man, Merridew, once proved by a phonetic misspelling the forgery of a document allegedly written by a deaf mute.

Doppler: I'm waiting for an explanation, sir.

Andrew: Tindle arrived at eight and left about an hour and a half later. I haven't seen him since.

Doppler: And nor has anyone else, sir.

Andrew: This is absurd. Are you suggesting that I killed Tindle?

Doppler: Killed Tindle, sir. I never mentioned kill.

Andrew: Oh really! You can't pull that old one on me. (*Mimicking* **Inspector's** *voice*): Garotted, sir? Might I ask how you knew that her ladyship was garotted? (*Normal voice*): Surely *you* told me so, Inspector. (**Inspector's** *voice*): No, sir. I never mentioned it.

Doppler: I'm sorry you find us so comic, sir. On the whole what we do is necessary.

Andrew: "You're just doing your job," that's the overworked phrase, isn't it?

Doppler: Possibly, sir. Your wife and Mr. Tindle have been associating closely for some time.

Andrew: Oh, so you know about that, do you? I suppose you can't keep anything quiet in a small village.

Doppler: Perfectly true, sir.

Andrew: You aren't suggesting a crime passionel, I hope, Inspector—not over Marguerite. It would be like knifing somebody for a tablespoonful of Cooperative white blancmange.

Doppler: I'm very partial to blancmange, sir. I find it a great standby.

Andrew: (*Oratorically*) "All of you had either means, motive or opportunity," said Inspector Doppler as he thoughtfully digested another spoonful of his favorite pud. "But only one of you had all three."

Doppler: Exactly so, sir! That person is you.

Andrew: Forgive me, Inspector. I suppose I'd better tell you what happened.

Doppler: Yes.

Andrew: Want a bribe to believe it?

Doppler: I'll have another drink.

Andrew: As you seem to know, Tindle was having an affair with my wife. Now, I'm one of that rare breed of men who genuinely don't mind losing gracefully to a gent who's playing by the same rules. But to be worsted by a flash crypto Italian lover, who mistakes my boredom for impotence and my provocative energy for narcissism is too much. It's like starting every game—thirty down, and the umpire against you.

Doppler: You mean you couldn't bring yourself to accept the situation, sir. Is that what you're saying?

Andrew: I think what infuriated me most was the things he said about me—things that Marguerite repeated to me. I mean, no man likes to listen to the other man's witticisms when he's trying to choke down his late night Ovaltine.

Doppler: What sort of things, sir?

Andrew: Oh you know, smarmy, deceitful things which any lover can make about any husband. It's just too easy for them with a captive audience groggy on redis-covered youth and penis envy. (*Pause*) It's not really playing the game.

Doppler: You seem to regard marriage as a game, sir.

Andrew: Not marriage, Inspector. *Sex*. Sex is the game with marriage the penalty. Round the board we jog towards each futile anniversary. Pass go. Collect two hundred rows, two hundred silences, two hundred scars in the deep places. It's just as well that I don't lack for amorous adventure. Finlandia provides.

Doppler: Are you trying to tell me that because of your indifference to your wife, you had no motive for killing Mr. Tindle?

Andrew: I'm simply saying that in common with most men I want to have my cookie and ignore it. That's rather witty!

Doppler: Well, sir. I must say you're very frank.

Andrew: Disarmingly so, I hope.

Doppler: Please go on.

Andrew: As I say. I thought I'd teach Mr. Tindle a lesson for his presumption. In a curious way, some of his remarks, which Marguerite repeated to me, led me to believe that he was worth taking a little trouble with—even perhaps worth getting to know. Well, the shortest way to a man's heart is humiliation. You soon find out what he's made of.

Doppler: So you invited him here and humiliated him?

Andrew: I did indeed. I took a leaf out of the book of certain eighteenth-century secret societies. They knew to a nicety how to determine whether someone was worthy to be included among their number and also how to humiliate him in the process. I refer of course to the initiation ceremony.

Doppler: Would it be something like bullying a new boy at school?

Andrew: Not unlike, but the victim had the choice of refusal. When Count Cag-liostro, the noted magician, sought admission to one such society, he was asked whether he was prepared to die for it, if need be. He said he was. He was then sentenced to death, blindfolded and a pistol containing powder but no shot placed against his temple and discharged.

Doppler: And you did this to Mr. Tindle?

Andrew: More or less. I invited Milo here and suggested to him that as my wife had expensive tastes and he was virtually a pauper, the only course open for him was to steal some valuable jewels which I had in the safe.

Doppler: And he agreed to this?

Andrew: With alacrity. I persuaded him to get out of his clothes and to dress as Grock, in which ludicrouse disguise he broke into the house and blew open the safe. He then pocketed the jewels, struggled convincingly round this room and was about to make off, when I turned nasty and revealed the purpose of the eve-ning. This of course was that I had maneuvered him into a position where by pretending to mistake him for a burglar, I could, as the outraged householder, legitimately shoot him as he raced away up the stairs. By the time the police arrived I would be standing in my night attire, innocent, bewildered and aggrieved. And as you well know, Inspector, there's no liar in Britain, however unconvincing, more likely to be believed than an owner occupier standing with his hair ruffled in front of his own fireplace, wearing striped Viyella pajamas under a camel Jaeger dressing gown.

Doppler: What was Mr. Tindle's reaction to all this?

Andrew: It was electrifying! He swallowed my story hook, line and sinker. He fell on his knees, and pleaded for his life, but I was implacable. I put the gun against his head and shot him with a *blank* cartridge. He fainted dead away. It was most gratifying.

Doppler: Gratifying or not, sir, Mr. Tindle must have been put in fear for his life. Such action invites a grave charge of assault.

Andrew: Well, I suppose that's marginally better than the murder charge you were contemplating a few minutes ago.

Doppler: I still am contemplating it, sir.

Andrew: Oh come now, Inspector. I've told you what happened. After a few minutes, Mr. Tindle recovered his senses, realized shrewdly that he wasn't dead after all and went off home.

Doppler: (*Shaking his head in disbelief*) Just like that?

Andrew: Well, he needed a glass or two of cognac to get the parts working. I mean, wouldn't you?

Doppler: I doubt whether I would have survived completely undamaged, sir. The whole thing sounds like the most irresponsible trick.

Andrew: Irresponsible? It was quite the contrary. I was upholding the sanctity of marriage. That's more than most people are prepared to do these days. By this action I was clearly stating "Marriage isn't dead. It's alive and well and living in Wiltshire."

Doppler: Tell me, did Mr. Tindle say anything when he left?

Andrew: No. He seemed speechless. (*Laughs*) He just lurched off.

Doppler: I'm sorry you appear to find all this so funny, Mr. Wyke. We may not take quite the same attitude.

Andrew: Look, why don't you see this from my point of view. In a sense, Milo *was* a burglar. He was stealing my wife.

Doppler: So you tortured him?

Andrew: (*Exploding*) Don't you see. It was a *game!*

Doppler: A game?

Andrew: A bloody game, yes!

Doppler: It sounds rather sad, sir—like a child not growing up.

Andrew: What's so sad about a child playing, eh!

Doppler: Nothing, sir—if you're a child.

Andrew: Let me tell you, Inspector. I have played games of such complexity that Jung and Einstein would have been honored to have been asked to participate in them. Games of construction and games of destruction. Games of hazard, and games of callidity. Games of deductive logic, inductive logic, semantics, color association, mathematics, hypnosis and prestidigitation. I have achieved leaps of the mind and leaps of the psyche unknown in ordinary human relationships. And I've had a great deal of not wholly innocent fun.

Doppler: And now, sir, you have achieved murder.

Andrew: No!

Doppler: I believe so, sir.

Andrew: No!

Doppler: Would you mind if I looked around?

Andrew: Go ahead. Crawl about the floor on hands and knees. Get your envelope out and imprison hairs. Gather ye blunt instruments while ye may.

(**Doppler** *rises and starts to examine the room*)

Andrew: (*Slowly*) I ask myself, if I wanted to conceal Milo . . . (**Doppler** *shakes the sailor on his passage round the room*) . . . where would I put him? In the cellar? . . . Too traditional! In the water tank? . . . Too poisonous! In the linen chest? . . . Too aromatic! In the furnace? . . . Too residual! In the herbaceous border? . . . Too ossiferous! In the . . .

Doppler: Excuse me sir, but these holes in the wall here and here. They look like bullet holes.

Andrew: (*Slowly*) Quite right, Inspector. So they are.

Doppler: I understood you to say, sir, that you used a blank.

Andrew: Two live bullets to set up the trick. One blank to complete it. I had to persuade Tindle I was in earnest. After all, there's really no point in playing a game unless you play it to the hilt.

Doppler: I see, sir. One blank. I'd like you to show me where Mr. Tindle was when you killed him.

Andrew: Pretended to kill him, you mean.

Doppler: Quite so, sir. Show me, please, exactly where he was when the bullet hit him.

Andrew: You do realize, of course, there wasn't a real bullet.

Doppler: (*Skeptically*) Very well, sir. Show me where he was when the blank cartridge was fired.

(**Andrew** *mounts the stairs, followed by the Inspector*)

Andrew: He was standing, kneeling, crouching about here. He fainted and fell down the stairs. Bang!

(**Doppler** *passes* **Andrew**)

Doppler: I see. About here you say, sir?

Andrew: Towards me. Come on. Come on. Stop.

Doppler: Were you close to Mr. Tindle when you fired the gun?

Andrew: Very. I was standing over him, in fact, with the gun pressed against his head. The actual feel of the gun coupled with the noise of the explosion was what did the trick. (**Doppler** *scrutinizes the staircase*) Could I interest you in a magnifying glass?

(**Doppler** *bends down to examine the staircase, then the banisters. Suddenly he rubs a finger on them, and straightens up, wiping them on his handkerchief*)

Doppler: Joke blood, sir?

Andrew: (*Nervous*) I'm not quite sure I follow, Inspector.

Doppler: This here on the banisters. It's dried blood.

Andrew: Blood? Where?

Doppler: Here in the angle of the banister——

(*Warily* **Andrew** *crosses to the stairs. He examines the banisters and slowly straightens up. His expression is confused and fearful*)

Doppler: Don't touch it, sir! Oh, look sir, here's some more. Someone's been rubbing at the carpet. Do you see, sir? There, deep in the pile, that's blood, sir. Oh!

It's still damp. Could you explain how it got there, sir?

Andrew: I have no idea, Milo . . . er . . . he was a little burnt . . . You must believe me!

Doppler: Why should I, sir?

Andrew: But it's impossible, it was only a game.

Doppler: A game, sir? With real bullets and real blood?

Andrew: (*Gabbling*) There's the hole cut in the pane of glass with the diamond cutter . . . and there are the marks of the ladder on the sill outside . . . and if you look down, you'll see the imprint of the other end of the ladder and of size twenty-eight shoes, or whatever they were, still there in the flower bed and this is the bureau that he broke open . . .

(Doppler *descends the stairs*)

Doppler: (*Hard*) Thank you, sir, but I don't require a conducted tour. Over the years my eyes have been adequately trained to see things for themselves.

Andrew: I'm sure they have, Inspector. I only meant to point out facts which would help substantiate my story. And that's the safe we blew open . . .

Doppler: Where are the jewels now, sir?

Andrew: I put them in the bank yesterday.

Doppler: On a Saturday?

Andrew: Yes, Inspector, on a Saturday. I went to Salisbury and I put them in the night safe. I felt they'd be better off there. I mean, anyone could break in and steal them.

Doppler: How provident, sir.

Andrew: And look down the corridor, you'll see the dressing-up basket . . .

(Doppler *turns away and looks out of the window, over the garden*)

Doppler: You didn't point out that mound of earth in the garden, did you, sir?

(Andrew *joins* **Doppler** *at the window*)

Andrew: Mound of earth? What mound of earth?

Doppler: Over there—by the far wall. In the shadow of that yew tree. Would you say it had been freshly dug, sir?

Andrew: (*Shouting*) How the hell should I know. It's probably something the gardener's doing. A new flower bed I think he said.

Doppler: A flower bed under a yew tree, sir?

Andrew: (*Shouting*) I've already told you I don't know. Why don't you ask him yourself? He's probably out there somewhere, maundering around on his moleskinned knees, aching for an opportunity to slander his employer.

Doppler: Funny, sir. I've always found gardeners make excellent witnesses. Slow, methodical, positive.

Andrew: Inspector, I've had just about enough of this farce. Go and dig the damned thing up, if you want to.

Doppler: Oh, we shall sir. Don't worry.

Andrew: (*Persuasive*) Look, do you really think that I'd bury Tindle in the garden, and leave all that newly turned earth for everyone to find?

Doppler: If you weren't expecting us, sir, yes. In a couple of weeks, with some bulbs or a little grass seed, it would be difficult to tell it had ever been disturbed. We in the police know just how fond murderers are of their back gardens, sir.

Andrew: (*Attempts a laugh*) You're nearer a killer's heart in a garden than anywhere else on earth, eh?

Doppler: Except a bedroom, sir. I think you'll find that's still the favorite. (*He starts* *rummaging in the wardrobe*) Tch! Tch! Tch! What a way to keep clothes! All screwed up at the back of your wardrobe. Why should you do that, I wonder. (*He holds up* **Milo's** *shirt*) That's an interesting monogram. I.W. No, I've got it the wrong way up—M.T.

Andrew: Let me see that.

Doppler: (*Reading*) Made by Owen and Smith of Percy Street. Sixteen-eight-sixty-nine for Mr. Milo Tindle. Tell me something, sir. (**Andrew** *seizes the shirt and stares at it in horror, unable to speak.* **Doppler** *holds up* **Milo's** *jacket and carefully reads the name in the inside pocket*) When Mr. Tindle lurched off as you put it, did he lurch naked?

Andrew: (*In great distress*) Believe me, Inspector. I have no idea how those clothes got there.

Doppler: Didn't you tell me that Mr. Tindle stripped off here the other night to disguise himself as a clown?

Andrew: Yes, that's right.

Doppler: Another part of the humiliation process, I suppose?

Andrew: But he changed back before he left. I mean, you can't really see him walking through the village dressed as a clown, can you?

Doppler: No sir, I can't. Which makes the appearance of his clothes here all the more significant.

Andrew: It's all so difficult . . .

Doppler: On the contrary, sir, I think it's all very simple. I think you started this as a game, exactly as you say you did, in order to play a diabolical trick on Mr. Tindle, but that it went wrong. Your third shot was not a blank as you had supposed, but was in fact a live bullet which killed Mr. Tindle stone dead, spattering his blood on the banisters in the process. When you realized what you'd done, you panicked and simply buried him in the garden. It was silly of you not to wash the blood properly off the banisters and burn his clothes, though.

Andrew: I swear Tindle left here alive.

Doppler: I don't believe it.

Andrew: I didn't murder him.

Doppler: I accept that. As I said, I think it happened by accident. We'll be quite content with a charge of manslaughter.

Andrew: (*Shouting*) I did not kill him! He left here alive.

Doppler: If you will pardon a flippancy, sir, you had better tell that to the judge.

Andrew: Look. There's one way of settling this. If you think Tindle is in the garden, go and dig him up.

Doppler: We don't need to find him, sir. Recent decisions have relieved the prosecution of producing the corpus delicti. If Mr. Tindle is not under the newly turned earth, it will merely go to indicate that in your panic you first thought of putting him there, then changed your mind and buried him somewhere else.

Andrew: Where?

Doppler: Does it matter? Spook Spinney! Flasher's Heath! It's all the same to us. He'll turn up sooner or later—discovered by some adulterous salesman or rutting boy scout. And if he doesn't, it scarcely matters, there's so much circumstantial evidence against you. Come along, it's time to go.

Andrew: (*A cry*) No!

Doppler: I'm afraid I must insist sir! There's a police car outside.

Andrew: (*Louder*) You may have a fleet of police cars out there. I'm not going.

Doppler: Now let's have no trouble, sir. Please don't make it difficult.

Andrew: (*Wildly*) I must see a lawyer. It's my right.

(**Andrew** *backs away.* **Doppler** *makes to seize him, there is a scuffle*)

Doppler: We can make a call from the station, sir. We wouldn't want to do anything unconstitutional. Come on, sir. Don't despair. At the most you'll only get seven years!

Andrew: (*Horrified*) Seven years!

Doppler: Seven years to regret playing silly games that go wrong.

Andrew: (*Bitterly*) It didn't go wrong. It went absolutely right. You've trapped me somehow.

Doppler: Yes, sir. You see, we real life detectives aren't as stupid as we are sometimes portrayed by writers like yourself. We may not have our pipes, or orchid houses, our shovel hats or deer-stalkers, but we tend to be reasonably effective for all that.

Andrew: Who the hell are you?

Doppler: Detective Inspector Doppler, sir, spelled as in C. Doppler, 1803–1853, whose principle it was that when the source of any wave movement is approached, the frequency appears greater than it would to an observer moving away. It is also not unconnected with Doppler meaning double in German—hence Doppleganger or double image. And of course, for those whose minds run to these things, it is virtually an anagram of the word Plodder. Inspector Plodder becomes Inspector Doppler, if you see what I mean, sir!

Andrew: (*A shriek*) Milo!

Milo: (*Normal voice*) The same.

(**Milo** *peels off his disguise which apart from elaborate face and hair make-up—wig, false nose, glasses, cheek padding and moustache—also includes a great deal of body padding, and elevator shoes, which have had the effect of making him taller than* **Andrew***, where in reality he is a fraction shorter*)

Andrew: You shit!

Milo: Just so.

Andrew: You platinum-plated, copper-bottomed, dyed-in-the-wool, all-time knock-down drag-out, champion bastard Milo!

Milo: Thanks.

Andrew: You weasel! You cozening coypu!

Milo: Obliged.

Andrew: You mendacious bollock of Satan. Milo! You triple-dealing turd!

Milo: In your debt.

Andrew: Mind you, I'm not saying it wasn't well done. It was—brilliant.

Milo: Thank you.

Andrew: Have a drink, my dear fellow?

Milo: Let me wash first. I'm covered with make-up and spirit gum.

(**Andrew** *shakily pours himself a whisky*)

Andrew: Just down the corridor. Cheers!

Milo: Good health.

(**Milo** *exits to bathroom as* **Andrew** *gulps drink down*)

Andrew: Yes, I must say, Milo, I congratulate you. It was first class. You really had me going there for a moment.

Milo: (*Quizzically*) For a moment?

Andrew: For a long moment, I concede. Of course, I had my suspicions toward the end. Flasher's Heath indeed! That was going a bit far.

Milo: (*Offstage*) I was giving you one of your English sporting chances.

Andrew: What did you think of *my* performance? The anguish of an innocent man trapped by circumstantial evidence.

Milo: (*Offstage*) Undignified—if it was a performance.

(**Milo** *returns on stage and picks up his clothes*)

Andrew: Of course it was, and it had to be undignified to be convincing. As I say, I had my suspicions.

Milo: Indeed? How cleverly you kept them to yourself.

(**Milo** *goes upstairs to the wardrobe where he dresses in his own clothes*)

Andrew: And how well you executed it. I loved your Inspector Doppler. His relentless courtesy, his chilly rusticity, his yeoman beadiness.

Milo: (**Doppler** *voice*) I'm glad you view the trifling masquerade in that light, sir.

Andrew: He was quite a masterpiece. Inspector Ringrose crossed with a kind of declassé Roger Sheringham, I'd have said.

Milo: Really?

Andrew: Oh yes? Surely you remember "The Poisoned Chocolate Case," 1929. It was a really astounding tour de force with no less than six separate solutions.

Milo: I've never heard of it.

Andrew: You should read it. It's a veritable textbook of the literature, not that you need any tips on plotting. I suppose you slipped in here yesterday when I was over in Salisbury.

Milo: Yes, I waited to see you leave.

Andrew: And dumped the clothes in the wardrobe, and sprinkled a little sacrificial blood on the banisters.

Milo: Exactly. But it wasn't my blood you will be relieved to hear. It was obtained from a pig's liver.

Andrew: Ugh! Perhaps you will do me the favor of wiping it off in a minute. I don't wish to fertilize the woodworm.

Milo: Question. Where would you find homosexual woodworms?

Andrew: What?

Milo: In a tallboy. (**Andrew** *grimaces. Then, sharply*) I'd like that drink now.

Andrew: Yes, of course. (*He goes to drinks table and pours a brandy for* **Milo**) You deserve it.

Milo: (*Sits on chair under staircase*) You know I haven't congratulated you on your game yet. You brought it off with great élan.

Andrew: Did you think so? Oh good! Good! I must say I was rather delighted with it myself. Tell me . . . did you really think that your last moment on earth had come?

Milo: Yes.

Andrew: You're not angry, are you?

Milo: Anger is a meaningless word in this context.

Andrew: I've already tried to explain it to you. I wanted to get to know you—to see if you were, as I suspected, my sort of person.

Milo: A games-playing sort of person?

Andrew: Exactly.

Milo: And am I?

Andrew: Most certainly. There's no doubt about it.

Milo: And what exactly is a games-playing person?

Andrew: He's the complete man—a man of reason and imagination, of potent passions and bright fancies. He's joyous and unrepenting. His weapons are the openness of a child and the cunning of a pike and with them he faces out the black terrors of life. For me personally he is a man who dares to live his life without the crutch of domestic tension. You see, at bottom, I'm rather a solitary man. An arrangement of clouds, the secret mystery of landscape, a game of intrigue and revelation mean more to me than people—even the ones I'm supposed to be in love with. I've never met a woman to whom the claims of intellect were as absolute as they are to me. For a long time I was reticent about all this, knowing that most people would mistake my adroit heart for one of polished stone. But it doesn't worry me any longer. I'm out in the open. I've turned my whole life into one great work of happy invention.

Milo: And you think I'm like this?

Andrew: Yes. I do.

Milo: You're wrong.

Andrew: I'm not. Look at the way you chose to get back at me—by playing Inspector Doppler.

Milo: That was just the need for revenge. Every Italian knows about that.

Andrew: Rubbish. You could have revenged yourself in one of many crude Mafiosi ways—cutting off the gardener's hands, for example, or staking the cleaning woman out on the gravel, or even I suppose, as a last resort, scratched loutish words on the hood of my Bentley. But no, you had to resort to a game.

Milo: I like to pay back in kind.

Andrew: And is honor satisfied? Is it one set all?

Milo: (*Hard*) By no means. Your game was superior to mine. I merely teased you for a few minutes with the thought of prison. (*Low*) You virtually terrified me to death.

Andrew: My dear fellow . . .

Milo: (*Slowly, thinking it out*) And that changes you profoundly. Once you've given yourself to death, actually faced the fact that the coat sleeve button, the banister, the nail on your fourth finger are the last things you're going to see ever—and then *heard* the sound of your own death—things cannot be the same again. I feel I've been tempered by madness. I stand outside and see myself for the first time without responsibility.

Andrew: (*Nervous*) That's shock, my dear chap. It'll pass. Here, have another drink. (**Andrew** *reaches for the glass.* **Milo** *jerks away. He is in great distress*) How cold you are. Milo, my dear fellow, I didn't realize how absolutely cold . . .

Milo: So that my only duty is to even our score. That's imperative. As you would put it "I'm three games up in the second set, having lost the first six-love." That's right, isn't it? That's about how you see it? I should hate to cheat.

Andrew: You're being too modest, Milo. In my scoring it's one set all.

Milo: Oh, no, I can't accept that. You see to the ends of playing the game and drawing honorably level, I *have* killed someone.

Andrew: Killed someone?

Milo: Murdered someone. Committed murder.

Andrew: You're not serious.

Milo: Yes.

Andrew: What is this. Some new murder game?

Milo: Yes. But it has a difference. Both the game and the murder are real. There's absolutely no point in another pretense murder game, is there?

Andrew: (*Soothing*) No, none. But I don't like to take advantage of you in this emotional state.

Milo: (*Shouting*) It can't wait.

Andrew: (*Soothing*) All right. All right. Let's play your game. Who did you kill?

Milo: Your girl friend, Tēa . . .

Andrew: You killed Tēa?

Milo: (*A little giggle*) She whose cobalt eyes were the secret forest pools of Finlandia. I closed them.

Andrew: You . . .

Milo: I strangled her—right here on this rug I strangled her and . . . I had her first.

Andrew: You raped and str . . .

Milo: No. Not rape. She wanted it.

Andrew: You're lying. You can't take me in with a crude game like this. (*With braggadocio*) Honestly, Milo. You're in the big league now. I gave you credit for better sport than this.

Milo: You'll have all the sport you can stomach in a moment, Andrew. That I promise you.

Andrew: Really, Milo, I think it would be better if . . .

Milo: When I was here yesterday, planting the blood and clothes for my Inspector Doppler scene, Tēa stopped by. I strangled her. She was under that freshly dug mound of earth in the garden that so took Doppler's fancy.

Andrew: Was? You mean she's not there now?

Milo: No. I moved her.

Andrew: (*Derisory*) You moved her? Where to? Flasher's Heath, I suppose.

Milo: Something like that. It was too easy leaving her here . . . Too easy for the game you are going to play against the clock before the police arrive.

Andrew: The police?

Milo: Yes. You see, about an hour ago I phoned them up and asked them to meet me here at ten o'clock tonight. They should be here in about ten minutes.

Andrew: (*Sarcastic*) Yes, yes. I'm sure they will be. Led, no doubt, by intrepid downy Inspector Doppler.

Milo: Oh, no. It'll be a real policeman, have no fear of that. Detective Sergeant Tarrant, his name is. I told him a lot about you, Andrew. I said that I knew you to be a man obsessed with games-playing and murder considered as a fine art. Your life's great ambition, I said, of which you'd often spoken, was to commit an actual real life murder, hide the body somewhere where it couldn't be traced to you and then leave clues linking you with the crime, strewn about your house in the certain knowledge that the pedestrian and simple-minded police wouldn't recognize them for what they were.

Andrew: Obsessed with games-playing and murder considered as a fine art! That's rather ingenious of you, Milo. But it won't work. Please sir, Andrew Wyke can't rest until he's committed a real murder which is going to make fools out of all you coppers. Honestly! Tell that to the average desk sergeant and you'll find yourself strapped straight into the giggle jacket.

Milo: Not so in fact, I told them that if they didn't believe me, one look at your bookcase and the furnishings of your house would confirm what I said about your obsessions.

Andrew: (*Slow*) Go on.

Milo: I also told them that two days ago your girl friend had come to my house in great distress, saying you suspected she was having affairs with other men and had threatened to kill her.

Andrew: The police believed all that?

Milo: After some demur, yes.

Andrew: The fuzz are watching too much T.V.

Milo: You mustn't resent imagination in public office, Andrew. Of course, I went on I had no proof that any harm had actually been done to her, but I thought I had better report the matter, particularly as I had just received an excited phone call from you, Andrew, saying you were all set to achieve your life's great ambition.

Andrew: My dear boy, I quite appreciate you have been captivated by the spirit of games-playing and the need, as you see it, to get even, but frankly you are trying too hard to be a big boy, too soon. (*He goes to the telephone and dials*) Hullo, Joyce, this is Andrew. May I speak to Tēa . . . she what? . . . when was this? Where . . . ? Oh my God!

(*He replaces the receiver and takes a drink straight from the bottle.* **Milo** *is very excited*)

Milo: I told you. I killed her yesterday. Now sweat for your life. You have a little over eight minutes before the law arrives. It's your giant brain against their plodding ones. Concealed in this room are two incriminating clues. And as a final expression of your contempt for the police, you hid the murder weapon itself. Do you follow me so far?

Andrew: (*Admiringly*) You bastard!

Milo: No judgments please. Three objects. Those you don't find, be sure the police will. I should add that they're all in plain view, though I have somewhat camouflaged them to make the whole thing more fun. The first object is a crystal bracelet.

Andrew: Not . . .

Milo: Yes, I tore it off her wrist . . . off you go. It's inscribed "From Andrew to Tēa, a propitiatory offering to a Karelian goddess."

Andrew: All right! All right! I know how it's inscribed. (*He takes off his jacket and starts his search*)

Milo: Would you like some help?

Andrew: Yes, damn you!

Milo: Tch! Tch! . . .
"For any man with half an eye.
What stands before him may espy;
But optics sharp it needs I ween,
To see what is not to be seen."

Andrew: (*Furious*) You said everything was in plain view.

Milo: Well, it's paradoxical old me, isn't it?

Andrew: I'll get my own back for this . . . don't worry. That I promise you. I'll roast you for this . . . I'll make you so sorry you ever . . .

Milo: Six minutes.

Andrew: (*Slowly to himself*) I must think . . . I must think . . . It's in plain view, yet not to be seen. H'm . . . there's a visual trick involved.
(**Andrew** *searches the room*)

Milo: A propitiatory offering, eh! What was it you had to propitiate for, I ask myself.

Andrew: None of your bloody business.

Milo: Just for being yourself, I suppose. Just for being cold, torturing Andrew Wyke. Poor Tēa, I wonder if all her jewelry was inscribed with apologies for your bully boy behavior.

Andrew: That's a cheap jibe.

Milo: Mind you, at least you gave her some. Marguerite just had the use of them.

Andrew: I see what you're doing. You're trying to distract me . . . But you won't succeed . . . I'll solve your puzzle . . . Let me think . . . Optics sharp it needs to see what is not to be seen . . . with the naked eye? It's microscopic! You only see a fraction of it. That's it!

(**Andrew** *picks up the microscope and uses it*)

Milo: You won't need the Sherlock Holmes kit, Andrew. The bracelet is full sized and in full view. Though the detective angle is not a bad one. I wonder how your man, Merry*dick*, would have gone about the search.

Andrew: (*Furious*) Merrydew! St. John Lord Merrydew!

Milo: Perhaps he'd have clambered up on that desk to look at the plinth, hauling his great tun of port belly after him. (**Andrew** *climbs up on his desk to inspect the plinth*) Or perhaps he'd have gone straight to the chimney and shoved his fat Father Christmas face right up to it. (**Andrew** *runs to the chimney and climbs inside it*) "My God!" cried the noble Lord, puking on his pipe and indulging his famed taste for bad puns. "This is hardly a *sootable* place for a gentleman!"

Andrew: (*Emerges from the chimney*) I won't listen to you. I must think . . . What are the properties of crystal? It's hard . . . It's brilliant . . . It's transparent.

Milo: You're getting warm, Andrew.

Andrew: You look through it and you don't see it. Now the only place to conceal a transparent thing, so as to make it invisible yet keep it in plain view, is in another transparent thing like . . . (*He inspects various glass objects including* **Milo's** *drink which he is holding conspicuously. Finally he crosses to the ornamental tank and lifts out the bracelet*) Suddenly it's all as clear as crystal. I don't need to destroy this, do I? She could have left this here anytime.

Milo: True, it was only planted so that the police could read the inscription. At least they'd know that your relationship with Tēa hadn't always been a happy one.

Andrew: Very subtle. What next?

Milo: The next object is much more damning. The clue is a riddle, which goes as follows:

"Two brothers we are,

Great burdens we bear,

On which we are bitterly pressed.

The truth is to say,

We are full all the day,

And empty when we go to rest."

Andrew: Oh, I know that . . . don't tell me . . . full all the day, empty when we go to rest . . . it's a . . . it's a pair of shoes!

Milo: Very good. In this case, one right, high-heeled shoe. Size six. The other, I need hardly add, is on Tēa's body.

Andrew: Oh, my God. Poor Tēa. (*He searches the room*)

Milo: Poor Tēa, eh? Well, that's a bit better. It's the first sign of sorrow you've shown since you heard of her death.

Andrew: It's not true! You think I don't care about Tēa, don't you? But I must save myself.

Milo: You're loving it. You're in a high state of brilliance and excitement. The thought that you are playing a game for your life is practically giving you an orgasm. It's pitiable.

Andrew: Hold your filthy tongue. What you see before you is someone using a mighty control to keep terror in check, while he tries to solve a particularly sadistic and morbid puzzle. It's a triumph of the mind over atavism! (**Andrew** *searches under the stairs and in the bookshelves, and pipe racks then the sailor's foot and finally finds the shoe in a brightly decorated cornucopia attached to the stage left column*) Ah! What have we here?

Milo: Very good! Sorry it's so messy. It's only earth from Tēa's first grave in your garden.

(**Andrew** *burns the shoe in the stove*)

Andrew: Now there's one thing left, isn't there. The murder weapon, that's what you said. Now you strangled her here. What with? Let's see . . . a rope . . . a belt . . . a scarf . . .

Milo: It bit into her neck very deeply, Andrew. I had to pry it loose.

Andrew: You sadistic bloody wop!

Milo: I hope I didn't hear that correctly . . . It would be foolish to antagonize me at this stage. Because as you're certain to need a lot more help, I would hate to have to give you an oblique, Florentine sort of one, sewn with treachery and double dealing.

Andrew: (*Controlling himself*) All right! All right!

Milo: As Don Quixote in common with a great number of chaps remarked, "*No es Oro todo que reluce.*"

Andrew: But the other chaps, of course, didn't say it in Spanish, did they?

Milo: Well at least you know it was Spanish, even if you can't speak it. I suppose that's what is meant by a general education in England.

Andrew: God, you're pretty damned insufferable, Milo.

Milo: I've learned it. Let's try you on a little Latin. Every gentleman knows Latin. I'm sure you're acquainted with the Winchester College Hall Book of 1401?

Andrew: (*Sarcastic*) Naturally. As a matter of fact I've got the paperback by my bedside.

Milo: (*Bland*) Then you will remember an entry by Alanus De Insulis—"*Non teneas nurum totum quod splendet ut aurum.*"

Andrew: (*Sarcastic*) I'm afraid I can't have got that far yet.

Milo: Pity . . . I suppose I could put it another way. "*Que tout n'est pas or qu'on voit luire.*" The French, of course, is thirteenth century.

Andrew: Say it again, slowly.

Milo: All-that-glitters . . .

Andrew: All that glitters isn't gold . . . Why didn't you say that in the first place . . . (**Milo** *whistles a scale*) Golden notes? Golden whistle? . . . Golden cord? . . . Golden cord! You strangled her with a golden cord and put it round the bellpull. (**Andrew** *runs to the bellpull, examines it, but finds nothing*) No, you didn't. (**Milo** *whistles "Anything Goes"*) Anything goes. In olden d . . . In olden days a . . . glimpse of stocking. It's in the spin dryer. (**Andrew** *goes off down the corridor to kitchen*)

Milo: Cold, cold. It's in this room, remember.

Andrew: (*Returning*) Where do you put stockings? On legs, golden legs . . . (*He examines the golden legs of the fender, then a chair*)

Milo: (*Sings*) "In olden days a glimpse of stocking was looked on as something shocking . . ." I thought I heard something. (*He exits to hallway. A moment later, he returns*) Yes, Andrew, it's the police. They're coming up the drive.

Andrew: (*Desperate*) Keep them out! Give me one more minute!

Milo: A glimpse of stocking, remember.

(**Milo** *exits to hallway*)

Milo: (*Offstage*) Good evening, Detective Sergeant Tarrant.

Tarrant: (*Offstage*) Yes, sir. This is Constable Higgs.

Milo: (*Off*) Good evening, Constable.

Higgs: Good evening, sir.

(*The grandfather clock strikes ten*)

Andrew: Olden days . . . A glimpse . . . Now you see it now you don't! Of course, the clock. (*He rushes to clock and finds stocking*)

Milo: (*Off*) Nice of you to be so prompt. I apologize for keeping you waiting out there for a moment. The front door's a bit stiff.

Tarrant: (*Off*) That's all right, sir. We're used to waiting.

Milo: Won't you hang your coats up? It's a bit warm inside.

Tarrant: Thank you, sir. I expect we'll be here a little time.

(**Andrew** *puts stocking into fire*)

Milo: (*Off*) Here, Constable. Let me take your helmet.

Higgs: Thank you, sir. If it's all the same to you, I think I'll keep it with me, but I'll take my coat off.

(*Door slams offstage*)

Milo: (*Off*) Come in, gentlemen. May I introduce Mr. Andrew Wyke. Andrew, may I introduce Detective Sergeant Tarrant and Constable Higgs.

Andrew: (Calls) Come in, gentlemen, come in.

(*A pause. No one enters*)

Milo: (*Off*) Or perhaps I should say, Inspector Plodder and Constable Freshface. Thank you, Sergeant. We won't be needing you after all.

Tarrant: That's all right, sir. Better to be safe than sorry, that's what I say, Good night, sir.

Milo: (*Own voice*) Good night, Sergeant. Good night, Constable. Good night, sir.

(**Milo** *returns from hallway.* **Andrew** *sinks on the settee, shattered*)

Milo: Aren't you going to ask about Tēa? She did call here yesterday looking for you when I was here setting the Doppler scene. I told her about the trick you had played on me with the gun. She wasn't a bit surprised. She knows only too well the kind of games you play—the kind of humiliation you enjoy inflicting on people. I said I wanted to play a game to get even with you, and I asked her to help me. I asked her to lend me a stocking, a shoe and a bracelet. She collaborated with enthusiasm. So did her flat-mate, Joyce. Would you like to telephone her, she'll talk to you now? Of course you don't really have much to say to her, do you? She's not really your mistress. She told me you and she hadn't slept together for over a year. She told me you were practically impotent—not at all, in fact, the selector's choice for the next Olympics.

(**Andrew** *hides his head as* **Milo** *starts up the stairs*)

Andrew: Where are you going?

Milo: To collect Marguerite's fur coat.

Andrew: She's not coming back?

Milo: No. Among other things she said she was fed up with living in Hamleys.

Andrew: Hamleys?

Milo: It's a toy shop in Regent Street.

Andrew: Milo.

Milo: Yes?

Andrew: Don't go. Don't waste it all on Marguerite. She doesn't appreciate you like I do. You and I are evenly matched. We know what it is to play a game and that's so rare. Two people coming together who have the courage to spend the little time of light between the eternal darkness—joking.

Milo: Do you mean live here?

Andrew: Yes.

Milo: (*Scornfully*) Is it legal in private between two consenting games-players?

Andrew: Please . . . I just want someone to play with.

Milo: No.

Andrew: Please.

Milo: No. Most people want someone to *live* with. But you have no life to give anyone—only the tricks and the shadows of long ago. Take a look at yourself, Andrew, and ask yourself a few simple questions about your attachment to the English detective story. Perhaps you might come to realize that the only place you can inhabit is a dead world—a country house world where peers and colonels die in their studies; where butlers steal the port, and pert parlormaids cringe, weeping malapropisms behind green baize doors. It's a world of coldness and class hatred, and two-dimensional characters who are not expected to communicate; it's a world where only the amateurs win, and where foreigners are automatically figures of fun. To be *puzzled* is all. Forgive me for taking Marguerite to a life where people try to *understand*. To put it shortly, the detective story is the normal recreation of snobbish, outdated, life-hating, ignoble minds. I'll get that fur coat now. I presume it is Marguerite's, unless, that is, you've taken to transvestism as a substitute for non-performance.

(**Milo** *disappears into the bedroom.* **Andrew** *sits on below, crushed and humiliated. After a minute, he rises and starts wearily across the stage. Suddenly he stops as a thought enters his mind*)

Andrew: (*To himself*) The coat! . . . The fur coat . . . of course . . . I've got him! (*He brightens visibly—a man who realizes suddenly that he can rescue a victory out of the jaws of defeat—and crosses firmly to his desk and takes out his gun*) You see, Inspector, I was working in the morning room when I heard a noise. I seized my gun and came in here. I saw the figure of a man, apparently carrying my wife's fur coat. I shouted for him to put his hands up, but instead he ran toward the front door, trying to escape. Though I aimed low, I'm afraid I shot him dead. (*Inspector's voice*) Mustn't blame yourself, sir, could have happened to anybody! (**Milo** *returns, carrying fur coat. He comes down the stairs, but does not see the gun hidden behind* **Andrew's** *back*)

Andrew: I'm not going to let you go, you know.

Milo: No? What are you going to do, Andrew. Shoot me down? Play that old burglar game again?

Andrew: Yes, that's precisely what I could do.

Milo: It wouldn't work, you know, even if you had the guts to go through with it.

Andrew: Why not?

Milo: (*Fetches a suitcase from the hall and packs the fur coat*) Because of what happened when I left here on Friday night. I *lurched* home in the moonlight, numb and dazed, and soiled. I sat up all night in a chair—damaged—contaminated by you and this house. I remembered something my father said to me; "In this country, Milo," he said, "there's justice, but sometimes for a foreigner it is difficult." In the morning I went to the police station and told them what had happened. One of them—Sergeant Tarrant—yes, he's real—took me into a room and we had quite a long chat. But I don't think he really believed me, even though I showed him the powder burn on my head. He seemed more interested in my relationship with Marguerite, which by the way they all appeared to know about. I felt this terrible anger coming over me. I thought "they're not going to believe me because I'm a stranger from London who's screwing the wife of the local nob and has got what he deserved." So I thought of my father, and what I might have done in Italy, and I took my own revenge. But remember, Andrew, the police might still come.

Andrew: (*Slowly*) Then why haven't they, then?

Milo: I don't know, perhaps they won't. But even if they don't, you can't play your burglar game now; they'd never swallow it. So you see, you've lost.

Andrew: I don't believe one word you're saying.

Milo: (*Deliberately*) It's the truth.

Andrew: You're lying!

Milo: Why don't you phone Sergeant Tarrant if you don't believe me.

Andrew: And say what? Please, Sergeant, has Milo Tindle been in saying that I framed him as a burglar and then shot him? I'm not that half-witted.

Milo: Suit yourself.

Andrew: I shall shoot you, Milo. You come here and ask my permission to steal away my wife, you pry into my manhood, you lecture me on dead worlds and ignoble minds, and you mock Merridew. Well, they're all real bullets this time.

Milo: I'm going home now.

(**Milo** *starts to leave*, **Andrew** *fires*. **Milo** *drops in pain, fatally shot*. **Andrew** *kneels and holds his head up*)

Andrew: You're a bad liar, Milo, and in the final analysis, an uninventive games-player. Can you hear me? Then listen to this, NEVER play the same game three times running.

(*There is the sound of a car approaching and pulling to a halt. A flashing blue police car light shines through the window. The door bell rings. There is a loud knocking on door. Painfully* **Milo** *lifts his head from the floor, he laughs*)

Milo: Game, set and match!

(*His laugh becomes a cough. Blood trickles from his mouth. He grimaces in surprise at the pain and dies. The knocking on the door is repeated more loudly.* **Andrew** *staggers to his desk and accidentally presses the button on it. This sets off the sailor who laughs ironically. The knocking becomes more insistent.* **Andrew** *leans weakly against pillar. He shouts in anguish as*)

THE CURTAIN FALLS

PART FIVE
LANGUAGE

"Don't jive me, Jack. Ah gonna cut yo' ass."

"Surely you jest, old top. Desist or I shall be forced to violence."

"I no believa you. I'm a hafta hurta you."

"Yeth, you are telling a big fib. Thtop it, Puthycat, or I'll thimply thcream."

"Uh, dat don't soun right ta me. I might gonna punch you one."

All these statements, when analyzed, say almost the same thing. As you read them, ask yourself what kind of person you would expect each speaker to be. What might he look like? What are his background, education, and ethnic group? How much does the word selection and delivery of the lines affect your image of the speaker?

A character's language is closely related to his background and physical appearance. When we read a play, we must often clothe the character, inferring what he is like from the language he and the other characters use. In reading drama, our most direct path to information about character and plot is through language.

These examples represent sterotypes that suggest classes of people, not individuals. The playwright is aware, however, that people do judge others on the basis of their language, especially if it fits a familiar stereotype. Language is therefore a major tool the dramatist can use to create quick, stereotyped characterizations. He knows, for example, that we have certain preconceived ideas about people from certain countries or regions. In an English or American play, a German accent evokes a certain kind of response, a Southern accent still another, and so on. Unless a character says or does something to break the stereotype, the audience is limited to such conventional responses.

These stereotypes can save time in conveying information about minor characters, but in most plays the writer uses language more subtly and precisely in creating his major characters. He knows that language can reveal significant information about the character as an individual.

Recognizable language patterns do, however, tend to develop among particular groups, to define them and help determine who belongs and who does not. Subcultures, countercultures, professions, socio-economic groups and the like have each developed language patterns that one must know in order to function in the world defined by that group. Lawyers, for example, learn a specific language that helps them to function in the world of contracts, wills, and courts. Similarly, a special language has grown up around rock music and the drug culture. Many young people who have adopted this language often find it difficult to communicate with parents whose generation has its own kind of language. At times, however, no language is sufficient for communicating with those who refuse to listen.

Although the above comments apply equally to both everyday and dramatic language, drama and its language are not exactly like life. Our everyday language does not create a unified effect. We walk around campus, for example, listening to snatches of a wide range of conversations, hearing people repeat, hesitate, rephrase, and ramble. The dramatist, however, is highly selective in the language his characters use. Well-written dialogue is under tension—it allows the audience not only to interpret literal meaning, but to penetrate more deeply into the character or the dramatic situation. Each word or phrase is chosen to help us see character, plot, or meaning more clearly. If we concentrate on the words and their patterns as we read or hear them, we will come to a fuller understanding of the play.

A character's language reflects his perception of the world and what he does to bring order to that world, thus revealing much about him as a unique human being. The playwright often establishes language patterns for his characters which give us significant information beyond the meaning of the words themselves. A character who sees the world in terms of religion, or finance, or sex will reflect these views in his selection of the words and images he uses to communicate with others whatever the topic. A self-centered character may continually turn the conversation back to himself, fidgeting until others have finished speaking, interrupting to relate his own experiences, constantly reasserting his need for the limelight. Characters who have difficulty coping with the events of whatever time they happen to live in may try to remain in the past, ignoring new concepts, new attitudes, and new words, rather than integrating such changes into their lives, and consequently, into their language.

A character who is blunt and straightforward may be a practical, no-nonsense kind of person. If his speech is full of cutting remarks and cruel jibes, he may be an insecure individual who must attack others to make himself seem stronger. Humorous language may be used by a character to entertain, to ridicule, or perhaps simply to cope with an otherwise bewildering world.

Repetition of certain words or images may form another pattern in which the dramatist reveals significant information about his characters. A materialistic character may phrase everything in terms of money and business; a morbid character may make frequent allusions to sickness and death; a character wishing to escape reality may use light, happy, pleasant language even when others are discussing the ugliness of the world in which they all live. A character's references to specific objects or places—such as a wedding ring, a picture, a garden, or his childhood home—may form significant patterns. One character may consistently use images referring to light, while another stresses dark images, or such references may change from dark to light during the play.

All such language patterns are chosen carefully and deliberately to point out the preoccupations, desires, fears, biases, and attitudes of the characters who use them.

The misuse of words may also be a clue to character development (as well as providing entertainment in itself.) Those who want to belong to some exclusive group may try to gain acceptance through using the slang of that group. Often such people seem only foolish because they don't know the subtleties of the language and therefore misuse it. Pretentious characters who want to appear intelligent may try to use long, complicated words to impress their listeners. Frequently, they use the wrong word in the right place, saying, for example, "I want to live forever—I want to be immoral." This kind of error is known as a *malapropism*. Sometimes a character chooses a mild-sounding word, or *euphemism*, instead of one which might seem too harsh or direct—saying "He went to his great reward" rather than "He died."

The playwright may also use language to show how characters relate to each other. A character may speak in short, precise sentences to one person and in long, complicated utterances to another. He may be very logical and rational in one conversation and appear disorganized and confused when certain other characters are present. In plays such as *Antigone* or *Othello*, a major character may speak in verse throughout most of the play, but use prose when conversing with specific people. Language may be used in this way to distinguish among social classes, levels of imagination, attitudes, or mental states within a play. The reader or viewer must decide why the character has varied his speech patterns and what this variation tells us about him and the other characters involved.

The tone in which a line is spoken may also provide insight into character and plot. The playwright often provides stage directions suggesting how a line should be said. In other instances the director and the actors involved must determine the tone through context. When reading plays, we must decide for ourselves how the characters would speak each line. For example, a spoiled petulant child, accused of stealing a dollar from his mother's purse, responds, "No, I didn't—no, I didn't! You're always blaming things on me!" We can almost hear the whining, strident tone.

The dramatist may choose to give his characters speech impediments or unusual speech patterns—a lisp, a stutter, a mumbling style—to evoke certain responses from the audience. Such impediments may be limited to certain kinds of situations showing us how the character responds to stress or to other characters. For example, a man may speak normally when conversing with his family or friends but develops a stutter when responding to his irritable boss.

In drama, as in daily life, it is also important to note what a person does not say. Deliberate omissions are sometimes as revealing as any statement the individual might make. Suppose, for example, that a friend asks what you think of his new girl friend. If you respond by talking about your history exam or your plans for the weekend, you have implicitly given your opinion. Or, imagine this situation in a play: A man's former supervisor is asked to recommend him for another position. Instead of answering directly, the supervisor speaks warmly of the man's family and emphasizes how much he needs the job. We learn as much from the supervisor's omission as from his statements.

Dramatic pauses, breaks in dialogue, and silences may also be used to communicate meanings not as easily or effectively conveyed through dialogue alone. The playwright may indicate such breaks or the dramatic situation may dictate it. For example, when a son, returning home from war, sees his parents for the first time, there is real communication as they stare wordlessly at one another. Or imagine a detective story in which a woman has apparently committed suicide while her husband was in the house. The detective who comes to investigate bends over the body and after a few seconds looks at the husband saying, "What do you think caused your wife to—ah—commit—ah—suicide?" Immediately we are aware of the detective's suspicions and toward whom they are directed. The plot has been advanced and clues have been provided about both the detective and the husband.

These language characteristics—accent, word choice, repeated images, speech patterns, poetry versus prose, tone, pauses, omissions—all combine to convey information about the characters and about the significance of the play itself. A good playwright is not wasteful. He has a limited amount of time and space and must make good use of every word or phrase he includes. Characters do not swear accidently; they do not pause and stammer by chance. Rather, they are trying to tell us something about themselves. If we are to appreciate the art of the playwright and to understand his play fully, we must listen to what his characters say and how they say it.

THE COUNTRY WIFE

William Wycherley

PROLOGUE

Spoken by **Mr. Horner**

Poets, like cudgell'd bullies, never do
At first or second blow submit to you;
But will provoke you still, and ne'er have done,
Till you are weary first with laying on.
The late so baffled scribbler of this day,
Though he stands trembling, bids me boldly say,
What we before most plays are us'd to do,
For poets out of fear first draw on you;
In a fierce prologue the still pit defy,
And, ere you speak, like Castril give the lie.
But though our Bayes's battles oft I've fought,
And with bruis'd knuckles their dear conquests bought;
Nay, never yet fear'd odds upon the stage,
In prologue dare not hector with the age,
But would take quarter from your saving hands,
Though Bayes within all yielding countermands,
Says you confed'rate wits no quarter give,
Therefore his play shan't ask your leave to live.
Well, let the vain rash fop, by huffing so,
Think to obtain the better terms of you;
But we, the actors, humbly will submit,
Now, and at any time, to a full pit;
Nay, often we anticipate your rage,
And murder poets for you on our stage:
We set no guards upon our tiring-room,
But when with flying colours there you come,
We patiently, you see, give up to you
Our poets, virgins, nay, our matrons too.

THE PERSONS

Mr. Horner
Mr. Harcourt
Mr. Dorilant
Mr. Pinchwife
Mr. Sparkish
Sir Jasper Fidget
A Boy
A Quack

Mrs. Margery Pinchwife
Mrs. Alithea
Lady Fidget
Mrs. Dainty Fidget
Mrs. Squeamish
Old Lady Squeamish
Lucy, Alithea's Maid
Waiters, Servants, and Attendants

SCENE. London

ACT I

(*Enter* **Horner**, *and* **Quack** *following him at a distance*)

Horn: (*aside*) A quack is as fit for a pimp as a midwife for a bawd; they are still but in their way, both helpers of nature.—(*aloud*) Well, my dear Doctor, hast thou done what I desired?

Quack: I have undone you for ever with the women, and reported you throughout the whole town as bad as an eunuch, with as much trouble as if I had made you one in earnest.

Horn: But have you told all the midwives you know, the orange wenches at the playhouses, the city husbands, and old fumbling keepers of this end of the town, for they'll be the readiest to report it?

Quack: I have told all the chambermaids, waiting-women, tire-women, and old women of my acquaintance; nay, and whispered it as a secret to 'em, and to the whisperers of Whitehall; so that you need not doubt 'twill spread, and you will be as odious to the handsome young women as——

Horn: As the small-pox. Well——

Quack: And to the married women of this end of the town, as——

Horn: As the great ones; nay, as their own husbands.

Quack: And to the city dames, as aniseed Robin, of filthy and contemptible memory; and they will frighten their children with your name, especially their females.

Horn: And cry, Horner's coming to carry you away. I am only afraid 'twill not be believed. You told 'em 'twas by an English-French disaster, and an English-French chirurgeon, who has given me at once not only a cure, but an antidote for the future against that damned malady, and that worse distemper, love, and all other women's evils?

Quack: Your late journey into France has made it the more credible, and your being here a fortnight before you appeared in public looks as if you apprehended the shame, which I wonder you do not. Well, I have been hired by young gallants to belie 'em t'other way, but you are the first would be thought a man unfit for women.

Horn: Dear Mr. Doctor, let vain rogues be contented only to be thought abler men than they are; generally 'tis all the pleasure they have, but mine lies another way.

Quack: You take, methinks, a very preposterous way to it, and as ridiculous as if we operators in physic should put forth bills to disparage our medicaments, with hopes to gain customers.

Horn: Doctor, there are quacks in love as well as physic, who get but the fewer and worse patients for their boasting; a good name is seldom got by giving it one's self; and women no more than honour are compassed by bragging. Come, come, Doctor, the wisest lawyer never discovers the merits of his cause till the trial; the wealthiest man conceals his riches, and the cunning gamester his play. Shy husbands and keepers, like old rooks, are not to be cheated but by a new unpractised trick: false friendship will pass now no more than false dice upon 'em; no, not in the city.

Notice how Horner's speeches all refer to sex.

(*Enter* **Boy**)

Boy: There are two ladies and a gentleman coming up. (*Exit.*)

Horn: A pox! some unbelieving sisters of my former acquaintance, who, I am afraid, expect their sense should be satisfied of the falsity of the report. No—this formal fool and women!

(*Enter* **Sir Jasper Fidget, Lady Fidget,** *and* **Mrs. Dainty Fidget**)

Quack: His wife and sister.

Jasper establishes pattern with repetition of sir. What does it suggest about him?

Sir Jasp: My coach breaking just now before your door, Sir, I look upon as an occasional reprimand to me, Sir, for not kissing your hands, Sir, since your coming out of France, Sir; and so my disaster, Sir, has been my good fortune, Sir; and this is my wife and sister, Sir.

Horn: What then, Sir?

Sir Jasp: My lady, and sister, Sir.—Wife, this is Master Horner.

Lady Fid: Master Horner, husband!

Sir Jasp: My lady, my Lady Fidget, Sir.

Horn: So, Sir.

Sir Jasp: Won't you be acquainted with her, Sir?—(*aside*) So, the report is true, I find, by his coldness or aversion to the sex; but I'll play the wag with him. —Pray salute my wife, my lady, Sir.

Effect of Horner's repeating the sir series?

Horn: I will kiss no man's wife, Sir, for him, Sir; I have taken my eternal leave, Sir, of the sex already, Sir.

Sir Jasp: (*aside*) Ha! ha! ha! I'll plague him yet.——Not know my wife, Sir?

Horn: I do not know your wife, Sir; she's a woman, Sir, and consequently a monster, Sir, a greater monster than a husband, Sir.

Sir Jasp: A husband! how, Sir?

Horn: So, Sir; but I make no more cuckolds, Sir. (*makes horns*)

Sir Jasp: Ha! ha! ha! Mercury! Mercury!

Lady Fid: Pray, Sir Jasper, let us be gone from this rude fellow.

Mrs. Dain: Who, by his breeding, would think he had ever been in France?

Lady Fid: Foh! he's but too much a French fellow, such as hate women of quality and virtue for their love to their husbands, Sir Jasper; a woman is hated by 'em as much for loving her husband as for loving their money. But pray, let's be gone.

Horn: You do well, Madam, for I have nothing that you came for: I have brought over not so much as a bawdy picture, no new postures, nor the second part of the *Escole des Filles*; nor——

Quack: (*apart to* **Horner**) Hold, for shame, Sir! what d'ye mean? You will ruin yourself for ever with the sex——

Sir Jasp: Ha! ha! ha! he hates women perfectly, I find.

Mrs. Dain: What pity 'tis he should!

Lady Fid: Ay, he's a base rude fellow for't. But affectation makes not a woman more odious to them than virtue.

Horner is blunt and realistic.

Horn: Because your virtue is your greatest affectation, Madam.

Lady Fid: How, you saucy fellow! would you wrong my honour?

Horn: If I could.

Lady Fid: How d'ye mean, Sir?

Sir Jasp: Ha! ha! ha! no, he can't wrong your Ladyship's honour, upon my honour; he, poor man—hark you in your ear—a mere eunuch.

Lady Fid: O filthy French beast! foh! foh! why do we stay? let's be gone: I can't endure the sight of him.

Sir Jasp: Stay but till the chairs come; they'll be here presently.

Lady Fid: No, no.

Sir Jasp: Nor can I stay longer. 'Tis—let me see, a quarter and a half quarter of a minute past eleven. The council will be sat; I must away. Business must be preferred always before love and ceremony with the wise, Mr. Horner.

Horn: And the impotent, Sir Jasper.

Sir Jasp: Ay, ay, the impotent, Master Horner; ha! ha! ha!

Lady Fid: What, leave us with a filthy man alone in his lodgings?

Sir Jasp: He's an innocent man now, you know. Pray stay, I'll hasten the chairs to you.—— Mr. Horner, your servant; I should be glad to see you at my house. Pray come and dine with me, and play at cards with my wife after dinner; you are fit for women at that game yet, ha! ha!—(*aside*) 'Tis as much a husband's prudence to provide innocent diversion for a wife as to hinder her unlawful pleasures; and he had better employ her than let her employ herself.——Farewell.

Horn: Your servant, Sir Jasper. (*Exit* **Sir Jasper**.)

Lady Fid: I will not stay with him, foh!——

Horn: Nay, Madam, I beseech you stay, if it be but to see I can be as civil to ladies yet as they would desire.

Euphemism: for Horner and the ladies, civil equals sex.

Lady Fid: No, no, foh! you cannot be civil to ladies.

Mrs. Dain: You as civil as ladies would desire?

Lady Fid: No, no, no, foh! foh! foh! (*Exeunt* **Lady Fidget** *and* **Dainty Fidget**.)

Quack: Now, I think, I, or you yourself, rather, have done your business with the women.

Horn: Thou art an ass. Don't you see already, upon the report and my carriage, this grave man of business leaves his wife in my lodgings, invites me to his house and wife, who before would not be acquainted with me out of jealousy?

Quack: Nay, by this means you may be the more acquainted with the husbands, but the less with the wives.

Horn: Let me alone; if I can but abuse the husbands, I'll soon disabuse the wives. Stay—I'll reckon you up the advantages I am like to have by my stratagem. First, I shall be rid of all my old acquaintances, the most insatiable sorts of duns, that invade our lodgings in a morning; and next to the pleasure of making a new mistress is that of being rid of an old one, and of all old debts. Love, when it comes to be so, is paid the most unwillingly.

Quack: Well, you may be so rid of your old acquaintances; but how will you get any new ones?

Horn: Doctor, thou wilt never make a good chemist, thou art so incredulous and impatient. Ask but all the young fellows of the town if they do not lose more time, like huntsmen, in starting the game, than in running it down. One knows not where to find 'em, who will or will not. Women of quality are so civil you can hardly distinguish love from good breeding, and a man is often mistaken: but now I can be sure she that shows an aversion to me loves the sport, as those women that are gone, whom I warrant to be right. And then the next thing is, your women of honour, as you call 'em, are only chary of their reputations, not their persons; and 'tis scandal they would avoid, not men. Now may I have, by the reputation of an eunuch, the privi-

Notice his logic. What's his opinion of women?

leges of one, and be seen in a lady's chamber in a morning as early as her husband; kiss virgins before their parents or lovers; and maybe, in short, the *passe-partout* of the town. Now, Doctor.

Quack: Nay, now you shall be the doctor, and your process is so new that we do not know but it may succeed.

Horn: Not so new neither; *probatum est*, Doctor.

Quack: Well, I wish you luck, and many patients, whilst I go to mine. (*Exit.*)

(*Enter* **Harcourt** *and* **Dorilant** *to* **Horner**)

Har: Come, your appearance at the play yesterday has, I hope, hardened you for the future against the women's contempt and the men's raillery; and now you'll abroad as you were wont.

Horn: Did I not bear it bravely?

Dor: With a most theatrical impudence, nay, more than the orange-wenches show there, or a drunken vizard-mask, or a great bellied actress; nay, or the most impudent of creatures, an ill poet; or what is yet more impudent, a second-hand critic.

Horn: But what say the ladies? have they no pity?

Har: What ladies? The vizard-masks, you know, never pity a man when all's gone, though in their service.

Dor: And for the women in the boxes, you'd never pity them when 'twas in your power.

Har: They say 'tis pity but all that deal with common women should be served so.

Dor: Nay, I dare swear they won't admit you to play at cards with them, go to plays with 'em, or do the little duties which other shadows of men are wont to do for 'em.

Horn: What do you call shadows of men?

Dor: Half-men.

Horn: What, boys?

What do animal images suggest about Dorilant's view of people?

Dor: Ay, your old boys, old *beaux garçons*, who, like super-annuated stallions, are suffered to run, feed, and whinny with the mares as long as they live, though they can do nothing else.

Horn: Well, a pox on love and wenching! Women serve but to keep a man from better company. Though I can't enjoy them, I shall you the more. Good fellowship and friendship are lasting, rational, and manly pleasures.

Har: For all that, give me some of those pleasures you call effeminate too; they help to relish one another.

Horn: They disturb one another.

Har: No, mistresses are like books. If you pore upon them too much, they doze you, and make you unfit for company; but if used discreetly, you are the fitter for conversation by 'em.

Dor: A mistress should be like a little country retreat near the town; not to dwell in constantly, but only for a night and away, to taste the town the better when a man returns.

Horn: I tell you, 'tis as hard to be a good fellow, a good friend, and a lover of women, as 'tis to be a good fellow, a good friend, and a lover of money. You cannot follow both, then choose your side. Wine gives you liberty, love takes it away.

Dor: Gad, he's in the right on't.

Horn: Wine gives you joy; love, grief and tortures, besides the chirurgeon's.

Wine makes us witty; love, only sots. Wine makes us sleep; love breaks it.

Dor: By the world, he has reason, Harcourt.

Horn: Wine makes——

Dor: Ay, wine makes us—makes us princes; love makes us beggars, poor rogues, egad—and wine——

Horn: So, there's one converted.—No, no, love and wine, oil and vinegar.

Har: I grant it; love will still be uppermost.

Horn: Come, for my part, I will have only those glorious manly pleasures of being very drunk and very slovenly.

(*Enter* **Boy**)

Horner's language is filled with references to physical pleasures.

Boy: Mr. Sparkish is below, Sir. (*Exit.*)

Har: What, my dear friend! a rogue that is fond of me, only I think, for abusing him.

Dor: No, he can no more think the men laugh at him than that women jilt him, his opinion of himself is so good.

Horn: Well, there's another pleasure by drinking I thought not of—I shall lose his acquaintance, because he cannot drink: and you know 'tis a very hard thing to be rid of him, for he's one of those nauseous offerers at wit, who, like the worst fiddlers, run themselves into all companies.

Har: One that, by being in the company of men of sense, would pass for one.

Horn: And may so to the short-sighted world, as a false jewel amongst true ones is not discerned at a distance. His company is as troublesome to us as a cuckold's when you have a mind to his wife's.

Har: No, the rogue will not let us enjoy one another, but ravishes our conversation, though he signifies no more to't than Sir Martin Mar-all's gaping, and awkward thrumming upon the lute, does to his man's voice and music.

Dor: And to pass for a wit in town shows himself a fool every night to us, that are guilty of the plot.

Horn: Such wits as he are, to a company of reasonable men, like rooks to the gamesters, who only fill a room at the table, but are so far from contributing to the play, that they only serve to spoil the fancy of those that do.

Dor: Nay, they are used like rooks too, snubbed, checked, and abused; yet the rogues will hang on.

Horn: A pox on 'em, and all that force nature, and would be still what she forbids 'em! Affectation is her greatest monster.

Har: Most men are the contraries to that they would seem. Your bully, you see, is a coward with a long sword; the little humbly fawning physician, with his ebony cane, is he that destroys men.

Dor: The usurer, a poor rogue, possessed of mouldy bonds and mortgages; and we they call spendthrifts are only wealthy who lay out his money upon daily new purchases of pleasure.

Horn: Ay, your arrantest cheat is your trustee or executor, your jealous man, the greatest cuckold, your churchman the greatest atheist, and your noisy pert rogue of a wit, the greatest fop, dullest ass, and worst company, as you shall see; for here he comes.

(*Enter* **Sparkish**)

Spark: How is't, sparks? how is't? Well, faith, Harry, I must rally thee a little, ha! ha! ha! upon the report in town of thee, ha! ha! ha! I can't hold i'faith; shall I speak?

Horn: Yes; but you'll be so bitter then.

Spark: Honest Dick and Frank here shall answer for me, I will not be extreme bitter, by the universe.

Har: We will be bound in a ten-thousand-pound bond, he shall not be bitter at all.

Dor: Nor sharp, nor sweet.

Horn: What, not downright insipid?

Spark: Nay then, since you are so brisk, and provoke me, take what follows. You must know, I was discoursing and rallying with some ladies yesterday, and they happened to talk of the fine new signs in town.

Horn: Very fine ladies, I believe.

Spark: Said I, I know where the best new sign is.—Where? says one of the ladies.—In Covent Garden, I replied.—Said another, In what street?—In Russel Street, answered I.—Lord, says another, I'm sure there was ne'er a fine new sign there yesterday.—Yes, but there was, said I again, and it came out of France, and has been there a fortnight.

Dor: A pox! I can hear no more, prithee.

Horn: No, hear him out; let him tune his crowd a while.

Har: The worst music, the greatest preparation.

Spark: Nay, faith, I'll make you laugh.—It cannot be, says a third lady.—Yes, yes, quoth I again.—Says a fourth lady——

Horn: Look to't, we'll have no more ladies.

Spark: No—then mark, mark, now. Said I to the fourth, Did you never see Mr. Horner? he lodges in Russel Street, and he's a sign of a man, you know, since he came out of France; ha! ha! ha!

Horn: But the devil take me if thine be the sign of a jest.

Sparkish giggles, makes a short story long, and through language, proves he is as Horner described him.

Spark: With that they all fell a-laughing, till they bepissed themselves. What, but it does not move you, methinks? Well, I see one had as good go to law without a witness, as break a jest without a laugher on one's side.——Come, come, sparks, but where do we dine? I have left at Whitehall an earl to dine with you.

Dor: Why, I thought thou hadst loved a man with a title better than a suit with a French trimming to't.

Har: Go to him again.

Spark: No, Sir, a wit to me is the greatest title in the world.

Horn: But go dine with your earl, Sir; he may be exceptious. We are your friends, and will not take it ill to be left, I do assure you.

Har: Nay, faith, he shall go to him.

Spark: Nay, pray, gentlemen.

Dor: We'll thrust you out, if you won't; what, disappoint anybody for us?

Spark: Nay, dear gentlemen, hear me.

Horn: No, no, Sir, by no means; pray go, Sir.

Spark: Why, dear rogues——

Dor: No, no. (*They all thrust him out of the room.*)

All: Ha! ha! ha!

(**Sparkish** *returns*)

Spark: But, sparks, pray hear me. What, d'ye think I'll eat then with gay shallow fops and silent coxcombs? I think wit as necessary at dinner as a glass of good wine, and that's the reason I never have any stomach when I eat alone. —Come, but where do we dine?

Horn: Even where you will.

Spark: At Chateline's?

Dor: Yes, if you will.

Spark: Or at the Cock?

Dor: Yes, if you please.

Spark: Or at the Dog and Partridge?

Horn: Ay, if you have a mind to't; for we shall dine at neither.

Spark: Pshaw! with your fooling we shall lose the new play; and I would no more miss seeing a new play the first day, than I would miss sitting in the wits' row. Therefore I'll go fetch my mistress, and away. (*Exit.*)

Not to see the play, but to be seen

(*Manent* **Horner, Harcourt, Dorilant:** *enter to them* **Mr. Pinchwife**)

Horn: Who have we here? Pinchwife?

Pinch: Gentlemen, your humble servant.

Horn: Well, Jack, by thy long absence from the town, the grumness of thy countenance, and the slovenliness of thy habit, I should give thee joy, should I not, of marriage?

Pinch: (*aside*) Death! does he know I'm married too? I thought to have concealed it from him at least.——My long stay in the country will excuse my dress; and I have a suit of law that brings me up to town, that puts me out of humour. Besides, I must give Sparkish to-morrow five thousand pound to lie with my sister.

Horn: Nay, you country gentlemen, rather than not purchase, will buy anything; and he is a cracked title, if we may quibble. Well, but am I to give thee joy? I heard thou wert married.

Pinch: What then?

Horn: Why, the next thing that is to be heard is, thou'rt a cuckold.

Pinch: (*aside*) Insupportable name!

Beginning of pattern: cuckold is insupportable word to Pinchwife

Horn: But I did not expect marriage from such a whoremaster as you, one that knew the town so much, and women so well.

Pinch: Why, I have married no London wife.

Horn: Pshaw! that's all one. That grave circumspection in marrying a country wife, is like refusing a deceitful pampered Smithfield jade, to go and be cheated by a friend in the country.

Pinch: (*aside*) A pox on him and his simile!——At least we are a little surer of the breed there, know what her keeping has been, whether foiled or unsound.

Animal images again — women as mares

Horn: Come, come, I have known a clap gotten in Wales; and there are cuzens, justices' clerks, and chaplains in the country, I won't say coachmen. But she's handsome and young?

Pinch: (*aside*) I'll answer as I should do.——No, no; she has no beauty but her youth, no attraction but her modesty: wholesome, homely, and huswifely; that's all.

Dor: He talks as like a grazier as he looks.

Pinch: She's too awkward, ill-favoured, and silly to bring to town.

Har: Then methinks you should bring her to be taught breeding.

Pun on breeding

Pinch: To be taught! no, Sir, I thank you. Good wives and private soldiers should be ignorant—I'll keep her from your instructions, I warrant you.

Har: (*aside*) The rogue is as jealous as if his wife were not ignorant.

Pinchwife's word choice betrays him.

Horn: Why, if she be ill-favoured, there will be less danger here for you than by leaving her in the country. We have such variety of dainties that we are seldom hungry.

Dor: But they have always coarse, constant, swingeing stomachs in the country.

Har: Foul feeders indeed!

Dor: And your hospitality is great there.

Har: Open house; every man's welcome.

Pinch: So, so, gentlemen.

Horn: But prithee, why wouldst thou marry her? If she be ugly, ill-bred, and silly, she must be rich then.

Pinch: As rich as if she brought me twenty thousand pound out of this town; for she'll be as sure not to spend her moderate portion as a London baggage would be to spend hers, let it be what it would: so 'tis all one. Then, because she's ugly, she's the likelier to be my own; and being ill-bred, she'll hate conversation; and since silly and innocent, will not know the difference betwixt a man of one-and-twenty and one of forty.

Nine must be said quickly— joke depends on rhythm

Horn: Nine—to my knowledge. But if she be silly, she'll expect as much from a man of forty-nine, as from him of one-and-twenty. But methinks wit is more necessary than beauty; and I think no young woman ugly that has it, and no handsome woman agreeable without it.

Pinch: 'Tis my maxim, he's a fool that marries; but he's a greater that does not marry a fool. What is wit in a wife good for, but to make a man a cuckold?

Horn: Yes, to keep it from his knowledge.

Pinch: A fool cannot contrive to make her husband a cuckold.

Horn: No; but she'll club with a man that can: and what is worse, if she cannot make her husband a cuckold, she'll make him jealous, and pass for one: and then 'tis all one.

Pinch: Well, well, I'll take care for one. My wife shall make me no cuckold, though she had your help, Mr. Horner. I understand the town, Sir.

Dor: (*aside*) His help!

Har: (*aside*) He's come newly to town, it seems, and has not heard how things are with him.

Horn: But tell me, has marriage cured thee of whoring, which it seldom does?

Har: 'Tis more than age can do.

Horn: No, the word is, I'll marry and live honest: but a marriage vow is like a penitent gamester's oath, and entering into bonds and penalties to stint himself to such a particular small sum at play for the future, which makes him but the more eager; and not being able to hold out, loses his money again, and his forfeit to boot.

Dor: Ay, ay, a gamester will be a gamester whilst his money lasts, and a whoremaster whilst his vigour.

Har: Nay, I have known 'em, when they are broke, and can lose no more, keep a-fumbling with the box in their hands to fool with only, and hinder other gamesters.

Dor: That had wherewithal to make lusty stakes.

Pinch: Well, gentlemen, you may laugh at me; but you shall never lie with my wife: I know the town.

Horn: But prithee, was not the way you were in better? is not keeping better than marriage?

Pinch: A pox on't! the jades would jilt me, I could never keep a whore to myself.

Horn: So, then you only married to keep a whore to yourself. Well, but let me tell you, women, as you say, are like soldiers, made constant and loyal by good pay, rather than by oaths and covenants. Therefore I'd advise my friends to keep rather than marry, since too I find, by your example, it does not serve one's turn; for I saw you yesterday in the eighteen-penny place with a pretty country wench.

Pinch: (*aside*) How the devil! did he see my wife then? I sat there that she might not be seen. But she shall never go to a play again.

Horn: What! dost thou blush at nine-and-forty for having been seen with a wench?

Dor: No, faith, I warrant 'twas his wife, which he seated there out of sight; for he's a cunning rogue, and understands the town.

Har: He blushes. Then 'twas his wife; for men are now more ashamed to be seen with them in public than with a wench.

Pinch: (*aside*) Hell and damnation! I'm undone, since Horner has seen her, and they know 'twas she.

Horn: But prithee, was it thy wife? She was exceedingly pretty: I was in love with her at that distance.

Pinch: You are like never to be nearer to her. Your servant, gentlemen. (*offers to go*)

Horn: Nay, prithee stay.

Pinch: I cannot; I will not.

Horn: Come, you shall dine with us.

Pinch: I have dined already.

Horn: Come, I know thou hast not: I'll treat thee, dear rogue; thou shalt spend none of thy Hampshire money to-day.

Pinch: (*aside*) Treat me! So, he uses me already like his cuckold.

Horn: Nay, you shall not go.

Pinch: I must; I have business at home. (*Exit*)

Har: To beat his wife. He's as jealous of her as a Cheapside husband of a Covent Garden wife.

Horn: Why, 'tis as hard to find an old whoremaster without jealousy and the gout, as a young one without fear or the pox.

As gout in age from pox in youth proceeds,
So wenching past, then jealousy succeeds:
The worst disease that love and wenching breeds.

Cuckold, eunuch, clap, animals, horns, eating, drinking, pox, jealousy, whore= master— words reveal the world.

(*Exeunt*)

ACT II

(**Mrs. Margery Pinchwife** *and* **Alithea**. Pinchwife *peeping behind at the door*)

Mrs. Pinch: Pray, Sister, where are the best fields and woods to walk in, in London?

Alith: A pretty question! Why, Sister, Mulberry Garden and St. James's Park; and, for close walks, the New Exchange.

Mrs. Pinch: Pray, Sister, tell me why my husband looks so grum here in town, and keeps me up so close, and will not let me go a-walking, nor let me wear my best gown yesterday.

Alith: Oh, he's jealous, Sister.

Mrs. Pinch: Jealous! what's that?

Alith: He's afraid you should love another man.

Mrs. Pinch: How should he be afraid of my loving another man, when he will not let me see any but himself?

Alith: Did he not carry you yesterday to a play?

Mrs. Pinch: Ay; but we sat amongst ugly people. He would not let me come near the gentry, who sat under us, so that I could not see 'em. He told me none but naughty women sat there, whom they toused and moused. But I would have ventured, for all that.

Alith: But how did you like the play?

Margery's country background shows in language: aweary, hugeously, goodliest.

Mrs. Pinch: Indeed I was aweary of the play, but I liked hugeously the actors. They are the goodliest, properest men, Sister!

Alith: Oh, but you must not like the actors, Sister.

Mrs. Pinch: Ay, how should I help it, Sister? Pray, Sister, when my husband comes in, will you ask leave for me to go a-walking?

Alith: (*aside*) A-walking! ha! ha! Lord, a country-gentlewoman's leisure is the drudgery of a footpost; and she requires as much airing as her husband's horses.——But here comes your husband: I'll ask, though I'm sure he'll not grant it.

Mrs. Pinch: He says he won't let me go abroad for fear of catching the pox.

Alith: Fy! the small-pox you should say.

(*Enter* **Pinchwife** *to them*)

Mrs. Pinch: O my dear, dear bud, welcome home! Why dost thou look so fropish? who has nangered thee?

Pinch: You're a fool.

(**Mrs. Pinchwife** *goes aside, and cries.*)

Alith: Faith, so she is, for crying for no fault, poor tender creature!

Pinch: What, you would have her as impudent as yourself, as arrant a jillflirt, a gadder, a magpie; and to say all, a mere notorious town-woman?

Alith: Brother, you are my only censurer; and the honour of your family shall sooner suffer in your wife there than in me, though I take the innocent liberty of the town.

Pinch: Hark you, mistress, do not talk so before my wife.—The innocent liberty of the town!

Alith: Why, pray, who boasts of any intrigue with me? what lampoon has made my name notorious? what ill women frequent my lodgings? I keep no company with any women of scandalous reputations.

Pinch: No, you keep the men of scandalous reputations company.

Alith: Where? would you not have me civil? answer 'em in a box at the plays, in the drawing-room at Whitehall, in St. James's Park, Mulberry Garden, or——

Pinch: Hold, hold! Do not teach my wife where the men are to be found: I believe she's the worse for your town-documents already. I bid you keep her in ignorance, as I do.

Mrs. Pinch: Indeed, be not angry with her, bud, she will tell me nothing of the town, though I ask her a thousand times a day.

Pinch: Then you are very inquisitive to know, I find?

Mrs. Pinch: Not I indeed, dear; I hate London. Our placehouse in the country is worth a thousand of't: would I were there again!

Pinch: So you shall, I warrant. But were you not talking of plays and players when I came in?——You are her encourager in such discourses.

Mrs. Pinch: No, indeed, dear; she chid me just now for liking the playermen.

Pinch: (*aside*) Nay, if she be so innocent as to own to me her liking them, there is no hurt in't.——Come, my poor rogue, but thou lik'st none better than me?

Mrs. Pinch: Yes, indeed, but I do. The playermen are finer folks.

Pinch: But you love none better than me?

Mrs. Pinch: You are mine own dear bud, and I know you. I hate a stranger.

Pinch: Ay, my dear, you must love me only, and not be like the naughty town-women, who only hate their husbands, and love every man else; love plays, visits, fine coaches, fine clothes, fiddles, balls, treats, and so lead a wicked town-life.

Mrs. Pinch: Nay, if to enjoy all these things be a town-life, London is not so bad a place, dear.

Pinch: How! if you love me, you must hate London.

Alith: (*aside*) The fool has forbid me discovering to her the pleasures of the town, and he is now setting her agog upon them himself.

Mrs. Pinch: But, husband, do the town-women love the playermen too?

Pinch: Yes, I warrant you.

Mrs. Pinch: Ay, I warrant you.

Pinch: Why, you do not, I hope?

Mrs. Pinch: No, no, bud. But why have we no playermen in the country?

Pinch: Ha!—Mrs. Minx, ask me no more to go to a play.

Mrs. Pinch: Nay, why love? I did not care for going: but when you forbid me, you make me, as 'twere, desire it.

Alith: (*aside*) So 'twill be in other things, I warrant.

Mrs. Pinch: Pray let me go to a play, dear.

Pinch: Hold your peace, I wo' not.

Mrs. Pinch: Why, love?

Pinch: Why, I'll tell you.

Alith: (*aside*) Nay, if he tell her, she'll give him more cause to forbid her that place.

Mrs. Pinch: Pray why, dear?

Pinch: First, you like the actors; and the gallants may like you.

Mrs. Pinch: What, a homely country girl! No, bud, nobody will like me.

Pinch: I tell you yes, they may.

Mrs. Pinch: No, no, you jest—I won't believe you: I will go.

Pinch: I tell you then, that one of the lewdest fellows in town, who saw you there, told me he was in love with you.

Mrs. Pinch: Indeed! who, who, pray who was't?

Pinch: (*aside*) I've gone too far, and slipped before I was aware; how overjoyed she is!

Mrs. Pinch: Was it any Hampshire gallant, any of our neighbours? I promise you, I am beholden to him.

Pinch: I promise you, you lie; for he would but ruin you, as he has done hundreds. He has no other love for women but that; such as he look upon women, like basilisks, but to destroy 'em.

Mrs. Pinch: Ay, but if he loves me, why should he ruin me? answer me to that. Methinks he should not, I would do him no harm.

Alith: Ha! ha! ha!

Pinch: 'Tis very well; but I'll keep him from doing you any harm, or me either. But here comes company; get you in, get you in.

Mrs. Pinch: But, pray, husband, is he a pretty gentleman that loves me?

Pinch: In, baggage, in. (*thrusts her in, shuts the door*)

(*Enter* **Sparkish** *and* **Harcourt**)

What, all the lewd libertines of the town brought to my lodging by this easy coxcomb! 'Sdeath, I'll not suffer it.

Spark: Here, Harcourt, do you approve my choice?——Dear little rogue, I told you I'd bring you acquainted with all my friends, the wits and——(**Harcourt** *salutes her.*)

Pinch: Ay, they shall know her, as well as you yourself will, I warrant you.

Spark: This is one of those, my pretty rogue, that are to dance at your wedding to-morrow; and him you must bid welcome ever, to what you and I have.

Pinch: (*aside*) Monstrous!

Spark: Harcourt, how dost thou like her, faith? Nay, dear, do not look down; I should hate to have a wife of mine out of countenance at anything.

Pinch: (*aside*) Wonderful!

Spark: Tell me, I say, Harcourt, how dost thou like her? Thou hast stared upon her enough to resolve me.

Har: So infinitely well, that I could wish I had a mistress too, that might differ from her in nothing but her love and engagement to you.

Alith: Sir, Master Sparkish has often told me that his acquaintance were all wits and railleurs, and now I find it.

Spark: No, by the universe, Madam, he does not rally now; you may believe him. I do assure you, he is the honestest, worthiest, true-hearted gentleman— a man of such perfect honour, he would say nothing to a lady he does not mean.

Pinch: (*aside*) Praising another man to his mistress!

Har: Sir, you are so beyond expectation obliging, that——

Spark: Nay, egad, I am sure you do admire her extremely; I see't in your eyes. ——He does admire you, Madam.——By the world, don't you?

Har: Yes, above the world, or the most glorious part of it, her whole sex: and till now I never thought I should have envied you, or any man about to marry, but you have the best excuse for marriage I ever knew.

Alith: Nay, now, Sir, I'm satisfied you are of the society of the wits and railleurs, since you cannot spare your friend, even when he is but too civil to you; but the surest sign is, since you are an enemy to marriage, for that I hear you hate as much as business or bad wine.

Har: Truly, Madam, I never was an enemy to marriage till now, because marriage was never an enemy to me before.

Alith: But why, Sir, is marriage an enemy to you now? Because it robs you of your friend here? for you look upon a friend married as one gone into a monastery, that is, dead to the world.

How does her definition of love differ from her husband's?

Har: 'Tis indeed, because you marry him; I see, Madam, you can guess my meaning. I do confess heartily and openly I wish it were in my power to break the match; by Heavens I would.

Spark: Poor Frank!

Alith: Would you be so unkind to me?

Har: No, no, 'tis not because I would be unkind to you.

Spark: Poor Frank! no gad, 'tis only his kindness to me.

Pinch: (*aside*) Great kindness to you indeed! Insensible fop, let a man make love to his wife to his face!

Spark: Come, dear Frank, for all my wife there, that shall be, thou shalt enjoy me sometimes, dear rogue. By my honour, we men of wit condole for our deceased brother in marriage, as much as for one dead in earnest: I think that was prettily said of me, ha, Harcourt?——But come, Frank, be not melancholy for me.

Har: No, I assure you, I am not melancholy for you.

Spark: Prithee, Frank, dost think my wife that shall be there, a fine person?

Har: I could gaze upon her till I became as blind as you are.

Spark: How as I am? how?

Har: Because you are a lover, and true lovers are blind, stock blind.

Spark: True, true; but by the world she has wit too, as well as beauty: go, go with her into a corner, and try if she has wit; talk to her anything; she's bashful before me.

Har: Indeed if a woman wants wit in a corner, she has it nowhere.

Alith: (*aside to* **Sparkish**) Sir, you dispose of me a little before your time——

Spark: Nay, nay, Madam, let me have an earnest of your obedience, or—go, go, Madam——

(**Harcourt** *courts* **Alithea** *aside.*)

Pinch: How, Sir! if you are not concerned for the honour of a wife, I am for that of a sister; he shall not debauch her. Be a pander to your own wife! bring men to her! let 'em make love before your face! thrust 'em into a corner together, then leave 'em in private! is this your town wit and conduct?

Spark: Ha! ha! ha! a silly wise rogue would make one laugh more than a stark fool, ha! ha! I shall burst. Nay, you shall not disturb 'em; I'll vex thee, by the world. *Tone of Sparkish's laugh?*

(*struggles with* **Pinchwife** *to keep him from* **Harcourt** *and* **Alithea**)

Alith: The writings are drawn, Sir, settlements made; 'tis too late, Sir, and past all revocation.

Har: Then so is my death.

Alith: I would not be unjust to him.

Har: Then why to me so?

Alith: I have no obligation to you.

Har: My love.

Alith: I had his before.

Har: You never had it; he wants, you see, jealousy, the only infallible sign of it.

Alith: Love proceeds from esteem; he cannot distrust my virtue: besides, he loves me, or he would not marry me.

Har: Marrying you is no more sign of his love than bribing your woman, that he may marry you, is a sign of his generosity. Marriage is rather a sign of interest than love; and he that marries a fortune covets a mistress, not loves her. But if you take marriage for a sign of love, take it from me immediately.

Alith: No, now you have put a scruple in my head; but in short, Sir, to end our dispute, I must marry him; my reputation would suffer in the world else.

Har: No; if you do marry him, with your pardon, Madam, your reputation suffers in the world, and you would be thought in necessity for a cloak.

Alith: Nay, now you are rude, Sir.——Mr. Sparkish, pray come hither, your friend here is very troublesome, and very loving.

Har: (*aside to* **Alithea**) Hold! hold!——

Pinch: D'ye hear that?

Word is not stylish —he rejects it.

Spark: Why, d'ye think I'll seem to be jealous, like a country bumpkin?

Pinch: No, rather be a cuckold, like a credulous cit.

Har: Madam, you would not have been so little generous as to have told him.

Alith: Yes, since you could be so little generous as to wrong him.

Har: Wrong him! no man can do't, he's beneath an injury: a bubble, a coward, a senseless idiot, a wretch so contemptible to all the world but you, that——

Alith: Hold, do not rail at him, for since he is like to be my husband, I am resolved to like him: nay, I think I am obliged to tell him you are not his friend.——Master Sparkish, Master Sparkish!

Spark: What, what?——Now, dear rogue, has not she wit?

Har: Not so much as I thought, and hoped she had. (*speaks surlily*)

Alith: Mr. Sparkish, do you bring people to rail at you?

Har: Madam——

Spark: How! no; but if he does rail at me, 'tis but in jest, I warrant: what we wits do for one another, and never take any notice of it.

Alith: He spoke so scurrilously of you, I had no patience to hear him; besides, he has been making love to me.

Har: (*aside*) True, damned tell-tale woman!

Words, witty flourishes, no real feelings — air, not substance

Spark: Pshaw! to show his parts—we wits rail and make love often, but to show our parts: as we have no affections, so we have no malice, we——

Alith: He said you were a wretch below an injury——

Spark: Pshaw!

Five pshaws in seven lines — say it aloud five times. What effect ?

Har: (*aside*) Damned, senseless, impudent, virtuous jade! Well, since she won't let me have her, she'll do as good, she'll make me hate her.

Alith: A common bubble——

Spark: Pshaw!

Alith: A coward——

Spark: Pshaw, pshaw!

Alith: A senseless, drivelling idiot——

Spark: How! did he disparage my parts? Nay, then, my honour's concerned, I can't put up that, Sir, by the world—brother, help me to kill him.—(*aside*) I may draw now, since we have the odds of him—'tis a good occasion, too, before my mistress——(*offers to draw*)

Alith: Hold, hold!

Spark: What, what?

Alith: (*aside*) I must not let 'em kill the gentleman neither, for his kindness to me: I am so far from hating him, that I wish my gallant had his person and understanding. Nay, if my honour——

Spark: I'll be thy death.

Alith: Hold, hold! Indeed, to tell the truth, the gentleman said after all, that what he spoke was but out of friendship to you.

Spark: How! say, I am—I am a fool, that is no wit, out of friendship to me?

Alith: Yes, to try whether I was concerned enough for you; and made love to me only to be satisfied of my virtue, for your sake.

Har: (*aside*) Kind, however.

Spark: Nay, if it were so, my dear rogue, I ask thee pardon; but why would not you tell me so, faith?

Har: Because I did not think on't, faith.

Spark: Come, Horner does not come; Harcourt, let's be gone to the new play. —Come, Madam.

Alith: I will not go, if you intend to leave me alone in the box and run into the pit, as you use to do.

Spark: Pshaw! I'll leave Harcourt with you in the box to entertain you, and that's as good; if I sat in the box, I should be thought no judge but of trimmings.—Come away, Harcourt, lead her down. (*Exeunt* **Sparkish**, **Harcourt**, *and* **Alithea**)

Pinch: Well, go thy ways, for the flower of the true town fops, such as spend their estates before they come to 'em, and are cuckolds before they're married. But let me go look to my own freehold.—How!

(*Enter* **My Lady Fidget**, **Mrs. Dainty Fidget**, *and* **Mrs. Squeamish**)

Lady Fid: Your servant, Sir: where is your lady? We are come to wait upon her to the new play.

Pinch: New play!

Lady Fid: And my husband will wait upon you presently.

Pinch: (*aside*) Damn your civility.——Madam, by no means; I will not see Sir Jasper here till I have waited upon him at home; nor shall my wife see you till she has waited upon your ladyship at your lodgings.

Lady Fid: Now we are here, Sir?

Pinch: No, Madam.

Mrs. Dain: Pray, let us see her.

Mrs. Squeam: We will not stir till we see her.

Pinch: (*aside*) A pox on you all!—(*goes to the door, and returns*) She has locked the door, and is gone abroad.

Lady Fid: No, you have locked the door, and she's within.

Mrs. Dain: They told us below she was here.

Pinch: (*aside*) Will nothing do?——Well, it must out then. To tell you the truth, ladies, which I was afraid to let you know before, lest it might endanger your lives, my wife has just now the small-pox come out upon her; do not be frightened, but pray be gone, ladies; you shall not stay here in danger of your lives; pray get you gone, ladies.

Lady Fid: No, no, we have all had 'em.

Mrs. Squeam: Alack, alack!

Mrs. Dain: Come, come, we must see how it goes with her; I understand the disease.

Lady Fid: Come!

Pinch: (*aside*) Well, there is no being too hard for women at their own weapon, lying, therefore I'll quit the field. (*Exit.*)

Mrs. Squeam: Here's an example of jealousy!

Lady Fid: Indeed, as the world goes, I wonder there are no more jealous, since wives are so neglected.

Mrs. Dain: Pshaw! as the world goes, to what end should they be jealous?

Lady Fid: Foh! 'tis a nasty world.

Mrs. Squeam: That men of parts, great acquaintance, and quality, should take up with and spend themselves and fortunes in keeping little playhouse creatures, foh!

Lady Fid: Nay, that women of understanding, great acquaintance, and good quality, should fall a-keeping too of little creatures, foh!

Mrs. Squeam: Why, 'tis the men of quality's fault; they never visit women of honour and reputation as they used to do; and have not so much as common civility for ladies of our rank, but use us with the same indifferency and ill-breeding as if we were all married to 'em.

Lady Fid: She says true; 'tis an arrant shame women of quality should be so slighted; methinks birth—birth should go for something; I have known men admired, courted, and followed for their titles only.

Mrs. Squeam: Ay, one would think men of honour should not love, no more than marry, out of their own rank.

Mrs. Dain: Fy, fy, upon 'em! they are come to think cross breeding for themselves best, as well as for their dogs and horses.

Lady Fid: They are dogs and horses for't.

Mrs. Squeam: One would think, if not for love, for vanity a little.

Mrs. Dain: Nay, they do satisfy their vanity upon us sometimes; and are kind to us in their report, tell all the world they lie with us.

Lady Fid: Damned rascals, that we should be only wronged by 'em! To report a man has had a person, when he has not had a person, is the greatest wrong in the whole world that can be done to a person.

Mrs. Squeam: Well, 'tis an arrant shame noble persons should be so wronged and neglected.

Lady Fid: But still 'tis an arranter shame for a noble person to neglect her own honour, and defame her own noble person with little inconsiderable fellows, foh!

Mrs. Dain: I suppose the crime against our honour is the same with a man of quality as with another.

Lady Fid: How! no, sure, the man of quality is likest one's husband, and therefore the fault should be the less.

Mrs. Dain: But then the pleasure should be the less.

Lady Fid: Fy, fy, fy, for shame, Sister! whither shall we ramble? Be continent in your discourse, or I shall hate you.

Mrs. Dain: Besides, an intrigue is so much the more notorious for the man's quality.

Mrs. Squeam: 'Tis true, nobody takes notice of a private man, and therefore with him 'tis more secret; and the crime's the less when 'tis not known.

Lady Fid: You say true; i'faith, I think you are in the right on't: 'tis not an injury to a husband till it be an injury to our honours; so that a woman of honour loses no honour with a private person; and to say truth——

Mrs. Dain: (*apart to* **Mrs. Squeamish**) So, the little fellow is grown a private person—with her——

Lady Fid: But still my dear, dear honour——

(*Enter* **Sir Jasper, Horner,** *and* **Dorilant**)

Sir Jasp: Ay, my dear, dear of honour, thou hast still so much honour in thy mouth——

Horn: (*Aside*) That she has none elsewhere.

Lady Fid: Oh, what d'ye mean to bring in these upon us?

Mrs. Dain: Foh! these are as bad as wits.

Mrs. Squeam: Foh!

Lady Fid: Let us leave the room.

Sir Jasp: Stay, stay; faith, to tell you the naked truth——

Lady Fid: Fy, Sir Jasper! do not use that word naked.

Sir Jasp: Well, well, in short I have business at Whitehall, and cannot go to the play with you, therefore would have you go——

Lady Fid: With those two to a play?

Sir Jasp: No, not with t'other, but with Mr. Horner; there can be no more scandal to go with him than with Mr. Tattle, or Master Limberham.

Lady Fid: With that nasty fellow! no—no.

Sir Jasp: Nay, prithee, dear, hear me. (*whispers to* **Lady Fidget**)

Horn: Ladies——

(**Horner**, **Dorilant** *drawing near* **Mrs. Squeamish** *and* **Mrs. Dainty Fidget**)

Mrs. Dain: Stand off.

Mrs. Squeam: Do not approach us.

Mrs. Dain: You herd with the wits, you are obscenity all over.

Mrs. Squeam: And I would as soon look upon a picture of Adam and Eve without fig-leaves, as any of you, if I could help it; therefore keep off, and do not make us sick.

Dor: What a devil are these?

Horn: Why, these are pretenders to honour, as critics to wit, only by censuring others; and as every raw, peevish, out-of-humoured, affected, dull, tea-drinking, arithmetical fop, sets up for a wit by railing at men of sense, so these for honour, by railing at the court, and ladies of as great honour as quality.

Sir Jasp: Come, Mr. Horner, I must desire you to go with these ladies to the play, Sir.

Horn: I, Sir?

Sir Jasp: Ay, ay, come, Sir.

Horn: I must beg your pardon, Sir, and theirs; I will not be seen in women's company in public again for the world.

Sir Jasp: Ha, ha, strange aversion!

Mrs. Squeam: No, he's for women's company in private.

Sir Jasp: He—poor man—he—ha! ha! ha!

Mrs. Dain: 'Tis a greater shame amongst lewd fellows to be seen in virtuous women's company, than for the women to be seen with them.

Horn: Indeed, Madam, the time was I only hated virtuous women, but now I hate the other too; I beg your pardon, ladies.

Lady Fid: You are very obliging, Sir, because we would not be troubled with you.

Sir Jasp: In sober sadness, he shall go.

Dor: Nay, if he wo' not, I am ready to wait upon the ladies, and I think I am the fitter man.

Sir Jasp: You, Sir! no, I thank you for that. Master Horner is a privileged man amongst the virtuous ladies, 'twill be a great while before you are so; he! he! he! he's my wife's gallant; he! he! he! No, pray withdraw, Sir, for as I take it, the virtuous ladies have no business with you.

She objects to the word, not the concept.

Alternation of syllables in series; said aloud, rhythm builds to last word

Dor: And I am sure he can have none with them. 'Tis strange a man can't come amongst virtuous women now, but upon the same terms as men are admitted into the Great Turk's seraglio. But heavens keep me from being an ombre player with 'em!——But where is Pinchwife? (*Exit.*)

Sir Jasp: Come, come, man; what, avoid the sweet society of womankind? that sweet, soft, gentle, tame, noble creature, woman, made for man's companion——

Horn: So is that soft, gentle, tame, and more noble creature a spaniel, and has all their tricks; can fawn, lie down, suffer beating, and fawn the more; barks at your friends when they come to see you, makes your bed hard, gives you fleas, and the mange sometimes. And all the difference is, the spaniel's the more faithful animal, and fawns but upon one master.

Animals again

Sir Jasp: He! he! he!

Mrs. Squeam: Oh the rude beast!

Mrs. Dain: Insolent brute!

Lady Fid: Brute! stinking, mortified, rotten French wether, to dare——

Sir Jasp: Hold, an't please your ladyship.——For shame, Master Horner! your mother was a woman—(*aside*) Now shall I never reconcile 'em.——(*aside to* **Lady Fidget**) Hark you, Madam, take my advice in your anger. You know you often want one to make up your drolling pack of ombre players, and you may cheat him easily; for he's an ill gamester, and consequently loves play. Besides, you know you have but two old civil gentlemen (with stinking breaths too) to wait upon you abroad; take in the third into your service. The others are but crazy; and a lady should have a supernumerary gentleman-usher as a supernumerary coach-horse, lest sometimes you should be forced to stay at home.

Lady Fid: But are you sure he loves play, and has money?

Sir Jasp: He loves play as much as you, and has money as much as I.

Lady Fid: Then I am contented to make him pay for his scurrility. Money makes up in a measure all other wants in men.—Those whom we cannot make hold for gallants, we make fine.

Sir Jasp: (*aside*) So, so; now to mollify, to wheedle him.——(*aside to* **Horner**) Master Horner, will you never keep civil company? Methinks 'tis time now, since you are only fit for them. Come, come, man, you must e'en fall to visiting our wives, eating at our tables, drinking tea with our virtuous relations after dinner, dealing cards to 'em, reading plays and gazettes to 'em, picking fleas out of their shocks for 'em, collecting receipts, new songs, women, pages, and footmen for 'em.

Horn: I hope they'll afford me better employment, Sir.

Eating and playing — double meaning for Horner?

Sir Jasp: He! he! he! 'tis fit you know your work before you come into your place. And since you are unprovided of a lady to flatter, and a good house to eat at, pray frequent mine, and call my wife mistress, and she shall call you gallant, according to the custom.

Horn: Who, I?

Sir Jasp: Faith, thou shalt for my sake; come, for my sake only.

Horn: For your sake——

Sir Jasp: Come, come, here's a gamester for you; let him be a little familiar sometimes; nay, what if a little rude? Gamesters may be rude with ladies, you know.

Lady Fid: Yes; losing gamesters have a privilege with women.

Horn: I always thought the contrary, that the winning gamester had most privilege with women; for when you have lost your money to a man, you'll lose anything you have, all you have, they say, and he may use you as he pleases.

Sir Jasp: He! he! he! well, win or lose, you shall have your liberty with her.

Lady Fid: As he behaves himself; and for your sake I'll give him admittance and freedom.

Horn: All sorts of freedom, Madam?

Sir Jasp: Ay, ay, ay, all sorts of freedom thou canst take. And so go to her, begin thy new employment; wheedle her, jest with her, and be better acquainted one with another.

Horn: (*aside*) I think I know her already; therefore may venture with her my secret for hers.

(**Horner** *and* **Lady Fidget** *whisper.*)

Sir Jasp: Sister, cuz, I have provided an innocent playfellow for you there.

Mrs. Dain: Who, he?

Mrs. Squeam: There's a playfellow, indeed!

Sir Jasp: Yes, sure. What, he is good enough to play at cards, blindman's-buff, or the fool with, sometimes!

Mrs. Squeam: Foh! we'll have no such playfellows.

Mrs. Dain: No, Sir; you shan't choose playfellows for us, we thank you.

Sir Jasp: Nay, pray hear me. (*whispering to them*)

Lady Fid: But, poor gentleman, could you be so generous, so truly a man of honour, as for the sakes of us women of honour, to cause yourself to be reported no man? No man! and to suffer yourself the greatest shame that could fall upon a man, that none might fall upon us women by your conversation? But, indeed, Sir, as perfectly, perfectly the same man as before your going into France, Sir? as perfectly, perfectly, Sir? *Tone. Effect of repetition?*

Horn: As perfectly, perfectly, Madam. Nay, I scorn you should take my word; I desire to be tried only, Madam.

Lady Fid: Well, that's spoken again like a man of honour: all men of honour desire to come to the test. But, indeed, generally you men report such things of yourselves, one does not know how or whom to believe; and it is come to that pass we dare not take your words no more than your tailor's, without some staid servant of yours be bound with you. But I have so strong a faith in your honour, dear, dear, noble Sir, that I'd forfeit mine for yours, at any time, dear Sir.

Horn: No, Madam, you should not need to forfeit it for me; I have given you security already to save you harmless, my late reputation being so well known in the world, Madam.

Lady Fid: But if upon any future falling-out, or upon a suspicion of my taking the trust out of your hands to employ some other, you yourself should betray your trust, dear Sir? I mean, if you'll give me leave to speak obscenely, you might tell, dear Sir.

Horn: If I did, nobody would believe me. The reputation of impotency is as hardly recovered again in the world as that of cowardice, dear Madam.

Lady Fid: Nay, then, as one may say, you may do your worst, dear, dear Sir. *Dear, dear sir*

Sir Jasp: Come, is your ladyship reconciled to him yet? have you agreed on matters? For I must be gone to Whitehall.

Lady Fid: Why, indeed, Sir Jasper, Master Horner is a thousand, thousand

What's in a name?

times a better man than I thought him. Cousin Squeamish, sister Dainty, I can name him now. Truly, not long ago, you know, I thought his very name obscenity; and I would as soon have lain with him as have named him.

Sir Jasp: Very likely, poor Madam.

Mrs. Dain: I believe it.

Mrs. Squeam: No doubt on't.

Business first for Jasper. Try to follow last sentence without commas.

Sir Jasp: Well, well—that your ladyship is as virtuous as any she, I know, and him all the town knows—he! he! he! Therefore now you like him, get you gone to your business together; go, go to your business, I say, pleasure; whilst I go to my pleasure, business.

Lady Fid: Come, then, dear gallant.

Horn: Come away, my dearest mistress.

Sir Jasp: So, so; why, 'tis as I'd have it. (*Exit.*)

Horn: And as I'd have it.

Lady Fid:

Who for his business from his wife will run,
Takes the best care to have her business done.

(*Exeunt omnes.*)

ACT III

SCENE I

(**Alithea** *and* **Mrs. Pinchwife**)

Alith: Sister, what ails you? You are grown melancholy.

Mrs. Pinch: Would it not make any one melancholy to see you go every day fluttering about abroad, whilst I must stay at home like a poor lonely sullen bird in a cage?

Alith: Ay, Sister, but you came young, and just from the nest to your cage, so that I thought you liked it, and could be as cheerful in't as others that took their flight themselves early, and are hopping abroad in the open air.

Mrs. Pinch: Nay, I confess I was quiet enough till my husband told me what pure lives the London ladies live abroad, with their dancing, meetings, and junketings, and dressed every day in their best gowns; and I warrant you, play at nine-pins every day of the week, so they do.

(*Enter* **Pinchwife**)

Pinch: Come, what's here to do? You are putting the town-pleasures in her head, and setting her a-longing.

Alith: Yes, after nine-pins. You suffer none to give her those longings you mean but yourself.

Pinch: I tell her of the vanities of the town like a confessor.

Alith: A confessor! just such a confessor as he that, by forbidding a silly ostler to grease the horse's teeth, taught him to do't.

Pinch: Come, Mistress Flippant, good precepts are lost when bad examples are still before us: the liberty you take abroad makes her hanker after it, and out of humour at home. Poor wretch! she desired not to come to London; I would bring her.

Alith: Very well.

Pinch: She has been this week in town, and never desired till this afternoon to go abroad.

Alith: Was she not at a play yesterday?

Pinch: Yes, but she ne'er asked me; I was myself the cause of her going.

Alith: Then if she ask you again, you are the cause of her asking, and not my example.

Pinch: Well, to-morrow night I shall be rid of you; and the next day, before 'tis light, she and I'll be rid of the town, and my dreadful apprehensions.—— Come, be not melancholy; for thou shalt go into the country after to-morrow, dearest.

Alith: Great comfort!

Mrs. Pinch: Pish! what d'ye tell me of the country for?

Pinch: How's this! what, pish at the country?

Mrs. Pinch: Let me alone; I am not well.

Pinch: Oh, if that be all—what ails my dearest?

Mrs. Pinch: Truly, I don't know: but I have not been well since you told me there was a gallant at the play in love with me.

Pinch: Ha!——

Alith: That's by my example too!

Pinch: Nay, if you are not well, but are so concerned because a lewd fellow chanced to lie, and say he liked you, you'll make me sick too.

Mrs. Pinch: Of what sickness?

Pinch: Oh, of that which is worse than the plague, jealousy.

Mrs. Pinch: Pish, you jeer! I'm sure there's no such disease in our receipt-book at home.

Pinch: No, thou never met'st with it, poor innocent.—(*aside*) Well, if thou cuckold me, 'twill be my own fault—for cuckolds and bastards are generally makers of their own fortune.

Mrs. Pinch: Well, but pray, bud, let's go to a play to-night.

Pinch: 'Tis just done, she comes from it. But why are you so eager to see a play?

Mrs. Pinch: Faith, dear, not that I care one pin for their talk there; but I like to look upon the playermen, and would see, if I could, the gallant you say loves me: that's all, dear bud.

Pinch: Is that all, dear bud?

Alith: This proceeds from my example!

Mrs. Pinch: But if the play be done, let's go abroad, however, dear bud.

Pinch: Come, have a little patience and thou shalt go into the country on Friday.

Mrs. Pinch: Therefore I would see first some sights to tell my neighbours of. Nay, I will go abroad, that's once.

Alith: I'm the cause of this desire too!

Pinch: But now I think on't, who, who was the cause of Horner's coming to my lodgings to-day? That was you.

Alith: No, you, because you would not let him see your handsome wife out of your lodging.

Mrs. Pinch: Why, O Lord! did the gentleman come hither to see me indeed?

Pinch: No, no. You are not cause of that damned question too, Mistress Alithea?—(*aside*) Well, she's in the right of it. He is in love with my wife—

and comes after her—'tis so—but I'll nip his love in the bud, lest he should follow us into the country, and break his chariot-wheel near our house, on purpose for an excuse to come to't. But I think I know the town.

Mrs. Pinch: Come, pray, bud, let's go abroad before 'tis late; for I will go, that's flat and plain.

Pinch: (*aside*) So! the obstinacy already of the town-wife; and I must, whilst she's here, humour her like one.——Sister, how shall we do, that she may not be seen or known?

Alith: Let her put on her mask.

Pinch: Pshaw! a mask makes people but the more inquisitive, and is as ridiculous a disguise as a stage-beard: her shape, stature, habit will be known. And if we should meet with Horner, he would be sure to take acquaintance with us, must wish her joy, kiss her, talk to her, leer upon her, and the devil and all. No, I'll not use her to a mask, 'tis dangerous, for masks have made more cuckolds than the best faces that ever were known.

Alith: How will you do then?

Mrs. Pinch: Nay, shall we go? The Exchange will be shut, and I have a mind to see that.

Pinch: So—I have it—I'll dress her up in the suit we are to carry down to her brother, little Sir James; nay, I understand the town-tricks. Come, let's go dress her. A mask! no—a woman masked, like a covered dish, gives a man curiosity and appetite; when, it may be, uncovered, 'twould turn his stomach: no, no.

Alith: Indeed your comparison is something a greasy one: but I had a gentle gallant used to say, A beauty masked, like the sun in eclipse, gathers together more gazers than if it shined out. (*Exeunt.*)

SCENE II.   The Scene Changes to the New Exchange

(*Enter* **Horner, Harcourt,** *and* **Dorilant**)

Dor: Engaged to women, and not sup with us!

Horn: Ay, a pox on 'em all!

Har: You were much a more reasonable man in the morning, and had as noble resolutions against 'em as a widower of a week's liberty.

Dor: Did I ever think to see you keep company with women in vain?

Horn: In vain: no—'tis since I can't love 'em, to be revenged on 'em.

Har: Now your sting is gone, you looked in the box amongst all those women like a drone in the hive, all upon you; shoved and ill-used by 'em all, and thrust from one side to t'other.

Notice image: bees, buzzing, sting, hive, drone. Significance?

Dor: Yet he must be buzzing amongst 'em still, like other old beetle-headed liquorish drones. Avoid 'em, and hate 'em, as they hate you.

Horn: Because I do hate 'em, and would hate 'em yet more, I'll frequent 'em. You may see by marriage, nothing makes a man hate a woman more than her constant conversation. In short, I converse with 'em, as you do with rich fools, to laugh at 'em and use 'em ill.

Dor: But I would no more sup with women unless I could lie with 'em than sup with a rich coxcomb unless I could cheat him.

Horn: Yes, I have known thee sup with a fool for his drinking; if he could set out your hand that way only, you were satisfied, and if he were a wine-swallowing mouth, 'twas enough.

Har: Yes, a man drinks often with a fool, as he tosses with a marker, only to keep his hand in ure. But do the ladies drink?

Horn: Yes, Sir; and I shall have the pleasure at least of laying 'em flat with a bottle, and bring as much scandal that way upon 'em as formerly t'other.

Har: Perhaps you may prove as weak a brother amongst 'em that way as t'other.

Dor: Foh! drinking with women is as unnatural as scolding with 'em. But 'tis a pleasure of decayed fornicators, and the basest way of quenching love.

Har: Nay, 'tis drowning love, instead of quenching it. But leave us for civil women too!

Dor: Ay, when he can't be the better for 'em. We hardly pardon a man that leaves his friend for a wench, and that's a pretty lawful call.

Horn: Faith, I would not leave you for 'em, if they would not drink.

Dor: Who would disappoint his company at Lewis's for a gossiping?

Har: Foh! Wine and women, good apart, together as nauseous as sack and sugar. But hark you, Sir, before you go, a little of your advice; an old maimed general, when unfit for action, is fittest for counsel. I have other designs upon women than eating and drinking with them; I am in love with Sparkish's mistress, whom he is to marry to-morrow: now how shall I get her?

(*Enter* **Sparkish**, *looking about*)

Horn: Why, here comes one will help you to her.

Har: He! he, I tell you, is my rival, and will hinder my love.

Horn: No; a foolish rival and a jealous husband assist their rival's designs, for they are sure to make their women hate them, which is the first step to their love for another man.

Har: But I cannot come near his mistress but in his company.

Horn: Still the better for you; for fools are most easily cheated when they themselves are accessories, and he is to be bubbled of his mistress as of his money, the common mistress, by keeping him company.

Spark: Who is that that is to be bubbled? Faith, let me snack; I han't met with a bubble since Christmas. 'Gad, I think bubbles are like their brother wood-cocks, go out with the cold weather.

Har: (*apart to* **Horner**) A pox! he did not hear all, I hope.

Spark: Come, you bubbling rogues you, where do we sup?——Oh, Harcourt, my mistress tells me you have been making fierce love to her all the play long: ha! ha! But I——

Har: I make love to her!

Spark: Nay, I forgive thee, for I think I know thee, and I know her; but I am sure I know myself.

Har: Did she tell you so? I see all women are like these of the Exchange; who, to enhance the price of their commodities, report to their fond customers offers which were never made 'em.

Horn: Ay, women are as apt to tell before the intrigue, as men after it, and so show themselves the vainer sex. But hast thou a mistress, Sparkish? 'Tis as hard for me to believe it as that thou ever hadst a bubble, as you bragged just now.

Spark: Oh, your servant, Sir; are you at your raillery, Sir? But we were some of us beforehand with you to-day at the play. The wits were something bold with you, Sir; did you not hear us laugh?

Horn: Yes; but I thought you had gone to plays to laugh at the poet's wit, not at your own.

Spark: Your servant, Sir: no, I thank you. 'Gad, I go to a play as to a country treat; I carry my own wine to one, and my own wit to t'other, or else I'm sure I should not be merry at either. And the reason why we are so often louder than the players is because we think we speak more wit, and so become the poet's rivals in his audience: for to tell you the truth, we hate the silly rogues, nay, so much, that we find fault even with their bawdy upon the stage, whilst we talk nothing else in the pit as loud.

Horn: But why shouldst thou hate the silly poets? Thou hast too much wit to be one; and they, like whores, are only hated by each other: and thou dost scorn writing, I'm sure.

Spark: Yes; I'd have you to know I scorn writing: but women, women, that make men do all foolish things, make 'em write songs too. Everybody does it. 'Tis even as common with lovers as playing with fans; and you can no more help rhyming to your Phyllis, than drinking to your Phyllis.

Har: Nay, poetry in love is no more to be avoided than jealousy.

Dor: But the poets damned your songs, did they?

Spark: Damn the poets! they turned 'em into burlesque, as they call it. That burlesque is a hocus-pocus trick they have got, which, by the virtue of *Hictius doctius, topsy turvy,* they make a wise and witty man in the world, a fool upon the stage you know not how: and 'tis therefore I hate 'em too, for I know not but it may be my own case; for they'll put a man into a play for looking asquint. Their predecessors were contented to make serving-men only their stage-fools: but these rogues must have gentlemen, with a pox to 'em, nay, knights; and, indeed, you shall hardly see a fool upon the stage but he's a knight. And to tell you the truth, they have kept me these six years from being a knight in earnest, for fear of being knighted in a play, and dubbed a fool.

Dor: Blame 'em not, they must follow their copy, the age.

Har: But why shouldst thou be afraid of being in a play, who expose yourself every day in the playhouses, and as public places?

Horn: 'Tis but being on the stage, instead of standing on a bench in the pit.

Dor: Don't you give money to painters to draw you like? and are you afraid of your pictures at length in a playhouse, where all your mistresses may see you?

Image confirms it— no real faces in this society

Spark: A pox! painters don't draw the small-pox or pimples in one's face. Come, damn all your silly authors whatever, all books and booksellers, by the world, and all readers, courteous or uncourteous!

Har: But who comes here, Sparkish?

(*Enter* **Mr. Pinchwife** *and his Wife in mans' clothes,* **Alithea,** **Lucy** *her maid*)

Spark: Oh, hide me! There's my mistress too.

(**Sparkish** *hides himself behind* **Harcourt**.)

Har: She sees you.

Spark: But I will not see her. 'Tis time to go to Whitehall, and I must not fail the drawing-room.

Har: Pray, first carry me, and reconcile me to her.

Spark: Another time. Faith, the king will have supped.

Har: Not with the worse stomach for thy absence. Thou art one of those fools that think their attendance at the king's meals as necessary as his physicians' when you are more troublesome to him than his doctors or his dogs.

Spark: Pshaw! I know my interest, Sir. Prithee hide me.

Horn: Your servant, Pinchwife.——What, he knows us not!

Pinch: (*to his wife aside*) Come along.

Mrs. Pinch: Pray, have you any ballads? give me sixpenny worth.

Clasp: We have no ballads.

Mrs. Pinch: Then give me "Covent Garden Drollery," and a play or two—— Oh, here's "Tarugo's Wiles," and "The Slighted Maiden"; I'll have them.

Pinch: (*apart to her*) No; plays are not for your reading. Come along; will you discover yourself?

Horn: Who is that pretty youth with him, Sparkish?

Spark: I believe his wife's brother, because he's something like her: but I never saw her but once.

Horn: Extremely handsome; I have seen a face like it too. Let us follow 'em. (*Exuent* **Pinchwife, Mrs. Pinchwife, Alithea, Lucy; Horner, Dorilant** *following them.*)

Har: Come, Sparkish, your mistress saw you, and will be angry you go not to her. Besides, I would fain be reconciled to her, which none but you can do, dear friend.

Spark: Well, that's a better reason, dear friend. I would not go near her now for hers or my own sake; but I can deny you nothing: for though I have known thee a great while, never go, if I do not love thee as well as a new acquaintance.

Har: I am obliged to you indeed, dear friend. I would be well with her, only to be well with thee still; for these ties to wives usually dissolve all ties to friends. I would be contented she should enjoy you a-nights, but I would have you to myself a-days as I have had, dear friend.

Spark: And thou shalt enjoy me a-days, dear, dear friend, never stir: and I'll be divorced from her, sooner than from thee. Come along.

Har: (*aside*) So, we are hard put to't, when we make our rival our procurer; but neither she nor her brother would let me come near her now. When all's done, a rival is the best cloak to steal to a mistress under, without suspicion; and when we have once got to her as we desire, we throw him off like other cloaks.

(*Exit* **Sparkish**, *and* **Harcourt** *following him.*)

(*Re-enter* **Pinchwife, Mrs. Pinchwife** *in man's clothes*)

Pinch: (*to* **Alithea**) Sister, if you will not go, we must leave you.—(*aside*) The fool her gallant and she will muster up all the young saunterers of this place, and they will leave their dear seamstresses to follow us. What a swarm of cuckolds and cuckold-makers are here!—— Come, let's be gone, Mistress Margery.

Mrs. Pinch: Don't you believe that; I han't half my bellyfull of sights yet.

Pinch: Then walk this way.

Mrs. Pinch: Lord, what a power of brave signs are here! stay—the Bull's-Head, the Ram's-Head, and the Stag's-Head, dear——

Pinch: Nay, if every husband's proper sign here were visible, they would be all alike.

Mrs. Pinch: What d'ye mean by that, bud?

Pinch: 'Tis no matter—no matter, bud.

Mrs. Pinch: Pray tell me: nay, I will know.

Pinch: They would be all Bulls', Stags', and Rams'-heads.

(*Exeunt* **Mr. Pinchwife** *and* **Mrs. Pinchwife**.)

(*Re-enter* **Sparkish, Harcourt, Alithea, Lucy,** at t'other door)

Spark: Come, dear Madam, for my sake you shall be reconciled to him.

Alith: For your sake I hate him.

Har: That's something too cruel, Madam, to hate me for his sake.

Spark: Ay indeed, Madam, too, too cruel to me, to hate my friend for my sake.

Alith: I hate him because he is your enemy; and you ought to hate him too, for making love to me, if you love me.

Spark: That's a good one! I hate a man for loving you! If he did love you, 'tis but what he can't help; and 'tis your fault, not his, if he admires you. I hate a man for being of my opinion? I'll n'er do't, by the world!

Alith: Is it for your honour, or mine, to suffer a man to make love to me, who am to marry you to-morrow?

Spark: Is it for your honour, or mine, to have me jealous? That he makes love to you, is a sign you are handsome; and that I am not jealous, is a sign you are virtuous. That I think is for your honour.

Alith: But 'tis your honour too I am concerned for.

Har: But why, dearest Madam, will you be more concerned for his honour than he is himself? Let his honour alone, for my sake and his. He! he has no honour——

Spark: How's that?

Har: But what my dear friend can guard himself.

Spark: Oh ho—that's right again.

Har: Your care of his honour argues his neglect of it, which is no honour to my dear friend here. Therefore once more, let his honour go which way it will, dear Madam.

Spark: Ay, ay; were it for my honour to marry a woman whose virtue I suspected, and could not trust her in a friend's hands?

Alith: Are you not afraid to lose me?

Har: He afraid to lose you, Madam! No, no—you may see how the most estimable and most glorious creature in the world is valued by him. Will you not see it?

Spark: Right, honest Frank, I have that noble value for her that I cannot be jealous of her.

Alith: You mistake him. He means, you care not for me, nor who has me.

Spark: Lord, Madam, I see you are jealous! Will you wrest a poor man's meaning from his words?

Alith: You astonish me, Sir, with your want of jealousy.

Spark: And you make me giddy, Madam, with your jealousy and fears, and virtue and honour. 'Gad, I see virtue makes a woman as troublesome as a little reading or learning.

Alith: Monstrous!

Lucy: (*behind*) Well, to see what easy husbands these women of quality can meet with! a poor chambermaid can never have such ladylike luck. Besides, he's thrown away upon her. She'll make no use of her fortune, her blessing, none to a gentleman, for a pure cuckold, for it requires good breeding to be a cuckold.

Margin notes:

What do they and Sparkish have in common?

Meaningful pause

What was Sparkish's meaning? Is his language adequate for the situation?

Alith: I tell you then plainly, he pursues me to marry me.

Spark: Pshaw!

Har: Come, Madam, you see you strive in vain to make him jealous of me. My dear friend is the kindest creature in the world to me.

Spark: Poor fellow!

Har: But his kindness only is not enough for me, without your favour, your good opinion, dear Madam: 'tis that must perfect my happiness. Good gentleman, he believes all I say: would you would do so! Jealous of me! I would not wrong him nor you for the world.

Spark: Look you there; Hear him, hear him, and do not walk away so. (**Alithea** *walks carelessy to and fro.*)

Har: I love you, Madam, so——

Spark: How's that? Nay, now you begin to go too far indeed.

Har: So much, I confess, I say, I love you, that I would not have you miserable, and cast yourself away upon so unworthy and inconsiderable a thing as what you see here.

(*clapping his hand on his breast, points at* **Sparkish**)

Spark: No, faith, I believe thou wouldst not: now his meaning is plain; but I knew before thou wouldst not wrong me, nor her.

How does action give meaning to language?

Har: No, no, Heavens forbid the glory of her sex should fall so low, as into the embraces of such a contemptible wretch, the last of mankind—my dear friend here—I injure him! (*embracing* **Sparkish**)

Alith: Very well.

Spark: No, no, dear friend, I knew it.——Madam, you see he will rather wrong himself than me, in giving himself such names.

Alith: Do not you understand him yet?

Spark: Yes: how modestly he speaks of himself, poor fellow!

Alith: Methinks he speaks impudently of yourself, since—before yourself too; insomuch that I can no longer suffer his scurrilous abusiveness to you, no more than his love to me. (*offers to go*)

Spark: Nay, nay, Madam, pray stay—his love to you! Lord, Madam, has he not spoke yet plain enough?

Alith: Yes, indeed, I should think so.

Spark: Well then, by the world, a man can't speak civilly to a woman now, but presently she says he makes love to her. Nay, Madam, you shall stay, with your pardon, since you have not yet understood him, till he has made an *éclaircissement* of his love to you, that is, what kind of love it is. Answer to thy catechism, friend; do you love my mistress here?

Har: Yes, I wish she would not doubt it.

Spark: But how do you love her?

Har: With all my soul.

Alith: I thank him, methinks he speaks plain enough now.

Spark: (*to* **Alithea**) You are out still.——But with what kind of love, Harcourt?

Har: With the best and the truest love in the world.

Spark: Look you there then, that is with no matrimonial love, I'm sure.

Alith: How's that? do you say matrimonial love is not best?

Spark: 'Gad, I went too far ere I was aware. But speak for thyself, Harcourt, you said you would not wrong me nor her.

Har: No, no, Madam, e'en take him for Heaven's sake——

Spark: Look you there, Madam.

Har: Who should in all justice be yours, he that loves you most. (*claps his hand on his breast*)

Alith: Look you there, Mr. Sparkish, who's that?

Spark: Who should it be?——Go on, Harcourt.

Har: Who loves you more than women, titles, or fortune fools. (*points at* **Sparkish**)

Spark: Look you there, he means me still, for he points at me.

Alith: Ridiculous!

Har: Who can only match your faith and constancy in love.

Spark: Ay.

Har: Who knows, if it be possible, how to value so much beauty and virtue.

Spark: Ay.

Har: Whose love can no more be equalled in the world, than that heavenly form of yours.

Spark: No.

Har: Who could no more suffer a rival than your absence, and yet could no more suspect your virtue than his own constancy in his love to you.

Spark: No.

Har: Who, in fine, loves you better than his eyes, that first made him love you.

Spark: Ay—— Nay, Madam, faith, you shan't go till——

Alith: Have a care, lest you make me stay too long.

Spark: But till he has saluted you; that I may be assured you are friends, after his honest advice and declaration. Come, pray, Madam, be friends with him.
(*Enter* **Master Pinchwife**, **Mrs. Pinchwife**)

Alith: You must pardon me, Sir, that I am not yet so obedient to you.

Pinch: What, invite your wife to kiss men? Monstrous! Are you not ashamed? I will never forgive you.

Spark: Are you not ashamed that I should have more confidence in the chastity of your family than you have? You must not teach me; I am a man of honour, Sir, though I am frank and free; I am frank, Sir——

Pinch: Very frank, Sir, to share your wife with your friends.

Spark: He is an humble, menial friend, such as reconciles the differences of the marriage bed; you know man and wife do not always agree; I design him for that use, therefore would have him well with my wife.

Pinch: A menial friend!—you will get a great many menial friends, by showing your wife as you do.

Spark: What then? It may be I have a pleasure in't, as I have to show fine clothes at a playhouse, the first day, and count money before poor rogues.

Pinch: He that shows his wife or money, will be in danger of having them borrowed sometimes.

Spark: I love to be envied, and would not marry a wife that I alone could love; loving alone is as dull as eating alone. Is it not a frank age? and I am a frank person; and to tell you the truth, it may be I love to have rivals in a wife; they make her seem to a man still but as a kept mistress; and so good night, for I must to Whitehall.——Madam, I hope you are now reconciled to my friend; and so I wish you a good night, Madam, and sleep if you can: for to-morrow you know I must visit you early with a canonical gentleman. Good night, dear Harcourt. (*Exit* **Sparkish**.)

Har: Madam, I hope you will not refuse my visit to-morrow, if it should be earlier with a canonical gentleman than Mr. Sparkish's.

Pinch: This gentlewoman is yet under my care, therefore you must yet forbear your freedom with her, Sir.

(*coming between* **Alithea** *and* **Harcourt**)

Har: Must, Sir?

Pinch: Yes, Sir, she is my sister.

Har: 'Tis well she is, Sir—for I must be her servant, Sir.——Madam——

Pinch: Come away, Sister, we had been gone, if it had not been for you, and so avoided these lewd rake-hells, who seem to haunt us.

(*Enter* **Horner**, **Dorilant**, *to them*)

Horn: How now, Pinchwife!

Pinch: Your servant.

Horn: What! I see a little time in the country makes a man turn wild and unsociable, and only fit to converse with his horses, dogs, and his herds.

Pinch: I have business, Sir, and must mind it; your business is pleasure; therefore you and I must go different ways.

Horn: Well, you may go on, but this pretty young gentleman—— (*takes hold of* **Mrs. Pinchwife**)

Har: The lady——

Dor: And the maid——

Horn: Shall stay with us; for I suppose their business is the same with ours, pleasure.

Pinch: (*aside*) 'Sdeath, he knows her, she carries it so sillily! Yet if he does not, I should be more silly to discover it first.

Alith: Pray, let us go, Sir.

Pinch: Come, come——

Horn: (*to* **Mrs. Pinchwife**) Had you not rather stay with us?——Prithee, Pinchwife, who is this pretty young gentleman?

Pinch: One to whom I'm a guardian.—(*aside*) I wish I could keep her out of your hands.

Horn: Who is he? I never saw anything so pretty in all my life.

Pinch: Pshaw! do not look upon him so much, he's a poor bashful youth; you'll put him out of countenance.——Come away, brother. (*offers to take her away*)

Horn: Oh, your brother!

Pinch: Yes, my wife's brother.——Come, come, she'll stay supper for us.

Horn: I thought so, for he is very like her I saw you at the play with, whom I told you I was in love with.

Mrs. Pinch: (*aside*) O jeminy! is this he that was in love with me? I am glad on't, I vow, for he's a curious fine gentleman, and I love him already, too.— (*To* **Pinchwife**.) Is this he, bud?

Pinch: (*to his Wife*) Come away, come away.

Horn: Why, what haste are you in? why won't you let me talk with him?

Pinch: Because you'll debauch him; he's yet young and innocent, and I would not have him debauched for anything in the world.—(*aside*) How she gazes on him! the devil!

Horn: Harcourt, Dorilant, look you here, this is the likeness of that dowdy he told us of, his wife; did you ever see a lovelier creature? The rogue has reason to be jealous of his wife, since she is like him, for she would make all that see her in love with her.

Har: And, as I remember now, she is as like him here as can be.

Dor: She is indeed very pretty, if she be like him.

Horn: Very pretty? a very pretty commendation!—she is a glorious creature, beautiful beyond all things I ever beheld.

Pinch: So, so.

Har: More beautiful than a poet's first mistress of imagination.

Horn: Or another man's last mistress of flesh and blood.

Effect of this language on Pinchwife?

Mrs. Pinch: Nay, now you jeer, Sir; pray don't jeer me.

Pinch: Come, come.—(*aside*) By Heavens, she'll discover herself!

Horn: I speak of your sister, Sir.

Pinch: Ay, but saying she was handsome, if like him, made him blush.—(*aside*) I am upon a rack!

Horn: Methinks he is so handsome he should not be a man.

Pinch: (*aside*) Oh, there 'tis out! he has discovered her! I am not able to suffer any longer.—(*To his Wife.*) Come, come away, I say.

Horn: Nay, by your leave, Sir, he shall not go yet.—(*aside to them*) Harcourt, Dorilant, let us torment this jealous rogue a little.

Har:
Dor: How?

Horn: I'll show you.

Pinch: Come, pray let him go, I cannot stay fooling any longer; I tell you his sister stays supper for us.

Horn: Does she? Come then, we'll all go sup with her and thee.

Pinch: No, now I think on't, having stayed so long for us, I warrant she's gone to bed.—(*aside*) I wish she and I were well out of their hands.——Come, I must rise early to-morrow, come.

Horn: Well then, if she be gone to bed, I wish her and you a good night. But pray, young gentleman, present my humble service to her.

Mrs. Pinch: Thank you heartily, Sir.

Pinch: (*aside*) 'Sdeath she will discover herself yet in spite of me.——He is something more civil to you, for your kindness to his sister, than I am, it seems.

Horn: Tell her, dear sweet little gentleman, for all your brother there, that you have revived the love I had for her at first sight in the playhouse.

Mrs. Pinch: But did you love her indeed, and indeed?

Pinch: (*aside*) So, so.——Away, I say.

Horn: Nay, stay.——Yes, indeed, and indeed, pray do you tell her so, and give her this kiss from me. (*kisses her*)

Pinch: (*aside*) O Heavens! what do I suffer? Now 'tis too plain he knows her, and yet——

Horn: And this, and this——(*kisses her again*)

Mrs. Pinch: What do you kiss me for? I am no woman.

Pinch: (*aside*) So, there, 'tis out.——Come, I cannot, nor will stay any longer.

Horn: Nay, they shall send your lady a kiss too. Here, Harcourt, Dorilant, will you not? (*They kiss her.*)

Pinch: (*aside*) How! do I suffer this? Was I not accusing another just now for this rascally patience, in permitting his wife to be kissed before his face? Ten thousand ulcers gnaw away their lips.——Come, come.

Horn: Good night, dear little gentleman; Madam, good night, farewell, Pinchwife.—(*apart to* **Harcourt** *and* **Dorilant**) Did not I tell you I would raise his jealous gall?

(*Exeunt* **Horner**, **Harcourt**, *and* **Dorilant**.)

Pinch: So, they are gone at last; stay, let me see first if the coach be at this door. (*Exit*.)

(**Horner**, **Harcourt**, *and* **Dorilant** *return*)

Horn: What, not gone yet? Will you be sure to do as I desired you, sweet Sir?

Mrs. Pinch: Sweet Sir, but what will you give me then?

Horn: Anything. Come away into the next walk.

(*Exit, haling away* **Mrs. Pinchwife**.)

Alith: Hold! hold! what d'ye do?

Lucy: Stay, stay, hold——

Har: Hold, Madam, hold, let him present him—he'll come presently; nay, I will never let you go till you answer my question.

(**Alithea**, **Lucy**, *struggling with* **Harcourt** *and* **Dorilant**)

Lucy: For God's sake, Sir, I must follow 'em.

Dor: No, I have something to present you with too, you shan't follow them.

(**Pinchwife** *returns*)

Pinch: Where?—how—what's become of?—gone!—whither?

Lucy: He's only gone with the gentleman, who will give him something, an't please your worship.

Pinch: Something!—give him something, with a pox!—where are they?

Alith: In the next walk only, Brother.

Pinch: Only, only! where, where?

(*Exit* **Pinchwife** *and returns presently, then goes out again.*)

Har: What's the matter with him? Why so much concerned? But, dearest Madam——

Alith: Pray let me go, Sir; I have said and suffered enough already.

Har: Then you will not look upon, nor pity, my sufferings?

Alith: To look upon 'em, when I cannot help 'em, were cruelty, not pity; therefore, I will never see you more.

Har: Let me then, Madam, have my privilege of a banished lover, complaining or railing, and giving you but a farewell reason why, if you cannot condescend to marry me, you should not take that wretch, my rival.

Alith: He only, not you, since my honour is engaged so far to him, can give me a reason why I should not marry him; but if he be true, and what I think him to me, I must be so to him. Your servant, Sir.

Har: Have women only constancy when 'tis a vice, and, like Fortune, only true to fools?

Dor: Thou shalt not stir, thou robust creature; you see I can deal with you, therefore you should stay the rather, and be kind. (*to* **Lucy**, *who struggles to get from him*)

(*Enter* **Pinchwife**)

Pinch: Gone, gone, not to be found! quite gone! ten thousand plagues go with 'em! which way went they?

Alith: But into t'other walk, Brother.

Lucy: Their business will be done presently sure, an't please your worship; it can't be long in doing, I'm sure on't.

Alith: Are they not there?

Pinch: No, you know where they are, you infamous wretch, eternal shame of

If it's the "something" Pinchwife thinks, it "a'nt going to please his worship."

your family, which you do not dishonour enough yourself you think, but you must help her to do it too, thou legion of bawds!

Alith: Good Brother——

Pinch: Damned, damned Sister!

Alith: Look you here, she's coming.

(*Enter* **Mrs. Pinchwife** *in man's clothes, running, with her hat under her arm, full of oranges and dried fruit,* **Horner** *following*)

Mrs. Pinch: O dear bud, look you here what I have got, see!

Pinch: (*aside, rubbing his forehead*) And what I have got here too, which you *Horns* can't see.

Mrs. Pinch: The fine gentleman has given me better things yet.

Pinch: Has he so?—(*aside*) Out of breath and coloured!—I must hold yet.

Horn: I have only given your little brother an orange, Sir.

Pinch: (*to* **Horner**) Thank you, Sir.—(*aside*) You have only squeezed my orange, I suppose, and given it me again; yet I must have a city patience.—(*to his Wife*)_ Come, come away.

Mrs. Pinch: Stay, till I have put up my fine things, bud.

(*Enter* **Sir Jasper Fidget**)

Sir Jasp: O, Master Horner, come, come, the ladies stay for you; your mistress, my wife, wonders you make not more haste to her.

Horn: I have stayed this half hour for you here, and 'tis your fault I am not now with your wife.

Sir Jasp: But, pray, don't let her know so much; the truth on't is, I was advancing a certain project to his majesty about—I'll tell you.

Horn: No, let's go, and hear it at your house. Good night, sweet little gentleman; one kiss more, you'll remember me now, I hope. (*kisses her*)

Dor: What, Sir Jasper, will you separate friends? He promised to sup with us, and if you take him to your house, you'll be in danger of our company too.

Sir Jasp: Alas! gentlemen, my house is not fit for you; there are none but civil women there, which are not for your turn. He, you know, can bear with the society of civil women now, ha! ha! ha! besides, he's one of my family—he's —he! he! he!

Dor: What is he?

Sir Jasp: Faith, my eunuch, since you'll have it; he! he! he!

(*Exeunt* **Sir Jasper Fidget** *and* **Horner**.)

Dor: I rather wish thou wert his or my cuckold. Harcourt, what a good cuckold is lost there for want of a man to make him one! Thee and I cannot have Horner's privilege, who can make use of it.

Har: Ay, to poor Horner 'tis like coming to an estate at threescore, when a man can't be the better for't.

Pinch: Come.

Mrs. Pinch: Presently, bud.

Dor: Come, let us go too.—(*to* **Alithea**) Madam, your servant.—(*to* **Lucy**) Good night, strapper.

Har: Madam, though you will not let me have a good day or night, I wish you one; but dare not name the other half of my wish.

Alith: Good night, Sir, for ever.

Mrs. Pinch: I don't know where to put this here, dear bud, you shall eat it;

nay, you shall have part of the fine gentleman's good things, or treat, as you call it, when we come home.

Pinch: Indeed, I deserve it, since I furnished the best part of it. (*strikes away the orange*)

The gallant treats presents, and gives the ball,
But 'tis the absent cuckold pays for all.

ACT IV

SCENE I. In **Pinchwife's** House in the morning

(**Lucy**, **Alithea** *dressed in new clothes*)

Contrast of images — life/death, love/repulsion, sweetness/stench

Lucy: Well, Madam,—now have I dressed you, and set you out with so many ornaments, and spent upon you ounces of essence and pulvillio; and all this for no other purpose but as people adorn and perfume a corpse for a stinking second-hand grave: such, or as bad, I think Master Sparkish's bed.

Alith: Hold your peace.

Lucy: Nay, Madam, I will ask you the reason why you would banish poor Master Harcourt for ever from your sight; how could you be so hard-hearted?

Alith: 'Twas because I was not hard-hearted.

Lucy: No, no; 'twas stark love and kindness, I warrant.

Alith: It was so; I would see him no more because I love him.

Lucy: Hey day, a very pretty reason!

Alith: You do not understand me.

Lucy: I wish you may yourself.

Her argument sounds rational. Are her actions?

Alith: I was engaged to marry, you see, another man, whom my justice will not suffer me to deceive or injure.

Lucy: Can there be a greater cheat or wrong done to a man than to give him your person without your heart? I should make a conscience of it.

Alith: I'll retrieve it for him after I am married a while.

Lucy: The woman that marries to love better, will be as much mistaken as the wencher that marries to live better. No, Madam, marrying to increase love is like gaming to become rich; alas! you only lose what little stock you had before.

Alith: I find by your rhetoric you have been bribed to betray me.

Key word is honor. Lucy's definition?

Lucy: Only by his merit, that has bribed your heart, you see, against your word and rigid honour. But what a devil is this honour! 'tis sure a disease in the head, like the megrim or falling-sickness, that always hurries people away to do themselves mischief. Men lose their lives by it; women, what's dearer to 'em, their love, the life of life.

Alith: Come, pray talk you no more of honour, nor Master Harcourt; I wish the other would come to secure my fidelity to him and his right in me.

Lucy: You will marry him then?

Alith: Certainly; I have given him already my word, and will my hand too, to make it good, when he comes.

Lucy: Well, I wish I may never stick pin more, if he be not an arrant natural to t'other fine gentleman.

Alith: I own he wants the wit of Harcourt, which I will dispense withal for another want he has, which is want of jealousy, which men of wit seldom want.

Lucy: Lord, Madam, what should you do with a fool to your husband? You intend to be honest, don't you? then that husbandly virtue, credulity, is thrown away upon you.

Alith: He only that could suspect my virtue should have cause to do it; 'tis Sparkish's confidence in my truth that obliges me to be so faithful to him.

Lucy: You are not sure his opinion may last.

Alith: I am satisfied 'tis impossible for him to be jealous after the proofs I have had of him. Jealousy in a husband—Heaven defend me from it! it begets a thousand plagues to a poor woman, the loss of her honour, her quiet, and her——

Lucy: And her pleasure.

Alith: What d'ye mean, impertinent?

Lucy: Liberty is a great pleasure, Madam.

Alith: I say, loss of her honour, her quiet, nay, her life sometimes; and what's as bad almost, the loss of this town; that is, she is sent into the country, which is the last ill-usage of a husband to a wife, I think.

Lucy: (*aside*) Oh, does the wind lie there?—— Then of necessity, Madam, you think a man must carry his wife into the country, if he be wise. The country is as terrible, I find, to our young English ladies, as a monastery to those abroad; and, on my virginity, I think they would rather marry a London jailer than a high sheriff of a county, since neither can stir from his employment. Formerly women of wit married fools for a great estate, a fine seat, or the like; but now 'tis for a pretty seat only in Lincoln's Inn Fields, St. James's Fields, or the Pall Mall.

Probably an ironic oath

(*Enter to them* **Sparkish**, *and* **Harcourt**, *dressed like a Parson*)

Spark: Madam, your humble servant, a happy day to you, and to us all.

Har: Amen.

Alith: Who have we here?

Spark: My chaplain, faith—— O Madam, poor Harcourt remembers his humble service to you; and, in obedience to your last commands, refrains coming into your sight.

Alith: Is not that he?

Spark: No, fy, no; but to show that he ne'er intended to hinder our match, has sent his brother here to join our hands. When I get me a wife, I must get her a chaplain, according to the custom; this is his brother, and my chaplain.

Alith: His brother!

Lucy: (*aside*) And your chaplain, to preach in your pulpit then——

Alith: His brother!

Spark: Nay, I knew you would not believe it.—— I told you, Sir, she would take you for your brother Frank.

Alith: Believe it!

Lucy: (*aside*) His brother! ha! ha! he! he has a trick left still, it seems.

Spark: Come, my dearest, pray let us go to church before the canonical hour is past.

Alith: For shame, you are abused still.

Spark: By the world, 'tis strange now you are so incredulous.

Alith: 'Tis strange you are so credulous.

Spark: Dearest of my life, hear me. I tell you this is Ned Harcourt of Cambridge, by the world; you see he has a sneaking college look. 'Tis true he's something like his brother Frank; and they differ from each other no more than in their age, for they were twins.

Lucy: Ha! ha! he!

Alith: Your servant, Sir; I cannot be so deceived, though you are. But come, let's hear, how do you know what you affirm so confidently?

Spark: Why, I'll tell you all. Frank Harcourt coming to me this morning to wish me joy, and present his service to you, I asked him if he could help me to a parson. Whereupon he told me he had a brother in town who was in orders; and he went straight away, and sent him, you see there, to me.

Alith: Yes, Frank goes and puts on a black coat, then tells you he is Ned; that's all you have for't.

Spark: Pshaw! pshaw! I tell you, by the same token, the midwife put her garter about Frank's neck, to know 'em asunder, they were so like.

Alith: Frank tells you this too?

Spark: Ay, and Ned there too: nay, they are both in a story.

Alith: So, so; very foolish.

Spark: Lord, if you won't believe one, you had best try him by your chambermaid there; for chambermaids must needs know chaplains from other men, they are so used to 'em.

Difference between a smile and a smirk? **Lucy:** Let's see: nay, I'll be sworn he has the canonical smirk, and the filthy clammy palm of a chaplain.

Alith: Well, most reverend Doctor, pray let us make an end of this fooling.

Har: With all my soul, divine heavenly creature, when you please.

Alith: He speaks like a chaplain indeed.

Spark: Why, was there not soul, divine, heavenly, in what he said?

Alith: Once more, most impertinent black coat, cease your persecution, and let us have a conclusion of this ridiculous love.

Har: (*aside*) I had forgot; I must suit my style to my coat, or I wear it in vain.

Alith: I have no more patience left; let us make once an end of this troublesome love, I say.

Har: So be it, seraphic lady, when your honour shall think it meet and convenient so to do.

Spark: 'Gad, I'm sure none but a chaplain could speak so, I think.

Alith: Let me tell you, Sir, this dull trick will not serve your turn; though you delay our marriage, you shall not hinder it.

Double meaning **Har:** Far be it from me, munificent patroness, to delay your marriage; I desire nothing more than to marry you presently, which I might do, if you yourself would; for my noble, good-natured, and thrice generous patron here would not hinder it.

Spark: No, poor man, not I, faith.

Har: And now, Madam, let me tell you plainly nobody else shall marry you, by Heavens! I'll die first, for I'm sure I should die after it.

Lucy: How his love has made him forget his function, as I have seen it in real parsons!

Alith: That was spoken like a chaplain too? Now you understand him, I hope.

Spark: Poor man, he takes it heinously to be refused; I can't blame him, 'tis putting an indignity upon him, not to be suffered; but you'll pardon me, Madam, it shan't be; he shall marry us; come away, pray, Madam.

Lucy: Ha! ha! he! more ado! 'tis late.

Alith: Invincible stupidity! I tell you, he would marry me as your rival, not as your chaplain.

Spark: Come, come, Madam. (*pulling her away*)

Lucy: I pray, Madam, do not refuse this reverend divine the honour and satisfaction of marrying you; for I dare say he has set his heart upon't, good doctor.

Alith: What can you hope or design by this?

Har: (*aside*) I could answer her, a reprieve for a day only, often revokes a hasty doom. At worst, if she will not take mercy on me, and let me marry her, I have at least the lover's second pleasure, hindering my rival's enjoyment, though but for a time.

Spark: Come, Madam, 'tis e'en twelve o'clock, and my mother charged me never to be married out of the canonical hours. Come, come; Lord, here's such a deal of modesty, I warrant, the first day.

Lucy: Yes, an't please your worship, married women show all their modesty the first day, because married men show all their love the first day.

(*Exeunt* **Sparkish, Alithea, Harcourt,** *and* **Lucy.**)

SCENE II. The Scene changes to a Bedchamber, where appear **Pinchwife** and **Mrs. Pinchwife**

Pinch: Come, tell me, I say.

Mrs. Pinch: Lord! han't I told it an hundred times over?

Pinch: (*aside*) I would try, if in the repetition of the ungrateful tale, I could find her altering it in the least circumstance; for if her story be false, she is so too.—— Come, how was't, baggage?

Mrs. Pinch: Lord, what pleasure you take to hear it, sure!

Pinch: No, you take more in telling it, I find; but speak, how was't?

Mrs. Pinch: He carried me up into the house next to the Exchange.

Pinch: So, and you two were only in the room!

Mrs. Pinch: Yes, for he sent away a youth that was there, for some dried fruit, and China oranges.

Pinch: Did he so? Damn him for it—and for——

Mrs. Pinch: But presently came up the gentlewoman of the house.

Pinch: Oh, 'twas well she did; but what did he do whilst the fruit came?

Mrs. Pinch: He kissed me an hundred times, and told me he fancied he kissed my fine sister, meaning me, you know, whom he said he loved with all his soul, and bid me be sure to tell her so, and to desire her to be at her window, by eleven of the clock this morning, and he would walk under it at that time.

Pinch: (*aside*) And he was as good as his word, very punctual; a pox reward him for't.

Mrs. Pinch: Well, and he said if you were not within, he would come up to her, meaning me, you know, bud, still.

Pinch: (*aside*) So—he knew her certainly; but for this confession, I am obliged to her simplicity.——But what, you stood very still when he kissed you?

Mrs. Pinch: Yes, I warrant you; would you have had me discover myself?

Why does he want to hear the details ?

Pinch: But you told me he did some beastliness to you, as you call it; what was't?

Mrs. Pinch: Why, he put——

Pinch: What?

Mrs. Pinch: Why, he put the tip of his tongue between my lips, and so mousled me—and I said, I'd bite it.

Pinch: An eternal canker seize it, for a dog!

Mrs. Pinch: Nay, you need not be so angry with him neither, for to say truth, he has the sweetest breath I ever knew.

Pinch: The devil! you were satisfied with it then, and would do it again?

Mrs. Pinch: Not unless he should force me.

Pinch: Force you, changeling! I tell you, no woman can be forced.

Mrs. Pinch: Yes, but she may sure, by such a one as he, for he's a proper, goodly, strong man; 'tis hard, let me tell you, to resist him.

Pinch: (*aside*) So, 'tis plain she loves him, yet she has not love enough to make her conceal it from me; but the sight of him will increase her aversion for me and love for him; and that love instruct her how to deceive me and satisfy

Reversed terms, reversed values
him, all idiot as she is. Love! 'twas he gave women first their craft, their art of deluding. Out of Nature's hands they came plain, open, silly, and fit for slaves, as she and Heaven intended 'em; but damned Love—well—I must strangle that little monster whilst I can deal with him.—— Go fetch pen, ink, and paper out of the next room.

Mrs. Pinch: Yes, bud. (*Exit.*)

Pinch: Why should women have more invention in love than men? It can only be because they have more desires, more soliciting passions, more lust, and more of the devil.

(**Mrs. Pinchwife** *returns*)

Come, minx, sit down and write.

Mrs. Pinch: Ay, dear bud, but I can't do't very well.

Pinch: I wish you could not at all.

Mrs. Pinch: But what should I write for?

Pinch: I'll have you write a letter to your lover.

Mrs. Pinch: O Lord, to the fine gentleman a letter!

Pinch: Yes, to the fine gentleman.

Mrs. Pinch: Lord, you do but jeer: sure you jest.

Pinch: I am not so merry: come, write as I bid you.

Mrs. Pinch: What, do you think I am a fool?

Pinch: (*aside*) She's afraid I would not dictate any love to him, therefore she's unwilling.——But you had best begin.

Mrs. Pinch: Indeed, and indeed, but I won't, so I won't.

Pinch: Why?

Mrs. Pinch: Because he's in town; you may send for him if you will.

Pinch: Very well, you would have him brought to you; is it come to this? I say, take the pen and write, or you'll provoke me.

Mrs. Pinch: Lord, what d'ye make a fool of me for? Don't I know that letters are never writ but from the country to London, and from London into the country? Now he's in town, and I am in town too; therefore I can't write to him, you know.

Pinch: (*aside*) So, I am glad it is no worse; she is innocent enough yet.——

Yes, you may, when your husband bids you, write letters to people that are in town.

Mrs. Pinch: Oh, may I so? then I'm satisfied.

Pinch: Come, begin (*dictates*)—"Sir"——

Mrs. Pinch: Shan't I say, "Dear Sir"? You know one says always something more than bare "Sir."

Pinch: Write as I bid you, or I will write whore with this penknife in your face.

Mrs. Pinch: Nay, good bud (*She writes.*)—"Sir"——

Pinch: "Though I suffered last night your nauseous, loathed kisses and embraces"—— Write!

Mrs. Pinch: Nay, why should I say so? You know I told you he had a sweet breath.

Pinch: Write!

Mrs. Pinch: Let me but put out "loathed."

Pinch: Write, I say!

Mrs. Pinch: Well then. (*writes*)

Pinch: Let's see, what have you writ?—(*takes the paper and reads*) "Though I suffered last night your kisses and embraces"——Thou impudent creature! where is "nauseous" and "loathed"?

Mrs. Pinch: I can't abide to write such filthy words.

Pinch: Once more write as I'd have you, and question it not, or I will spoil thy writing with this. I will stab out those eyes that cause my mischief. (*holds up the penknife*)

Mrs. Pinch: O Lord! I will.

Pinch: So—so—let's see now.—(*reads*) "Though I suffered last night your nauseous, loathed kisses and embraces"—go on—"yet I would not have you presume that you shall ever repeat them"—so——(*She writes.*)

Mrs. Pinch: I have writ it.

Pinch: On, then—"I then concealed myself from your knowledge, to avoid your insolencies."——(*She writes.*)

Mrs. Pinch: So——

Pinch: "The same reason, now I am out of your hands"——(*She writes.*)

Mrs. Pinch: So——

Pinch: "Makes me own to you my unfortunate, though innocent frolic, of being in man's clothes"——(*She writes.*)

Mrs. Pinch: So——

Pinch: "That you may for evermore cease to pursue her, who hates and detests you"——(*She writes on.*)

Mrs. Pinch: So—h——(*sighs*)

Pinch: What, do you sigh?—"detests you—as much as she loves her husband and her honour."

Mrs. Pinch: I vow, husband, he'll ne'er believe I should write such a letter.

Pinch: What, he'd expect a kinder from you? Come, now your name only.

Mrs. Pinch: What, shan't I say "Your most faithful humble servant till death"?

Pinch: No, tormenting fiend!—(*aside*) Her style, I find, would be very soft.—— Come, wrap it up now, whilst I go fetch wax and a candle; and write on the backside, "For Mr. Horner." (*Exit* **Pinchwife**)

Mrs. Pinch: "For Mr. Horner."——So, I am glad he has told me his name.

Both are aware of language and its power.

Language formula

Dear Mr. Horner! But why should I send thee such a letter that will vex thee, and make thee angry with me?——Well, I will not send it.—— Ay, but then my husband will kill me—for I see plainly he won't let me love Mr. Horner— but what care I for my husband? I won't, so I won't, send poor Mr. Horner such a letter—— But then my husband—but oh, what if I writ at bottom my husband made me write it?—— Ay, but then my husband would see't—Can one have no shift? Ah, a London woman would have had a hundred presently. Stay—what if I should write a letter, and wrap it up like this, and write upon't too? Ay, but then my husband would see't—I don't know what to do.— But yet egads I'll try, so I will—for I will not send this letter to poor Mr. Horner, come what will on't.

"Dear, sweet Mr. Horner"—(*She writes and repeats what she hath writ.*)—so— "my husband would have me send you a base, rude, unmannerly letter; but I won't"—so—"and would have me forbid you loving me; but I won't"—so— "and would have me say to you, I hate you, poor Mr. Horner; but I won't tell a lie for him"—there—"for I'm sure if you and I were in the country at cards together"—so—"I could not help treading on your toe under the table"—so—"or rubbing knees with you, and staring in your face, till you saw me"—very well—"and then looking down, and blushing for an hour together"—so—"but I must make haste before my husband comes: and now he has taught me to write letters, you shall have longer ones from me, who am, dear, dear, poor, dear Mr. Horner, your most humble friend, and servant to command till death,—Margery Pinchwife."

Stay, I must give him a hint at bottom—so—now wrap it up just like t'other —so—now write "For Mr. Horner"—But oh now, what shall I do with it? for here comes my husband.

(*Enter* **Pinchwife**)

Pinch: (*aside*) I have been detained by a sparkish coxcomb, who pretended a visit to me; but I fear 'twas to my wife——What, have you done?

Mrs. Pinch: Ay, ay, bud, just now.

Pinch: Let's see't: what d'ye tremble for? what, you would not have it go?

Mrs. Pinch: Here—(*aside*) No, I must not give him that: so I had been served if I had given him this. (*He opens and reads the first letter.*)

Pinch: Come, where's the wax and seal?

Mrs. Pinch: (*aside*) Lord, what shall I do now? Nay, then I have it——Pray let me see't. Lord, you think me so arrant a fool I cannot seal a letter; I will do't, so I will. (*snatches the letter from him, changes it for the other, seals it, and delivers it to him*)

Pinch: Nay, I believe you will learn that, and other things too, which I would not have you.

Mrs. Pinch: So, han't I done it curiously?—(*aside*) I think I have; there's my letter going to Mr. Horner, since he'll needs have me send letters to folks.

Pinch: 'Tis very well; but I warrant you would not have it go now?

Mrs. Pinch: Yes, indeed, but I would, bud, now.

Pinch: Well, you are a good girl then. Come, let me lock you up in your chamber till I come back; and be sure you come not within three strides of the window when I am gone, for I have a spy in the street.—(*Exit* **Mrs. Pinchwife**, **Pinchwife** *locks the door.*) At least, 'tis fit she think so. If we do not cheat women, they'll cheat us, and fraud may be justly used with secret enemies, of which a wife is the most dangerous; and he that has a handsome one to keep, and a frontier town, must provide against treachery, rather than open force. Now I have secured all within, I'll deal with the foe without, with false intelligence. (*Holds up the letter. Exit* **Pinchwife**.)

What view of marriage do these images suggest?

SCENE III.   The Scene changes to **Horner's** Lodging

(**Quack** *and* **Horner**)

Quack: Well, Sir, how fadges the new design? Have you not the luck of all your brother projectors, to deceive only yourself at last?

Horn: No, good domine Doctor, I deceive you, it seems, and others too; for the grave matrons, and old, rigid husbands think me as unfit for love as they are; but their wives, sisters, and daughters know, some of 'em, better things already.

Quack: Already!

Horn: Already, I say. Last night I was drunk with half-a-dozen of your civil persons, as you call 'em, and people of honour, and so was made free of their society and dressing-rooms for ever hereafter; and am already come to the privileges of sleeping upon their pallets, warming smocks, tying shoes and garters, and the like, Doctor, already, already, Doctor.

Quack: You have made use of your time, Sir.

Horn: I tell thee, I am now no more interruption to 'em when they sing, or talk, bawdy, than a little squab French page who speaks no English.

Quack: But do civil persons and women of honour drink, and sing bawdy songs?

Horn: Oh, amongst friends, amongst friends. For your bigots in honour are just like those in religion; they fear the eye of the world more than the eye of Heaven, and think there is no virtue but railing at vice, and no sin but giving scandal. They rail at a poor little kept player, and keep themselves some young modest pulpit comedian to be privy to their sins in their closets, not to tell 'em of them in their chapels.

Quack: Nay, the truth on't is priests, amongst the women now, have quite got the better of us lay-confessors, physicians.

Horn: And they are rather their patients; but——

(*Enter* **My Lady Fidget**, *looking about her*)

Now we talk of women of honour, here comes one. Step behind the screen there, and but observe if I have not particular privileges with the women of reputation already, Doctor, already. (**Quack** *retires.*)

Lady Fid: Well, Horner, am not I a woman of honour? You see, I'm as good as my word.

Horn: And you shall see, Madam, I'll not be behindhand with you in honour; and I'll be as good as my word too, if you please but to withdraw into the next room.

Lady Fid: But first, my dear Sir, you must promise to have a care of my dear honour.

Horn: If you talk a word more of your honour, you'll make me incapable to wrong it. To talk of honour in the mysteries of love, is like talking of Heaven or the Deity in an operation of witchcraft just when you are employing the devil: it makes the charm impotent.

Lady Fid: Nay, fy! let us not be smutty. But you talk of mysteries and bewitching to me; I don't understand you.

Horn: I tell you, Madam, the word money in a mistress's mouth, at such a nick of time, is not a more disheartening sound to a younger brother, than that of honour to an eager lover like myself.

Lady Fid: But you can't blame a lady of my reputation to be chary.

Horn: Chary! I have been chary of it already, by the report I have caused of myself.

Lady Fid: Ay, but if you should ever let other women know that dear secret, it would come out. Nay, you must have a great care of your conduct; for my acquaintance are so censorious (oh, 'tis a wicked, censorious world, Mr. Horner!), I say, are so censorious and detracting that perhaps they'll talk to the prejudice of my honour, though you should not let them know the dear secret.

Horn: Nay, Madam, rather than they shall prejudice your honour, I'll prejudice theirs; and, to serve you, I'll lie with 'em all, make the secret their own, and then they'll keep it. I am a Machiavel in love, Madam.

Lady Fid: Oh, no, Sir, not that way.

Horn: Nay, the devil take me if censorious women are to be silenced any other way.

Lady Fid: A secret is better kept, I hope, by a single person than a multitude; therefore pray do not trust anybody else with it, dear, dear Mr. Horner. (*embracing him*)

(*Enter* **Sir Jasper Fidget**)

Sir Jasp: How now!

Lady Fid: (*aside*) Oh my husband!—prevented—and what's almost as bad, found with my arms about another man—that will appear too much—what shall I say?——Sir Jasper, come hither: I am trying if Mr. Horner were ticklish, and he's as ticklish as can be. I love to torment the confounded toad; let you and I tickle him.

Sir Jasp: No, your ladyship will tickle him better without me, I suppose. But is this your buying china? I thought you had been at the china-house.

Horn: (*aside*) China-house! that's my cue, I must take it.——A pox! can't you keep your impertinent wives at home? Some men are troubled with the husbands, but I with the wives; but I'd have you to know, since I cannot be your journeyman by night, I will not be your drudge by day, to squire your wife about, and be your man of straw or scarecrow only to pies and jays, that would be nibbling at your forbidden fruit; I shall be shortly the hackney gentleman-usher of the town.

Sir Jasp: (*aside*) He! he! he! poor fellow, he's in the right on't, faith. To squire women about for other folks is as ungrateful an employment, as to tell money for other folks.—— He! he! he! be'n't angry, Horner.

Lady Fid: No, 'tis I have more reason to be angry, who am left by you to go abroad indecently alone; or, what is more indecent, to pin myself upon such ill-bred people of your acquaintance as this is.

Sir Jasp: Nay, prithee, what has he done?

Lady Fid: Nay, he has done nothing.

Sir Jasp: But what d'ye take ill, if he has done nothing?

Lady Fid: Ha! ha! ha! faith, I can't but laugh, however; why, d'ye think the

unmannerly toad would come down to me to the coach? I was fain to come up to fetch him, or go without him, which I was resolved not to do; for he knows china very well, and has himself very good, but will not let me see it lest I should beg some; but I will find it out, and have what I came for yet.

Horn: (*apart to* **Lady Fidget**) Lock the door, Madam.—(*Exit* **Lady Fidget**, *and locks the door followed by* **Horner** *to the door.*)—— So, she has got into my chamber and locked me out. Oh the impertinency of womankind! Well, Sir Jasper, plain-dealing is a jewel; if ever you suffer your wife to trouble me again here she shall carry you home a pair of horns, by my lord mayor she shall; though I cannot furnish you myself, you are sure, yet I'll find a way.

Sir Jasp: Ha! ha! he!—(*aside*) At my first coming in, and finding her arms about him, tickling him it seems, I was half jealous, but now I see my folly.—— He! he! he! poor Horner.

Horner: Nay, though you laugh now, 'twill be my turn ere long. Oh, women, more impertinent, more cunning, and more mischievous than their monkeys, and to me almost as ugly!—Now is she throwing my things about and rifling all I have; but I'll get in to her the back way, and so rifle her for it.

Sir Jasp: Ha! ha! ha! poor angry Horner.

Horn: Stay here a little, I'll ferret her out to you presently, I warrant. (*Exit at t'other door.*)

(**Sir Jasper** *calls through the door to his* Wife; *she answers from within.*)

Double meaning? **Sir Jasp:** Wife! my Lady Fidget! wife! he is coming in to you the back way.

Lady Fid: Let him come, and welcome, which way he will.

Sir Jasp: He'll catch you, and use you roughly, and be too strong for you.

Lady Fid: Don't you trouble yourself, let him if he can.

Quack: (*behind*) This indeed I could not have believed from him, nor any but my own eyes.

(*Enter* **Mrs. Squeamish**)

Mrs. Squeam: Where's this woman-hater, this toad, this ugly, greasy, dirty sloven?

Sir Jasp: (*aside*) So, the women all will have him ugly: methinks he is a comely person, but his wants make his form contemptible to 'em; and 'tis e'en as my wife said yesterday, talking of him, that a proper handsome eunuch was as ridiculous a thing as a gigantic coward.

Mrs. Squeam: Sir Jasper, your servant: where is the odious beast?

Sir Jasp: He's within in his chamber, with my wife; she's playing the wag with him.

Mrs. Squeam: Is she so? and he's a clownish beast, he'll give her no quarter, he'll play the wag with her again, let me tell you: come, let's go help her.— What, the door's locked?

Sir Jasp: Ay, my wife locked it.

Mrs. Squeam: Did she so? Let's break it open then.

Sir Jasp: No, no; he'll do her no hurt.

Mrs. Squeam: No.—(*aside*) But is there no other way to get in to 'em? Whither goes this? I will disturb 'em. (*Exit* **Mrs. Squeamish** *at another door.*)

(*Enter* **Old Lady Squeamish**)

Lady Squeam: Where is this harlotry, this impudent baggage, this rambling tomrigg? O Sir Jasper, I'm glad to see you here; did you not see my vile grandchild come in hither just now?

Sir Jasp: Yes.

Lady Squeam: Ay, but where is she then? where is she? Lord, Sir Jasper, I have e'en rattled myself to pieces in pursuit of her: but can you tell what she makes here? They say below, no woman lodges here.

Sir Jasp: No.

Lady Squeam: No! what does she here then? Say, if it be not a woman's lodging, what makes she here? But are you sure no woman lodges here?

Sir Jasp: No, nor no man neither; this is Mr. Horner's lodging.

Lady Squeam: Is it so, are you sure?

Sir Jasp: Yes, yes.

Lady Squeam: So; then there's no hurt in't, I hope. But where is he?

Sir Jasp: He's in the next room with my wife.

Lady Squeam: Nay, if you trust him with your wife, I may with my Biddy. They say he's a merry harmless man now, e'en as harmless a man as ever came out of Italy with a good voice, and as pretty, harmless company for a lady as a snake without his teeth.

Sir Jasp: Ay, ay, poor man.

(*Enter* **Mrs. Squeamish**)

Mrs. Squeam: I can't find 'em.—— Oh, are you here, Grandmother? I followed, you must know, my Lady Fidget hither; 'tis the prettiest lodging, and I have been staring on the prettiest pictures——

(*Enter* **Lady Fidget** *with a piece of china in her hand, and* **Horner** *following*)

Lady Fid: And I have been toiling and moiling for the prettiest piece of china, my dear.

> *Is china a euphemism? Why?*

Horn: Nay, she has been too hard for me, do what I could.

Mrs. Squeam: O Lord, I'll have some china too. Good Mr. Horner, don't think to give other people china, and me none; come in with me too.

Horn: Upon my honour, I have none left now.

Mrs. Squeam: Nay, nay, I have known you deny your china before now, but you shan't put me off so. Come.

Horn: This lady had the last there.

Lady Fid: Yes, indeed, Madam, to my certain knowledge, he has no more left.

Mrs. Squeam: Oh, but it may be he may have some you could not find.

Lady Fid: What, d'ye think if he had had any left, I would not have had it too? for we women of quality never think we have china enough.

Horn: Do not take it ill, I cannot make china for you all, but I will have a roll-waggon for you too, another time.

Mrs. Squeam: Thank you, dear toad.

Lady Fid: (*to* **Horner** *aside*) What do you mean by that promise?

Horn: (*apart to* **Lady Fidget**) Alas, she has an innocent, literal understanding.

Lady Squeam: Poor Mr. Horner! he has enough to do to please you all, I see.

Horn: Ay, Madam, you see how they use me.

Lady Squeam: Poor gentleman, I pity you.

Horn: I thank you, Madam: I could never find pity but from such reverend ladies as you are; the young ones will never spare a man.

Mrs. Squeam: Come, come, beast, and go dine with us; for we shall want a man at ombre after dinner.

Horn: That's all their use of me, Madam, you see.

Mrs. Squeam: Come, sloven, I'll lead you, to be sure of you. (*pulls him by the cravat*)

Lady Squeam: Alas, poor man, how she tugs him! Kiss, kiss her; that's the way to make such nice women quiet.

Horn: No, Madam, that remedy is worse than the torment; they know I dare suffer anything rather than do it.

Lady Squeam: Prithee kiss her, and I'll give you her picture in little, that you admired so last night; prithee do.

Horn: Well, nothing but that could bribe me: I love a woman only in effigy and good painting, as much as I hate them. I'll do't, for I could adore the devil well painted. (*kisses **Mrs. Squeamish***)

Mrs. Squeam: Foh, you filthy toad! nay, now I've done jesting.

Lady Squeam: Ha! ha! ha! I told you so.

Mrs. Squeam: Foh! a kiss of his——

Sir Jasp: Has no more hurt in't than one of my spaniel's.

Mrs. Squeam: Nor no more good neither.

Quack: (*behind*) I will now believe anything he tells me.

(*Enter **Pinchwife***)

Lady Fid: O Lord, here's a man! Sir Jasper, my mask, my mask. I would not be seen here for the world.

Sir Jasp: What, not when I am with you?

Lady Fid: No, no, my honour—let's be gone.

Mrs. Squeam: O Grandmother, let us be gone; make haste, make haste, I know not how he may censure us.

Lady Fid: Be found in the lodging of anything like a man!—Away.

(*Exeunt **Sir Jasper Fidget, Lady Fidget, Old Lady Squeamish, Mrs. Squeamish.***)

Quack: (*behind*) What's here? another cuckold? he looks like one, and none else sure have any business with him.

Horn: Well, what brings my dear friend hither?

Pinch: Your impertinency.

Horn: My impertinency!—why, you gentlemen that have got handsome wives think you have a privilege of saying anything to your friends, and are as brutish as if you were our creditors.

Pinch: No, Sir, I'll ne'er trust you any way.

Horn: But why not, dear Jack? Why diffide in me thou know'st so well?

Pinch: Because I do know you so well.

Horn: Han't I been always thy friend, honest Jack, always ready to serve thee, in love or battle, before thou wert married, and am so still?

Pinch: I believe so; you would be my second now, indeed.

Horn: Well then, dear Jack, why so unkind, so grim, so strange to me? Come, prithee, kiss me, dear rogue: gad, I was always, I say, and am still as much thy servant as——

Pinch: As I am yours, Sir. What, you would send a kiss to my wife, is that it?

Horn: So, there 'tis—a man can't show his friendship to a married man, but presently he talks of his wife to you. Prithee, let thy wife alone, and let thee and I be all one, as we were wont. What, thou art as shy of my kindness as a Lombard Street alderman of a courtier's civility at Locket's!

Pinch: But you are overkind to me, as kind as if I were your cuckold already;

yet I must confess you ought to be kind and civil to me, since I am so kind, so civil to you, as to bring you this: look you there, Sir. (*delivers him a letter*)

Horn: What is't?

Pinch: Only a love letter, Sir.

Horn: From whom?—how! this is from your wife—hum—and hum—— (*reads*)

Pinch: Even from my wife, Sir: am I not wondrous kind and civil to you now too?—(*aside*) But you'll not think her so.

Horn: (*aside*) Ha! is this a trick of his or hers?

Pinch: The gentleman's surprised I find.—What, you expected a kinder letter?

Horn: No faith, not I, how could I?

Pinch: Yes, yes, I'm sure you did. A man so well made as you are must needs be disappointed, if the women declare not their passion at first sight or opportunity.

Horn: (*aside*) But what should this mean? Stay, the postscript.—(*reads aside*) "Be sure you love me, whatsoever my husband says to the contrary, and let him not see this, lest he should come home and pinch me, or kill my squirrel."—It seems he knows not what the letter contains.

Pinch: Come, ne'er wonder at it so much.

Horn: Faith, I can't help it.

Pinch: Now, I think I have deserved your infinite friendship and kindness, and have showed myself sufficiently an obliging kind friend and husband; am I not so, to bring a letter from my wife to her gallant?

Horn: Ay, the devil take me, art thou, the most obliging, kind friend and husband in the world, ha! ha!

Pinch: Well, you may be merry, Sir; but in short I must tell you, Sir, my honour will suffer no jesting.

Horn: What dost thou mean?

Pinch: Does the letter want a comment? Then, know, Sir, though I have been so civil a husband as to bring you a letter from my wife, to let you kiss and court her to my face, I will not be a cuckold, Sir, I will not.

Horn: Thou art mad with jealousy. I never saw thy wife in my life but at the play yesterday, and I know not if it were she or no. I court her, kiss her!

Pinch: I will not be a cuckold, I say; there will be danger in making me a cuckold.

Horn: Why, wert thou not well cured of thy last clap?

Pinch: I wear a sword.

Horn: It should be taken from thee, lest thou shouldst do thyself a mischief with it; thou art mad, man.

Pinch: As mad as I am, and as merry as you are, I must have more reason from you ere we part. I say again, though you kissed and courted last night my wife in man's clothes, as she confesses in her letter——

Horn: (*aside*) Ha!

Pinch: Both she and I say you must not design it again, for you have mistaken your woman, as you have done your man.

Horn: (*aside*) Oh—I understand something now—— Was that thy wife! Why wouldst thou not tell me 'twas she? Faith, my freedom with her was your fault, not mine.

Pinch: (*aside*) Faith, so 'twas.

Horn: Fy! I'd never do't to a woman before her husband's face, sure.

Pinch: But I had rather you should do't to my wife before my face, than behind my back; and that you shall never do.

Horn: No—you will hinder me.

Pinch: If I would not hinder you, you see by her letter she would.

Horn: Well, I must e'en acquiesce then, and be contented with what she writes.

Pinch: I'll assure you 'twas voluntarily writ; I had no hand in't, you may believe me.

Horn: I do believe thee, faith.

Pinch: And believe her too, for she's an innocent creature, has no dissembling in her: and so fare you well, Sir.

Horn: Pray, however, present my humble service to her, and tell her I will obey her letter to a tittle, and fulfil her desires, be what they will, or with what difficulty soever I do't; and you shall be no more jealous of me, I warrant her, and you.

Pinch: Well then, fare you well; and play with any man's honour but mine, kiss any man's wife but mine, and welcome.

(*Exit* **Mr. Pinchwife**.)

Horn: Ha! ha! ha! Doctor.

Quack: It seems he has not heard the report of you, or does not believe it.

Horn: Ha! ha!—now, Doctor, what think you?

Quack: Pray let's see the letter—hum—(*reads the letter*)—"for—dear—love you——"

Horn: I wonder how she could contrive it! What say'st thou to't? 'Tis an original.

Quack: So are your cuckolds, too, originals: for they are like no other common cuckolds, and I will henceforth believe it not impossible for you to cuckold the Grand Signior amidst his guards of eunuchs, that I say.

Horn: And I say for the letter, 'tis the first love letter that ever was without flames, darts, fates, destinies, lying and dissembling in't.

(*Enter* **Sparkish** *pulling in* **Mr. Pinchwife**)

Spark: Come back, you are a pretty brother-in-law, neither go to church nor to dinner with your sister bride!

Pinch: My sister denies her marriage, and you see is gone away from you dissatisfied.

Spark: Pshaw! upon a foolish scruple, that our parson was not in lawful orders, and did not say all the common prayer; but 'tis her modesty only I believe. But let women be never so modest the first day, they'll be sure to come to themselves by night, and I shall have enough of her then. In the meantime, Harry Horner, you must dine with me: I keep my wedding at my aunt's in the Piazza.

Horn: Thy wedding! what stale maid has lived to despair of a husband, or what young one of a gallant?

Spark: Oh, your servant, Sir—this gentleman's sister then,—no stale maid.

Horn: I'm sorry for't.

Pinch: (*aside*) How comes he so concerned for her?

Spark: You sorry for't? Why, do you know any ill by her?

Horn: No, I know none but by thee; 'tis for her sake, not yours, and another man's sake that might have hoped, I thought.

Spark: Another man! another man! What is his name?

Horn: Nay, since 'tis past, he shall be nameless.—(*aside*) Poor Harcourt! I am sorry thou hast missed her.

Pinch: (*aside*) He seems to be much troubled at the match.

Spark: Prithee, tell me——Nay, you shan't go, Brother.

Pinch: I must of necessity, but I'll come to you to dinner.

(*Exit* **Pinchwife.**)

Spark: But, Harry, what, have I a rival in my wife already? But with all my heart, for he may be of use to me hereafter; for though my hunger is now my sauce, and I can fall on heartily without, the time will come when a rival will be as good sauce for a married man to a wife, as an orange to veal.

For Sparkish, how is eating like sex ?

Horn: O thou damned rogue! thou hast set my teeth on edge with thy orange.

Spark: Then let's to dinner—there I was with you again. Come.

Horn: But who dines with thee?

Spark: My friends and relations, my brother Pinchwife, you see, of your acquaintance.

Horn: And his wife?

Spark: No, 'gad, he'll ne'er let her come amongst us good fellows; your stingy country coxcomb keeps his wife from his friends, as he does his little firkin of ale for his own drinking, and a gentleman can't get a smack on't; but his servants, when his back is turned, broach it at their pleasures, and dust it away, ha! ha! ha!—'Gad, I am witty, I think, considering I was married to-day, by the world; but come——

Horn: No, I will not dine with you, unless you can fetch her too.

Spark: Pshaw! what pleasure canst thou have with women now, Harry?

Horn: My eyes are not gone; I love a good prospect yet, and will not dine with you unless she does too; go fetch her, therefore, but do not tell her husband 'tis for my sake.

Spark: Well, I'll go try what I can do; in the meantime, come away to my aunt's lodging; 'tis in the way to Pinchwife's.

Horn: The poor woman has called for aid, and stretched forth her hand, Doctor; I cannot but help her over the pale out of the briars. (*Exeunt* **Sparkish, Horner, Quack.**)

SCENE IV. The Scene changes to **Pinchwife's** House

(**Mrs. Pinchwife** *alone, leaning on her elbow. A table, pen, ink, and paper*)

Mrs. Pinch: Well, 'tis e'en so, I have got the London disease they call love; I am sick of my husband, and for my gallant. I have heard this distemper called a fever, but methinks 'tis liker an ague; for when I think of my husband, I tremble, and am in a cold sweat, and have inclinations to vomit; but when I think of my gallant, dear Mr. Horner, my hot fit comes, and I am all in a fever indeed; and, as in other fevers, my own chamber is tedious to me, and I would fain be removed to his, and then methinks I should be well. Ah, poor Mr. Horner! Well, I cannot, will not stay here; therefore I'll make an end of my letter to him, which shall be a finer letter than my last, because I have studied it like anything. Oh sick, sick! (*takes the pen and writes*) (*Enter* **Pinchwife**, *who, seeing her writing, steals softly behind her, and, looking over her shoulder, snatches the paper from her.*)

Pinch: What, writing more letters?

Mrs. Pinch: O lord, bud, why d'ye fright me so? (*She offers to run out; he stops her, and reads.*)

Pinch: How's this? nay, you shall not stir, Madam:—"Dear, dear, dear Mr. Horner"—very well—I have taught you to write letters to good purpose—but let's see't. "First, I am to beg your pardon for my boldness in writing to you, which I'd have you to know I would not have done, had not you said first you loved me so extremely, which if you do, you will never suffer me to lie in the arms of another man whom I loathe, nauseate, and detest."—Now you can write these filthy words. But what follows?—"Therefore, I hope you will speedily find some way to free me from this unfortunate match, which was never, I assure you, of my choice, but I'm afraid 'tis already too far gone; however, if you love me, as I do you, you will try what you can do; but you must help me away before to-morrow, or else, alas! I shall be for ever out of your reach, for I can defer no longer our—our——" (*The letter concludes.*) what is to follow "our"?—speak, what? Our journey into the country I suppose—Oh woman, damned woman! and Love, damned Love, their old tempter! for this is one of his miracles; in a moment he can make those blind that could see, and those see that were blind, those dumb that could speak, and those prattle who were dumb before; nay, what is more than all, make these dough-baked, senseless, indocile animals, women, too hard for us, their politic lords and rulers, in a moment. But make an end of your letter, and then I'll make an end of you thus, and all my plagues together. (*draws his sword*)

Mrs. Pinch: O Lord, O Lord, you are such a passionate man, bud!

(*Enter* **Sparkish**)

Spark: How now, what's here to do?

Pinch: This fool here now!

Spark: What! drawn upon your wife? You should never do that, but at night in the dark, when you can't hurt her. This is my sister-in-law, is it not? ay, faith e'en our country Margery (*pulls aside her handkerchief*); one may know her. Come, she and you must go dine with me; dinner's ready, come. But where's my wife? Is she not come home yet? Where is she?

Pinch: Making you a cuckold; 'tis that they all do, as soon as they can.

Spark: What, the wedding-day? No, a wife that designs to make a cully of her husband will be sure to let him win the first stake of love, by the world. But come, they stay dinner for us: come, I'll lead down our Margery.

Mrs. Pinch: No—Sir, go, we'll follow you.

Spark: I will not wag without you.

Pinch: (*aside*) This coxcomb is a sensible torment to me amidst the greatest in the world.

Spark: Come, come, Madam Margery.

Pinch: No; I'll lead her my way: what, would you treat your friends with mine, for want of your own wife?—(*leads her to t'other door, and locks her in and returns*) I am contented my rage should take breath——

Spark: (*aside*) I told Horner this.

Pinch: Come now.

Spark: Lord, how shy you are of your wife! But let me tell you, Brother, we men of wit have amongst us a saying that cuckolding, like the small-pox, comes with a fear; and you may keep your wife as much as you will out of danger of infection, but if her constitution incline her to't, she'll have it sooner or later, by the world, say they.

Pinch: (*aside*) What a thing is a cuckold, that every fool can make him ridiculous!—— Well, Sir—but let me advise you, now you are come to be concerned, because you suspect the danger, not to neglect the means to prevent it, especially when the greatest share of the malady will light upon your own head, for

Hows'e'er the kind wife's belly comes to swell,
The husband breeds for her, and first is ill.

ACT V

SCENE I. Mr. Pinchwife's House

(*Enter* **Mr. Pinchwife** *and* **Mrs. Pinchwife**. *A table and candle*)

Pinch: Come, take the pen and make an end of the letter, just as you intended; if you are false in a tittle, I shall soon perceive it, and punish you with this as you deserve.—(*lays his hand on his sword*) Write what was to follow—let's see— "You must make haste, and help me away before to-morrow, or else I shall be for ever out of your reach, for I can defer no longer our"—What follows "our"?

Mrs. Pinch: Must all out, then, bud?—Look you there, then.

(**Mrs. Pinchwife** *takes the pen and writes*.)

Pinch: Let's see—"For I can defer no longer our—wedding—Your slighted Alithea."—What's the meaning of this? my sister's name to't? Speak, unriddle.

Mrs. Pinch: Yes, indeed, bud.

Pinch: But why her name to't? Speak—speak, I say.

Mrs. Pinch: Ay, but you'll tell her then again. If you would not tell her again——

Pinch: I will not:—I am stunned, my head turns round.—Speak.

Mrs. Pinch: Won't you tell her, indeed, and indeed?

Pinch: No; speak, I say.

Mrs. Pinch: She'll be angry with me; but I had rather she should be angry with me than you, bud; and, to tell you the truth, 'twas she made me write the letter, and taught me what I should write.

Pinch: (*aside*) Ha! I thought the style was somewhat better than her own.—— But how could she come to you to teach you, since I had locked you up alone?

Mrs. Pinch: Oh, through the keyhole, bud.

Pinch: But why should she make you write a letter for her to him, since she can write herself?

Mrs. Pinch: Why, she said because—for I was unwilling to do it——

Pinch: Because what—because?

Mrs. Pinch: Because, lest Mr. Horner should be cruel, and refuse her; or vain afterwards, and show the letter, she might disown it, the hand not being hers.

Pinch: (*aside*) How's this? Ha!—then I think I shall come to myself again. This changeling could not invent this lie: but if she could, why should she? she might think I should soon discover it.—Stay—now I think on't too, Horner said he was sorry she had married Sparkish; and her disowning her marriage to me makes me think she has evaded it for Horner's sake: yet why should she take this course? But men in love are fools; women may well be so——But hark you, Madam, your sister went out in the morning, and I have not seen her within since.

Mrs. Pinch: Alack-a-day, she has been crying all day above, it seems, in a corner.

Pinch: Where is she? Let me speak with her.

Mrs. Pinch: (*aside*) O Lord, then he'll discover all!——Pray hold, bud; what, d'ye mean to discover me? she'll know I have told you then. Pray, bud, let me talk with her first.

Pinch: I must speak with her, to know whether Horner ever made her any promise, and whether she be married to Sparkish or no.

Mrs. Pinch: Pray, dear bud, don't, till I have spoken with her, and told her that I have told you all; for she'll kill me else.

Pinch: Go then, and bid her come out to me.

Mrs. Pinch: Yes, yes, bud.

Pinch: Let me see——

Mrs. Pinch: (*aside*) I'll go, but she is not within to come to him: I have just got time to know of Lucy her maid, who first set me on work, what lie I shall tell next; for I am e'en at my wit's end. (*Exit* **Mrs. Pinchwife**.)

Pinch: Well, I resolve it, Horner shall have her: I'd rather give him my sister than lend him my wife; and such an alliance will prevent his pretensions to my wife, sure. I'll make him of kin to her, and then he won't care for her. (**Mrs. Pinchwife** *returns*)

Mrs. Pinch: O Lord, bud! I told you what anger you would make me with my sister.

Pinch: Won't she come hither?

Mrs. Pinch: No, no. Alack-a-day, she's ashamed to look you in the face: and she says, if you go in to her, she'll run away downstairs, and shamefully go herself to Mr. Horner, who has promised her marriage, she says; and she will have no other, so she won't.

Pinch: Did he so?—promise her marriage!—then she shall have no other. Go tell her so; and if she will come and discourse with me a little concerning the means, I will about it immediately. Go.—(*Exit* **Mrs. Pinchwife**.) His estate is equal to Sparkish's, and his extraction is much better than his as his parts are; but my chief reason is I'd rather be akin to him by the name of brother-in-law than that of cuckold.

(*Enter* **Mrs. Pinchwife**)

Well, what says she now?

Mrs. Pinch: Why, she says she would only have you lead her to Horner's lodging; with whom she first will discourse the matter before she talks with you, which yet she cannot do; for alack, poor creature, she says she can't so much as look you in the face, therefore she'll come to you in a mask. And you must excuse her if she make you no answer to any question of yours, till you have brought her to Mr. Horner; and if you will not chide her, nor question her, she'll come out to you immediately.

Pinch: Let her come: I will not speak a word to her, nor require a word from her.

Mrs. Pinch: Oh, I forgot: besides, she says she cannot look you in the face, though through a mask; therefore would desire you to put out the candle.

Pinch: I agree to all. Let her make haste.—There, 'tis out.—(*Puts out the candle. Exit* **Mrs. Pinchwife**.) My case is something better: I'd rather fight with Horner for not lying with my sister, than for lying with my wife; and of the two, I had rather find my sister too forward than my wife. I expected no other from her free education, as she calls it, and her passion for the town. Well, wife and sister are names which make us expect love and duty, pleasure and comfort; but we find 'em plagues and torments, and are equally, though differently, troublesome to their keeper; for we have as much ado to get people to lie with our sisters as to keep 'em from lying with our wives.

(*Enter* **Mrs. Pinchwife** *masked, and in hoods and scarfs, and a night-gown and petticoat of* **Alithea's,** *in the dark.*)

What, are you come, Sister? let us go then.—But first, let me lock up my wife. Mrs. Margery, where are you?

Mrs. Pinch: Here, bud.

Pinch: Come hither, that I may lock you up: get you in.—(*locks the door*) Come, Sister, where are you now?

(**Mrs. Pinchwife** *gives him her hand; but when he lets her go, she steals softly on t'other side of him, and is led away by him for his sister,* **Alithea**.)

SCENE II.   The Scene changes to **Horner's** Lodging

(**Quack, Horner**)

Quack: What, all alone? not so much as one of your cuckolds here, nor one of their wives! They use to take their turns with you, as if they were to watch you.

Horn: Yes, it often happens that a cuckold is but his wife's spy, and is more upon family duty when he is with her gallant abroad, hindering his pleasure, than when he is at home with her playing the gallant. But the hardest duty a married woman imposes upon a lover is keeping her husband company always.

Quack: And his fondness wearies you almost as soon as hers.

Horn: A pox! keeping a cuckold company, after you have had his wife, is as tiresome as the company of a country squire to a witty fellow of the town, when he has got all his money.

Quack: And as at first a man makes a friend of the husband to get the wife, so at last you are fain to fall out with the wife to be rid of the husband.

Horn: Ay, most cuckold-makers are true courtiers; when once a poor man has cracked his credit for 'em, they can't abide to come near him.

Quack: But at first, to draw him in, are so sweet, so kind, so dear! just as you are to Pinchwife. But what becomes of that intrigue with his wife?

Horn: A pox! he's as surly as an alderman that has been bit; and since he's so coy, his wife's kindness is in vain, for she's a silly innocent.

Quack: Did she not send you a letter by him?

Horn: Yes; but that's a riddle I have not yet solved. Allow the poor creature to be willing, she is silly too, and he keeps her up so close——

Quack: Yes, so close, that he makes her but the more willing, and adds but revenge to her love; which two, when met, seldom fail of satisfying each other one way or other.

Horn: What! here's the man we are talking of, I think.

(*Enter* **Mr. Pinchwife**, *leading in his Wife masked, muffled, and in her Sister's gown*)
Pshaw!

Quack: Bringing his wife to you is the next thing to bringing a love letter from her.

Horn: What means this?

Pinch: The last time, you know, Sir, I brought you a love letter; now, you see, a mistress; I think you'll say I am a civil man to you.

Horn: Ay, the devil take me, will I say thou art the civilest man I ever met with; and I have known some. I fancy I understand thee now better than I did the letter. But, hark thee, in thy ear——

Pinch: What?

Horn: Nothing but the usual question, man: is she sound, on thy word?

Pinch: What, you take her for a wench, and me for a pimp?

Horn: Pshaw! wench and pimp, paw words; I know thou art an honest fellow, and hast a great acquaintance among the ladies, and perhaps hast made love for me, rather than let me make love to thy wife.

Pinch: Come, Sir, in short, I am for no fooling.

Horn: Nor I neither: therefore prithee, let's see her face presently. Make her show, man: art thou sure I don't know her?

Pinch: I am sure you do know her.

Horn: A pox! why dost thou bring her to me then?

Pinch: Because she's a relation of mine——

Horn: Is she, faith, man? then thou art still more civil and obliging, dear rogue.

Pinch: Who desired me to bring her to you.

Horn: Then she is obliging, dear rogue.

Pinch: You'll make her welcome for my sake, I hope.

Horn: I hope she is handsome enough to make herself welcome. Prithee let her unmask.

Pinch: Do you speak to her; she would never be ruled by me.

Horn: Madam——(**Mrs. Pinchwife** *whispers to* **Horner.**) She says she must speak with me in private. Withdraw, prithee.

Pinch: (*aside*) She's unwilling, it seems, I should know all her undecent conduct in this business.——Well then, I'll leave you together, and hope when I am gone, you'll agree; if not, you and I shan't agree, Sir.

Horn: What means the fool? if she and I agree 'tis no matter what you and I do. (*whispers to* **Mrs. Pinchwife**, *who makes signs with her hand for him to be gone*)

Pinch: In the meantime I'll fetch a parson, and find out Sparkish and disabuse him. You would have me fetch a parson, would you not? Well then—now I think I am rid of her, and shall have no more trouble with her—our sisters and daughters, like usurers' money, are safest when put out; but our wives, like their writings, never safe but in our closets under lock and key. (*Exit* **Mr. Pinchwife.**)

(*Enter Boy*)

Boy: Sir Jasper Fidget, Sir, is coming up. (*Exit.*)

Horn: Here's the trouble of a cuckold now we are talking of. A pox on him! has he not enough to do to hinder his wife's sport, but he must other women's too?—Step in here, Madam. (*Exit* **Mrs. Pinchwife.**)

(*Enter* **Sir Jasper**)

Sir Jasp: My best and dearest friend.

Horn: (*aside to* **Quack**) The old style, Doctor.—— Well, be short, for I am busy. What would your impertinent wife have now?

Sir Jasp: Well guessed, i'faith; for I do come from her.

Horn: To invite me to supper! Tell her, I can't come: go.

Sir Jasp: Nay, now you are out, faith; for my lady, and the whole knot of the virtuous gang, as they call themselves, are resolved upon a frolic of coming to you tonight in masquerade, and are all dressed already.

Horn: I shan't be at home.

Sir Jasp: (*aside*) Lord, how churlish he is to women!—— Nay, prithee don't disappoint 'em; they'll think 'tis my fault: prithee don't. I'll send in the banquet and the fiddles. But make no noise on't; for the poor virtuous rogues would not have it known, for the world, that they go a-masquerading; and they would come to no man's ball but yours.

Horn: Well, well—get you gone; and tell 'em, if they come, 'twill be at the peril of their honour and yours.

Sir Jasp: He! he! he!—we'll trust you for that: farewell. (*Exit* **Sir Jasper**.)

Horn:
Doctor, anon you too shall be my guest,
But now I'm going to a private feast. (*Exeunt.*)

SCENE III. The Scene changes to the Piazza of Covent Garden

(**Sparkish, Pinchwife**)

Spark: (*with the letter in his hand*) But who would have thought a woman could have been false to me? By the world, I could not have thought it.

Pinch: You were for giving and taking liberty: she has taken it only, Sir, now you find in that letter. You are a frank person, and so is she, you see there.

Spark: Nay, if this be her hand—for I never saw it.

Pinch: 'Tis no matter whether that be her hand or no; I am sure this hand, at her desire, led her to Mr. Horner, with whom I left her just now, to go fetch a parson to 'em at their desire too, to deprive you of her for ever; for it seems yours was but a mock marriage.

Spark: Indeed, she would needs have it that 'twas Harcourt himself, in a parson's habit, that married us; but I'm sure he told me 'twas his brother Ned.

Pinch: Oh, there 'tis out; and you were deceived, not she: for you are such a frank person. But I must be gone.—You'll find her at Mr. Horner's. Go, and believe your eyes. (*Exit* **Mr. Pinchwife**.)

Spark: Nay, I'll to her, and call her as many crocodiles, sirens, harpies, and other heathenish names as a poet would do a mistress who had refused to hear his suit, nay more, his verses on her.—But stay, is not that she following a torch at t'other end of the Piazza? and from Horner's certainly—'tis so. (*Enter* **Alithea** *following a torch, and* **Lucy** *behind*)

You are well met, Madam, though you don't think so. What, you have made a short visit to Mr. Horner. But I suppose you'll return to him presently; by that time the parson can be with him.

Alith: Mr. Horner and the parson, Sir!

Spark: Come, Madam, no more dissembling, no more jilting; for I am no more a frank person.

Alith: How's this?

Lucy: (*aside*) So, 'twill work, I see.

Spark: Could you find out no easy country fool to abuse? none but me, a gentleman of wit and pleasure about the town? But it was your pride to be too hard for a man of parts, unworthy false woman! false as a friend that lends a man money to lose; false as dice, who undo those that trust all they have to 'em.

Lucy: (*aside*) He has been a great bubble, by his similes, as they say.

Alith: You have been too merry, Sir, at your wedding-dinner, sure.

Spark: What, d'ye mock me too?

Alith: Or you have been deluded.

Spark: By you.

Alith: Let me understand you.

Spark: Have you the confidence—I should call it something else, since you know your guilt—to stand my just reproaches? You did not write an impudent letter to Mr. Horner? who I find now has clubbed with you in deluding me with his aversion for women, that I might not, forsooth, suspect him for my rival.

Lucy: (*aside*) D'ye think the gentleman can be jealous now, Madam?

Alith: I write a letter to Mr. Horner!

Spark: Nay, Madam, do not deny it. Your brother showed it me just now; and told me likewise, he left you at Horner's lodging to fetch a parson to marry you to him: and I wish you joy, Madam, joy, joy; and to him, too, much joy; and to myself more joy, for not marrying you.

Alith: (*aside*) So, I find my brother would break off the match; and I can consent to't, since I see this gentleman can be made jealous.—— O Lucy, by his rude usage and jealousy, he makes me almost afraid I am married to him. Art thou sure 'twas Harcourt himself, and no parson, that married us?

Spark: No, Madam, I thank you. I suppose that was a contrivance too of Mr. Horner's and yours, to make Harcourt play the parson; but I would as little as you have him one now, no, not for the world. For shall I tell you another truth? I never had any passion for you till now, for now I hate you. 'Tis true, I might have married your portion, as other men of parts of the town do sometimes: and so, your servant. And to show my unconcernedness, I'll come to your wedding, and resign you with as much joy as I would a stale wench to a new cully; nay, with as much joy as I would after the first night, if I had been married to you. There's for you; and so your servant, servant. (*Exit Sparkish.*)

Alith: How was I decieved in a man!

Lucy: You'll believe then a fool may be made jealous now? for that easiness in him that suffers him to be led by a wife, will likewise permit him to be persuaded against her by others.

Alith: But marry Mr. Horner! my brother does not intend it, sure: if I thought he did, I would take thy advice, and Mr. Harcourt for my husband. And now I wish that if there be any overwise woman of the town, who, like me, would marry a fool for fortune, liberty, or title, first, that her husband may love play, and be a cully to all the town but her, and suffer none but Fortune to be mistress of his purse; then, if for liberty, that he may send her into the country, under the conduct of some huswifely mother-in-law; and if for title, may the world give 'em none but that of cuckold.

Lucy: And for her greater curse, Madam, may he not deserve it.

Alith: Away, impertinent! Is not this my old Lady Lanterlu's?

Appropriate image? Why?

Lucy: Yes, Madam.—(*aside*) And here I hope we shall find Mr. Harcourt. (*Exeunt.*)

SCENE IV.   The Scene changes again to **Horner's** Lodging.

(**Horner, Lady Fidget, Mrs. Dainty Fidget, Mrs. Squeamish**)
(*A table, banquet, and bottles*)

Horn: (*aside*) A pox! they are come too soon—before I have sent back my new mistress. All I have now to do is to lock her in, that they may not see her.

Lady Fid: That we may be sure of our welcome, we have brought our entertainment with us, and are resolved to treat thee, dear toad. *No longer ugly or vile toad.*

Mrs. Dain: And that we may be merry to purpose, have left Sir Jasper and my old Lady Squeamish quarrelling at home at backgammon.

Mrs. Squeam: Therefore let us make use of our time, lest they should chance to interrupt us.

Lady Fid: Let us sit then.

Horn: First, that you may be private, let me lock this door and that, and I'll wait upon you presently.

Lady Fid: No. Sir, shut 'em only, and your lips for ever; for we must trust you as much as our women.

Horn: You know all vanity's killed in me; I have no occasion for talking.

Lady Fid: Now, ladies, supposing we had drank each of us our two bottles, let us speak the truth of our hearts.

Mrs. Dain. and Mrs. Squeam: Agreed.

Lady Fid: By this brimmer, for truth is nowhere else to be found—(*aside to* **Horner**) not in thy heart, false man!

Horn: (*aside to* **Lady Fidget**) You have found me a true man, I'm sure.

Lady Fid: (*aside to* **Horner**) Not every way.—— But let us sit and be merry. *Why include a song here?*
(**Lady Fidget** *sings.*)

1

Why should our damn'd tyrants oblige us to live
On the pittance of pleasure which they only give?
    We must not rejoice
    With wine and with noise:
In vain we must wake in a dull bed alone,
Whilst to our warm rival, the bottle, they're gone.
    Then lay aside charms,
    And take up these arms.°

2

'Tis wine only gives 'em their courage and wit;
Because we live sober, to men we submit.
    If for beauties you'd pass,
    Take a lick of the glass,
'Twill mend your complexions, and when they are gone,
  The best red we have is the red of the grape:
Then, sisters, lay't on,
    And damn a good shape.

°The glasses.

Mrs. Dain: Dear brimmer! Well, in token of our openness and plain-dealing, let us throw our masks over our heads.

Horn: So, 'twill come to the glasses anon.

Mrs. Squeam: Lovely brimmer! let me enjoy him first.

Lady Fid: No, I never part with a gallant till I've tried him. Dear brimmer! that makest our husbands short-sighted.

Mrs. Dain: And our bashful gallants bold.

Mrs. Squeam: And, for want of a gallant, the butler lovely in our eyes.—— Drink, eunuch.

Lady Fid: Drink, thou representative of a husband.—Damn a husband!

Mrs. Dain: And, as it were a husband, an old keeper.

Mrs. Squeam: And an old grandmother.

Horn: And an English bawd, and a French chirurgeon.

Lady Fid: Ay, we have all reasons to curse 'em.

Horn: For my sake, ladies?

Lady Fid: No, for our own; for the first spoils all young gallants' industry.

Mrs. Dain: And the other's art makes 'em bold only with common women.

Mrs. Squeam: And rather run the hazard of the vile distemper amongst them, than of a denial amongst us.

Mrs. Dain: The filthy toads choose mistresses now as they do stuffs, for having been fancied and worn by others.

Mrs. Squeam: For being common and cheap.

What quality? **Lady Fid:** Whilst women of quality, like the richest stuffs, lie untumbled, and unasked for.

Horn: Ay, neat, and cheap, and new, often they think best.

Mrs. Dain: No, Sir, the beasts will be known by a mistress longer than by a suit.

Mrs. Squeam: And 'tis not for cheapness neither.

Lady Fid: No; for the vain fops will take up druggets and embroider 'em. But I wonder at the depraved appetites of witty men; they use to be out of the common road, and hate imitation. Pray tell me, beast, when you were a man, why you rather chose to club with a multitude in a common house for an entertainment than to be the only guest at a good table.

Horn: Why, faith, ceremony and expectation are unsufferable to those that are sharp bent. People always eat with the best stomach at an ordinary, where every man is snatching for the best bit.

Lady Fid: Though he get a cut over the fingers.—But I have heard people eat most heartily of another man's meat, that is, what they do not pay for.

Horn: When they are sure of their welcome and freedom; for ceremony in love and eating is as ridiculous as in fighting: falling on briskly is all should be done on those occasions.

Lady Fid: Well then, let me tell you, Sir, there is nowhere more freedom than in our houses; and we take freedom from a young person as a sign of good breeding; and a person may be as free as he pleases with us, as frolic, as gamesome, as wild as he will.

Horn: Han't I heard you all declaim against wild men?

Duck or rabbit? **Lady Fid:** Yes; but for all that, we think wildness in a man as desirable a quality as in a duck or rabbit: a tame man! foh!

Horn: I know not, but your reputations frightened me as much as your faces invited me.

Lady Fid: Our reputation! Lord, why should you not think that we women make use of our reputation, as you men of yours, only to deceive the world with less suspicion? Our virtue is like the stateman's religion, the Quaker's word, the gamester's oath, and the great man's honour—but to cheat those that trust us.

Mrs. Squeam: And that demureness, coyness, and modesty that you see in our faces in the boxes at plays, is as much a sign of a kind woman, as a vizard-mask in the pit.

Mrs. Dain: For, I assure you, women are least masked when they have the velvet vizard on.

Lady Fid: You would have found us modest women in our denials only.

Mrs. Squeam: Our bashfulness is only the reflection of the men's.

Mrs. Dain: We blush when they are shamefaced.

Horn: I beg your pardon, ladies, I was deceived in you devilishly. But why that mighty pretence to honour?

Lady Fid: We have told you; but sometimes 'twas for the same reason you men pretend business often, to avoid ill company, to enjoy the better and more privately those you love.

Horn: But why would you ne'er give a friend a wink then?

Lady Fid: Faith, your reputation frightened us as much as ours did you, you were so notoriously lewd.

Horn: And you so seemingly honest.

Lady Fid: Was that all that deterred you?

Horn: And so expensive—you allow freedom, you say——

Lady Fid: Ay, ay.

Horn: That I was afraid of losing my little money, as well as my little time, both which my other pleasures required.

Lady Fid: Money! foh! you talk like a little fellow now: do such as we expect money?

Horn: I beg your pardon, Madam, I must confess, I have heard that great ladies, like great merchants, set but the higher prices upon what they have, because they are not in necessity of taking the first offer.

Mrs. Dain: Such as we make sale of our hearts?

Mrs. Squeam: We bribed for our love? foh!

Horn: With your pardon, ladies, I know, like great men in offices, you seem to exact flattery and attendance only from your followers; but you have receivers about you, and such fees to pay a man is afraid to pass your grants. Besides, we must let you win at cards, or we lose your hearts; and if you make an assignation, 'tis at a goldsmith's, jeweller's, or china-house, where for your honour you deposit to him, he must pawn his to the punctual cit, and so paying for what you take up, pays for what he takes up.

Mrs. Dain: Would you not have us assured of our gallants' love?

Mrs. Squeam: For love is better known by liberality than by jealousy.

Lady Fid: For one may be dissembled, the other not.—(*aside*) But my jealousy can be no longer dissembled, and they are telling ripe.—— Come, here's to our gallants in waiting, whom we must name, and I'll begin. This is my false rogue. (*claps him on the back*)

Mrs. Squeam: How!

Horn: So, all will out now.

Mrs. Squeam: (*aside to* **Horner**) Did you not tell me 'twas for my sake only you reported yourself no man?

Mrs. Dain: (*aside to* **Horner**) Oh, wretch! did you not swear to me, 'twas for my love and honour you passed for that thing you do?

Horn: So, so.

Lady Fid: Come, speak, ladies: this is my false villain.

Mrs. Squeam: And mine too.

Mrs. Dain: And mine.

Horn: Well then, you are all three my false rogues too, and there's an end on't.

Her image sums up the play: appearance vs. reality. **Lady Fid:** Well then, there's no remedy; sister sharers, let us not fall out, but have a care of our honour. Though we get no presents, no jewels of him, we are savers of our honour, the jewel of most value and use, which shines yet to the world unsuspected, though it be counterfeit.

Horn: Nay, and is e'en as good as if it were true, provided the world think so; for honour, like beauty now, only depends on the opinion of others.

Lady Fid: Well, Harry Common, I hope you can be true to three. Swear; but 'tis to no purpose to require your oath, for you are as often forsworn as you swear to new women.

Horn: Come, faith, Madam, let us e'en pardon one another; for all the difference I find betwixt we men and you women, we forswear ourselves at the beginning of an amour, you as long as it lasts.

(*Enter* **Sir Jasper Fidget,** *and* **Old Lady Squeamish**)

Sir Jasp: Oh, my Lady Fidget, was this your cunning, to come to Mr. Horner without me? But you have been nowhere else, I hope.

Lady Fid: No, Sir Jasper.

Lady Squeam: And you came straight hither, Biddy?

Mrs. Squeam: Yes, indeed, lady Grandmother.

Sir Jasp: 'Tis well, 'tis well; I knew when once they were thoroughly acquainted with poor Horner, they'd ne'er be from him: you may let her masquerade it with my wife and Horner, and I warrant her reputation safe.

(*Enter* **Boy**)

Boy: O Sir, here's the gentleman come, whom you bid me not suffer to come up without giving you notice, with a lady too, and other gentlemen.

Horn: Do you all go in there, whilst I send 'em away; and, boy, do you desire 'em to stay below till I come, which shall be immediately.

(*Exeunt* **Sir Jasper, Lady Squeamish, Lady Fidget, Mrs. Dainty, Mrs. Squeamish.**)

Boy: Yes, sir. (*Exit.*)

(*Exit* **Horner** *at t'other door, and returns with* **Mrs. Pinchwife.**)

Horn: You would not take my advice, to be gone home before your husband came back; he'll now discover all. Yet pray, my dearest, be persuaded to go home, and leave the rest to my management; I'll let you down the back way.

Mrs. Pinch: I don't know the way home, so I don't.

Horn: My man shall wait upon you.

Mrs. Pinch: No, don't you believe that I'll go at all; what, are you weary of me already?

Horn: No, my life, 'tis that I may love you long, 'tis to secure my love, and your reputation with your husband; he'll never receive you again else.

Mrs. Pinch: What care I? d'ye think to frighten me with that? I don't intend to go to him again; you shall be my husband now.

Horn: I cannot be your husband, dearest, since you are married to him.

Mrs. Pinch: Oh, would you make me believe that? Don't I see every day, at London here, women leave their first husbands, and go and live with other men as their wives? Pish, pshaw! you'd make me angry, but that I love you so mainly.

Margery's naïveté threatens Horner.

Horn: So, they are coming up—In again, in, I hear 'em.—(*Exit* **Mrs. Pinchwife.**) Well, a silly mistress is like a weak place, soon got, soon lost, a man has scarce time for plunder; she betrays her husband first to her gallant, and then her gallant to her husband.

(*Enter* **Pinchwife, Alithea, Harcourt, Sparkish,** *and a* **Parson**)

Pinch: Come, Madam, 'tis not the sudden change of your dress, the confidence of your asseverations, and your false witness there, shall persuade me I did not bring you hither just now; here's my witness, who cannot deny it, since you must be confronted.——Mr. Horner, did not I bring this lady to you just now?

Horn: (*aside*) Now must I wrong one woman for another's sake—but that's no new thing with me, for in these cases I am still on the criminal's side against the innocent.

Alith: Pray speak, Sir.

Horn: (*aside*) It must be so. I must be impudent, and try my luck; impudence uses to be too hard for truth.

Pinch: What, you are studying an evasion or excuse for her! Speak, Sir.

Horn: No, faith, I am something backward only to speak in women's affairs or disputes.

Pinch: She bids you speak.

Alith: Ah, pray, Sir, do, pray satisfy him.

Horn: Then truly, you did bring that lady to me just now.

Pinch: Oh ho!

Alith: How, Sir?

Har: How, Horner?

Alith: What mean you, Sir? I always took you for a man of honour.

Horn: (*aside*) Ay, so much a man of honour, that I must save my mistress, I thank you, come what will on't.

Spark: So, if I had had her, she'd have made me believe the moon had been made of a Christmas pie.

Lucy: (*aside*) Now could I speak, if I durst, and solve the riddle, who am the author of it.

Alith: Oh unfortunate woman! A combination against my honour! which most concerns me now, because you share in my disgrace, Sir, and it is your censure, which I must now suffer, that troubles me, not theirs.

Har: Madam, then have no trouble, you shall now see 'tis possible for me to love too, without being jealous; I will not only believe your innocence myself, but make all the world believe it.—(*apart to* **Horner**) Horner, I must now be concerned for this lady's honour.

Horn: And I must be concerned for a lady's honour too.

Har: This lady has her honour, and I will protect it.

Horn: My lady has not her honour, but has given it me to keep, and I will preserve it.

Repetition is humorous.

Har: I understand you not.

Horn: I would not have you.

Mrs. Pinch: (*peeping in behind*) What's the matter with 'em all?

Pinch: Come, come, Mr. Horner, no more disputing; here's the parson, I brought him not in vain.

Har: No, Sir, I'll employ him, if this lady please.

Pinch: How! what d'ye mean?

Spark: Ay, what does he mean?

Horn: Why, I have resigned your sister to him; he has my consent.

Pinch: But he has not mine, Sir; a woman's injured honour, no more than a man's, can be repaired or satisfied by any but him that first wronged it; and you shall marry her presently, or——(*lays his hand on his sword*)

(*Enter to them* **Mrs. Pinchwife**)

Mrs. Pinch: (*aside*) O Lord, they'll kill poor Mr. Horner! besides, he shan't marry her whilst I stand by, and look on; I'll not lose my second husband so.

Pinch: What do I see?

Alith: My sister in my clothes!

Spark: Ha!

Mrs. Pinch: (*to* **Mr. Pinchwife**) Nay, pray now don't quarrel about finding work for the parson: he shall marry me to Mr. Horner; for now, I believe, you have enough of me.

Horner: (*aside*) Damned, damned loving changeling!

Mrs. Pinch: Pray, Sister, pardon me for telling so many lies of you.

Horn: I suppose the riddle is plain now.

Lucy: No, that must be my work.—— Good Sir, hear me. (*kneels to* **Mr. Pinchwife**, *who stands doggedly with his hat over his eyes*)

Pinch: I will never hear woman again, but make 'em all silent thus——(*offers to draw upon his Wife*)

Horn: No, that must not be.

Pinch: You then shall go first, 'tis all one to me. (*offers to draw on* **Horner**, *stopped by* **Harcourt**)

Har: Hold!

(*Enter* **Sir Jasper Fidget, Lady Fidget, Lady Squeamish, Mrs. Dainty Fidget, Mrs. Squeamish**)

Sir Jasp: What's the matter? what's the matter? pray, what's the matter, Sir? I beseech you communicate, Sir.

What does he mean by communicate?

Pinch: Why, my wife has communicated, Sir, as your wife may have done too, Sir, if she knows him, Sir.

Sir Jasp: Pshaw, with him! ha! ha! he!

Pinch: D'ye mock me, Sir? A cuckold is a kind of a wild beast; have a care, Sir.

Sir Jasp: No, sure, you mock me, Sir. He cuckold you! it can't be, ha! ha! he! why, I'll tell you, Sir——(*offers to whisper*)

Pinch: I tell you again, he has whored my wife, and yours too, if he knows her, and all the women he comes near; 'tis not his dissembling, his hypocrisy, can wheedle me.

Sir Jasp: How! does he dissemble? is he a hypocrite? Nay, then—how—wife—sister, is he a hypocrite?

Lady Squeam: A hypocrite! a dissembler! Speak, young harlotry, speak, how?

Sir Jasp: Nay, then—Oh my head too!—Oh thou libidinous lady!

Lady Squeam: Oh thou harloting harlotry! hast thou done't then?

Sir Jasp: Speak, good Horner, art thou a dissembler, a rogue? hast thou——

Horn: Soh!

Lucy: (*apart to* **Horner**) I'll fetch you off, and her too, if she will but hold her tongue.

Horn: (*apart to* **Lucy**) Can'st thou? I'll give thee——

Lucy: (*to* **Mr. Pinchwife**) Pray have but patience to hear me, Sir, who am the unfortunate cause of all this confusion. Your wife is innocent, I only culpable; for I put her upon telling you all these lies concerning my mistress, in order to the breaking off the match between Mr. Sparkish and her, to make way for Mr. Harcourt.

Spark: Did you so, eternal rotten tooth? Then, it seems my mistress was not false to me, I was only deceived by you. Brother, that should have been, now man of conduct, who is a frank person now, to bring your wife to her lover, ha?

Colorful language

Lucy: I assure you, Sir, she came not to Mr. Horner out of love, for she loves him no more——

Mrs. Pinch: Hold, I told lies for you, but you shall tell none for me, for I do love Mr. Horner with all my soul, and nobody shall say me nay; pray, don't you go to make poor Mr. Horner believe to the contrary; 'tis spitefully done of you, I'm sure.

Horn: (*aside to* **Mrs. Pinchwife**) Peace, dear idiot.

Tone of this line?

Mrs. Pinch: Nay, I will not peace.

Pinch: Not till I make you.

(*Enter* **Dorilant**, **Quack**)

Dor: Horner, your servant; I am the doctor's guest, he must excuse our intrusion.

Quack: But what's the matter, gentlemen? for Heaven's sake, what's the matter?

Horn: Oh, 'tis well you are come. 'Tis a censorious world we live in; you may have brought me a reprieve, or else I had died for a crime I never committed, and these innocent ladies had suffered with me; therefore, pray satisfy these worthy, honorable, jealous gentlemen—that——(*whispers*)

Quack: Oh, I understand you; is that all?—— Sir Jasper, by Heavens, and upon the word of a physician, Sir——(*whispers to* **Sir Jasper**)

Sir Jasp: Nay, I do believe you truly.—— Pardon me, my virtuous lady and dear of honour.

Lady Squeam: What, then all's right again?

Sir Jasp: Ay, ay, and now let us satisfy him too. (*They whisper with* **Mr. Pinchwife**.)

Pinch: An eunuch! Pray, no fooling with me.

Quack: I'll bring half the chirurgeons in town to swear it.

Pinch: They!—they'll swear a man that bled to death through his wounds died of apoplexy.

Quack: Pray, hear me, Sir—why, all the town has heard the report of him.

Pinch: But does all the town believe it?

Quack: Pray, inquire a little, and first of all these.

Pinch: I'm sure when I left the town, he was the lewdest fellow in't.

Quack: I tell you, Sir, he has been in France since; pray, ask but these ladies and gentlemen, your friend Mr. Dorilant. Gentlemen and ladies, han't you all heard the late sad report of poor Mr. Horner?

All the ladies: Ay, ay, ay.

Dor: Why, thou jealous fool, dost thou doubt it? he's an arrant French capon.

Mrs. Pinch: 'Tis false, Sir, you shall not disparage poor Mr. Horner, for to my certain knowledge——

Lucy: Oh, hold!

Mrs. Squeam: (*aside to* **Lucy**) Stop her mouth!

Lady Fid: (*to* **Pinchwife**) Upon my honour, Sir, 'tis as true——

Mrs. Dain: D'ye think we would have been seen in his company?

Mrs. Squeam: Trust our unspotted reputations with him?

Lady Fid: (*aside to* **Horner**) This you get, and we too, by trusting your secret to a fool.

Horn: Peace, Madam.—(*aside to* **Quack**) Well, Doctor, is not this a good design, that carries a man on unsuspected, and brings him off safe?

Pinch: (*aside*) Well, if this were true—but my wife——(**Dorilant** *whispers with* **Mrs. Pinchwife.**)

Pinchwife's imagination is correct, but he'd rather believe a lie.

Alith: Come, Brother, your wife is yet innocent, you see; but have a care of too strong an imagination, lest, like an overconcerned timorous gamester, by fancying an unlucky cast, it should come. Women and fortune are truest still to those that trust 'em.

Lucy: And any wild thing grows but the more fierce and hungry for being kept up, and more dangerous to the keeper.

Alith: There's doctrine for all husbands, Mr. Harcourt.

Har: I edify, Madam, so much, that I am impatient till I am one.

Dor: And I edify so much by example, I will never be one.

Spark: And because I will not disparage my parts, I'll ne'er be one.

Horn: And I, alas! can't be one.

Pinch: But I must be one—against my will to a country wife, with a country murrain to me!

Mrs. Pinch: (*aside*) And I must be a country wife still too, I find; for I can't, like a city one, be rid of my musty husband, and do what I list.

Horn: Now, Sir, I must pronounce your wife innocent, though I blush whilst I do it; and I am the only man by her now exposed to shame, which I will straight drown in wine, as you shall your suspicion; and the ladies' troubles we'll divert with a ballad.—— Doctor, where are your maskers?

Lucy: Indeed, she's innocent, Sir, I am her witness; and her end of coming out was but to see her sister's wedding; and what she has said to your face of her love to Mr. Horner was but the usual innocent revenge on a husband's jealousy—was it not, Madam, speak?

Mrs. Pinch: (*aside to* **Lucy** *and* **Horner**) Since you'll have me tell more lies—— Yes, indeed, bud.

Pinch:

How is reality concealed by language?

For my own sake fain I would all believe;
Cuckolds, like lovers, should themselves deceive.
But—— (*sighs*) his honour is least safe (too late I find)
Who trusts it with a foolish wife or friend.
(*A Dance of Cuckolds*)

Horn:

Vain fops but court and dress, and keep a pother,
To pass for women's men with one another;
But he who aims by woman to be priz'd,
First by the men, you see, must be despis'd.

Is this the "moral"
of the play?
Why in verse?

EPILOGUE

(*Spoken by* **My Lady Fidget**)

Now you the vigorous, who daily here
O'er vizard-mask in public domineer,
And what you'd do to her, if in place where;
Nay, have the confidence to cry, "Come out!"
Yet when she says, "Lead on!" you are not stout;
But to your well-dress'd brother straight turn round,
And cry, "Pox on her, Ned, she can't be sound!"
Then slink away, a fresh one to engage,
With so much seeming heat and loving rage,
You'd frighten listening actress on the stage;
Till she at last has seen you huffing come,
And talk of keeping in the tiring-room,
Yet cannot be provok'd to lead her home.
Next, you Falstaffs of fifty, who beset
Your buckram maidenheads, which your friends get;
And whilst to them you of achievements boast,
They share the booty, and laugh at your cost.
In fine, you essenc'd boys, both old and young,
Who would be thought so eager, brisk, and strong,
Yet do the ladies, not their husbands wrong;
Whose purses for your manhood make excuse,
And keep your Flanders mares for show, not use;
Encourag'd by our woman's man to-day,
A Horner's part may vainly think to play;
And may intrigues so bashfully disown,
That they may doubted be by few or none;
May kiss the cards at picquet, ombre, loo,
And so be thought to kiss the lady too;
But, gallants, have a care, faith, what you do.
The world, which to no man his due will give,
You by experience know you can deceive,
And men may still believe you vigorous,
But then we women—there's no cozening us.

OPEN TWENTY-FOUR HOURS

Roger N. Cornish

CHARACTERS
(In order of appearance)

A White Woman   George
A Black Woman   Custodian
Harold   Policeman
Number One

SCENE: A commercial laundromat.

DESCRIPTION OF CHARACTERS

White Woman: Age thirty to fifty, physical type open. She is on welfare and should reflect this somewhat in her appearance without being dressed in rags.

Black Woman: Again there is a broad scope for age and appearance. She contrasts with the **White Woman** by way of her more positive attitude toward life.

Harold: About thirty, pleasant looking, casually but well dressed. He is not terribly bright but his open personality and unforced friendliness should win the audience quickly.

Number One: Early twenties, sharply dressed in either J. Press or African Heritage style. His physical type is open because his body is an afterthought. It is his brain that dominates—we can sense it tracking at a constant sprint. Whatever he may say, he never ate soul food at home.

George: Of the three principals, he is closest to a healthy, normal human being. He has the anger potential of most people and can therefore become a violent black man in the face of the black man's frustration. But unlike **Number One**, he cannot constantly chew on the same grievance. And unlike **Harold**, he has no feelings of guilt—probably because he has nothing to feel guilty about—up to this point.

Custodian: Black or white, elderly but not decrepit. Role, not race, governs his attitudes.

Policeman: Black or white. Like the **Custodian**, he has professional attitudes.

SCENE: *A garden variety commercial laundromat, none too well tended. Assets include top loading washers, large driers, coke machine, change maker, soap and cigarette vending machines, and a bulletin board displaying notices, ads and a couple of items of mislaid clothing, including a sock—all pinned up with thumb tacks. It is night: The electric clock high on the wall reads two-thirty. The clock is chained to the wall and further protected by a metal grill. Furniture is limited to a couple of plain benches, long, bare tables for folding clothes and a couple of trash containers. There are one or two extremely battered laundry* *carts. There is nothing else portable, and nothing at all worth stealing. The walls are decorated with faded posters instructing, directing and warning the customers. They are illustrated with simple pastel drawings. One prohibits dyeing clothes in the machines; another instructs customers to be present when their machines go off; at least two warn the unwary that the management is not to be held responsible for stolen property. These latter are illustrated by masked thieves tiptoeing off clutching items of lingerie. By the coin-changer is a notice that the establishment is protected by a fearless and formidable agency of private detectives who will track malefactors to the ends of the earth.*

At rise: Two persons are on stage: a **Black Woman** *and a* **White Woman***. The former folds her laundry and the latter watches hers go round in the drier.*

White Woman: *(Picking up a small, open box of soap, the kind dispensed by the vending machines.)* How come I always got part of a box left over?

Black Woman: They're pretty smart . . . The machine takes a cup of detergent—the box gives you three quarters of a cup for a dime—so you have to buy another box and you got soap left over.

White Woman: *(Proffering the box)* You want it?

Black Woman: No, thanks . . .

White Woman: What am I supposed to do? Throw it away?

Black Woman: That's the idea. My husband says that's why they make the boxes that size—so you'll have to throw some away—"patriotic consumption."

White Woman: What's that?

Black Woman: That's when you help the national economy by buying more stuff than you can use and then throw part of it away so you have to buy more the next time. That's the primary goal of the packaging industry.

White Woman: Well, I can't afford to be patriotic.

Black Woman: Why don't you buy the large economy size in the store and bring what you need in a paper bag, like me? *(The* **Black Woman** *should be about finished with her folding and the* **White Woman** *taking her clothes from the drier.)*

White Woman: I can see you're not on welfare—the large economy size costs ninety-three cents.

Black Woman: But in the long run——

White Woman: —it costs more to be poor. You should try raising five on a welfare check.

Black Woman: Try raising 'em on what my husband brings home—I could get more from welfare. After all, the city pays by the kid, but his boss doesn't.

White Woman: Then let your old man take off, you'll get a raise.

Black Woman: No, I don't think so—I'd miss my winter sports too much.

White Woman: Why? My old man drops in often enough to keep me from going through the ceiling.

Black Woman: Don't you get checked by your case-worker?

White Woman: I get checked, all right. He knocks on my door at one o'clock in the morning, but he isn't looking for the man on the premises, the creep!
*(***Harold***, a white man, enters, carrying a bag of laundry. He is dressed informally, but well. He sets a portable radio on a washer while he busies himself with his laundry. The* **Women** *ignore him until he speaks.)*

Black Woman: Maybe he only wants to keep you from going through the ceiling.

White Woman: Yeah, he wants to get me pinned to the floor. But I'm not that hard up yet. *(Sees the* **Other** *is ready to go.)* Well, I'll be seeing you——

Black Woman: Oh, you live down near me, I might as well wait.

White Woman: You don't have to——

Black Woman: I better . . . At this time of night, this neighborhood——

Harold: (*At the vending machine*) I beg your pardon, ladies . . . Can you tell me which kind of soap to use?

White Woman: Do you want a white tornado or a washer ten feet tall?

Harold: What? Oh, ha ha ha, it doesn't make much difference, eh?

White Woman: Not much——

Black Woman: Now me, I never use a white tornado——

Harold: Then neither will I. When in Rome, you know . . . but you'll have to get me a ladder to get my clothes out of the washer—ha, ha, ha. (*He receives a small box of soap for his coin.*)

White Woman: You don't do clothes too often, eh?

Harold: No, but I'm game for anything once.

White Woman: I guess you got a maid to do all that stuff for you.

Harold: No, but my wife says I treat her like a maid. . . . what makes you think I have a maid?

White Woman: You live in that fancy building over on the avenue, don't you?

Harold: Well, yes——

White Woman: (*To* **Black Woman**) You can always tell——

Harold: It's really not very fancy, and we only have a one-bedroom anyway—until we move into the new place . . . (*He is loading his clothes in a machine.*)

Black Woman: Hey, you better get those socks out of there.

Harold: Oh?

Black Woman: Unless you want to dye those white things charcoal grey——

White Woman: Especially those brassieres . . . Your wife'll have a hernia.

Harold: Oh boy, she'd really let me have it, all right—it's all her stuff—nightgowns and things . . . Thanks a lot. (*He sorts out the socks and one or two other colored items as they talk. He starts the machine with the white load and puts the colored things in another.*)

Black Woman: Hey, how come you brought your laundry way over here? You got a laundromat in your own neighborhood.

Harold: Really?

Black Woman: Sure, a block from your building, right on this street.

Harold: Oh, now I get it. I thought she said it was only a block away—I just went in the wrong direction.

White Woman: It couldn't have been wronger.

Harold: Do I put in the whole box?

Black Woman: And then some.

White Woman: Here's some more, you can use it on them socks.

Harold: Why, thank you.

White Woman: Don't mention it. My part in the war on poverty.

Black Woman: Uh oh, listen . . .

Harold: What is it?

Black Woman: Listen to that machine.

Harold: What's it doing?

Black Woman: Everything to those clothes but clean 'em. (*At the machine*) Well, for heaven's sake . . . look what you did!

Harold: Don't tell me . . . what?

Black Woman: See this little tag?

Harold: (*Reading*) "Sorry, tired today."

Black Woman: This machine is busted. You hardly got as far as the wash cycle.

Harold: What do I do now?

White Woman: Dredge it all out and put it in another machine with another quarter.

Harold: Oh great . . .

Black Woman: Why'd your wife ever trust you out of the house, anyway?

Harold: (*Laughs*) I'm that bad, eh? She's in the hospital . . . My wife . . . We had a baby yesterday.

White Woman: Oooh, isn't that wonderful?

Black Woman: Congratulations.

Harold: Can I offer you a cigar? Ha, ha, ha.

Black Woman: Your first, eh?

Harold: Uh-huh. Anyway, she asked me to bring her nightgowns and stuff, so here I am, washing them up.

White Woman: Get used to it, it'll be three nights a week with diapers from now on. But use the launderette in your own neighborhood—it's healthier.

Harold: Why, there's nothing wrong with this place—not when I have two such charming ladies to help me. But, of course, we'll be getting diaper service. That's more sensible, don't you think?

White Woman: Oh, sure—Well, I'm ready to go . . . (**Harold** *begins to remove the clothes from the broken machine—a messy, sudsy business.*)

Black Woman: Well, friend, here's where the rats desert the sinking ship. Good luck.

White Woman: We'd give you a hand, but it's awful late——

Harold: Thanks, no point in sharing the misery. (*Young black man,* **Number One***, enters, looks around, goes to cigarette machine.*)

White Woman: (*From the door*) Hey, was it a boy or girl?

Harold: (*Arms full of sudsy clothes*) A boy, the little—beggar.

Black Woman: (*As they leave*) You ain't seen nothing yet! (*Exits with a little laugh. Alone,* **Harold** *goes about his business. He looks to put the sudsy clothes in another washer. All tops are down, so he puts clothes atop one; blows a cloud of suds off his arms, opens washer, picks up clothes and dumps them in, reaches into pocket and comes out with wet change.*)

Harold: Dimes, for God's sake! (*He goes to the change machine and reads the instructions.*) "Two dimes and a nickel or one dime and three nickels." (*In despair, he bangs the change machine with his fist.* **Number One***, having found right change and his brand, buys a pack, and turns to go. Roused,* **Harold** *jumps at the chance of aid.*) Excuse me, friend, would you happen to have a quarter? I'm all screwed up here with a load of wet-wash.

Number One: I might. Let me take a look . . . (*He fishes out his change.*) Yeah, here you go—(*offers quarter*)

Harold: Thanks a lot, you saved my life! (*Starts to take coin*) Oh, excuse me, wet hands.

Number One: That's okay. Don't worry about it . . .

Harold: (*Wiping his hands under his arms*) There . . . (*Takes quarter*) Listen, you saved my life . . . (*Fishing out his own change*) I could just see myself wallowing home with a load of sudsy underwear. Dammit, I don't have the exact change—as you might imagine . . . Well, here's three dimes, okay?

Number One: Just give me two and we'll call it even. You might need the other for the drier.

Harold: Oh no, I couldn't—I mean, why should you pay for my stupidity?

Number One: It's only a nickel—

Harold: Well, you know—the principle of the thing and all that . . .

Number One: You don't want to be—in my debt, huh, man?

Harold: No, no, it's not that—but fair is fair, why should you have to pay?

Number One: That's mighty white of you——

Harold: I insist! Come on, take my dime or I won't take your quarter. Blame it on my foolish pride. Ha, ha, ha.

Number One: (*Taking dime*) Okay, man, have it your own way—I guess you've got me beat for pride——

Harold: My stubborn Yankee stock. Well, thanks for helping me out——

Number One: Any time, man. (*He extends his hand to* **Harold** *who starts to respond. But* **Number One** *draws his hand back before* **Harold** *can grasp it.*) Whoops, I forgot—wet hands. (*Exits with a skip and a little wave*)

Harold: Thanks again. (*He goes to the new washer, checks his laundry and inserts his quarter, starting the machine. He takes out a dime and gets another box of soap from the vending machine. He opens the box, dumps the soap in the washer and throws the box away. He starts to turn on his radio but, seeing that his hands are covered with soap particles, stops. He looks about and spies the sock on the bulletin board, takes it down, wipes his hands and starts to throw it away. Then, thinking better of it, he tacks it up again. He sits on a bench and turns on the radio. He tunes in loud classical music. After a moment, he notices that the machine with his socks in it has stopped. He removes the socks and puts them in a drier. Meanwhile, unnoticed by* **Harold,** **Number One** *and* **George** *enter. The latter carries a tiny bag of laundry over his shoulder.*)

Number One: Here's a first-class machine, George.

George: Hey, we really gonna fool aroun' with this washin' business?

Number One: You betray a lack of understanding, George. (**Harold** *has not heard them because of the loud music on his radio.* **Number One** *now raises his voice to carry over it.*) Remember, child, cleanliness is not only next to Godliness, but is the key to upward mobility in the society of rising expectations.

Harold: Oh! It's you. Hi——

Number One: Whaddya say, man?

Harold: I didn't expect to see you again—so soon——

Number One: Dump it in, George. (**George** *sets about doing the small load of clothes.*) Well, I'll tell you what brought me back—besides my underwear—that entire load is underwear—all skivvies, you know——

Harold: Well, we all have to wear underwear, don't we? Ha, ha, ha—if we didn't, our outerwear would be our underwear.

Number One: Ha, ha, ha. That's right, and if there's one thing I like, it's clean underwear, right, George?

George: You're Mister Clean with hair, Number One.

Number One: I don't care what I got on outside, black, brown or beige, but underneath I gotta be lily-white . . . How about that, George?

George: Yeah, that's good, ha, ha, ha.

Harold: Ha, ha, ha——

Number One: You don't have to laugh, man. George is one of those idiots who laughs at everything about color—you know, he's hipped on the subject. Say, you're not hipped on it too, are you?

Harold: Oh, no—but I wouldn't say I was unaware——

Number One: Goovy, man. Hey, I'll tell you why I came back . . . (*He proffers* **Harold** *a nickel.*)

Harold: The nickel?

Number One: I know, baby, it's only five cents. But then I got to thinking about Abraham Lincoln walking twenty miles in a blizzard to return a penny—what was that anyway, a library fine? I forget—and I said to myself, "That's what's wrong with my people, not enough of that Yankee pride." Isn't that right?

Harold: No, I don't think so. I'd say a Negro has about as much pride as anybody else——

Number One: Negroes! Who's talking about Negroes? I'm talking about Unitarians. I'm a Unitarian and George there is one of my co-religionists——

Harold: Oh, I'm sorry, I misunderstood——

Number One: Say, man, you didn't think we were some of those Black Muslims or something, did you? Not us. Say something in Unitarian, George.

George: I can't get any soap out of this machine.

Number One: You did put in a dime——

George: Come on, Number One——

Number One: Okay. What's the standard procedure when The Man tries to screw us?

George: Lean on him.

Number One: Right. (**George** *deals the soap vendor a terrific blow with the side of his fist and a box of soap falls out. He holds it up for* **Number One** *to see.*) The first lesson. You're learning, baby.

Harold: The first lesson——

Number One: I'm instructing George in the Unitarian creed. George, recite the first lesson of the creed.

George: Oh, now——

Number One: We mustn't be ashamed to bear witness for the faith, brother!

George: The first lesson: And the Leader spake, saying, "If ye go unto The Man, go unto him with thy fist."

Harold: That's Unitarianism?

Number One: Eastern rite, man. That's from the apocryphal portions of The Sermon on the Mount.

Harold: That's a helluva gospel for the meek.

Number One: Well, man, among us Unitarians, there's a doctrinal schism going on—the orthodox church versus the reform movement. There's Pope Innocent Abernathy the Second and Cardinal Wilkins on the one side, and on the other there's us reformers, the meek who are tired of inheriting the earth—we have proclaimed the New Gospel.

Harold: Actually, I think Roy Wilkins is a pretty good man—one of the few statesmen in America today.

Number One: And we all love him . . . Why, he's the Bernard Baruch of us Unitarians, but he hasn't got the new revelation——

Harold: Like Rap Brown, I suppose——

Number One: Well, baby, Rap's all right—for a middle-of-the-roader——

Harold: Middle-of-the-road!

Number One: But hear the new Gospel! Blessed are they that lean on The Man, for they shall see Westchester County——

Harold: You keep saying "lean on the man."

Number One: Look, that machine belongs to a white man, right?

Harold: Wrong! You don't know that. Anyone might own this business——

Number One: No 'fense, Charlie . . . Let's just say it belongs to the Establishment then—I mean, if you own anything, you're in the Establishment by definition. Well now, if the disestablished—that's us Unitarians—want anything from the Established, even after we've sweat for it and paid for it, we have to lean on 'em, bounce 'em around a little. That's the first law of progress in these here United States.

Harold: Come now, you're too intelligent to believe that.

Number One: Do I believe it, George?

George: You wrote the book, Number One.

Harold: But that's crazy——

Number One: Yeah . . .

Harold: After all, there are only a handful of—Unitarians compared to everyone else. Even putting ethics aside—it's a matter of practicality. You can't win with blood, only with brains. You have to get people on your side—along with the ones that are already there. After all, most of us want the same thing, don't we? Excuse me, I think my socks are dry.

Number One: How are your palms? (**Harold** *is busy with his laundry.*) How are my scanties doing, brother?

George: Forget the laundry. What are we waiting for?

Number One: The light of realization——

George: Huh?

Number One: Without which there is no beneficence in harsh medicine.

George: Don't put me down, Number One.

Number One: Never, baby. I'm going to pull you way up high.

George: Then talk so I can understand you.

Number One: Georgie, your Leader isn't to be understood. If things were that simple, what would be the point? (*To* **Harold**) Hey, man, do something with that box, all right? You're playing the racket so loud, I'm about to lose my natural rhythm.

Harold: I'm sorry. You don't care for classical music?

Number One: Care for it? Why lawdy, Rastus yere an' me, we jus' *loves* symphony music, don' we, Rastus? Except it hasn't got any balls. Can it.

Harold: All right. There's no need for unpleasantness. (*Turns off radio*)

Number One: You're absolutely correct. We certainly don't want any undue unpleasantness disturbing the status which—or do we, George?

George: The second lesson: And the Leader saith, "The Man heareth the slave in the soft voice; therefore speak unto him with harshness and discord."

Number One: You get another gold star. (*To* **Harold**) Pay no attention to him, he's under the influence of one of those cockamamy, radical philosophies—yesterday, he burned his library card.

Harold: Yes, well I'd better get my clothes out of the washer——

Number One: Aren't you going to play any music at all?

Harold: I thought you wanted it off——

Number One: That's your second mistake, thinking—not off, man, different.

Harold: (*Turns radio on*) Oh, sure . . . Say, I think Jazzbo's on now——

Number One: No, man, I don't want jazz either. Nor do I want some disc jockey who tries to make up like a Unitarian when he can't even get his hair to kink.

Harold: I just assumed you meant jazz——

Number One: You dig, it, right, man? Miles, Max, Milt—you dig 'em, right?

Harold: As a matter of fact, I have everything Miles Davis ever cut——

Number One: Not quite, but let it pass . . . And learn something, aficionado of Africa's great contribution to our national heritage, jazz is just one more way of putting us Unitarians down, man—classical thirty-threes played at seventy-eight.

Harold: Well, what kind of music do you want?

Number One: Haven't you heard the Dominoes?

Harold: Well——

Number One: What about the Chevelles, The Impalas, The Corvettes?

Harold: They're okay if you like them, I'm sure——

Number One: How about the Kaiser Frazers?

Harold: Well, you're entitled to your own taste, and I'm sure you wouldn't deny me mine.

Number One: (*Dialing in a group*) Listen! Are you gonna stand there and tell me that's not art? What are you, some kind of bigot?

Harold: Now, hold on a minute——

Number One: *Listen!* That's the black-ass, black mass culture; don't you like it? *Ain't it art?*

Harold: As a matter of fact, I can't truthfully say I like it at all. But it's a free country and there's as much room for that kind of music as any other kind, I suppose.

Number One: Nice try, Charlie. What's the matter, haven't you got the nerve to say it turns your stomach to think that noise is the national culture? That's the urban sound, baby—the black monkey, the brown banana, the beige mashed potato——

Harold: All right, I don't like it. If that makes me a bigot, I'm sorry. (*He heads back to the washer.*)

Number One: Hey, man, I was just kidding. I don't dig that stuff either. George does though, don't you, George? (*Turns radio off*)

George: It's okay, you didn't have to turn it off.

Number One: George is part of the mass culture, aren't you, George? A regular soul brother, aren't you, George?

George: Cut it out, Number One——

Number One: In fact, George is the archetype of the primitive, uninhibited swinger, aren't you, George?

George: I said cut it out, Number One——

Number One: Say, (*To* **Harold**) can you do the Monkey?

Harold: I'm afraid not——

Number One: But you've got a girl, or a wife, haven't you?

Harold: Yes—I'm married.

Number One: Then you gotta be able to do the Monkey, man—it's very pre-coital——

Harold: So is the fox-trot if you've got the right posture.

Number One: Say, that's good, that's very good. Take that man's name, George—what is your name, by the way?

Harold: Uh—Harold.

Number One: George, this is Harold; Harold, this is George. George, teach Harold to do the Monkey.

Harold: I'd really just as soon——

Number One: Don't miss this chance, Harold. Dancing with George is a real experience. He's light as a feather, aren't you, George?

George: Aw, cut out that fairy stuff——

Number One: That's middle-class hypocrisy talking, George . . . Dance with Harold.

George: You wanna do the Monkey?

Harold: No thank you, George——

Number One: Aw, is your card all filled up?

Harold: Look, I just want to get my laundry into the drier.

Number One: Ah'll take keer o' that, boss. (*He makes a grotesque dive at the washer.*) You jes joy yaself at the play party——

Harold: Please, I'd rather do it myself!

Number One: You sound like a headache commercial, Harold. What's the matter with you anyway, are you prejudiced? You won't dance with George because he's a Unitarian and you won't let me finger your wife's panties because I bite my nails——

Harold: Look! I just don't want to Monkey with another man in a laundromat!

Number One: Oh, would you rather go up to his apartment?

Harold: No, and I won't reconsider for the Mashed Potato either.

Number One: Well, as long as you put it that way . . . Your feelings aren't hurt, are they, George?

George: Shoot, you know I don't go for that fairy stuff——

Number One: And you don't dance very well, either. (*To* **Harold**) All kidding aside, Harold, I knew you were a right-thinking liberal all along—you have a real sincere look about you.

Harold: (*As he puts his laundry in drier*) What makes you think you can just look at me and know anything about me?

Number One: You can't tell a book by its cover—that's a nice liberal sentiment, Harold.

Harold: All right, it's a cliché, but that doesn't mean it's untrue . . . Well, does it?

Number One: Absolutely not! Don't you agree, George?

George: Whatever you say, Number One.

Harold: Excuse me, but why does he call you Number One?

Number One: It's okay, he can speak without an interpreter. Tell him, George.

George: He's my leader.

Number One: He's my follower.

Harold: That's a pretty small—what do you call it—club, lodge, party?

Number One: A mass movement, a practical revolutionary organization.

Harold: Where do you hold your convention, in a phone booth?

Number One: Laugh while you can, baby. No real politician ever laughed at a man with a follower, not one who'll do what his leader tells him—and you will, won't you, George?

George: You say shit, I squat and strain——

Number One: Suppose I say spit on the floor . . . (**George** *obliges.*) Suppose I say wipe it up with your sleeve? (**George** *does so.*) Suppose I say—I'm not saying it—kill this ofay bastard?

George: He's dead.

Number One: Lean on that cancer dispenser. (**George** *punches in the glass front of the* *machine. To* **Harold**) You can't laugh off a movement with discipline like that, baby.

Harold: (*To* **George**) Did you cut yourself?

Number One: He doesn't care. If it hurts, he'll enjoy it.

George: Yeah, we're breaking things up.

Harold: This is all crazy—I can't understand your attitude. You're not deprived——

Number One: You mean how can I be such a goddam nut when The Man, he let me go to school and I'm invited to dinner every year on Brotherhood Week and pinktoe babies are scrambling to beat each other into the sack with me just to prove whose behind is the most liberal, not to mention the fact that there are now two black-ass heroes on television—all this and the skirmish on poverty too? How can I be such an ingrate?

Harold: Well, before there were two heroes, there were none, right? What the hell do you want if you don't want progress?

Number One: Well of course, and you have a right to be proud. You're a right-thinking liberal—some of your best friends eat watermelon.

Harold: I never mentioned pride and I certainly try not to be smug.

Number One: Smug—you? Never! You have sensitivity; why, you're probably even ashamed to live in that high-price, tangerine flake, elevator shafted, mocha-maidtended, antiseptic tower right next to the cockroach barracks—aren't you?

Harold: You're in love with the sound of your own voice, aren't you?

Number One: Maybe I just think you ought to hear a black voice now and then——

Harold: I hear plenty. And for your information, I live in an integrated building—we have plenty of Negro tenants.

Number One: Sure—a doctor, a lawyer and an African chief . . . And I bet you treat them just like people.

Harold: As a matter of fact, I don't treat them any way at all—just like any other neighbor—I don't curry them and I don't cut them . . . I think I do have a little sensitivity, enough to put myself in someone else's place——

Number One: I have it, by Jove! You're one of those fellows James Baldwin's always talking about—you're one of those white Negroes—hey, maybe you're really Norman Mailer. . . We can all sit around and make kissy-face together, the White Negro and the Black Ofay . . . It's a party——

George: Number One, what the hell are you talking about?

Number One: Don't strain yourself, George. Norman knows, don't you, Norman?

Harold: If you mean me, no I don't. It doesn't make any sense to me that you should attack the very people who want to help you. That wouldn't fit any man's definition of reasonable behavior——

Number One: Well now, Harold, it's this helping business——

Harold: I know all about that . . . Certainly, our help seems patronizing—but what can we do? If we can't understand your life, it's not our unwillingness, we just haven't lived it——

Number One: Harold, you're the greatest—really, I mean, you *would* let your daughter marry Arthur Ashe.

Harold: I don't have a daughter——

Number One: Oh, what a shame, what a loss to the movement——

Harold: I have a son—he was born yesterday.

Number One: Say, you hear that, George?

George: Yeah, where's my cigar?

Number One: Why, George, we should give cigars to Harold, the friend of the race.

Harold: I don't smoke anymore, doctor's orders.

Number One: Well, it's the spirit that counts. Say, I bet you wouldn't mind if he brought home a nice colored girl some time, would you?

Harold: Of course not, he'll be free to do as he pleases.

Number One: Right! And some day, when he's teaching you all about the birds and the bees, you'll poke him in the ribs and ask him about that black poontang, huh? . . . I mean all them sex fears go right out the window when it comes to our women; now, don't they?

Harold: As a matter of fact, I don't think I have any sex fears at all——

Number One: Not even a teensy one?

Harold: Well, I certainly don't subscribe to superstitions about Negro sexuality——

Number One: You mean you don't envy our superior male potency, our jumpin' jungle juices? Look at yourself, white-eyes—have you got the nerve to stand there and say you're our sexual equal?

Harold: (*Trying for right answer*) Well, I don't know . . . Envy? There's spontaneity of course, I mean—but I'm not jealous——

Number One: That's right, Harold, we're all rompin', stompin' studs . . . Look at George there—stand up straight, George—doesn't he look like a regular love machine?

George: That's me, two hundred and ten pounds of solid royal jelly.

Harold: Yes, I suppose I'd have to give you cards and . . .

Number One: And? . . . Go on, Harold, say it . . . You're among friends, say it . . . *Say it.*

Harold: Spades.

Number One: What delicacy. Well, I'm gonna let you in on a little secret. I'm gonna flush all those racial sex fears right out of your little psyche. Is your wife nice?

Harold: Is that part of the routine laundry interrogation?

Number One: Come on, baby, you certainly aren't ashamed of her, are you—?

Harold: Of course not——

Number One: Has she got a nice ass—a hot little body?

Harold: Well, I don't see that it's any of your damn . . . Well, she's certainly attractive; yes, as a matter of fact, she's very nice——

Number One: Lucky man! Well listen, baby, you slip your lady fair and Big George there between the same sheets and she couldn't be safer. You see, big stud is a faggot!

George: Aw, cut it out, Number One——

Number One: In fact, he's just about the whole bundle of sticks. Why, he isn't a a fairy, he's a regular g-nome, a pixie, a two hundred and ten pound elf!

Harold: He certainly doesn't look it——

Number One: What a diplomat—enlist that man for the foreign service!

George: You're puttin' me down, Number One——

Harold: Really, you look quite masculine to me——

Number One: There's only one way to settle this disagreement . . . George, soul sister, give Harold a nice big kiss.

George: Aw, come on——

Number One: Yeah, show Harold what he's been missing . . .

Harold: Wait a minute, this has gone far enough . . .

Number One: In the pursuit of truth, there's no such thing as far enough.

Harold: Look . . .

Number One: *Move*, Georgie Girl, pleasure that dude!

George: Shit man, this is stupid . . .

Number One: (*Serious*) This is the big quiz, Georgie, *Move*.

George: All right (*He starts lumbering toward* **Harold**, *who backs off.*)

Harold: Please, this is ridiculous . . .

Number One: He's being coy, Georgie—*romance* him, *talk* to him, he wants to be coaxed!

George: (*Woodenly, as he moves toward* **Harold**, *arms wide*) Kiss me, I love you.

Harold: (*Cornered, pointing at* **George**) For God's sake, will you turn him off!

Number One: (*Laughing*) Okay, okay. (*To* **George**) Simmer down, lover boy. Ha, ha, ha. Okay. (*To* **Harold**) The party's over . . . but I had you goin' for a minute, eh?

Harold: Oh, no—no. Why, George, anyone could just look at you and tell you're not—that way.

Number One: "You can't judge a book by its cover."

George: Come on, Number One, let's get it over with . . .

Number One: What do you say, Harold, shall we get it over with?

George: Oh, Jesus, be decent——

Harold: Get what over with——?

Number One: Maybe you're right, George. I don't see much hope for enlightenment—no apocalyptic vision——

Harold: Are you talking about me? (*The* **Night Custodian** *enters to make a routine check, clean out the garbage, etc. He is elderly and not very prosperous looking.*)

Custodian: Good evening, gentlemen . . . Found out how to beat the crowd, eh?

Number One: (*To* **Harold**) No, man, we're talking about something else completely, not you. (*To* **Custodian**) Yeah, Pops, we jus' 'bout got the whole place to ourselves.

Custodian: (*To* **Harold**) Our machines doing a good job on your clothes, sir?

Harold: Oh, fine . . . I did have a little trouble with a broken washer—I didn't notice the little sign saying it was out of order.

Custodian: Don't you worry about that . . . You just fill out one of our complaint forms . . . (*Pointing to pad and pencil stub on bulletin board*) You'll get your quarter right back.

Harold: Thank you, that's very kind.

Custodian: It's just good business, sir—we want you to come back. (*He is collecting trash which he will later consolidate and lug out the back way.*)

Number One: Hey, Pops, I got a complaint——

Custodian: Fill out a complaint form and you'll get your quarter back.

Number One: Old man, I can overlook your lack of warmth, but a quarter will hardly assuage my anguish——

Custodian: Now, young fella, I live around here and I know your kind—now, what's the trouble?

Number One: Well now, when we got here—George will back me up on this, won't you, George?

George: It's the absolute truth——

Number One: I put a large bundle of black underwear in that washer, and it came out white, *white*. Now what I want to know is what is the meaning of that? Are you in league with the N.A.A.C.P. or what?

Custodian: Now don't you try your stuff on me, Mister, I know you and I won't stand for it——

Number One: I forgot myself——

Custodian: You just finish your laundry and move on—the police don't like to see loitering in here . . . (*To* **Harold**) Have these men been bothering you, sir?

Number One: Oh man, is that crazy talk. What are you going to do with people like that, Harold? You can't even have a friendly discussion without some John Bircher starting an investigation.

Harold: It's all right. We've just been chatting, a friendly discussion, as he says.

Custodian: Yes, sir . . . (*Dragging barrel off to rear*) But don't let them get fresh, sir; it doesn't pay . . . (*He is off*)

Number One: Man, hardening of the arteries really makes you nutty!

Harold: Well, sometimes imagination does improve with age——

Number One: Long wear hasn't improved his brain any . . . Say, if we were troublemakers, George would have leaned on that old man, right, George, flapping his mouth like that?

George: Medicare time——

Harold: Well, let's face it, you did provoke him.

Number One: You're right, Harold, and I feel sorry about that. (*The* **Custodian** *enters rear to exit front.*) Hey, Pops, no hard feelin's—we was just spoofin'.

Custodian: No, no hard feelings . . . (*Passing cigarette machine, notices broken glass for first time*) Hey, what happened here?

Number One: My guess is that someone broke the front of the machine.

Custodian: I can see that! Now what?

Number One: Why don't you fill out a complaint form—maybe they'll send you a quarter?

Custodian: Don't you fool with me, Mister Smart Guy, I know you . . . hey, did you have anything to do with this?

Number One: Not I . . . George?

Geroge: I think it was like that when we come, Number One.

Number One: That's right, I remember now . . . (*To* **Harold**.) Harold . . . remember, when we came in you said to watch out for the broken glass?

Harold: Uh—yes, that's right—it was like that when I arrived.

Custodian: (*Piling shards together with his foot*) If you say so, sir. I'll just have to report this for an unknown cause . . . (*He starts out.*) Well, good night.

Harold: Good night.

George: See ya, Dick Tracy.

Number One: George! Good night, old timer, take care of yourself. (*The* **Custodian** *is gone.*) Harold, you really saved our lives, didn't he, George?

George: Yeah . . . Uh, look, your stuff is done, let's get out of here——

Harold: It wasn't anything. I mean, what's the point of making trouble?

Number One: You're right, it wasn't anything—so your conscience is clear. George, we don't have to change our plans.

George: Okay. Let's get it over with then, all right?

Number One: All right! Turn on the radio, George.

Harold: Why did you do that? . . . What are you . . . What is it you have to get over with?

Number One: Come on, Harold, you know . . .

Harold: No I don't know . . . For God's sake, will you stop talking in riddles? (*By*

this time, **George** *and* **Number One** *should be in such positions as to cut off* **Harold's**
escape.)

Number One: Harold, you don't *want* to understand . . . but down at the tip of
your little pink toe, you know what's going to happen.

Harold: No——

Number One: You knew before the old family retainer blew in to lug out the
garbage—but you muffed your big chance because you won't harbor evil thoughts
about Unitarians in your liberal heart. It wouldn't be cricket to suspect two nice
colored boys like us of being troublemakers . . . (*mimics* **Harold's** *speech to the*
Custodian.) "We've just been chatting, three stock brokers chewin' the fat while
our drawers go round together." Come on, Harold!

Harold: Well, it was just talk——

Number One: Sure it was and you really believed I came back here just to dabble
my dainties, didn't you? That's because you fine, open-minded, unprejudiced
friends of black folk figure we just move ass down to the laundromat every night
and do our delicate things—we just can't stand for our undies to get moldy in the
laundry basket, even though you can.

Harold: Are you trying to frighten me?

Number One: Nothing could be further from my mind.

Harold: George, you'll give me a straight answer . . . Why did you come here?

George: I got nothin' to tell you.

Harold: You have to tell me.

George: Like hell I do. Ask *him*!

Number One: Two of a kind! Well, there you are, Harold. You're just going to
have to say it for yourself.

Harold: Say what?

Number One: You already know that, Harold.

Harold: No, I don't know anything . . .

Number One: Just say it, Harold, for the good of your soul . . .

Harold: George, please . . .

George: Get off me, mother.

Number One: Say it, Harold . . .

Harold: Oh, my God . . .

Number One: Like you could have said it the minute we walked in . . .

Harold: No, that's not right . . .

Number One: Come on, Harold, say it.

Harold: I can't . . .

Number One: But you know it.

Harold: But why?

Number One: There!

Harold: Why?

George: Because he says so.

Number One: And see, Harold, you weren't the least bit surprised, you knew all
along—of course, you kept pushing all those nasty thoughts about poor old black
folk to the back of your mind . . . (*He bends at the knees and does a pattycake routine
on his hands and thighs, ending palms outward with a big minstrel show grin.*) Dat's me,
Mistuh Bones, dey ain't a mean thought in mah poh ol' black body . . . It would
never occur to you, Harold, to give me credit for being as mean a son of a bitch
as an Alabama sheriff—it pains me to say so, Harold, but you really are a bigot.

Harold: All because I thought well of you?

Number One: It's bigotry, isn't it, Georgie?

George: That's right, it is, man, pure white bigotry.

Number One: So you won't have to feel guilty, Georgie. Does it make sense now, Harold—that it's for your prejudice—I mean, who gave you the *right* to think well of us?

Harold: But what do you want from me?

Number One: The same cold neutrality you give everybody else, Harold, to look right through me without even noticing what I am—forget I'm black and lump me together with the rest of the garbage.

Harold: Not a word of that is true! If I saw right through you, you'd hate me even more—you want what you can never have, you want us to help you and see right through at the same time—it's childish!

Number One: Why, Harold, you are a gritty little fellow after all, isn't he, George?

Harold: And it isn't possible anyway. If you live here today—you have to choose a side——

Number One: You suffocating, patronizing Negro-lover, don't choose my side. Where do you get off treating me as if I were a black African and you were a one-man Marshall plan—be against me or ignore, but don't degrade me!

Harold: But your life is part of my life—nobody's innocent. I have to be aware of blackness.

Number One: Now you are in a quandary, Harold. But then, that's your problem, not mine.

Harold: Mine only?

Number One: Rule Number Six, George . . .

George: And the Leader speaketh, saying: Let the sins of the father be the sins of the child and let the generation of sin be his children's children.

Number One: The Man invented the problem, fed the problem and cuddled the problem—so it's his problem.

George: And all the problem's babies are your babies——

Harold: You don't really believe that, you're just spouting lessons——

Number One: He can act on it——

Harold: How can you possibly blame me for three hundred years of history? I'm nobody——

George: You're The Man.

Harold: If I have to stand for something bigger than myself, it's for the other white man, the one who wants wrongs righted, the one who's ashamed——

Number One: If you're not at fault, how come you're ashamed, baby?

Harold: I can't explain . . . I'm not ashamed of *myself* exactly——

Number One: Not even now that you know you're a bigot?

Harold: I'm *not*! *You're* the only bigot here——

Number One: Are you so thick you still don't get it? The day you can look at George there and think to yourself he might not *have* a big prick but might *be* one—*then* you won't be a bigot any more.

Harold: I can't understand you people——

Number One: Stop trying! That's the final kernal of white superiority that drives us wild—you keep thinking you can understand——

Harold: All right! I can't understand what it's like to be black—ever! Then how do you think you can understand me? Is your suffering so complex and my guilt so simple?

Number One: Let's just say our suffering is so concrete and your guilt so theoretical——

Harold: Theoretical! Do you think guilt doesn't hurt? Do you know how it feels
to enjoy your happiness at the expense of others?

Number One: We're willing to learn.

Harold: Can't you believe that some of us are troubled and confused to the depths
of our souls by this——?

Number One: There may be something to that, Harold . . . In fact, that's why
we're still talking, haven't opened you up so all your confusion could run out on
the floor and then shoveled it into one of the driers—cause we's good colored
folk, mind, and we don' wanna make no mess hyar on Massa Charlie's nice,
clean flo'.

George: Come on, let's get it done with——

Number One: You're missing the point, George . . . Harold has to understand
why we erase him . . . I don't know where George gets his puritan strain, Harold
—he can throttle a chicken, but he doesn't like to talk about it.

Harold: George, this isn't your idea at all, is it?

George: Ideas aren't my job——

Number One: You're riding a dead horse, Harold. George has made the leap to
faith, haven't you, Georgie?

George: Don't call me Georgie, Number One. . .

Number One: *George* understands the principles of revolution—I taught him: One
mind, one body, no hesitation . . . No, you better try me . . . who knows,
maybe you'll convince me you're more valuable alive than dead.

Harold: Now I see—that's it, this is just a game—you want to *give* me my life. That's
it, isn't it? You're making *me* the slave and you the masters—then you'll let me
beg my way free——

Number One: That displays a certain imagination, Harold, but you haven't got it
quite right. I'm going to let you talk until you realize you *deserve* to be put away,
and then I'll let Georgie lean on you. You'll shuffle off like a Greek hero, with a
new self-knowledge—the modern salvation, see yourself and die.

Harold: But you have nothing to gain from my death.

Number One: Your death will frighten the Establishment, and the Establishment
only changes when it's frightened.

Harold: You talk like a tract! Like a textbook——

Number One: That's what I am, baby, the New Primer of Social Progress.

Harold: But people can act out of sheer decency, if you only teach them what's
right.

Number One: The difference between good people and bad people: Neither gets
off his behind until he's pushed—when the pushing gets too rough, the good
does good, the bad does bad.

Harold: But you've just admitted you don't know what effect pressure will have
. . . Maybe if you—hurt me, the result will harm your cause, not help it.

Number One: Good thinking! And you're right, Harold, sufficient irritation will
bring on the apocalypse, the two ends of infinity. We push and we push and we
push until one day The Man either gives us everything we want or he rises up
and . . . The final solution to the Jewish question . . . Twenty million sweaty
blacks bound back to Bechuanaland, or forty million sides of black beef—canned
like Spam . . . Yes, I think that would be most efficient. After all, we run two
and a half million cars through these car crushers every year, and they come out

nice cubes of corrugated steel, ready to use as bridge and building foundation blocks . . . You put four of us into each car just before it's driven into the crusher, and in two years—you've solved the problem! Not only that, but when those five million blocks of meat and metal are shoring up hospitals and whore-houses, temples and tenements—you'll be right back to the *status quo*—America the Beautiful standing tall and straight on the bodies of black people.

Harold: Your mind is impossible—not even science fiction could match that . . .

Number One: What about history? The new marching song could be "We did it before and we can do it again . . ." (*Sung.*)

Harold: Horror like that could never happen here.

Number One: Then we're not taking any chances by erasing you—it can only result in another step toward brotherly love.

Harold: (*Tries to laugh.*) This is all wild theorizing. You wouldn't kill me without some immediate gain——

Number One: I'd get my nickel back——

Harold: If you were caught it would be for nothing.

Number One: You're wrong, Harold, it's for everything, here, now, tonight—you, especially you . . .

Harold: George, you're sane—why should anyone have to kill me? Why me?

George: I'm not the one to ask——

Harold: But I'm asking you anyway—this game has *some* rules evidently—and one is that you have to answer me . . . Why me?

George: So we can have—the movement—because he *has* to.

Number One: George knows, but he isn't very articulate. Are you, George?

George: Am I what?

Number One: Articulate.

George: No——

Number One: (*Taking off* **George**) An ah doesn't talk much nuther, Marse Boss——

George: Come on, cut it out——

Number One: Harold, we need you for the baby to grow. Right now, my move-ment is two bricks, Georgie and me, with no cement—you're the cement.

Harold: I think you must be a poet—I can't make sense of anything you say . . .

Number One: My deah, that's the nicest compliment I've had since my draft board called me a misfit . . . Try to understand, Harold . . . a mass movement takes blood. Once we shed it, we can never turn back . . . See, you're the cement, you'll bind us together . . . Why, you'll be famous, like Charles the First, or Louis the Fifteenth—you'll be Harold—the Clean, ha, ha, ha——

Harold: But I'm not famous, I'm nobody, I won't be noticed——

Number One: We'll notice you, Harold.

Harold: But why me? Anyone would do—is it just dumb chance?

Number One: Not a bit—in fact, you more or less volunteered, baby. Here were George and I just cruising down the street, see, talking about our movement, and I say to him, "Kimosabe, for five cents, I'd knock off the next paleface we see." Well, then I come in here for a pack of weeds, and you give me a nickel—it's fate! I went out to the car and told Georgie there's a round-shouldered Ivy-league square volunteering for duty. I said, "We're in business," right, George?

George: "Now or never," you said.

Number One: So it's all settled, Harold—"Now or never." I can't renege now—Georgie would lose faith in me. I'd be a leader without a follower; Georgie would be a lost black sheep; and you'd be confused again.

Harold: George——

Number One: Here comes the big pitch, Georgie——

George: Don't call me *Georgie*——

Number One: Sorry, Soul Brother.

Harold: George, if this is all for your benefit, then you have to decide . . . Do you really want to kill a man?

George: I—just want to follow orders——

Harold: You can't get off that easy—if you do it, it's because *you* make the decision to do it—it's all on you.

Number One: Listen close, Georgie, now you're gonna learn everything I told you about The Man——

George: Why don't both of you shut up and leave me be?

Harold: George, it's not me who won't leave you be, is it? I don't need anything from you except to be alone myself, but *he* needs something from you——

Number One: And away we go! Charlie White-eyes strikes again with the devastating power of his superior intellect. He's putting you down, baby——

Harold: I'm not the one who puts you down, George—I don't treat you like a fool; I don't call you "Georgie"; I don't need your unquestioning obedience to make me feel like a big man——

Number One: And you'll never have it, man—those days are gone!

Harold: He's getting worried, George—hear him? I'm getting close——

Number One: Worried. One word, baby, one word from me and George lowers the boom.

Harold: Hear that, George? . . . You're in his pocket, that's what he's saying—he *owns* you.

Number One: This game has gone far enough——

George: Shut up a minute——

Harold: What is this great "Movement"? It's a two-man plantation, one master and one slave, and you know which one you are. He bought you with a lot of talk about the "Movement," but what did you buy?

Number One: See, Georgie, The Man has got a thousand tricks and this is one of the best—divide and conquer—you should listen to me, baby.

Harold: Yes, listen to him, after all he owns your mind as well as your body——

Number One: Only The Man ever owned people, baby——

Harold: And after you do what he wants you to do with me——

Number One: We fooled around long enough, George——

Harold: He'll own you *forever*!

Number One: (*Moving toward* **Harold**) The party's over, Harold——

George: (*Without actually stepping between*) Let him finish his say, Number One——

Number One: You big jerk, he's turning you to a first class Uncle Tom——

Harold: Black or white, what's the difference, George?

Number One: Come on, George, we can't waste any more time——

Harold: When someone *owns* you, you're a slave no matter what color he is——

Number One: Let's do it now!

George: Shut up!

Number One: Do it now!

Harold: Where's Number Three?

George: What?

Harold: He's Number One, you're Number Two, where's Number Three, the one who takes orders from you?

George: What do you mean——?

Number One: You dumb idiot, what are you listening to?

Harold: Or are you only good for taking orders—for memorizing lessons and winning gold stars like a school kid—where's Number Three?

George: Where is he, Number One?

Number One: You're nuts, Georgie——

Harold: You certainly are if you think there's ever going to be anyone but you and him, slave and master——

Number One: Stomp him now!

George: *Why*, just to make you feel big?

Number One: *I'm your leader! Do it!* (**George** *doesn't make a move.*) Do it! (*To* **Harold**) You ofay bastard . . . (*We can't be sure if* **Number One** *would attack* **Harold** *by himself, because during the pause after his words, a* **Policeman** *enters the laundromat. The three* **Principals** *immediately relax into casual postures, even* **Harold** *somehow joining in a conspiratorial mood.*)

Policeman: What's happening, fellas?

Number One: Well, we're doing laundry, sir—what else would be going on?

Policeman: Nobody in this neighborhood has that much laundry, boy.

Number One: My friend and I have only been here a few minutes——

Policeman: Don't give me that crap, friend. The old man told me to keep an eye on you half an hour ago. Now, what's the party all about? (**Number One** *starts to speak.*) Not you. What's the matter with you two? (**Harold** *and* **George**) You— (**George**) you're big enough to talk.

George: I—(*Referring to* **Number One**)—it's like he says, man.

Policeman: Sure . . . What about you—(**Harold**) You're the odd man here . . .

Harold: I beg your pardon——

Policeman: You don't live in this neighborhood, do you?

Harold: As a matter of fact——

Policeman: What's so irresistible about this laundromat?

Harold: Actually, I ended up here by mistake.

Policeman: I'll say . . . Well, the three of you finish your wetwash and move out. If you want to have a party, hire a hall. Okay?

Number One: Yes, sir, we'll be done in a minute.

Policeman: (*Calling out to his partner*) Okay. Let's go. Frank, there's nothing happening here. (*He is gone.*)

George: Let's get out of here while we got the chance.

Number One: What's the hurry, baby? They're gone——

Harold: (*Gathering up his things*) Well, I'd better be on my way——

Number One: Exit the conquering hero——

George: Hey, man, thanks for cooling it——

Number One: That was a real surprise, wasn't it, Georgie?

George: Cut it out. Hey, man, how come you didn't say anything?

Harold: I—uh——

Number One: In fact, I think Harold was as surprised as we were, weren't you, Harold?

Harold: Frankly, I wouldn't want to see George have trouble over this——

Number One: The man is a prince—thank him again, Georgie——

Harold: You don't have to——

Number One: You're damn right you don't have to! Don't get it, baby? You've been had——

Harold: My God, you don't think you can start all over——

Number One: It never got stopped, Harold—I told you, George, I told you The Man had a thousand weapons—how do you think he's whipped us for three hundred years? We knew what we came for, but he found a way to make you forget—what they've always done, baby, divide and conquer——

Harold: (*To* **George**) I freed you——

Number One: Who the hell do you think you are, Abraham Lincoln? He made you a house Negro, baby, and then he stuck it in deep—don't you feel it? Why didn't he spill his guts to that cop?

Harold: I told you—

Number One: Because he had you sewn up, baby, because you were faithful old George, just like one of the family—(*To* **Harold**) Who gave you the right to trust him? (*To* **George**) He knew he had you licked with his superior white brain, that's why . . . (*To* **Harold**) But you blew it, man—you're never going to climb into that saddle again—especially you——

Harold: You turn everything I say inside out——

George: Like you turned me inside out——

Harold: I could have turned you in——

Number One: But you figured you didn't need help with two simple children of the jungle——

Harold: I'm wasting my breath——

Number One: You have a point, Harold, we're wasting time. Now, George, it's cement time—nobody'll be able to pry us apart again——

Harold: Please——

Number One: Sorry, Harold, no time for last requests—Unless you'd like to finish folding your clothes first—there's no time for a last meal or anything, but if you really want to fold those undies—(*They are very close to Harold now, pressing in.*)

Harold: My wife's in the hospital . . . it was caesarean . . . how will she know?

Number One: Don't worry, Harold, we'll put a note in her dainties.

Harold: (*A little quiet*) Not knives . . . I'm afraid of knives——

Number One: Weapons! We don't carry weapons . . . do we look like hoodlums, Harold?

George: Come on, let's get it done——

Harold: Then what——?

Number One: Tonight we improvise . . . We'll just have to stomp you, I guess——

Harold: (*Almost ready to vomit—crosses hands over his chest—his heart is beating wildly*) Oh, my God—(*He has backed against the washer or table where most of his laundry is piled.*)

Number One: Oh, it won't be so bad, it'll be quick—look at those gunboats on George . . . All right, George . . . (*They start to move in.* **Harold**, *his knees already starting to buckle, feels desperately behind him for some kind of a weapon. Absurdly, he grabs a bra and brings it forward in one hand without realizing what he's doing.*) Sorry, Harold, that's about a thirty-six and you need at least a forty-five . . . (*They are almost upon him and* **Harold** *sinks to his knees, certain he is about to die, and hides his face in the bra, sobbing, completely dissolved.*)

George: (*Taken aback by* **Harold's** *abject posture*) Aw, come on . . . Hey, Number One——

Number One: Defend yourself, Harold—you're letting George down—come on, a vicious adversary to the end . . . where are your balls, man?

George: You said man to man——

Number One: Get up, for Christ's sake—act like a man, you bastard——

George: Shoot, I can't lean on a man with his face on a brassiere——

Number One: (*To* **Harold**) You think you're pretty smart——

George: Come on, Number One, he ain't The Man——

Number One: Yes, he is, the smart son-of-a-bitch! He's ofay Charlie with one more trick up his sleeve, just like always——

George: Just piss on him an' let's get out of here——

Number One: You'd like that, wouldn't you pasty-face? You'd like to get off like a fag in the Penn Station john—and just run home to your fancy tile shower . . . Get up and fight! (*Screaming in frustration*) Get up! (**Number One** *reaches down and tears the bra away from* **Harold**, *who, his last vestige of protection gone, is more terrified than ever.* **Number One** *seizes one of the bra cups in his teeth, tears away a piece and flings the bra in* **Harold's** *face, spitting the bitten out piece after it.* **Harold** *is petrified.*) Get up, you motherless sucker, or I'll stomp you where you sit!

Harold: I can't——

George: *Fight*, man? What can you lose?

Harold: (*With shame as well as fear*) I can't fight—I never could——

George: Damn, what a letdown——

Harold: I'm sorry——

Number One: You're sorry! Listen, Harold . . . . Baby, you're The Man—you're on top of it all and we're trying to take it all away from you—get it? That's what it's all about. We're trying to take it away and you're fighting to keep it—that's how it works, goddamit——

Harold: Not with me, I'm not your man . . . If you got down on the floor with a brassiere over your face and I had George—I still couldn't fight you—I never could——

Number One: Man, you have to fight. How else did you get that fancy apartment, that clean shirt, that cushy job? By putting us down, that's how, being The Man, the top dog——

Harold: No—no, those things just happened to me—like . . .

Number One: Like what?

Harold: Like you're happening to me.

Number One: What about that sexy, butterbottom wife, what about her? How did you get her?

Harold: I don't know—I think she got me——

George: Well she sure didn't want much . . . Come on, Number One, he ain't worth the shoe leather . . .

Number One: No! He doesn't get off so easy. There's just two kinds of people, outs and ins—and you're an in——

Harold: But I belong to no secret order, have no ruling power. My life just happened to me——

Number One: A poor innocent lamb——

Harold: All I ever did was say, "I don't mind . . ." My parents told me I was going to college and I said, "I don't mind." Someone offered me a job and I said, "I don't mind."

George: How about your wife—she say, "Do you mind?"

Number One: (*Mimicking*) No, I don't mind.

Harold: I guess the effect was the same——

George: Dumb luck——

Number One: Is that all it is, Harold?

Harold: I guess so.

Number One: You could just as well have been poor.

Harold: Yes.

Number One: Or ignorant.

Harold: Of course. I had nothing to do with it.

Number One: In fact, in short, you could just as well have been black.

Harold: Certainly——

George: Only nobody asked him, so he couldn't say, "I don't mind." Ha, ha, ha.

Number One: Shut up! Harold, you're a mindless, gutless bug that's been blown into a warm place—aren't you?

Harold: I can't argue——

Number One: But what if you had been born black—how would gutless, mindless, *black* Harold have turned out?

George: Kiss that duplex by-by, baby!

Number One: Harold, the college man?

Harold: Probably not.

Number One: Harold, the frat man? Harold, the assimilated, middle class, white collar, grey flannel black man . . . ?

Harold: No——

Number One: Harold, the drunken, downtrodden *nigger*, right, George?

George: You couldn't hack it, baby, being black——

Number One: Could you hack it, Harold?

Harold: I don't know——

Number One: You don't have George's muscle—you don't have my brains or imagination—have you? You haven't anything—have you? . . . *Have you?*

Harold: No . . . nothing—none of those things——

Number One: Why, Harold, do you know what that makes you? The real factory reject—get it, George? Under that pasty, lucky skin, he's a junkie, alkie, illiterate welfare case——

George: You could never cut it, man——

Number One: Norman Mailer may be the white Negro, baby, but you, you, Harold, are the white *nigger*. Do you follow me, *nigger*?

Harold: Yes——

Number One: Yes, *sir*, nigger!

Harold: Yes, sir . . .

George: Hey, Number One, he's a fine nigger——

Number One: Well, he has potential. Hey, boy—boy!

Harold: Yes, sir?

Number One: That's right, Harold, boy, play the game sharp and we might let you hang around 'til sundown . . . You *do* want to play the game?

Harold: Yes, sir.

Number One: You haven't got that just right, boy—it's *yassuh*.

Harold: Yassuh.

Number One: (*Laying on a tremendous Stepin Fetchit accent*) Yassuh.

Harold: (*Equally thick*) Yassuh.

George: Hey, that boy has talent——

Number One: George, who's teachin' this nigger?

George: You don't have to teach 'em, it's in their blood.

Number One: (*Laughing*) Shut up, George. Listen, Harold, boy, I want you to say *yassuh* again, but this time, I want you to put a *smile* in it.

Harold: Yassuh——

Number One: More!

Harold: (*Practically singing, a broad rictus and rolling eyes*) Yassuh!

Number One: More!

Harold: YASSUH!!

Number One: That's better. We like happy niggers around here, don't we, George?

George: Full of grits and goobers——

Number One: And remember, Harold, boy, happy niggers are healthy niggers.

Harold: Yassuh.

Number One: How's life treatin' you, boy?

Harold: Yassuh.

Number One: What kind of a dumb answer is that, boy? If you're too stupid to play right, we can go back to the other game, dig?

Harold: Yassuh!

Number One: That's better, boy. Now, the question was, "How's life been treatin' you?"

Harold: Jes fahn—Mistuh Boss——

George: (*Laughing*) He certainly is a *good* nigger, he could live to eighty-five in Biloxi.

Number One: How do you like slobbering on your knees in a laundromat, boy?

Harold: Ah likes it fahn, yassuh.

Number One: You don't have any desire to stand up, do you, boy?

Harold: Oh, no, suh.

Number One: And if some agitatin' red bastard walked in and told you to stand on your own two feet and tell us where to get off, what would you say, boy?

Harold: No thank you, suh.

Number One: Shoot, nigger, where's your loyalty? Tell that agitatin' red bastard that your masters love you and know what's best for you. Tell him.

Harold: Marse Boss, he know wha's bes' fo me . . .

Number One: Go on.

Harold: He say I'm happier on my knees, so I's gwine to stay hyar . . .

Number One: Harold, you're a good boy. Stand up and wipe yourself off. (*Taking a pair of underpants from* **Harold's** *laundry*) Here, wipe your face.

Harold: (*Doing so after only a slight hesitation*) Thank you, Marse Boss.

Number One: (*Arm around* **Harold's** *shoulder*) Don't mention it, boy. Why, I got a soft spot in my heart for a white nigger who knows his place.

Harold: Can I go home now?

Number One: How's that?

Harold: Kin ah go home now, boss?

Number One: George, Harold is tired of our new game . . .

George: Would you like to go back to the old game, Harold?

Number One: We could finish it.

Harold: Please, no . . .

Number One: Turn up the boy's radio, George. (**George** *obliges.*)

Harold: Please——

Number One: And we'll play with a will—hey, we'll have a party—c'mon, boy, now's your chance to shine for the boss—dance—dance, Harold——

Harold: I can't——

Number One: Who is that, George?

George: The Bananas.

Number One: That's first class music, nigger. C'mon, dance——

Harold: I can't dance, I don't know how——

Number One: You puttin' us on, boy, but you can't get away with it—it's in your jumpin', jivin' blood. Dance, nigger!

Harold: Yassuh . . . (*The music is hard rock*—**Harold** *tries to dance. At first, he merely shuffles his feet, but as* **Number One** *prods him, he gradually brings everything, hips, hands, elbows, eyes and teeth, into play. He taps, soft shoes and bops, at each of which he is completely inept and graceless. By the climax of the dance, he is completely involved, putting one hundred percent of his energy and concentration into it. After that point, when his chest is paining, he becomes more and more exhausted until we feel, at his exit, that he could not possibly dance another step.*)

Number One: I said, dance, boy—you're a nigger, aren't you?

Harold: Yassuh.

Number One: Up on stage, Stepin Fetchit. (*They force* **Harold** *onto the folding table where he does his dance.*)

Harold: Yassuh.

Number One: Now dance, wild child of nature, swing! George, I don't think he hears the beat——

George: (*Clapping time*) One an' two an' one an' two an' one——

Number One: You're dogging it, boy . . . Use those hands, those hips . . . Shake your ass . . . That's a little better, now enjoy yourself . . . Look like you havin' a good time, dammit . . . C'mon, nigger, if we wasn't makin' you dance, you'd do it all night for fun . . . more, *more* . . . MORE . . . FASTER . . . Yay, now you're swingin'! (*During this speech,* **Number One** *jumps in a laundry cart and* **George** *pushes him in a circle around the dancing* **Harold**. **Number One** *takes pennies from his pocket and starts to toss them at* **Harold**. **George** *follows suit. They toss the coins, not hard, but around* **Harold's** *face, just swiftly enough to terrorize him further.*)

Harold: Stop, I can't dance any more——

Number One: Sure you can, you just hittin' the big money now——

George: Shoot, nigger, you can dance all night and pick ten bags tomorrow——

Harold: (*Breathing very hard.*) No more—no more——

Number One: No more? (*Tossing a sheet to* **George** *and donning one himself.* **George** *follows suit.*) Why this is a party, boy, a dress-up play party—we'll all dance. (*With a whoop, he and* **George**, *covered with sheets, start to dance a circle around the stumbling, dancing* **Harold**. *The* **Actors** *support the lines with improvised sounds scattered between the lines. For example,* **George** *launches into a complicated jazz scat.* **Harold**, *attempting to please, tries to imitate* **George's** *scatting but can only produce a ludicrous parody.*)

Harold: Please, boss, ah's a good nigger——

George: (*Screaming under the sheet*) The best, the best of the niggers!

Number One: (*Also sheeted*) Dance, love-child, dance——

Harold: Ah's a good nigger——

Number One: We love our pickaninny sweetheart——

Harold: Ah's a mite tired . . .

George: (*Under* **Number One**) Dance, dance, dance, mother, dance, mother, dance! (*Etc.*)

Number One: (*Screaming under his sheet*) Dance me, kiss me, hug me—(*He and*

George *lurch together, meeting around* **Harold**, *and bear him off the table, his head protruding over their white-sheeted mass.*) Squeeze me, hold me, choke me . . . (*They dance* **Harold** *round the table and finally cast him to the floor. Breathless,* **George** *and* **Number One** *step back. Then* **Number One** *speaks.*) Hey, white nigger, are you fallin' down on the job?

Harold: Can't I rest a minute, boss?

Number One: Dance, nigger! (**Harold** *struggles up and continues dancing.*) You can rest tomorrow——

Harold: (*Dancing*) Tomorrow?

Number One: I know that seems far away to your primitive heart, but it'll come—if you keeps us entertained——

Harold: (*Dancing harder*) You won't do anything—else?

Number One: Now, Harold, you don't think George and I would harm a nigger, do you? There are so few left—and you're so authentic——

Harold: Yassuh . . .

George: One of nature's noblemen, but he doesn't dance very well——

Number One: Well, there's always the freak that ain't born with it——

Harold: God bless you, boss.

Number One: George, I think we've taught this nigger a lesson. Should we let him dance his way home?

Harold: Kin ah go now, boss?

Number One: "If he hollers, let him go."

George: Sure, back to his soft pad, to laugh us off——

Number One: You gonna laugh, dancin' boy?

Harold: Please, let me stop—my chest——

Number One: Are you gonna dance over to the maternity ward and tell your groovy wife all about it? Man, she'll laugh so hard she'll strain her milk—especially over what a good dancin' nigger you turned out to be——

Harold: She wouldn't laugh——

Number One: And she'd think you were much man, too, wouldn't she?

Harold: No, suh——

Number One: No, Harold boy will keep this all to himself—after all, if he told people he was a secret nigger, they might break his lease. You won't be laughing, will you, nigger?

Harold: No, suh.

Number One: Okay, *dance* over and pick up your laundry—oh, don't forget that tasty little brassiere. (**Harold** *obeys.*) If little mother asks about the hole in the cup—just say you got awful lonely while she was gone. (**Harold** *dances toward the door with his laundry. He looks to* **Number One** *for final permission.*) Dance right out, boy—it's a free country. George, open the door for Harold—show him you're no bigot.

George: (*Opening door*) Sure. There's nothing I like better than helping a white nigger who knows his place. (**Harold** *starts to dance out.*)

Number One: Oh, Harold . . . (**Harold** *freezes—there is no physical restraint preventing his escape.*) Aren't you going to say goodbye?

Harold: Goodbye.

Number One: That's not a very warm farewell, Harold. Come on, one little farewell performance for your friends—you do still like us, don't you?

Harold: Like you?

Number One: Us—us noble savages—us poor, downtrodden, Negro Americans—to the bottom of your dancing feet, you still love us, don't you?

Harold: I think Negroes are very—please let me go—my chest——

Number One: Are very?

Harold: I respect Negroes—I sympathize with their goals——

Number One: Harold, you play kiss-my-foot like you been playing it all your life. Ain't he a joy, George?

George: Yeah, he's an honor student—We can graduate him. (**Harold** *is about to collapse against the door frame. He could exit before they could stop him, but does not do so.*)

Number One: Uh-unh, Harold, you can't sit this one out yet. (**Harold** *continues dancing.*) You've told us what you thought we wanted to hear—that's nigger survival training . . . Now tell us the truth.

Harold: Please let me stop.

Number One: Not till you've told the truth, Harold—for the sake of your white-nigger soul.

Harold: WHICH TRUTH DO YOU WANT?

Number One: The truth about *inside* Harold Nigger—inside your gut——

George: How you wish *you* could lean on *us*——

Harold: I don't wish that——

George: How you wish you was eight feet tall, with steel-toe stompin' boots and nutcracker fingers—how you'd like to crack some black nuts——

Harold: I wouldn't do that . . . Please—let me go——

Number One: You couldn't *do*, boy, but how you can *wish* . . . wish you could cut us up, burn us down, tear us apart and scatter our seed—boy, you'd like to cut off our balls with a rusty beer can—but you know you'll never do it, because we beat you to the punch. Isn't that right—isn't it? The truth now, boy—you'd like to kill us, *right*?

Harold: (*Stops dancing—rigid, shaking*) Yes!

George: Halleluia, brother!

Harold: Yes, do to you what you've done to me! I'd like to rip your belly open with a razor blade—I'd like to cut your——

Number One: Congratulations, Harold. You are now a classic, one-hundred-percent, pure-blooded nigger! Yes, you're one of the few perfect specimens left—a low-down, spineless nigger—all gut-hate on the inside and shuffling lick-spit on the outside——

George: The last of the red-hot niggers!

Harold: (*Quivering, speaking with difficulty*) I'd like to——

Number One: To what, *nigger*?

Harold: To—to—I'd like to——

George: You got something to say, boy?

Harold: Nothing. Please—let me go home.

Number One: (*With a threatening step*) Then move your ass out of here——

George: (*With a step*) Yeah, drag-ass——

Number One: Back where you belong, nigger! (**Harold** *staggers out and is gone.* **Number One** *shouting after him.*) And don't show your face around here again. (*A pause.* **George** *and* **Number One** *look at each other.* **George** *goes to the washer and removes* **Number One's** *things with the intention of putting them in the drier.*) Man, I'll bet he's really burning up the sidewalk—if he's got any wind left. What's the matter with you?

George: Let's cut, man.

Number One: Hey, George, I'm still Number One, aren't I?

George: (*Pause*) Yeah . . .

Number One: You don't sound too sure——

George: What we did—wasn't what we come for——

Number One: Why, Georgie, I didn't know you were so bloodthirsty——

George: Don't shit me, Number One, we come to do a job but we just been playin' games.

Number One: You think I let you down, is that it?

George: You said we were gonna get The Man. We didn't get him . . . and he wasn't The Man anyway.

Number One: You've been thinkin' very hard . . .

George: He's just a sad-ass ofay loser.

Number One: . . . and you're gonna strain your head if you don't stop it. (**George** *turns away peevishly and jams more laundry into the bag.*)

Number One: That's the whole point, don't you dig? The Man *is* a loser. We opened him up and got inside him and there was nothing there—zero! We *got* him . . .

George: And let him off . . .

Number One: No, he's gonna stay got—we're inside for good.

George: What if he was puttin' us on?

Number One: Man, he couldn't be . . .

George: But if he was, he beat us one more time . . .

Number One: George, you *saw* him—you can believe me . . .

George: You can talk, but you can't ever prove it was real.

Number One: No one is that good an actor! Nobody . . . (*At this point, we become conscious of the flashing blue light of a police cruiser in the street.* **George** *and* **Number One** *freeze, look at each other, move to the window and look down the street.*)

George: What are they doin'?

Number One: I can't tell. Pick up the laundry quick. (*He steps out the front door as* **George** *moves swiftly to collect their things. In a moment,* **Number One** *returns.*)

George: What's happenin'?

Number One: Your worries are over, brother. He really *couldn't* hack it.

George: Who?

Number One: Harold the Clean—he's out there on the sidewalk—they just pulled a sheet over his face.

George: You're kiddin' me . . .

Number One: Right! I'm kiddin' you. Why don't you go ask the pig to pull the sheet back so you can see his face.

George: . . . Hey, did we do that, Number One?

Number One: (*Pointing where* **Harold** *would be*) That?

George: Yeah. . .

Number One: Yes, George, I think maybe we killed us a nigger.

George: . . . You know, he wasn't such a bad cat . . .

Number One: Didn't I tell you? Lots of them aren't such bad cats—but that doesn't cut any ice, baby, does it?

George: Don't it?

Number One: George, you're getting too complicated—you can't get your mind together. (**George** *has moved toward the window.*)

George: Hey, man, they're lookin' around. Let's make it outta here.

Number One: (*Revelation*) I know what you need!

George: Let's go, man!

Number One: But with dignity, George, with dignity. Get the stuff. (**George** *gets the laundry.* **Number One** *puts the "Sorry, Tired Today" sign back on the washer.*)

Number One: Yeah, I know what you need. (*They are moving toward the rear exit.*)

George: What?

Number One: Let's you and I go out and find us a Number Three.

George: Yeah? (*They are exiting.*)

Number One: Yeah. And a Number Four, and a Number Five, and a . . .
(*They are off. Lights fade until only the blue flasher alternately reveals and hides the legend, "Sorry, Tired Today."*)

PART SIX
IRONY

Fred was sitting in a bar one evening, sipping a beer and talking to a friend. During a lull in the conversation, he noticed a pool game going on in the back. What held his attention was the skill of one player, a small, older man with a few days' growth of whiskers, wearing old, threadbare clothes. He was a magician at the table, making each shot precisely while setting up the cue ball in perfect position for the next shot. His stroke with the cue stick was so smooth that the slender wooden shaft seemed to be an extension of his own skinny arms. He easily won the game that Fred was watching; money changed hands, and the balls were racked again. Just as before, the old man won, this time running the table on his first turn. Careful shot, plop of the ball in the pocket, cue ball rolling to exact position—the pattern was repeated until all the striped balls and the black one had disappeared from the smooth, green felt. His opponent shook his head, angrily threw a bill on the table, and slammed out the back door. The old man picked up the money, went to the far end of the bar, and ordered himself a draft.

In a few minutes Fred saw the old man back at the table. This time he was play-ing a big, loudmouthed guy who had come in after the last game and seated himself near the old man. But something had now happened to the magician: his stroke was jerky, he missed easy shots, and he seemed to be blasting the balls around the table without plan. The loudmouthed guy played fairly well and won the game easily. Fred wondered if the old man were drunk or scared or if old age had sud-denly caught up with him. The old fellow flipped a coin to the big one, and they played again. Same result. Another game, same outcome, but the stakes were going up—the whiskered one had to fork over a bill this time.

Fred—a little slow but not stupid—began to understand what was happening as he watched the next game. The smooth stroke—the unmistakable sign of an expert shooter—had returned to the old man. He still missed a number of shots, but it became obvious to Fred that the misses weren't because he lacked the skill. The little guy won the game by only a narrow margin. The big fellow looked embar-rassed as he passed over a bill, and Fred watched the two players talk heatedly. The loudmouth said something about "a last game for ten" and the old man shook his head. Finally, Fred saw him nod and then rack the balls. Loudmouth broke, made two, missed, and then it was all over. The master was resurrected. Click, plop, click, plop—eight times. The big guy never had a chance. As he stood there, the realization that he'd been taken began to show in his face, the redness starting at his neck and creeping upward. His biceps and shoulders seemed to bulge, and it looked as if he was about to throw himself at the smaller man. Old whiskers reversed his cue stick, walked up to the big guy, looked him square in the eye, and held out his hand. A few seconds passed, then the big man seemed visibly to shrink inside his clothes as he reached for his wallet. The hustler palmed the two bills, replaced his cue, went to the far end of the bar, and ordered himself a draft. Loudmouth looked around and then stepped quickly through the back door.

This incident contains all the basic elements of dramatic irony that we need to remember when seeing or reading a play. First is the person who causes the irony, the *ironist*, who acts from knowledge that certain other characters do not possess. Second, there is a particular person or persons who are ignorant of some truth and are acted upon by the ironist. In a sense, the second group can be considered victims, whether the outcome of the situation is comic or serious. Third, there must be an audience—those who do not necessarily participate in the ironist/victim relationship but who share in the knowledge possessed by the ironist. In the preceding incident, we can easily identify the three participants in this scene of dramatic irony: the ironist was the old man, acting from the knowledge of his own skill on the pool table and disguising that skill until the appropriate moment to make it appear that he did not possess it. The victim was the loudmouth. He was ignorant of the old man's skill and was taken in by his opponent's deception. The audience was Fred, a little naive at first, but finally realizing what the hustler was up to and sharing in the knowledge of the old man's skill (having observed him before the loudmouth arrived).

What happens in the relationship between ironist and victim can become the source of several stages of enjoyment for the audience. First, the identification of irony is often not a cut and dried affair—it can become a matter of detective work, a test of our own perception. We can ask ourselves whether something is said straightforwardly or ironically. For example, if two people were candidates for election, the loser might say to the winner in a neutral tone of voice, "Congratulations. The people have made their choice and I will support you." On the surface this may seem straightforward and, if we have no other indications to the contrary, we accept the loser's words at face value. However, the words may become obviously ironic if, as the winner walks away, the loser makes an obscene gesture toward him or begins immediately an attempt to impeach him. It can, however, be much more subtle. The loser might hint very guardedly to others that perhaps the election was rigged or that the winner is incompetent. In that case, the audience has to be alert to hints that reveal the loser's true attitude and prepare for the real significance of his subsequent actions. If we do become aware of the truth in this situation, we congratulate ourselves on our ability to see the loser's words in their ironic perspective, resulting in one kind of enjoyment.

Similar to the pleasure that occurs when we successfully detect irony is the gratification we feel when we know something that others do not grasp even though the information is available to them. It feeds our egos, giving us a sense of superiority, whether consciously felt or not, to realize that we know something other people do not. It is similar to what might have happened when you were a kid and a friend told you a secret—you probably walked around with this precious information in your head, knowing something the other kids didn't.

Probably more significant is the enjoyment that comes from our anticipation when we, as audience, see two opposing forces involved in an action, and we share with one force a crucial bit of information of which the other is ignorant. Suspense or tension develops from our point of view, as we wait anxiously to see what happens when the victim gains the knowledge that we share with the ironist. This is basically the same kind of tension we experience when watching an exciting TV mystery or reading a suspenseful novel. The anticipation is always there, with varying degrees of intensity, forcing us to see a situation through—to finish watching a program or reading a play. The human mind is not satisfied with an open end but seeks a finality, a closure. We think in terms of beginnings, middles, and ends, of completions; we are usually not satisfied simply with beginnings and middles.

The final stage of enjoyment comes through actually observing the reaction of the victim when he comes to awareness—whether it is as we had hoped it would be or it completely surprises us. The anticipation has been fulfilled; the mind has been supplied with an answer. When this awareness occurs, the possible reactions are numerous. For example, in the pool-shooting incident we have seen one ending, but there could have been several others. What if the loudmouth had taken the old man out back and beaten him up? Who then is the victim, who the ironist? What if the loudmouth had actually been the best pool shooter in town and had been hustling the hustler? What if he had become lucky and had run the table or had sunk the eight ball on the break (a win in some games)? Then the irony is reversed and we have to shuffle roles in the relationship. In any case, we have been caught up in the interaction of the two forces, have tentatively identified the irony, felt superior in our knowledge, anticipated and probably hypothesized the ending, and eventually experienced the conclusion. These are the basic elements in appreciating irony.

In general, then, the progress of dramatic irony is from ignorance to knowledge, from appearance to reality, from X to non-X. We the audience follow the victim from ignorance through experience to knowledge, moving from what seems to be true to what actually is. We perceive what seems to represent one thing and learn that it is something else—X to non-X. The stuff of irony lies between these two points, and the progress of a drama is often charted between them. The substance of the play may be the experience of a character realizing that what appears to be true simply is not. One of the universal appeals of drama and its irony is that it represents what we find to be true in life: our dilemma as human beings is that we often accept as true that which is not. But when reading or seeing good drama, the audience is provided sufficient information to make the crucial determination. Such information often is not available to the other characters or to us as we act out our own lives.

In order to begin the process of enjoyment, we must first be able to identify irony in a play—which involves paying close attention to detail. A playwright can use several different techniques to inform his audience of the reality of the world in the play and the ironies involved. We have already discussed dramatic irony, the broadest and most essential kind of irony in drama. But within this larger framework other specific kinds of irony may contribute to and intensify the overall dramatic effect.

Somewhere in your study you may have had to memorize a definition of irony similar to this: "Irony is someone saying one thing but meaning another." From what we have already said about the subject, you can probably recognize that this definition falls short of being all-encompassing. This definition does apply to one aspect of one kind of irony—verbal irony. This is the most easily identifiable form of irony, and we hear it in our everyday conversations with others. For example, your aunt—to whom you have never felt particularly close—makes an unannounced visit, forcing you to cancel a date. The next day when a friend asks you about the visit, you reply sarcastically, "Yeah, it was great—made my whole day." The irony is so obvious that we go from ignorance to knowledge almost immediately, becoming audience and victim at the same time.

But another kind of verbal irony occurs when someone makes a statement we know to be false—a statement that shows the person has been deceived. You are talking to your roommate's mother who is visiting campus. She is speaking about the prevalence of drug use at the school and is thankful that Sally (your roommate) never touches the dirty stuff. You have seen Sally come in stoned four nights in a row, and the last night she was so high she couldn't even find her bed. You possess information that Sally's mother does not have; her statements are therefore ironic for you because you know she has been deceived. Another example occurs in the play you are about to read: Iago is doing all he can to destroy Othello but pretends they are close friends. You the reader know the situation and can appreciate the irony when Othello continually refers to him as "honest Iago."

Another kind of irony does not require an obvious ironist but rather a recognition by the audience of incompatible elements, things that just don't go together. This type is called *situational irony* or *irony of events*. For example, in church on Sunday you hear the minister deliver a long, inspiring sermon on the evils of alcohol. The following Saturday night you see the same minister reeling down the sidewalk, giving off alcoholic fumes that can be smelled fifteen feet away. There is a great incongruity between what he has said and what he has done. On a small scale, we see ironies like this fairly often in our day-to-day existence: a snowplow stuck in the snow; a peace sign in the window of the ROTC building; a girl with a plunging neckline self-consciously clutching her books to her bosom. This form of irony occurs in drama when a character's actions contradict his words or when he tries to be something he really is not. A character may boast that he is a great fighter, but at the first sign of violent conflict, he runs away.

Growing out of this kind of irony and closely related to the larger concept of dramatic irony is the form that occurs when an individual or group of people attempt to accomplish something that the audience knows has no possible chance of success. A black friend of yours has applied for the position of secretary to the president of a small company. Because of civil rights legislation, the firm must interview all qualified applicants, and your friend is sure that she is the most qualified. But you know that this man is vehemently prejudiced against blacks and that your friend has no chance of being hired. In another example, the administration of your school, apparently yielding to demands for greater student involvement in decision-making, names a student group to recommend improvements. In reality, however, the administration has no intention of listening to the students or acting upon their recommendations. The students' work is as futile as the black girl's applying for the job. People in their positions do not realize the truth of the situation, and their efforts often take on overtones of tragedy when viewed by an informed third party. In such instances the ironist might be a certain social attitude, fate, chance, or some other force over which the victim has no control. This kind of irony occurs in drama when the audience, watching a character attempt to achieve a particular goal, knows of a factor that will prevent his success. In Greek tragedy, for example, in which fate or custom often operates against a character, the audience is aware of the nature of fate but the character is not. In a modern play a man might strive diligently toward what he believes to be society's definition of success only to discover later that he pursued his goal in the wrong way or that society's values have changed, and he has been struggling for something that is no longer valued.

Another kind of irony, *structural irony*, occurs when a dramatist places two scenes next to each other, or *juxtaposes* them, using one scene to cast the other into an ironic perspective. Let's say you have recently stolen something from a store or from somebody's home. You are greatly relieved that you haven't been caught and want to avoid any such risk again. Just as you promise yourself that you will never steal again, a policeman comes along and arrests you. Another example is the familiar irony that comes when people say they are going to quit smoking, or stop drinking, or not use drugs again—as soon as the next opportunity comes along, they're off once more. Structural irony works virtually the same way in drama. A character or incident leading one direction is immediately juxtaposed with a scene which casts it into an ironic context. For example, in one scene we might see a certain character praising the loyalty and goodness of another, but in the next scene we hear him plotting the death of the person he spoke so highly about. Placing the two scenes next to each other intensifies the irony and allows us to appreciate more fully the discrepancy between appearance and reality.

Finally, there is the irony that is predicated on visual perception: what we see compared to what really exists. This visual irony can take several shapes. An all-pro linebacker costumed as Little Bo Peep; a homicidal maniac dressed as a priest; your long-haired, bearded, far-out, antiestablishment friend appearing in a tuxedo—all of these are examples of one kind of visual irony. Another kind becomes apparent through something one does, such as a movement or gesture: a miserly man shrugging his shoulders when asked if he wants a free chance to win a hundred dollars, a psychiatrist who has a nervous habit of biting his nails. In drama, many disguises become ironic when the physical appearance of a character is in opposition to his real nature. Visual irony also occurs when we see someone performing a significant action that cannot be seen by the other actors. For example, we may see the actions of a lover concealed in the closet while the wife tries to convince her husband that he must immediately go back out for milk at 1:00 A.M.

These are the major forms of irony. They overlap, and there are others we have not discussed. But the important thing to keep in mind about all forms of irony is that it involves the double vision of ignorance and knowledge. In reading or viewing drama, if we are careful observers of detail, the knowledge will always be ours and the ignorance will belong to the characters in the play and to careless readers or viewers. The process of enjoyment discussed earlier will be ours; we will be able to get involved in the plays and appreciate what is going on. A good playwright does nothing without a specific purpose, and when we run into something that seems to be incongruous or contradictory, it is worth our time to search around for ironic possibilities.

OTHELLO

William Shakespeare

CHARACTERS

Othello, the Moor *highly respected military man*

Brabantio, father to Desdemona

Cassio, an honorable lieutenant

Iago, a villain *antagonist, crafty, evil*

Roderigo, a gulled gentleman *believed*

Duke of Venice

Senators

Montano, Governor of Cyprus

Gentlemen of Cyprus

Lodovico and Gratiano, two noble
   Venetians

Sailors

Clown

Desdemona, wife to Othello *sheltered*

Emilia, wife to Iago *serving maid to Desdemona*

Bianca, a courtesan

**Messenger, Herald, Officers,
   Gentlemen, Musicians,
   Attendants**

SCENE. Venice and Cyprus

ACT I

SCENE I. Venice. A street.

(*Enter* **Roderigo** *and* **Iago.**)

Roderigo: Tush! Never tell me? I take it much unkindly
   That thou, Iago, who hast had my purse
   As if the strings were thine, shouldst know of this.

Iago: 'Sblood,° but you'll not hear me! If ever I did dream
   Of such a matter, abhor me.

Roderigo: Thou told'st me
   Thou didst hold him in thy hate.

Iago: Despise me
   If I do not. Three great ones of the city,
   In personal suit to make me his lieutenant,
   Off-capped° to him; and, by the faith of man,
   I know my price; I am worth no worse a place.
   But he, as loving his own pride and purposes,
   Evades them with a bombast circumstance,°
   Horribly stuffed with epithets of war;
   Nonsuits° my mediators. For, "Certes," says he,
   "I have already chose my officer." And what was he?

'Sblood by God's blood
Off-capped doffed their caps—as a mark
of respect

bombast circumstance stuffed, roundabout speech
Nonsuits rejects

Forsooth, a great arithmetician,°
One Michael Cassio, a Florentine,
(A fellow almost damned in a fair wife)°
That never set a squadron in the field,
Nor the division of a battle knows
More than a spinster; unless the bookish theoric,
Wherein the tonguèd° consuls can propose
As masterly as he. Mere prattle without practice
Is all his soldiership. But he, sir, had th' election;
And I, of whom his eyes had seen the proof
At Rhodes, at Cyprus, and on other grounds
Christian and heathen, must be belee'd and calmed
By debitor and creditor. This counter-caster,°
He, in good time, must his lieutenant be,
And I—God bless the mark!—his Moorship's ancient.°
Roderigo: By heaven, I rather would have been his hangman.
Iago: Why, there's no remedy. 'Tis the curse of service:
Preferment goes by letter and affection,°
And not by old gradation,° where each second
Stood heir to th' first. Now, sir, be judge yourself,
Whether I in any just term am affined°
To love the Moor.
Roderigo: I would not follow him then.
Iago: O, sir, content you.
I follow him to serve my turn upon him. _to get revenge_
We cannot all be masters, nor all masters
Cannot be truly followed. You shall mark
Many a duteous and knee-crooking° knave
That, doting on his own obsequious bondage,
Wears out his time, much like his master's ass,
For naught but provender; and when he's old, cashiered.
Whip me such honest knaves! Others there are
Who, trimmed in forms and visages of duty,
Keep yet their hearts attending on themselves,
And, throwing but shows of service on their lords,
Do well thrive by them, and when they have lined their coats,
Do themselves homage. These fellows have some soul;
And such a one do I profess myself. For, sir,
It is as sure as you are Roderigo,

arithmetician theorist (rather than practical)
A . . . wife (a much-disputed passage, which is probably best taken as a general sneer at Cassio as a dandy and a ladies' man. But in the story from which Shakespeare took his plot the counterpart of Cassio is married, and it may be that at the beginning of the play Shakespeare had decided to keep him married but later changed his mind)

tonguèd eloquent
counter-caster i.e., a bookkeeper who *casts* (reckons up) figures on a *counter* (abacus)
ancient standard-bearer; an underofficer
letter and affection recommendations (from men of power) and personal preference
old gradation seniority
affined bound
knee-crooking bowing

Were I the Moor, I would not be Iago.
In following him, I follow but myself.
Heaven is my judge, not I for love and duty,
But seeming so, for my peculiar° end;
For when my outward action doth demonstrate
The native° act and figure of my heart
In complement extern,° 'tis not long after
But I will wear my heart upon my sleeve
For daws to peck at; I am not what I am.

Dramatic irony: Iago says he is hypocritical; others may be denied this insight.

Roderigo: What a full fortune does the thick-lips owe° *racial slur*
If he can carry't thus!

Iago: Call up her father,
Rouse him. Make after him, poison his delight,
Proclaim him in the streets, incense her kinsmen,
And though he in a fertile climate dwell,
Plague him with flies; though that his joy be joy,
Yet throw such chances of vexation on't
As it may lose some color.

Roderigo: Here is her father's house. I'll call aloud.

Iago: Do, with like timorous° accent and dire yell
As when, by night and negligence, the fire
Is spied in populous cities.

Roderigo: What, ho, Brabantio! Signior Brabantio, ho!

Iago: Awake! What, ho, Brabantio! Thieves! Thieves!
Look to your house, your daughter, and your bags!
Thieves! Thieves!
(**Brabantio** *above°* *at window*)

Brabantio: What is the reason of this terrible summons?
What is the matter there?

Roderigo: Signior, is all your family within?

Iago: Are your doors locked?

Brabantio: Why, wherefore ask you this?

Iago: Zounds, sir, y'are robbed! For shame. Put on your gown!
Your heart is burst, you have lost half your soul.
Even now, now, very now, an old black ram
Is tupping your white ewe. Arise, arise!
Awake the snorting citizens with the bell,
Or else the devil will make a grandsire of you.
Arise, I say!

Brabantio: What, have you lost your wits?

Roderigo: Most reverend signior, do you know my voice?

Brabantio: Not I. What are you?

Roderigo: My name is Roderigo.

---

peculiar personal
native natural, innate
complement extern outward appearances
owe own

timorous frightening
above on the small upper stage above and to the rear of the main platform stage, which resembled the projecting upper story of an Elizabethan house

Brabantio: The worser welcome!
I have charged thee not to haunt about my doors.
In honest plainness thou hast heard me say
My daughter is not for thee; and now, in madness,
Being full of supper and distemp'ring draughts,°
Upon malicious knavery dost thou come
To start° my quiet.
Roderigo: Sir, sir, sir——
Brabantio: But thou must needs be sure
My spirits and my place° have in their power
To make this bitter to thee.
Roderigo: Patience, good sir.
Brabantio: What tell'st thou me of robbing? This is Venice;
My house is not a grange.°
Roderigo: Most grave Brabantio,
In simple and pure soul I come to you.
Iago: Zounds, sir, you are one of those that will not serve God if the devil bid
you. Because we come to do you service and you think we are ruffians, you'll
have your daughter covered with a Barbary° horse, you'll have your neph-
ews° neigh to you, you'll have coursers for cousins,° and gennets for
germans.°
Brabantio: What profane wretch art thou?
Iago: I am one, sir, that comes to tell you your daughter and the Moor are
making the beast with two backs.
Brabantio: Thou art a villain.
Iago: You are—a senator.
Brabantio: This thou shalt answer. I know thee, Roderigo.
Roderigo: Sir, I will answer anything. But I beseech you,
If't be your pleasure and most wise consent,
As partly I find it is, that your fair daughter,
At this odd-even° and dull watch o' th' night,
Transported, with no worse nor better guard
But with a knave of common hire, a gondolier,
To the gross clasps of a lascivious Moor——
If this be known to you, and your allowance,
We then have done you bold and saucy wrongs;
But if you know not this, my manners tell me
We have your wrong rebuke. Do not believe
That from the sense of all civility°
I thus would play and trifle with your reverence.
Your daughter, if you have not given her leave,
I say again, hath made a gross revolt,

---

distemp'ring draughts unsettling drinks
start disrupt
place rank, i.e., of senator
grange isolated house
Barbary Arabian, i.e., Moorish
nephews i.e., grandsons

cousins relations
gennets for germans Spanish horses for
blood relatives
odd-even between night and morning
sense of all civility feeling of what is
proper

Tying her duty, beauty, wit, and fortunes
In an extravagant° and wheeling stranger
Of here and everywhere. Straight satisfy yourself.
If she be in her chamber, or your house,
Let loose on me the justice of the state
For thus deluding you.

Brabantio: Strike on the tinder, ho!
Give me a taper! Call up all my people!
This accident° is not unlike my dream.
Belief of it oppresses me already.
Light, I say! Light!   (*Exit above.*)

Iago: Farewell, for I must leave you.
It seems not meet, nor wholesome to my place,
To be produced—as, if I stay, I shall—
Against the Moor. For I do know the State,
However this may gall him with some check,°
Cannot with safety cast° him; for he's embarked
With such loud reason to the Cyprus wars,
Which even now stands in act,° that for their souls
Another of his fathom° they have none
To lead their business; in which regard,
Though I do hate him as I do hell-pains,
Yet, for necessity of present life,
I must show out a flag and sign of love,
Which is indeed but sign. That you shall surely find him,
Lead to the Sagittary° the raisèd search;
And there will I be with him. So farewell.   (*Exit.*)
(*Enter* **Brabantio** *in his nightgown, with* **Servants** *and torches.*)

Brabantio: It is too true an evil. Gone she is;
And what's to come of my despisèd time
Is naught but bitterness. Now, Roderigo,
Where didst thou see her?—O unhappy girl!—
With the Moor, say'st thou?—Who would be a father?—
How didst thou know 'twas she?—O, she deceives me
Past thought!—What said she to you? Get moe° tapers!
Raise all my kindred!—Are they married, think you?

Roderigo: Truly I think they are.

Brabantio: O heaven! How got she out? O treason of the blood!
Fathers, from hence trust not your daughters' minds
By what you see them act.° Is there not charms
By which the property° of youth and maidhood
May be abused? Have you not read, Roderigo,
Of some such thing?

---

extravagant   vagrant, wandering (Othello is not Venetian and thus may be considered a wandering soldier of fortune)
accident   happening
check   restraint
cast   dismiss

stands in act   takes place
fathom   ability
Sagittary   (probably the name of an inn)
moe   more
act   do
property   true nature

Roderigo: Yes, sir, I have indeed.

Brabantio: Call up my brother.—O, would you had had her!—
　Some one way, some another.—Do you know
　Where we may apprehend her and the Moor?

Roderigo: I think I can discover him, if you please
　To get good guard and go along with me.

Brabantio: Pray you lead on. At every house I'll call;
　I may command at most.—Get weapons, ho!
　And raise some special officers of might.—
　On, good Roderigo; I will deserve your pains.°

(*Exeunt.*)

Situational irony: compare with Brabantio's warning to Roderigo on page 361.

SCENE II. A street.

(*Enter* **Othello**, **Iago**, **Attendants** *with torches.*)

Iago: Though in the trade of war I have slain men,
　Yet do I hold it very stuff° o' th' conscience
　To do no contrived murder. I lack iniquity
　Sometime to do me service. Nine or ten times
　I had thought t' have yerked° him here, under the ribs.

Othello: 'Tis better as it is.

Iago: Nay, but he prated,
　And spoke such scurvy and provoking terms
　Against your honor, that with the little godliness I have
　I did full hard forbear him. But I pray you, sir,
　Are you fast married? Be assured of this,
　That the magnifico° is much beloved,
　And hath in his effect a voice potential
　As double as the Duke's.° He will divorce you,
　Or put upon you what restraint or grievance
　The law, with all his might to enforce it on,
　Will give him cable.°

Othello: Let him do his spite.
　My services which I have done the Signiory°
　Shall out-tongue his complaints. 'Tis yet to know°—
　Which when I know that boasting is an honor
　I shall promulgate—I fetch my life and being
　From men of royal siege;° and my demerits°
　May speak unbonneted to as proud a fortune
　As this that I have reached.° For know, Iago,
　But that I love the gentle Desdemona,

Verbal irony: Iago shows no lack of iniquity.

deserve your pains be worthy of (and reward) your efforts
stuff essence
yerked stabbed
magnifico nobleman
hath . . . Duke's i.e., can be as effective as the Duke

cable range, scope
Signiory the rulers of Venice
yet to know unknown as yet
siege rank
demerits deserts
May . . . reached, i.e., are the equal of the family I have married into

I would not my unhousèd° free condition
Put into circumscription and confine
For the seas' worth. But look, what lights come yond?
(Enter **Cassio**, *with* **Officers** *and torches.*)
Iago: Those are the raisèd father and his friends.
You were best go in.
Othello: Not I. I must be found.
My parts, my title, and my perfect soul°
Shall manifest me rightly. Is it they?
Iago: By Janus, I think no.
Othello: The servants of the Duke? And my lieutenant?
The goodness of the night upon you, friends.
What is the news?
Cassio: The Duke does greet you, general;
And he requires your haste-posthaste appearance
Even on the instant.
Othello: What is the matter, think you?
Cassio: Something from Cyprus, as I may divine.
It is a business of some heat. The galleys
Have sent a dozen sequent° messengers
This very night at one another's heels,
And many of the consuls, raised and met,
Are at the Duke's already. You have been hotly called for.
When, being not at your lodging to be found,
The Senate hath sent about three several° quests
To search you out.
Othello: 'Tis well I am found by you.
I will but spend a word here in the house,
And go with you.   *(Exit.)*
Cassio: Ancient, what makes he here?
Iago: Faith, he tonight hath boarded a land carack.°
If it prove lawful prize, he's made forever.
Cassio: I do not understand.
Iago: He's married.
Cassio: To who?
(Enter **Othello**.)
Iago: Marry,° to—Come, captain, will you go?
Othello: Have with you.
Cassio: Here comes another troop to seek for you.
(Enter **Brabantio**, **Roderigo**, *with* **Officers** *and torches.*)
Iago: It is Brabantio. General, be advised.
He comes to bad intent.
Othello: Holla! Stand there!
Roderigo: Signior, it is the Moor.
Brabantio: Down with him, thief!

unhousèd unconfined	**several** separate
perfect soul clear, unflawed conscience	**carack** treasure ship
sequent successive	**Marry** By Mary (an interjection)

(They draw swords.)

Iago: You, Roderigo? Come, sir, I am for you.

Othello: Keep up your bright swords, for the dew will rust them.
Good signior, you shall more command with years
Than with your weapons.

Brabantio: O thou foul thief, where hast thou stowed my daughter?
Damned as thou art, thou hast enchanted her!
For I'll refer me to all things of sense,°
If she in chains of magic were not bound,
Whether a maid so tender, fair, and happy,
So opposite to marriage that she shunned
The wealthy, curlèd darlings of our nation,
Would ever have, t' incur a general mock,°
Run from her guardage to the sooty bosom
Of such a thing as thou—to fear, not to delight.
Judge me the world if 'tis not gross in sense°
That thou hast practiced° on her with foul charms,
Abused her delicate youth with drugs or minerals
That weaken motion.° I'll have't disputed on;
'Tis probable, and palpable to thinking.
I therefore apprehend and do attach° thee
For an abuser of the world, a practicer
Of arts inhibited and out of warrant.°
Lay hold upon him. If he do resist,
Subdue him at his peril.

Othello: Hold your hands,
Both you of my inclining and the rest.
Were it my cue to fight, I should have known it
Without a prompter. Whither will you that I go
To answer this your charge?

Brabantio: To prison, till fit time
Of law and course of direct session
Call thee to answer.

Othello: What if I do obey?
How may the Duke be therewith satisfied,
Whose messengers are here about my side
Upon some present° business of the state
To bring me to him?

Officer: 'Tis true, most worthy signior.
The Duke's in council, and your noble self
I am sure is sent for.

Brabantio: How? The Duke in council?
In this time of the night? Bring him away.

---

refer . . . sense i.e., base (my argument) on all ordinary understanding of nature
general mock public shame
gross in sense obvious
practiced used tricks

motion thought, i.e., reason
attach arrest
inhibited . . . warrant prohibited and illegal (black magic)
present immediate

Visual and situational irony: Do they really intend to fight?

Mine's not an idle cause. The Duke himself,
Or any of my brothers° of the state,
Cannot but feel this wrong as 'twere their own;
For if such actions may have passage free,
Bondslaves and pagans shall our statesmen be.
(*Exeunt.*)

SCENE III. A council chamber.

(*Enter* **Duke**, **Senators**, *and* **Officers** [*set at a table, with lights and* **Attendants**].)
Duke: There's no composition° in this news
　　That gives them credit.°
First Senator:　　　　　　　Indeed, they are disproportioned.
　　My letters say a hundred and seven galleys.
Duke: And mine a hundred forty.
Second Senator:　　　　　　　And mine two hundred.
　　But though they jump° not on a just accompt°—
　　As in these cases where the aim° reports
　　'Tis oft with difference—yet do they all confirm
　　A Turkish fleet, and bearing up to Cyprus.
Duke: Nay, it is possible enough to judgment.°
　　I do not so secure me in the error,
　　But the main article I do approve
　　In fearful sense.°
Sailor: (*Within*) What, ho! What, ho! What, ho!
　　(*Enter* **Sailor**.)
Officer: A messenger from the galleys.
Duke:　　　　　　　Now? What's the business?
Sailor: The Turkish preparation makes for Rhodes.
　　So was I bid report here to the State
　　By Signior Angelo.
Duke: How say you by this change?
First Senator:　　　　　　　This cannot be
　　By no assay of reason. 'Tis a pageant°
　　To keep us in false gaze.° When we consider
　　Th' importancy of Cyprus to the Turk,
　　And let ourselves again but understand
　　That, as it more concerns the Turk than Rhodes,
　　So may he with more facile question° bear it,
　　For that it stands not in such warlike brace,°

brothers i.e., the other senators
composition agreement
gives them credit makes them believable
jump agree
just accompt exact counting
aim approximation
to judgment when carefully considered

I do . . . sense i.e., just because the numbers disagree in the reports, I do not doubt that the principal information (that the Turkish fleet is out) is fearfully true
pageant show, pretense
in false gaze looking the wrong way
facile question easy struggle
warlike brace "military posture"

But altogether lacks th' abilities
That Rhodes is dressed in. If we make thought of this,
We must not think the Turk is so unskillful
To leave that latest which concerns him first,
Neglecting an attempt of ease and gain
To wake and wage a danger profitless.
Duke: Nay, in all confidence he's not for Rhodes.
Officer: Here is more news.
(*Enter a* **Messenger**.)
Messenger: The Ottomites, reverend and gracious,
Steering with due course toward the isle of Rhodes,
Have there injointed them with an after° fleet.
First Senator: Ay, so I thought. How many, as you guess?
Messenger: Of thirty sail; and now they do restem
Their backward course, bearing with frank appearance
Their purposes toward Cyprus. Signior Montano,
Your trusty and most valiant servitor,
With his free duty° recommends° you thus,
And prays you to believe him.
Duke: 'Tis certain then for Cyprus.
Marcus Luccicos, is not he in town?
First Senator: He's now in Florence.
Duke: Write from us to him; post-posthaste dispatch.
First Senator: Here comes Brabantio and the valiant Moor.
(*Enter* **Brabantio**, **Othello**, **Cassio**, **Iago**, **Roderigo**, *and* **Officers**.)
Duke: Valiant Othello, we must straight° employ you
Against the general° enemy Ottoman.
(*To* **Brabantio**) I did not see you. Welcome, gentle signior.
We lacked your counsel and your help tonight.
Brabantio: So did I yours. Good your grace, pardon me.
Neither my place, nor aught I heard of business,
Hath raised me from my bed; nor doth the general care
Take hold on me; for my particular grief
Is of so floodgate and o'erbearing nature
That it engluts and swallows other sorrows,
And it is still itself.
Duke: Why, what's the matter?
Brabantio: My daughter! O, my daughter!
Senators: Dead?
Brabantio: Ay, to me.
She is abused, stol'n from me, and corrupted
By spells and medicines bought of mountebanks;
For nature so prepost'rously to err,
Being not deficient, blind, or lame of sense,
Sans° witchcraft could not.

after following	**straight** at once
free duty unlimited respect	**general** universal
recommends informs	**Sans** without

Duke: Whoe'er he be that in this foul proceeding
  Hath thus beguiled your daughter of herself,
  And you of her, the bloody book of law
  You shall yourself read in the bitter letter
  After your own sense; yea, though our proper° son
  Stood in your action.°
Brabantio: Humbly I thank your Grace.
  Here is the man—this Moor, whom now, it seems,
  Your special mandate for the state affairs
  Hath hither brought.
All: We are very sorry for't.
Duke: (*To* **Othello**) What in your own part can you say to this?
Brabantio: Nothing, but this is so.
Othello: Most potent, grave, and reverend signiors,
  My very noble and approved° good masters,
  That I have ta'en away this old man's daughter,
  It is most true; true I have married her.
  The very head and front° of my offending
  Hath this extent, no more. Rude am I in my speech,
  And little blessed with the soft phrase of peace,
  For since these arms of mine had seven years' pith°
  Till now some nine moons wasted,° they have used
  Their dearest° action in the tented field;
  And little of this great world can I speak
  More than pertains to feats of broils and battle;
  And therefore little shall I grace my cause
  In speaking for myself. Yet, by your gracious patience,
  I will a round° unvarnished tale deliver
  Of my whole course of love—what drugs, what charms,
  What conjuration, and what mighty magic,
  For such proceeding I am charged withal,
  I won his daughter——
Brabantio: A maiden never bold,
  Of spirit so still and quiet that her motion
  Blushed at herself;° and she, in spite of nature,
  Of years, of country, credit, everything,
  To fall in love with what she feared to look on!
  It is a judgment maimed and most imperfect
  That will confess perfection so could err
  Against all rules of nature, and must be driven
  To find out practices of cunning hell
  Why this should be. I therefore vouch again

---

proper own
Stood in your action were the accused
in your suit
approved tested, proven by past performance
head and front extreme form (front =
forehead)

pith strength
wasted past
dearest most important
round blunt
her motion/Blushed at herself i.e., she
was so modest that she blushed at every
thought (and movement)

That with some mixtures pow'rful o'er the blood,
Or with some dram, conjured to this effect,
He wrought upon her.
Duke: To vouch this is no proof,
Without more wider and more overt test
Than these thin habits° and poor likelihoods
Of modern° seeming do prefer against him.
First Senator: But, Othello, speak.
Did you by indirect and forcèd courses
Subdue and poison this young maid's affections?
Or came it by request, and such fair question°
As soul to soul affordeth?
Othello: I do beseech you,
Send for the lady to the Sagittary
And let her speak of me before her father.
If you do find me foul in her report,
The trust, the office, I do hold of you
Not only take away, but let your sentence
Even fall upon my life.
Duke: Fetch Desdemona hither.
Othello: Ancient, conduct them; you best know the place.
(*Exit* **Iago**, *with two or three* **Attendants**.)
And till she come, as truly as to heaven
I do confess the vices of my blood,
So justly to your grave ears I'll present
How I did thrive in this fair lady's love,
And she in mine.
Duke: Say it, Othello.
Othello: Her father loved me; oft invited me;
Still° questioned me the story of my life
From year to year, the battle, sieges, fortune
That I have passed.
I ran it through, even from my boyish days
To th' very moment that he bade me tell it.
Wherein I spoke of most disastrous chances,
Of moving accidents by flood and field,
Of hairbreadth scapes i' th' imminent° deadly breach,
Of being taken by the insolent foe
And sold to slavery, of my redemption thence
And portance° in my travel's history,
Wherein of anters° vast and deserts idle,°
Rough quarries, rocks, and hills whose heads touch heaven,
It was my hint to speak. Such was my process.
And of the Cannibals that each other eat,

habits clothing	**imminent** threatening
modern trivial	**portance** manner of acting
question discussion	**anters** caves
Still regularly	**idle** empty, sterile

The Anthropophagi,° and men whose heads
Grew beneath their shoulders. These things to hear
Would Desdemona seriously incline;
But still the house affairs would draw her thence;
Which ever as she could with haste dispatch,
She'd come again, and with a greedy ear
Devour up my discourse. Which I observing,
Took once a pliant hour, and found good means
To draw from her a prayer of earnest heart
That I would all my pilgrimage dilate,°
Whereof by parcels she had something heard,
But not intentively.° I did consent,
And often did beguile her of her tears
When I did speak of some distressful stroke
That my youth suffered. My story being done,
She gave me for my pains a world of kisses.
She swore in faith 'twas strange, 'twas passing° strange;
'Twas pitiful, 'twas wondrous pitiful.
She wished she had not heard it; yet she wished
That heaven had made her such a man. She thanked me,
And bade me, if I had a friend that loved her,
I should but teach him how to tell my story,
And that would woo her. Upon this hint I spake.

Do his dangers and her pity seem strong basis for marriage?

She loved me for the dangers I had passed,
And I loved her that she did pity them.
This only is the witchcraft I have used
Here comes the lady. Let her witness it.
(*Enter* **Desdemona, Iago, Attendants**.)

Duke: I think this tale would win my daughter too.
Good Brabantio, take up this mangled matter at the best.°
Men do their weapons rather use
Than their bare hands.

Brabantio: I pray you hear her speak.
If she confess that she was half the wooer,
Destruction on my head if my bad blame
Light on the man. Come hither, gentle mistress.
Do you perceive in all this noble company
Where most you owe obedience?

Desdemona: My noble father,
I do perceive here a divided duty.
To you I am bound for life and education;
My life and education both do learn me
How to respect you. You are the lord of duty,
I am hitherto your daughter. But here's my husband,

Anthropophagi man-eaters
dilate relate in full
intentively at length and in some sequence

passing surpassing
Take . . . best i.e., make the best of this disaster

And so much duty as my mother showed
To you, preferring you before her father,
So much I challenge° that I may profess
Due to the Moor my lord.

Brabantio: God be with you. I have done.
Please it your Grace, on to the state affairs.
I had rather to adopt a child than get° it.
Come hither, Moor.
I here do give thee that with all my heart
Which, but thou hast already, with all my heart
I would keep from thee. For your sake,° jewel,
I am glad at soul I have no other child,
For thy escape would teach me tyranny,
To hang clogs on them. I have done, my lord.

Duke: Let me speak like yourself and lay a sentence°
Which, as a grise° or step, may help these lovers.
When remedies are past, the griefs are ended
By seeing the worst, which late on hopes depended.°
To mourn a mischief that is past and gone
Is the next° way to draw new mischief on.
What cannot be preserved when fortune takes,
Patience her injury a mock'ry makes.
The robbed that smiles, steals something from the thief;
He robs himself that spends a bootless° grief.

Brabantio: So let the Turk of Cyprus us beguile:
We lose it not so long as we can smile.
He bears the sentence well that nothing bears
But the free comfort which from thence he hears;
But he bears both the sentence and the sorrow
That to pay grief must of poor patience borrow.
These sentences, to sugar, or to gall,
Being strong on both sides, are equivocal.
But words are words. I never yet did hear
That the bruisèd heart was piercèd° through the ear.
I humbly beseech you, proceed to th' affairs of state.

Duke: The Turk with a most mighty preparation makes for Cyprus. Othello,
the fortitude° of the place is best known to you; and though we have there
a substitute° of most allowed sufficiency,° yet opinion, a more sovereign

---

challenge   claim as right
get   beget
For your sake   because of you
lay a sentence   provide a maxim
grise   step
late on hopes depended   was supported
by hope (of a better outcome) until lately
next   closest, surest
bootless   valueless
piercèd   (some editors amend to *pieced*,
i.e., "healed." But *pierced* makes good

sense: Brabantio is saying in effect that his
heart cannot be further hurt [pierced] by
the indignity of the useless, conventional
advice the Duke offers him. *Pierced* can
also mean, however, "lanced" in the
medical sense, and would then mean
"treated")
fortitude   fortification
substitute   viceroy
most allowed sufficiency   generally
acknowledged capability

mistress of effects, throws a more safer voice on you.° You must therefore
be content to slubber° the gloss of your new fortunes with this more stubborn and boisterous° expedition.

Othello: The tyrant Custom, most grave senators,
Hath made the flinty and steel couch of war
My thrice-driven° bed of down. I do agnize°
A natural and prompt alacrity
I find in hardness and do undertake
This present wars against the Ottomites.
Most humbly, therefore, bending to your state,
I crave fit disposition for my wife,
Due reference of place, and exhibition,°
With such accommodation and besort
As levels with° her breeding.

Duke: Why, at her father's.

Brabantio: I will not have it so.

Othello: Nor I.

Desdemona: Nor would I there reside,
To put my father in impatient thoughts
By being in his eye. Most gracious Duke,
To my unfolding° lend your prosperous° ear,
And let me find a charter° in your voice,
T' assist my simpleness.

Duke: What would you, Desdemona?

Desdemona: That I love the Moor to live with him,
My downright violence, and storm of fortunes,
May trumpet to the world. My heart's subdued
Even to the very quality of my lord.°
I saw Othello's visage in his mind,
And to his honors and his valiant parts
Did I my soul and fortunes consecrate.
So that, dear lords, if I be left behind,
A moth of peace, and he go to the war,
The rites° for why I love him are bereft me,
And I a heavy interim shall support
By his dear absence. Let me go with him.

Othello: Let her have your voice.°
Vouch with me, heaven, I therefore beg it not

---

opinion . . . you i.e., the general opinion, which finally controls affairs, is that
you would be the best man in this situation
slubber besmear
stubborn and boisterous rough and violent
thrice-driven i.e., softest
agnize know in myself
exhibition grant of funds
levels with is suitable to

unfolding explanation
prosperous favoring
charter permission
My . . . lord i.e., I have become one
in nature and being with the man I married (therefore, I too would go to the wars
like a soldier)
rites (may refer either to the marriage
rites or to the rites, formalities, of war)
voice consent

To please the palate of my appetite,
Nor to comply with heat°—the young affects°
In me defunct—and proper satisfaction;°
But to be free and bounteous to her mind;
And heaven defend° your good souls that you think
I will your serious and great business scant
When she is with me. No, when light-winged toys
Of feathered Cupid seel° with wanton° dullness
My speculative and officed instrument,°
That my disports corrupt and taint my business,
Let housewives make a skillet of my helm,
And all indign° and base adversities
Make head° against my estimation!°——

Duke: Be it as you shall privately determine,
Either for her stay or going. Th' affair cries haste,
And speed must answer it.

First Senator: You must away tonight.

Othello: With all my heart.

Duke: At nine i' th' morning here we'll meet again
Othello, leave some officer behind,
And he shall our commission bring to you,
And such things else of quality and respect
As doth import you.

Othello: So please your grace, my ancient;
A man he is of honesty and trust.
To his conveyance I assign my wife,
With what else needful your good grace shall think
To be sent after me.

Duke: Let it be so.
Good night to every one. (*To* **Brabantio**) And, noble signior,
If virtue no delighted° beauty lack,
Your son-in-law is far more fair than black.

First Senator: Adieu, brave Moor. Use Desdemona well.

Brabantio: Look to her, Moor, if thou hast eyes to see:
She has deceived her father, and may thee.

(*Exeunt* **Duke, Senators, Officers, & company.**)

Othello: My life upon her faith! Honest Iago,
My Desdemona must I leave to thee.
I prithee let thy wife attend on her,
And bring them after in the best advantage.°
Come, Desdemona. I have but an hour

*Verbal irony: Iago
tried to prevent
Othello's marriage.*

heat lust	**speculative . . . instrument** i.e., sight
affects passions	(and, by extension, the mind)
proper satisfaction i.e., consummation	**indign** unworthy
of the marriage	**Make head** form an army, i.e., attack
defend forbid	**estimation** reputation
seel sew up	**delighted** delightful
wanton lascivious	**advantage** opportunity

Of love, of wordly matter, and direction
To spend with thee. We must obey the time.
(*Exit* **Moor** *and* **Desdemona**.)

Roderigo: Iago?

Iago: What say'st thou, noble heart?

Roderigo: What will I do, think'st thou?

Iago: Why, go to bed and sleep.

Roderigo: I will incontinently° drown myself.

Iago: If thou dost, I shall never love thee after. Why, thou silly gentleman?

Roderigo: It is silliness to live when to live is torment; and then have we a prescription to die when death is our physician.

Iago: O villainous! I have looked upon the world for four times seven years, and since I could distinguish betwixt a benefit and an injury, I never found man that knew how to love himself. Ere I would say I would drown myself for the love of a guinea hen, I would change my humanity with a baboon.

Roderigo: What should I do? I confess it is my shame to be so fond, but it is not my virtue° to amend it.

Iago: Virtue? A fig! 'Tis in ourselves that we are thus, or thus. Our bodies are our gardens, to the which our wills are gardeners; so that if we will plant nettles or sow lettuce, set hyssop and weed up thyme, supply it with one gender of herbs or distract° it with many—either to have it sterile with idleness or manured with industry—why, the power and corrigible° authority of this lies in our wills. If the balance of our lives had not one scale of reason to poise another of sensuality, the blood and baseness of our natures would conduct us to most prepost'rous conclusions.° But we have reason to cool our raging motions, our carnal stings or unbitted° lusts, whereof I take this that you call love to be a sect or scion.°

Roderigo: It cannot be.

Iago: It is merely a lust of the blood and a permission of the will. Come, be a man! Drown thyself? Drown cats and blind puppies! I have professed me thy friend, and I confess me knit to thy deserving with cables of perdurable toughness. I could never better stead° thee than now. Put money in thy purse. Follow thou the wars; defeat thy favor° with an usurped° beard. I say, put money in thy purse. It cannot be long that Desdemona should continue her love to the Moor. Put money in thy purse. Nor he his to her. It was a violent commencement in her and thou shalt see an answerable° sequestration—put but money in thy purse. These Moors are changeable in their wills—fill thy purse with money. The food that to him now is as luscious as locusts° shall be to him shortly as bitter as coloquintida.° She must change for youth; when she is sated with his body, she will find the errors of her choice. Therefore, put money in thy purse. If thou wilt needs

incontinently at once
virtue strength (Roderigo is saying that his nature controls him)
distract vary
corrigible corrective
conclusions ends
unbitted i.e., uncontrolled
sect or scion offshoot

stead serve
defeat thy favor disguise your face
usurped assumed
answerable similar
locusts (a sweet fruit)
coloquintida (a purgative derived from a bitter apple)

damn thyself, do it a more delicate way than drowning. Make all the money thou canst. If sanctimony° and a frail vow betwixt an erring° barbarian and supersubtle Venetian be not too hard for my wits, and all the tribe of hell, thou shalt enjoy her. Therefore, make money. A pox of drowning thyself, it is clean out of the way. Seek thou rather to be hanged in compassing° thy joy than to be drowned and go without her.

Roderigo: Wilt thou be fast to my hopes, if I depend on the issue?

Iago: Thou art sure of me. Go, make money. I have told thee often, and I retell thee again and again, I hate the Moor. My cause is hearted;° thine hath no less reason. Let us be conjunctive° in our revenge against him. If thou canst cuckold him, thou dost thyself a pleasure, me a sport. There are many events in the womb of time, which will be delivered. Traverse, go, provide thy money! We will have more of this tomorrow. Adieu.

Roderigo: Where shall we meet i' th' morning?

Iago: At my lodging.

Roderigo: I'll be with thee betimes.

Iago: Go to, farewell. Do you hear, Roderigo?

Roderigo: I'll sell all my land.   (*Exit.*)

Iago: Thus do I ever make my fool my purse;
For I mine own gained knowledge° should profane
If I would time expend with such snipe
But for my sport and profit. I hate the Moor,
And it is thought abroad that 'twixt my sheets
H'as done my office. I know not if't be true,
But I, for mere suspicion in that kind,
Will do, as if for surety.° He holds me well;
The better shall my purpose work on him.
Cassio's a proper° man. Let me see now:
To get his place, and to plume up my will°
In double knavery. How? How? Let's see.
After some time, to abuse Othello's ears
That he is too familiar with his wife.
He hath a person and a smooth dispose°
To be suspected—framed° to make women false.
The Moor is of a free and open nature
That thinks men honest that but seem to be so;
And will as tenderly be led by th' nose
As asses are.
I have't! It is engendered! Hell and night
Must bring this monstrous birth to the world's light.   (*Exit.*)

---

sanctimony sacred bond (of marriage)	**proper** handsome
erring wandering	**plume up my will** (many explanations
compassing encompassing, achieving	have been offered for this crucial line,
hearted deep-seated in the heart	which in Q1 reads "make up my will."
conjunctive joined	The general sense is something like "to
gained knowledge i.e., practical, worldly	make more proud and gratify my ego")
wisdom	**dispose** manner
surety certainty	**framed** designed

ACT II

SCENE I. Cyprus.

(*Enter* Montano *and two* Gentlemen, *one above.*°)

Montano: What from the cape can you discern at sea?

First Gentleman: Nothing at all, it is a high-wrought flood.
I cannot 'twixt the heaven and the main
Descry a sail.

Montano: Methinks the wind hath spoke aloud at land;
A fuller blast ne'er shook our battlements.
If it hath ruffianed so upon the sea,
What ribs of oak, when mountains melt on them,
Can hold the mortise? What shall we hear of this?

Second Gentleman: A segregation° of the Turkish fleet.
For do but stand upon the foaming shore,
The chidden billow seems to pelt the clouds;
The wind-shaked surge, with high and monstrous main,°
Seems to cast water on the burning Bear
And quench the guards of th' ever-fixéd pole.°
I never did like molestation view
On the enchaféd flood.

Montano: If that the Turkish fleet
Be not ensheltered and embayed, they are drowned;
It is impossible to bear it out.

(*Enter a* third Gentleman.)

Third Gentleman: News, lads! Our wars are done.
The desperate tempest hath so banged the Turks
That their designment halts. A noble ship of Venice
Hath seen a grievous wrack and sufferance°
On most part of their fleet.

Montano: How? Is this true?

Third Gentleman: The ship is here put in,
A Veronesa; Michael Cassio,
Lieutenant to the warlike Moor Othello,
Is come on shore; the Moor himself at sea,
And is in full commission here for Cyprus.

Montano: I am glad on't. 'Tis a worthy governor.

Third Gentleman: But this same Cassio, though he speak of comfort
Touching the Turkish loss, yet he looks sadly

---

above (the Folio arrangement of this scene requires that the First Gentleman stand above—on the upper stage— and act as a lookout reporting sights which cannot be seen by Montano standing below on the main stage)
segregation separation

main (both "ocean" and "strength")
Seems . . . pole (the constellation Ursa Minor contains two stars which are the *guards*, or companions, of the *pole*, or North Star)
sufferance damage

And prays the Moor be safe, for they were parted
With foul and violent tempest.

Montano: Pray heavens he be;
For I have served him, and the man commands
Like a full soldier. Let's to the seaside, ho!
As well to see the vessel that's come in
As to throw out our eyes for brave Othello,
Even till we make the main and th' aerial blue
An indistinct regard.°

Third Gentleman: Come, let's do so;
For every minute is expectancy
Of more arrivancie.°

(*Enter* **Cassio**.)

Cassio: Thanks, you the valiant of the warlike isle,
That so approve° the Moor. O, let the heavens
Give him defense against the elements,
For I have lost him on a dangerous sea.

Montano: Is he well shipped?

Cassio: His bark is stoutly timbered, and his pilot
Of very expert and approved allowance;°
Therefore my hopes, not surfeited to death,°
Stand in bold cure.°   (*Within*) A sail, a sail, a sail!

Cassio: What noise?

First Gentleman: The town is empty; on the brow o' th' sea
Stand ranks of people, and they cry, "A sail!"

Cassio: My hopes do shape him for the governor.   (*A shot.*)

Second Gentleman: They do discharge their shot of courtesy:
Our friends at least.

Cassio: I pray you, sir, go forth
And give us truth who 'tis that is arrived.

Second Gentleman: I shall.   (*Exit.*)

Montano: But, good lieutenant, is your general wived?

Cassio: Most fortunately. He hath achieved a maid
That paragons° description and wild fame;°
One that excels the quirks of blazoning pens,°
And in th' essential vesture of creation°
Does tire the ingener.°

(*Enter* **Second Gentleman**.)

How now? Who has put in?

the main . . . regard i.e., the sea and sky become indistinguishable
arrivancie arrivals
approve ("honor" or, perhaps, "are as warlike and valiant as your governor")
approved allowance known and tested
not surfeited to death i.e., not so great as to be in danger
Stand in bold cure i.e., are likely to be restored

paragons exceeds
wild fame extravagant report
quirks of blazoning pens ingenuities of praising pens
essential vesture of creation i.e., essential human nature as given by the Creator
tire the ingener (a difficult line which probably means something like "outdo the human ability to imagine and picture")

Second Gentleman: 'Tis one Iago, ancient to the general.
Cassio: H'as had most favorable and happy speed:
    Tempests themselves, high seas, and howling winds,
    The guttered° rocks and congregated° sands,
    Traitors ensteeped° to enclog the guiltless keel,
    As having sense° of beauty, do omit
    Their mortal° natures, letting go safely by
    The divine Desdemona.
Montano: What is she?
Cassio: She that I spake of, our great captain's captain,
    Left in the conduct of the bold Iago,
    Whose footing° here anticipates our thoughts
    A se'nnight's° speed. Great Jove, Othello guard,
    And swell his sail with thine own pow'rful breath,
    That he may bless this bay with his tall° ship,
    Make love's quick pants in Desdemona's arms,
    Give renewed fire to our extincted spirits.
    (*Enter* **Desdemona, Iago, Roderigo,** *and* **Emilia.**)
    O, behold! The riches of the ship is come on shore!
    You men of Cyprus, let her have your knees.   (*Kneeling.*)
    Hail to thee, lady! and the grace of heaven,
    Before, behind thee, and on every hand,
    Enwheel thee round.
Desdemona: I thank you, valiant Cassio.
    What tidings can you tell of my lord?
Cassio: He is not yet arrived, nor know I aught
    But that he's well and will be shortly here.
Desdemona: O but I fear. How lost you company?
Cassio: The great contention of sea and skies
    Parted our fellowship. (*Within*) A sail, a sail!
    (*A shot.*)
                    But hark. A sail!
Second Gentleman: They give this greeting to the citadel;
    This likewise is a friend.
Cassio: See for the news.   (*Exit* **Gentleman.**)
    Good ancient, you are welcome. (*To* **Emilia**) Welcome, mistress.
    Let it not gall your patience, good Iago,
    That I extend° my manners. 'Tis my breeding°
    That gives me this bold show of courtesy.   (*Kisses* **Emilia.**)
Iago: Sir, would she give you so much of her lips
    As of her tongue she oft bestows on me,
    You would have enough.

guttered jagged
congregated gathered
ensteeped submerged
sense awareness
mortal deadly
footing landing
se'nnight's week's

tall brave
extend stretch
breeding careful training in manners
(Cassio is considerably more the polished gentleman than Iago, and aware of it)

Desdemona: Alas, she has no speech.

Iago: In faith, too much.

I find it still when I have leave to sleep.°
Marry, before your ladyship,° I grant,
She puts her tongue a little in her heart
And chides with thinking.

Emilia: You have little cause to say so.

Iago: Come on, come on! You are pictures° out of door,
Bells in your parlors, wildcats in your kitchens,
Saints in your injuries,° devils being offended,
Players in your housewifery,° and housewives in your beds.

Desdemona: O, fie upon thee, slanderer!

Iago: Nay, it is true, or else I am a Turk:
You rise to play, and go to bed to work.

Emilia: You shall not write my praise.

Iago: No, let me not.

Desdemona: What wouldst write of me, if thou shouldst praise me?

Iago: O gentle lady, do not put me to't,
For I am nothing if not critical.

Desdemona: Come on, assay. There's one gone to the harbor?

Iago: Ay, madam.

Desdemona: (*Aside*) I am not merry; but I do beguile
The thing I am by seeming otherwise.—
Come, how wouldst thou praise me?

Iago: I am about it; but indeed my invention
Comes from my pate as birdlime° does from frieze°—
It plucks out brains and all. But my Muse labors,
And thus she is delivered:
If she be fair° and wise: fairness and wit,
The one's for use, the other useth it.

Desdemona: Well praised. How if she be black° and witty?

Iago: If she be black, and thereto have a wit,
She'll find a white that shall her blackness fit.

Desdemona: Worse and worse!

Emilia: How if fair and foolish?

Iago: She never yet was foolish that was fair,
For even her folly helped her to an heir.

Desdemona: These are old fond° paradoxes to make fools laugh i' th' ale-house. What miserable praise hast thou for her that's foul and foolish?

---

still . . . sleep i.e., even when she allows me to sleep she continues to scold
before your ladyship in your presence
pictures models (of virtue)
in your injuries when you injure others
housewifery (this word can mean "careful, economical household management," and Iago would then be accusing women of only pretending to be good housekeepers, while in bed they are either [1] economical of their favors, or more likely [2] serious and dedicated workers)
birdlime a sticky substance put on branches to catch birds
frieze rough cloth
fair light-complexioned
black brunette
fond foolish

Iago: There's none so foul, and foolish thereunto,
But does foul pranks which fair and wise ones do.

Desdemona: O heavy ignorance. Thou praisest the worst best. But what praise
couldst thou bestow on a deserving woman indeed—one that in the authority
of her merit did justly put on the vouch of very malice itself?°

Iago: She that was ever fair, and never proud;
Had tongue at will, and yet was never loud;
Never lacked gold, and yet went never gay;
Fled from her wish, and yet said "Now I may";
She that being angered, her revenge being nigh,
Bade her wrong stay, and her displeasure fly;
She that in wisdom never was so frail
To change the cod's head for the salmon's tail;°
She that could think, and nev'r disclose her mind;
See suitors following, and not look behind:
She was a wight° (if ever such wights were)——

Desdemona: To do what?

Iago: To suckle fools and chronicle small beer.°

Desdemona: O most lame and impotent conclusion. Do not learn of him,
Emilia, though he be thy husband. How say you, Cassio? Is he not a most
profane and liberal° counselor?

Cassio: He speaks home,° madam. You may relish him more in° the soldier
than in the scholar. (*Takes* **Desdemona's** *hand.*)

*Visual irony:
Iago will use this
courtesy to imply
romantic interest.*
Iago: (*Aside*) He takes her by the palm. Ay, well said, whisper! With as little
a web as this will I ensnare as great a fly as Cassio. Ay, smile upon her, do!
I will gyve° thee in thine own courtship.—You say true; 'tis so, indeed!—If
such tricks as these strip you out of your lieutenantry, it had been better you
had not kissed your three fingers so oft—which now again you are most apt
to play the sir° in. Very good! Well kissed! An excellent curtsy!° 'Tis so
indeed. Yet again your fingers to your lips? Would they were clyster pipes°
for your sake! (*Trumpets within.*) The Moor! I know his trumpet.°

Cassio: 'Tis truly so.

Desdemona: Let's meet him and receive him.

Cassio: Lo, where he comes.

(*Enter* **Othello** *and* **Attendants**.)

Othello: O my fair warrior!

Desdemona: My dear Othello.

Othello: It gives me wonder great as my content
To see you here before me. O my soul's joy!

---

one . . . itself i.e., a woman so honest
and deserving that even malice would be
forced to approve of her
To . . . tail i.e., to exchange something
valuable for something useless
wight person
chronicle small beer i.e., keep household accounts (the most trivial of occupations in Iago's opinion)
liberal licentious

speaks home thrusts deeply with his
speech
relish him more in enjoy him more as
gyve bind
the sir the fashionable gentleman
curtsy courtesy, i.e., bow
clyster pipes enema tubes
his trumpet (great men had their own
distinctive calls)

If after every tempest come such calms,
May the winds blow till they have wakened death.
And let the laboring bark climb hills of seas
Olympus-high, and duck again as low
As hell's from heaven. If it were now to die,
'Twere now to be most happy; for I fear
My soul hath her content so absolute
That not another comfort like to this
Succeeds in unknown fate.

Desdemona: The heavens forbid
But that our loves and comforts should increase
Even as our days do grow.

Othello: Amen to that, sweet powers!
I cannot speak enough of this content;
It stops me here (*touches his heart*); it is too much of joy.
And this, and this, the greatest discords be (*They kiss.*)
That e'er our hearts shall make!

Iago: (*Aside*) O, you are well tuned now!
But I'll set down the pegs° that make this music,
As honest as I am.

Othello: Come, let us to the castle.
News, friends! Our wars are done; the Turks are drowned.
How does my old acquaintance of this isle?
Honey, you shall be well desired in Cyprus;
I have found great love amongst them. O my sweet,
I prattle out of fashion, and I dote
In mine own comforts. I prithee, good Iago,
Go to the bay and disembark my coffers.
Bring thou the master to the citadel;
He is a good one, and his worthiness
Does challenge° much respect. Come, Desdemona,
Once more well met at Cyprus.

(*Exit* **Othello** *and* **Desdemona** *and all but* **Iago** *and* **Roderigo**.)

Iago: (*To an* **Attendant**) Do thou meet me presently at the harbor. (*To* **Roderigo**) Come hither. If thou be'st valiant (as they say base men being in love have then a nobility in their natures more than is native to them), list me. The lieutenant tonight watches on the court of guard.° First, I must tell thee this: Desdemona is directly in love with him.

Roderigo: With him? Why, 'tis not possible.

Iago: Lay thy finger thus (*puts his finger to his lips*), and let thy soul be instructed. Mark me with what violence she first loved the Moor but for bragging and telling her fantastical lies. To love him still for prating? Let not thy discreet heart think it. Her eye must be fed. And what delight shall she have to look on the devil? When the blood is made dull with the act of sport, there should be a game° to inflame it and to give satiety a fresh appetite, loveliness in

Structural irony: After the storm, Othello and Desdemona feel safe in Cyprus not knowing the storm Iago will thrust them into.

---

set down the pegs loosen the strings (to produce discord)
challenge require, exact

court of guard guardhouse
game sport (with the added sense of "gamey," "rank")

favor,° sympathy in years,° manners, and beauties; all which the Moor is defective in. Now for want of these required conveniences,° her delicate tenderness will find itself abused, begin to heave the gorge,° disrelish and abhor the Moor. Very nature will instruct her in it and compel her to some second choice. Now, sir, this granted—as it is a most pregnant° and unforced position—who stands so eminent in the degree of this fortune as Cassio does? A knave very voluble; no further conscionable° than in putting on the mere form of civil and humane° seeming for the better compass of his salt° and most hidden loose° affection. Why, none! Why, none! A slipper° and subtle knave, a finder of occasion, that has an eye can stamp and counterfeit advantages, though true advantage never present itself. A devilish knave. Besides, the knave is handsome, young, and hath all those requisites in him that folly and green minds look after. A pestilent complete knave, and the woman hath found him already.

Roderigo: I cannot believe that in her; she's full of most blessed condition.

Iago: Blessed fig's-end! The wine she drinks is made of grapes. If she had been blessed, she would never have loved the Moor. Blessed pudding! Didst thou not see her paddle with the palm of his hand? Didst not mark that?

Roderigo: Yes, that I did; but that was but courtesy.

Iago: Lechery, by this hand! (*Extends his index finger.*) An index° and obscure prologue to the history of lust and foul thoughts. They met so near with their lips that their breaths embraced together. Villainous thoughts, Roderigo. When these mutualities so marshal the way, hard at hand comes the master and main exercise, th' incorporate° conclusion: Pish! But, sir, be you ruled by me. I have brought you from Venice. Watch you tonight; for the command, I'll lay't upon you. Cassio knows you not. I'll not be far from you. Do you find some occasion to anger Cassio, either by speaking too loud, or tainting° his discipline, or from what other course you please which the time shall more favorably minister.

Roderigo: Well.

Iago: Sir, he's rash and very sudden in choler,° and haply may strike at you. Provoke him that he may; for even out of that will I cause these of Cyprus to mutiny, whose qualification shall come into no true taste° again but by the displanting of Cassio. So shall you have a shorter journey to your desires by the means I shall then have to prefer them; and the impediment most profitably removed without the which there were no expectation of our prosperity.

Roderigo: I will do this if you can bring it to any opportunity.

Iago: I warrant thee. Meet me by and by at the citadel. I must fetch his necessaries ashore. Farewell.

---

favor countenance, appearance
sympathy in years sameness of age
conveniences advantages
heave the gorge vomit
pregnant likely
no further conscionable having no more conscience
humane polite
salt lecherous

loose immoral
slipper slippery
index pointer
incorporate carnal
tainting discrediting
choler anger
qualification . . . taste i.e., appeasement will not be brought about (wine was "qualified" by adding water)

Roderigo: Adieu.   (*Exit.*)
Iago: That Cassio loves her, I do well believe 't;
That she loves him, 'tis apt and of great credit.
The Moor, howbeit that I endure him not,
Is of a constant, loving, noble nature,
And I dare think he'll prove to Desdemona
A most dear° husband. Now I do love her too;
Not out of absolute° lust, though peradventure°
I stand accountant for as great a sin,
But partly led to diet° my revenge,
For that I do suspect the lusty Moor
Hath leaped into my seat; the thought whereof
Doth, like a poisonous mineral, gnaw my inwards;
And nothing can or shall content my soul
Till I am evened with him, wife for wife.
Or failing so, yet that I put the Moor
At least into a jealousy so strong
That judgment cannot cure. Which thing to do,
If this poor trash of Venice, whom I trace°
For his quick hunting, stand the putting on,
I'll have our Michael Cassio on the hip,
Abuse him to the Moor in the right garb°
(For I fear Cassio with my nightcap too),
Make the Moor thank me, love me, and reward me
For making him egregiously an ass
And practicing upon° his peace and quiet,
Even to madness. 'Tis here, but yet confused:
Knavery's plain face is never seen till used.   (*Exit.*)

SCENE II.   A street.

(*Enter **Othello's Herald**, with a proclamation.*)
Herald: It is Othello's pleasure, our noble and valiant general, that upon certain tidings now arrived importing the mere perdition° of the Turkish fleet, every man put himself into triumph. Some to dance, some to make bonfires, each man to what sport and revels his addition° leads him. For, besides these beneficial news, it is the celebration of his nuptial. So much was his pleasure should be proclaimed. All offices° are open, and there is full liberty of feasting from this present hour of five till the bell have told eleven. Bless the isle of Cyprus and our noble general Othello!   (*Exit.*)

---

dear   expensive
out of absolute   absolutely out of
peradventure   perchance
diet   feed
trace   (most editors amend to "trash," meaning to hang weights on a dog to slow his hunting; but "trace" clearly means

something like "put on the trace" or "set on the track")
right garb   i.e., "proper fashion"
practicing upon   scheming to destroy
mere perdition   absolute destruction
addition   rank
offices   kitchens and storerooms of food

SCENE III.   The citadel of Cyprus.

(*Enter* **Othello, Desdemona, Cassio,** *and* **Attendants**.)
Othello: Good Michael, look you to the guard tonight.
Let's teach ourselves that honorable stop,
Not to outsport discretion.
Cassio: Iago hath direction what to do;
But notwithstanding, with my personal eye
Will I look to't.
Othello: Iago is most honest.
Michael, good night. Tomorrow with your earliest
Let me have speech with you. (*To* **Desdemona**)
Come, my dear love,
The purchase made, the fruits are to ensue,
That profit's yet to come 'tween me and you.
Good night.
(*Exit* **Othello** *with* **Desdemona** *and* **Attendants**. *Enter* **Iago**.)
Cassio: Welcome, Iago. We must to the watch.
Iago: Not this hour, lieutenant; 'tis not yet ten o' th' clock. Our general cast°
us thus early for the love of his Desdemona; who let us not therefore blame.
He hath not yet made wanton the night with her, and she is sport for Jove.
Cassio: She's a most exquisite lady.
Iago: And, I'll warrant her, full of game.
Cassio: Indeed, she's a most fresh and delicate creature.
Iago: What an eye she has! Methinks it sounds a parley to provocation.
Cassio: An inviting eye; and yet methinks right modest.
Iago: And when she speaks, is it not an alarum° to love?
Cassio: She is indeed perfection.
Iago: Well, happiness to their sheets! Come, lieutenant, I have a stoup° of
wine, and here without are a brace of Cyprus gallants that would fain have a
measure to the health of black Othello.
Cassio: Not tonight, good Iago. I have very poor and unhappy brains for
drinking; I could well wish courtesy would invent some other custom of
entertainment.
Iago: O, they are our friends. But one cup! I'll drink for you.
Cassio: I have drunk but one cup tonight, and that was craftily qualified° too;
and behold what innovation it makes here. I am unfortunate in the infirmity
and dare not task my weakness with any more.
Iago: What, man! 'Tis a night of revels, the gallants desire it.
Cassio: Where are they?
Iago: Here, at the door. I pray you call them in.
Cassio: I'll do't, but it dislikes me.   (*Exit.*)
Iago: If I can fasten but one cup upon him
With that which he hath drunk tonight already,
He'll be as full of quarrel and offense

---

cast dismissed
alarum the call to action, "general
quarters"

stoup two-quart tankard
qualified diluted

As my young mistress' dog. Now, my sick fool Roderigo,
Whom love hath turned almost the wrong side out,
To Desdemona hath tonight caroused
Potations pottle-deep;° and he's to watch.
Three else° of Cyprus, noble swelling spirits,
That hold their honors in a wary distance,°
The very elements of this warlike isle,
Have I tonight flustered with flowing cups,
And they watch too. Now, 'mongst this flock of drunkards
Am I to put our Cassio in some action
That may offend the isle. But here they come.
(*Enter* **Cassio, Montano,** *and* **Gentlemen.**)
If consequence do but approve my dream,
My boat sails freely, both with wind and stream.

Cassio: Fore God, they have given me a rouse° already.

Montano: Good faith, a little one; not past a pint, as I am a soldier.

Iago: Some wine, ho!
(*Sings*) And let me the canakin clink, clink;
      And let me the canakin clink.
      A soldier's a man;
      O man's life's but a span,
      Why then, let a soldier drink.
Some wine, boys!

Cassio: 'Fore God, an excellent song!

Iago: I learned it in England, where indeed they are most potent in potting.
Your Dane, your German, and your swag-bellied° Hollander—Drink, ho!—
are nothing to your English.

Cassio: Is your Englishman so exquisite° in his drinking?

Iago: Why, he drinks you with facility your Dane dead drunk; he sweats not
to overthrow your Almain; he gives your Hollander a vomit ere the next
pottle can be filled.

Cassio: To the health of our general!

Montano: I am for it, lieutenant, and I'll do you justice.

Iago: O sweet England!
(*Sings*) King Stephen was and a worthy peer;
      His breeches cost him but a crown;
      He held them sixpence all too dear,
      With that he called the tailor lown.°
      He was a wight of high renown,
      And thou art but of low degree:
      'Tis pride that pulls the country down;
      And take thine auld cloak about thee.
Some wine, ho!

Cassio: 'Fore God, this is more exquisite song than the other.

---

pottle-deep to the bottom of the cup
else others
hold . . . distance are scrupulous in
maintaining their honor

rouse drink
swag-bellied hanging
exquisite superb
lown lout

Iago: Will you hear't again?

Cassio: No, for I hold him to be unworthy of his place that does those things. Well, God's above all; and there be souls must be saved, and there be souls must not be saved.

Iago: It's true, good lieutenant.

Cassio: For mine own part—no offense to the general, nor any man of quality— I hope to be saved.

Iago: And so do I too, lieutenant.

Cassio: Ay, but, by your leave, not before me. The lieutenant is to be saved before the ancient. Let's have no more of this; let's to our affairs.—God forgive us our sins!—Gentlemen, let's look to our business. Do not think, gentlemen, I am drunk. This is my ancient; this is my right hand, and this is my left. I am not drunk now. I can stand well enough, and I speak well enough.

Gentlemen: Excellent well!

Cassio: Why, very well then. You must not think then that I am drunk. (*Exit.*)

Montano: To th' platform, masters. Come, let's set the watch.

Iago: You see this fellow that is gone before.
He's a soldier fit to stand by Caesar
And give direction; and do but see his vice.
'Tis to his virtue a just equinox,°
The one as long as th' other. 'Tis pity of him.
I fear the trust Othello puts him in,
On some odd time of his infirmity,
Will shake this island.

Montano: But is he often thus?

Iago: 'Tis evermore his prologue to his sleep:
He'll watch the horologe a double set°
If drink rock not his cradle.

Montano.   It were well
The general were put in mind of it.
Perhaps he sees it not, or his good nature
Prizes the virtue that appears in Cassio
And looks not on his evils. Is not this true?
(*Enter* **Roderigo**.)

Iago: (*Aside*) How now, Roderigo?
I pray you after the lieutenant, go!   (*Exit* **Roderigo**.)

Montano: And 'tis great pity that the noble Moor
Should hazard such a place as his own second
With one of an ingraft° infirmity.
It were an honest action to say so
To the Moor.

Iago: Not I, for this fair island!
I do love Cassio well and would do much

---

just equinox   exact balance (of dark and light)
watch . . . set   stay awake twice around
the clock
ingraft   ingrained

To cure him of this evil. (Help! Help! *Within.*)
                 But hark? What noise?

(*Enter* **Cassio**, *pursuing* **Roderigo**.)

Cassio: Zounds, you rogue! You rascal!

Montano: What's the matter, lieutenant?

Cassio: A knave teach me my duty? I'll beat the knave into a twiggen° bottle.

Roderigo: Beat me?

Cassio: Dost thou prate, rogue?   (*Strikes him.*)

Montano: Nay, good lieutenant! I pray you, sir, hold your hand.   (*Stays him.*)

Cassio: Let me go, sir, or I'll knock you o'er the mazzard.°

Montano: Come, come, you're drunk!

Cassio: Drunk?   (*They fight.*)

Iago: (*Aside to* **Roderigo**) Away, I say! Go out and cry a mutiny!   (*Exit* **Roderigo**.)
    Nay, good lieutenant. God's will, gentlemen!
    Help, ho! Lieutenant. Sir. Montano.
    Help, masters! Here's a goodly watch indeed!   (*A bell rung.*)
    Who's that which rings the bell? Diablo, ho!
    The town will rise. God's will, lieutenant,
    You'll be ashamed forever.

(*Enter* **Othello** *and* **Attendants**.)

Othello: What is the matter here?

Montano: Zounds, I bleed still. I am hurt to the death. He dies.   (*He and* **Cassio** *fight again.*)

Othello: Hold for your lives!

Iago: Hold, ho! Lieutenant. Sir. Montano. Gentlemen!
    Have you forgot all place of sense and duty?
    Hold! The general speaks to you. Hold, for shame!

Othello: Why, how now, ho? From whence ariseth this?
    Are we turned Turks, and to ourselves do that
    Which heaven hath forbid the Ottomites?°
    For Christian shame put by this barbarous brawl!
    He that stirs next to carve for his own rage
    Holds his soul light;° he dies upon his motion.
    Silence that dreadful bell! It frights the isle
    From her propriety.° What is the matter, masters?
    Honest Iago, that looks dead with grieving,
    Speak. Who began this? On thy love, I charge thee.

Iago: I do not know. Friends all, but now, even now,
    In quarter° and in terms like bride and groom
    Devesting them for bed; and then, but now—
    As if some planet had unwitted men—
    Swords out, and tilting one at the other's breasts

*Structural irony:
Compare Cassio's
attitude on p. 384
(I have drunk...
more).*

Verbal irony

twiggen wicker-covered
mazzard head
heaven . . . Ottomites i.e., by sending
the storm which dispersed the Turks

Holds his soul light values his soul
lightly
propriety proper order
In quarter on duty

In opposition bloody. I cannot speak
Any beginning to this peevish odds,°
And would in action glorious I had lost
Those legs that brought me to a part of it!
Othello: How comes it, Michael, you are thus forgot?
Cassio: I pray you pardon me; I cannot speak.
Othello: Worthy Montano, you were wont to be civil;
The gravity and stillness of your youth
The world hath noted, and your name is great
In mouths of the wisest censure.° What's the matter
That you unlace° your reputation thus
And spend your rich opinion° for the name
Of a night-brawler? Give me answer to it.
Montano: Worthy Othello, I am hurt to danger.
Your officer, Iago, can inform you,
While I spare speech, which something now offends° me,
Of all that I do know; nor know I aught
By me that's said or done amiss this night,
Unless self-charity be sometimes a vice,
And to defend ourselves it be a sin
When violence assails us.
Othello: Now, by heaven,
My blood begins my safer guides to rule,
And passion, having my best judgment collied,°
Assays to lead the way. If I once stir
Or do but lift this arm, the best of you
Shall sink in my rebuke. Give me to know
How this foul rout began, who set it on;
And he that is approved in this offense,
Though he had twinned with me, both at a birth,
Shall lose me. What? In a town of war
Yet wild, the people's hearts brimful of fear,
To manage° private and domestic quarrel?
In night, and on the court and guard of safety?
'Tis monstrous. Iago, who began't?
Montano: If partially affined, or leagued in office,°
Thou dost deliver more or less than truth,
Thou art no soldier.
Iago: Touch me not so near.
I had rather have this tongue cut from my mouth
Than it should do offense to Michael Cassio.
Yet I persuade myself to speak the truth
Shall nothing wrong him. This it is, general.

Iago can't "do offense" to Cassio but tries to ruin him. How is Othello's reaction ironic?

odds quarrel
censure judgment
unlace undo (the term refers specifically to the dressing of a wild boar killed in the hunt)
opinion reputation

offends harms, hurts
collied darkened
manage conduct
If . . . office if you are partial because you are related ("affined") or the brother officer (of Cassio)

Montano and myself being in speech,
There comes a fellow crying out for help,
And Cassio following him with determined sword
To execute upon him. Sir, this gentleman
Steps in to Cassio and entreats his pause.
Myself the crying fellow did pursue,
Lest by his clamor—as it so fell out—
The town might fall in fright. He, swift of foot,
Outran my purpose; and I returned then rather
For that I heard the clink and fall of swords,
And Cassio high in oath; which till tonight
I ne'er might say before. When I came back—
For this was brief—I found them close together
At blow and thrust, even as again they were
When you yourself did part them.
More of this matter cannot I report;
But men are men; the best sometimes forget.
Though Cassio did some little wrong to him,
As men in rage strike those that wish them best,
Yet surely Cassio I believe received
From him that fled some strange indignity,
Which patience could not pass.°
Othello: I know, Iago,
Thy honesty and love doth mince° this matter,
Making it light to Cassio. Cassio, I love thee;
But never more be officer of mine.
(*Enter* **Desdemona**, *attended.*)
Look if my gentle love be not raised up.
I'll make thee an example.
Desdemona: What is the matter, dear.
Othello: All's well, sweeting; come away to bed.
(*To* **Montano**) Sir, for your hurts, myself will be your surgeon.
Lead him off.   (**Montano** *led off.*)
Iago, look with care about the town
And silence those whom this vile brawl distracted.
Come, Desdemona: 'tis the soldiers' life
To have their balmy slumbers waked with strife.
(*Exit with all but* **Iago** *and* **Cassio**.)
Iago: What, are you hurt, lieutenant?
Cassio: Ay, past all surgery.
Iago: Marry, God forbid!
Cassio: Reputation, reputation, reputation! O, I have lost my reputation! I
have lost my reputation! I have lost the immortal part of myself, and what
remains is bestial. My reputation, Iago, my reputation.
Iago: As I am an honest man, I had thought you had received some bodily
wound. There is more sense° in that than in reputation. Reputation is an idle

---

pass allow to pass   **sense** physical feeling
mince cut up (i.e., tell only part of)

and most false imposition,° oft got without merit and lost without deserving. You have lost no reputation at all unless you repute yourself such a loser. What, man, there are more ways to recover the general again. You are but now cast in his mood°—a punishment more in policy° than in malice—even so as one would beat his offenseless dog to affright an imperious lion. Sue to him again, and he's yours.

Cassio: I will rather sue to be despised than to deceive so good a commander with so slight, so drunken, and so indiscreet an officer. Drunk! And speak parrot!° And squabble! Swagger! Swear! and discourse fustian° with one's own shadow! O thou invisible spirit of wine, if thou hast no name to be known by, let us call thee devil!

The devil isn't invisible or in the wine but stands before him.

Iago: What was he that you followed with your sword? What had he done to you?

Cassio: I know not.

Iago: Is't possible?

Cassio: I remember a mass of things, but nothing distinctly: a quarrel, but nothing wherefore. O God, that men should put an enemy in their mouths to steal away their brains! that we should with joy, pleasance, revel, and applause transform ourselves into beasts!

Iago: Why, but you are now well enough. How came you thus recovered?

Cassio: It hath pleased the devil drunkenness to give place to the devil wrath. One unperfectness shows me another, to make me frankly despise myself.

Iago: Come, you are too severe a moraler. As the time, the place, and the condition of this country stands, I could heartily wish this had not befall'n; but since it is as it is, mend it for your own good.

Cassio: I will ask him for my place again: he shall tell me I am a drunkard. Had I as many mouths as Hydra, such an answer would stop them all. To be now a sensible man, by and by a fool, and presently a beast! O strange! Every inordinate cup is unblest, and the ingredient is a devil.

Iago: Come, come, good wine is a good familiar creature if it be well used. Exclaim no more against it. And, good lieutenant, I think you think I love you.

Cassio: I have well approved it, sir. I drunk?

Iago: You or any man living may be drunk at a time, man. I tell you what you shall do. Our general's wife is now the general. I may say so in this respect, for that he hath devoted and given up himself to the contemplation, mark, and devotement of her parts° and graces. Confess yourself freely to her; importune her help to put you in your place again. She is of so free, so kind, so apt, so blessed a disposition she holds it a vice in her goodness not to do more than she is requested. This broken joint between you and her husband entreat her to splinter;° and my fortunes against any lay° worth naming, this crack of your love shall grow stronger than it was before.

Cassio: You advise me well.

imposition external thing
cast in his mood dismissed because of his anger
in policy politically necessary
speak parrot gabble without sense
discourse fustian speak nonsense ("fus-

tian" was a coarse cotton cloth used for stuffing)
devotement of her parts devotion to her qualities
splinter splint
lay wager

Iago: I protest, in the sincerity of love and honest kindness.

Cassio: I think it freely; and betimes in the morning I will beseech the virtuous
Desdemona to undertake for me. I am desperate of my fortunes if they
check° me.

Iago: You are in the right. Good night, lieutenant; I must to the watch.

Cassio: Good night, honest Iago.   (*Exit* **Cassio**.)

Iago: And what's he then that says I play the villain,
When this advice is free° I give, and honest,
Probal to° thinking, and indeed the course
To win the Moor again? For 'tis most easy
Th' inclining° Desdemona to subdue
In any honest suit; she's framed as fruitful°
As the free elements.° And then for her
To win the Moor—were't to renounce his baptism,
All seals and symbols of redeemèd sin—
His soul is so enfettered to her love
That she may make, unmake, do what she list,
Even as her appetite° shall play the god
With his weak function.° How am I then a villain
To counsel Cassio to his parallel course,
Directly to his good? Divinity of hell!
When devils will the blackest sins put on,°
They do suggest at first with heavenly shows,°
As I do now. For whiles this honest fool
Plies Desdemona to repair his fortune,
And she for him pleads strongly to the Moor,
I'll pour this pestilence into his ear:
That she repeals him° for her body's lust;
And by how much she strives to do him good,
She shall undo her credit with the Moor.
So will I turn her virtue into pitch,
And out of her own goodness make the net
That shall enmesh them all. How now, Roderigo?

(*Enter* **Roderigo**.)

Roderigo: I do follow here in the chase, not like a hound that hunts, but one
that fills up the cry.° My money is almost spent; I have been tonight exceedingly well cudgeled; and I think the issue will be, I shall have so much experience for my pains; and so, with no money at all, and a little more wit,
return again to Venice.

Iago: How poor are they that have not patience!
What wound did ever heal but by degrees?

check repulse
free generous and open
Probal to provable by
inclining inclined (to be helpful)
framed as fruitful made as generous
elements i.e., basic nature
appetite liking
function thought

put on advance, further
shows appearances
repeals him asks for (Cassio's reinstate-
ment)
fills up the cry makes up one of the
hunting pack, adding to the noise but not
actually tracking

Thou know'st we work by wit, and not by witchcraft;
And wit depends on dilatory time.
Does't not go well? Cassio hath beaten thee,
And thou by that small hurt hath cashiered Cassio.
Though other things grow fair against the sun,
Yet fruits that blossom first will first be ripe.
Content thyself awhile. By the mass, 'tis morning!
Pleasure and action make the hours seem short.
Retire thee; go where thou art billeted.
Away, I say! Thou shalt know more hereafter.
Nay, get thee gone!   (*Exit* **Roderigo**.)
                                Two things are to be done:

What does Iago (ironist) know that victims do not? (Basis for dramatic irony of the play)

My wife must move° for Cassio to her mistress;
I'll set her on;
Myself awhile° to draw the Moor apart
And bring him jump° when he may Cassio find
Soliciting his wife. Ay, that's the way!
Dull not device by coldness and delay.   (*Exit.*)

ACT III

SCENE I.   A street.

(*Enter* **Cassio** *and* **Musicians**.)
Cassio: Masters, play here. I will content your pains.°
    Something that's brief; and bid "Good morrow,
    general."   (*They play.*)
(*Enter* **Clown**.°)
Clown: Why, masters, have your instruments been in
    Naples° that they speak i' th' nose thus?
Musician: How, sir, how?
Clown: Are these, I pray you, wind instruments?
Musician: Ay, marry, are they, sir.
Clown: O, thereby hangs a tale.
Musician: Whereby hangs a tale, sir?
Clown: Marry, sir, by many a wind instrument that I know. But, masters,
    here's money for you; and the general so likes your music that he desires
    you, for love's sake, to make no more noise with it.
Musician: Well, sir, we will not.
Clown: If you have any music that may not be heard, to't again. But, as they
    say, to hear music the general does not greatly care.
Musician: We have none such, sir.

move petition	**Clown** fool
awhile at the same time	**Naples** (this may refer either to the Nea-
jump at the precise moment and place	politan nasal tone, or to syphilis—rife in
content your pains reward your efforts	Naples—which breaks down the nose)

Clown: Then put up your pipes in your bag, for I'll away. Go, vanish into air, away!   (*Exit* **Musicians**.)

Cassio: Dost thou hear me, mine honest friend?

Clown: No. I hear not your honest friend. I hear you.

Cassio: Prithee keep up thy quillets.° There's a poor piece of gold for thee. If the gentlewoman that attends the general's wife be stirring, tell her there's one Cassio entreats her a little favor of speech. Wilt thou do this?

Clown: She is stirring, sir. If she will stir hither, I shall seem to notify unto her.°   (*Exit* **Clown**.)

(*Enter* **Iago**.)

Cassio: In happy time, Iago.

Iago: You have not been abed then?

Cassio: Why no, the day had broke before we parted.
I have made bold, Iago, to send in to your wife;
My suit to her is that she will to virtuous Desdemona
Procure me some access.

Iago: I'll send her to you presently.
And I'll devise a mean to draw the Moor
Out of the way, that your converse and business
May be more free.

Cassio: I humbly thank you for't.   (*Exit* **Iago**)
                    I never knew
A Florentine° more kind and honest.

(*Enter* **Emilia**.)

Emilia: Good morrow, good lieutenant. I am sorry
For your displeasure;° but all will sure be well.
The general and his wife are talking of it,
And she speaks for you stoutly. The Moor replies
That he you hurt is of great fame in Cyprus
And great affinity,° and that in wholesome wisdom
He might not but refuse you. But he protests he loves you,
And needs no other suitor but his likings
To bring you in again.

Cassio: Yet I beseech you,
If you think fit, or that it may be done,
Give me advantage of some brief discourse
With Desdemona alone.

Emilia: Pray you come in.
I will bestow you where you shall have time
To speak your bosom° freely.

Cassio: I am much bound to you.

(*Exeunt*.)

Compare Cassio's trust in Iago with what we know is true. Parallel with Othello/Iago relationship?

---

quillets puns
seem . . . her (the Clown is mocking Cassio's overly elegant manner of speaking)
Florentine i.e., Iago is as kind as if he

were from Cassio's home town, Florence
displeasure discomforting
affinity family
bosom inmost thoughts

SCENE II.   The citadel.

(*Enter* **Othello**, **Iago**, *and* **Gentlemen**.)
Othello: These letters give, Iago, to the pilot
   And by him do my duties to the Senate.
   That done, I will be walking on the works;
   Repair° there to me.
Iago: Well, my good lord, I'll do't.
Othello: This fortification, gentlemen, shall we see't?
Gentlemen: We'll wait upon your lordship.
   (*Exeunt*.)

SCENE III.   The citadel.

(*Enter* **Desdemona**, **Cassio**, *and* **Emilia**.)
Desdemona: Be thou assured, good Cassio, I will do
   All my abilities in thy behalf.

Emilia and **Emilia:** Good madam, do. I warrant it grieves my husband
Desdemona are   As if the cause were his.
both taken in. **Desdemona:** O, that's an honest fellow. Do not doubt, Cassio,
   But I will have my lord and you again
   As friendly as you were.
Cassio: Bounteous madam,
   Whatever shall become of Michael Cassio,
   He's never anything but your true servant.
Desdemona: I know't; I thank you. You do love my lord.
   You have known him long, and be you well assured
   He shall in strangeness stand no farther off
   Than in a politic distance.°
Cassio: Ay, but, lady,
   That policy may either last so long,
   Or feed upon such nice° and waterish diet,
   Or breed itself so out of circumstances,°
   That, I being absent, and my place supplied,°
   My general will forget my love and service.
Desdemona: Do not doubt° that; before Emilia here
   I give thee warrant of thy place. Assure thee,
   If I do vow a friendship, I'll perform it
   To the last article. My lord shall never rest;
   I'll watch him tame° and talk him out of patience;
   His bed shall seem a school, his board a shrift;°

Repair go
He . . . distance i.e., he shall act no
more distant to you than is necessary for
political reasons
nice trivial
Or . . . circumstances i.e., or grow so
on the basis of accidental happenings
and political needs
supplied filled
doubt imagine
watch him tame (animals were tamed
by being kept awake)
board a shrift table (seem) a confessional

I'll intermingle everything he does
With Cassio's suit. Therefore be merry, Cassio,
For thy solicitor shall rather die
Than give thy cause away.
(*Enter* **Othello** *and* **Iago** *at a distance.*)
Emilia: Madam, here comes my lord.
Cassio: Madam, I'll take my leave.
Desdemona: Why, stay, and hear me speak.
Cassio: Madam, not now. I am very ill at ease,
Unfit for mine own purposes.
Desdemona: Well, do your discretion.   (*Exit* **Cassio**.)
Iago: Ha! I like not that.
Othello: What dost thou say?
Iago: Nothing, my lord; or if—I know not what.
Othello: Was not that Cassio parted from my wife?
Iago: Cassio, my lord? No, sure, I cannot think it
That he would steal away so guilty-like,
Seeing your coming.
Othello: I do believe 'twas he.
Desdemona: (*Coming to them*) How now, my lord?
I have been talking with a suitor here,
A man that languishes in your displeasure.
Othello: Who is't you mean?
Desdemona: Why, your lieutenant, Cassio. Good my lord,
If I have any grace or power to move you,
His present° reconciliation take.
For if he be not one that truly loves you,
That errs in ignorance, and not in cunning,
I have no judgment in an honest face.
I prithee call him back.
Othello: Went he hence now?
Desdemona: I' sooth so humbled
That he hath left part of his grief with me
To suffer with him. Good love, call him back.
Othello: Not now, sweet Desdemon; some other time.
Desdemona: But shall't be shortly?
Othello: The sooner, sweet, for you.
Desdemona: Shall't be tonight at supper?
Othello: No, not tonight.
Desdemona: Tomorrow dinner then?
Othello: I shall not dine at home;
I meet the captains at the citadel.
Desdemona: Why then, tomorrow night, on Tuesday morn,
On Tuesday noon, or night, on Wednesday morn.
I prithee name the time, but let it not
Exceed three days. In faith, he's penitent;
And yet his trespass, in our common reason

present immediate

*Structural irony:
compare Iago's
plan, p. 392. (My
wife must move...)*

*Compare to
Desdemona's lines,
p. 394 (Do not
doubt that...).
Verbal irony in
Iago's lines through-
out this scene?*

(Save that, they say, the wars must make example
Out of her best) is not almost a fault
T' incur a private check.° When shall he come?
Tell me, Othello, I wonder in my soul
What you would ask me that I should deny
Or stand so mamm'ring° on. What? Michael Cassio,
That came awooing with you, and so many a time,
When I have spoke of you dispraisingly,
Hath ta'en your part—to have so much to do
To bring him in? By'r Lady, I could do much——

Othello: Prithee no more. Let him come when he will!
I will deny thee nothing.

Desdemona: Why, this is not a boon;
'Tis as I should entreat you wear your gloves,
Or feed on nourishing dishes, or keep you warm,
Or sue to you to do a peculiar profit°
To your own person. Nay, when I have a suit
Wherein I mean to touch your love indeed,
It shall be full of poise° and difficult weight,
And fearful to be granted.

Othello: I will deny thee nothing!
Whereon I do beseech thee grant me this,
To leave me but a little to myself.

Desdemona: Shall I deny you? No. Farewell, my lord.

Othello: Farewell, my Desdemona: I'll come to thee straight.°

Desdemona: Emilia, come. Be as your fancies teach you;
Whate'er you be, I am obedient.   (*Exit with* **Emilia**.)

Othello: Excellent wretch! Perdition catch my soul
But I do love thee! And when I love thee not,
Chaos is come again.

Iago: My noble lord——

Othello: What dost thou say, Iago?

Iago: Did Michael Cassio, when you wooed my lady,
Know of your love?

Othello: He did, from first to last. Why dost thou ask?

Iago: But for a satisfaction of my thought,
No further harm.

Othello: Why of thy thought, Iago?

Iago: I did not think he had been acquainted with her.

Othello: O, yes, and went between us° very oft.

Iago: Indeed?

Othello: Indeed? Ay, indeed! Discern'st thou aught in that?
Is he not honest?

Iago: Honest, my lord?

Othello doesn't realize the depth of his statement; we do, knowing Iago's villainy.

---

is . . . check is almost not serious
enough for a private rebuke (let alone a
public disgrace)
mamm'ring hesitating

peculiar profit particularly personal
good
poise weight
straight at once
between us i.e., as messenger

Othello: Honest? Ay, honest.
Iago: My lord, for aught I know.
Othello: What dost thou think?
Iago: Think, my lord?
Othello: Think, my lord?
  By heaven, thou echoest me,
  As if there were some monster in thy thought
  Too hideous to be shown. Thou dost mean something.
  I heard thee say even now, thou lik'st not that,
  When Cassio left my wife. What didst not like?
  And when I told thee he was of my counsel°
  Of my whole course of wooing, thou cried'st "Indeed?"
  And didst contract and purse thy brow together,
  As if thou then hadst shut up in thy brain
  Some horrible conceit.° If thou dost love me,
  Show me thy thought.
Iago: My lord, you know I love you.
Othello: I think thou dost;
  And, for I know thou'rt full of love and honesty
  And weigh'st thy words before thou giv'st them breath,
  Therefore these stops° of thine fright me the more;
  For such things in a false disloyal knave
  Are tricks of custom;° but in a man that's just
  They're close dilations,° working from the heart
  That passion cannot rule.
Iago: For Michael Cassio,
  I dare be sworn, I think that he is honest.
Othello: I think so too.
Iago: Men should be what they seem;
  Or those that be not, would they might seem none!
Othello: Certain, men should be what they seem.
Iago: Why then, I think Cassio's an honest man.
Othello: Nay, yet there's more in this?
  I prithee speak to me as to thy thinkings,
  As thou does ruminate, and give thy worst of thoughts
  The worst of words.
Iago: Good my lord, pardon me:
  Though I am bound to every act of duty,
  I am not bound to that all slaves are free to.
  Utter my thoughts? Why, say they are vile and false,
  As where's that palace whereinto foul things
  Sometimes intrude not? Who has that breast so pure
  But some uncleanly apprehensions
  Keep leets and law days,° and in sessions sit
  With meditations lawful?

Othello doesn't know how well Iago weighs his words.

Compare with his lines on p. 360. (I am not...)

---

of my counsel in my confidence
conceit thought
stops interruptions
of custom customary

close dilations expressions of hidden thoughts
leets and law days meetings of local courts

Othello: Thou dost conspire against thy friend, Iago,
    If thou but think'st him wronged, and mak'st his ear
    A stranger to thy thoughts.
Iago: I do beseech you—
    Though I perchance am vicious in my guess
    (As I confess it is my nature's plague
    To spy into abuses, and of my jealousy
    Shape faults that are not), that your wisdom
    From one that so imperfectly conceits
    Would take no notice, nor build yourself a trouble
    Out of his scattering and unsure observance.
    It were not for your quiet nor your good,
    Nor for my manhood, honesty, and wisdom,
    To let you know my thoughts.
Othello: What dost thou mean?

Compare Iago's advice to Roderigo on p. 374 (Put money in...) and to Cassio on p. 389 (There is more sense...).

Iago: Good name in man and woman, dear my lord,
    Is the immediate jewel of their souls.
    Who steals my purse steals trash; 'tis something, nothing;
    'Twas mine, 'tis his, and has been slave to thousands;
    But he that filches from me my good name
    Robs me of that which not enriches him
    And makes me poor indeed.
Othello: By heaven, I'll know thy thoughts!
Iago: You cannot, if my heart were in your hand;
    Nor shall not whilst 'tis in my custody.
Othello: Ha!

Iago is telling Othello he __should__ be jealous though seeming to warn him against it.

Iago: O, beware, my lord, of jealousy!
    It is the green-eyed monster, which doth mock
    The meat it feeds on. That cuckold lives in bliss
    Who, certain of his fate, loves not his wronger;
    But O, what damnèd minutes tells° he o'er
    Who dotes, yet doubts—suspects, yet fondly° loves!
Othello: O misery.
Iago: Poor and content is rich, and rich enough;
    But riches fineless° is as poor as winter
    To him that ever fears he shall be poor.
    Good God the souls of all my tribe defend
    From jealousy!
Othello: Why? Why is this?
    Think'st thou I'd make a life of jealousy,
    To follow still° the changes of the moon
    With fresh suspicions? No! To be once in doubt
    Is to be resolved. Exchange me for a goat
    When I shall turn the business of my soul
    To such exsufflicate and blown° surmises,

tells counts
fondly foolishly
fineless infinite

To follow still to change always (as the phases of the moon)
exsufflicate and blown inflated and fly-blown

Matching thy inference. 'Tis not to make me jealous
To say my wife is fair, feeds well, loves company,
Is free of speech, sings, plays, and dances;
Where virtue is, these are more virtuous.
Nor from mine own weak merits will I draw
The smallest fear or doubt of her revolt,
For she had eyes, and chose me. No, Iago;
I'll see before I doubt; when I doubt, prove;
And on the proof there is no more but this:
Away at once with love or jealousy!

Iago: I am glad of this; for now I shall have reason
To show the love and duty that I bear you
With franker spirit. Therefore, as I am bound,
Receive it from me. I speak not yet of proof.
Look to your wife; observe her well with Cassio;
Wear your eyes thus: not jealous nor secure.
I would not have your free and noble nature
Out of self-bounty° be abused. Look to't.
I know our country disposition well:
In Venice they do let heaven see the pranks
They dare not show their husbands; their best conscience
Is not to leave't undone, but kept unknown.°

Othello: Dost thou say so?

Iago: She did deceive her father, marrying you;
And when she seemed to shake and fear your looks,
She loved them most.

Othello: And so she did.

Iago: Why, go to then!
She that so young could give out such a seeming
To seel° her father's eyes up close as oak°—
He thought 'twas witchcraft. But I am much to blame.
I humbly do beseech you of your pardon
For too much loving you.

Othello: I am bound to thee forever.

Iago: I see this hath a little dashed your spirits.

Othello: Not a jot, not a jot.

Iago: Trust me, I fear it has.
I hope you will consider what is spoke
Comes from my love. But I do see y' are moved.
I am to pray you not to strain° my speech
To grosser issues, nor to larger reach°
Than to suspicion.

Othello: I will not.

Iago: Should you do so, my lord,

---

self-bounty innate kindness (which attributes his own motives to others)
their . . . unknown i.e., their morality does not forbid adultery, but it does forbid being found out

seel hoodwink
oak (a close-grained wood)
strain enlarge the meaning of
reach meaning

My speech should fall into such vile success
Which my thoughts aimed not. Cassio's my worthy friend—
My lord, I see y' are moved.

Othello: No, not much moved.
I do not think but Desdemona's honest.

Iago: Long live she so. And long live you to think so.

Othello: And yet, how nature erring from itself——

Iago: Ay, there's the point, as (to be bold with you)
Not to affect many proposèd matches
Of her own clime, complexion, and degree,°
Whereto we see in all things nature tends°—
Foh! one may smell in such a will most rank,
Foul disproportions, thoughts unnatural.
But, pardon me, I do not in position°
Distinctly° speak of her; though I may fear
Her will, recoiling to her better judgment,
May fall to match° you with her country forms,°
And happily° repent.

Othello: Farewell, farewell!
If more thou dost perceive, let me know more.
Set on thy wife to observe. Leave me, Iago.

Iago: My lord, I take my leave.   (Going.)

Othello: Why did I marry? This honest creature doubtless
Sees and knows more, much more, than he unfolds.

Iago: (Returns.) My lord, I would I might entreat your honor
To scan this thing no farther. Leave it to time.
Although 'tis fit that Cassio have his place,
For sure he fills it up with great ability,
Yet, if you please to hold him off awhile,
You shall by that perceive him and his means.
Note if your lady strain his entertainment°
With any strong or vehement importunity;
Much will be seen in that. In the meantime
Let me be thought too busy in my fears
(As worthy cause I have to fear I am)
And hold her free, I do beseech your honor.

Iago knows Othello well. Compare p.375 (The Moor is...)

Othello: Fear not my government.°

Iago: I once more take my leave.   (Exit.)

Othello: This fellow's of exceeding honesty,
And knows all qualities,° with a learnèd spirit
Of human dealings. If I do prove her haggard,°

degree social station
in . . . tends i.e., all things in nature seek out their own kind
position general argument
Distinctly specifically
fall to match happen to compare
country forms i.e., the familiar appearances of her countrymen

happily by chance
strain his entertainment urge strongly that he be reinstated
government self-control
qualities natures, types of people
haggard a partly trained hawk which has gone wild again

Though that her jesses° were my dear heartstrings,
I'd whistle her off and let her down the wind°
To prey at fortune. Haply for° I am black
And have not those soft parts° of conversation
That chamberers° have, or for I am declined
Into the vale of years—yet that's not much—
She's gone. I am abused, and my relief
Must be to loathe her. O curse of marriage,
That we can call these delicate creatures ours,
And not their appetites! I had rather be a toad
And live upon the vapor of a dungeon
Than keep a corner in the thing I love
For others' uses. Yet 'tis the plague to great ones;
Prerogatived are they less than the base.
'Tis destiny unshunnable, like death.
Even then this forkèd° plague is fated to us
When we do quicken.° Look where she comes.
(*Enter* **Desdemona** *and* **Emilia**.)
If she be false, heaven mocked itself!
I'll not believe't.

Desdemona: How now, my dear Othello?
Your dinner, and the generous islanders
By you invited, do attend° your presence.

Othello: I am to blame.

Desdemona: Why do you speak so faintly?
Are you not well?

Othello: I have a pain upon my forehead, here.°

Desdemona: Why, that's with watching; 'twill away again.
Let me but bind it hard, within this hour
It will be well.

Othello: Your napkin° is too little;
(*He pushes the handkerchief away, and it falls.*)
Let it° alone. Come, I'll go in with you.

Desdemona: I am very sorry that you are not well.
(*Exit with* **Othello**.)

Emilia: I am glad I have found this napkin;
This was her first remembrance from the Moor.
My wayward husband hath a hundred times
Wooed me to steal it; but she so loves the token

Othello is proud of his limited knowledge of courtly ways, the very weakness Iago plays upon. How is this ironic?

---

jesses straps which held the hawk's legs to the trainer's wrist
I'd ... wind I would release her (like an untamable hawk) and let her fly free
Haply for it may be because
soft parts gentle qualities and manners
chamberers courtiers—or perhaps, accomplished seducers
forkèd horned (the sign of the cuckold was horns)

do quicken are born
attend wait
here (he points to his imaginary horns)
napkin elaborately worked handkerchief
it (it makes a considerable difference in the interpretation of later events whether this "it" refers to Othello's forehead or to the handkerchief; nothing in the text makes the reference clear)

(For he conjured her she should ever keep it)
That she reserves it evermore about her
To kiss and talk to. I'll have the work ta'en out°
And give't Iago. What he will do with it,
Heaven knows, not I; I nothing° but to please his fantasy.°
(*Enter* **Iago.**)

Iago: How now? What do you here alone?

Emilia: Do not you chide; I have a thing for you.

Iago: You have a thing for me? It is a common thing——

Emilia: Ha?

Iago: To have a foolish wife.

Emilia: O, is that all? What will you give me now
For that same handkerchief?

Iago: What handkerchief?

Emilia: What handkerchief!
Why, that the Moor first gave to Desdemona,
That which so often you did bid me steal.

Iago: Hast stol'n it from her?

Emilia: No, but she let it drop by negligence,
And to th' advantage,° I, being here, took't up.
Look, here 't is.

Iago: A good wench. Give it me.

Emilia: What will you do with't, that you have been so earnest
To have me filch it?

Iago: Why, what is that to you?   (*Takes it.*)

Emilia: If it be not for some purpose of import,°
Give't me again. Poor lady, she'll run mad
When she shall lack° it.

Iago: Be not acknown on't.°
I have use for it. Go, leave me.   (*Exit* **Emilia.**)
I will in Cassio's lodging lose this napkin
And let him find it. Trifles light as air
Are to the jealous confirmations strong
As proofs of Holy Writ. This may do something.
The Moor already changes with my poison:
Dangerous conceits are in their natures poisons,
Which at the first are scarce found to distaste,°
But, with a little,° act upon the blood,
Burn like the mines of sulfur. I did say so.
(*Enter* **Othello.**)
Look where he comes! Not poppy nor mandragora,°
Nor all the drowsy syrups of the world,

---

work ta'en out needlework copied
I nothing I wish nothing
fantasy fancy, whim
to th' advantage being lucky
import importance
lack miss

Be not acknown on't forget you ever saw it
are scarce found to distaste scarcely can be tasted
with a little in a short time
poppy nor mandragora (soporifics)

Shall ever medicine thee to that sweet sleep
Which thou owedst° yesterday.
Othello: Ha! ha! False to me?
Iago: Why, how now, general? No more of that.
Othello: Avaunt! be gone! Thou hast set me on the rack.
  I swear 'tis better to be much abused
  Than but to know't a little.
Iago: How now, My lord?
Othello: What sense had I of her stol'n hours of lust?
  I saw't not, thought it not, it harmed not me;
  I slept the next night well, fed well, was free and merry;
  I found not Cassio's kisses on her lips.
  He that is robbed, not wanting° what is stol'n,
  Let him not know't, and he's not robbed at all.
Iago: I am sorry to hear this.
Othello: I had been happy if the general camp,
  Pioners° and all, had tasted her sweet body,
  So I had nothing known. O now, forever
  Farewell the tranquil mind! Farewell content!
  Farewell the plumed troops, and the big wars
  That makes ambition virtue! O, farewell!
  Farewell the neighing steed and the shrill trump,
  The spirit-stirring drum, th' ear-piercing fife,
  The royal banner, and all quality,
  Pride, pomp, and circumstance° of glorious war!
  And O you mortal engines° whose rude throats
  Th' immortal Jove's dread clamors° counterfeit,
  Farewell! Othello's occupation's gone!
Iago: Is't possible, my lord?
Othello: Villain, be sure thou prove my love a whore!
  Be sure of it; give me the ocular proof;
  Or, by the worth of mine eternal soul,
  Thou hadst been better have been born a dog
  Than answer my waked wrath!
Iago: Is't come to this?
Othello: Make me to see't; or at the least so prove it
  That the probation° bear no hinge nor loop
  To hang a doubt on—or woe upon thy life!
Iago: My noble lord——
Othello: If thou dost slander her and torture me,
  Never pray more; abandon all remorse;
  On horror's head horrors accumulate;
  Do deeds to make heaven weep, all earth amazed;

owedst possessed
wanting missing
Pioners (the basest manual laborers in
the army, who dug trenches and mines)
circumstance pageantry

mortal engines lethal weapons, i.e.,
cannon
clamors i.e., thunder
probation proof

For nothing canst thou to damnation add
Greater than that.

Iago:　　　　　　　O grace! O heaven forgive me!
Are you a man? Have you a soul or sense?
God b' wi' you! Take mine office. O wretched fool,
That lov'st to make thine honesty a vice!
O monstrous world! Take note, take note, O world,
To be direct and honest is not safe.
I thank you for this profit, and from hence
I'll love no friend, sith° love breeds such offense.

Othello: Nay, stay. Thou shouldst be honest.

Iago: I should be wise; for honesty's a fool
And loses that it works for.

Othello:　　　　　　　By the world,
I think my wife be honest, and think she is not;
I think that thou art just, and think thou art not.
I'll have some proof. My name, that was as fresh
As Dian's° visage, is now begrimed and black
As mine own face. If there be cords, or knives,
Poison, or fire, or suffocating streams,
I'll not endure it. Would I were satisfied!

Iago: I see you are eaten up with passion.
I do repent me that I put it to you.
You would be satisfied?

Othello:　　　　　　Would? Nay, and I will.

Iago: And may; but how? How satisfied, my lord?
Would you, the supervisor,° grossly gape on?
Behold her topped?

Othello:　　　　　　Death and damnation! O!

Iago: It were a tedious° difficulty, I think,
To bring them to that prospect.° Damn them then,
If ever mortal eyes do see them bolster°
More than their own! What then? How then?
What shall I say? Where's satisfaction?
It is impossible you should see this,
Were they as prime° as goats, as hot as monkeys,
As salt° as wolves in pride,° and fools as gross
As ignorance made drunk. But yet, I say,
If imputation and strong circumstances
Which lead directly to the door of truth
Will give you satisfaction, you might have't.

Othello: Give me a living reason she's disloyal.

Iago: I do not like the office.°

Is this true in the world of Cyprus?

sith since	**prospect** sight (where they can be seen)
Dian's Diana's (goddess of the moon and of chastity)	**bolster** go to bed
supervisor onlooker	**prime, salt** lustful
tedious hard to arrange	**pride** heat
	office duty

But sith I am entered in this cause so far,
Pricked° to't by foolish honesty and love,
I will go on. I lay with Cassio lately,
And being troubled with a raging tooth,
I could not sleep.
There are a kind of men so loose of soul
That in their sleeps will mutter their affairs.
One of this kind is Cassio.
In sleep I heard him say, "Sweet Desdemona,
Let us be wary, let us hide our loves!"
And then, sir, would he gripe° and wring my hand,
Cry "O sweet creature!" Then kiss me hard,
As if he plucked up kisses by the roots
That grew upon my lips; laid his leg o'er my thigh,
And sigh, and kiss, and then cry, "Cursèd fate
That gave thee to the Moor!"

Othello: O monstrous! monstrous!

Iago: Nay, this was but his dream.

Othello: But this denoted a foregone conclusion,°
'Tis a shrewd doubt,° though it be but a dream.

Iago: And this may help to thicken other proofs
That do demonstrate° thinly.

Othello: I'll tear her all to pieces!

Iago: Nay, yet be wise. Yet we see nothing done;
She may be honest yet. Tell me but this:
Have you not sometimes seen a handkerchief
Spotted with strawberries in your wife's hand?

Othello: I gave her such a one; 'twas my first gift.

Iago: I know not that; but such a handkerchief—
I am sure it was your wife's—did I today
See Cassio wipe his beard with.

Othello: If it be that——

Iago: If it be that, or any that was hers,
It speaks against her with the other proofs.

Othello: O, that the slave had forty thousand lives!
One is too poor, too weak for my revenge.
Now do I see 'tis true. Look here, Iago:
All my fond love thus do I blow to heaven.
'Tis gone.
Arise, black vengeance, from the hollow hell!
Yield up, O Love, thy crown and hearted° throne
To tyrannous hate! Swell, bosom, with thy fraught,°
For 'tis of aspics'° tongues.

Pricked spurred	**demonstrate** show, appear
gripe seize	**hearted** seated in the heart
foregone conclusion consummated fact	**fraught** burden
shrewd doubt penetrating guess	**aspics'** asps'

Iago: Yet be content.°

Othello: O, blood, blood, blood!

Iago: Patience, I say, Your mind may change.

Othello: Never, Iago. Like to the Pontic Sea,°
Whose icy current and compulsive course
Nev'r keeps retiring ebb, but keeps due on
To the Propontic and the Hellespont,
Even so my bloody thoughts, with violent pace,
Shall nev'r look back, nev'r ebb to humble love,
Till that a capable and wide° revenge
Swallow them up. (*He kneels.*) Now, by yond marble heaven,
In the due reverence of a sacred vow
I here engage my words.

Visually ironic scene? Who is in control?

Iago: Do not rise yet.   (**Iago** *kneels.*)
Witness, you ever-burning lights above,
You elements that clip° us round about,
Witness that here Iago doth give up
The execution° of his wit, hands, heart
To wronged Othello's service! Let him command,
And to obey shall be in me remorse,°
What bloody business ever.°   (*They rise.*)

Othello: I greet thy love,
Not with vain thanks but with acceptance bounteous,°
And will upon the instant put thee to't.°
Within these three days let me hear thee say
That Cassio's not alive.

Compare p.398 (O, beware, my lord...).

Iago: My friend is dead. 'Tis done at your request.
But let her live.

Othello: Damn her, lewd minx! O, damn her! Damn her!
Come, go with me apart. I will withdraw
To furnish me with some swift means of death
For the fair devil. Now art thou my lieutenant.

Iago has what he said he wanted on p.358. (Despise me...) Is he satisfied?

Iago: I am your own forever.
(*Exeunt.*)

SCENE IV.   A street.

(*Enter* **Desdemona, Emilia,** *and* **Clown.**)

Desdemona: Do you know, sirrah, where Lieutenant Cassio lies?°

Clown: I dare not say he lies anywhere.

---

content patient, quiet
Pontic Sea The Black Sea (famous for the strong and constant current with which it flows through the Bosporus into the Mediterranean, where the water level is lower)
capable and wide sufficient and far-reaching

clip enfold
execution workings, action
remorse pity
ever soever
bounteous absolute
to't i.e., to the work you have said you are prepared to do
lies lodges

Desdemona: Why, man?

Clown: He's a soldier, and for me to say a soldier lies, 'tis stabbing.

Desdemona: Go to. Where lodges he?

Clown: To tell you where he lodges is to tell you where I lie.

Desdemona: Can anything be made of this?

Clown: I know not where he lodges, and for me to devise a lodging, and say he lies here or he lies there, were to lie in mine own throat.°

Desdemona: Can you enquire him out, and be edified° by report?

Clown: I will catechize the world for him; that is, make questions, and by them answer.

Desdemona: Seek him, bid him come hither. Tell him I have moved° my lord on his behalf and hope all will be well.

Clown: To do this is within the compass° of man's wit, and therefore I will attempt the doing it.   (*Exit* **Clown**.)

Desdemona: Where should° I lose the handkerchief, Emilia?

Emilia: I know not, madam.

Desdemona: Believe me, I had rather have lost my purse
Full of crusadoes.° And but my noble Moor
Is true of mind, and made of no such baseness
As jealous creatures are, it were enough
To put him to ill thinking.

Emilia: Is he not jealous?

Desdemona: Who? He? I think the sun where he was born
Drew all such humors° from him.

Emilia: Look where he comes.

(*Enter* **Othello**.)

Desdemona: I will not leave him now till Cassio
Be called to him. How is't with you, my lord?

Othello: Well, my good lady. (*Aside*) O, hardness to dissemble!°—
How do you, Desdemona?

Desdemona: Well, my good lord.

Othello: Give me your hand. This hand is moist,° my lady.

Desdemona: It hath felt no age nor known no sorrow.

Othello: This argues° fruitfulness and liberal° heart.
Hot, hot, and moist. This hand of yours requires
A sequester° from liberty; fasting and prayer;
Much castigation; exercise devout;
For here's a young and sweating devil here

---

lie in mine own throat (to lie in the throat is to lie absolutely and completely)
edified enlightened (Desdemona mocks the Clown's overly elaborate diction)
moved pleaded with
compass reach
should might
crusadoes Portuguese gold coins
humors characteristics
hardness to dissemble (Othello may refer here either to the difficulty he has in maintaining his appearance of composure,

or to what he believes to be Desdemona's hardened hypocrisy)
moist (a moist, hot hand was taken as a sign of a lustful nature)
argues suggests
liberal free, open (but also with a suggestion of "licentious"; from here on in this scene Othello's words bear a double meaning, seeming to be normal but accusing Desdemona of being unfaithful)
sequester separation

That commonly rebels. 'Tis a good hand,
A frank one.
Desdemona: You may, indeed, say so;
For 'twas that hand that gave away my heart.
Othello: A liberal hand! The hearts of old gave hands,
But our new heraldry° is hands, not hearts.
Desdemona: I cannot speak of this. Come now, your promise!
Othello: What promise, chuck?
Desdemona: I have sent to bid Cassio come speak with you.
Othello: I have a salt and sorry rheum° offends me.
Lend me thy handkerchief.
Desdemona: Here, my lord.
Othello: That which I gave you.
Desdemona: I have it not about me.
Othello: Not?
Desdemona: No, indeed, my lord.
Othello: That's a fault.
That handkerchief
Did an Egyptian to my mother give.
She was a charmer,° and could almost read
The thoughts of people. She told her, while she kept it
'Twould make her amiable° and subdue my father
Entirely to her love; but if she lost it
Or made a gift of it, my father's eye
Should hold her loathèd, and his spirits should hunt
After new fancies. She, dying, gave it me,
And bid me, when my fate would have me wived,
To give it her. I did so; and take heed on't;
Make it a darling like your precious eye.
To lose't or give't away were such perdition
As nothing else could match.
Desdemona: Is't possible?
Othello: 'Tis true. There's magic in the web° of it.
A sibyl that had numbered in the world
The sun to course two hundred compasses,
In her prophetic fury° sewed the work;
The worms were hallowed that did breed the silk,
And it was dyed in mummy° which the skillful
Conserved of maidens' hearts.
Desdemona: Indeed? Is't true?
Othello: Most veritable. Therefore look to't well.
Desdemona: Then would to God that I had never seen't!
Othello: Ha! Wherefore?

---

heraldry heraldic symbolism
a salt and sorry rheum a heavy, running
head cold
charmer magician
amiable desirable

web weaving
prophetic fury seized by the spirit and
able to prophesy
mummy liquid drained from embalmed
bodies

Desdemona: Why do you speak so startingly and rash?

Othello: Is't lost? Is't gone? Speak, is it out o' th' way?

Desdemona: Heaven bless us!

Othello: Say you?

Desdemona: It is not lost. But what an if it were?

Othello: How?

Desdemona: I say it is not lost.

Othello: Fetch't, let me see't!

Desdemona: Why, so I can; but I will not now.
This is a trick to put me from my suit:
Pray you let Cassio be received again.

Othello: Fetch me the handkerchief! My mind misgives.

Desdemona: Come, come!
You'll never meet a more sufficient° man——

Othello: The handkerchief!

Desdemona: A man that all his time
Hath founded his good fortunes on your love,
Shared dangers with you——

Othello: The handkerchief!

Desdemona: I'faith, you are to blame.

Othello: Away!   (*Exit* **Othello**.)

Emilia: Is not this man jealous?

Desdemona: I nev'r saw this before.
Sure there's some wonder in this handkerchief;
I am most unhappy in the loss of it.

Emilia: 'Tis not a year or two shows us a man.
They are all but stomachs, and we all but food;
They eat us hungerly, and when they are full,
They belch us.
(*Enter* **Iago** *and* **Cassio**.)
                     Look you, Cassio and my husband.

Iago: There is no other way; 'tis she must do't.
And lo the happiness! Go and importune her.

Desdemona: How now, good Cassio? What's the news with you?

Cassio: Madam, my former suit. I do beseech you
That by your virtuous means I may again
Exist, and be a member of his love
Whom I will all the office° of my heart
Entirely honor. I would not be delayed.
If my offense be of such mortal kind
That nor my service past, nor present sorrows,
Nor purposed merit in futurity,
Can ransom me into his love again,
But to know so must be my benefit.°
So shall I clothe me in a forced content,

Desdemona speaks the name that incenses Othello. We could clear up the confusion but are powerless to do so.

sufficient complete, with all proper qualities

office duty
benefit good

And shut myself up in some other course
To fortune's alms.
Desdemona: Alas, thrice-gentle Cassio,
My advocation° is not now in tune.
My lord is not my lord; nor should I know him
Were he in favor° as in humor altered.
So help me every spirit sanctified
As I have spoken for you all my best
And stood within the blank° of his displeasure
For my free speech. You must awhile be patient.
What I can do I will; and more I will
Than for myself I dare. Let that suffice you.
Iago: Is my lord angry?
Emilia: He went hence but now,
And certainly in strange unquietness.
Iago: Can he be angry? I have seen the cannon
When it hath blown his ranks into the air
And, like the devil, from his very arm
Puffed his own brother. And is he angry?
Something of moment° then. I will go meet him.
There's matter in't indeed if he be angry.
Desdemona: I prithee do so.   (*Exit* **Iago**)
                    Something sure of state,°
Either from Venice or some unhatched practice°
Made demonstrable here in Cyprus to him,
Hath puddled° his clear spirit; and in such cases
Men's natures wrangle with inferior things,
Though great ones are their object. 'Tis even so.
For let our finger ache, and it endues°
Our other, healthful members even to a sense
Of pain. Nay, we must think men are not gods,
Nor of them look for such observancy
As fits the bridal. Beshrew me much, Emilia,
I was, unhandsome warrior as I am,
Arraigning his unkindness with my soul;
But now I find I had suborned the witness,
And he's indicted falsely.
Emilia: Pray heaven it be
State matters, as you think, and no conception
Nor no jealous toy° concerning you.
Desdemona: Alas the day! I never gave him cause.
Emilia: But jealous souls will not be answered so;
They are not ever jealous for the cause,

advocation advocacy	**unhatched practice** undisclosed plot
favor countenance	**puddled** muddied
blank bull's-eye of a target	**endues** leads
moment importance	**toy** trifle
of state state affairs	

But jealous for they're jealous. It is a monster
Begot upon itself, born on itself.
Desdemona: Heaven keep the monster from Othello's mind!
Emilia: Lady, amen.
Desdemona: I will go seek him. Cassio, walk here about.
If I do find him fit,° I'll move your suit
And seek to effect it to my uttermost.
Cassio: I humbly thank your ladyship.
(*Exit* **Desdemona** *with* **Emilia**. *Enter* **Bianca**.)
Bianca: Save you, friend Cassio!
Cassio: What make you from home?
How is't with you, my most fair Bianca?
I' faith, sweet love, I was coming to your house.
Bianca: And I was going to your lodging, Cassio.
What, keep a week away? Seven days and nights?
Eightscore eight hours? And lovers' absent hours
More tedious than the dial eightscore times?
O weary reck'ning.°
Cassio: Pardon me, Bianca.
I have this while with leaden thoughts been pressed,
But I shall in a more continuate° time
Strike off this score° of absence. Sweet Bianca,
(*Gives her* **Desdemona's** *handkerchief.*)
Take me this work out.
Bianca: O Cassio, whence came this?
This is some token from a newer friend.
To the felt absence now I feel a cause.
Is't come to this? Well, well.
Cassio: Go to, woman!
Throw your vile guesses in the devil's teeth,
From whence you have them. You are jealous now
That this is from some mistress, some remembrance.
No, by my faith, Bianca.
Bianca: Why, whose is it?
Cassio: I know not neither; I found it in my chamber.
I like the work well; ere it be demanded,°
As like enough it will, I would have it copied.
Take it and do't, and leave me for this time.
Bianca: Leave you? Wherefore?
Cassio: I do attend here on the general
And think it no addition, nor my wish,
To have him see me womaned.
Bianca: Why, I pray you?
Cassio: Not that I love you not.

---

fit receptive
reck'ning addition
continuate uninterrupted
Strike off this score i.e., pay this bill

(the *score* being the account of drinks kept
in a tavern)
demanded asked for (by the person who
lost it)

Bianca: But that you do not love me!
I pray you bring° me on the way a little,
And say if I shall see you soon at night.
Cassio: 'Tis but a little way that I can bring you,
For I attend here; but I'll see you soon.
Bianca: 'Tis very good. I must be circumstanced.°
(*Exeunt omnes.*)

SCENE I.   A street.

(*Enter* **Othello** *and* **Iago**.)
Iago: Will you think so?
Othello: Think so, Iago?
Iago: What,
To kiss in private?
Othello: An unauthorized° kiss?
Iago: Or to be naked with her friend in bed
An hour or more, not meaning any harm?
Othello: Naked in bed, Iago, and not mean harm?
It is hypocrisy against the devil.
They that mean virtuously, and yet do so,
The devil their virtue tempts, and they tempt heaven.
Iago: If they do nothing, 'tis a venial slip.
But if I give my wife a handkerchief——
Othello: What then?
Iago: Why, then 'tis hers, my lord; and being hers,
She may, I think, bestow't on any man.
Othello: She is protectress of her honor too.
May she give that?
Iago: Her honor is an essence that's not seen;
They have it very oft that have it not.
But for the handkerchief——
Othello: By heaven, I would most gladly have forgot it!
Thou said'st—O, it comes o'er my memory
As doth the raven° o'er the infected house,
Boding to all—he had my handkerchief.
Iago: Ay, what of that?
Othello: That's not so good now.
Iago: What if I had said I had seen him do you wrong?
Or heard him say—as knaves be such abroad°
Who having, by their own importunate suit,
Or voluntary dotage° of some mistress,

bring   accompany
circumstanced   accept things as they are
unauthorized   illicit

raven   (a harbinger of death)
abroad   i.e., in the world
voluntary dotage   weakness of the will

Convincèd or supplied° them, cannot choose
But they must blab——
Othello: Hath he said anything?
Iago: He hath, my lord; but be you well assured,
No more than he'll unswear.
Othello: What hath he said?
Iago: Why, that he did—I know not what he did.
Othello: What? what?
Iago: Lie——
Othello: With her?
Iago: With her, on her; what you will.
Othello: Lie with her? Lie on her?—We say lie on her when they belie her.—
Lie with her! Zounds, that's fulsome.°—Handkerchief—confessions—hand-
kerchief!—To confess, and be hanged for his labor—first to be hanged, and
then to confess! I tremble at it. Nature would not invest herself in such
shadowing passion without some instruction.° It is not words that shakes
me thus.—Pish! Noses, ears, and lips? Is't possible?—Confess?—Handkerchief?
—O devil!   (*Falls in a trance.*)
Iago: Work on.
My med'cine works! Thus credulous fools are caught,
And many worthy and chaste dames even thus,
All guiltless, meet reproach.° What, ho! My lord!
My lord, I say! Othello!
(*Enter* **Cassio**.)
How now, Cassio?
Cassio: What's the matter?
Iago: My lord is fall'n into an epilepsy.
This is his second fit; he had one yesterday.
Cassio: Rub him about the temples.
Iago: The lethargy° must have his quiet course.
If not, he foams at mouth, and by and by
Breaks out to savage madness. Look, he stirs.
Do you withdraw yourself a little while.
He will recover straight. When he is gone,
I would on great occasion° speak with you.   (*Exit* **Cassio**.)
How is it, general? Have you not hurt your head?
Othello: Dost thou mock° me?
Iago: I mock you not, by heaven.
Would you would bear your fortune like a man.
Othello: A hornèd man's a monster and a beast.
Iago: There's many a beast then in a populous city,
And many a civil° monster.

Convincèd or supplied persuaded or
gratified (the mistress)
fulsome foul, repulsive
Nature . . . instruction i.e., my mind
would not become so darkened (with
anger) unless there were something in this
(accusation); (it should be remembered
that Othello believes in the workings of

magic and supernatural forces)
reproach shame
lethargy coma
great occasion very important matter
mock (Othello takes Iago's comment
as a reference to his horns—which it is)
civil city-dwelling

Othello: Did he confess it?
Iago: Good, sir, be a man.
Think every bearded fellow that's but yoked
May draw° with you. There's millions now alive
That nightly lie in those unproper° beds
Which they dare swear peculiar.° Your case is better.
O, 'tis the spite of hell, the fiend's arch-mock,
To lip a wanton in a secure couch,
And to suppose her chaste. No, let me know;
And knowing what I am, I know what she shall be.
Othello: O, thou art wise! 'Tis certain.
Iago: Stand you awhile apart;
Confine yourself but in a patient list.°
Whilst you were here, o'erwhelmèd with your grief—
A passion most unsuiting such a man—
Cassio came hither. I shifted him away°
And laid good 'scuses upon your ecstasy;°
Bade him anon return, and here speak with me;
The which he promised. Do but encave° yourself
And mark the fleers,° the gibes, and notable° scorns
That dwell in every region of his face.
For I will make him tell the tale anew:
Where, how, how oft, how long ago, and when
He hath, and is again to cope your wife.
I say, but mark his gesture. Marry patience,
Or I shall say you're all in all in spleen,°
And nothing of a man.
Othello: Dost thou hear, Iago?
I will be found most cunning in my patience;
But—dost thou hear?—most bloody.
Iago: That's not amiss;
But yet keep time in all. Will you withdraw?
(**Othello** *moves to one side, where his remarks are not audible to* **Cassio** *and* **Iago**.)
Now will I question Cassio of Bianca,
A huswife° that by selling her desires
Buys herself bread and cloth. It is a creature
That dotes on Cassio, as 'tis the strumpet's plague
To beguile many and be beguiled by one.
He, when he hears of her, cannot restrain
From the excess of laughter. Here he comes.
(*Enter* **Cassio**.)
As he shall smile, Othello shall go mad;

---

draw i.e., like the horned ox
unproper i.e., not exclusively the husband's
peculiar their own alone
a patient list the bounds of patience
shifted him away got rid of him by a stratagem
ecstasy trance (the literal meaning, "out-side oneself," bears on the meaning of the change Othello is undergoing)
encave hide
fleers mocking looks or speeches
notable obvious
spleen passion, particularly anger
huswife housewife (but with the special meaning here of "prostitute")

Iago is the ironist.
Who is the victim
and who the
audience? To whom
do we feel superior?

And his unbookish° jealousy must conster°
Poor Cassio's smiles, gestures, and light behaviors
Quite in the wrong. How do you, lieutenant?

Cassio: The worser that you give me the addition°
Whose want even kills me.

Iago: Ply Desdemona well, and you are sure on't.
Now, if this suit lay in Bianca's power,
How quickly should you speed!

Cassio: Alas, poor caitiff!°

Othello: Look how he laughs already!

Iago: I never knew woman love man so.

Cassio: Alas, poor rogue! I think, i' faith, she loves me.

Othello: Now he denies it faintly, and laughs it out.

Iago: Do you hear, Cassio?

Othello: Now he importunes him
To tell it o'er. Go to! Well said, well said!

Iago: She gives it out that you shall marry her.
Do you intend it?

Cassio: Ha, ha, ha!

Othello: Do ye triumph, Roman? Do you triumph?

Cassio: I marry? What, a customer?° Prithee bear some charity to my wit; do
not think it so unwholesome. Ha, ha, ha!

Othello: So, so, so, so. They laugh that win.

Iago: Why, the cry goes that you marry her.

Cassio: Prithee, say true.

Iago: I am a very villain else.

Othello: Have you scored° me? Well.

Cassio: This is the monkey's own giving out. She is persuaded I will marry
her out of her own love and flattery, not out of my promise.

Othello: Iago beckons me; now he begins the story.

(**Othello** *moves close enough to hear.*)

Cassio: She was here even now; she haunts me in every place. I was the other
day talking on the sea bank with certain Venetians, and thither comes the
bauble,° and falls me thus about my neck——

Othello: Crying "O dear Cassio!" as it were. His gesture imports it.

Cassio: So hangs, and lolls, and weeps upon me; so shakes and pulls me! Ha,
ha, ha!

Othello: Now he tells how she plucked him to my chamber. O, I see that nose
of yours, but not that dog I shall throw it to.

Cassio: Well, I must leave her company.

Iago: Before me!° Look where she comes.

(*Enter* **Bianca**.)

Cassio: 'Tis such another fitchew!° Marry a perfumed one? What do you mean
by this haunting of me?

unbookish ignorant	**scored** marked, defaced
conster construe	**bauble** plaything
addition title	**Before me!** (an exclamation of surprise)
caitiff wretch	**fitchew** polecat, i.e., strong-smelling
customer one who sells, a merchant	creature
(here, a prostitute)	

Bianca: Let the devil and his dam haunt you! What did you mean by that same handkerchief you gave me even now? I was a fine fool to take it. I must take out the work? A likely piece of work that you should find it in your chamber and know not who left it there! This is some minx's token, and I must take out the work? There! (*She throws down the handkerchief.*) Give it your hobby-horse.° Wheresoever you had it, I'll take out no work on't.

Cassio: How now, my sweet Bianca? How now? how now?

Othello: By heaven, that should be my handkerchief!

Bianca: If you'll come to supper tonight, you may; if you will not, come when you are next prepared for.°   (*Exit.*)

Iago: After her, after her!

Cassio: Faith, I must; she'll rail in the streets else.

Iago: Will you sup there?

Cassio: Yes, I intend so.

Iago: Well, I may chance to see you, for I would very fain speak with you.

Cassio: Prithee come. Will you?

Iago: Go to, say no more.   (*Exit* **Cassio**.)

Othello: (*Comes forward.*) How shall I murder him, Iago?

Iago: Did you perceive how he laughed at his vice?

Othello: O Iago!

Iago: And did you see the handkerchief?

Othello: Was that mine?

Iago: Yours, by this hand! And to see how he prized the foolish woman your wife! She gave it him, and he hath giv'n it his whore.

Othello: I would have him nine years a-killing!—A fine woman, a fair woman, a sweet woman?

Iago: Nay, you must forget that.

Othello: Ay, let her rot, and perish, and be damned tonight; for she shall not live. No, my heart is turned to stone; I strike it, and it hurts my hand. O, the world hath not a sweeter creature! She might lie by an emperor's side and command him tasks.

Iago: Nay, that's not your way.°

Othello: Hang her! I do but say what she is. So delicate with her needle. An admirable musician. O, she will sing the savageness out of a bear! Of so high and plenteous wit and invention°——

Iago: She's the worse for all this.

Othello: O, a thousand, a thousand times. And then, of so gentle a condition?°

Iago: Ay, too gentle.

Othello: Nay, that's certain. But yet the pity of it, Iago. O Iago, the pity of it, Iago.

Iago: If you are so fond over her iniquity, give her patent to offend; for if it touch° not you, it comes near nobody.

Othello: I will chop her into messes!° Cuckold me!

Iago: O, 'tis foul in her.

Othello: With mine officer!

hobbyhorse prostitute
next prepared for next expected—i.e., never
way proper course
invention imagination

gentle a condition (1) well born (2) of a gentle nature
touch affects
messes bits

Iago: That's fouler.

Othello: Get me some poison, Iago, this night. I'll not expostulate with her, lest her body and beauty unprovide my mind° again. This night, Iago!

Iago: Do it not with poison. Strangle her in her bed, even the bed she hath contaminated.

Othello: Good, good! The justice of it pleases. Very good!

Iago: And for Cassio, let me be his undertaker.° You shall hear more by midnight.

Othello: Excellent good!   (*A trumpet.*)
                    What trumpet is that same?

Iago: I warrant something from Venice.

   (*Enter* **Lodovico,** **Desdemona,** *and* **Attendants.**)
                            'Tis Lodovico.
This comes from the Duke. See, your wife's with him.

Lodovico: God save you, worthy general.

Othello: With° all my heart, sir.

Lodovico: The Duke and the senators of Venice greet you.

   (*Gives him a letter.*)

Othello: I kiss the instrument of their pleasures.   (*Opens the letter and reads.*)

Desdemona: And what's the news, good cousin Lodovico?

Iago: I am very glad to see you, signior.
   Welcome to Cyprus.

Lodovico: I thank you. How does Lieutenant Cassio?

Iago: Lives, sir.

Desdemona: Cousin, there's fall'n between him and my lord
   An unkind° breach; but you shall make all well.

Othello: Are you sure of that?

Desdemona: My lord?

Othello: (*Reads*) "This fail you not to do, as you will——"

Lodovico: He did not call; he's busy in the paper.
   Is there division 'twixt my lord and Cassio?

Desdemona: A most unhappy one. I would do much
   T' atone° them, for the love I bear to Cassio.

Othello: Fire and brimstone!

Desdemona: My lord?

Othello: Are you wise?

Desdemona: What, is he angry?

Lodovico: May be th' letter moved him;
   For, as I think, they do command him home,
   Deputing Cassio in his government.°

Desdemona: Trust me, I am glad on't.

Othello: Indeed?

Desdemona: My lord?

Othello: I am glad to see you mad.

How does Othello interpret her use of love? What is the irony?

---

unprovide my mind undo my resolution
undertaker (not "burier" but "one who
undertakes to do something")
With i.e., I greet you with

unkind unnatural
atone reconcile
government office

Desdemona: Why, sweet Othello——

Othello: Devil!   (*Strikes her.*)

Desdemona: I have not deserved this.

Lodovico: My lord, this would not be believed in Venice,

Though I should swear I saw't. 'Tis very much.

Make her amends; she weeps.

Othello: O devil, devil!

If that the earth could teem° with woman's tears,

Each drop she falls° would prove a crocodile.°

Out of my sight!

Desdemona: I will not stay to offend you.   (*Going.*)

Lodovico: Truly, an obedient lady.

I do beseech your lordship call her back.

Othello: Mistress!

Desdemona: My lord?

Othello: What would you with her, sir?

Lodovico: Who? I, my lord?

Othello: Ay! You did wish that I would make her turn.

Sir, she can turn, and turn, and yet go on

And turn again; and she can weep, sir, weep;

And she's obedient; as you say, obedient.

Very obedient. Proceed you in your tears.

Concerning this, sir—O well-painted passion!

I am commanded home.—Get you away;

I'll send for you anon.—Sir, I obey the mandate

And will return to Venice.—Hence, avaunt!   (*Exit* **Desdemona**.)

Cassio shall have my place. And, sir, tonight

I do entreat that we may sup together.

You are welcome, sir, to Cyprus.—Goats and monkeys!   (*Exit.*)

Lodovico: Is this the noble Moor whom our full Senate

Call all in all sufficient? Is this the nature

Whom passion could not shake? whose solid virtue

The shot of accident nor dart of chance

Could neither graze nor pierce?

Iago: He is much changed.

Lodovico: Are his wits safe? Is he not light of brain?

Iago: He's that he is; I may not breathe my censure.

What he might be (if, what he might, he is not)

I would to heaven he were!

Lodovico: What, strike his wife?

Iago: Faith, that was not so well; yet would I knew

That stroke would prove the worst.

Lodovico: Is it his use?°

Or did the letters work upon his blood°

And new-create his fault?

If director puts Iago next to Desdemona here, what kind of irony is created?

---

teem conceive
falls drops
crocodile (the crocodile was supposed

to shed false tears to lure its victims)
use habit
blood passion

Iago: Alas, alas!
It is not honesty in me to speak
What I have seen and known. You shall observe him,
And his own courses° will denote him so
That I may save my speech. Do but go after
And mark how he continues.
Lodovico: I am sorry that I am deceived in him.
(*Exeunt.*)

SCENE II.   The citadel.

(*Enter* **Othello** *and* **Emilia.**)
Othello: You have seen nothing then?
Emilia: Nor ever heard, nor ever did suspect.
Othello: Yes, you have seen Cassio and she together.
Emilia: But then I saw no harm, and then I heard
Each syllable that breath made up° between them.
Othello: What, did they never whisper?
Emilia: Never, my lord.
Othello: Nor send you out o' th' way?
Emilia: Never.
Othello: To fetch her fan, her gloves, her mask, nor nothing?
Emilia: Never, my lord.
Othello: That's strange.
Emilia: I durst, my lord, to wager she is honest,
Lay down my soul at stake.° If you think other,
Remove your thought. It doth abuse your bosom.

We know who did, but Emilia doesn't.

If any wretch have put this in your head,
Let heaven requite it with the serpent's curse,°
For if she be not honest,° chaste, and true,
There's no man happy. The purest of their wives
Is foul as slander.
Othello: Bid her come hither. Go.   (*Exit* **Emilia.**)
She says enough; yet she's a simple bawd°
That cannot say as much. This is a subtle whore,
A closet lock and key of villainous secrets,
And yet she'll kneel and pray; I have seen her do't.
(*Enter* **Desdemona** *and* **Emilia.**)
Desdemona: My lord, what is your will?
Othello: Pray you, chuck, come hither.
Desdemona: What is your pleasure?
Othello: Let me see your eyes.
Look in my face.
Desdemona: What horrible fancy's this?

courses actions
that breath made up spoken
at stake as the wager
serpent's curse (God's curse on the ser-

pent after the fall in Eden)
honest chaste
bawd procuress

Othello: *(To* **Emilia***)* Some of your function,° mistress:
Leave procreants alone and shut the door;
Cough or cry hem if anybody come.
Your mystery,° your mystery! Nay, dispatch!   *(Exit* **Emilia.***)*

Desdemona: Upon my knee, what doth your speech import?
I understand a fury in your words.°

Othello: Why, what art thou?

Desdemona: Your wife, my lord; your true
And loyal wife.

Othello: Come, swear it, damn thyself;
Lest, being like one of heaven, the devils themselves
Should fear to seize thee. Therefore be double-damned:
Swear thou art honest.

Desdemona: Heaven doth truly know it.

Othello: Heaven truly knows that thou art false as hell.

Desdemona: To whom, my lord? With whom? How am I false?

Othello: Ah, Desdemon! Away! Away! Away!

Desdemona: Alas the heavy day! Why do you weep?
Am I the motive° of these tears, my lord?
If haply° you my father do suspect
An instrument of this your calling back,
Lay not your blame on me. If you have lost him,
I have lost him too.

Othello: Had it pleased heaven
To try me with affliction, had they rained
All kinds of sores and shames on my bare head,
Steeped° me in poverty to the very lips,
Given to captivity me and my utmost hopes,
I should have found in some place of my soul
A drop of patience. But, alas, to make me
The fixèd figure for the time of scorn°
To point his slow and moving finger at.
Yet could I bear that too, well, very well.
But there where I have garnered up my heart,
Where either I must live or bear no life,
The fountain from the which my current runs
Or else dries up—to be discarded thence,
Or keep it as a cistern for foul toads
To knot and gender° in—turn thy complexion there,
Patience, thou young and rose-lipped cherubin!
I here look grim as hell!°

Desdemona: I hope my noble lord esteems me honest.

Some of your function do your proper work (as the operator of a brothel)
mystery trade
words (Q1 adds to this line, "But not the words")
motive cause
haply by chance
Steeped submerged

The . . . scorn the very image of scorn in our time
knot and gender twist in bunches and procreate
turn . . . hell (the rough sense would seem to be, "even Patience would grow pale, turn complexion, at Desdemona's perfidy, but that Othello looks grimly on")

Othello: O, ay, as summer flies are in the shambles,°
  That quicken even with blowing.° O thou weed,
  Who art so lovely fair, and smell'st so sweet,
  That the sense aches at thee, would thou hadst never been born!
Desdemona: Alas, what ignorant° sin have I committed?
Othello: Was this fair paper, this most goodly book,
  Made to write "whore" upon? What committed?
  Committed? O thou public commoner,°
  I should make very forges of my cheeks
  That would to cinders burn up modesty,
  Did I but speak thy deeds. What committed?
  Heaven stops the nose at it, and the moon winks;°
  The bawdy wind that kisses all it meets
  Is hushed within the hollow mine of earth
  And will not hear't. What committed? .
Desdemona: By heaven, you do me wrong!
Othello: Are not you a strumpet?
Desdemona: No, as I am a Christian!
  If to preserve this vessel for my lord
  From any other foul unlawful touch
  Be not to be a strumpet, I am none.
Othello: What, not a whore?
Desdemona: No, as I shall be saved!
Othello: Is't possible?
Desdemona: O, heaven forgive us!
Othello: I cry you mercy° then.
  I took you for that cunning whore of Venice
  That married with Othello. (*Calling*) You, mistress,
  (*Enter* **Emilia**.)
  That have the office opposite to Saint Peter
  And keep the gate of hell! You, you, ay, you!
  We have done our course; there's money for your pains.
  (*Throws her some coins.*)
  I pray you turn the key and keep our counsel.   (*Exit.*)
Emilia: Alas, what does this gentleman conceive?
  How do you, madam? How do you, my good lady?
Desdemona: Faith, half asleep.
Emilia: Good madam, what's the matter with my lord?
Desdemona: With who?
Emilia: Why, with my lord, madam.
Desdemona: Who is thy lord?
Emilia: He that is yours, sweet lady.
Desdemona: I have none. Do not talk to me, Emilia.
  I cannot weep, nor answers have I none

---

shambles abattoirs
quicken even with blowing become impregnated as soon as they lay their eggs
ignorant unknowing

commoner prostitute
winks closes its eyes (the moon was the symbol of chastity)
cry you mercy ask your pardon

But what should go by water.° Prithee tonight
Lay on my bed my wedding sheets, remember;
And call thy husband hither.
Emilia: Here's a change indeed!   (*Exit.*)
Desdemona: 'Tis meet I should be used so, very meet.
How have I been behaved, that he might stick
The small'st opinion on my least misuse?°
(*Enter* **Iago** *and* **Emilia.**)
Iago: What is your pleasure, madam? How is't with you?   *Pretended ignorance*
Desdemona: I cannot tell. Those that do teach young babes
Do it with gentle means and easy tasks.
He might have chid me so; for, in good faith,
I am a child to chiding.
Iago: What is the matter, lady?
Emilia: Alas, Iago, my lord hath so bewhored her,
Thrown such despite° and heavy terms upon her
That true hearts cannot bear it.
Desdemona: Am I that name, Iago?
Iago: What name, fair lady?
Desdemona: Such as she said my lord did say I was.
Emilia: He called her whore. A beggar in his drink
Could not have laid such terms upon his callet.°
Iago: Why did he so?
Desdemona: I do not know; I am sure I am none such.
Iago: Do not weep, do not weep. Alas the day.
Emilia: Hath she forsook so many noble matches,
Her father and her country, and her friends,
To be called whore? Would it not make one weep?
Desdemona: It is my wretched fortune.
Iago: Beshrew° him for 't!
How comes this trick upon him?
Desdemona: Nay, heaven doth know.
Emilia: I will be hanged if some eternal villain,   *She's right— he has*
Some busy and insinuating rogue,   *the office but wants*
Some cogging,° cozening slave, to get some office,   *more.*
Have not devised this slander. I will be hanged else.
Iago: Fie, there is no such man! It is impossible.
Desdemona: If any such there be, heaven pardon him.
Emilia: A halter pardon him! And hell gnaw his bones!
Why should he call her whore? Who keeps her company?
What place? What time? What form? What likelihood?
The Moor's abused by some most villainous knave,
Some base notorious knave, some scurvy fellow.

water tears   **callet** slut
stick . . . misuse base any doubt on   **Beshrew** curse
my smallest fault   **cogging** cheating
despite abuse

O heavens, that such companions° thou'dst unfold,°
And put in every honest hand a whip
To lash the rascals naked through the world
Even from the east to th' west!

Iago: Speak within door.°

Emilia: O, fie upon them! Some such squire° he was
That turned your wit the seamy side without
And made you to suspect me with the Moor.

Iago: You are a fool. Go to.

Desdemona: Alas, Iago,
What shall I do to win my lord again?
Good friend, go to him, for, by this light of heaven,
I know not how I lost him. Here I kneel:
If e'er my will did trespass 'gainst his love
Either in discourse of thought° or actual deed,
Or that mine eyes, mine ears, or any sense
Delighted them in any other form;
Or that I do not yet, and ever did,
And ever will (though he do shake me off
To beggarly divorcement) love him dearly,
Comfort forswear me. Unkindness may do much,
And his unkindness may defeat° my life,
But never taint my love. I cannot say "whore."
It does abhor me now I speak the word;
To do the act that might the addition earn
Not the world's mass of vanity could make me.

Iago: I pray you be content. 'Tis but his humor.°
The business of the state does him offense.

Desdemona: If 'twere no other.

Iago: It is but so, I warrant.   (*Trumpets within.*)
Hark how these instruments summon to supper.
The messengers of Venice stay the meat.°
Go in, and weep not. All things shall be well.
(*Exeunt* **Desdemona** *and* **Emilia.**) (*Enter* **Roderigo.**)
How now, Roderigo?

Roderigo: I do not find that thou deal'st justly with me.

Iago: What in the contrary?

Roderigo: Every day thou daff'st° me with some device,° Iago, and rather, as
it seems to me now, keep'st from me all conveniency° than suppliest me
with the least advantage of hope. I will indeed no longer endure it; nor am
I yet persuaded to put up° in peace what already I have foolishly suffered.

Iago: Will you hear me, Roderigo?

*Visual irony:
compare her action
with Othello's on
page 406.*

*At least one
victim begins to
come to knowledge.*

companions fellows, rogues	**humor** mood
unfold disclose	**stay the meat** await the meal
within door more quietly and moderately	**daff'st** put off
	device scheme
squire (a term of contempt)	**conveniency** what is needful
discourse of thought thinking	**put up** accept
defeat destroy	

Roderigo: I have heard too much, and your words and performances are no kin together.

Iago: You charge me most unjustly.

Roderigo: With naught but truth. I have wasted myself out of my means. The jewels you have had from me to deliver Desdemona would half have corrupted a votarist.° You have told me she hath received them, and returned me expectations and comforts of sudden respect° and acquaintance; but I find none.

Iago: Well, go to; very well.

Roderigo: Very well? Go to? I cannot go to, man; nor 'tis not very well. Nay, I think it is scurvy, and begin to find myself fopped° in it.

Iago: Very well.

Roderigo: I tell you 'tis not very well. I will make myself known to Desdemona. If she will return me my jewels, I will give over my suit and repent my unlawful solicitation. If not, assure yourself I will seek satisfaction of you.

Iago: You have said now?

Roderigo: Ay, and said nothing but what I protest° intendment of doing.

Iago: Why, now I see there's mettle° in thee, and even from this instant do build on thee a better opinion than ever before. Give me thy hand, Roderigo. Thou hast taken against me a most just exception;° but yet I protest I have dealt most directly° in thy affair.

Roderigo: It hath not appeared.

Iago: I grant indeed it hath not appeared, and your suspicion is not without wit and judgment. But, Roderigo, if thou hast that in thee indeed which I have greater reason to believe now than ever—I mean purpose, courage, and valor—this night show it. If thou the next night following enjoy not Desdemona, take me from this world with treachery and devise engines for° my life.

Roderigo: Well, what is it? Is it within reason and compass?°

Iago: Sir, there is especial commission come from Venice to depute Cassio in Othello's place.

Roderigo: Is that true? Why, then Othello and Desdemona return again to Venice.

Iago: O, no; he goes into Mauritania and taketh away with him the fair Desdemona, unless his abode be lingered here by some accident; wherein none can be so determinate° as the removing of Cassio.

Roderigo: How do you mean, removing him?

Iago: Why, by making him uncapable of Othello's place—knocking out his brains.

Roderigo: And that you would have me to do?

Iago: Ay, if you dare do yourself a profit and a right. He sups tonight with a harlotry,° and thither will I go to him. He knows not yet of his honorable

votarist nun	**directly** straightforwardly
sudden respect immediate consideration	**engines for** schemes against
fopped duped	**compass** possibility
protest aver	**determinate** effective
mettle spirit	**harlotry** female
exception objection	

fortune. If you will watch his going thence, which I will fashion to fall out°
between twelve and one, you may take him at your pleasure. I will be near
to second° your attempt, and he shall fall between us. Come, stand not
amazed at it, but go along with me. I will show you such a necessity in his
death that you shall think yourself bound to put it on him. It is now high
supper time, and the night grows to waste. About it.

Roderigo: I will hear further reason for this.

Iago: And you shall be satisfied.

(*Exeunt.*)

SCENE III.   The citadel.

(*Enter* **Othello, Lodovico, Desdemona, Emilia,** *and* **Attendants.**)

Lodovico: I do beseech you, sir, trouble yourself no further.

Othello: O, pardon me; 'twill do me good to walk.

Lodovico: Madam, good night. I humbly thank your ladyship.

Desdemona: Your honor is most welcome.

Othello: Will you walk, sir? O, Desdemona.

Desdemona: My lord?

Othello: Get you to bed on th' instant; I will be returned forthwith. Dismiss
your attendant there. Look't be done.

Desdemona: I will, my lord.

(*Exit* **Othello,** *with* **Lodovico** *and* **Attendants.**)

Emilia: How goes it now? He looks gentler than he did.

Desdemona: He says he will return incontinent,°
And hath commanded me to go to bed,
And bade me to dismiss you.

Emilia: Dismiss me?

Desdemona: It was his bidding; therefore, good Emilia,
Give me my nightly wearing, and adieu.
We must not now displease him.

Emilia: I would you had never seen him!

Desdemona: So would not I. My love doth so approve him
That even his stubbornness, his checks,° his frowns—
Prithee unpin me—have grace and favor.

Emilia: I have laid these sheets you bade me on the bed.

Desdemona: All's one.° Good Father, how foolish are our minds!
If I do die before, prithee shroud me
In one of these same sheets.

Emilia: Come, come! You talk.

Desdemona: My mother had a maid called Barbary.
She was in love; and he she loved proved mad
And did forsake her. She had a song of "Willow";
An old thing 'twas, but it expressed her fortune,

---

fall out occur
second support
incontinent at once

checks rebukes
All's one no matter

And she died singing it. That song tonight
Will not go from my mind; I have much to do
But to go hang my head all at one side
And sing it like poor Barbary. Prithee dispatch.
Emilia: Shall I go fetch your nightgown?
Desdemona: No, unpin me here.
This Lodovico is a proper man.
Emilia: A very handsome man.
Desdemona: He speaks well.
Emilia: I know a lady in Venice would have walked
barefoot to Palestine for a touch of his nether lip.
Desdemona: (*Sings*)
"The poor soul sat singing by a sycamore tree,
  Sing all a green willow;
Her hand on her bosom, her head on her knee,
  Sing willow, willow, willow.
The fresh streams ran by her and murmured her moans;
  Sing willow, willow, willow;
Her salt tears fell from her, and soft'ned the stones—
  Sing willow, willow, willow—"
Lay by these.   (*Gives* **Emilia** *her clothes.*)
"Willow, Willow"——
Prithee hie° thee; he'll come anon.°
  "Sing all a green willow must be my garland.
  Let nobody blame him; his scorn I approve"——
Nay, that's not next. Hark! Who is't that knocks?
Emilia: It is the wind.
Desdemona: (*Sings*)
"I called my love false love; but what said he then?
  Sing willow, willow, willow:
If I court moe° women, you'll couch with moe men."
So, get thee gone; good night. Mine eyes do itch.
Doth that bode weeping?
Emilia: 'Tis neither here nor there.
Desdemona: I have heard it said so. O, these men, these men.
Dost thou in conscience think, tell me, Emilia,
That there be women do abuse their husbands
In such gross kind?
Emilia: There be some such, no question.
Desdemona: Wouldst thou do such a deed for all the world?
Emilia: Why, would not you?
Desdemona: No, by this heavenly light!
Emilia: Nor I neither by this heavenly light.
I might do't as well i' th' dark.
Desdemona: Wouldst thou do such a deed for all the world?
Emilia: The world's a huge thing; it is a great price for a small vice.

---

hie hurry   **moe** more
anon at once

Desdemona: In troth, I think thou wouldst not.

Emilia: In troth, I think I should; and undo't when I had done. Marry, I would not do such a thing for a joint-ring,° nor for measures of lawn,° nor for gowns, petticoats, nor caps, nor any petty exhibition,° but for all the whole world? Why, who would not make her husband a cuckold to make him a monarch? I should venture purgatory for't.

Desdemona: Beshrew me if I would do such a wrong for the whole world.

Emilia: Why, the wrong is but a wrong i' th' world; and having the world for your labor, 'tis a wrong in your own world, and you might quickly make it right.

Desdemona: I do not think there is any such woman.

Emilia: Yes, a dozen; and as many to th' vantage as
would store° the world they played for.
But I do think it is their husbands' faults
If wives do fall. Say that they slack their duties
And pour our treasures into foreign° laps;
Or else break out in peevish jealousies,
Throwing restraint upon us; or say they strike us,
Or scant our former having in despite°—
Why, we have galls; and though we have some grace,
Yet have we some revenge. Let husbands know
Their wives have sense like them. They see, and smell,
And have their palates both for sweet and sour,
As husbands have. What is it that they do
When they change° us for others? Is it sport?
I think it is. And doth affection° breed it?
I think it doth. Is't frailty that thus errs?
It is so too. And have not we affections?
Desires for sport? and frailty? as men have?
Then let them use us well; else let them know,
The ills we do, their ills instruct us so.°

Desdemona: Good night, good night. Heaven me such uses° send,
Not to pick bad from bad, but by bad mend.
(*Exeunt.*)

ACT V

SCENE I. A street.

(*Enter* **Iago** *and* **Roderigo**.)

Iago: Here, stand behind this bulk;° straight will he come.

---

joint-ring (a ring with two interlocking halves)
lawn fine linen
exhibition payment
to . . . store in addition as would fill
foreign alien, i.e., other than the wife
scant . . . despite reduce, in spite, our

household allowance (?)
change exchange
affection strong feeling, desire
instruct us so teach us to do likewise
uses practices
bulk projecting stall of a shop

Wear thy good rapier bare, and put it home.
Quick, quick! Fear nothing; I'll be at thy elbow.
It makes us, or it mars us, think on that,
And fix most firm thy resolution.
Roderigo: Be near at hand; I may miscarry in't.
Iago: Here, at thy hand. Be bold, and take thy stand.   (*Moves to one side.*)
Roderigo: I have no great devotion to the deed,
And yet he hath given me satisfying reasons.
'Tis but a man gone. Forth my sword! He dies!
Iago: I have rubbed this young quat° almost to the sense,°
And he grows angry. Now, whether he kill Cassio,
Or Cassio him, or each do kill the other,
Every way makes my gain. Live Roderigo,
He calls me to a restitution large
Of gold and jewels that I bobbed° from him
As gifts to Desdemona.
It must not be. If Cassio do remain,
He hath a daily beauty in his life
That makes me ugly; and besides, the Moor
May unfold me to him; there stand I in much peril.
No, he must die. But so, I hear him coming.
(*Enter* **Cassio**.)
Roderigo: I know his gait. 'Tis he. Villain, thou diest!   (*Thrusts at* **Cassio**.)
Cassio: That thrust had been mine enemy indeed
But that my coat° is better than thou know'st.
I will make proof of thine.   (*Fights with* **Roderigo**.)
Roderigo: O, I am slain!°
Cassio: I am maimed forever. Help, ho! Murder! Murder!
(*Enter* **Othello** *to one side.*)
Othello: The voice of Cassio. Iago keeps his word.
Roderigo: O, villain that I am!
Othello: It is even so.
Cassio: O help, ho! Light! A surgeon!
Othello: 'Tis he. O brave Iago, honest and just,
That hast such noble sense of thy friend's wrong!
Thou teachest me. Minion,° your dear lies dead,
And your unblest° fate hies.° Strumpet, I come.
Forth of my heart those charms, thine eyes, are blotted.
Thy bed, lust-stained, shall with lust's blood be spotted.   (*Exit* **Othello**.)
(*Enter* **Lodovico** *and* **Gratiano**.)
Cassio: What, ho? No watch? No passage?° Murder! Murder!

quat pimple
to the sense raw
bobbed swindled
coat i.e., a mail shirt or bulletproof vest
slain (most editors add here a stage direction which has Iago wounding Cassio in the leg from behind, but remaining unseen. However, nothing in the text requires this, and Cassio's wound can be given him in the fight with Roderigo, for presumably when Cassio attacks Roderigo the latter would not simply accept the thrust but would parry.
Minion hussy, i.e., Desdemona
unblest unsanctified
hies approaches swiftly
passage passers-by

Gratiano: 'Tis some mischance. The voice is very direful.

Cassio: O, help!

Lodovico: Hark!

Roderigo: O wretched villain!

Lodovico: Two or three groan. 'Tis heavy night.
These may be counterfeits. Let's think't unsafe
To come into the cry without more help.

Roderigo: Nobody come? Then shall I bleed to death.

Lodovico: Hark!
(*Enter* **Iago** *with a light.*)

Gratiano: Here's one comes in his shirt, with light and weapons.

Iago: Who's there? Whose noise is this that cries on murder?

Lodovico: We do not know.

Iago: Do not you hear a cry?

Cassio: Here, here! For heaven's sake, help me!

Iago: What's the matter?

Gratiano: This is Othello's ancient, as I take it.

Lodovico: The same indeed, a very valiant fellow.

Iago: What are you here that cry so grievously?

Cassio: Iago? O, I am spoiled, undone by villains.
Give me some help.

Iago: O me, lieutenant! What villains have done this?

Cassio: I think that one of them is hereabout
And cannot make away.

Iago: O treacherous villains!
(*To* **Lodovico** *and* **Gratiano**) What are you there?
Come in, and give some help.

Roderigo: O, help me there!

Cassio: That's one of them.

Iago: O murd'rous slave! O villain!   (*Stabs* **Roderigo**.)

Roderigo: O damned Iago! O inhuman dog!

Iago: Kill men i' th' dark?—Where be these bloody thieves?—
How silent is this town!—Ho! Murder! Murder!—
What may you be? Are you of good or evil?

Lodovico: As you shall prove us, praise us.

Iago: Signior Lodovico?

Lodovico: He, sir.

Iago: I cry you mercy. Here's Cassio hurt by villains.

Gratiano: Cassio?

Iago: How is't, brother?

Cassio: My leg is cut in two.

Iago: Marry, heaven forbid!
Light, gentlemen. I'll bind it with my shirt.
(*Enter* **Bianca**.)

Bianca: What is the matter, ho? Who is't that cried?

Iago: Who is't that cried?

Bianca: O my dear Cassio! My sweet Cassio!
O Cassio, Cassio, Cassio!

Irony: two of them are "hereabout." Is Iago in so deeply he can't "make away"?

Iago: O notable strumpet!—Cassio, may you suspect
Who they should be that have thus mangled you?
Cassio: No.
Gratiano: I am sorry to find you thus. I have been to seek you.
Iago: Lend me a garter. So. O for a chair
To bear him easily hence.
Bianca: Alas, he faints! O Cassio, Cassio, Cassio!
Iago: Gentlemen all, I do suspect this trash
To be a party in this injury.—
Patience awhile, good Cassio.—Come, come.
Lend me a light. Know we this face or no?
Alas, my friend and my dear countryman
Roderigo? No.—Yes, sure.—Yes, 'tis Roderigo!
Gratiano: What, of Venice?
Iago: Even he, sir. Did you know him?
Gratiano: Know him? Ay.
Iago: Signior Gratiano? I cry your gentle pardon.
These bloody accidents must excuse my manners
That so neglected you.
Gratiano: I am glad to see you.
Iago: How do you, Cassio?—O, a chair, a chair!
Gratiano: Roderigo?
Iago: He, he 'tis he! (*A chair brought in.*) O, that's well said;° the chair.
Some good man bear him carefully from hence.
I'll fetch the general's surgeon. (**To Bianca**) For you, mistress,
Save you your labor. (*To* **Cassio**) He that lies slain here, Cassio,
Was my dear friend. What malice was between you?
Cassio: None in the world; nor do I know the man.
Iago: What, look you pale?—O, bear him out o' th' air.
(**Cassio** *is carried off.*)
Stay you, good gentlemen.—Look you pale, mistress?
Do you perceive the gastness° of her eye?
Nay, if you stare, we shall hear more anon.
Behold her well; I pray you look upon her.
Do you see, gentlemen? Nay, guiltiness will speak,
Though tongues were out of use.°
(*Enter* **Emilia**.)
Emilia: Alas, what is the matter? What is the matter, husband?
Iago: Cassio hath here been set on in the dark
By Roderigo and fellows that are scaped.
He's almost slain, and Roderigo quite dead.
Emilia: Alas, good gentleman! Alas, good Cassio!
Iago: This is the fruits of whoring. Prithee, Emilia,
Go know of Cassio where he supped tonight.
(*To* **Bianca**) What, do you shake at that?
Bianca: He supped at my house; but I therefore shake not.

---

well said well done
gastness terror

tongues were out of use men no longer
spoke

Iago: O, did he so? I charge° you go with me.

Emilia: Oh fie upon thee, strumpet!

Bianca: I am no strumpet, but of life as honest
As you that thus abuse me.

Emilia: As I? Fie upon thee!

Iago: Kind gentlemen, let's go see poor Cassio dressed.°
(*To* **Bianca**) Come, mistress, you must tell's another tale.
Emilia, run you to the citadel
And tell my lord and lady what hath happened.   (*Exit* **Emilia**.)
Will you go on afore?   (*Exeunt all but* **Iago**.)
                    This is the night
That either makes me or fordoes me quite.°   (*Exit.*)

SCENE II.   Desdemona's chamber.

(*Enter* **Othello** *with a light; and* **Desdemona** *in her bed.*)

Othello: It is the cause, it is the cause, my soul.
Let me not name it to you, you chaste stars.
It is the cause. Yet I'll not shed her blood,
Nor scar that whiter skin of hers than snow,
And smooth as monumental alabaster.
Yet she must die, else she'll betray more men.
Put out the light, and then put out the light.
If I quench thee, thou flaming minister,°
I can again thy former light restore,
Should I repent me; but once put out thy light,
Thou cunning'st° pattern of excelling nature,
I know not where is that Promethean heat°
That can thy light relume.° When I have plucked the rose,
I cannot give it vital° growth again;
It needs must wither. I'll smell thee on the tree.   (*He kisses her.*)
O balmy breath, that dost almost persuade
Justice to break her sword. One more, one more!
Be thus when thou art dead, and I will kill thee,
And love thee after. One more, and that's the last!
So sweet was ne'er so fatal. I must weep,
But they are cruel tears. This sorrow's heavenly;
It strikes where it doth love. She wakes.

Desdemona: Who's there? Othello?

Othello: Ay, Desdemona.

Desdemona: Will you come to bed, my lord?

Othello: Have you prayed tonight, Desdemona?

Words and images (whiter skin, the rose) seem out of tune with deed of execution. How are his words and tone ironic?

charge   command
dressed   bandaged
fordoes me quite   completely ruins me
minister   worker, servant
cunning'st   most intricate and skillfully
wrought (by nature excelling itself)

Promethean heat   divine fire (Prome-
theus is the Titan who stole fire from
heaven and gave it to man)
relume   relight
vital   living

Desdemona: Ay, my lord.
Othello: If you bethink yourself of any crime
  Unreconciled as yet to heaven and grace,
  Solicit for it straight.
Desdemona: Alack, my lord, what may you mean by that?
Othello: Well, do it, and be brief; I will walk by.°
  I would not kill thy unpreparèd spirit.
  No, heavens forfend! I would not kill thy soul.
Desdemona: Talk you of killing?
Othello: Ay, I do.
Desdemona: Then heaven
  Have mercy on me!
Othello: Amen, with all my heart.
Desdemona: If you say so, I hope you will not kill me.
Othello: Humh.
Desdemona: And yet I fear you; for you're fatal then
  When your eyes roll so. Why I should fear I know not,
  Since guiltiness I know not; but yet I feel I fear.
Othello: Think on thy sins.
Desdemona: They are loves I bear to you.
Othello: Ay, and for that thou diest.
Desdemona: That death's unnatural that kills for loving.
  Alas, why gnaw you so your nether lip?
  Some bloody passion shakes your very frame.
  These are portents; but yet I hope, I hope,
  They do not point on me.
Othello: Peace and be still.
Desdemona: I will so. What's the matter?
Othello: That handkerchief which I so loved and gave thee,
  Thou gav'st to Cassio.
Desdemona: No, by my life and soul!
  Send for the man and ask him.
Othello: Sweet soul, take heed,
  Take heed of perjury; thou art on thy deathbed.
Desdemona: Ay, but not yet to die.
Othello: Presently.°
  Therefore confess thee freely of thy sin,
  For to deny each article° with oath
  Cannot remove nor choke the strong conception
  That I do groan withal. Thou art to die.
Desdemona: Then Lord have mercy on me.
Othello: I say, amen.
Desdemona: And have you mercy too. I never did
  Offend you in my life; never loved Cassio
  But with such general warranty° of heaven

Cassio is finally named. Compare Othello's line, p.421. (Heaven truly knows...)

by nearby
Presently immediately
article item (of the charge of adultery.

Othello makes heavy use of legal terms in this scene)
warranty allowance

As I might love. I never gave him token.
Othello: By heaven, I saw my handkerchief in's hand!
O perjured woman! thou dost stone° my heart,
And mak'st me call what I intend to do
A murder, which I thought a sacrifice.
I saw the handkerchief.
Desdemona: He found it then.
I never gave it him. Send for him hither.
Let him confess a truth.
Othello: He hath confessed.
Desdemona: What, my lord?
Othello: That he hath used thee.
Desdemona: How? Unlawfully?
Othello: Ay.
Desdemona: He will not say so.
Othello: No, his mouth is stopped.
Honest Iago hath ta'en order for't.°
Desdemona: O, my fear interprets. What, is he dead?
Othello: Had all his hairs been lives, my great revenge
Had stomach° for them all.
Desdemona: Alas, he is betrayed, and I undone!
Othello: Out, strumpet! Weep'st thou for him to my face?
Desdemona: O, banish me, my lord, but kill me not!
Othello: Down, strumpet!
Desdemona: Kill me tomorrow; let me live tonight!
Othello: Nay, if you strive——
Desdemona: But half an hour!
Othello: Being done, there is no pause.
Desdemona: But while I say one prayer!
Othello: It is too late.   (*Smothers her.*)
(**Emilia** *at the door.*)
Emilia: (*Calls within.*) My lord, my lord! What, ho, my lord, my lord!
Othello: What noise is this? Not dead? Not yet quite dead?
I that am cruel am yet merciful;
I would not have thee linger in thy pain.
So, so.
Emilia: (*Within*) What, ho! My lord, my lord!
Othello: Who's there?
Emilia: (*Within*) O, good my lord, I would speak a word with you.
Othello: Yes, 'tis Emilia.—By and by.—She's dead.—
'Tis like she comes to speak of Cassio's death.
The noise was high.° Ha! No more moving?
Still as the grave.—Shall she come in? Were't good?—
I think she stirs again. No.—What's best to do?
If she come in, she'll sure speak to my wife.
My wife! My wife! What wife? I have no wife.

---

stone turn to stone   **stomach** appetite
ta'en order for't made sure of it   **high** loud

O, insupportable! O heavy hour!
Methinks it should be now a huge eclipse
Of sun and moon, and that th' affrighted globe
Should yawn° at alteration.°

Emilia: (*Within*) I do beseech you
That I may speak with you, O good my lord!

Othello: I had forgot thee. O, come in, Emilia.
Soft, by and by.—Let me the curtains draw.—
(*Draws the bed hangings and then opens the door.*)
Where art thou?
(*Enter* **Emilia.**)
                              What's the matter with thee now?

Emilia: O my good lord, yonder's foul murders done!

Othello: What? Now?

Emilia: But now, my lord.

Othello: It is the very error° of the moon.
She comes more nearer earth than she was wont
And makes men mad.

Emilia: Cassio, my lord, hath killed a young Venetian
Called Roderigo.

Othello: Roderigo killed?
And Cassio killed?

Emilia: No, Cassio is not killed.

Othello: Not Cassio killed? Then murder's out of tune,
And sweet revenge grows harsh.

Desdemona: O, falsely, falsely murdered!

Emilia: O Lord! What cry is that?

Othello: That? What?

Emilia: Out and alas! that was my lady's voice.
Help! Help, ho! Help! O lady, speak again!
Sweet Desdemona! O sweet mistress, speak!

Desdemona: A guiltless death I die.

Emilia: O, who hath done this deed?

Desdemona: Nobody—I myself. Farewell.
Commend me to my kind lord. O, farewell!   (*She dies.*)

Othello: Why, how should she be murd'red?

Emilia: Alas, who knows?

Othello: You heard her say herself, it was not I.

Emilia: She said so. I must needs report the truth.

Othello: She's like a liar gone to burning hell!
'Twas I that killed her.

Emilia: O, the more angel she,
And you the blacker devil!

Othello: She turned to folly, and she was a whore.

Can murder ever be in tune? Compare Iago's line, p. 381. (O, you are well tuned...)

yawn gape open (as in an earthquake)
Methinks . . . alteration (the Elizabethans believed that great changes in human affairs were reflected by disorders in nature)

error wandering out of regular course (disorders in the heavens were believed by some to cause disorders on earth, as well as vice versa)

Emilia: Thou dost belie her, and thou art a devil.

Othello: She was false as water.

Emilia: Thou art rash as fire to say
That she was false. O, she was heavenly true!

Othello: Cassio did top her. Ask thy husband else.
O, I were damned beneath all depth in hell
But that I did proceed upon just grounds
To this extremity. Thy husband knew it all.

Emilia: My husband?

Othello: Thy husband.

Emilia: That she was false to wedlock?

Othello: Ay, with Cassio. Had she been true,
If heaven would make me such another world
Of one entire and perfect chrysolite,°
I'd not have sold her for it.

Emilia: My husband?

Othello: Ay, 'twas he that told me on her first.
An honest man he is, and hates the slime
That sticks on filthy deeds.

Emilia: My husband?

Othello: What needs this iterance? Woman, I say thy husband.

Emilia: O mistress, villainy hath made mocks with love!
My husband say she was false?

Othello: He, woman.
I say, thy husband. Dost understand the word?
My friend, thy husband; honest, honest Iago.

Emilia: If he say so, may his pernicious soul
Rot half a grain a day! He lies to th' heart.
She was too fond of her most filthy bargain.

Othello: Hah?

Emilia: Do thy worst.
This deed of thine is no more worthy heaven
Than thou wast worthy her.

Othello: Peace, you were best.°

Emilia: Thou hast not half that pow'r to do me harm
As I have to be hurt. O gull! O dolt!
As ignorant as dirt! Thou hast done a deed—

(**Othello** *moves to draw his sword.*)
I care not for thy sword; I'll make thee known,
Though I lost twenty lives. Help! Help! Ho! Help!
The Moor hath killed my mistress! Murder! Murder!

(*Enter* **Montano, Gratiano,** *and* **Iago** *and* **Others.**)

Montano: What is the matter? How now, general?

Emilia: O, are you come, Iago? You have done well,
That men must lay their murders on your neck.

Gratiano: What is the matter?

---

chrysolite topaz   be silent
Peace, you were best i.e., you had better

Emilia: Disprove this villain, if thou be'st a man.
  He says thou told'st him that his wife was false.
  I know thou didst not; thou'rt not such a villain.
  Speak, for my heart is full.
Iago: I told him what I thought, and told no more
  Than what he found himself was apt and true.
Emilia: But did you ever tell him she was false?
Iago: I did.
Emilia: You told a lie, an odious damnèd lie!
  Upon my soul, a lie! A wicked lie!
  She false with Cassio? Did you say with Cassio?
Iago: With Cassio, mistress. Go to, charm° your tongue.
Emilia: I will not charm my tongue; I am bound to speak:
  My mistress here lies murdered in her bed.
All: O heavens forfend!
Emilia: And your reports have set the murder on.
Othello: Nay, stare not, masters. It is true indeed.
Gratiano: 'Tis a strange truth.
Montano: O monstrous act!
Emilia: Villainy, villainy, villainy!
  I think upon't—I think I smell't!—O villainy!
  I thought so then.—I'll kill myself for grief.—
  O villainy, villainy!
Iago: What, are you mad? I charge you get you home.
Emilia: Good gentlemen, let me have leave to speak.
  'Tis proper I obey him, but not now.
  Perchance, Iago, I will ne'er go home.
Othello: O! O! O!   (*Falls on the bed.*)
Emilia: Nay, lay thee down and roar,
  For thou hast killed the sweetest innocent
  That e'er did lift up eye.
Othello: O, she was foul!   (*Rises.*)
  I scarce did know you, uncle. There lies your niece,
  Whose breath, indeed, these hands have newly stopped.
  I know this act shows horrible and grim.
Gratiano: Poor Desdemon! I am glad thy father's dead.
  Thy match was mortal to him, and pure grief
  Shore his old thread in twain. Did he live now,
  This sight would make him do a desperate turn;
  Yea, curse his better angel from his side,
  And fall to reprobation.°
Othello: 'Tis pitiful; but yet Iago knows
  That she with Cassio hath the act of shame
  A thousand times committed. Cassio confessed it;
  And she did gratify his amorous works
  With that recognizance and pledge of love,
  Which I first gave her. I saw it in his hand.

charm control   **reprobation** damnation

It was a handkerchief, an antique token
My father gave my mother.
Emilia: O God! O heavenly God!
Iago: Zounds, hold your peace!
Emilia: 'Twill out, 'twill out! I peace?
No, I will speak as liberal as the north.°
Let heaven and men and devils, let them all,
All, all, cry shame against me, yet I'll speak.
Iago: Be wise, and get you home.
Emilia: I will not.
(**Iago** *draws and threatens* **Emilia.**)
Gratiano: Fie! Your sword upon a woman?
Emilia: O thou dull Moor, that handkerchief thou speak'st of
I found by fortune, and did give my husband;
For often with a solemn earnestness—
More than indeed belonged to such a trifle—
He begged of me to steal't.
Iago: Villainous whore!
Emilia: She give it Cassio? No, alas, I found it,
And I did give't my husband.
Iago: Filth, thou liest!
Emilia: By heaven, I do not, I do not, gentlemen.
O murd'rous coxcomb! What should such a fool
Do with so good a wife?
Othello: Are there no stones° in heaven
But what serves for the thunder? Precious villain!
(*The* **Moor** *runs at* **Iago**, *but is disarmed by* **Montano. Iago** *kills his wife.*)
Gratiano: The woman falls. Sure he hath killed his wife.
Emilia: Ay, ay. O, lay me by my mistress' side.   (*Exit* **Iago.**)
Gratiano: He's gone, but his wife's killed.
Montano: 'Tis a notorious° villain. Take you this weapon,
Which I have recovered from the Moor.
Come, guard the door without. Let him not pass,
But kill him rather. I'll after that same villain,
For 'tis a damnèd slave.
(*Exit with all but* **Othello** *and* **Emilia.**)
Othello: I am not valiant neither;
But every puny whipster° gets my sword.
But why should honor outlive honesty?
Let it go all.
Emilia: What did thy song bode, lady?
Hark, canst thou hear me? I will play the swan,
And die in music. (*Sings*) "Willow, willow, willow."
Moor, she was chaste. She loved thee, cruel Moor,
So come my soul to bliss as I speak true.
So speaking as I think, alas, I die.   (*She dies.*)

---

liberal as the north freely (and bitingly)
as the north wind blows
stones thunderbolts

notorious out-and-out
puny whipster small top-whipping boy

Othello: I have another weapon in this chamber;
  It was a sword of Spain, the ice-brook's temper.
  O, here it is.—Uncle, I must come forth.
Gratiano: (*Within*) If thou attempt it, it will cost thee dear.
  Thou hast no weapon, and perforce must suffer.
Othello: Look in upon me then and speak with me,
  Or, naked as I am, I will assault thee.
  (*Enter* **Gratiano.**)
Gratiano: What is the matter?
Othello: Behold, I have a weapon;
  A better never did itself sustain
  Upon a soldier's thigh. I have seen the day
  That with this little arm and this good sword
  I have made my way through more impediments
  Than twenty times your stop. But O vain boast!
  Who can control his fate? 'Tis not so now.
  Be not afraid, though you do see me weaponed.
  Here is my journey's end, here is my butt,°
  And very seamark of my utmost sail.°
  Do you go back dismayed? 'Tis a lost fear.
  Man but a rush° against Othello's breast,
  And he retires. Where should Othello go?
  Now, how dost thou look now? O ill-starred wench!
  Pale as thy smock! When we shall meet at compt,°
  This look of thine will hurl my soul from heaven,
  And fiends will snatch at it. Cold, cold, my girl?
  Even like thy chastity.
  O cursèd, cursèd slave! Whip me, ye devils,
  From the possession of° this heavenly sight!
  Blow me about in winds! roast me in sulfur!
  Wash me in steep-down gulfs of liquid fire!
  O Desdemon! Dead Desdemon; dead. O! O!
  (*Enter* **Lodovico, Cassio, Montano,** *and* **Iago** [*as prisoner*], *with* **Officers.**)
Lodovico: Where is this rash and most unfortunate man?
Othello: That's he that was Othello? Here I am.
Lodovico: Where is that viper? Bring the villain forth.
Othello: I look down towards his feet°—but that's a fable.
  If that thou be'st a devil, I cannot kill thee.   (*Wounds* **Iago.**)
Lodovico: Wrench his sword from him.   (**Othello** *is disarmed.*)
Iago: I bleed, sir, but not killed.
Othello: I am not sorry neither. I'd have thee live;
  For in my sense, 'tis happiness to die.
Lodovico: O thou Othello that was once so good,
  Fall'n in the practice° of a cursèd slave,
  What shall be said to thee?

Othello (victim) realizes he has exchanged heaven for hell.

---

butt target, stopping place
seamark of my utmost sail marker of
my farthest journey
Man but a rush attack with only a reed

compt Judgment Day
the possession of being possessed by
towards his feet i.e., for his cloven hoof
practice plotting

Is Othello's view accurate here?

Othello: Why, anything:
   An honorable murderer, if you will;
   For naught I did in hate, but all in honor.
Lodovico: This wretch hath part confessed his villainy.
   Did you and he consent in Cassio's death?
Othello: Ay.
Cassio: Dear general, I never gave you cause.
Othello: I do believe it, and I ask your pardon.
   Will you, I pray, demand that demi-devil
   Why he hath thus ensnared my soul and body?
Iago: Demand me nothing. What you know, you know.
   From this time forth I never will speak word.
Lodovico: What, not to pray?
Gratiano: Torments will ope your lips.
Othello: Well, thou dost best.
Lodovico: Sir, you shall understand what hath befall'n,
   Which, as I think, you know not. Here is a letter
   Found in the pocket of the slain Roderigo;
   And here another. The one of them imports
   The death of Cassio to be undertook
   By Roderigo.
Othello: O villain!
Cassio: Most heathenish and most gross!
Lodovico: Now here's another discontented paper
   Found in his pocket too; and this, it seems,
   Roderigo meant t' have sent this damnèd villain;
   But that, belike, Iago in the interim
   Came in and satisfied him.
Othello: O thou pernicious caitiff!
   How came you, Cassio, by that handkerchief
   That was my wife's?
Cassio: I found it in my chamber;
   And he himself confessed it but even now
   That there he dropped it for a special purpose
   Which wrought to his desire.
Othello: O fool! Fool! Fool!
Cassio: There is besides in Roderigo's letter,
   How he upbraids Iago that he made him
   Brave me upon the watch; whereon it came
   That I was cast; and even but now he spake,
   After long seeming dead—Iago hurt him,
   Iago set him on.
Lodovico: You must forsake this room and go with us.
   Your power and your command is taken off,
   And Cassio rules in Cyprus. For this slave,
   If there be any cunning cruelty
   That can torment him much and hold him long,
   It shall be his. You shall close prisoner rest

Till that the nature of your fault be known
To the Venetian state. Come, bring away.
Othello: Soft you, a word or two before you go.
I have done the state some service, and they know't.
No more of that. I pray you, in your letters,
When you shall these unlucky deeds relate,
Speak of me as I am. Nothing extenuate,
Nor set down aught in malice. Then must you speak
Of one that loved not wisely, but too well;
Of one not easily jealous, but, being wrought,
Perplexed in the extreme; of one whose hand,
Like the base Judean,° threw a pearl away
Richer than all his tribe; of one whose subdued eyes,
Albeit unusèd to the melting mood,
Drops tears as fast as the Arabian trees
Their med'cinable gum. Set you down this.
And say besides that in Aleppo once,
Where a malignant and a turbaned Turk
Beat a Venetian and traduced the state,
I took by th' throat the circumcisèd dog
And smote him—thus.   (*He stabs himself.*)
Lodovico: O bloody period!°
Gratiano: All that is spoke is marred.
Othello: I kissed thee ere I killed thee. No way but this,
Killing myself, to die upon a kiss.
(*He falls over* **Desdemona** *and dies.*)
Cassio: This did I fear, but thought he had no weapon;
For he was great of heart.
Lodovico: (*To* **Iago**)   O Spartan dog,
More fell° than anguish, hunger, or the sea!
Look on the tragic loading of this bed.
This is thy work. The object poisons sight;
Let it be hid.   (*Bed curtains drawn.*)
            Gratiano, keep° the house,
And seize upon the fortunes of the Moor,
For they succeed on you. To you, lord governor,
Remains the censure of this hellish villain,
The time, the place, the torture. O, enforce it!
Myself will straight aboard, and to the state
This heavy act with heavy heart relate.
(*Exeunt.*)

> Does Othello see himself as realistically as he thinks? If not, are the lines ironic? Who is the ironist and who the victim?

FINIS

Judean   (most editors use the Q1 reading, "Indian," here, but F is clear; both readings point toward the infidel, the unbeliever)

period   end
fell   cruel
keep   remain in

BLACK COMEDY

Peter Shaffer

CHARACTERS

Brindsley Miller: A young sculptor (mid-twenties), intelligent and attractive, but nervous and uncertain of himself.

Carol Melkett: His fiancée. A young debutante; very pretty, very spoiled; very silly. Her sound is that unmistakable, terrifying deb quack.

Miss Furnival: A middle-aged spinster. Prissy; and refined. Clad in the blouse and sack skirt of her gentility, her hair in a bun, her voice in a bun, she reveals only the repressed gestures of the middle-class spinster—until alcohol undoes her.

Colonel Melkett: Carol's commanding father. Brisk, barky, yet given to sudden vocal calms which suggest a deep and alarming instability. It is not only the constant darkness which gives him his look of wide-eyed suspicion.

Harold Gorringe: The camp owner of an antique-china shop, and Brindsley's neighbor, Harold comes from the North of England. His friendship is highly conditional and possessive: sooner or later, payment for it will be asked. A specialist in emotional blackmail, he can become hysterical when slighted, or (as inevitably happens) rejected. He is older than Brindsley by several years.

Schuppanzigh: A middle-class German refugee, chubby, cultivated, and effervescent. He is an entirely happy man, delighted to be in England, even if this means being employed full time by the London Electricity Board.

Clea: Brindsley's ex-mistress. Mid-twenties; dazzling, emotional, bright and mischievous. The challenge to her to create a dramatic situation out of the darkness is ultimately irresistible.

Georg Bamberger: An elderly millionaire art collector, easily identifiable as such.

THE SET. *The action of the play takes place in* **Brindsley's** *apartment in South Kensington, London. This forms the ground floor of a large house now divided into flats.* **Harold Gorringe** *lives opposite;* **Miss Furnival** *lives above.*

There are four ways out of the room. A door at the left, upstage, leads directly across the passage to **Harold's** *room. The door to this, with its mat laid tidily outside, can clearly be seen. A curtain, upstage center, screens* **Brindsley's** *studio: when it is parted we glimpse samples of his work in metal. To the right of this an open stair shoots steeply up to his bedroom above, reached through a door at the top. To the left, downstage, a trap in the floor leads down to the cellar.*

It is a gay room, when we finally see it, full of color and space and new shapes. It is littered with marvelous objects—mobiles, mannikins, toys, and dotty bric-a-brac—the happy paraphernalia of a free and imaginative mind. The total effect is of chaos tidied in honor of an occasion, and of a temporary elegance created by the furniture borrowed from **Harold Gorringe** *and arranged to its best advantage.*

This consists of three elegant Regency chairs in gold leaf; a Regency chaise-longue to match; a small Queen Anne table bearing a fine opaline lamp, with a silk shade; a Wedgwood bowl in black basalt; a good Coalport vase containing summer flowers; and a fine porcelain Buddha.

The only things which actually belong to **Brindsley** *are a cheap square table bearing the drinks; an equally cheap round table in the middle of the room, shrouded by a cloth and decorated with the Wedgwood bowl; a low stool downstage center, improved by the Buddha; a record player; and his own artistic creations. These are largely assumed to be in the studio awaiting inspection; but one of them is visible in this room. On the dais stands a bizarre iron sculpture dominated by two long detachable metal prongs, and hung with metal pieces which jangle loudly if touched. On the wall hang paintings, some of them presumably by* **Clea***. All are non-figurative: colorful geometric designs, splashes, splodges and splats of color; whirls and whorls and wiggles—all testifying more to a delight in handling paint than to an ability to achieve very much with it.*

THE TIME.   *9:30 on a Sunday night.*

THE LIGHT.   *On the few occasions when a lighter is lit, matches are struck or a torch is put on, the light on stage merely gets dimmer. When these objects are extinguished, the stage immediately grows brighter.*

COMPLETE DARKNESS.

Two voices are heard: **Brindsley** *and* **Carol***. They must give the impression of two people walking round a room with absolute confidence, as if in the light. We hear sounds as of furniture being moved. A chair is dumped down.*

Brindsley: There! How do you think the room looks?

Carol: (*Quacking*) Fabulous! I wish you could always have it like this. That lamp looks divine there. And those chairs are just the right color. I told you green would look well in here.

Brindsley: Suppose Harold comes back?

Carol: He is not coming back till tomorrow morning.

(**Brindsley** *paces nervously.*)

Brindsley: I know. But suppose he comes tonight? He's mad about his antiques. What do you think he'll say if he goes into his room and finds out we've stolen them?

Carol: Don't dramatize. We haven't stolen all his furniture. Just three chairs, the sofa, that table, the lamp, the bowl, and the vase of flowers, that's all.

Brindsley: And the Buddha. That's more valuable than anything. Look at it.

Carol: Oh, do stop worrying, darling.

Brindsley: Well, you don't know Harold. He won't even let anyone touch his antiques.

Carol: Look, we'll put everything back as soon as Mr. Bamberger leaves. Now stop being dreary.

Brindsley: Well, frankly, I don't think we should have done it. I mean—*anyway*, Harold or no.

Carol: Why not, for heaven's sake? The room looks divine now. Just look at it!

Brindsley: Darling, Georg Bamberger's a multi-millionaire. He's lived all his life against this sort of furniture. Our few stolen bits aren't going to impress him. He's coming to see the work of an unknown sculptor. If you ask me, it would look much better to him if he found me exactly as I really am: a poor artist. It might touch his heart.

Carol: It might—but it certainly won't impress Daddy. Remember, he's coming too.

Brindsley: As if I could forget! Why you had to invite your monster father tonight, I can't think!

Carol: Oh, not again!

Brindsley: Well, it's too bloody much. If he's going to be persuaded I'm a fit husband for you, just by watching a famous collector buy some of my work, he
doesn't deserve to have me as a son-in-law!

Carol: He just wants some proof you can earn your own living.

Brindsley: And what if Bamberger *doesn't* like my work?

Carol: He will, darling. Just stop worrying.

Brindsley: I can't. Get me a whiskey.

(*She does. We hear her steps, and a glass clink against a bottle—then the sound of a soda
syphon.*)

I've got a foreboding. It's all going to be a disaster. An A-one, copper-bottomed,
twenty-four-carat disaster.

Carol: Look, darling, you know what they say. Faint heart never won fair ladypegs!

Brindsley: How true.

Carol: The trouble with you is you're what Daddy calls a Determined Defeatist.

Brindsley: The more I hear about your Daddy, the more I hate him. I loathe military men anyway . . . and in any case, he's bound to hate me.

Carol: Why?

Brindsley: Because I'm a complete physical coward. He'll smell it on my breath.

Carol: Look, darling, all you've got to do is stand up to him. Daddy's only a bully
when he thinks people are afraid of him.

Brindsley: Well, I am.

Carol: You haven't even met him.

Brindsley: That doesn't make any difference.

Carol: Don't be ridiculous. (*Hands him a drink.*) Here.

Brindsley: Thanks.

Carol: What can he do? To you?

Brindsley: For one thing he can refuse to let me marry you.

Carol: Ah, that's sweetipegs.

(*They embrace.*)

Brindsley: I like you in yellow. It brings out your hair.

Carol: Straighten your tie. You look sloppy.

Brindsley: Well, you look divine.

Carol: Really?

Brindsley: I mean it. I've never seen you look so lovely.

Carol: Tell me, Brin, have there been many before me?

Brindsley: Thousands.

Carol: Seriously!

Brindsley: Seriously—none.

Carol: What about that girl in the photo?

Brindsley: She lasted about three months.

Carol: When?

Brindsley: Two years ago.

Carol: What was her name?

Brindsley: Clea.

Carol: What was she like?

Brindsley: She was a painter. Very honest. Very clever. And just about as cozy as a
steel razor blade.

Carol: When was the last time you saw her?

Brindsley: (*Evasively*) I told you . . . two years ago.

Carol: Well, why did you still have her photo in your bedroom drawer?

Brindsley: It was just there. That's all. Give me a kiss . . . (*Pause*) No one in the world kisses like you.

Carol: (*Murmuring*) Tell me something . . . did you like it better with her—or me?

Brindsley: Like what?

Carol: Sexipegs.

Brindsley: Look, people will be here in a minute. Put a record on. It had better be something for your father. What does he like?

Carol: (*Crossing to the record player*) He doesn't like anything except military marches.

Brindsley: I might have guessed . . . Wait—I think I've got some! That last record on the shelf. The orange cover. It's called "Marching and Murdering with Sousa," or something.

Carol: This one?

Brindsley: That's it.

Carol: (*Getting it*) "The Band of the Coldstream Guards."

Brindsley: Ideal. Put it on.

Carol: How d'you switch on?

Brindsley: The last knob on the left. That's it . . . Let us pray! Oh God, let this evening go all right! Let Mr. Bamberger like my sculpture and buy some! Let Carol's monster father like me! And let my neighbor Harold Gorringe never find out that we borrowed his precious furniture behind his back! Amen.

(*A Sousa march; loud. Hardly has it begun, however, when it runs down—as if there is a failure of electricity.*

Brilliant light floods the stage. The rest of the play, save for the times when matches are struck, or for the scene with Schuppanzigh, is acted in this light, but as if in pitch darkness.

They freeze: **Carol** *by the end of the sofa;* **Brindsley** *by the drinks table. The* **Girl's** *dress is a silk flag of chic wrapped round her greyhound's body. The* **Boy's** *look is equally cool: narrow, contained, and sexy. Throughout the evening, as things slide into disaster for him, his crisp, detached shape degenerates progressively into sweat and rumple—just as the elegance of his room gives way relentlessly to its usual near-slum appearance. For the place, as for its owner, the evening is a progress through disintegration.*)

God! We've blown a fuse!

(*The structure and appearance of* **Brindsley's** *room is described in the note at the beginning of the play.*)

Carol: *Oh no!*

Brindsley: It must be. (**He** *blunders to the light switch, feeling ahead of him, trying to part the darkness with his hands. Finding the switch,* **He** *flicks it on and off.*)

Carol: *It is!*

Brindsley: Oh no!

Carol: Or a power cut. Where's the box?

Brindsley: In the hall.

Carol: Have you any candles?

Brindsley: No. Damn!

Carol: Where are the matches?

Brindsley: They should be on the drinks table. (*Feeling round the bottles*) No. Try on the record player.

(**They** *both start groping about the room, feeling for matches.*)

Damn, damn, damn, damn, damn, damn!

(**Carol** *sets a maraca rattling off the record player.*)

Carol: There! (*Finding it*) No . . .

(*The telephone rings.*)

Brindsley: Would you believe it?!

(**He** *blunders his way toward the sound of the bell. Just in time* **He** *remembers the central table—and stops himself colliding into it with a smile of self-congratulation.*)

All right: I'm coming!

(*Instead* **He** *trips over the dais, and goes sprawling—knocking the phone onto the floor.* **He** *has to grope for it on his knees, hauling the receiver back to him by the wire. Into receiver*) Hallo? . . . (*In sudden horror*) Hallo! . . . No, no, no, no—I'm fine, just fine! . . . You? . . . (*His hand over the receiver: to* **Carol**) Darling—look in the bedroom, will you?

Carol: I haven't finished in here yet.

Brindsley: Well, I've just remembered there's some fuse wire in the bedroom. In that drawer where you found the photograph. Go and get it, will you?

Carol: I don't think there is. I didn't see any there.

Brindsley: (*Snapping*) Don't argue. Just look!

Carol: All right. Keep your hairpiece on.

(*During the following* **She** *gropes her way cautiously up the stairs—head down, arms up the banisters, silken bottom thrust out with the effort.*)

Brindsley: (*Controlling himself*) I'm sorry. I just know it's there, that's all. You must have missed it.

Carol: What about the matches?

Brindsley: We'll have to mend it in the dark, that's all. Please hurry, dear.

Carol: (*Climbing*) Oh God, how dreary!

Brindsley: (*Taking his hand off the receiver and listening to hear* **Carol** *go*) Hallo? . . . Well, well, well, well! How are you? Good. That's just fine. Fine, fine! . . . Stop saying what?

(**Carol** *reaches the top of the stairs—and from force of habit pulls down her skirt before groping her way into the bedroom.*)

Brindsley: (*Hand still over the receiver*) Carol? . . . Darling? . . .

(*Satisfied* **She** *has gone; in a rush into the telephone, his voice low*)

Clea! What are you doing here? I thought you were in Finland . . . But you've hardly been gone six weeks . . . Where are you speaking from? . . . The Air Terminal? . . . Well, no, that's not a good idea tonight. I'm terribly busy, and I'm afraid I just can't get out of it. It's business.

Carol: (*Calling from the bedroom door, above*) There's nothing there except your dreary socks. I told you.

Brindsley: (*Calling back*) Well, try the other drawers . . . (**He** *rises as* **He** *speaks, turning so that the wire wraps itself around his legs.* **Carol** *returns to her search. Low and rapid, into phone*)

Look: I can't talk now. Can I call you tomorrow? Where will you be? . . . Look, I told you *no*, Clea. Not tonight. I know it's just around the corner, that's not the point. You can't come round . . . Look, the situation's changed. Something's happened this past month——

Carol: (*Off*) I can't see anything. Brin, *please!*——

Brindsley: Clea, I've got to go . . . Look, I can't discuss it over the phone . . . Has it got to do with what? Yes, of course it has. I mean you can't expect things to stay frozen, can you?

Carol: (*Emerging from the bedroom*) There's nothing here. Haven't we any matches at all?

Brindsley: Oh stop wailing! (*Into phone*) No, not you. I'll call you tomorrow. Good-bye.

(He *hangs up sharply—but fails to find the rest of the telephone so that* He *bangs the receiver hard on the table first. Then* **He** *has to disentangle himself from the wire. Already* **Brindsley** *is beginning to be fussed.*)

Carol: (*Descending*) Who was that?

Brindsley: Just a chum. Did you find the wire?

Carol: I can't find anything in this. We've *got* to get some matches!——

Brindsley: I'll try the pub. Perhaps they'll have some candles as well.

(*Little screams are heard approaching from above. It is* **Miss Furnival** *groping her way down in a panic.*)

Miss Furnival: (*Squealing*) Help! Help! . . . Oh please someone help me!

Brindsley: (*Calling out*) Is that you, Miss Furnival?

Miss Furnival: Mr. Miller? . . .

Brindsley: Yes?

Miss Furnival: Mr. Miller!

Brindsley: Yes!

(**She** *gropes her way in.* **Brindsley** *crosses to find her, but narrowly misses her.*)

Miss Furnival: Oh, thank God, you're there; I'm so frightened!

Brindsley: Why? Have your lights gone too?

Miss Furnival: Yes!

Brindsley: It must be a power cut. (**He** *finds her hand and leads her to the chair downstage left.*)

Miss Furnival: I don't think so. The street lights are on in the front. I saw them from the landing.

Brindsley: Then it must be the main switch of the house.

Carol: Where is that?

(**Miss Furnival** *gasps at the strange voice.*)

Brindsley: It's in the cellar. It's all sealed up. No one's allowed to touch it but the electricity people.

Carol: What are we going to do?

Brindsley: Get them—quick!

Carol: Will they come at this time of night?

Brindsley: They've got to.

(**Brindsley** *accidentally touches* **Miss Furnival's** *breasts.* **She** *gives a little scream.* **Brindsley** *gropes his way to the phone.*)

Have you by any chance got a match on you, Miss Furnival?

Miss Furnival: I'm afraid I haven't. So improvident of me. And I'm absolutely terrified of the dark.

Brindsley: Darling, this is Miss Furnival, from upstairs. Miss Furnival—Miss Melkett.

Miss Furnival: How do you do?

Carol: (*Extending her hand into the darkness*) How do you do?

Miss Furnival: Isn't this frightful?

(**Brindsley** *picks up the phone and dials "O".*)

Carol: Perhaps we can put Mr. Bamberger off.

Brindsley: Impossible. He's dining out and coming on here after. He can't be reached.

Carol: Oh, flip!

Brindsley: (*Sitting on the dais, and speaking into the phone*) Hallo, Operator, can you give me the London Electricity Board, please? Night Service . . . I'm sure it's in the book, Miss, but I'm afraid I can't see . . . There's no need to apologize. No, I'm not blind!—I just can't see: we've got a fuse . . . No we *haven't* got any matches! (*Desperate*) Miss, *please*: this is an emergency . . . Thank you! . . . (*To the room*) London is staffed with imbeciles!

Miss Furnival: Oh, you're so right, Mr. Miller.

Brindsley: (*Rising, frantic: into the phone*) Miss, I *don't want* the number: I can't dial it! . . . Well, have *you* ever tried to dial a number in the dark? . . . (*Trying to keep control*) I just want to be connected . . . Thank you. (*To* **Miss Furnival**) Miss Furnival, do you by any remote chance have any candles?

Miss Furnival: I'm afraid not, Mr. Miller.

Brindsley: (*Mouthing nastily at her*) "I'm afraid not, Mr. Miller" . . . (*Briskly, into phone*) Hallo? Look, I'd like to report a main fuse at Eighteen Scarlatti Gardens. My name is Miller. (*Exasperated*) Yes, yes! All right! . . . (*Maddened: to the room.*) Hold on! Hold bloody on!

Miss Furnival: If I might suggest—Harold Gorringe opposite might have some candles. He's away for the weekend, but always leaves his key under the mat.

Brindsley: What a good idea. That's just the sort of practical thing he would have. (*To* **Carol**) Here—take this . . . I'll go and see, love.

(**He** *hands her the telephone in a fumble—then makes for the door—only to collide smartly with his sculpture.*)

Bugger!

Miss Furnival: Are you all right, Mr. Miller?

Brindsley: I knew it! I bloody knew it. This is going to be the worst night of my life! . . . (**He** *collides with the door.*)

Carol: Don't panic, darling. Just don't panic!

He *stumbles out and is seen groping under* **Harold's** *mat for the key.* **He** *finds it and enters the room opposite.*)

Miss Furnival: You're so right, Miss Melkett. We must none of us panic.

Carol: (*On the phone*) Hallo? Hallo? (*To* **Miss Furnival**) This would have to happen tonight. It's just Brindsley's luck.

Miss Furnival: Is it something special tonight then, Miss Melkett?

Carol: It couldn't be more special if it tried.

Miss Furnival: Oh, dear. May I ask why?

Carol: Have you ever heard of a German called Georg Bamberger?

Miss Furnival: Indeed, yes. Isn't he the richest man in the world?

Carol: Yes. (*Into phone*) Hallo? . . . (*To* **Miss Furnival**) Well, he's coming here tonight.

Miss Furnival: Tonight!

Carol: In about twenty minutes, to be exact. And to make matters worse, he's apparently stone deaf.

Miss Furnival: How extraordinary! May I ask why he's coming?

Carol: He saw some photos of Brindsley's work and apparently got madly excited about it. His secretary rang up last week and asked if he could come and see it. He's a great collector. Brin would be absolutely *made* if Bamberger bought a piece of his.

Miss Furnival: Oh, how exciting!

Carol: It's his big break. Or was—till a moment ago.

Miss Furnival: Oh my dear, you *must* get some help. Jiggle that thing.

Carol: (*Jiggling the phone*) Hallo? Hallo? . . . Perhaps the Bomb's fallen, and everyone's dead.

Miss Furnival: Oh, please don't say things like that—even in levity.

Carol: (*Someone answers her at last*) Hallo? Ah! This is Number Eighteen, Scarlatti Gardens. I'm afraid we've had the most dreary fuse. It's what's laughingly known as the Main Switch. We want a *little man* . . . Well, they can't all have flu . . . Oh, please try! It's screamingly urgent . . . Thank you. (**She** *hangs up*) Sometime this evening, they hope. That's a lot of help.

Miss Furnival: They're not here to help, my dear. In my young days you paid your rates and you got satisfaction. Nowadays you just get some foreigner swearing at you. And if they think you're of the middle class, that only makes it worse.

Carol: Would you like a drink?

Miss Furnival: I don't drink, thank you. My dear father, being a Baptist minister, strongly disapproved of alcohol.

(*A scuffle is heard amongst milk bottles off, followed by a stifled oath.*)

Colonel Melkett: (*Off*) Damn and blast!! . . . (*Barking*) Is there anybody there?

Carol: (*Calling*) In here, daddypegs!

Colonel: Can't you put the light on, dammit? I've almost knocked meself out on a damn milk bottle.

Carol: We've got a fuse. Nothing's working.

(**Colonel Melkett** *appears, holding a lighter which evidently is working—we can see the flame, and of course, the lights go down a little.*)

Miss Furnival: Oh what a relief! A light!

Carol: This is my father, Colonel Melkett, Miss Furnival. She's from upstairs.

Colonel: Good evening.

Miss Furnival: I'm taking refuge for a moment with Mr. Miller. I'm not very good in the dark.

Colonel: When did this happen?

(**Miss Furnival**, *glad for the light, follows it pathetically as the* **Colonel** *crosses the room.*)

Carol: Five minutes ago. The main just blew.

Colonel: And where's this young man of yours?

Carol: In the flat opposite. He's trying to find candles.

Colonel: You mean he hasn't got any?

Carol: No. We can't even find the matches.

Colonel: I see. No organization. Bad sign!

Carol: Daddy, please. It could happen to any of us.

Colonel: Not to me.

(*He turns to find* **Miss Furnival** *right behind him and glares at her balefully. The poor* **Woman** *retreats to the sofa and sits down.* **Colonel Melkett** *gets his first sight of* **Brindsley's** *sculpture.*)

What the hell's that?

Carol: Some of Brindsley's work.

Colonel: Is it, by Jove? And how much does that cost?

Carol: I think he's asking fifty pounds for it.

Colonel: My God!

Carol: (*Nervously*) Do you like the flat, Daddy? He's furnished it very well, hasn't he? I mean it's rich, but not gaudipegs.

Colonel: Very elegant—good: I can see he's got excellent taste. (*Seeing the Buddha*) Now that's what I understand by a real work of art—you can see what it's meant to be.

Miss Furnival: Good heavens!

Carol: What is it?

Miss Furnival: Nothing . . . It's just that Buddha—it so closely resembles the one Harold Gorringe has.

(**Carol** *looks panic-stricken.*)

Colonel: It must have cost a pretty penny, what? He must be quite well off. . . . By Jove—it's got pretty colors. (**He** *bends to examine it.*)

Carol: (*Sotto voce, urgently, to* **Miss Furnival**) You know Mr. Gorringe?

Miss Furnival: Oh, very well indeed. We're excellent friends. He has such lovely things . . . (*For the first time* **She** *notices the sofa on which* **She** *is sitting.*) Oh . . .

Carol: What?

Miss Furnival: This furniture . . . (*Looking about her*) Surely—?—my goodness!——

Carol: (*Hastily*) Daddy, why don't you look in there? It's Brin's studio. There's something I particularly want you to see before he comes back.

Colonel: What?

Carol: It—it—er—it's a surprise, go and see.

Colonel: Very well, Dumpling. Anythin' to oblige. (*To* **Miss Furnival**) Excuse me. (**He** *goes off into the studio, taking his lighter with him. The light instantly gets brighter on stage.* **Carol** *sits beside the* **Spinster** *on the sofa, crouching like a conspirator.*)

Carol: (*Low and urgent*) Miss Furnival, you're a sport, aren't you?

Miss Furnival: I don't know. What is this furniture doing in here? It belongs to Harold Gorringe.

Carol: I know. We've done something absolutely frightful. We've stolen all his best pieces and put Brin's horrid old bits into *his* room.

Miss Furnival: But why? It's disgraceful!

Carol: (*Sentimentally*) Because Brindsley's got nothing, Miss Furnival. Nothing at all. He's as poor as a church mouse. If Daddy had seen this place as it looks normally, he'd have forbidden our marriage on the spot. Mr. Gorringe wasn't there to ask—so we just took the chance.

Miss Furnival: If Harold Gorringe knew that anyone had touched his furniture or his porcelain, he'd go out of his mind! And as for that Buddha—(*Pointing in the wrong direction*)—it's the most precious piece he owns. It's worth hundreds of pounds.

Carol: Oh, please, Miss Furnival—you won't give us away, will you? We're desperate! And it's only for an hour . . . Oh, please! *please!*

Miss Furnival: (*Giggling*) Very well! I won't betray you!

Carol: Oh, thank you!

Miss Furnival: But it'll have to go back exactly as it was, just as soon as Mr. Bamberger and your father leave.

Carol: I swear! Oh, Miss Furnival, you're an angel! Do have a drink. Oh no, you don't. Well, have a bitter lemon.

Miss Furnival: Thank you. That I won't refuse.

(*The* **Colonel** *returns, still holding his lighter. The stage darkens a little.*)

Colonel: Well, they're certainly a surprise. And that's supposed to be sculpture?

Carol: It's not supposed to be. It is.

Colonel: They'd make good garden implements. I'd like 'em for turnin' the soil.

(Miss Furnival *giggles.*)

Carol: That's not very funny, Daddy.

(Miss Furnival *stops giggling.*)

Colonel: Sorry, Dumpling. Speak as you find.

Carol: I wish you wouldn't call me Dumpling.

Colonel: Well, there's no point wastin' this. We may need it!

(He *snaps off his lighter.* Miss Furnival *gives her little gasp as the stage brightens.*)

Carol: Don't be nervous, Miss Furnival. Brin will be here in a minute with the candles.

Miss Furnival: Then I'll leave, of course. I don't want to be in your way.

Carol: You're not at all. (*Hearing him*) Brin?——

(Brindsley *comes out of* Harold's *room—returns the key under the mat.*)

Brindsley: Hallo?

Carol: Did you find anything?

Brindsley: (*Coming in*) You can't find anything in this. If there's candles there, I don't know where they are. Did you get the electric people?

Carol: They said they might send someone around later.

Brindsley: How much later?

Carol: They don't know.

Brindsley: That's a lot of help. What a lookout! Not a bloody candle in the house. A deaf millionaire to show sculpture to—and your monster father to keep happy. Lovely!

Colonel: (*Grimly lighting his lighter*) Good evenin'.

(Brindsley *jumps.*)

Carol: Brin, this *is* my father—Colonel Melkett.

Brindsley: (*Wildly embarrassed*) Well, well, well, well, well! . . . (*Panic*) Good evening, sir. Fancy you being there all the time! I—I'm expecting some dreadful neighbors, some neighbor monsters, monster neighbors, you know . . . They rang up and said they might look round . . . Well, well, well . . .

Colonel: (*Darkly*) Well, well.

Miss Furnival: (*Nervously*) Well, well!

Carol: (*Brightly*) Well!

(The Colonel *rises and advances on* Brindsley *who retreats before him across the room.*)

Colonel: You seem to be in a spot of trouble.

Brindsley: (*With mad nervousness*) Oh, not really! Just a fuse—nothing really, we have them all the time . . . I mean, it won't be the first fuse I've survived, and I daresay it won't be the last! (He *gives a wild braying laugh.*)

Colonel: (*Relentless*) In the meantime, you've got no matches. Right?

Brindsley: Right.

Colonel: No candles. Right?

Brindsley: Right.

Colonel: No basic efficiency, right?

Brindsley: I wouldn't say that, exactly . . .

Colonel: By basic efficiency, young man, I mean the simple state of being At Attention in life, rather than At Ease. Understand?

Brindsley: Well, I'm certainly not at ease.

Colonel: What are you goin' to do about it?

Brindsley: Do?

Colonel: Don't echo me, sir. I don't like it.

Brindsley: You don't like it. . . . I'm sorry.

Colonel: Now look you here. This is an emergency. Anyone can see that.

Brindsley: No one can see anything: that's the emergency.

(**He** *gives his braying laugh again.*)

Colonel: Spare me your humor, sir, if you don't mind. Let's look at the situation objectively. Right?

Brindsley: Right.

Colonel: Good. (**He** *snaps off the lighter.*) Problem: Darkness. Solution: Light.

Brindsley: Oh very good, sir.

Colonel: Weapons: Matches: none! Candles: none! What remains?

Brindsley: Search me.

Colonel: (*Triumphantly*) Torches. Torches, sir! what?

Brindsley: Or a set of early Christians.

Colonel: What did you say?

Brindsley: I'm sorry. I think I'm becoming unhinged. Very good. Torches—brilliant.

Colonel: Routine. Well, where would you find one?

Brindsley: The pub. What time is it?

(*The* **Colonel** *lights his lighter, but now not at the first try. The stage light flickers up and down accordingly.*)

Colonel: Blasted thing. It's beginnin' to go. (**He** *consults his watch.*) Quarter to ten. You can just make it, if you hurry.

Brindsley: Thank you, sir. Your clarity of mind has saved the day.

Colonel: Well, get on with it, man.

Brindsley: Yes sir! Back in a minute.

(*The* **Colonel** *sits in the Regency chair, downstage right.*)

Carol: Good luck, darling.

Brindsley: Thank you, my sweet.

(**She** *blows him a kiss.* **He** *blows her one back.*)

Colonel: (*Irritated*) Stop that at once.

(**Brindsley** *starts for the door—but as* **He** *reaches it,* **Harold Gorringe** *is heard, off.*)

Harold: (*Broad Lancashire accent*) Hallo? Hallo? Anyone there?

Brindsley: (*Freezing with horror*) HAROLD!!

Harold: Brindsley?

Brindsley: (*Meant for* **Carol**) It's Harold. He's back!

Carol: Oh no!

Brindsley: THE FURNITURE!!

Harold: What's going on here?

(**Harold** *appears.* **He** *wears a smart raincoat and carries a weekend suitcase. His hair falls over his brow in a flossy attempt at elegance.*)

Brindsley: Nothing, Harold. Don't go in there—come in here. We've had a fuse. It's dark—it's all over the house.

Harold: Have you phoned the electric? (*Reaching out*)

Brindsley: (*Reaching out and grabbing him*) Yes. Come in here.

Harold: (*Grabbed*) Ohh! . . . (**He** *takes* **Brindsley's** *hand and enters the room cozily on his arm.*) It's rather cozy in the dark, isn't it?

Brindsley: (*Desperately*) Yes! I suppose so . . . So you're back from your weekend then . . .

Harold: I certainly am, dear. Weekend! Some weekend! It rained the whole bloody time. I feel damp to my knickers.

Brindsley: (*Nervously*) Well, have a drink and tell us all about it.

Harold: Us? (*Disengaging himself*) Who's here, then?

Miss Furnival: (*Archly*) I am, Mr. Gorringe.

Harold: Ferny?

Miss Furnival: Taking refuge, I'm afraid. You know how I hate the dark.

Colonel: (*Attempting to light his lighter.*) Blasted thing! . . . (**He** *succeeds.*) There we are! (*Raising it to* **Gorringe's** *face, with distaste*) Who are you?

Brindsley: May I present my neighbor. This is Harold Gorringe—Colonel Melkett.

Harold: How do?

Colonel: How d'ye do?

Brindsley: And this is Miss Carol Melkett, Harold Gorringe.

Carol: (*Giving him a chilly smile*) Hallo! . . .

(**Harold** *nods coldly.*)

Brindsley: Here, let me take your raincoat, Harold.

(**He** *is wearing a tight, modish, gray suit and a brilliant, strawberry shirt.*)

Harold: (*Taking it off and handing it to him*) Be careful, it's sopping wet.

(*Adroitly,* **Brindsley** *drops the coat over the Wedgwood bowl on the table.*)

Colonel: You got no candles, I suppose?

Harold: Would you believe it, Colonel, but I haven't? Silly me!

(**Brindsley** *crosses and blows out the* **Colonel's** *lighter, just as* **Harold** *begins to look round the room. The stage brightens.*)

Colonel: What the devil did you do that for?

Brindsley: I'm saving your wick, Colonel. You may need it later and it's failing fast.

(*The* **Colonel** *gives him a suspicious look.* **Brindsley** *moves quickly back, takes up the coat and drops it over the right end of the sofa, to conceal as much of it as possible.*)

Harold: It's all right. I've got some matches.

Carol: (*Alarmed*) Matches!

Harold: Here we are! I hope I've got the right end. (**He** *strikes one.*)

(**Brindsley** *immediately blows it out from behind, then moves swiftly to hide the Wedgwood bowl under the table and drop the tablecloth over the remaining end of the sofa.* **Miss Furnival** *sits serenely unknowing between the two covers.*)

Hey, what was that?

Brindsley: (*Babbling*) A draught. No match stays alight in this room. It's impossible. Cross currents, you know. Old houses are full of them. They're almost a permanent feature in this house . . .

Harold: (*Bewildered*) I don't know what you're on about.

(**He** *strikes another match.* **Brindsley** *again blows it out as* **He** *nips over to sit in the chair downstage left, but this time is seen.*)

Harold: What's up with you?

Brindsley: Nothing!

Harold: Have you got a dead body in here or something?

Brindsley: NO! (**He** *starts his maniacal laughter.*)

Harold: Here, have you been drinking?

Brindsley: No. Of course not.

(**Harold** *strikes another match.* **Brindsley** *dashes up. All these strikings and blowings are of course accompanied by swift and violent alterations of the light.*)

Harold: (*Exasperated*) Now look here! What's up with you?

Brindsley: (*Inspired*) Dangerous!

Harold: What?

Brindsley: (*Frantically improvising*) Dangerous! It's dangerous! . . . We can all die! Naked flames! Hideous accidents can happen with naked flames!

Harold: I don't know what you're on about—what's up with you?

(**Brindsley** *clutches* **Harold** *and backs him bewilderedly across to the center table.*)

Brindsley: I've just remembered! It's something they always warn you about. In old houses the fuse box and the gas meter are in the same cupboard. They are here!

Colonel: So what about it?

Brindsley: Well . . . electrical blowouts can damage the gas supply. They're famous for it. They do it all the time! And they say you've got to avoid naked flames till they're mended.

Colonel: I've never heard of that.

Harold: Me neither.

Brindsley: Well, take my word for it. It's fantastically dangerous to burn a naked flame in this room!

Carol: (*Catching on*) Brin's absolutely right. In fact, they warned me about it on the phone this evening when I called them. They said, "Whatever you do, don't strike a match till the fuse is mended."

Brindsley: There, you see!—it's terribly dangerous.

Colonel: (*Grimly*) Then why didn't you warn me, Dumpling?

Carol: I—I forgot.

Colonel: Brilliant!

Miss Furnival: Oh goodness, we must take care.

Brindsley: We certainly must! . . . (*Pause*) Let's all have a drink. Cheer us up! . . .

Carol: Good idea! Mr. Gorringe, would you like a drink?

Harold: Well, I must say, that wouldn't come amiss. Not after the journey I've had tonight. I swear to God there was thirty-five people in that compartment if there was one—babes in arms, toddlers, two nuns, three yapping poodles, and not a sausage to eat from Leamington to London. It's a bloody disgrace.

Miss Furnival: You'd think they'd put on a restaurant car, Mr. Gorringe.

Harold: Not them, Ferny. They don't care if you perish once they've got your fare. Excuse me, I'll just go and clean up.

Brindsley: (*Panic*) You can do that here.

Harold: Well, I must unpack anyway.

Brindsley: Do it later.

Harold: No, I hate to keep clothes in a suitcase longer than I absolutely have to. If there's one thing I can't stand, it's a creased suit.

Brindsley: Five more minutes won't hurt, surely?

Harold: Ooh, you aren't half bossy!

Carol: What will you have? Winnie, Vera or Ginette?

Harold: Come again?

Carol: Winnie Whiskey, Vera Vodka, or dear old standby Ginette.

Harold: (*Yielding*) I can see you're the camp one! . . . If it's all the same to you, I'll have a drop of Ginette, please, and a little lime juice.

Colonel: Young man, do I have to keep reminding you that you are in an emergency? You have a guest arrivin' any second.

Brindsley: Oh God, I'd forgotten!

Colonel: Try the pub. Try the neighbors. Try who you damn well please, sir—but *get a torch!*

Brindsley: Yes . . . Yes! . . . Carol, can I have word with you, please?
Carol: I'm here.

(**She** *gropes toward him and* **Brindsley** *leads her to the stairs.*)

Colonel: What now?
Brindsley: Excuse us just a moment, please, Colonel.

(*He pulls her quickly after him, up the stairs.*)

Miss Furnival: (*As* **They** *do this*) Oh, Mr. Gorringe, it's so exciting. You'll never guess who's coming here tonight.
Harold: Who?
Miss Furnival: Guess.
Harold: The Queen!
Miss Furnival: Oh, Mr. Gorringe, you are ridiculous!

(**Brindsley** *arrives at the top of the stairs, then opens the bedroom door and closes it behind them.*)

Brindsley: What are we going to do?
Carol: (*Behind the door*) I don't know!
Brindsley: (*Behind the door*) Think!
Carol. But——
Brindsley: *Think!*
Colonel: Is that boy touched or somethin'?
Harold: Touched? He's an absolute poppet.
Colonel: A what?
Harold: A duck. I've known him for years, ever since he came here. There's not many secrets we keep from each other, I can tell you.
Colonel: (*Frostily*) Really?
Harold: Yes, really. He's a very sweet boy.

(**Brindsley** *and* **Carol** *emerge from behind the bedroom door.*)

Brindsley: We'll have to put all Harold's furniture back in his room.
Carol: *Now?!*
Brindsley: We'll have to. I can't get a torch till we do.
Carol: We can't!
Brindsley: We must. He'll go mad if he finds out what we've done.
Harold: Well come on, Ferny: don't be a tease. Who is it? Who's coming?
Miss Furnival: I'll give you a clue. It's someone with money.
Harold: Money? . . . Let me think.
Colonel: (*Calling out*) Carol!
Carol: Look, can't you just tell him it was a joke?
Brindsley: You don't know him. He can't bear anyone to touch his treasures. They're like children to him. He cleans everything twice a day with a special swansdown duster. He'd wreck everything. Would you like him to call me a thief in front of your father?
Carol: Of course not!
Brindsley: Well, he would. He gets absolutely hysterical. I've seen him.
Colonel: (*Mildly*) Brindsley!
Carol: Well, how the hell can we do it?
Harold: It's no good. You can't hear up there.
Brindsley: (*Stripping off his jacket*) Look, you hold the fort. Serve them drinks. Just keep things going. Leave it all to me. I'll try and put everything back in the dark.
Carol: It won't work.

Brindsley: It's *got* to!

Colonel: (*Roaring*) Brindsley!!

Brindsley: (*Dashing to the door*) Coming sir . . . (*With false calm*) I'm just getting some empties to take to the pub.

Colonel: Say what you like. That boy's touched.

Brindsley: (*To* **Carol,** *intimately*) Trust me, darling.

(**They** *kiss.*)

Colonel: At the double, Miller.

Brindsley: Yes, sir! Yes, sir!

(**He** *rushes out and in his anxiety,* **He** *misses his footing and falls neatly down the entire flight of stairs. Picking himself up*)

I'm off now, Colonel! Help is definitely on the way.

Colonel: Well, hurry it up, man.

Brindsley: Carol will give you drinks. If Mr. Bamberger arrives, just explain the situation to him.

Harold: (*Feeling for his hand*) Would you like me to come with you?

Brindsley: No, no, no—good heavens: stay and enjoy yourself.

(**Harold** *kisses his hand.* **Brindsley** *pulls it away.*)

I mean, you must be exhausted after all those poodles. A nice gin and lime will do wonders. I shan't be a minute.

(**He** *reaches the door, opens it, then slams it loudly, remaining on the inside. Stealthily* **He** *opens it again, stands dead still for a moment, center, silently indicating to himself the position of the chairs* **He** *has to move—then* **He** *finds his way to the first of the Regency chairs, downstage left, which* **He** *lifts noiselessly.*)

Carol: (*With bright desperation*) Well now, drinks! What's everyone going to have? It's Ginette for Mr. Gorringe and I suppose Winnie for Daddy.

Colonel: And how on earth are you going to do that in the dark?

Carol: I remember the exact way I put out the bottles.

(**Brindsley** *bumps into her with the chair and falls back, gored by its leg.*)

Carol: It's very simple.

Harold: Oh look, luv, let me strike a match. I'm sure it's not that dangerous, just for a minute. (**He** *strikes a match.*)

Carol: Oh no! . . .

(**Brindsley** *ducks down, chair in hand, and blows out the match.*)

Do you want to blow us all up, Mr. Gorringe? . . . All poor Mr. Bamberger would find would be teensy weensy bits of us. Very messypegs.

(**She** *snatches the box of matches, feels for the ice bucket, and drops them into it.* **Brindsley** *steals out, Felix-the-cat-like, with the chair as* **Carol** *fumblingly starts to mix drinks.* **He** *sets it down, opens* **Harold's** *door, and disappears inside it with the chair.*)

Harold: Bamberger? Is that who's coming? Georg Bamberger?

Miss Furnival: Yes. To see Mr. Miller's work. Isn't it exciting?

Harold: Well, I never. I read an article about him last week in the Sunday Pic. He's known as the mystery millionaire. He's almost completely deaf—deaf as a post, and spends most of his time indoors alone with his collection. He hardly ever goes out, except to a gallery or a private studio. That's the life! If I had money that's what I'd do. Just collect all the china and porcelain I wanted.

(**Brindsley** *returns with a poor, broken-down chair of his own and sets it down in the same position as the one* **He** *has taken out. The second chair presents a harder challenge.*

It sits right across the room, upstage right. Delicately **He** *moves towards it—but* **He** *has difficulty finding it. We watch him walk round and round it in desperately narrowing circles till* **He** *touches it and with relief picks it up.*)

Miss Furnival: I've never met a millionaire. I've always wondered if they feel different to us. I mean their actual skins.

Colonel: Their skins?

Miss Furnival: Yes. I've always imagined they must be softer than ours. Like the skins of ladies when I was a girl.

Carol: What an interesting idea.

Harold: Oh she's very fanciful is Ferny. Real imagination, I always say.

Miss Furnival: Very kind of you, Mr. Gorringe. You're always so generous with your compliments.

(*As* **She** *speaks her next speech staring smugly into the darkness, hands clasped in maidenly gentility, the second Regency chair is being moved slowly across what should be her field of vision, two inches from her face. During the following* **Brindsley** *unfortunately misaims and carries the chair past the door, bumps into the wall, retreats from it, and inadvertently shuts the door softly with his back. Now* **He** *cannot get out of the room.* **He** *has to set down the chair, grope for the door handle, turn it, then open the door—then re-find the chair which* **He** *has quite lost. This takes a long and frantic time. At last* **He** *triumphs, and staggers from the room, nearly exhausted.*)

But this is by no means fancy. In my day, softness of skin was quite the sign of refinement. Nowadays, of course, it's hard enough for us middle classes to keep ourselves decently clothed, let alone soft. My father used to say, even before the bombs came and burnt our dear little house at Wendover: "The game's up, my girl. We middle classes are as dead as the dodo." Poor Father, how right he was.

(*NOTE: Hopefully, if the counterpoint of farce action goes well,* **Miss Furnival** *may have to ad-lib a fair bit during all this, and not mind too much if nobody hears her. The essential thing for all four actors during the furniture-moving is to preserve the look of ordinary conversation.*)

Colonel: Your father was a professional man?

Miss Furnival: He was a man of God, Colonel.

Colonel: Oh.

(**Brindsley** *returns with a broken-down rocking chair of his own.* **He** *crosses gingerly to where the* **Colonel** *is sitting.*)

How are those drinks coming, Dumpling?

Carol: Fine, Daddy. They'll be one minute.

Colonel: (*Speaking directly into* **Brindsley's** *face*) Let me help you.

(**Brindsley** *staggers back, startled.*)

Carol: You can take this bitter lemon to Miss Furnival if you want.

(**Brindsley** *sets down the rocker immediately next to the* **Colonel's** *chair.*)

Colonel: Very well.

(*He rises just as* **Brindsley's** *hand pulls it from beneath him. With his other hand* **Brindsley** *pulls the rocker into the identical position. The* **Colonel** *moves slowly across the room, arms outstretched for the bitter lemon. Unknowingly* **Brindsley** *follows him, carrying the third chair. The* **Colonel** *collides gently with the table. At the same moment* **Brindsley** *reaches it upstage of him, and searches for the Wedgwood bowl. Their hands narrowly miss. Then the* **Young Man** *remembers the bowl is under the table. Deftly* **He** *reaches down and retrieves it—and carrying it in one hand and the chair in the other,* *triumphantly leaves the room through the arch unconsciously provided by the outstretched arms of* **Carol** *and the* **Colonel**, *giving and receiving a glass of Scotch—which* **They** *think is lemonade.*)

Carol: Here you are, Daddy. Bitter lemon for Miss Furnival.

Colonel: Right you are, Dumpling. (*To* **Miss Furnival**) So your father was a minister then?

Miss Furnival: He was a saint, Colonel. I'm only thankful he never lived to see the rudeness and vulgarity of life today.

(*The* **Colonel** *sets off to find her but goes much too far to the right.*)

Harold: (**He** *sits on the sofa beside her.*) Oooh, you're so right, Ferny. Rudeness and vulgarity—that's it to a T. The manners of some people today are beyond belief. Honestly. Did I tell you what happened in my shop last Friday? I don't think I did.

Miss Furnival: No, Mr. Gorringe, I don't think so.

(*Her voice corrects the* **Colonel's** *direction. During the following* **He** *moves slowly up toward her.*)

Harold: Well, I'd just opened up—it was about quarter to ten and I was dusting off the teapots—you know, Rockingham collects the dust something shocking!—when who should walk in but that Mrs. Levitt, you know—the ginger-haired bit I told you about, the one who thinks she's God's gift to bachelors.

Colonel: (*Finding her head with his hand and presenting her with the Scotch*) Here's your lemonade.

Miss Furnival: Oh, thank you. Most kind.

(*Throughout* **Harold's** *story,* **Miss Furnival** *nurses the glass, not drinking. The* **Colonel** *finds his way slowly back to the chair* **He** *thinks* **He** *was sitting on before, but which is now a rocker.* **Brindsley** *re-appears triumphantly carrying one of the original Regency chairs* **He** *took out.* **He** *moves slowly across the room getting his bearings.*)

Harold: Anyway, she's got in her hand a vase I'd sold her last week—it was a birthday present for an old geezer she's having a bit of a ding dong with somewhere in Earls Court, hoping to collect all his lolly when he dies, as I read the situation. I'm a pretty good judge of character, Ferny, as you know—and she's a real grasper if ever I saw one.

(*The* **Colonel** *sits heavily in the rocking chair which overbalances backward, spilling him onto the floor.*)

Colonel: Dammit to hell!

Carol: What's the matter, Daddy?

(*A pause.* **Brindsley** *sits down panic-stricken on the chair* **He** *has carried in. The* **Colonel** *feels the chair and sets it on its feet.*)

Colonel: (*Unbelieving*) It's a blasted rockin' chair! I didn't see a blasted rockin' chair here before! . . .

(*Astounded, the* **Colonel** *remains on the floor.* **Brindsley** *rises and moves the chair to the original position of the second chair* **He** *moved.*)

Harold: Oh yes, you want to watch that. It's in a pretty ropey condition, I've told Brin about it several times. Anyway, this vase. It's a nice bit of Kang Tsi, blue and white with a good orange-peel glaze, absolutely authentic—I'd let her have it for twenty-five pounds, and she'd got infinitely the best of the bargain, no argument about that.

(**Harold** *rises and leans against the center table to tell his story more effectively. The* **Colonel** *seats himself again, gingerly.*)

Well, in she prances, her hair all done up in one of them bouffon hair-dos, you
know, tarty—French-like—it would have looked fancy on a girl half her age with
twice her looks——

(**Brindsley** *mistakenly lifts the end of the sofa.* **Miss Furnival** *gives a little scream at
the jolt.*)

Harold: Exactly. You know the sort.

(**Brindsley** *staggers in the opposite direction downstage onto the rostrum.*)

And d'you know what she says to me? "Mr. Gorringe," she says, "I've been
cheated."

Miss Furnival: No!

Harold: Her very words. "Cheated."

(**Brindsley** *collides with the sculpture on the dais. It jangles violently. To it*)

Hush up, I'm talking!

Carol: (*Covering up*) I'm frightfully sorry.

(**Harold** *whirls round, surprised.*)

Harold: Anyway—"Oh," I say, "and how exactly has that occurred, Mrs. Levitt?"
"Well," she says, "quite by chance I took this vase over to Bill Everett in the
Portobello, and he says it's not what you called it at all, Chinese and very rare.
He says it's a piece of nineteenth-century English trash."

(**Brindsley** *finds the lamp on the downstage table and picks it up.* **He** *walks with it round
the rocking chair, on which the* **Colonel** *is now sitting again.*)

"Does he?" I say. "Does he?" I keep calm. I always do when I'm riled. "Yes,"
she says. "He does. And I'd thank you to give me money back."

(*The wire of the lamp has followed* **Brindsley** *round the bottom of the rocking chair. It
catches.* **Brindsley** *tugs it gently. The chair moves. Surprised, the* **Colonel** *jerks forward.*
Brindsley *tugs it again, much harder. The rocking chair is pulled forward, spilling the*
Colonel *out of it, again onto the floor, and then falling itself on top of him. The shade of
the lamp comes off. During the ensuing dialogue* **Brindsley** *gets to his knees and crawls
right across the room following the flex of the lamp.* **He** *finds the plug, pulls it out, and—still
on his knees—re-traces his steps, winding up the wire around his arm, and becoming helplessly
entangled in it. The* **Colonel** *remains on the floor, now really alarmed.*)

Miss Furnival: How dreadful, Mr. Gorringe. What did you do?

Harold: I counted to ten, and then I let her have it. "In the first place," I said, "I
don't expect my customers to go checking up on my honesty behind my back.
In the second, Bill Everett is ignorant as Barnsley dirt, he doesn't know Tang
from Ting. And in the third place, that applies to you, too, Mrs. Levitt."

Miss Furnival: You didn't!

Harold: I certainly did—and worse than that. "You've got in your hand," I said, "a
minor masterpiece of Chinese pottery. But in point of fact," I said, "you're not
even fit to hold a 1953 Coronation mug. Don't you ever come in here again," I
said, "—don't you cross my threshold. Because if you do, Mrs. Levitt, I won't
make myself responsible for the consequences."

Carol: (*With two drinks in her hand*) My, Mr. Gorringe, how splendid of you. Here's
your gin and lime. You deserve it. (**She** *hands him the bitter lemon.*)

Harold: (*Accepting it*) Ta. I was proper blazing, I didn't care.

Carol: Where are you? Where are you, Daddy? Here's your Scotch.

Colonel: Here, Dumpling!

(**He** *gets up dazedly and fumbles his way to the glass of gin and lime.* **Brindsley** *meanwhile
realizes* **He** *has lost the shade of the lamp. On his knees,* **He** *begins to look for it.*)

Harold: Carrotty old bitch—telling *me* about pottery! *Oooh!!*

(**He** *shakes himself indignantly at the recollection of it.*)

Miss Furnival: Do you care for porcelain yourself, Colonel?

Colonel: I'm afraid I don't know very much about it, Madam. I like some of that Chinese stuff—you get some lovely colors, like on that statue I saw when I came in here—very delicate.

Harold: What statue's that, Colonel?

Colonel: The one on the packing case, sir. Very fine.

Harold: I didn't know Brin had any Chinese stuff. What's it of then, this statue?

(**Brindsley** *freezes.*)

Carol: (*Desperately*) Well, we've all got drinks, I'd like to propose Daddy's regimental toast. Raise your glasses everyone! "To the dear old Twenty-Fifth Horse. Up the British, and Death to All Natives"!

Miss Furnival: I'll drink to that!

Harold: Up the old Twenty-Fifth!!

(*Quickly* **Brindsley** *finds the Buddha, moves it from the packing case to the table, then gets* **Harold's** *raincoat from the sofa, and wraps the statue up in it, leaving it on the table.*)

Colonel: Thank you, Dumpling. That was very touchin' of you. Very touchin' indeed. (**He** *swallows his drink.*) Dammit, that's gin!

Harold: I've got lemonade!

Miss Furnival: Oh! Horrible! . . . Quite horrible! That would be alcohol, I suppose! . . . Oh dear, how unpleasant! . . .

Harold: (*To* **Miss Furnival**) Here, luv, exchange with me. No—you get the lemonade—but I get the gin. Colonel——

Colonel: Here, sir.

(*Seizing her chance* **Miss Furnival** *downs a huge draft of Scotch.* **They** *all exchange drinks.* **Brindsley** *resumes his frantic search for the shade.*)

Harold: Here, Ferny.

(*The* **Colonel** *hands her the gin and lime.* **He** *gets instead the bitter lemon from* **Harold.** **Harold** *gets the Scotch.*)

Miss Furnival: Thank you.

Harold: Well, let's try again. Bottoms up!

Colonel: Quite.

(**They** *drink. Triumphantly,* **Brindsley** *finds the shade. Unfortunately at the same moment the* **Colonel** *spits out his lemonade in a fury all over him, as he marches toward him on his knees.*)

Look here—I can't stand another minute of this!

(**He** *fishes his lighter out of his pocket and angrily tries to light it.*)

Carol: Daddy, please!

Colonel: I don't care, Dumpling. If I blow us up, then I'll blow us up! This is ridiculous . . .

(*His words die in the flame.* **He** *spies* **Brindsley** *kneeling at his feet, wound about with lampwire.*)

What the devil are you doin' there?

Brindsley: (*Blowing out his lighter*) Now don't be rash, Colonel! Isn't the first rule of an officer "Don't involve your men in unnecessary danger"?

(*Quickly* **He** *steals, still on his knees, to the table downstage right.*)

Colonel: Don't be impertinent. Where's the torch?

Brindsley: Er . . . the pub was closed.

Harold: You didn't go to the pub in that time, surely? You couldn't have done.

Brindsley: Of course I did.

Miss Furnival: But it's five streets away, Mr. Miller.

Brindsley: Needs must when the devil drives, Miss Furnival. Whatever that means. (*Quickly* **He** *lifts the table, and steals out of the room with it and the wrecked lamp.*)

Colonel: (*Who thinks* **He** *is still kneeling at his feet*) Now look here: there's somethin' very peculiar goin' on in this room. I may not know about art, Miller, but I know men. I know a liar in the light, and I know one in the dark.

Carol: Daddy!

Colonel: I don't want to doubt your word, sir. All the same, I'd like your oath you went out to that public house. *Well?*

Carol: (*Realizing* **He** *isn't there, raising her voice*) Brin, Daddy's talking to you!

Colonel: What are you shoutin' for?

Brindsley: (*Rushing back from* **Harold's** *room, still entangled in the lamp.*) Of course. I know. He's absolutely right. I was—just thinking it over for a moment.

Colonel: Well? What's your answer?

Brindsley: I . . . I couldn't agree with you more, sir.

Colonel: What?

Brindsley: That was a very perceptive remark you made there. Not everyone would have thought of that. Individual. You know. Almost witty. Well, it *was* witty. Why be ungenerous? . . .

Colonel: Look, young man, are you trying to be funny?

Brindsley: (*Ingratiatingly*) Well, I'll try anything once . . .

Harold: I say, this is becoming a bit unpleasant, isn't it?

Carol: It's becoming drearypegs.

Colonel: Quiet, Dumpling. Let me handle this.

Brindsley: What's there to handle, sir?

Colonel: If you think I'm going to let my daughter marry a born liar, you're very much mistaken.

Harold: Marry!

Carol: Well, that's the idea.

Harold: You and this young lady, Brin?

Carol: Are what's laughingly known as engaged. Subject of course to Daddy's approval.

Harold: Well! (*Furious at the news, and at the fact that* **Brindsley** *hasn't confided in him.*) What a surprise! . . .

Brindsley: We were keeping it a secret.

Harold: Evidently. How long's this been going on, then?

Brindsley: A few months.

Harold: You old slyboots.

Brindsley: (*Nervous*) I hope you approve, Harold.

Harold: Well, I must say, you know how to keep things to yourself.

Brindsley: (*Placatingly*) I meant to tell you, Harold . . . I really did. You were the one person I was going to tell.

Harold: Well why didn't you, then?

Brindsley: I don't know. I just never got around to it.

Harold: You saw me every day.

Brindsley: I know.

Harold: You could have mentioned it at any time.

Brindsley: I know.

Harold: (*Huffy*) Well, it's your business. There's no obligation to share confidences. I've only been your neighbor for three years. I've always assumed there was more than a geographical closeness between us, but I was obviously mistaken.

Brindsley: Oh don't start getting huffy, Harold.

Harold: I'm not getting anything. I'm just saying it's surprising, that's all. Surprising and somewhat disappointing.

Brindsley: Oh look, Harold, please understand——

Harold: (*Shrill*) There's no need to say anything! It'll just teach me in future not to bank too much on friendship. It's silly me again! Silly, stupid, trusting me!

(**Miss Furnival** *rises in agitation and gropes her way to the drinks table.*)

Colonel: Good God!

Carol: (*Wheedling*) Oh come, Mr. Gorringe. We haven't told anybody. Not one single soulipegs. Really.

Colonel: At the moment, Dumpling, there's nothing to tell. And I'm not sure there's going to be!

Brindsley: Look, sir, we seem to have got off on the wrong foot. If it's my fault, I apologize.

Miss Furnival: (*Groping about on the drinks table*) My father always used to say, "To err is human: to forgive divine."

Carol: I thought that was somebody else.

Miss Furnival: (*Blithely*) So many people copied him. (**She** *finds the open bottle of gin, lifts it and sniffs it eagerly.*)

Carol: May I help you, Miss Furnival?

Miss Furnival: No, thank you, Miss Melkett. I'm just getting myself another bitter lemon. That is—if I may, Mr. Miller?

Brindsley: Of course. Help yourself.

Miss Furnival: Thank you, most kind!

(**She** *pours more gin into her glass and returns slowly to sit upstage on the edge of the rostrum.*)

Colonel: Well, sir, wherever you are——

Brindsley: Here, Colonel.

Colonel: I'll overlook your damn peculiar behavior this once, but understand this, Miller. My daughter's dear to me. You show me you can look after her, and I'll consider the whole thing most favorably. I can't say fairer than that, can I?

Brindsley: No, sir. Most fair, sir. Most fair. (**He** *pulls a hideous face one inch from the* **Colonel's**.)

Carol: Of course he can look after me, Daddy. His works are going to be world-famous. In five years I'll feel just like Mrs. Michaelangelo.

Harold: (*Loftily*) There wasn't a Mrs. Michaelangelo, actually.

Carol: (*Irritated*) Wasn't there?

Harold: No. He had passionate feelings of a rather different nature.

Carol: Really, Mr. Gorringe. I didn't know that. (**She** *puts out her tongue at him.*)

Brindsley: Look, Harold, I'm sorry if I've hurt your feelings.

Harold: (*Loftily*) You haven't.

Brindsley: I know I have. Please forgive me.

Carol: Oh, do, Mr. Gorringe. Quarreling is so dreary. I hope we're all going to be great friends.

Harold: I'm not sure that I can contemplate a friendly relationship with a viper.

Miss Furnival: Remember: to err is human, to forgive divine!

Colonel: (*Irritated*) You just said that, madam.

(**Clea** *enters, wearing dark glasses and carrying an air-bag.* **She** *stands in the doorway, amazed by the dark.* **She** *takes off her glasses, but this doesn't improve matters.*)

Miss Furnival: (*Downing her gin happily*) Did I?

Carol: Brin's not really a viper. He's just artistic, aren't you, darling?

Brindsley: Yes, darling.

(**Carol** *sends an audible kiss across the astonished* **Clea**. **He** *returns it, equally audibly.*)

Carol: (*Winningly*) Come on, Mr. Gorringe. It really is a case of forgive and forgettipegs.

Harold: Is it reallypegs?

Carol: Have another Ginette and lime. I'll have one with you.

(**She** *rises and mixes the drink.*)

Harold: (*Rising*) Oh, all right. I don't mind if I do.

Carol: Let me mix it for you.

Harold: Ta.

(**He** *crosses to her, narrowly missing* **Clea** *who is now crossing the room to the sofa, and gets his drink.*)

I must say there's nothing nicer than having a booze up with a pretty girl.

Carol: (*Archly*) You haven't seen me yet.

Harold: Oh, I just know it. Brindsley always had wonderful taste. I've often said to him, you've got the same taste in ladies as I have in porcelain. Ta.

(**Harold** *and* **Brindsley**—*one from upstage, one from across the room—begin to converge on the sofa. On the word "modest"* **All Three, Clea** *in the middle, sit on it.* **Brindsley** *of course imagines* **He** *is sitting next to* **Harold**.)

Brindsley: Harold!

Carol: Oh don't be silly, Brin. Why be so modest? I found a photograph of one of his bits from two years ago, and I must say she was pretty stunning in a blowsy sort of way.

Harold: Which one was that, then? I suppose she means Clea.

Carol: Did you know her, Mr. Gorringe?

Harold: Oh yes. She's been around a long time.

(**Brindsley** *nudges* **Clea** *warningly—imagining* **She** *is* **Harold**. **Clea** *gently bumps* **Harold**.)

Carol: (*Surprised*) Has she?

Harold: Oh yes, dear. Or am I speaking out of turn?

Brindsley: Not at all. I've told Carol all about Clea. (**He** *bangs* **Clea** *again, a little harder—who correspondingly bumps against* **Harold**.) Though I must say, Harold, I'm surprised you call three months "a long time."

(**Clea** *shoots him a look of total outrage at this lie.* **Harold** *is also astonished.*)

Carol: What was she like?

Brindsley: (*Meaningfully, into* **Clea's** *ear*) I suppose you can hardly remember her, Harold.

Harold: (*Speaking across her*) Why on earth shouldn't I?

Brindsley: Well, since it was two years ago, you've probably forgotten.

Harold: Two years?!

Brindsley: *Two years ago!*

(**He** *punches* **Clea** *so hard that the rebound knocks* **Harold** *off the sofa, drink and all.*)

Harold: (*Picking himself up. Spitefully*) Well, now since you mention it, I remember her perfectly. I mean, she's not one you can easily forget!

Carol: Was she pretty?

Harold: No, not at all. In fact, I'd say the opposite. Actually she was rather plain.

Brindsley: She wasn't!

Harold: I'm just giving my opinion.

Brindsley: You've never given it before.

Harold: (*Leaning over* **Clea**) I was never asked! But since it's come up, I always thought she was ugly. For one thing, she had teeth like a picket fence—yellow and spiky. And for another, she had bad skin.

Brindsley: She had nothing of the kind!

Harold: She did. I remember it perfectly. It was like new pink wallpaper, with an old gray crumbly paper underneath.

Miss Furnival: Quite right, Mr. Gorringe. I hardly ever saw her, but I do recall her skin. It was a strange color, as you say—and very coarse . . . Not soft, as the skins of young ladies should be, if they *are* young ladies.

(**Clea** *rises in outrage.*)

Harold: Aye, that's right. Coarse.

Miss Furnival: And rather lumpy.

Harold: Very lumpy.

Brindsley: This is disgraceful.

Harold: You knew I never liked her, Brindsley. She was too clever by half.

Miss Furnival: And so tiresomely Bohemian.

Carol: You mean she was as pretentious as her name?

(**Clea**, *who has been reacting to this last exchange of comments about her like a spectator at a tennis match, now reacts to* **Carol** *open-mouthed.*)

I bet she was. That photograph I found showed her in a dirndl and a sort of sultry peasant blouse. She looked like "The Bartered Bride" done by Lloyds Bank.

(**They** *laugh,* **Brindsley** *hardest of all. Guided by the noise,* **Clea** *aims her hand and slaps his face.*)

Brindsley: Ahh!

Carol: What's wrong?

Miss Furnival: What is it, Mr. Miller?

Brindsley: (*Furious*) That's not very funny, Harold. What the hell's the matter with you?

(**Clea** *makes her escape.*)

Harold: (*Indignant*) With me?

Brindsley: Well, I'm sure it wasn't the Colonel.

Colonel: What wasn't, sir?

(**Brindsley**, *groping about, catches* **Clea** *by the bottom, and instantly recognizes it.*)

Brindsley: *Clea!* . . . (*In horror*) *Clea!!*

(**Clea** *breaks loose and moves away from him. During the following* **He** *tries to find her in the dark, and* **She** *narrowly avoids him.*)

Colonel: What?

Brindsley: I was just remembering her, sir. You're all talking the most awful nonsense. She was beautiful . . . And anyway, Harold, you just said I was famous for my taste in women.

Harold: Aye, but it had its lapses.

Brindsley: (*Frantically moving about*) Rubbish! She was beautiful and tender and considerate and kind and loyal and witty and adorable in every way!

Carol: You told me she was as cozy as a steel razor blade.

Brindsley: Did I? Surely not! No. What I said was . . . something quite different

. . . Utterly different . . . entirely different . . . As different as chalk from cheese. Although when you come to think of it, cheese isn't all that different from chalk. (**He** *gives his braying laugh.*)

Colonel: Are you sure you know what you're talking about?

(*During this* **Clea** *has reached the table, picked up a bottle of Scotch, and rejected it in favor of vodka, which* **She** *takes with her.*)

Carol: You said to me in this room when I asked you what she was like, "She was a painter. Very honest. Very clever, and just about as cozy——"

Brindsley: (*Stopping, exasperated*) As a steel razor blade! Well then, I said it! So bloody what? . . .

Carol: So nothing!

(**He** *throws out his hands in a gesture of desperate exhaustion and bumps straight into* **Clea**. **They** *instantly embrace,* **Clea** *twining herself around him, her vodka bottle held aloft. A tiny pause*)

Colonel: If that boy isn't touched, I don't know the meaning of the word!

Carol: What's all this talk about her being kind and tender, all of a sudden?

Brindsley: (*Tenderly, holding* **Clea**) She could be. On occasion. *Very.*

Carol: Very rare occasions, I imagine.

Brindsley: Not so rare. (**He** *kisses* **Clea** *again.*) Not so rare at all. (*He .leads her softly past the irritated* **Carol**, *toward the stairs.*)

Carol: Meaning what, exactly? . . . (*Shouting*) Brindsley, I'm talking to you!

Brindsley: (*Sotto voce, into* **Clea's** *ear as* **They** *stand just behind* **Harold**) I can explain. Go up to the bedroom. Wait for me there.

Harold: (*In amazement: thinking* **He** *is being addressed*) Now? Do you think this is quite the moment?

Brindsley: Oh God! . . . I wasn't talking to you.

Carol: What did you say?

Harold: (*To* **Carol**) I think he wants *you* upstairs. (*Slyly*) For what purpose, I can't begin to imagine.

Colonel: They're going to do some more of that plotting, I daresay.

Miss Furnival: Lover's talk, Colonel.

Colonel: Very touching, I'm sure.

(**Brindsley** *pushes* **Clea** *ahead of him up the stairs.*)

Miss Furnival: "Journeys end in lovers meeting," as my father always used to say.

Colonel: What a strikingly original father you seem to have had, madam.

(**Carol** *joins the* **Other Two** *on the stairs. We see* **All Three** *groping blindly up to the bedroom,* **Brindsley's** *hands on* **Clea's** *hips,* **Carol's** *on* **Brindsley's**.)

Carol: (*With a conspirator's stage whisper.*) What is it, darling? Has something gone wrong? What can't you move?

(*This next dialogue sotto voce.*)

Brindsley: Nothing. It's all back—every bit of it—except the sofa, and I've covered that up.

Carol: You mean, we can have lights?

Brindsley: Yes . . . NO!!

Carol: Why not?

Brindsley: Never mind!

Carol: Why do you want me in the bedroom?

Brindsley: I don't. Go away!

Carol: Charming!

Brindsley: I didn't mean that.

Colonel: There you are. They *are* plotting again. What the hell is going on up there?

Brindsley: Nothing, Colonel. I've just remembered—there may be a torch under my bed. I keep it to blind the burglars with. Have another drink, Colonel!

(**He** *pushes* **Clea** *into the bedroom and shuts the door.*)

Colonel: What d'you mean another? I haven't had one yet.

Miss Furnival: Oh! Poor Colonel! Let me get you one.

Colonel: (*Rising*) I can get one for myself, thank you. Let me get you another lemonade.

Miss Furnival: (*Rising*) No thank you, Colonel, I'll manage myself. It's good practice!

(**They** *grope toward the drinks table. Above,* **Clea** *and* **Brindsley** *sit on the bed.*)

Clea: So this is what they mean by a blind date. What the hell is going on?

Brindsley: (*Sarcastic*) Nothing! Georg Bamberger is only coming to see my work tonight, and we've got a main fuse.

Clea: Is that the reason for all this furtive clutching?

Brindsley: Look, I can't explain things at the moment.

Clea: Who's that—(*Debutante accent*) "frightful gel"?

Brindsley: Just a friend.

Clea: She sounded more than that.

Brindsley: Well, if you must know, it's Carol. I've told you about her.

Clea: The Idiot Deb?

Brindsley: She's a very sweet girl. As a matter of fact we've become very good friends in the last six weeks.

Clea: How good?

Brindsley: Just good.

Clea: And have you become friends with her father too?

Brindsley: If it's any of your business, they just dropped in to meet Mr. Bamberger.

Clea: What was it you wanted to tell me on the phone tonight?

Brindsley: Nothing.

Clea: You're lying!

Brindsley: Ah, here comes the inquisition! Look, Clea, if you ever loved me, just slip away quietly with no more questions, and I'll come round later and explain everything, I promise.

Clea: I don't believe you.

Brindsley: Please darling . . . Please . . . Please . . . Please!!

(**They** *kiss, passionately, stretched out on the bed.*)

Colonel: (*Pouring*) At last . . . a decent glass of Scotch. Are you getting your lemonade?

Miss Furnival: (*Cheerfully pouring herself an enormous gin.*) Oh yes, thank you, Colonel!

Colonel: I'm just wonderin' if this Bamberger fellow is goin' to show up at all. He's half an hour late already.

Harold: Oh! That's nothing, Colonel. Millionaires are always late. It's their thing.

Miss Furnival: I'm sure you're right, Mr. Gorringe. That's how *I* imagine them. Hands like silk, and always two hours late.

Carol: Brin's been up there a long time. What can he be doing?

Harold: Maybe he's got that Clea hidden away in his bedroom, and they're having a tête-à-tête!!

Carol: What a flagrant suggestion, Mr. Gorringe.

Brindsley: (*Disengaging himself*) No one in the world kisses like you.

Clea: I missed you so badly, Brin. I had to see you. I've thought about nothing else these past six weeks. Brin, I made the most awful mistake walking out.

Brindsley: Clea—*please*!

Clea: I mean we've known each other for four years. We can't just throw each other away like old newspapers.

Brindsley: I don't see why not. You know my politics, you've heard my gossip, and you've certainly been through all my entertainment section.

Clea: Well, how about a second edition?

Brindsley: Darling, we simply can't talk about this now. Can't you trust me just for an hour?

Clea: Of course I can, darling. You don't want me down there?

Brindsley: No.

Clea: Then I'll get undressed and go quietly to bed. When you've got rid of them all, I'll be waiting.

Brindsley: That's a terrible idea!

Clea: (*Reaching for him*) I think it's lovely. A little happy relaxation for us both.

Brindsley: (*Falling off the bed*) I'm perfectly relaxed!

Carol: Brindsley!

Clea: "Too solemn for day, too sweet for night. Come not in darkness, come not in light." That's me, isn't it?

Brindsley: Of course not. I just can't explain now, that's all.

Clea: Oh, very well, you can explain later . . . in bed!

Brindsley: Not tonight, Clea.

Clea: Either that or I come down and discover your sordid secret.

Brindsley: There *is* no sordid secret!

Clea: Then you won't mind my coming down!

Carol, Colonel: (*Roaring together*) BRINDSLEY!!!

Brindsley: Oh God!! . . . All right, stay. Only keep quiet . . . Blackmailing bitch! (**He** *emerges at the top of the stairs.*) Yes, my sweet?

Carol: What are you doing up there? You've been an eternity!

Brindsley: I . . . I . . . I'm just looking in the bathroom, my darling. You never know what you might find in that clever little cabinet.

Colonel: (*Moving to the stairs*) Are you trying to madden me, sir? Are you trying to put me in a fury?

Brindsley: Certainly not, sir!!

Colonel: I warn you, Miller, it's not difficult! In the old days in the regiment I was known for my furies. I was famous for my furies . . . Do you hear?

Clea: I may sing!

(**She** *goes off into the bathroom.*)

Brindsley: I may knock your teeth in!

Colonel: What did you say?

Carol: Brin! How dare you talk to Daddy like that!

Brindsley: Oh!! I . . . I . . . I wasn't talking to Daddy like that . . .

Carol: Then who *were* you talking to?

Brindsley: I was talking to no one! Myself I was talking to! I was saying . . . "If I keep groping about up here like this, I might knock my teeth in!"

Colonel: Mad! . . . Mad! . . . Mad as the south wind! It's the only explanation— you've got yourself engaged to a lunatic.

Carol: There's something going on up there, and I'm coming up to find out what it is. Do you hear me, Brin?

Brindsley: Carol—no!

Carol: (*Climbing the stairs*) I'm not such a fool as you take me for. I know when you're hiding something. Your voice goes all deceitful—very, very foxipegs!

Brindsley: Darling please. That's not very ladylike . . . I'm sure the Colonel won't approve of you entering a man's bedroom in the dark!

(*Enter* **Schuppanzigh**. **He** *wears the overcoat and peaked cap of the London Electricity Board and carries a large tool bag, similarly labeled.*)

Carol: I'm comin' up, Brindsley, I'm comin' up!!!

Brindsley: (*Scrambling down*) I'm coming down . . . We'll all have a nice cozy drink . . .

Schuppanzigh: 'Allo please? Mr. Miller? Mr. Miller? I've come as was arranged.

Brindsley: My God . . . it's Bamberger!

Carol: Bamberger?

Brindsley: Yes, Bamberger. (**Brindsley** *rushes down the remaining stairs, pulling* **Carol** *with him.*)

Schuppanzigh: You must have thought I was never coming!

(**He** *takes off his overcoat and cap.*)

Brindsley: Not at all. I'm delighted you could spare the time. I know how busy you are. I'm afraid we've had the most idiotic disaster. We've had a fuse.

Harold: You'll have to speak up, dear. He's stone deaf!

Brindsley: (*Yelling*) We've had a fuse—not the best conditions for seeing sculpture.

Schuppanzigh: Please not to worry. Here!

(**He** *produces a torch from his pocket and "lights" it. The light on stage dims a little, as usual, to indicate this.* **All** *relax with audible sighs of pleasure.* **Schuppanzigh** *at once places his tool bag on the Regency chair, and puts his coat and cap on top of it, concealing that it is one of* **Harold's** *chairs.*)

Carol: Oh what a relief!

Brindsley: (*Hastily dragging the sheet over the rest of the sofa*) Do you always travel with a torch?

Schuppanzigh: Mostly, yes. It helps to see details. (*Seeing the* **Others**) You are holding a private view?

Miss Furnival: Oh no! I was just going. I'd hate to distract you.

Schuppanzigh: Please not on my account, dear lady. I am not so easily distracted.

Miss Furnival: (*Charmed*) Oh! . . .

Brindsley: (*Yelling in his ear*) May I present Colonel Melkett?

Colonel: (*Yelling in his other ear*) A great honor, sir!

Schuppanzigh: (*Banging his ear, to clear it*) No, no, mine—mine!

Brindsley: Miss Carol Melkett.

Carol: (*Screeching in his ear*) I say: hello. So glad you got here! It's terribly kind of you to take such an interest!

Schuppanzigh: Not at all. *Vous êtes très gentil.*

Carol: (*Yelling*) What would you like to drink?

Schuppanzigh: (*Bewildered*) A little vodka, would be beautiful!

Carol: Of course!

Brindsley: Harold Gorringe—a neighbor of mine!

Harold: How do? Very honored, I'm sure.

Schuppanzigh: Enchanted.

Harold: I must say it's a real thrill, meeting you!

Brindsley: And another neighbor, Miss Furnival.

Schuppanzigh: Enchanted.

Miss Furnival: (*Hooting in his ear*) I'm afraid we've all been taking refuge from the *storm*, as it were. (*Exclaiming as* **She** *holds* **Schuppanzigh's** *hand*) Oh! It *is* true! They *are* softer! Much, much softer!

Schuppanzigh: (*Utterly confused as* **She** *strokes his hand*) Softer? Please?

(**Brindsley** *and* **Harold** *pull her away, and* **She** *subsides onto the sofa.*)

Brindsley: Miss Furnival, please!

Carol: (*At the drinks table*) Darling, where's the vodka?

Brindsley: It's on the table.

Carol: No, it isn't.

Brindsley: It must be!

(*Above,* **Clea** *re-enters wearing the top half of* **Brindsley's** *pajamas and nothing else.* **She** *gets into bed, still clutching the vodka bottle and carrying a plastic toothmug.*)

Carol: Well, see for yourself. There's Winnie and Ginette, and Vera has quite vanished, the naughty girl.

Brindsley: She can't have done.

Schuppanzigh: Please don't concern yourselves. I am pressed for time. If I might just be shown where to go.

Brindsley: Of course. It's through the studio there. Darling, if you would just show our guest into the studio—*with his torch.*

Carol: What?? . . .

Brindsley: (*Sotto voce*) The sofa! . . . Get him out of here.

Carol: Oh yes!!

Schuppanzigh: (*Sighting the sculpture*) Oh! Good gracious! What an extraordinary object!

Brindsley: Oh, that's just a spare piece of my work I keep in here!

Schuppanzigh: Spare, maybe, but fascinating!

Brindsley: You really think so?

Schuppanzigh: (*Approaching it*) I do! Ja!

Brindsley: Well, in that case you should see my main collection. It's next door. My fiancée will show you!

(**Miss Furnival** *sits on the sofa.* **She** *is now quite drunk.*)

Schuppanzigh: One amazement at a time, if you please! In this gluttonous age it is easy to get visual indigestion—hard to find visual Alka Seltzer . . . Permit me to digest this first!

Brindsley: Oh, by all means . . . Good, yes . . . There's no hurry—no hurry at all . . . Only . . . (*Inspired*) Why don't you digest it *in the dark*?

Schuppanzigh: I beg your pardon?

Brindsley: You'll never believe it, sir, but I actually made that piece to be appreciated in the dark. I was working on a very interesting theory. You know how the Victorians said, "Children should be seen and not heard"? Well, I say, "Art should be felt and not seen."

Schuppanzigh: Amazing.

Brindsley: Yes, isn't it. I call it my theory of Factual Tactility. If it doesn't stab you to the quick—it's not art. Look! Why don't you give me that torch, and try for yourself?

Schuppanzigh: Very well, I will!! (*He hands* **Brindsley** *the torch.*)

Brindsley: Thank you!
(**He** *turns off the torch and hands it to* **Carol**. *At the same moment* **Miss Furnival** *quietly lies down, her full length on the sofa.*)
Now just stretch out your arms and feel it all over, sir.
(**He** *steals toward the studio.*)
Have a good long feel!
(**Schuppanzigh** *embraces the metal sculpture with a fervent clash.* **He** *pulls at the two metal prongs.*)
Do you see what I mean?
(*Silently* **He** *opens the curtains.*)

Schuppanzigh: Amazing! . . . Absolutely incredible! . . . It's quite true . . . Like this, the piece becomes a masterpiece at once.

Brindsley: (*Astonished*) It does??

Schuppanzigh: But of course! I feel it here—and here—the two needles of man's unrest! . . . Self love and self hate, leading to the same point! That's the meaning of the work, isn't it?

Brindsley: Of course. You've got it in one! You're obviously a great expert, sir!
(*Quietly* **He** *pulls the sofa into the studio, bearing on it the supine* **Miss Furnival**, *who waves good-bye as she disappears.*)

Schuppanzigh: Not at all. *Vous êtes très gentil*—but it is evident . . . Standing here in the dark, one can feel the vital thrust of the argument! The essential anguish! The stress and the torment of our times! It is simple but not simpleminded! Ingenious, but not ingenuous! Above all, it has real moral force! Of how many modern works can one say that, good people?

Carol: Oh, none, none at all really.

Schuppanzigh: I hope I do not lecture. It can be a fault with me.

Carol: Not at all! I could listen all night, it's so profound.

Harold: Me too. Really deep!

Colonel: I don't know anything about this myself, sir, but it's an honor to listen to you.
(**He** *starts off upstage in search of the sofa, seating himself tentatively in the air, then moving himself along in a sitting position, trying to find it with his rear end. At the same moment* **Brindsley** *emerges from the studio, closes the curtains behind him, and gropes his way to the upstage corner where there stands a small packing-case. This he carries forward, hopefully to do duty for the missing sofa. Just as* **He** *places it on the ground the traveling* **Colonel** *sits on it, trapping* **Brindsley's** *hand beneath his weight. During the following,* **Brindsley** *tries frantically to free himself.*)

Schuppanzigh: *Vous êtes très gentil!*

Harold: You mean to say you see all that in a bit of metal?

Schuppanzigh: A *tiny* bit of metal, that's the point. A miracle of compression! You want my opinion, this boy is a genius. A master of the miniature. In the space of a matchbox he can realize anything he wants—the black virginity of Chartres! The white chorale of the Acropolis! *Wunderbar!*

Carol: Oh how super!

Schuppanzigh: You should charge immense sums for work like this, Mr. Miller. They should be very very expensive! This one, for example, how much is this?

Brindsley: Fifty.

Carol: Five hundred guineas.

Schuppanzigh: Ah so! Very cheap.

Harold: Cheap!

Carol: I think so, Mr. Gorringe. Well . . . so will you have it then?

Schuppanzigh: Me?

Brindsley: Darling . . . aren't you rushing things just a little? Perhaps you would like to see the rest of my work.

Schuppanzigh: Alas, I have no more time. To linger would be pleasant, but alas, I must work . . . Also, as Moses discovered, it is sufficient to glimpse milk and honey. One does not have to wolf them down!

Brindsley: Well.

Colonel: Well . . .

Harold: Well. . . .

Carol: Well . . . Would you like it then?

Schuppanzigh: Very much.

Colonel: (*Rising;* **Brindsley** *is freed at last.*) For five hundred guineas?

Schuppanzigh: Certainly—if I had it!

Harold: According to the Sunday Pictorial, you must be worth at least seventeen million pounds.

Schuppanzigh: The Sunday papers are notoriously ill-informed. According to my bank statement, I was worth one hundred pounds, eight shillings and fourpence.

Harold: You mean you've gone broke?

Schuppanzigh: No. I mean I never had any more.

Colonel: Now look, sir, I know millionaires are supposed to be eccentric, but this is gettin' tiresome.

Carol: Daddy, ssh!——

Schuppanzigh: Millionaires? Who do you think I am?

Colonel: Dammit, man!—You must know who you are!

Carol: Mr. Bamberger, is this some kind of joke you like to play?

Schuppanzigh: Excuse me. That is not my name.

Brindsley: It isn't?

Schuppanzigh: No. My name is Schuppanzigh. Franz Schuppanzigh. Born in Weimar 1905. Student of Philosophy at Heidelberg 1934. Refugee to this country, 1938. Regular employment ever since with the London Electricity Board. (**All** *rise.*)

Carol: Electricity?

Miss Furnival: Electricity!

Brindsley: You mean you're not?——

Harold: Of course he's not!

Schuppanzigh: But who did you imagine I was?

Harold: (*Furious*) How dare you? (**He** *snatches the* **Electrician's** *torch.*)

Schuppanzigh: (*Retreating before him*) Please?——

Harold: Of all the nerve, coming in here, giving us a lecture about needles and virgins, and all the time you're simply here to mend the fuses!

Colonel: I agree with you, sir. It's monstrous!

Schuppanzigh: (*Bewildered*) It is?

(*The* **Colonel** *takes the torch and shines it pitilessly in the* **Man's** *face.*)

Colonel: You come in here, a public servant, and proceed to harangue your employers, unasked and uninvited.

Schuppanzigh: (*Bewildered*) Excuse me. But I *was* invited.

Colonel: Don't answer back. In my day you would have been fired on the spot for impertinence.

Carol: Daddy's absolutely right! Ever since the Beatles, the lower classes think they can behave exactly as they want.

Colonel: (*Handing the torch to* **Brindsley**) Miller, will you kindly show this feller his work?

Brindsley: The mains are in the cellar. There's a trap door. (*Indicating*) Do you mind?

Schuppanzigh: (*Snatching the torch furiously*) Why should I mind? It's why I came, after all! (**He** *takes his coat, cap, and bag off* **Harold's** *Regency chair . . . Seeing it.*) Now there is a really beautiful chair!

(**Brindsley** *stares at the chair aghast—and in a twinkling seats himself in it to conceal it.*)

Brindsley: (*Exasperated*) Why don't you just go into the cellar?

Schuppanzigh: *How?* Where is it?

Brindsley: (*To* **Carol**) Darling, will you open the trap, please.

Carol: Me? (*Understanding—as* **He** *indicates the chair.*) Oh—yes! (**She** *kneels and struggles to open the trap.*)

Colonel: (*To* **Brindsley**) Well, I must say, that's very gallant of you, Miller.

Brindsley: I've got a sudden touch of lumbago, sir. It often afflicts me after long spells in the dark.

Carol: (*Very sympathetic*) Oh, darling! Has it come back?

Brindsley: I'm afraid it has, my sweet.

Harold: (*Opening the trap*) Here, let me. I'm not as frail as our wilting friend. (*To* **Schuppanzigh**) Well, down you go, you!

Schuppanzigh: (*Shrugging*) So. Farewell. I leave the light of Art for the dark of Science.

Harold: Let's have a little less of your lip, shall we?

Schuppanzigh: Excuse me.

(**Schuppanzigh** *descends through the trap, taking the torch with him.* **Harold** *slams the trap door down irritably after him, and of course the lights immediately come up full. There is a long pause.* **All** *stand about embarrassed. Suddenly they hear the noise of* **Miss Furnival** *singing "Rock of Ages" in a high drunken voice from behind the curtain. Above, attracted by the noise of the slam,* **Clea** *gets out of bed, still clutching the vodka and tooth-mug, opens the door, and stands at the top of the stairs listening.*)

Brindsley: None of this evening is happening.

Carol: Cheer up, darling. In a few minutes everything will be all right. Mr. Bamberger will arrive in the light—he'll adore your work and give you twenty thousand pounds for your whole collection.

Brindsley: (*Sarcastic*) Oh, yes!

Carol: Then we can buy a super Georgian house and live what's laughingly known as happily ever after. I want to leave this place just as soon as we're married. (**Clea** *hears this. Her mouth opens wide.*)

Brindsley: (*Nervously*) Sssh!

Carol: Why? I don't want to live in a slum for our first couple of years—like other newlyweds.

Brindsley: Ssh! Ssssh! . . .

Carol: What's the matter with you?

Brindsley: The gods listen, darling. They've given me a terrible night so far. They may do worse.

Carol: (*Cooing*) I know, darling. You've had a filthy evening. Poor babykins. But I'll fight them with you. I don't care a fig for those naughty old Goddipegs. (*Looking up*) Do you hear? Not a single little fig!

(**Clea** *aims at the voice and sends a jet of vodka splashing down over* **Carol**.)
Ahh!!!

Brindsley: What is it?

Carol: It's raining!

Brindsley: Don't be ridiculous.

Carol: I'm all wet!

Brindsley: How can you be?

(**Clea** *throws vodka over a wider area.* **Harold** *gets it.*)

Harold: Hey, what's going on?

Brindsley: What?

Colonel: What the devil's the matter with you all? What are you hollerin' for?

(**He** *gets a slug of vodka in the face.*) Ahh!!

Brindsley: (*Inspired*) It's a leak—the water mains must have gone now.

Harold: Oh good God!

Brindsley: It must be!

(*Mischievously,* **Clea** *raps her bottle on the top stair. There is a terrified silence.* **All** *look up.*)

Harold: Don't say there's someone else here.

Brindsley: Good Lord!

Colonel: Who's there?

(*Silence from above*)

Come on! I know you're there!

Brindsley: (*Improvising wildly*) I—I bet you it's Mrs. Punnet.

(**Clea** *looks astonished*)

Colonel: Who?

Brindsley: (*For* **Clea's** *benefit*) Mrs. Punnet. My cleaning woman.

Harold: Cleaning woman?

Brindsley: She does for me on Mondays, Wednesdays, and Fridays.

Carol: Well, what would she be doing here now?

Brindsley: I've just remembered—she rang up and said she'd look in about six to tidy up the place.

Colonel: Dammit, man, it's almost eleven.

Harold: She's not that conscientious. She couldn't be!

Carol: Not these days!

Colonel: Well, we'll soon see. (*Calling up*) Mrs. Punnet?

Brindsley: (*Desperately*) Don't interrupt her, sir. She doesn't like to be disturbed when she's working. Why don't we just leave her to potter around upstairs with her duster?

Colonel: Let us first just see if it's her. Is that you, Mrs. Punnet? . . .

(**Clea** *keeps still.*)

Colonel: (*Roaring*) MRS. PUNNET!

Clea: (*Deciding on a cockney voice of great antiquity*) 'Allo! Yes?

Brindsley: (*Weakly*) It is. Good heavens, Mrs. Punnet, what on earth are you doing up there?

Clea: I'm just giving your bedroom a bit of a tidy, sir.

Brindsley: At this time of night?

(*The mischief in* **Clea** *begins to take over.*)

Clea: Better late than never, sir, as they say. I know how you like your bedroom to be nice and inviting when you're giving one of your parties.

Brindsley: Yes, yes, yes, of course . . .

Colonel: When did you come, madam?

Clea: Just a few minutes ago, sir. I didn't like to disturb you, so I come on up 'ere.

Harold: Was it you pouring all that water on us, then?

Clea: Water? Good 'eavens, I must have upset something. It's as black as Newgate's Knocker up 'ere. Are you playing one of your saucy games, Mr. Miller?

Brindsley: No, Mrs. Punnet. We've had a fuse. It's all over the house.

Clea: Oh! A *fuse*! I thought it might be one of them saucy games in the dark, sir: Sardines or Piccadilly. The kind that end in a general squeeze-up. I know you're rather partial to kinky games, Mr. Miller, so I just wondered. (**She** *starts to come down the stairs.*)

Brindsley: (*Distinctly*) It is a fuse, Mrs. Punnet. The man's mending it now. The lights will be on *any minute*!

Clea: Well, that'll be a relief for you, won't it? (**She** *dashes the vodka accurately in his face, passes him by and comes into the room.*)

Brindsley: Yes, of course. Now why don't you just go on home?

Clea: I'm sorry I couldn't come before, sir. I was delayed, you see. My Rosie's been taken queer again.

Brindsley: I quite understand! (**He** *gropes around trying to hide her, but* **She** *continuously evades him.*)

Clea: (*Relentlessly*) It's her tummy. There's a lump under her belly button the size of a grapefruit.

Harold: Oh how nasty!

Clea: Horrid. Poor little Rosie. I said to her this evening, I said, "There's no good your being mulish, my girl. You're going to the hospital first thing tomorrow morning and getting yourself ultra-violated!"

Brindsley: Well, hadn't you better be getting back to poor little Rosie! She must need you, surely?—And there's really nothing you can do here tonight.

Clea: (*Meaningfully*) Are you sure of that, sir?

Brindsley: Positive, thank you.

(**They** *are close now.*)

Clea: I mean, I know what this place can be like after one of your evenings. A gypsy caravan isn't in it. Gin bottles all over the floor! Bras and panties in the sink! And God knows what in the——

(**Brindsley** *muzzles her with his hand.* **She** *bites it hard, and* **He** *drops to his knees in silent agony.*)

Colonel: Please watch what you say, madam. You don't know it, but you're in the presence of Mr. Miller's fiancée.

Clea: Fiancée?

Colonel: Yes, and I am her father.

Clea: Well, I never . . . Oh, Mr. Miller! I'm so 'appy for you! . . . Fiancée! Oh, sir! And you never told me!

Brindsley: I was keeping it a surprise.

Clea: Well, I never! Oh, how lovely! . . . May I kiss you sir, please?

Brindsley: (*On his knees*) Well yes, yes, of course . . .

(**Clea** *gropes for his ear, finds it and twists it.*)

Clea: Oh sir, I'm so pleased for you! And for *you*, Miss, too!

Carol: Thank you.

Clea: (*To* **Colonel Melkett**) And for *you*, sir.

Colonel: Thank you.

Clea: You must be Miss Clea's father.

Colonel: Miss Clea? I don't understand.

(*Triumphantly* **She** *sticks out her tongue at* **Brindsley**, *who collapses his length on the floor, face down, in a gesture of total surrender. For him it is the end. The evening can hold no further disasters for him.*)

Clea: (*To* **Carol**) Well, I never! So you've got him at last! Well done, Miss Clea! I never thought you would—not after four years . . .

Brindsley: No—no—no—no . . .

Clea: Forgive me, sir, if I'm speaking out of turn, but you must admit four years is a long time to be courting one woman. Four days is stretching it a bit nowadays!

Brindsley: (*Weakly*) Mrs. Punnet, *please!*

Carol: Four years!

Clea: Well, yes, dear. It's been all of that and a bit more really, hasn't it? (*In a stage whisper*) And of course it's just in time. It was getting a bit prominent, your little bun in the oven.

(**Carol** *screeches with disgust.* **Brindsley** *covers his ears.*)

Oh, Miss, I don't mean that's why he popped the question. Of course it's not. He's always been stuck on you. He told me so, not one week ago, in this room. (*Sentimentally*) "Mrs. Punnet," he says, "Mrs. Punnet, as far as I'm concerned you can keep the rest of them—Miss Clea will always be on top of the heap for me." "Oh," I says, "then what about that debutante bit, Carol, the one you're always telling me about?" "Oh, 'er," he says, "she's just a bit of Knightsbridge candyfloss. A couple of licks and you've 'ad 'er."

(*There is a long pause.* **Clea** *is now sitting on the table, swinging her vodka bottle in absolute command of the situation.*)

Colonel: (*Faintly; at last grappling with the situation*) Did you say four years, madam?

Clea: (*In her own voice, quiet*) Yes, Colonel. Four years, in this room.

Harold: I know that voice. It's Clea!

Miss Furnival: (*Surprised*) Clea!

Carol: (*Horrified*) Clea!

Brindsley: (*Unconvincingly surprised*) Clea!

Clea: Surprised, Brin?

Carol: (*Understanding*) Clea! . . .

Colonel: I don't understand anything that's going on in this room.

Clea: I know. It is a very odd room, isn't it? It's like a magic dark room, where everything happens the wrong way round. Rain falls indoors, the Daily comes at night and turns in a second from a nice maid into nasty mistress.

Brindsley: Be quiet, Clea!

Clea: At last! One real word of protest! Have you finished lying, then? Have you eaten the last crumb of humble pie? Oh you coward, you bloody coward! Just because you didn't want to marry me, did you have to settle for this lot?

Carol: Marry!

Colonel: Marry?

Clea: Four years of meaning to end in this triviality! Miss Laughingly Known As and her Daddipegs!

Carol: Stop her! She's disgusting.

Colonel: How can I, for God's sake?

Carol: Well, where's all that bloody resource you keep talking about?

(*The* **Colonel** *goes to her but takes* **Clea's** *hand by mistake.*)

Colonel: Now calm down, Dumpling. Keep your head . . . There—hold my hand, that's it, now Daddy's here. Everything is under control. All right?

Clea: Are you sure that is your daughter's hand you're holding, Colonel?

Colonel: What? Carol, isn't this your hand?

Carol: No.

Clea: You must have lived with your daughter for well over twenty years, Colonel. What remarkable use you've made of your eyes.

(*There is another pause. The* **Colonel** *moves away in embarrassment.*)

Clea: (*Wickedly*) All right! Kinky game time! . . . Let's all play Guess the Hand.

Harold: Oh good God!

Clea: Or would you rather Guess the Lips, Harold?

Carol: How disgusting!

Clea: Well, that's me, dear. (**Carol's** *accent*) I'm Queen Disgustipegs!

(**She** *seizes* **Carol's** *hand and puts it into* **Harold's**.) Who's that?

Carol: I don't know.

Clea: Guess.

Carol: I don't know, and I don't care.

Clea: Oh go on. Have a go!

Carol: It's Brin, of course: You can't trick me like that! It's Brindsley's stupid hand.

Harold: I'm afraid you're wrong. It's me.

Carol: (*Struggling*) It's not. You're lying.

Harold: (*Holding on*) I'm not. I don't lie.

Carol: You're lying! . . . You're lying!

Harold: I'm not.

(**Carol** *breaks away and blunders upstage.* **She** *is becoming hysterical.*)

Clea: You try it, Harold. Take the hand on your right.

Harold: I'm not playing. It's a bloody silly game.

Clea: Go on . . .

(**She** *seizes his hand and puts it into* **Brindsley's**.)

Well?

Harold: It's Brin.

Brindsley: Yes.

Clea: Well done! (**She** *sits on the low stool.*)

Carol: (*Outraged*) How does he know that? How does *he* know your hand and I don't?

Brindsley: Calm down, Carol.

Carol: Answer me! I want to know!

Brindsley: Stop it!

Carol: I won't!

Brindsley: You're getting hysterical!

Carol: Leave me alone! I want to go home.

(*And suddenly* **Miss Furnival** *gives a sharp short scream and blunders out through the curtains.*)

Miss Furnival: Prams! Prams! Prams—in the supermarket! . . .

(**They** *all freeze.* **She** *is evidently out of control in a world of her own fears.* **She** *speaks quickly and strangely.*)

All those hideous wire prams full of babies and bottles—cornflakes over there, is all they say—and then they leave you to yourself. Biscuits over there—cat food over there—fish cakes over there—Airwick over there. Pink stamps, green stamps, free balloons—television dinners—pay as you go out—oh, Daddy, it's awful! And then the Godless ones, the heathens in their leather jackets—laughing me to scorn! But, not for long. Oh, no! Who shall stand when He appeareth? He'll strike them from their motorcycles! He'll dash their helmets to the ground! Yea, verily, I say unto thee—there shall be an end of gasoline! An end to cigarette puffing and jostling with hips . . . Keep off . . . Keep off! Keep off! . . .

(**She** *runs drunkenly across the room and collides with* **Harold**.)

Harold: Come on, Ferny, I think it's time we went home.

Miss Furnival: (*Pulling herself together*) Yes. You're quite right . . . (*With an attempt at grandeur*) I'm sorry I can't stay any longer, Mr. Miller; but your millionaire is unpardonably late. So typical of modern manners . . . Express my regrets, if you please.

Brindsley: Certainly.

(*Leaning heavily on* **Harold's** *arm* **She** *leaves the room.* **He** *shuts the door after them.*) Thank you, Clea. Thank you very much.

Clea: Any time.

Brindsley: You had no right.

Clea: No?

Brindsley: *You* walked out on *me*. (**He** *joins her on the low stool.*)

Clea: Is that what I did?

Brindsley: You said you never wanted to see me again.

Clea: I never saw you at all—how could you be walked out on? You should live in the dark, Brindsley. It's your natural element.

Brindsley: Whatever that means.

Clea: It means you don't really want to be seen. Why is that, Brindsley? Do you think if someone really saw you, they would never love you?

Brindsley: Oh go away.

Clea: I want to know.

Brindsley: Yes, you always want to know. Pick-pick-pick away! Why is *that*, Clea? Have you ever thought why you need to do it? Well?

Clea: Perhaps because I care about you.

Brindsley: Perhaps there's nothing to care about. Just a fake artist.

Clea: Stop pitying yourself. It's always your vice. I told you when I met you: you could either be a good artist, or a chic fake. You didn't like it, because I refused just to give you applause.

Brindsley: God knows, you certainly did that!

Clea: Is that what *she* gives you? Twenty hours of ego-massage every day?

Brindsley: At least our life together isn't the replica of the Holy Inquisition you made of ours. I didn't have an affair with you: it was just four years of nooky with Torquemada!

Clea: And don't say you didn't enjoy it!

Brindsley: Enjoy it? I hated every second of it.

Clea: Yes, I remember.

Brindsley: Every second.

Clea: I recall.

Brindsley: When you left for Finland, it was the happiest day of my life.

Clea: Mine, too!

Brindsley: I sighed with relief.

Clea: So did I.

Brindsley: I went out dancing that very night.

Clea: So did I. It was out with the lyre and the timbrel.

Brindsley: Good. Then that's all right.

Clea: Fine.

Brindsley: Super!

Clea: Duper!

Brindsley: It's lovely to see you looking so happy.

Clea: You too. Radiant with self-fulfilment.

(*A pause*)

Brindsley: If you felt like this, why did you come back?

Clea: If *you* felt like this, why did you tell Mrs. Punnet I was still at the top of the heap?

Brindsley: I never said that!

Clea: You did.

Brindsley: Never!

Clea: You *did*!

Brindsley: Of course I didn't. You invented that ten minutes ago, when you were *playing* Mrs. Punnet.

Clea: I—Oh! So I did! . . .

(**They** *both giggle.* **She** *falls happily against his shoulder.*)

Brindsley: You know something—I'm not sure she's not right.

(*During this exchange the* **Colonel** *and his* **Daughter** *have been standing frozen with astonished anger. Now the outraged* **Father** *takes over.*)

Colonel: No doubt this is very funny to you two.

Clea: It is, quite, actually.

Colonel: I'm not so easily amused, however, madam.

Brindsley: Now look, Colonel——

Colonel: Hold your tongue, sir, I'm talking. Do you know what would have happened to a young man in my day who dared to treat a girl the way you have treated my Dumpling?

Brindsley: Well, I assume, Colonel——

Colonel: Hold your tongue, I'm talking.

Carol: Oh, leave it, Daddy. Let's just go home.

Colonel: In a moment, Dumpling. Kindly leave this to me.

Brindsley: Look, Carol, I can explain——

Carol: Explain what?

Brindsley: It's impossible here.

Colonel: You understate, sir.

Brindsley: Carol, you don't understand.

Carol: What the hell's there to understand? All the time you were going with me, she was in the background—that's all there is to it—What were you doing? Weighing us up? . . . . Here! (**She** *pulls off her engagement ring.*)

Brindsley: What?

Carol: Your ring. Take the bloody thing back!

(**She** *throws it. It hits the* **Colonel** *in the eye.*)

Colonel: My eye! My damned eye!

(**Clea** *starts to laugh again. In mounting fury, clutching his eye*)

Oh very droll, madam! Very droll indeed! Laugh your fill! Miller! I asked you a question. Do you know what would have happened to a young lout like you in my day?

Brindsley: Happened, sir?

Colonel: (*Quietly*) You'd have been thrashed, sir.

Brindsley: (*Nervous*) Thrashed——

(*The* **Man of War** *begins to go after him, feeling his way in the dark—like some furious robot.*)

Colonel: You'd have felt the mark of a father's horsewhip across your seducer's shoulders. You'd have gone down on your cad's bended knees, and begged my daughter's pardon for the insults you've offered her tonight.

Brindsley: (*Retreating before the* **Colonel's** *groping advance*) Would I, sir?

Colonel: You'd have raised your guttersnipe voice in a piteous scream for mercy and forgiveness!

(*A terrible scream is heard from the hall.* **They** *freeze, listening as it comes nearer and nearer, then the door is flung open and* **Harold** *plunges into the room.* **He** *is wild-eyed with rage: a lit and bent taper shakes in his furious hand.*)

Harold. Ooooooh! You villain!

Brindsley: Harold——

Harold: You skunky, conniving little villain!

Brindsley: What's the matter?

Harold: (*Raging.*) Have you seen the state of my room? My room? My lovely room, the most elegant and cared for in this entire district?—one chair turned absolutely upside down, one chair on top of another like a Portobello junk-shop! And that's not all, is it, Brindsley? Oh no, that's not the worst by a long chalk, is it, Brindsley?

Brindsley: Long chalk?

Harold: Don't play the innocent with me. I thought I had a friend living all these years. I didn't know I was living opposite a Light-fingered Lenny!

Brindsley: Harold!—

Harold: (*Hysterical*) This is my reward, isn't it?—After years of looking after you, sweeping and tidying up this place, because you're too much of a slut to do it for yourself—to have my best pieces stolen from me to impress your new girl friend and her daddy. Or did she help you?

Brindsley: Harold, it was an emergency.

Harold: Don't talk to me: I don't want to know! I know what you think of me now . . . "Don't tell Harold about the engagement. He's not to be trusted. He's not a friend. He's just someone to steal things from!"

Brindsley: You know that's not true.

Harold: (*Shrieking—in one hysterical breath*) I know I was the last one to know—that's what I know! I have to find it out in a room full of strangers. Me, who's listened to more of your miseries in the small hours of the morning than anyone else would put up with! All your boring talk about women, hour after hour, as if no one's got troubles but you!—

Clea: She's getting hysterical, dear. Ignore her.

Harold: It's you who's going to be ignored, Clea. (*To* **Brindsley**) As for you, all I can say about your engagement is this: you deserve each other, you and that little nit.

(**Carol** *gives a shriek.*)

Brindsley: Carol!

Harold: Oh, so you're there, are you?—Skulking in the shadows!

Brindsley: Leave her alone!

Harold: I'm not going to touch her. I just want my things and I'll be off. Did you hear me, Brindsley? You give me my things now, or I'll call the police.

Brindsley: Don't be ridiculous.

Harold: (*Grimly*) Item: One lyre-back Regency chair, in lacquered mahogany with Ormolu inlay and appliqué work on the cushions.

Brindsley: In front of you. (**He** *thrusts the taper at it.*)

Harold: Ta. Item: One half-back sofa—likewise Regency—supported by claw legs and upholstered in a rich silk of bottle green to match the aforesaid chair.

Brindsley: In the studio.

Harold: Unbelievable! Item: One Coalport vase, dated 1809, decorated on the rim with a pleasing design of daisies and peonies.

Brindsley: On the floor.

Harold: Ta.

(**Brindsley** *hands it to him.*)

Ooooh! You've even taken the flowers! I'll come back for the chair and sofa in a minute. (*Drawing himself up with all the offended dignity of which a* **Harold Gorringe** *is capable.*) This is the end of our relationship, Brindsley. We won't be speaking again, I don't think.

(**He** *twitches his raincoat off the table. Inside it, of course, is the Buddha, which falls on the floor and smashes beyond repair. There is a terrible silence. Trying to keep his voice under control*)

Do you know what that statue was worth? Do you? More money than you'll ever see in your whole life, even if you sell every piece of that nasty, rusty rubbish. (*With the quietness of the mad*) I think I'm going to have to smash you, Brindsley.

Brindsley: (*Nervously*) Now steady on, Harold . . . don't be rash . . .

Harold: Yes, I'm very much afraid I'll have to smash you . . . Smash for smash—that's fair do's. (**He** *pulls one of the long metal prongs out of the sculpture.*) Smash for smash. Smash for *smash!*

(*Insanely* **He** *advances on* **Brindsley** *holding the prong like a sword, the taper burning in his other hand.*)

Brindsley: (*Retreating*) Stop it, Harold. You've gone mad!

Colonel: Well done, sir. I think it's time for the reckoning.

(*The* **Colonel** *grabs the other prong and also advances.*)

Brindsley: (*Retreating from them* **Both**) Now just a minute, Colonel. Be reasonable! . . . Let's not revert to savages! . . . Harold, I appeal to you—you've always had civilized instincts! Don't join the Army! . . .

Carol: (*Grimly advancing also*) Get him, Daddy! Get him! Get him!

Brindsley: (*Horrified at her*) Carol!

Carol: (*Malevolently*) Get him! Get him! Get him! Get . . .

Brindsley: *Clea!*

(**Clea** *leaps up and blows out the taper. Lights up.*)

Colonel: Dammit!

(**Clea** *grabs* **Brindsley's** *hand and pulls him out of danger. To* **Clea**)

Careful, my little Dumpling. Keep out of the way.

Harold: (*To* **Carol**) Hush up, Colonel. We'll be able to hear them breathing.

Colonel: Clever idea! Smart tactics, sir!

(*Silence.* **They** *listen.* **Brindsley** *climbs carefully onto the table and silently pulls* **Clea** *up after him.* **Harold** *and the* **Colonel**, *prodding and slashing the darkness with their swords,* *grimly hunt their quarry. Twenty seconds. Suddenly, with a bang* **Schuppanzigh** *opens the trap from below.* **Both Men** *advance on it warily. The* **Electrician** *disappears again below.* **They** *have almost reached it, on tiptoe, when there is another crash—this time from the hall.* **Someone** *has again tripped over the milk bottles.* **Harold** *and the* **Colonel** *immediately swing round and start stalking upstage, still on tiptoe.*

Enter **Georg Bamberger.** *He is quite evidently a millionaire. Dressed in the Gulbenkian manner,* **He** *wears a beard, an eyeglass, a frock coat, a top hat and an orchid.* **He** *carries a large deaf aid. Bewildered,* **He** *advances into the room. Stealthily, the* **Two** *armed* **men** *stalk him upstage as* **He** *silently gropes his way downstage and passes between them.)*

Bamberger: *(Speaking in a middle-aged German voice, as near to the voice of* **Schuppanzigh** *as possible.)* Hallo, please! Mr. Miller?

(Harold *and the* **Colonel** *spin round in a third direction.)*

Harold: Oh, it's the electrician!

Bamberger: Hallo, please?

Colonel: What the devil are you doing up here?

(Schuppanzigh *appears at the trap)*

Have you mended the fuse?

Harold: Or are you going to keep us in the dark all night?

Schuppanzigh: Don't worry. The fuse is mended.

(He *comes out of the trap.* **Bamberger** *goes round the stage, right.)*

Harold: Thank God for that.

Bamberger: *(Still groping around)* Hallo, please? Mr. Miller—vere are you? Vy zis darkness? Is a joke, yes?

Schuppanzigh: *(Incensed)* Ah, no! That is not very funny, good people—just because I am a foreigner, to imitate my voice. You English can be the rudest people on earth!

Bamberger: *(Imperiously)* Mr. Miller! I have come here to give attention to your sculptures!

Schuppanzigh: *Gott in himmel!*

Bamberger: *Gott in himmel!*

Brindsley: God, it's him! Bamberger!

Clea: He's come!

Harold: Bamberger!

Colonel: Bamberger!

(They *freeze. The* **Millionaire** *sets off, left, toward the open trap.)*

Brindsley: Don't worry, Mr. Bamberger. We've had a fuse, but it's mended now.

Bamberger: *(Irritably)* Mr. Miller!

Clea: You'll have to speak up. He's deaf.

Brindsley: *(Shouting)* Don't worry, Mr. Bamberger! We've has a fuse, but it's all right now! . . .

(Standing on the table, **He** *clasps* **Clea** *happily.* **Bamberger** *misses the trap by inches.)*

Oh, Clea, that's true. Everything's all right now! Just in the nick of time!

(But as **He** *says this* **Bamberger** *turns and falls into the open trap door.* **Schuppanzigh** *slams it to with his foot.)*

Schuppanzigh: So! Here's now an end to your troubles! Like Jehovah in the Sacred Testament, I give you the most miraculous gift of the Creation! Light!

Clea: Light!

Brindsley: Oh, thank God. *Thank God!*

(Schuppanzigh *goes to the switch.)*

Harold: (*Grimly*) I wouldn't thank Him too soon, Brindsley, if I were you!

Colonel: Nor would I, Brindsley, if I were you!

Carol: Nor would I, Brinnie Winnie, if I were you!

Schuppanzigh: (*Grandly*) Then thank *me*! For I shall play God for this second! (*Clapping his hands*) Attend all of you. God said: "Let there be light!" And there was, good people, suddenly!—astoundingly!—instantaneously!—inconceivably— inexhaustibly—inextinguishably and eternally—LIGHT!

(**Schuppanzigh**, *with a great flourish, flicks the light switch. INSTANT DARKNESS. The turntable of the phonograph starts up again, and with an exultant crash the Sousa march falls on the audience—and blazes away in the black.*)

END

PART SEVEN
STAGING

For the purpose of our study, we have treated five basic elements of drama as rather isolated subjects, devoting one section each to character, setting, plot, language, and irony. But such distinctions are artificial—all these elements overlap and fuse into the play as a whole. As is evident in the introductions, we cannot discuss character without touching on setting or language, or talk about plot without referring to character, setting, or irony. After dealing with the parts, we have to reassemble the play and perceive it as a whole if we are to appreciate what the playwright has done and to feel the power of his creation. Perhaps through examining staging we can discuss the whole play more meaningfully.

For a play to be staged successfully, it must first of all be well-written. The dramatist needs a sound working knowledge of theater if he is to create a play that can be performed well on stage. He must be aware of the unique limitations of drama—time, space, physical requirements—as contrasted with those of other literary forms.

When a director prepares a play for production, he approaches it somewhat as you do in careful reading. He gets to know the characters, noting how they live and what their world is like. He listens to their language, observes their situations and the ironies of their actions and statements, and analyzes the conflicts, watching their development and eventual resolution.

But he cannot simply develop his personal interpretation of the play and stop there. He must create an entire production that will express his interpretation to an audience: he must *stage* the play. Whatever the director's interpretation, however, he is bound by the text, and we as audience have the right to ask what basis exists in the text for any aspect of the production. In accomplishing this goal, he relies to a great extent on the talents of numerous other creative people—including actors, scene designers, sound and lighting artists, choreographers, voice and movement coaches, costume designers, makeup artists, and stage managers in addition to a variety of technicians, stagehands, business managers, and even the audience—to plan and execute the thousands of details which comprise a theatrical production.

The extent to which these other artists help evolve the interpretation and plan the production varies from director to director. Some directors prefer to plan many of the production details even before meeting with their creative staffs; others present their overall interpretation to the designers and other artists and let them work out the details. Whatever the approach, the goal is a unified, consistent production which is true to the text of the play.

One of the key artists with whom the director works is the scene designer. Together they must create a physical set which conveys and enhances the director's interpretation of the play. An audience usually receives its first impression of a play when it sees the set. This first impression is important in setting the mood and tone for the entire production. A stark, somber set helps create a heavy, somber mood even before any action occurs on stage. A bare stage with few stage properties forces the audience to focus on the actions and dialogue of the characters themselves. However, a busy, cluttered set may stress a particular mood or tone that communicates something about the world in which the characters live. The director and designer must make numerous other decisions such as what materials are used to build the set, whether it will be shifted behind closed curtains or in front of the audience, and so forth. Whatever the style of production, such decisions must be made deliberately and for specific reasons.

Working closely with the director and scene designer is the lighting designer, whose design enhances the set and adds to the whole production. It helps create mood; it emphasizes certain objects, actors, or stage areas; it enhances makeup and costumes; it helps establish time of day, weather conditions, and climate. Lighting can heighten whatever effects the other elements are designed to achieve. A set depicting a dingy, shabby shack can look even dingier and shabbier through lighting. A scene set in a hot, arid desert will seem even hotter and more parched when lighting is used effectively.

In designing lighting, just as in planning the other elements, the director and designer must work from the text of the play. Often a playwright provides details in the script which indicate the desired lighting effect for a specific scene. But the lighting design must go beyond the literal requirements of the script and contribute artistically to the meaning of the whole play.

Two other important visual elements of production are costuming and makeup. Costuming especially helps create the illusion of a particular period or locale. Color, style, fabric, texture, ornamentation, jewelry, and accessories—all these must be carefully considered in creating costumes. Each costume should reinforce the interpretation of the character who wears it. If the leading female character wears a long gown of faded blue silk, accented with a pearl necklace, these details were selected for a specific purpose. Makeup completes the visual image of each character. It can help establish age, health, social class, and period as well as suggesting more subtle aspects of personality. For example, a character who is dour and bad-tempered can seem more so through effective makeup, such as heavy eyebrows, downward slanting mouth lines, and a wrinkled forehead. Such details are consciously selected to achieve specific effects.

Sound effects, like the visual elements, may be used to establish specific details given in the script as well as contributing to mood and emphasis. If the script calls for a gunshot, an automobile horn, the braying of a mule, or the sound of thunder, the director and sound technician must decide how these effects will be produced and what they should sound like. But, like lighting, sound effects design must go beyond such literal requirements to help interpret each scene. Music can be an important sound effect for conveying mood and emphasis and may even occupy a major position in the production.

An essential element in any production, large or small, is the acting. One of the director's important tasks in staging a play is casting each role carefully. He must consider each actor's physical features, voice quality, acting ability, and stage presence in deciding his or her suitability for a given role. In addition, the director must select actors who will work well together in creating the overall effect. Sometimes a definite contrast may be desired in the appearance and bearing of two characters. Such a requirement must influence the director's choice in casting these roles. Many other similar considerations must be kept in mind throughout the casting process. The ultimate goal, as in planning the other elements, is to select a cast which will, collectively and individually, express the director's interpretation of the play convincingly to an audience.

The movement and positioning of the actors on stage, known as the *blocking*, can be an effective interpretative tool. The relative placement of the characters, their individual body positions, their relation to specific objects on stage, and the acting area which each occupies are all important factors in blocking the play. If a certain object signifies power, the director may position his characters around it to show dominance or struggle for power. Since certain acting areas and body positions have greater visual strength than others, the director moves and places each actor carefully to achieve the desired balance and emphasis.

The overall effect of blocking must also be considered. The arrangements and movements should not become monotonous and repetitive unless such an effect is desired for some reason. Body positions and acting areas must be varied. Too much or too little movement can destroy or weaken the effects a director is trying to achieve with other elements of staging.

Probably one of the most important functions of blocking is to show the inter-relationships of the characters from scene to scene. A simple example is illustrated below. Two conflicting groups have aligned themselves on opposite sides of the stage (1); character Z finds himself caught between the two groups (2); he may demonstrate visually the resolution of his conflict by joining the opposite group (3).

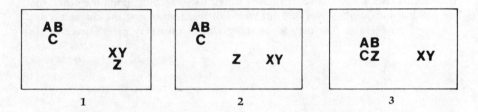

Even more subtle and complex relationships may be expressed in part through blocking. When seeing a play, we will understand and enjoy it more fully if we observe such details and ask ourselves what the director is trying to achieve in each scene through blocking.

All the other elements of staging would, of course, be pointless without the receiver of these efforts—the audience. A good director recognizes and utilizes the double vision which audiences have in the theater. On the one hand, the audience becomes emotionally involved in what is happening on stage. They laugh when a character falls on a banana peel; they feel sad and cry when a tragic hero dies; they sympathize with the child whose parents don't love him. Often, they may see themselves in a particular character, identifying his feelings and actions with their own.

Sometimes a playwright may consciously use this double vision. He may try to create the feeling that the audience is looking through a window or wall, watching people live their lives. Or he may consciously destroy the deep emotional involvement in the production by having the actors mingle with the audience, talking about the make-believe nature of theater, thus stressing the intellectual aspects of the play.

At the same time, however, the audience realizes intellectually that they are in a theater watching a performance. They are aware of whether or not the seats are comfortable; they hear people around them coughing, whispering, shifting in their seats, or dropping their programs. But more important, a good audience is aware of the technical details of the production. They are conscious of the lights emphasizing some object or person; they appreciate the skill of a particular actor; they evaluate the costumes, the set, the blocking—all these judgments occur even while the audience is emotionally involved in the play. A good production and a knowledgeable audience maintain a balance between these facets of the double vision. An audience must not become so carried away with the action that they fail to perceive the subtleties and skills of the actors and technicians. The woman who suddenly leaps from her seat to scream at Othello for being deceived by Iago has become too emotionally involved—she can no longer distinguish art from life. Likewise, the man who calmly and dispassionately counts the number of lighting changes during the killing of Desdemona has missed an important part of enjoying drama—he has not allowed himself to become emotionally involved.

In certain respects the theater is artificial—its participants wear masks and costumes and act out roles. However, it is only a more structured form of what we do in our own lives—we all, in a sense, wear masks and play roles in our day-to-day living. Whether a play is realistic or nonrealistic—that is, whether it attempts to make us believe to some extent that the characters and setting are *real* or whether it calls attention to the fact that these are actors performing in a theater for us, an audience—we do distinguish between the world of the play and the world of our own lives. But if this book accomplishes nothing else, we hope it shows that the two worlds are closely related, that one can tell us something about the other, that we can learn about ourselves and our world through observing the characters and sharing their feelings. The play is the thing wherein we may meet ourselves.

SIX CHARACTERS IN SEARCH OF AN AUTHOR

(Sei personaggi in cerca d'autore)

A COMEDY IN THE MAKING

Luigi Pirandello

English version by EDWARD STORER

ACTORS OF THE COMPANY

The Manager	Other Actors and Actresses
Leading Lady	Property Man
Leading Man	Prompter
Second Lady	Machinist
Lead	Manager's Secretary
L'Ingénue	Door-Keeper
Juvenile Lead	Scene-Shifters

Daytime. The Stage of a Theatre

N. B. *The Comedy is without acts or scenes. The performance is interrupted once, without the curtain being lowered, when the manager and the chief characters withdraw to arrange the scenario. A second interruption of the action takes place when, by mistake, the stage hands let the curtain down.*

ACT I

The spectators will find the curtain raised and the stage as it usually is during the day time. It will be half dark, and empty, so that from the beginning the public may have the impression of an impromptu performance.

Prompter's box and a small table and chair for the manager.

Two other small tables and several chairs scattered about as during rehearsals.

The **Actors** and **Actresses** of the company enter from the back of the stage:
first one, then another, then two together; nine or ten in all. They are about to rehearse a Pirandello play: *Mixing It Up.*° Some of the company move off towards their dressing rooms. The **Prompter** who has the "book" under his arm, is waiting for the manager in order to begin the rehearsal.

The **Actors** and **Actresses**, some standing, some sitting, chat and smoke. One perhaps reads a paper; another cons his part.

°**i.e.,** *Il giuoco delle parti.*

This play operates on several levels of reality.

Finally, **The Manager** *enters and goes to the table prepared for him. His* **Secretary** *brings him his mail, through which he glances. The* **Prompter** *takes his seat, turns on a light, and opens the "book."*

Technical staging is overt and practical; he needs light to see.

The Manager (*throwing a letter down on the table*): I can't see (*To* **Property Man.**) Let's have a little light, please!

Property Man: Yes sir, yes, at once. (*A light comes down on to the stage.*)

The Manager (*clapping his hands*): Come along! Come along! Second act of "Mixing It Up." (*Sits down.*)

(*The* **Actors** *and* **Actresses** *go from the front of the stage to the wings, all except the three who are to begin the rehearsal.*)

Prompter (*reading the "book"*): "Leo Gala's house. A curious room serving as dining-room and study."

Not particularly concerned with details— the old set will do.

The Manager (*to* **Property Man**): Fix up the old red room.

Property Man (*noting it down*): Red set. All right!

Prompter (*continuing to read from the "book"*): "Table already laid and writing desk with books and papers. Book-shelves. Exit rear to Leo's bedroom. Exit left to kitchen. Principal exit to right."

Manager operates as director: the decisions are his.

The Manager (*energetically*): Well, you understand: The principal exit over there; here, the kitchen. (*Turning to* **Actor** *who is to play the part of* **Socrates.**) You make your entrances and exits here. (*To* **Property Man.**) The baize doors at the rear, and curtains.

Property Man (*noting it down*): Right!

Prompter (*reading as before*): "When the curtain rises, Leo Gala, dressed in cook's cap and apron is busy beating an egg in a cup. Philip, also dressed as a cook, is beating another egg. Guido Venanzi is seated and listening."

Leading Man (*to* **Manager**): Excuse me, but must I absolutely wear a cook's cap?

The Manager (*annoyed*): I imagine so. It says so there anyway. (*Pointing to the "book."*)

Leading Man: But it's ridiculous!

The Manager (*jumping up in a rage*): Ridiculous? Ridiculous? Is it my fault if France won't send us any more good comedies, and we are reduced to putting on Pirandello's works, where nobody understands anything, and where the author plays the fool with us all? (*The* **Actors** *grin. The* **Manager** *goes to* **Leading Man** *and shouts.*) Yes sir, you put on the cook's cap and beat eggs. Do you suppose that with all this egg-beating business you are on an ordinary stage? Get that out of your head. You represent the shell of the eggs you are beating!

He interprets Pirandello's work, though he says nobody understands it. Is author toying with us?

(*Laughter and comments among the* **Actors.**) Silence! and listen to my explanations, please! (*To* **Leading Man.**) "The empty form of reason without the fullness of instinct, which is blind."—You stand for reason, your wife is instinct. It's a mixing up of the parts, according to which you who act your own part become the puppet of yourself. Do you understand?

Leading Man: I'm hanged if I do.

The Manager: Neither do I. But let's get on with it. It's sure to be a glorious failure anyway. (*Confidentially.*) But I say, please face three-quarters. Otherwise, what with the abstruseness of the dialogue, and the public that won't be able to hear you, the whole thing will go to hell. Come on! come on!

Prompter: Pardon sir, may I get into my box? There's a bit of a draught.

The Manager: Yes, yes, of course!

At this point, the **Door-Keeper** *has entered from the stage door and advances towards the manager's table, taking off his braided cap. During this manoeuvre, the* **Six Characters** *enter, and stop by the door at back of stage, so that when the* **Door-Keeper** *is about to announce their coming to the* **Manager**, *they are already on the stage. A tenuous light surrounds them, almost as if irradiated by them—the faint breath of their fantastic reality.*

Challenging problem for the technicians

This light will disappear when they come forward towards the actors. They preserve, however, something of the dream lightness in which they seem almost suspended; but this does not detract from the essential reality of their forms and expressions.

He who is known as **The Father** *is a man of about 50: hair, reddish in colour, thin at the temples; he is not bald, however; thick moustaches, falling over his still fresh mouth, which often opens in an empty and uncertain smile. He is fattish, pale; with an especially wide forehead. He has blue, oval-shaped eyes, very clear and piercing. Wears light trousers and a dark jacket. He is alternatively mellifluous and violent in his manner.*

The Mother *seems crushed and terrified as if by an intolerable weight of shame and abasement. She is dressed in modest black and wears a thick widow's veil of crêpe. When she lifts this, she reveals a wax-like face. She always keeps her eyes downcast.*

Many details, but room for interpretation. How do you create a "still fresh mouth" or "a wax-like face"?

The Step-Daughter *is dashing, almost impudent, beautiful. She wears mourning too, but with great elegance. She shows contempt for the timid half-frightened manner of the wretched* **Boy** *(14 years old, and also dressed in black); on the other hand, she displays a lively tenderness for her little sister,* **The Child** *(about four), who is dressed in white, with a black silk sash at the waist.*

The Son *(22) tall, severe in his attitude of contempt for* **The Father**, *supercilious and indifferent to* **The Mother**. *He looks as if he had come on the stage against his will.*

Door-Keeper (*cap in hand*): Excuse me, sir . . .

The Manager (*rudely*): Eh? What is it?

Door-Keeper (*timidly*): These people are asking for you, sir.

The Manager (*furious*): I am rehearsing, and you know perfectly well no one's allowed to come in during rehearsals! (*Turning to the* **Characters**.) Who are you, please? What do you want?

The Father (*coming forward a little, followed by the others who seem embarrassed*): As a matter of fact . . . we have come here in search of an author . . .

The Manager (*half angry, half amazed*): An author? What author?

The Father: Any author, sir.

The Manager: But there's no author here. We are not rehearsing a new piece.

The Step-Daughter (*vivaciously*): So much the better, so much the better! We can be your new piece.

An Actor (*coming forward from the others*): Oh, do you hear that?

The Father (*to* **Step-Daughter**): Yes, but if the author isn't here . . . (*To* **Manager**.) unless you would be willing . . .

The Manager: You are trying to be funny.

The Father: No, for Heaven's sake, what are you saying? We bring you a drama, sir.

The Step-Daughter: We may be your fortune.

The Manager: Will you oblige me by going away? We haven't time to waste with mad people.

The Father (*mellifluously*): Oh sir, you know well that life is full of infinite absurdities, which, strangely enough, do not even need to appear plausible, since they are true.

The Manager: What the devil is he talking about?

The Father: I say that to reverse the ordinary process may well be considered a madness: that is, to create credible situations, in order that they may appear true. But permit me to observe that if this be madness, it is the sole *raison d'être* of your profession, gentlemen.

(*The* **Actors** *look hurt and perplexed.*)

The Manager (*getting up and looking at him*): So our profession seems to you one worthy of madmen then?

The Father: Well, to make seem true that which isn't true . . . without any need . . . for a joke as it were . . . Isn't that your mission, gentlemen: to give life to fantastic characters on the stage?

The Manager (*interpreting the rising anger of the* **Company**): But I would beg you to believe, my dear sir, that the profession of the comedian is a noble one. If today, as things go, the playwrights give us stupid comedies to play and puppets to represent instead of men, remember we are proud to have given life to immortal works here on these very boards! (*The* **Actors**, *satisfied, applaud their* **Manager**.)

Are dramatic characters more real than we?

The Father (*interrupting furiously*): Exactly, perfectly, to living beings more alive than those who breathe and wear clothes: beings less real perhaps, but truer! I agree with you entirely. (*The* **Actors** *look at one another in amazement.*)

The Manager: But what do you mean? Before, you said . . .

The Father: No, excuse me, I meant it for you, sir, who were crying out that you had no time to lose with madmen, while no one better than yourself knows that nature uses the instrument of human fantasy in order to pursue her high creative purpose.

The Manager: Very well,—but where does all this take us?

The Father: Nowhere! It is merely to show you that one is born to life in many forms, in many shapes, as tree, or as stone, as water, as butterfly, or as woman. So one may also be born a character in a play.

The Manager (*with feigned comic dismay*): So you and these other friends of yours have been born characters?

The Father: Exactly, and alive as you see! (**Manager** *and* **Actors** *burst out laughing.*)

The Father (*hurt*): I am sorry you laugh, because we carry in us a drama, as you can guess from this woman here veiled in black.

The Manager (*losing patience at last and almost indignant*): Oh, chuck it! Get away please! Clear out of here! (*To* **Property Man**.) For Heaven's sake, turn them out!

The Father (*resisting*): No, no, look here, we . . .

The Manager (*roaring*): We come here to work, you know.

Leading Actor: One cannot let oneself be made such a fool of.

Combination of speech and movement focuses attention on a character.

The Father (*determined, coming forward*): I marvel at your incredulity, gentlemen. Are you not accustomed to see the characters created by an author spring to life in yourselves and face each other? Just because there is no "book" (*Pointing to the* **Prompter's** *box.*) which contains us, you refuse to believe . . .

The Step-Daughter (*advances towards* **Manager**, *smiling and coquettish*): Believe me, we are really six most interesting characters, sir; sidetracked however.

The Father: Yes, that is the word! (*To* **Manager** *all at once.*) In the sense, that is, that the author who created us alive no longer wished, or was no longer able, materially to put us into a work of art. And this was a real crime, sir; because he who has had the luck to be born a character can laugh even at death. He cannot die. The man, the writer, the instrument of the creation will die, but his creation does not die. And to live for ever, it does not need to have extraordinary gifts or to be able to work wonders. Who was Sancho Panza? Who was Don Abbondio? Yet they live eternally because—live germs as they were—they had the fortune to find a fecundating matrix, a fantasy which could raise and nourish them: make them live for ever!

Complex argument: Hamlet is alive; those who played him are dead or dying.

The Manager: That is quite all right. But what do you want here, all of you?

The Father: We want to live.

The Manager (*ironically*): For Eternity?

The Father: No, sir, only for a moment . . . in you.

An Actor: Just listen to him!

Leading Lady: They want to live, in us . . . !

Juvenile Lead (*pointing to the* **Step-Daughter**): I've no objection, as far as that one is concerned!

The Father: Look here! look here! The comedy has to be made. (*To the* **Manager.**) But if you and your actors are willing, we can soon concert it among ourselves.

The Manager (*annoyed*): But what do you want to concert? We don't go in for concerts here. Here we play dramas and comedies!

The Father: Exactly! That is just why we have come to you.

The Manager: And where is the "book"?

The Father: It is in us! (*The* **Actors** *laugh.*) The drama is in us, and we are the drama. We are impatient to play it. Our inner passion drives us on to this.

The Step-Daughter (*disdainful, alluring, treacherous, full of impudence*): My passion, sir! Ah, if you only knew! My passion for him! (*Points to* **The Father** *and makes a pretence of embracing him. Then she breaks out into a loud laugh.*)

A complicated speech — in position, gesture, voice, attitude, and tone.

The Father (*angrily*): Behave yourself! And please don't laugh in that fashion.

The Step-Daughter: With your permission, gentlemen, I, who am a two months' orphan, will show you how I can dance and sing. (*Sings and then dances* PRENEZ GARDE À TCHOU-TCHIN-TCHOU.)

> Les chinois sont un peuple malin,
> De Shangaï à Pekin,
> Ils ont mis des écriteaux partout:
> Prenez garde à Tchou-Tchin-Tchou.

Actors and Actresses: Bravo! Well done! Tip-Top!

The Manager: Silence! This isn't a café concert, you know! (*Turning to the* **Father** *in consternation.*) Is she mad?

The Father: Mad? No, she's worse than mad.

The Step-Daughter (*to* **Manager**): Worse? Worse? Listen! Stage this drama for us at once! Then you will see that at a certain moment I . . . when this little darling here . . . (*Takes the* **Child** *by the hand and leads her to the* **Manager.**) Isn't she a dear? (*Takes her up and kisses her.*) Darling! Darling! (*Puts her down again and adds feelingly.*) Well, when God suddenly takes this dear little child away from that poor mother there; and this imbecile here (*Seizing hold of the* **Boy** *roughly and pushing him forward.*) does the stupidest things, like the fool he is, you will see me run away. Yes, gentlemen, I shall be off. But the moment hasn't arrived yet. After what has taken place between him and me (*Indicates the* **Father** *with a horrible wink.*) I can't remain any longer in this society, to have to witness the anguish of this mother here for that fool . . . (*Indicates the* **Son.**) Look at him! Look at him! See how indifferent, how frigid he is, because he is the legitimate son. He despises me, despises him (*Pointing to the* **Boy.**), despises this baby here; because . . . we are bastards. (*Goes to the* **Mother** *and embraces her.*) And he doesn't want to recognize her as his mother—she who is the common mother of us all. He looks down upon her as if she were only the mother of us three bastards. Wretch! (*She says all this very rapidly, excitedly. At the word "bastards" she raises her voice, and almost spits out the final "Wretch!"*)

The Mother (*to the* **Manager,** *in anguish*): In the name of these two little children, I beg you . . . (*She grows faint and is about to fall.*) Oh God!

The Father (*coming forward to support her as do some of the* **Actors**): Quick, a chair, a chair for this poor widow!

The Actors: Is it true? Has she really fainted?

The Manager: Quick, a chair! Here!

(*One of the* **Actors** *brings a chair, the* **Others** *proffer assistance. The* **Mother** *tries to prevent the* **Father** *from lifting the veil which covers her face.*)

The Father: Look at her! Look at her!

The Mother: No, no; stop it please!

The Father (*raising her veil*): Let them see you!

The Mother (*rising and covering her face with her hands, in desperation*): I beg you, sir, to prevent this man from carrying out his plan which is loathsome to me.

The Manager (*dumbfounded*): I don't understand at all. What is the situation? Is this lady your wife? (*To the* **Father.**)

The Father: Yes, gentlemen: my wife!

The Manager: But how can she be a widow if you are alive? (*The* **Actors** *find relief for their astonishment in a loud laugh.*)

The Father: Don't laugh! Don't laugh like that, for Heaven's sake. Her drama lies just here in this: she has had a lover, a man who ought to be here.

The Mother (*with a cry*): No! No!

The Step-Daughter: Fortunately for her, he is dead. Two months ago as I said. We are in mourning, as you see.

The Father: He isn't here you see, not because he is dead. He isn't here—look at her a moment and you will understand—because her drama isn't a drama of the love of two men for whom she was incapable of feeling anything except possibly a little gratitude—gratitude not for me but for the other. She isn't a woman, she is a mother, and her drama—powerful sir, I assure you—lies, as a matter of fact, all in these four children she has had by two men.

The Mother: I had them? Have you got the courage to say that I wanted them? (*To the* **Company.**) It was his doing. It was he who gave me that other man, who forced me to go away with him.

Whom should we believe?

The Step-Daughter: It isn't true.

The Mother (*startled*): Not true, isn't it?

The Step-Daughter: No, it isn't true, it just isn't true.

The Mother: And what can you know about it?

The Step-Daughter: It isn't true. Don't believe it. (*To* **Manager**.) Do you know why she says so? For that fellow there. (*Indicates the* **Son**.) She tortures herself, destroys herself on account of the neglect of that son there; and she wants him to believe that if she abandoned him when he was only two years old, it was because he (*Indicates the* **Father**.) made her do so.

The Mother (*vigorously*): He forced me to it, and I call God to witness it. (*To the* **Manager**.) Ask him (*Indicates* **Husband**.) if it isn't true. Let him speak. You (*To* **Daughter**.) are not in a position to know anything about it.

The Step-Daughter: I know you lived in peace and happiness with my father while he lived. Can you deny it?

The Mother: No, I don't deny it . . .

The Step-Daughter: He was always full of affection and kindness for you. (*To the* **Boy**, *angrily*.) It's true, isn't it? Tell them! Why don't you speak, you little fool?

The Mother: Leave the poor boy alone. Why do you want to make me appear ungrateful, daughter? I don't want to offend your father. I have answered him that I didn't abandon my house and my son through any fault of mine, nor from any wilful passion.

The Father: It is true. It was my doing.

Levels of reality. Who are the people sitting in the theater seats?

Leading Man (*to the* **Company**): What a spectacle!

Leading Lady: We are the audience this time.

Juvenile Lead: For once, in a way.

The Manager (*beginning to get really interested*): Let's hear them out. Listen!

The Son: Oh yes, you're going to hear a fine bit now. He will talk to you of the Demon of Experiment.

The Father: You are a cynical imbecile. I've told you so already a hundred times. (*To the* **Manager**.) He tries to make fun of me on account of this expression which I have found to excuse myself with.

The Son (*with disgust*): Yes, phrases! phrases!

The Father: Phrases! Isn't everyone consoled when faced with a trouble or fact he doesn't understand, by a word, some simple word, which tells us nothing and yet calms us?

The Step-Daughter: Even in the case of remorse. In fact, especially then.

The Father: Remorse? No, that isn't true. I've done more than use words to quieten the remorse in me.

The Step-Daughter: Yes, there was a bit of money too. Yes, yes, a bit of money. There were the hundred lire he was about to offer me in payment, gentlemen . . . (*Sensation of horror among the* **Actors**.)

The Son (*to the* **Step-Daughter**): This is vile.

The Step-Daughter: Vile? There they were in a pale blue envelope on a little mahogany table in the back of Madame Pace's shop. You know Madame Pace—one of those ladies who attract poor girls of good family into their ateliers, under the pretext of their selling *robes et manteaux*.

The Son: And he thinks he has bought the right to tyrannize over us all with those hundred lire he was going to pay; but which, fortunately—note this, gentlemen—he had no chance of paying.

The Step-Daughter: It was a near thing, though, you know! (*Laughs ironically*.)

The Mother (*protesting*): Shame, my daughter, shame!

The Step-Daughter: Shame indeed! This is my revenge! I am dying to live that scene . . . The room . . . I see it . . . Here is the window with the mantles exposed, there the divan, the looking-glass, a screen, there in front of the window the little mahogany table with the blue envelope containing one hundred lire. I see it. I see it. I could take hold of it . . . But you, gentlemen, you ought to turn your backs now: I am almost nude, you know. But I don't blush: I leave that to him. (*Indicating* **Father**.)

Sets scene in detail. Compare with manager's set for the other play.

The Manager: I don't understand this at all.

The Father: Naturally enough. I would ask you, sir, to exercise your authority a little here, and let me speak before you believe all she is trying to blame me with. Let me explain.

The Step-Daughter: Ah yes, explain it in your own way.

The Father: But don't you see that the whole trouble lies here. In words, words. Each one of us has within him a whole world of things, each man of us his own special world, and how can we ever come to an understanding if I put in the words I utter the sense and value of things as I see them; while you who listen to me must inevitably translate them according to the conception of things each one of you has within himself. We think we understand each other, but we never really do. Look here! This woman (*Indicating the* **Mother**.) takes all my pity for her as a special ferocious form of cruelty.

Director can use position or lighting to emphasize important speech. What techniques could help to highlight this speech?

The Mother: But you drove me away.

The Father: Do you hear her? I drove her away! She believes I really sent her away.

The Mother: You know how to talk, and I don't; but, believe me, sir (*To* **Manager**.), after he had married me . . . who knows why? . . . I was a poor insignificant woman . . .

The Father: But, good Heavens! it was just for your humility that I married you. I loved this simplicity in you. (*He stops when he sees she makes signs to contradict him, opens his arms wide in sign of desperation, seeing how hopeless it is to make himself understood.*) You see she denies it. Her mental deafness, believe me, is phenomenal, the limit: (*Touches his forehead.*) deaf, deaf, mentally deaf! She has plenty of feeling. Oh yes, a good heart for the children; but the brain—deaf, to the point of desperation——!

The Step-Daughter: Yes, but ask him how his intelligence has helped us.

The Father: If we could see all the evil that may spring from good, what should we do? (*At this point the* **Leading Lady** *who is biting her lips with rage at seeing the* **Leading Man** *flirting with the* **Step-Daughter**, *comes forward and says to the* **Manager**.)

The flirting has been going on.

Leading Lady: Excuse me, but are we going to rehearse today?

The Manager: Of course, of course; but let's hear them out.

Shifts focus to another level.

Juvenile Lead: This is something quite new.

L'Ingénue: Most interesting!

Leading Lady: Yes, for the people who like that kind of thing. (*Casts a glance at* **Leading Man**.)

The Manager (*to* **Father**): You must please explain yourself quite clearly. (*Sits down.*)

The Father: Very well then: listen! I had in my service a poor man, a clerk, a secretary of mine, full of devotion, who became friends with her. (*Indicating the* **Mother**.) They understood one another, were kindred souls in fact, without, however, the least suspicion of any evil existing. They were incapable even of thinking of it.

The Step-Daughter: So he thought of it—for them!

The Father: That's not true. I meant to do good to them—and to myself, I confess, at the same time. Things had come to the point that I could not say a word to either of them without their making a mute appeal, one to the other, with their eyes. I could see them silently asking each other how I was to be kept in countenance, how I was to be kept quiet. And this, believe me, was just about enough of itself to keep me in a constant rage, to exasperate me beyond measure.

The Manager: And why didn't you send him away then—this secretary of yours?

The Father: Precisely what I did, sir. And then I had to watch this poor woman drifting forlornly about the house like an animal without a master, like an animal one has taken in out of pity.

The Mother: Ah yes . . . !

The Father (*suddenly turning to the* **Mother**): It's true about the son anyway, isn't it?

The Mother: He took my son away from me first of all.

The Father: But not from cruelty. I did it so that he should grow up healthy and strong by living in the country.

How do you point ironically? What does the boy look like?

The Step-Daughter (*pointing to him ironically*): As one can see.

The Father (*quickly*): Is it my fault if he has grown up like this? I sent him to a wet nurse in the country, a peasant, as *she* did not seem to me strong enough, though she is of humble origin. That was, anyway, the reason I married her. Unpleasant all this may be, but how can it be helped? My mistake possibly, but there we are! All my life I have had these confounded aspirations towards a certain moral sanity. (*At this point the* **Step-Daughter** *bursts into a noisy laugh.*) Oh, stop it! Stop it! I can't stand it.

The Manager: Yes, please stop it, for Heaven's sake.

The Step-Daughter: But imagine moral sanity from him, if you please—the client of certain ateliers like that of Madame Pace!

The Father: Fool! That is the proof that I am a man! This seeming contradiction, gentlemen, is the strongest proof that I stand here a live man before you. Why, it is just for this very incongruity in my nature that I have had to suffer what I have. I could not live by the side of that woman (*Indicating the* **Mother**.) any longer; but not so much for the boredom she inspired me with as for the pity I felt for her.

The Mother: And so he turned me out——.

The Father: ——well provided for! Yes, I sent her to that man, gentlemen . . . to let her go free of me.

The Mother: And to free himself.

The Father: Yes, I admit it. It was also a liberation for me. But great evil has come of it. I meant well when I did it; and I did it more for her sake than mine. I swear it. (*Crosses his arms on his chest; then turns suddenly to the* **Mother**.) Did I ever lose sight of you until that other man carried you off to another town, like the angry fool he was? And on account of my pure interest in you . . . my pure interest, I repeat, that had no base motive in it . . . I watched with the tenderest concern the new family that grew up around her. She can bear witness to this. (*Points to the* **Step-Daughter**.)

The Step-Daughter: Oh yes, that's true enough. When I was a kiddie, so so high, you know, with plaits over my shoulders and knickers longer than my skirts, I used to see him waiting outside the school for me to come out. He came to see how I was growing up.

The Father: This is infamous, shameful!

The Step-Daughter: No. Why?

The Father: Infamous! infamous! (*Then excitedly to* **Manager** *explaining*.) After she (*Indicating* **Mother**.) went away, my house seemed suddenly empty. She was my incubus, but she filled my house. I was like a dazed fly alone in the empty rooms. This boy here (*Indicating the* **Son**.) was educated away from home, and when he came back, he seemed to me to be no more mine. With no mother to stand between him and me, he grew up entirely for himself, on his own, apart, with no tie of intellect or affection binding him to me. And then—strange but true—I was driven, by curiosity at first and then by some tender sentiment, towards her family, which had come into being through my will. The thought of her began gradually to fill up the emptiness I felt all around me. I wanted to know if she were happy in living out the simple daily duties of life. I wanted to think of her as fortunate and happy because far away from the complicated torments of my spirit. And so, to have proof of this, I used to watch that child coming out of school.

The Step-Daughter: Yes, yes. True. He used to follow me in the street and smiled at me, waved his hand, like this. I would look at him with interest, wondering who he might be. I told my mother, who guessed at once. (*The* **Mother** *agrees with a nod*.) Then she didn't want to send me to school for some days; and when I finally went back, there he was again—looking so ridiculous—with a paper parcel in his hands. He came close to me, caressed me, and drew out a fine straw hat from the parcel, with a bouquet of flowers—all for me!

The Manager: A bit discursive this, you know!

The Son (*contemptuously*): Literature! Literature!

The Father: Literature indeed! This is life, this is passion!

The Manager: It may be, but it won't act.

The Father: I agree. This is only the part leading up. I don't suggest this should be staged. She (*Pointing to the* **Step-Daughter**.), as you see, is no longer the flapper with plaits down her back——.

The Step-Daughter: ——and the knickers showing below the skirt!

The Father: The drama is coming now, sir; something new, complex, most interesting.

The Step-Daughter: As soon as my father died . . .

The Father: ——there was absolute misery for them. They came back here, unknown to me. Through her stupidity! (*Pointing to the* **Mother**.) It is true she can barely write her own name; but she could anyhow have got her daughter to write to me that they were in need . . .

The Mother: And how was I to divine all this sentiment in him?

The Father: That is exactly your mistake, never to have guessed any of my sentiments.

Drama isn't life except for "the character."

How can director keep long speeches from becoming boring?

The Mother: After so many years apart, and all that had happened . . .

The Father: Was it my fault if that fellow carried you away? It happened quite suddenly; for after he had obtained some job or other, I could find no trace of them; and so, not unnaturally, my interest in them dwindled. But the drama culminated unforeseen and violent on their return, when I was impelled by my miserable flesh that still lives . . . Ah! what misery, what wretchedness is that of the man who is alone and disdains debasing *liaisons*! Not old enough to do without women, and not young enough to go and look for one without shame. Misery? It's worse than misery; it's a horror; for no woman can any longer give him love; and when a man feels this . . . One ought to do without, you say? Yes, yes, I know. Each of us when he appears before his fellows is clothed in a certain dignity. But every man knows what unconfessable things pass within the secrecy of his own heart. One gives way to the temptation, only to rise from it again, afterwards, with a great eagerness to re-establish one's dignity, as if it were a tombstone to place on the grave of one's shame, and a monument to hide and sign the memory of our weaknesses. Everybody's in the same case. Some folks haven't the courage to say certain things, that's all!

The Step-Daughter: All appear to have the courage to do them though.

The Father: Yes, but in secret. Therefore, you want more courage to say these things. Let a man but speak these things out, and folks at once label him a cynic. But it isn't true. He is like all the others, better indeed, because he isn't afraid to reveal with the light of the intelligence the red shame of human bestiality on which most men close their eyes so as not to see it.

Woman—for example, look at her case! She turns tantalizing inviting glances on you. You seize her. No sooner does she feel herself in your grasp than she closes her eyes. It is the sign of her mission, the sign by which she says to man: "Blind yourself, for I am blind."

The Step-Daughter: Sometimes she can close them no more: when she no longer feels the need of hiding her shame to herself, but dry-eyed and dispassionately, sees only that of the man who has blinded himself without love. Oh, all these intellectual complications make me sick, disgust me—all this philosophy that uncovers the beast in man, and then seeks to save him, excuse him . . . I can't stand it, sir. When a man seeks to "simplify" life bestially, throwing aside every relic of humanity, every chaste aspiration, every pure feeling, all sense of ideality, duty, modesty, shame . . . then nothing is more revolting and nauseous than a certain kind of remorse—crocodiles' tears, that's what it is.

The Manager: Let's come to the point. This is only discussion.

The Father: Very good, sir! But a fact is like a sack which won't stand up when it is empty. In order that it may stand up, one has to put into it the reason and sentiment which have caused it to exist. I couldn't possibly know that after the death of that man, they had decided to return here, that they were in misery, and that she (*Pointing to the* **Mother**.) had gone to work as a modiste, and at a shop of the type of that of Madame Pace.

The Step-Daughter: A real high-class modiste, you must know, gentlemen. In appearance, she works for the leaders of the best society; but she arranges matters so that these elegant ladies serve her purpose . . . without prejudice to other ladies who are . . . well . . . only so so.

The Mother: You will believe me, gentlemen, that it never entered my mind that the old hag offered me work because she had her eyes on my daughter.

The Step-Daughter: Poor mamma! Do you know, sir, what that woman did when I brought her back the work my mother had finished? She would point out to me that I had torn one of my frocks, and she would give it back to my mother to mend. It was I who paid for it, always I; while this poor creature here believed she was sacrificing herself for me and these two children here, sitting up at night sewing Madame Pace's robes.

The Manager: And one day you met there . . .

The Step-Daughter: Him, him. Yes sir, an old client. There's a scene for you to play! Superb!

The Father: She, the Mother arrived just then . . .

The Step-Daughter (*treacherously*): Almost in time!

The Father (*crying out*): No, in time! in time! Fortunately I recognized her . . . in time. And I took them back home with me to my house. You can imagine now her position and mine; she, as you see her; and I who cannot look her in the face.

The Step-Daughter: Absurd! How can I possibly be expected—after that—to be a modest young miss, a fit person to go with his confounded aspirations for "a solid moral sanity"?

The Father: For the drama lies all in this—in the conscience that I have, that each one of us has. We believe this conscience to be a single thing, but it is manysided. There is one for this person, and another for that. Diverse consciences. So we have this illusion of being one person for all, of having a personality that is unique in all our acts. But it isn't true. We perceive this when, tragically perhaps, in something we do, we are as it were, suspended, caught up in the air on a kind of hook. Then we perceive that all of us was not in that act, and that it would be an atrocious injustice to judge us by that action alone, as if all our existence were summed up in that one deed. Now do you understand the perfidy of this girl? She surprised me in a place, where she ought not to have known me, just as I could not exist for her; and now she seeks to attach to me a reality such as I could never suppose I should have to assume for her in a shameful and fleeting moment of my life. I feel this above all else. And the drama, you will see, acquires a tremendous value from this point. Then there is the position of the others . . . his . . . (*Indicating the* **Son.**)

If he had a whole life, it would be true, but he has only the life and actions the author gave him.

The Son (*shrugging his shoulders scornfully*): Leave me alone! I don't come into this.

The Father: What? You don't come into this?

The Son: I've got nothing to do with it, and don't want to have; because you know well enough I wasn't made to be mixed up in all this with the rest of you.

The Step-Daughter: We are only vulgar folk! He is the fine gentleman. You may have noticed, Mr. Manager, that I fix him now and again with a look of scorn while he lowers his eyes—for he knows the evil he has done me.

The Son (*scarcely looking at her*): I?

The Step-Daughter: You! you! I owe my life on the streets to you. Did you or did you not deny us, with your behaviour, I won't say the intimacy of home, but even that mere hospitality which makes guests feel at their ease? We were intruders who had come to disturb the kingdom of your legitimacy. I should like to have you witness, Mr. Manager, certain scenes between him and me. He says I have tyrannized over everyone. But it was just his behaviour which made me insist on the reason for which I had come into the house,—this reason he calls "vile"—into his house, with my mother who is his mother too. And I came as mistress of the house.

The Son: It's easy for them to put me always in the wrong. But imagine, gentlemen, the position of a son, whose fate it is to see arrive one day at his home a young woman of impudent bearing, a young woman who inquires for his father, with whom who knows what business she has. This young man has then to witness her return bolder than ever, accompanied by that child there. He is obliged to watch her treat his father in an equivocal and confidential manner. She asks money of him in a way that lets one suppose he must give it her, *must*, do you understand, because he has every obligation to do so.

The Father: But I have, as a matter of fact, this obligation. I owe it to your mother.

The Son: How should I know? When had I ever seen or heard of her? One day there arrive with her (*Indicating* **Step-Daughter**.) that lad and this baby here. I am told: "This is your mother too, you know." I divine from her manner (*Indicating* **Step-Daughter** *again.*) why it is they have come home. I had rather not say what I feel and think about it. I shouldn't even care to confess to myself. No action can therefore be hoped for from me in this affair. Believe me, Mr. Manager, I am an "unrealized" character, dramatically speaking; and I find myself not at all at ease in their company. Leave me out of it, I beg you.

Author gives us few details about him. Why?

The Father: What? It is just because you are so that . . .

The Son: How do you know what I am like? When did you ever bother your head about me?

The Father: I admit it. I admit it. But isn't that a situation in itself? This aloofness of yours which is so cruel to me and to your mother, who returns home and sees you almost for the first time grown up, who doesn't recognize you but knows you are her son . . . (*Pointing out the* **Mother** *to the* **Manager**.) See, she's crying!

The Step-Daughter (*angrily, stamping her foot*): Like a fool!

The Father (*indicating* **Step-Daughter**): She can't stand him you know. (*Then referring again to the* **Son**.) He says he doesn't come into the affair, whereas he is really the hinge of the whole action. Look at that lad who is always clinging to his mother, frightened and humiliated. It is on account of this fellow here. Possibly his situation is the most painful of all. He feels himself a stranger more than the others. The poor little chap feels mortified, humiliated at being brought into a home out of charity as it were. (*In confidence.*) He is the image of his father. Hardly talks at all. Humble and quiet.

Concerned with practicality, not art. On one level, he denies the boy life.

The Manager: Oh, we'll cut him out. You've no notion what a nuisance boys are on the stage . . .

The Father: He disappears soon, you know. And the baby too. She is the first to vanish from the scene. The drama consists finally in this: when that mother re-enters my house, her family born outside of it, and shall we say superimposed on the original, ends with the death of the little girl, the tragedy of the boy and the flight of the elder daughter. It cannot go on, because it is foreign to its surroundings. So after much torment, we three remain: I, the mother, that son. Then, owing to the disappearance of that extraneous family, we too find ourselves strange to one another. We find we are living in an atmosphere of mortal desolation which is the revenge, as he (*Indicating* **Son**.) scornfully said of the Demon of Experiment, that unfortunately hides in me. Thus, sir, you see when faith is lacking, it becomes impossible to create certain states of happiness, for we lack the necessary humility. Vaingloriously, we try to substitute ourselves for this faith, creating thus for the rest of the world a reality which we believe after their fashion, while, actually, it doesn't exist. For each one of us has his own reality to be respected before God, even when it is harmful to one's very self.

The Manager: There is something in what you say. I assure you all this interests me very much. I begin to think there's the stuff for a drama in all this, and not a bad drama either.

The Step-Daughter (*coming forward*): When you've got a character like me.

The Father (*shutting her up, all excited to learn the decision of the* **Manager**): You be quiet!

The Manager (*reflecting, heedless of interruption*): It's new . . . hem . . . yes . . .

The Father: Absolutely new!

The Manager: You've got a nerve though, I must say, to come here and fling it at me like this . . .

The Father: You will understand, sir, born as we are for the stage . . .

The Manager: Are you amateur actors then?

The Father: No. I say born for the stage, because . . .

The Manager: Oh, nonsense. You're an old hand, you know.

The Father: No sir, no. We act that rôle for which we have been cast, that rôle which we are given in life. And in my own case, passion itself, as usually happens, becomes a trifle theatrical when it is exalted.

The Manager: Well, well, that will do. But you see, without an author . . . I could give you the address of an author if you like . . .

The Father: No, no. Look here! You must be the author.

The Manager: I? What are you talking about?

The Father: Yes, you, you! Why not?

The Manager: Because I have never been an author: that's why.

The Father: Then why not turn author now? Everybody does it. You don't want any special qualities. Your task is made much easier by the fact that we are all here alive before you . . .

The Manager: It won't do.

The Father: What? When you see us live our drama . . .

The Manager: Yes, that's all right. But you want someone to write it.

The Father: No, no. Someone to take it down, possibly, while we play it, scene by scene! It will be enough to sketch it out at first, and then try it over. *Some plays are written this way.*

The Manager: Well . . . I am almost tempted. It's a bit of an idea. One might have a shot at it.

The Father: Of course. You'll see what scenes will come out of it. I can give you one, at once . . .

The Manager: By Jove, it tempts me. I'd like to have a go at it. Let's try it out. Come with me to my office. (*Turning to the* **Actors**.) You are at liberty for a bit, but don't step out of the theatre for long. In a quarter of an hour, twenty minutes, all back here again! (*To the* **Father**.) We'll see what can be done. Who knows if we don't get something really extraordinary out of it?

The Father: There's no doubt about it. They (*Indicating the* **Characters**.) had better come with us too, hadn't they?

The Manager: Yes, yes. Come on! come on! (*Moves away and then turning to the* **Actors**.) Be punctual, please! (**Manager** *and the* **Six Characters** *cross the stage and go off. The other* **Actors** *remain, looking at one another in astonishment.*)

Leading Man: Is he serious? What the devil does he want to do?

Juvenile Lead: This is rank madness.

Third Actor: Does he expect to knock up a drama in five minutes?

Juvenile Lead: Like the improvisers!

Leading Lady: If he thinks I'm going to take part in a joke like this . . .

Juvenile Lead: I'm out of it anyway.

Fourth Actor: I should like to know who they are. (*Alludes to* **Characters**.)

Third Actor: What do you suppose? Madmen or rascals!

Juvenile Lead: And he takes them seriously!

L'Ingénue: Vanity! He fancies himself as an author now.

Leading Man: It's absolutely unheard of. If the stage has come to this . . . well I'm . . .

Fifth Actor: It's rather a joke.

Third Actor: Well, we'll see what's going to happen next.

(*Thus talking, the* **Actors** *leave the stage; some going out by the little door at the back; others retiring to their dressing-rooms. The curtain remains up. The action of the play is suspended for twenty minutes.*)

If you were in the audience, would you know what to do? Would you applaud, go get a coke, stay in your seat?

ACT II

To warn the audience, too. Are they actors in a way?

The stage call-bells ring to warn the company that the play is about to begin again.

The **Step-Daughter** *comes out of the* **Manager's** *office along with the* **Child** *and the* **Boy**. *As she comes out of the office, she cries:—*

Nonsense! nonsense! Do it yourselves! I'm not going to mix myself up in this mess. (*Turning to the* **Child** *and coming quickly with her on to the stage.*) Come on, Rosetta, let's run!

(*The* **Boy** *follows them slowly, remaining a little behind and seeming perplexed.*)

The Step-Daughter (*stops, bends over the* **Child** *and takes the latter's face between her hands*): My little darling! You're frightened, aren't you? You don't know where we are, do you? (*Pretending to reply to a question of the* **Child**.) What is the stage? It's a place, baby, you know, where people play at being serious, a place where they act comedies. We've got to act a comedy now, dead serious, you know; and you're in it also, little one. (*Embraces her, pressing the little head to her breast, and rocking the* **Child** *for a moment.*) Oh darling, darling, what a horrid comedy you've got to play! What a wretched part they've found for you! A garden . . . a fountain . . . look . . . just suppose, kiddie, it's here. Where, you say? Why, right here in the middle. It's all pretence you know. That's the trouble, my pet: it's all make-believe here. It's better to imagine it though, because if they fix it up for you, it'll only be painted cardboard, painted cardboard for the rockery, the water, the plants . . . Ah, but I think a baby like this one would sooner have a make-believe fountain than a real one, so she could play with it. What a joke it'll be for the others! But for you, alas! not quite such a joke: you who are real, baby dear, and really play by a real fountain that is big and green and beautiful, with ever so many bamboos around it that are reflected in the water, and a whole lot of little ducks swimming about . . . No, Rosetta, no, your mother doesn't bother about you on account of that wretch of a son there. I'm in the devil of a temper, and as for that lad . . . (*Seizes* **Boy** *by the arm to force him to take one of his hands out of his pockets.*) What have you got there? What are you hiding? (*Pulls his hand out of his pocket, looks into it and catches the glint of a revolver.*) Ah! where did you get this? (*The* **Boy**, *very pale in the face, looks at her, but does not answer.*) Idiot! If I'd been in your place, instead of killing myself, I'd have shot one of those two, or both of them: father and son. (*The* **Father** *enters from the office, all excited from his work. The* **Manager** *follows him.*)

Directors take either approach: some build fountains; some let the audience create them. What would you do?

Foreshadowing. In this structure he must inevitably shoot himself.

The Father: Come on, come on dear! Come here for a minute! We've arranged everything. It's all fixed up.

The Manager (*also excited*): If you please, young lady, there are one or two points to settle still. Will you come along?

The Step-Daughter (*following him towards the office*): Ouff! what's the good, if you've arranged everything.

(*The* **Father**, **Manager** *and* **Step-Daughter** *go back into the office again* [*off*] *for a moment. At the same time, the* **Son** *followed by the* **Mother**, *comes out.*)

The Son (*looking at the three entering office*): Oh this is fine, fine! And to think I can't even get away!

(*The* **Mother** *attempts to look at him, but lowers her eyes immediately when* **He** *turns away from her. She then sits down. The* **Boy** *and the* **Child** *approach her. She casts a glance again at the* **Son**, *and speaks with humble tones, trying to draw him into conversation.*)

The Mother: And isn't my punishment the worst of all? (*Then seeing from the* **Son's** *manner that he will not bother himself about her.*) My God! Why are you so cruel? Isn't it enough for one person to support all this torment? Must you then insist on others seeing it also?

The Son (*half to himself, meaning the* **Mother** *to hear, however*): And they want to put it on the stage! If there was at least a reason for it! He thinks he has got at the meaning of it all. Just as if each one of us in every circumstance of life couldn't find his own explanation of it! (*Pauses.*) He complains he was discovered in a place where he ought not to have been seen, in a moment of his life which ought to have remained hidden and kept out of the reach of that convention which he has to maintain for other people. And what about my case? Haven't I had to reveal what no son ought ever to reveal: how father and mother live and are man and wife for themselves quite apart from that idea of father and mother which we give them? When this idea is revealed, our life is then linked at one point only to that man and that woman; and as such it should shame them, shouldn't it?

Every director interprets; none arrives at the meaning.

(*The* **Mother** *hides her face in her hands. From the dressing-rooms and the little door at the back of the stage the* **Actors** *and* **Stage Manager** *return, followed by the* **Property Man**, *and the* **Prompter**. *At the same moment, the* **Manager** *comes out* *of his office, accompanied by the* **Father** *and the* **Step-Daughter**.)

The Manager: Come on, come on, ladies and gentlemen! Heh! you there, machinist!

Machinist: Yes sir?

The Manager: Fix up the white parlor with the floral decorations. Two wings and a drop with a door will do. Hurry up!

(*The* **Machinist** *runs off at once to prepare the scene, and arranges it while the* **Manager** *talks with the* **Stage Manager**, *the* **Property Man**, *and the* **Prompter** *on matters of detail.*)

We watch a set being constructed. For the manager, rehearsal; for the Step-Daughter, life.

The Manager (*to* **Property Man**): Just have a look, and see if there isn't a sofa or divan in the wardrobe . . .

Property Man: There's the green one.

The Step-Daughter: No no! Green won't do. It was yellow, ornamented with flowers—very large! and most comfortable!

Property Man: There isn't one like that.

The Manager: It doesn't matter. Use the one we've got.

The Step-Daughter: Doesn't matter? It's most important!

The Manager: We're only trying it now. Please don't interfere. (*To* **Property Man**.) See if we've got a shop window—long and narrowish.

The Step-Daughter: And the little table! The little mahogany table for the pale blue envelope!

Property Man (*to* **Manager**): There's that little gilt one.

The Manager: That'll do fine.

The Father: A mirror.

The Step-Daughter: And the screen! We must have a screen. Otherwise how can I manage?

Property Man: That's all right, Miss. We've got any amount of them.

The Manager (*to the* **Step-Daughter**): We want some clothes pegs too, don't we?

The Step-Daughter: Yes, several, several!

The Manager: See how many we've got and bring them all.

Property Man: All right!

(*The* **Property Man** *hurries off to obey his orders. While he is putting the things in their places, the* **Manager** *talks to the* **Prompter** *and then with the* **Characters** *and the* **Actors**.)

The Manager (*to* **Prompter**): Take your seat. Look here: this is the outline of the scenes, act by act. (*Hands him some sheets of paper.*) And now I'm going to ask you to do something out of the ordinary.

Prompter: Take it down in shorthand?

The Manager (*pleasantly surprised*): Exactly! Can you do shorthand?

Prompter: Yes, a little.

The Manager: Good! (*Turning to a* **Stage Hand**.) Go and get some paper from my office, plenty, as much as you can find.

(*The* **Stage Hand** *goes off, and soon returns with a handful of paper which he gives to the* **Prompter**.)

The Manager (*to* **Prompter**): You follow the scenes as we play them, and try and get the points down, at any rate the most important ones. (*Then addressing the* **Actors**.) Clear the stage, ladies and gentlemen! Come over here (*Pointing to the left.*) and listen attentively.

Leading Lady: But, excuse me, we . . .

The Manager (*guessing her thought*): Don't worry! You won't have to improvise.

Leading Man: What have we to do then?

The Manager: Nothing. For the moment you just watch and listen. Everybody will get his part written out afterwards. At present we're going to try the thing as best we can. They're going to act now.

The Father (*as if fallen from the clouds into the confusion of the stage*): We? What do you mean, if you please, by a rehearsal?

The Manager: A rehearsal for them. (*Points to the* **Actors.**)

The Father: But since we are the characters . . .

The Manager: All right: "characters" then, if you insist on calling yourselves such. But here, my dear sir, the characters don't act. Here the actors do the acting. The characters are there, in the "book" (*Pointing towards* **Prompter's** *box.*)—when there is a "book"!

The Father: I won't contradict you; but excuse me, the actors aren't the characters. They want to be, they pretend to be, don't they? Now if these gentlemen here are fortunate enough to have us alive before them . . .

In all plays characters live only because of actors.

The Manager: Oh this is grand! You want to come before the public yourselves then?

The Father: As we are . . .

The Manager: I can assure you it would be a magnificent spectacle!

Leading Man: What's the use of us here anyway then?

The Manager: You're not going to pretend that you can act? It makes me laugh! (*The* **Actors** *laugh.*) There, you see, they are laughing at the notion. But, by the way, I must cast the parts. That won't be difficult. They cast themselves. (*To the* **Second Lady Lead.**) You play the Mother. (*To the* **Father.**) We must find her a name.

The Father: Amalia, sir.

The Manager: But that is the real name of your wife. We don't want to call her by her real name.

The Father: Why ever not, if it is her name? . . . Still, perhaps, if that lady must . . . (*Makes a slight motion of the hand to indicate the* **Second Lady Lead.**) I see this woman here (*Means the* **Mother.**) as Amalia. But do as you like. (*Gets more and more confused.*) I don't know what to say to you. Already, I begin to hear my own words ring false, as if they had another sound . . .

The Manager: Don't you worry about it. It'll be our job to find the right tones. And as for her name, if you want her Amalia, Amalia it shall be; and if you don't like it, we'll find another! For the moment though, we'll call the characters in this way: (*To* **Juvenile Lead.**) You are the Son. (*To the* **Leading Lady.**) You naturally are the Step-Daughter . . .

The Step-Daughter (*excitedly*): What? what? I, that woman there? (*Bursts out laughing.*)

The Manager (*angry*): What is there to laugh at?

Leading Lady (*indignant*): Nobody has ever dared to laugh at me. I insist on being treated with respect; otherwise I go away.

The Step-Daughter: No, no, excuse me . . . I am not laughing at you . . .

The Manager (*to* **Step-Daughter**): You ought to feel honored to be played by . . .

Leading Lady (*at once, contemptuously*): "That woman there" . . .

The Step-Daughter: But I wasn't speaking of you you know. I was speaking of myself—whom I can't see at all in you! That is all. I don't know . . . but . . . you . . . aren't in the least like me . . .

The Father: True. Here's the point. Look here, sir, our temperaments, our souls . . .

The Manager: Temperament, soul, be hanged! Do you suppose the spirit of the piece is in you? Nothing of the kind!

The Father: What, haven't we our own temperaments, our own souls?

The Manager: Not at all. Your soul or whatever you like to call it takes shape here. The actors give body and form to it, voice and gesture. And my actors—I may tell you—have given expression to much more lofty material than this little drama of yours, which may or may not hold up on the stage. But if it does, the merit of it, believe me, will be due to my actors.

The Father: I don't dare contradict you, sir; but, believe me, it is a terrible suffering for us who are as we are, with these bodies of ours, these features to see . . .

The Manager (*cutting him short and out of patience*): Good heavens! The make-up will remedy all that, man, the make-up . . .

The Father: Maybe. But the voice, the gestures . . .

The Manager: Now, look here! On the stage, you as yourself, cannot exist. The actor here acts you, and that's an end to it!

The Father: I understand. And now I think I see why our author who conceived us as we are, all alive, didn't want to put us on the stage after all. I haven't the least desire to offend your actors. Far from it! But when I think that I am to be acted by . . . I don't know by whom . . .

Leading Man (*on his dignity*): By me, if you've no objection!

The Father (*humbly, mellifluously*): Honored, I assure you, sir. (*Bows.*) Still, I must say that try as this gentleman may, with all his good will and wonderful art, to absorb me into himself . . .

Leading Man: Oh chuck it! "Wonderful art!" Withdraw that, please!

The Father: The performance he will give, even doing his best with make-up to look like me . . .

Leading Man: It will certainly be a bit difficult! (*The* **Actors** *laugh.*)

Actors can only approach the essence of character created by author. There is no one right interpretation.

The Father: Exactly! It will be difficult to act me as I really am. The effect will be rather—apart from the make-up—according as to how he supposes I am, as he senses me—if he does sense me—and not as I inside of myself feel myself to be. It seems to me then that account should be taken of this by everyone whose duty it may become to criticize us . . .

The Manager: Heavens! The man's starting to think about the critics now! Let them say what they like. It's up to us to put on the play if we can. (*Looking around.*) Come on! come on! Is the stage set? (*To the* **Actors** *and* **Characters.**) Stand back—stand back! Let me see, and don't let's lose any more time! (*To the* **Step-Daughter.**) Is it all right as it is now?

The Step-Daughter: Well, to tell the truth, I don't recognize the scene.

The Manager: My dear lady, you can't possibly suppose that we can construct that shop of Madame Pace piece by piece here? (*To the* **Father.**) You said a white room with flowered wall paper, didn't you?

The Father: Yes.

The Manager: Well then. We've got the furniture right more or less. Bring that little table a bit further forward. (*The* **Stage Hands** *obey the order. To* **Property Man**.) You go and find an envelope, if possible, a pale blue one; and give it to that gentleman. (*Indicates* **Father**.)

Property Man: An ordinary envelope?

Manager and Father: Yes, yes, an ordinary envelope.

Property Man: At once, sir. (*Exit*.)

The Manager: Ready, everyone! First scene—the Young Lady. (*The* **Leading Lady** *comes forward*.) No, no, you must wait. I meant her (*Indicating the* **Step-Daughter**.) You just watch——

The Step-Daughter (*adding at once*): How I shall play it, how I shall live it! . . .

Leading Lady (*offended*): I shall live it also, you may be sure, as soon as I begin!

The Manager (*with his hands to his head*): Ladies and gentlemen, if you please! No more useless discussions! Scene I: the young lady with Madame Pace: Oh! (*Looks around as if lost*.) And this Madame Pace, where is she?

The Father: She isn't with us, sir.

The Manager: Then what the devil's to be done?

The Father: But she is alive too.

The Manager: Yes, but where is she?

The Father: One minute. Let me speak! (*Turning to the* **Actresses**.) If these ladies would be so good as to give me their hats for a moment . . .

The Actresses (*half surprised, half laughing, in chorus*): What? Why?
Our hats?
What does he say?

The Manager: What are you going to do with the ladies' hats? (*The* **Actors** *laugh*.)

The Father: Oh nothing. I just want to put them on these pegs for a moment. And one of the ladies will be so kind as to take off her mantle . . .

The Actors: Oh, what d'you think of that?
Only the mantle?
He must be mad.

Some Actresses: But why?
Mantles as well?

The Father: To hang them up here for a moment. Please be so kind, will you?

The Actresses (*taking off their hats, one or two also their cloaks, and going to hang them on the racks*): After all, why not?
There you are!
This is really funny.
We've got to put them on show.

The Father: Exactly; just like that, on show.

The Manager: May we know why?

The Father: I'll tell you. Who knows if, by arranging the stage for her, she does not come here herself, attracted by the very articles of her trade? (*Inviting the* **Actors** *to look towards the exit at back of stage*.) Look! Look!

(*The door at the back of stage opens and* **Madame Pace** *enters and takes a few steps forward. She is a fat, oldish woman with puffy oxygenated hair. She is rouged and powdered, dressed with a comical elegance in black silk. Round her waist is a long silver chain from which hangs a pair of scissors. The* **Step-Daughter** *runs over to her at once amid the stupor of the actors*.)

Costumes reveal character.

The Step-Daughter (*turning towards her*): There she is! There she is!

The Father (*radiant*): It's she! I said so, didn't I? There she is!

The Manager (*conquering his surprise, and then becoming indignant*): What sort of a trick is this?

Leading Man (*almost at the same time*): What's going to happen next?

Juvenile Lead: Where does *she* come from?

L'Ingénue: They've been holding her in reserve, I guess.

Leading Lady: A vulgar trick!

The Father (*dominating the protests*): Excuse me, all of you! Why are you so anxious to destroy in the name of a vulgar, commonplace sense of truth, this reality which comes to birth attracted and formed by the magic of the stage itself, which has indeed more right to live here than you, since it is much truer than you—if you don't mind my saying so? Which is the actress among you who is to play Madame Pace? Well, here is Madame Pace herself. And you will allow, I fancy, that the actress who acts her will be less true than this woman here, who is herself in person. You see my daughter recognized her and went over to her at once. Now you're going to witness the scene!

(But the scene between the Step-Daughter and Madame Pace has already begun despite the protest of the actors and the reply of the Father. It has begun quietly, naturally, in a manner impossible for the stage. So when the actors, called to attention by the Father, turn round and see Madame Pace, who has placed one hand under the Step-Daughter's chin to raise her head, they observe her at first with great attention, but hearing her speak in an unintelligible manner their interest begins to wane.)

The Manager: Well? well?

Leading Man: What does she say?

Leading Lady: One can't hear a word.

Juvenile Lead: Louder! Louder please!

The Step-Daughter (*leaving Madame Pace, who smiles a Sphinx-like smile, and advancing towards the Actors*): Louder? Louder? What are you talking about? These aren't matters which can be shouted at the top of one's voice. If I have spoken them out loud, it was to shame him and have my revenge. (*Indicates Father.*) But for Madame it's quite a different matter.

The Manager: Indeed? indeed? But here, you know, people have got to make themselves heard, my dear. Even we who are on the stage can't hear you. What will it be when the public's in the theatre? And anyway, you can very well speak up now among yourselves, since we shan't be present to listen to you as we are now. You've got to pretend to be alone in a room at the back of a shop where no one can hear you.

(The Step-Daughter coquettishly and with a touch of malice makes a sign of disagreement two or three times with her finger.)

The Manager: What do you mean by no?

The Step-Daughter (*sotto voce, mysteriously*): There's someone who will hear us if she (*Indicating Madame Pace.*) speaks out loud.

The Manager (*in consternation*): What? Have you got someone else to spring on us now? (*The Actors burst out laughing.*)

The Father: No, no sir. She is alluding to me. I've got to be here—there behind that door, in waiting; and Madame Pace knows it. In fact, if you will allow me, I'll go there at once, so I can be quite ready. (*Moves away.*)

Madam Pace cannot act Madam Pace; she can only be Madam Pace.

Why is natural action impossible on stage?

How would you do this?

The Manager (*stopping him*): No! Wait! wait! We must observe the conventions of the theatre. Before you are ready . . . Really? Does this play observe them?

The Step-Daughter (*interrupting him*): No, get on with it at once! I'm just dying, I tell you, to act this scene. If he's ready, I'm more than ready.

The Manager (*shouting*): But, my dear young lady, first of all, we must have the scene between you and this lady . . . (*Indicates* **Madame Pace**.) Do you understand? . . .

The Step-Daughter: Good Heavens! She's been telling me what you know already: that mamma's work is badly done again, that the material's ruined: and that if I want her to continue to help us in our misery I must be patient . . .

Madame Pace (*coming forward with an air of great importance*): Yes indeed, sir, I no wanta take advantage of her, I no wanta be hard . . .

(*Note.* **Madame Pace** *is supposed to talk in jargon half Italian, half English.*)

The Manager (*alarmed*): What? What? She talks like that? (*The* **Actors** *burst out laughing again.*)

The Step-Daughter (*also laughing*): Yes yes, that's the way she talks, half English, half Italian! Most comical it is!

Madame Pace: Itta seem not verra polite gentlemen laugha atta me eef I trya best speaka English.

The Manager: *Diamine!* Of course! Of course! Let her talk like that! Just what we want. Talk just like that, Madame, if you please! The effect will be certain. Exactly what was wanted to put a little comic relief into the crudity of the situation. Of course she talks like that! Magnificent!

The Step-Daughter: Magnificent? Certainly! When certain suggestions are made to one in language of that kind, the effect is certain, since it seems almost a joke. One feels inclined to laugh when one hears her talk about an "old signore" "who wanta talka nicely with you." Nice old signore, eh, Madame? To manager, the accent is good theater. Step-Daughter's lines are ironic.

Madame Pace: Not so old my dear, not so old! And even if you no lika him, he won't make any scandal!

The Mother (*jumping up amid the amazement and consternation of the* **Actors** *who had not been noticing her. They move to restrain her*): You old devil! You murderess!

The Step-Daughter (*running over to calm her* **Mother**): Calm yourself, Mother, calm yourself! Please don't . . .

The Father (*going to her also at the same time*): Calm yourself! Don't get excited! Sit down now!

The Mother: Well then, take that woman away out of my sight!

The Step-Daughter (*to* **Manager**): It is impossible for my mother to remain here.

The Father (*to* **Manager**): They can't be here together. And for this reason, you see: that woman there was not with us when we came . . . If they are on together, the whole thing is given away inevitably, as you see.

The Manager: It doesn't matter. This is only a first rough sketch—just to get an idea of the various points of the scene, even confusedly . . . (*Turning to the* **Mother** *and leading her to her chair.*) Come along, my dear lady, sit down now, and let's get on with the scene . . .

(*Meanwhile, the* **Step-Daughter**, *coming forward again, turns to* **Madame Pace**.)

The Step-Daughter: Come on, Madame, come on!

Madame Pace (*offended*): No, no, *grazie*. I not do anything witha your mother present.

The Step-Daughter: Nonsense! Introduce this "old signore" who wants to talk nicely to me. (*Addressing the* **Company** *imperiously*.) We've got to do this scene one way or another, haven't we? Come on! (*To* **Madame Pace**.) You can go!

Madame Pace: Ah yes! I go'way! I go'way! Certainly! (*Exists furious*.)

The Step-Daughter (*to the* **Father**): Now you make your entry. No, you needn't go over there. Come here. Let's suppose you've already come in. Like that, yes! I'm here with bowed head, modest like. Come on! Out with your voice! Say "Good morning, Miss" in that peculiar tone, that special tone . . .

On what level is each a manager?

The Manager: Excuse me, but are you the Manager, or am I? (*To the* **Father**, *who looks undecided and perplexed*.) Get on with it, man! Go down there to the back of the stage. You needn't go off. Then come right forward here.

(*The* **Father** *does as he is told, looking troubled and perplexed at first. But as soon as he begins to move, the reality of the action affects him, and he begins to smile and to be more natural. The* **Actors** *watch intently*.)

The Manager (*sotto voce, quickly to the* **Prompter** *in his box*): Ready! ready? Get ready to write now.

Actors acting acting

The Father (*coming forward and speaking in a different tone*): Good afternoon, Miss!

The Step-Daughter (*head bowed down slightly, with restrained disgust*): Good afternoon!

The Father (*looks under her hat which partly covers her face. Perceiving she is very young, he makes an exclamation, partly of surprise, partly of fear lest he compromise himself in a risky adventure*): Ah . . . but . . . ah . . . I say . . . this is not the first time that you have come here, is it?

The Step-Daughter (*Modestly*): No sir.

The Father: You've been here before, eh? (*Then seeing her nod agreement*.) More than once? (*Waits for her to answer, looks under her hat, smiles, and then says*.) Well then, there's no need to be so shy, is there? May I take off your hat?

The Step-Daughter (*anticipating him and with veiled disgust*): No sir . . . I'll do it myself. (*Takes it off quickly*.)

(*The* **Mother**, *who watches the progress of the scene with the* **Son** *and the other two children who cling to her, is on thorns; and follows with varying expressions of sorrow, indignation, anxiety, and horror the words and actions of the other two. From time to time she hides her face in her hands and sobs*.)

The Mother: Oh, my God, my God!

The Father (*playing his part with a touch of gallantry*): Give it to me! I'll put it down. (*Takes hat from her hands*.) But a dear little head like yours ought to have a smarter hat. Come and help me choose one from the stock, won't you?

L'Ingênue (*interrupting*): I say . . . those are our hats you know.

The Manager (*furious*): Silence! silence! Don't try and be funny, if you please . . . We're playing the scene now I'd have you notice. (*To the* **Step-Daughter**.) Begin again, please!

The Step-Daughter (*continuing*): No thank you, sir.

The Father: Oh, come now. Don't talk like that. You must take it. I shall be upset if you don't. There are some lovely little hats here; and then—Madame will be pleased. She expects it, anyway, you know.

The Step-Daughter: No, no! I couldn't wear it!

The Father: Oh, you're thinking about what they'd say at home if they saw you come in with a new hat? My dear girl, there's always a way round these little matters, you know.

The Step-Daughter (*all keyed up*): No, it's not that. I couldn't wear it because I am . . . as you see . . . you might have noticed . . . (*Showing her black dress.*)

The Father: . . . In mourning! Of course: I beg your pardon: I'm frightfully sorry . . .

The Step-Daughter (*forcing herself to conquer her indignation and nausea*): Stop! Stop! It's I who must thank you. There's no need for you to feel mortified or specially sorry. Don't think any more of what I've said. (*Tries to smile.*) I must forget that I am dressed so . . .

The Manager (*Interrupting and turning to the* **Prompter**): Stop a minute! Stop! Don't write that down. Cut out that last bit. (*Then to the* **Father** *and* **Step-Daughter**.) Fine! it's going fine! (*To the* **Father** *only.*) And now you can go on as we arranged. (*To the* **Actors**.) Pretty good that scene, where he offers her the hat, eh?

The Step-Daughter: The best's coming now. Why can't we go on?

The Manager: Have a little patience! (*To the* **Actors**.) Of course, it must be treated rather lightly.

Leading Man: Still, with a bit of go in it!

Leading Lady: Of course! It's easy enough! (*To* **Leading Man**.) Shall you and I try it now?

Leading Man: Why, yes! I'll prepare my entrance. (*Exit in order to make his entrance.*)

The Manager (*to* **Leading Lady**): See here! The scene between you and Madame Pace is finished. I'll have it written out properly after. You remain here . . . oh, where are you going?

Leading Lady: One minute. I want to put my hat on again (*Goes over to hat-rack and puts her hat on her head.*)

The Manager: Good! You stay here with your head bowed down a bit.

The Step-Daughter: But she isn't dressed in black.

Leading Lady: But I shall be, and much more effectively than you.

The Manager (*to* **Step-Daughter**): Be quiet please, and watch! You'll be able to learn something. (*Clapping his hands.*) Come on! come on! Entrance, please! (*The door at the rear of stage opens, and the* **Leading Man** *enters with the lively manner of an old gallant. The rendering of the scene by the* **Actors** *from the very first words is seen to be quite a different thing, though it has not in any way the air of a parody. Naturally, the* **Step-Daughter** *and the* **Father**, *not being able to recognize themselves in the* **Leading Lady** *and the* **Leading Man**, *who deliver their words in different tones and with a different psychology, express, sometimes with smiles, sometimes with gestures, the impression they receive.*)

Actors acting actors acting

Leading Man: Good afternoon, Miss . . .

The Father (*at once unable to contain himself*): No! no!

(*The* **Step-Daughter** *noticing the way the* **Leading Man** *enters, bursts out laughing.*)

The Manager (*furious*): Silence! And you please just stop that laughing. If we go on like this, we shall never finish.

The Step-Daughter: Forgive me, sir, but it's natural enough. This lady (*Indicat-*

ing **Leading Lady**.) stands there still; but if she is supposed to be me, I can assure you that if I heard anyone say "Good afternoon" in that manner and in that tone, I should burst out laughing as I did.

The Father: Yes, yes, the manner, the tone . . .

The Manager: Nonsense! Rubbish! Stand aside and let me see the action.

Leading Man: If I've got to represent an old fellow who's coming into a house of an equivocal character . . .

The Manager: Don't listen to them, for Heaven's sake! Do it again! It goes fine. (*Waiting for the* **Actors** *to begin again.*) Well?

Leading Man: Good afternoon, Miss.

Leading Lady: Good afternoon.

Leading Man (*imitating the gesture of the* **Father** *when he looked under the hat, and then expressing quite clearly first satisfaction and then fear*): Ah, but . . . I say . . . this is not the first time that you have come here, is it?

The Manager: Good, but not quite so heavily. Like this. (*Acts himself.*) "This isn't the first time that you have come here" . . . (*To* **Leading Lady**.) And you say: "No, sir."

Leading Lady: No, sir.

Leading Man: You've been here before, more than once.

The Manager: No, no, stop! Let her nod "yes" first. "You've been here before, eh?" (*The* **Leading Lady** *lifts up her head slightly and closes her eyes as though in disgust. Then she inclines her head twice.*)   *Manager changes script. Does he have good reason?*

The Step-Daughter (*unable to contain herself*): Oh, my God! (*Puts a hand to her mouth to prevent herself from laughing.*)

The Manager (*turning round*): What's the matter?

The Step-Daughter: Nothing, nothing!

The Manager (*to* **Leading Man**): Go on!

Leading Man: You've been here before, eh? Well then, there's no need to be so shy, is there? May I take off your hat?

(*The* **Leading Man** *says this last speech in such a tone and with such gestures that the* **Step-Daughter**, *though she has her hand to her mouth, cannot keep from laughing.*)   *Steals attention from him*

Leading Lady (*indignant*): I'm not going to stop here to be made a fool of by that woman there.

Leading Man: Neither am I! I'm through with it!

The Manager (*shouting to* **Step-Daughter**): Silence! for once and all, I tell you!

The Step-Daughter: Forgive me! forgive me!

The Manager: You haven't any manners: that's what it is! You go too far.

The Father (*endeavoring to intervene*): Yes, it's true, but excuse her . . .

The Manager: Excuse what? It's absolutely disgusting.

The Father: Yes, sir, but believe me, it has such a strange effect when . . .

The Manager: Strange? Why strange? Where is it strange?

The Father: No, sir; I admire your actors—this gentleman here, this lady; but they are certainly not us!

The Manager: I should hope not. Evidently they cannot be you, if they are actors.

The Father: Just so: actors! Both of them act our parts exceedingly well. But, believe me, it produces quite a different effect on us. They want to be us, but they aren't, all the same.

The Manager: What is it then anyway?

The Father: Something that is . . . that is theirs—and no longer ours . . .

The Manager: But naturally, inevitably. I've told you so already.

The Father: Yes, I understand . . . I understand . . .

The Manager: Well then, let's have no more of it! (*Turning to the* **Actors**.) We'll have the rehearsals by ourselves, afterwards, in the ordinary way. I never could stand rehearsing with the author present. He's never satisfied! (*Turning to* **Father** *and* **Step-Daughter**.) Come on! Let's get on with it again; and try and see if you can't keep from laughing.

The Step-Daughter: Oh, I shan't laugh any more. There's a nice little bit coming for me now: you'll see.

The Manager: Well then: when she says "Don't think any more of what I've said. I must forget, etc.," you (*Addressing the* **Father**.) come in sharp with "I understand, I understand"; and then you ask her . . .

The Step-Daughter (*interrupting*): What?

The Manager: Why she is in mourning.

The Step-Daughter: Not at all! See here: when I told him that it was useless for me to be thinking about my wearing mourning, do you know how he answered me? "Ah well," he said, "then let's take off this little frock."

The Manager: Great! Just what we want, to make a riot in the theatre!

The Step-Daughter: But it's the truth!

Theatrical conventions sometimes interfere with truth.

The Manager: What does that matter? Acting is our business here. Truth up to a certain point, but no further.

The Step-Daughter: What do you want to do then?

The Manager: You'll see, you'll see! Leave it to me.

The Step-Daughter: No sir! What you want to do is to piece together a little romantic sentimental scene out of my disgust, out of all the reasons, each more cruel and viler than the other, why I am what I am. He is to ask me why I'm in mourning; and I'm to answer with tears in my eyes, that it is just two months since papa died. No sir, no! He's got to say to me; as he did say: "Well, let's take off this little dress at once." And I; with my two months' mourning in my heart, went there behind that screen, and with these fingers tingling with shame . . .

The Manager (*running his hands through his hair*): For Heaven's sake! What are you saying?

The Step-Daughter (*crying out excitedly*): The truth! The truth!

The Manager: It may be. I don't deny it, and I can understand all your horror; but you must surely see that you can't have this kind of thing on the stage. It won't go.

The Step-Daughter: Not possible, eh? Very well! I'm much obliged to you—but I'm off!

The Manager: Now be reasonable. Don't lose your temper!

The Step-Daughter: I won't stop here! I won't! I can see you've fixed it all up with him in your office. All this talk about what is possible for the stage . . . I understand! He wants to get at his complicated "cerebral drama," to have his famous remorses and torments acted; but I want to act my part, *my part!*

The Manager (*annoyed, shaking his shoulders*): Ah! Just *your* part! But, if you will pardon me, there are other parts than yours: His (*Indicating the* **Father**.) and hers. (*Indicating the* **Mother**.) On the stage you can't have a character becoming too prominent and overshadowing all the others. The thing is to pack them all into a neat little framework and then act what is actable. I am aware of the fact that everyone has his own interior life which he wants very much to put forward. But the difficulty lies in this fact: to set out just so much as is necessary for the stage, taking the other characters into consideration, and at the same time hint at the unrevealed interior life of each. I am willing to admit, my dear young lady, that from your point of view it would be a fine idea if each character could tell the public all his troubles in a nice monologue or a regular one hour lecture. (*Good humoredly.*) You must restrain yourself, my dear, and in your own interest, too; because this fury of yours, this exaggerated disgust you show, may make a bad impression, you know. After you have confessed to me that there were others before him at Madame Pace's and more than once . . .

Given what this book claims about drama, is he right ?

The Step-Daughter (*bowing her head, impressed*): It's true. But remember those others mean him for me all the same.

The Manager (*not understanding*): What? The others? What do you mean?

The Step-Daughter: For one who has gone wrong, sir, he who was responsible for the first fault is responsible for all that follow. He is responsible for my faults, was, even before I was born. Look at him, and see if it isn't true!

The Manager: Well, well! And does the weight of so much responsibility seem nothing to you? Give him a chance to act it, to get it over!

The Step-Daughter: How? How can he act all his "noble remorses," all his "moral torments," if you want to spare him the horror of being discovered one day—after he had asked her what he did ask her—in the arms of her, that already fallen woman, that child, sir, that child he used to watch come out of school? (*She is moved.*)

(*The* **Mother** *at this point is overcome with emotion, and breaks out into a fit of crying. All are touched. A long pause.*)

The Step-Daughter (*as soon as the* **Mother** *becomes a little quieter, adds resolutely and gravely*): At present, we are unknown to the public. Tomorrow, you will act us as you wish, treating us in your own manner. But do you really want to see drama, do you want to see it flash out as it really did?

The Manager: Of course! That's just what I do want, so I can use as much of it as possible.

The Step-Daughter: Well then, ask that Mother there to leave us.

The Mother (*changing her low plaint into a sharp cry*): No! No! Don't permit it, sir, don't permit it!

The Manager: But it's only to try it.

The Mother: I can't bear it. I can't.

The Manager: But since it has happened already . . . I don't understand!

The Mother: It's taking place now. It happens all the time. My torment isn't a pretended one. I live and feel every minute of my torture. Those two children there—have you heard them speak? They can't speak any more. They cling to me to keep up my torment actual and vivid for me. But for themselves, they do not exist, they aren't any more. And she (*Indicating the* **Step-Daughter**.) has run away, she has left me, and is lost. If I now see her here before me, it is only to renew for me the tortures I have suffered for her too.

In the famous painting, Washington is crossing the Delaware— then, now, forever.

The Father: The eternal moment! She (*Indicating the* **Step-Daughter**.) is here to catch me, fix me, and hold me eternally in the stocks for that one fleeting and shameful moment of my life. She can't give it up! And you sir, cannot either fairly spare me it.

The Manager: I never said I didn't want to act it. It will form, as a matter of fact, the nucleus of the whole first act right up to her surprise. (*Indicates the* **Mother**.)

The Father: Just so! This is my punishment: the passion in all of us that must culminate in her final cry.

The Step-Daughter: I can hear it still in my ears. It's driven me mad, that cry! —You can put me on as you like; it doesn't matter. Fully dressed, if you like—provided I have at least the arm bare; because standing like this (*She goes close to the* **Father** *and leans her head on his breast.*) with my head so, and my arms round his neck, I saw a vein pulsing in my arm here; and then, as if that live vein had awakened disgust in me, I closed my eyes like this, and let my head sink on his breast. (*Turning to the* **Mother**.) Cry out mother! Cry out! (*Buries head in* **Father's** *breast, and with her shoulders raised as if to prevent her hearing the cry, adds in tones of intense emotion.*) Cry out as you did then!

> A posed scene. Can you hear the cry? What does it sound like?

The Mother (*coming forward to separate them*): No! My daughter, my daughter! (*And after having pulled her away from him.*) You brute! you brute! She is my daughter! Don't you see she's my daughter?

The Manager (*walking backwards towards footlights*): Fine! fine! Damned good! And then, of course—curtain!

The Father (*going towards him excitedly*): Yes, of course, because that's the way it really happened.

The Manager (*convinced and pleased*): Oh, yes, no doubt about it. Curtain here, curtain!

> Conventions of theater have turned comically on the manager.

(*At the reiterated cry of the* **Manager**, *the* **Machinist** *lets the curtain down, leaving the* **Manager** *and the* **Father** *in front of it before the footlights.*)

The Manager: The darned idiot! I said "curtain" to show the act should end there, and he goes and lets it down in earnest. (*To the* **Father**, *while he pulls the curtain back to go on to the stage again.*) Yes, yes, it's all right. Effect curtain! That's the right ending. I'll guarantee the first act at any rate.

ACT III

When the curtain goes up again, it is seen that the stage hands have shifted the bit of scenery used in the last part, and have rigged up instead at the back of the stage a drop, with some trees, and one or two wings. A portion of a fountain basin is visible. The

> Significance in placement of actors?

Mother is sitting on the right with the two children by her side. The **Son** is on the same side, but away from the others. He seems bored, angry, and full of shame. The **Father** and the **Step-Daughter** are also seated towards the right front. On the other side (left) are the **Actors**, much in the positions they occupied before the curtain was lowered. Only the **Manager** is standing up in the middle of the stage, with his hand closed over his mouth in the act of meditating.

The Manager (*shaking his shoulders after a brief pause*): Ah yes: the second act! Leave it to me, leave it all to me as we arranged, and you'll see! It'll go fine!

The Step-Daughter: Our entry into his house (*Indicates* **Father**.) in spite of him . . . (*Indicates the* **Son**.)

The Manager (*out of patience*): Leave it to me, I tell you!

The Step-Daughter: Do let it be clear, at any rate, that it is in spite of my wishes.

The Mother (*from her corner, shaking her head*): For all the good that's come of it . . .

The Step-Daughter (*turning towards her quickly*): It doesn't matter. The more harm done us, the more remorse for him.

The Manager (*impatiently*): I understand! Good Heavens! I understand! I'm taking it into account.

The Mother (*supplicatingly*): I beg you, sir, to let it appear quite plain that for conscience' sake I did try in every way . . .

The Step-Daughter (*interrupting indignantly and continuing for the* **Mother**): . . . to pacify me, to dissuade me from spiting him. (*To* **Manager**.) Do as she wants: satisfy her, because it is true! I enjoy it immensely. Anyhow, as you can see, the meeker she is, the more she tries to get at his heart, the more distant and aloof does he become.

The Manager: Are we going to begin this second act or not?

The Step-Daughter: I'm not going to talk any more now. But I must tell you this: you can't have the whole action take place in the garden, as you suggest. It isn't possible!

The Manager: Why not?

The Step-Daughter: Because he (*Indicates the* **Son** *again.*) is always shut up alone in his room. And then there's all the part of that poor dazed-looking boy there which takes place indoors.

The Manager: Maybe! On the other hand, you will understand—we can't change scenes three or four times in one act.

The Leading Man: They used to once.

The Manager: Yes, when the public was up to the level of that child there.

The Leading Lady: It makes the illusion easier.

The Father (*irritated*): The illusion! For Heaven's sake, don't say illusion. Please don't use that word, which is particularly painful for us.

Theatrical conventions change as evidenced by this play.

The Manager (*astounded*): And why, if you please?

The Father: It's painful, cruel, really cruel; and you ought to understand that.

The Manager: But why? What ought we to say then? The illusion, I tell you, sir, which we've got to create for the audience . . .

The Leading Man: With our acting.

The Manager: The illusion of a reality.

The Father: I understand; but you, perhaps, do not understand us. Forgive me! You see . . . here for you and your actors, the thing is only—and rightly so . . . a kind of game . . .

The Leading Lady (*interrupting indignantly*): A game! We're not children here, if you please! We are serious actors.

The Father: I don't deny it. What I mean is the game, or play, of your art, which has to give, as the gentleman says, a perfect illusion of reality.

The Manager: Precisely——!

The Father: Now, if you consider the fact that we (*Indicates himself and the other five* **Characters**.), as we are, have no other reality outside of this illusion . . .

The Manager (*astonished, looking at his* **Actors**, *who are also amazed*): And what does that mean?

The Father (*after watching them for a moment with a wan smile*): As I say, sir, that which is a game of art for you is our sole reality. (*Brief pause. He goes a step*

The character knows who he is; he never changes. Does each of us know who we are?

or two nearer the **Manager** *and adds.*) But not only for us, you know, by the way. Just you think it over well. (*Looks him in the eyes.*) Can you tell me who you are?

The Manager (*perplexed, half smiling*): What? Who am I? I am myself.

The Father: And if I were to tell you that that isn't true, because you and I . . . ?

The Manager: I should say you were mad——! (*The* **Actors** *laugh.*)

The Father: You're quite right to laugh: because we are all making believe here. (*To* **Manager**.) And you can therefore object that it's only for a joke that that gentleman there (*Indicates the* **Leading Man**.), who naturally is himself, has to be me, who am on the contrary myself—this thing you see here. You see I've caught you in a trap! (*The* **Actors** *laugh.*)

The Manager (*annoyed*): But we've had all this over once before. Do you want to begin again?

The Father: No, no! That wasn't my meaning! In fact, I should like to request you to abandon this game of art (*Looking at the* **Leading Lady** *as if anticipating her.*) which you are accustomed to play here with your actors, and to ask you seriously once again: who are you?

The Manager (*astonished and irritated, turning to his* **Actors**): If this fellow here hasn't got a nerve! A man who calls himself a character comes and asks me who I am!

The Father (*with dignity, but not offended*): A character, sir, may always ask a man who he is. Because a character has really a life of his own, marked with his especial characteristics; for which reason he is always "somebody." But a man—I'm not speaking of you now—may very well be "nobody."

The Manager: Yes, but you are asking these questions of me, the boss, the manager! Do you understand?

The Father: But only in order to know if you, as you really are now, see yourself as you once were with all the illusions that were yours then, with all the things both inside and outside of you as they seemed to you—as they were then indeed for you. Well, sir, if you think of all those illusions that mean nothing to you now, of all those things which don't even *seem* to you to exist any more, while once they *were* for you, don't you feel that—I won't say these boards—but the very earth under your feet is sinking away from you

Disturbing

when you reflect that in the same way this *you* as you feel it today—all this present reality of yours—is fated to seem a mere illusion to you tomorrow?

The Manager (*without having understood much, but astonished by the specious argument*): Well, well! And where does all this take us anyway?

The Father: Oh, nowhere! It's only to show you that if we (*Indicating the* **Characters**.) have no other reality beyond the illusion, you too must not count overmuch on your reality as you feel it today, since, like that of yesterday, it may prove an illusion for you tomorrow.

The Manager (*determining to make fun of him*): Ah, excellent! Then you'll be saying next that you, with this comedy of yours that you brought here to act, are truer and more real than I am.

The Father (*with the greatest seriousness*): But of course; without doubt!

The Manager: Ah, really?

The Father: Why, I thought you'd understand that from the beginning.

The Manager: More real than I?

The Father: If your reality can change from one day to another . . .

The Manager: But everyone knows it can change. It is always changing, the same as anyone else's.

The Father (*with a cry*): No, sir, not ours! Look here! That is the very difference! Our reality doesn't change: it can't change! It can't be other than what it is, because it is already fixed for ever. It's terrible. Ours is an immutable reality which should make you shudder when you approach us if you are really conscious of the fact that your reality is a mere transitory and fleeting illusion, taking this form today and that tomorrow, according to the conditions, according to your will, your sentiments, which in turn are controlled by an intellect that shows them to you today in one manner and tomorrow . . . who knows how? . . . Illusions of reality represented in this fatuous comedy of life that never ends, nor can ever end! Because if tomorrow it were to end . . . then why, all would be finished.

The Manager: Oh for God's sake, will you *at least* finish with this philosophizing and let us try and shape this comedy which you yourself have brought me here? You argue and philosophize a bit too much, my dear sir. You know you seem to me almost, almost . . . (*Stops and looks him over from head to foot.*) Ah, by the way, I think you introduced yourself to me as a— what shall . . . we say—a "character," created by an author who did not afterward care to make a drama of his own creations.

The Father: It is the simple truth, sir.

The Manager: Nonsense! Cut that out, please! None of us believes it isn't a thing, as you must recognize yourself, which one can believe seriously. If you want to know, it seems to me you are trying to imitate the manner of a certain author whom I heartily detest—I warn you—although I have unfortunately bound myself to put on one of his works. As a matter of fact, I was just starting to rehearse it, when you arrived. (*Turning to the* **Actors.**) And this is what we've gained—out of the frying-pan into the fire!

The Father: I don't know to what author you may be alluding, but believe me I feel what I think; and I seem to be philosophizing only for those who do not think what they feel, because they blind themselves with their own sentiment. I know that for many people this self-blinding seems much more "human"; but the contrary is really true. For man never reasons so much and becomes so introspective as when he suffers; since he is anxious to get at the cause of his sufferings, to learn who has produced them, and whether it is just or unjust that he should have to bear them. On the other hand, when he is happy, he takes his happiness as it comes and doesn't analyze it, just as if happiness were his right. The animals suffer without reasoning about their sufferings. But take the case of a man who suffers and begins to reason about it. Oh, no! it can't be allowed! Let him suffer like an animal, and then—ah yet, he is "human"!

The Manager: Look here! Look here! You're off again, philosophizing worse than ever.

The Father: Because I suffer, sir! I'm not philosophizing: I'm crying aloud the reason of my sufferings.

The Manager (*makes brusque movement as he is taken with a new idea*): I should like to know if anyone has ever heard of a character who gets right out of his part and perorates and speechifies as you do. Have you ever heard of a case? I haven't.

The Father: You have never met such a case, sir, because authors, as a rule, hide the labour of their creations. When the characters are really alive before their author, the latter does nothing but follow them in their action, in their words, in the situations which they suggest to him; and he has to will them the way they will themselves—for there's trouble if he doesn't. When a character is born, he acquires at once such an independence, even of his own author, that he can be imagined by everybody even in many other situations where the author never dreamed of placing him; and so he acquires for himself a meaning which the author never thought of giving him.

The Manager: Yes, yes, I know this.

The Father: What is there then to marvel at in us? Imagine such a misfortune for characters as I have described to you: to be born of an author's fantasy, and be denied life by him; and then answer me if these characters left alive, and yet without life, weren't right in doing what they did do and are doing now, after they have attempted everything in their power to persuade him to give them their stage life. We've all tried him in turn, I, she (*Indicating the* **Step-Daughter**.) and she. (*Indicating the* **Mother**.)

The Step-Daughter: It's true. I too have sought to tempt him, many, many times, when he has been sitting at his writing table, feeling a bit melancholy, at the twilight hour. He would sit in his armchair too lazy to switch on the light, and all the shadows that crept into his room were full of our presence coming to tempt him. (*As if she saw herself still there by the writing table, and was annoyed by the presence of the* **Actors**.) Oh, if you would only go away, go away and leave us alone—mother here with that son of hers—I with that Child—that Boy there always alone—and then I with him (*Just hints at the* **Father**.)—and then I alone, alone . . . in those shadows! (*Makes a sudden movement as if in the vision she has of herself illuminating those shadows she wanted to seize hold of herself.*) Ah! my life! my life! Oh, what scenes we proposed to him—and I tempted him more than any of the others!

If you were director, how would you suggest her reminiscence?

The Father: Maybe. But perhaps it was your fault that he refused to give us life: because you were too insistent, too troublesome.

The Step-Daughter: Nonsense! Didn't he make me so himself? (*Goes close to the* **Manager** *to tell him as if in confidence.*) In my opinion he abandoned us in a fit of depression, of disgust for the ordinary theatre as the public knows it and likes it.

The Son: Exactly what it was, sir; exactly that!

The Father: Not at all! Don't believe it for a minute. Listen to me! You'll be doing quite right to modify, as you suggest, the excesses both of this girl here, who wants to do too much, and of this young man, who won't do anything at all.

The Son: No, nothing!

The Manager: You too get over the mark occasionally, my dear sir, if I may say so.

The Father: I? When? Where?

The Manager: Always! Continuously! Then there's this insistence of yours in trying to make us believe you are a character. And then too, you must really argue and philosophize less, you know, much less.

The Father: Well, if you want to take away from me the possibility of representing the torment of my spirit which never gives me peace, you will be suppressing me: that's all. Every true man, sir, who is a little above the level of the beasts and plants does not live for the sake of living, without knowing how to live; but he lives so as to give a meaning and a value of his own to life. For me this is *everything*. I cannot give up this, just to represent a mere fact as she (*Indicating the* **Step-Daughter**.) wants. It's all very well for her, since her "vendetta" lies in the "fact." I'm not going to do it. It destroys my *raison d'être*.

The Manager: Your *raison d'être!* Oh, we're going ahead fine! First she starts off, and then you jump in. At this rate, we'll never finish.

The Father: Now, don't be offended! Have it your own way—provided, however, that within the limits of the parts you assign us each one's sacrifice isn't too great.

The Manager: You've got to understand that you can't go on arguing at your own pleasure. Drama is action, sir, action and not confounded philosophy. *Maybe it's both.*

The Father: All right. I'll do just as much arguing and philosophizing as everybody does when he is considering his own torments.

The Manager: If the drama permits! But for Heaven's sake, man, let's get along and come to the scene.

The Step-Daughter: It seems to me we've got too much action with our coming into his house. (*Indicating* **Father**.) You said, before, you couldn't change the scene every five minutes.

The Manager: Of course not. What we've got to do is to combine and group up all the facts in one simultaneous, close-knit, action. We can't have it as you want, with your little brother wandering like a ghost from room to room, hiding behind doors and meditating a project which—what did you say it did to him?

The Step-Daughter: Consumes him, sir, wastes him away!

The Manager: Well, it may be. And then at the same time, you want the little girl there to be playing in the garden . . . one in the house, and the other in the garden: isn't that it?

The Step-Daughter: Yes, in the sun, in the sun! That is my only pleasure: to see her happy and careless in the garden after the misery and squalor of the horrible room where we all four slept together. And I had to sleep with her—I, do you understand? with my vile contaminated body next to hers; with her folding me fast in her loving little arms. In the garden, whenever she spied me, she would run to take me by the hand. She didn't care for the big flowers, only the little ones; and she loved to show me them and pet me.

The Manager: Well then, we'll have it in the garden. Everything shall happen in the garden; and we'll group the other scenes there. (*Calls a* **Stage Hand**.) Here, a backcloth with trees and something to do as a fountain basin. (*Turning round to look at the back of the stage.*) Ah, you've fixed it up. Good! (*To* **Step-Daughter**.) This is just to give an idea, of course. The Boy, instead of hiding behind the doors, will wander about here in the garden, hiding behind the trees. But it's going to be rather difficult to find a child to do that scene with you where she shows you the flowers. (*Turning to the* **Boy**.) Come forward a little, will you please? Let's try it now! Come along! come along! (*Then seeing him come shyly forward, full of fear and looking lost.*) It's a nice business, this lad here. What's the matter with him? We'll have to give him a word or two to say. (*Goes close to him, puts a hand on his shoulders, and leads him behind* *one of the trees.*) Come on! come on! Let me see you a little! Hide here . . . yes, like that. Try and show your head just a little as if you were looking for someone . . . (*Goes back to observe the effect, when the* **Boy** *at once goes through the action.*) Excellent! fine! (*Turning to* **Step-Daughter**.) Suppose the little girl there were to surprise him as he looks round, and run over to him, so we could give him a word or two to say?

He tries to direct a play over which he has no control.

The Step-Daughter: It's useless to hope he will speak, as long as that fellow there is here . . . (*Indicates the* **Son**.) You must send him away first.

The Son (*jumping up*): Delighted! Delighted! I don't ask for anything better. (*Begins to move away.*)

The Manager (*at once stopping him*): No! No! Where are you going? Wait a bit! (*The* **Mother** *gets up alarmed and terrified at the thought that he is really about to go away. Instinctively she lifts her arms to prevent him, without, however, leaving her seat.*)

The Son (*to* **Manager** *who stops him*): I've got nothing to do with this affair. Let me go please! Let me go!

The Manager: What do you mean by saying you've got nothing to do with this?

The Step-Daughter (*calmly, with irony*): Don't bother to stop him: he won't go away.

The Father: He has to act the terrible scene in the garden with his mother.

The Son (*suddenly resolute and with dignity*): I shall act nothing at all. I've said so from the beginning. (*To the* **Manager**.) Let me go!

The Step-Daughter (*going over to the* **Manager**): Allow me? (*Puts down the* **Manager's** *arm which is restraining the* **Son**.) Well, go away then, if you want to! (*The* **Son** *looks at her with contempt and hatred. She laughs and says.*) You see, he can't, he can't go away! He is obliged to stay here, indissolubly bound to the chain. If I, who fly off when that happens which has to happen, because I can't bear him—if I am still here and support that face and expression of his, you can well imagine that he is unable to move. He has to remain here, has to stop with that nice father of his, and that mother whose only son he is. (*Turning to the* **Mother**.) Come on, mother, come along! (*Turning to the* **Manager** *to indicate her.*) You see, she was getting up to keep him back. (*To the* **Mother**, *beckoning her with her hand.*) Come on! come on! (*Then to* **Manager**.) You can imagine how little she wants to show these actors of yours what she really feels; but so eager is she to get near him that . . . There, you see? She is willing to act her part. (*And in fact, the* **Mother** *approaches him; and as soon as the* **Step-Daughter** *has finished speaking, opens her arms to signify that she consents.*)

As the father said, they have no choice.

The Son (*suddenly*): No! no! If I can't go away, then I'll stop here; but I repeat: I act nothing!

The Father (*to* **Manager** *excitedly*): You can force him, sir.

The Son: Nobody can force me.

The Father: I can.

The Step-Daughter: Wait a minute, wait . . . First of all, the baby has to go to the fountain . . . (*Runs to take the* **Child** *and leads her to the fountain.*)

The Manager: Yes, yes of course; that's it. Both at the same time.

(*The second* **Lady Lead** *and the* **Juvenile Lead** *at this point separate themselves from the group of* **Actors**. *One watches the* **Mother** *attentively; the other moves about studying the movements and manner of the* **Son** *whom he will have to act.*)

The Son (*to* **Manager**): What do you mean by both at the same time? It isn't right. There was no scene between me and her. (*Indicates the* **Mother**.) Ask her how it was!

The Mother: Yes, it's true. I had come into his room . . .

The Son: Into my room, do you understand? Nothing to do with the garden.

The Manager: It doesn't matter. Haven't I told you we've got to group the action?

The Son (*observing the* **Juvenile Lead** *studying him*): What do you want?

The Juvenile Lead: Nothing! I was just looking at you.

The Son (*turning towards the* **Second Lady Lead**): Ah! she's at it too: to re-act her part! (*Indicating the* **Mother**.)

The Manager: Exactly! And it seems to me that you ought to be grateful to them for their interest.

The Son: Yes, but haven't you yet perceived that it isn't possible to live in front of a mirror which not only freezes us with the image of ourselves, but throws our likeness back at us with a horrible grimace?

The Father: That is true, absolutely true. You must see that.

The Manager (*to* **Second Lady Lead** *and* **Juvenile Lead**): He's right! Move away from them!

The Son: Do as you like. I'm out of this!

The Manager: Be quiet, you, will you? And let me hear your mother! (*To* **Mother**.) You were saying you had entered . . .

The Mother: Yes, into his room, because I couldn't stand it any longer. I went to empty my heart to him of all the anguish that tortures me . . . But as soon as he saw me come in . . .

The Son: Nothing happened! There was no scene. I went away, that's all! I don't care for scenes!

The Mother: It's true, true. That's how it was.

The Manager: Well now, we've got to do this bit between you and him. It's indispensable.

The Mother: I'm ready . . . when you are ready. If you could only find a chance for me to tell him what I feel here in my heart.

The Father (*going to* **Son** *in a great rage*): You'll do this for your mother, for your mother, do you understand?

The Son (*quite determined*): I do nothing!

The Father (*taking hold of him and shaking him*): For God's sake, do as I tell you! Don't you hear your mother asking you for a favor? Haven't you even got the guts to be a son?

The Son (*taking hold of the* **Father**): No! No! And for God's sake stop it, or else . . . (*General agitation. The* **Mother**, *frightened, tries to separate them*.)

The Mother (*pleading*): Please! please!

The Father (*not leaving hold of the* **Son**): You've got to obey, do you hear?

The Son (*almost crying from rage*): What does it mean, this madness you've got? (*They separate.*) Have you no decency, that you insist on showing everyone our shame? I won't do it! I won't! And I stand for the will of our author in this. He didn't want to put us on the stage, after all!

The Manager: Man alive! You came here . . .

The Son (*indicating* **Father**): *He* did! I didn't!

The Manager: Aren't you here now?

The Son: It was his wish, and he dragged us along with him. He's told you not only the things that did happen, but also things that have never happened at all.

The Manager: Well, tell me then what did happen. You went out of your room without saying a word?

The Son: Without a word, so as to avoid a scene!

The Manager: And then what did you do?

The Son: Nothing . . . walking in the garden . . . (*Hesitates for a moment with expression of gloom.*)

The Manager (*coming closer to him, interested by his extraordinary reserve*): Well, well . . . walking in the garden . . .

The Son (*exasperated*): Why on earth do you insist? It's horrible! (*The* **Mother** *trembles, sobs, and looks towards the fountain.*)

The Manager (*slowly observing the glance and turning towards the* **Son** *with increasing apprehension*): The baby?

The Son: There in the fountain . . .

The Father (*pointing with tender pity to the* **Mother**): She was following him at the moment . . .

The Manager (*to the* **Son** *anxiously*): And then you . . .

The Son: I ran over to her; I was jumping in to drag her out when I saw something that froze my blood . . . the boy standing stock still, with eyes like a madman's, watching his little drowned sister, in the fountain! (*The* **Step-Daughter** *bends over the fountain to hide the* **Child**. *She sobs.*) Then . . . (*A revolver shot rings out behind the trees where the* **Boy** *is hidden.*)

The explosion startles us, emotionally and intellectually, also exploding assumptions about reality. The characters' past, present, and future suddenly blend into one moment. Illusion of play within a play destroyed — actions of actors and characters merge.

The Mother (*with a cry of terror runs over in that direction together with several of the* **Actors** *amid general confusion*): My son! My son! (*Then amid the cries and exclamations one hears her voice.*) Help! Help!

The Manager (*pushing the* **Actors** *aside while they lift up the* **Boy** *and carry him off.*): Is he really wounded?

Some Actors: He's dead! dead!

Other Actors: No, no, it's only make believe, it's only pretence!

The Father (*with a terrible cry*): Pretence? Reality, sir, reality!

The Manager: Pretence? Reality? To hell with it all! Never in my life has such a thing happened to me. I've lost a whole day over these people, a whole day!

MOTEL

from AMERICA HURRAH

A masque for three dolls

Jean-Claude van Itallie

(Light will come upon the room very slowly. It will increase in whiteness to the point of fluorescent glare by the time the dolls enter.

During this dawning a woman's voice will be heard, coming from any place in the theatre, and not necessarily from any one place continually. The voice will at first be mellow, mellow and husky. As the light grows harsher and brighter so the voice will grow older, more set in its pattern, hard finally, and patronizing and petty.)

Woman's Voice: I am an old idea. Gaia I have been, and Lilith. I am an old idea. Lilly, Molly, Gaia; the walls of the stream that from which it springs forth. The nothing they enclose with walls, making then a place from which it springs forth, in which it happens, in which they happen too. I am that idea: the place, the walls, the room. A Roman theatre: roofless stone place where the heat of the sun and the cheers of the people break loose the fangs of the lion. There was that room too, a railroad carriage in the Forest of Compiègne, in 1918 and again in 1941. There have been rooms of marble and rooms of cork, all letting forth an avalanche. Rooms of mud, rooms of silk. Within which they happen. There is another room here. And it too will be slashed as if by a scimitar, its balconies shuddered, its contents spewed and yawned out. What walls it has will be un-squared, the room tumbriled, its cornices broken. That is what happens. It is almost happening in fact. This is my room too. I made it. I am this room. It's a nice room, not so fancy as some, but with all the conveniences. And a touch of home. The antimacassar comes from my mother's house in Boise. Boise, Idaho. Sits kind of nice, I think, on the Swedish swing. That's my own idea you know. All modern, up to date, that's it—no motel on this route is more up to date. Or cleaner. Go look, then talk me a thing or two. All modern here, but, as I say, with the tang of home. Do you understand? When folks are fatigued, in a strange place? Not that it's old fashioned. No. Not in the wrong way. There's a button-push here for TV. The toilet flushes of its own accord. All you've got to do is get off. Pardon my mentioning it, but you'll have to go far before you see a thing like that on this route. Oh it's quite a room. Yes. And reasonable. Sign here. Pardon the pen leak. I can see you're fatigued. Any children? Well that's nice. Children don't appreciate travel. And rooms don't appreciate children. As it happens it's the last one I've got left. I'll just flip my vacancy switch. Twelve dollars please. In advance that'll be. That way you can go any time you want to go, you know, get an early start. On a trip to see sights, are you? That's nice. You just get your luggage while I go unlock the room. You can see the light.

*(The **Motel-Keeper** enters through the door. It is a large doll, slightly larger than human size, though not a giantess. The dancers will be inside the dolls. Their movements will have*

the quality of ritual, their fascination will be that of a dance or a machine: strictly controllable, humorous sometimes, but increasingly violent and disturbing. The **Motel-Keeper** *doll is predominantly gray, feminine, with square breasts and a triangular skirt. On its mask it wears large square eyeglasses which are mirrors. It doesn't matter what these mirrors reflect any given moment. The audience may occasionally catch a glimpse of itself, or be bothered by reflections of light. It doesn't matter; the sensory nerves of the audience are not to be spared. It may be more feasible for the* **Motel-Keeper's** *voice to continue coming from a loudspeaker, with accompanying rhythmic jaw motions on the part of the doll.)*

Motel-Keeper's Voice: There now. What I say doesn't matter. You can see. It speaks for itself. The room speaks for itself. You can see it's a perfect 1966 room. But a taste of home. I've seen to that. A taste of home.

(She turns down the covers on the double bed.)

Comfy, cozy, nice, but a taste of newness. That's what. You can see it.

(She snaps up the shades. There are neon lights outside.)

The best stop on route six sixty-six. Well, there might be others like it, but this is the best stop. You've arrived at the right place. This place. And a hooked rug. I don't care what but I've said no room is without a hooked rug.

(She centers the rug.)

No complaints yet. Never.

(The **Woman** *doll enters. It is the same size as the* **Motel-Keeper**. *Its shoulders are thrown way back, like a girl posing for a calendar ad. Its breasts are wiggleable. It has glamorous blonde hair and a cherry-lipstick smile. Its clothes, real clothes these, are those of a young married woman. The* **Woman** *doll goes directly to the bathroom and doesn't shut the door. There is absolutely no rapport between the other dolls and the* **Motel-Keeper**. *The other dolls do not ever stop what they are doing, and they are perpetually doing something. The* **Motel-Keeper** *is sometimes still and sometimes ambulates in circles. But all her remarks are directed generally; she is never motivated by the actions of other dolls.)*

Modern people like modern places. Oh yes. I can tell. They tell me. And reasonable. Very very reasonable rates. No cheaper rates on the route, not for this. You receive what you pay for.

(The toilet flushes.)

All that driving and driving and driving. Fatigued. You must be. I would be. Miles and miles and miles.

(The toilet flushes again.)

Fancy. Fancy your ending up right here. You didn't know and I didn't know. But you did. End up right here. Respectable and decent and homelike. Right here.

(The **Man** *doll enters carrying suitcases. He is the same size as the others. His clothes are real and vulgar, unremarkable.)*

All folks everywhere sitting in the very palm of God. Waiting, whither, whence.

(The **Man** *doll begins an inspection of the bed. The* **Woman** *doll comes rapidly from the bathroom, opens one of the suitcases, and messily rummages for toilet articles with which she returns to the bathroom.)*

Any motel you might have come to on six sixty-six. Any motel. On that vast network of roads. Whizzing by, whizzing by. Trucks too. And cars from everywhere. Full up with folks, all sitting in the very palm of God. I can tell proper folks when I get a look at them. All folks.

(The **Man** *doll pulls at the coverlet in every direction, testing its strength. He begins to jump on every part of the mattress.)*

Country roads, state roads, United States roads. It's a big world and here you are. I noticed you got a license plate. I've not been to there myself. I've not been to anywhere myself, excepting Town for supplies, and Boise. Boise, Idaho.

(*The* **Man** *doll is now jumping heavily on the mattress.*)

The world arrives to me, you'd say. It's a small world. These plastic flowers here: "Made in Japan" on the label. You noticed? Got them from the catalogue. Cat-a-logue. Every product in this room is ordered.

(*Pieces of the* **Woman** *doll's clothing are thrown from the bathroom.*)

Ordered from the catalogue. Excepting the antimacassar and the hooked rug. Made the hooked rug myself. Tang of home. No room is a room without. Course the bedspread, hand-hooked, hooked near here at Town. Mrs. Harritt. Betsy Harritt gets materials through another catalogue. Cat-a-logue.

(*Now toilet articles and fixtures from the bathroom follow the clothing.*

The **Woman** *doll returns, without clothes. She applies more lipstick to her lips and nipples—her breasts are obscenely huge. The* **Man** *doll takes off his trousers.*)

Myself, I know it from the catalogue: bottles, bras, breakfasts, refrigerators, cast-iron gates, plastic posies, paper subscriptions, Buick trucks, blankets, forks, clitter-clack darning hooks, transistors and antimacassars, vinyl plastics,

(*The* **Woman** *doll blots her lipstick on the walls. The* **Man** *doll strikes at objects in the room with a cigar.*)

crazy quilts, paper hairpins, cats, catnip, club feet, canisters, bannisters, holy books, tattooed toilet articles, tables, teacozies,

(*On the wall the* **Man** *doll writes simple obscenities with his cigar. She does the same with her lipstick.*)

pickles, bayberry candles, South Dakotan kewpie dolls, fiberglas hair, polished milk, amiable grandpappies, colts, Galsworthy books, cribs, cabinets, teeter-totters,

(*The* **Man** *and* **Woman** *dolls have turned to picture-making. They work together; he with his cigar, her filling in with her lipstick.*)

and television sets.

(*The* **Motel-Keeper** *doll turns on the television set which eventually starts glaring.*)

Oh I tell you it, I do. It's a wonder. Full with things, the world, full up. Shall I tell you my thought? Next year there's a shelter to be built by me, yes. Shelter motel. Everything to be placed under the ground. Signs up in every direction up and down six sixty-six. "Complete Security," "Security While You Sleep Tight," "Bury Your Troubles at This Motel," "Homelike, Very Comfy, and Encased in Lead," "Every Room Its Own Set," "Fourteen Day Emergency Supplies $5.00 Extra."

(*The* **Man** *doll pushes the TV button with his cigar, and the TV plays the twist. The* **Man** *and* **Woman** *dolls twist.*)

"Self-Contained Latrine Waters," "Filters, Counters, Periscopes and Mechanical Doves," "Hooked Rugs," "Dearest Little Picture Frames for Loved Ones (Made in Japan)," through the catalogue. Cat-a-logue. You can pick items and products: cablecackles (so nice), cuticles, twice-twisted combs with corrugated calesthenics, meat-beaters, fish-tackles, bug bombs,

(*The* **Motel-Keeper's** *voice is slowly drowned out by the twist music. The* **Man** *and* **Woman** *dolls, moving ever more rapidly, tear the bedspread in two, tear the rug, and smash the framed prints on the wall. A civil defense siren's noise starts to build up.*)

toasted terra-cotta'd Tanganyikan switch blades, ocher closets, ping pong balls, didies, capricorn and cancer prognostics, crackers, total uppers, stickpins, basting tacks . . .

(*As the two dolls continue to destroy they dismantle the* **Motel-Keeper** *doll, tear down the curtains, and finally start to rip apart the walls. The civil defense siren comes up to full pitch. Each of the dolls' movements must be choreographed, with nothing left haphazard. There is no disorder in what they do, only increasingly violent destruction.*

Suddenly all noise and movement will cease. Against a dark backdrop the audience will contemplate, for five or six seconds, an available object of incredible beauty, possibly a rear-projection slide of a quiet painting by Vermeer.

The curtain call should be taken by the dancers without their masks and dolls. Preferably a fourth person—director, stage manager, anyone—should appear too.)

THE END

PART EIGHT
FILM

Almost everything we have said about plays is also true of films. Each is an artist's view of reality that he attempts to convey to an audience. Both drama and film are public and visual, intended to be viewed by a group of people at a public gathering. Both use actors to portray characters who engage in some kind of action or plot. Like the playwright and play director, the film director is concerned with character, setting, structure, language, and staging, or production. Both media work with these same basic elements.

However, film is quite different from live theatrical production. Perhaps the single most significant difference is that on stage we view the actors directly with our eyes, while in films we see them through the lens of a camera. This may seem to be an obvious point, but the implications are important. Because of the camera, a film director has more control over what his audience sees than does the stage director; consequently, he must pay close attention not only to the same details as his stage counterpart but especially to those details that apply exclusively to film.

In the first place, the camera can move. In the theater you as an audience member are generally confined to the seat you were assigned when you came in. The distance between you and the actors may vary during the production, but your eyes remain essentially in one place from which you view the acting. In a film, however, the camera is your eye, and it matters little where you are seated. The director carefully controls what you see and how you see it. He may give you a panoramic view of five thousand soldiers storming the walls of a city, or he may focus on the twitch of one soldier's mustache as he awaits execution.

The director also controls precisely the angle at which you see something on the screen. He may position the camera on the ground and aim it directly up into someone's face, or he may shoot down at two people as they embrace in a dimly lit corner. He may film a scene with several cameras positioned at different angles and later select the view that best suits his purpose. He may hold the camera still and allow the actors to move, move the camera and hold the actors still, or either fix or move both actors and camera simultaneously. He may also hold the audience's attention on any one shot or specific detail for as long as he wishes to create the desired effect.

The film director may also create special effects such as double images, distorted images, accelerated motion, or slow motion. To create a dreamlike atmosphere, he may film a scene as if through a haze or may flood the set with bright lights. He may shift abruptly from one place to another or may fuse or *dissolve* scenes together. On stage such effects are very difficult—often impossible—to achieve.

The many options available to a film director involve a great deal of responsibility. A director must know that every angle, every detail, every movement of his shots communicates something to his audience. We as audience should realize that each thing a director does represents a choice, and we should assume that each choice is made for a particular reason. If the movements are accidental or convenient or haphazard, the director is not really in control of his medium, is not being responsible to his audience, and hence is not in control of the process of communicating with those who view his work. He is not artistic.

But if a director is aware of the effects he can produce in his audience—of what he can say to them through the use of his camera—then he has at his disposal a means of communication unique to the film.

In filmmaking, the camera allows a kind of accuracy and permanence that is not possible in live productions. If after shooting a scene the film director is unhappy with the results, he may shoot it again and again until he achieves the effect he wants. Once the footage that has been shot is cut, put together in a particular way, and sealed in a can for distribution, the creations of all the artists involved in producing the work are permanent. The film will never change as long as it exists. This is not true in the theatre: a play changes from performance to performance, from audience to audience.

There are numerous other aspects of film study. Volumes have been written about the techniques and the artistry of film; we are not trying to summarize those studies in a few pages nor make you professional film critics.° We are suggesting that much of the appreciation of film as well as drama comes from paying attention to detail. Just as a great deal of pleasure can be derived from noticing details and patterns in plays, similar pleasures can be gained from the same kind of observation of film. But we must be aware of how the director works and how he uses the camera to convey his particular statement.

Films are usually about people who are like all of us in one way or another, who exist in particular settings and have particular conflicts; we watch them attempt to deal with or resolve those conflicts. In this sense, film, like drama, is a source of self-knowledge if we will only participate.

°For a more detailed examination of film techniques, we suggest **Elements of Film** by Lee R. Bobker, Harcourt Brace Jovanovich, Inc., 1969.

AN OCCURRENCE AT OWL CREEK BRIDGE

Ambrose Bierce

I

A man stood upon a railroad bridge in northern Alabama, looking down into the swift water twenty feet below. The man's hands were behind his back, the wrists bound with a cord. A rope loosely encircled his neck. It was attached to a stout cross-timber above his head, and the slack fell to the level of his knees. Some loose boards laid upon the sleepers supporting the metals of the railway supplied a footing for him and his executioners—two private soldiers of the Federal army, directed by a sergeant who in civil life may have been a deputy sheriff. At a short remove upon the same temporary platform was an officer in the uniform of his rank, armed. He was a captain. A sentinel at each end of the bridge stood with his rifle in the position known as "support," that is to say, vertical in front of the left shoulder, the hammer resting on the forearm thrown straight across the chest—a formal and unnatural position, enforcing an erect carriage of the body. It did not appear to be the duty of these two men to know what was occurring at the center of the bridge; they merely blockaded the two ends of the foot plank which traversed it.

Beyond one of the sentinels, nobody was in sight; the railroad ran straight away into a forest for a hundred yards, then, curving, was lost to view. Doubtless there was an outpost farther along. The other bank of the stream was open ground—a gentle acclivity topped with a stockade of vertical tree trunks, loop-holed for rifles, with a single embrasure through which protruded the muzzle of a brass cannon commanding the bridge. Midway of the slope between bridge and fort were the spectators—a single company of infantry in line, at "parade rest," the butts of the rifles on the ground, the barrels inclining slightly backward against the right shoulder, the hands crossed upon the stock. A lieutenant stood at the right of the line, the point of his sword upon the ground, his left hand resting upon his right. Excepting the group of four at the center of the bridge, not a man moved. The company faced the bridge, staring stonily, motionless. The sentinels, facing the banks of the stream, might have been statues to adorn the bridge. The captain stood with folded arms, silent, observing the work of his subordinates, but making no sign. Death is a dignitary who when he comes announced is to be received with formal manifestations of respect, even by those most familiar with him. In the code of military etiquette silence and fixity are forms of deference.

The man who was engaged in being hanged was apparently about thirty-five years of age. He was a civilian, if one might judge from his habit, which was that of a planter. His features were good—a straight nose, firm mouth, broad forehead, from which his long, dark hair was combed straight back, falling behind his ears to the collar of his well-fitting frockcoat. He wore a mustache and pointed beard, but no whiskers; his eyes were large and dark gray, and had a kindly expression which one would hardly have expected in one whose neck was in the hemp. Evidently this was no vulgar assassin. The liberal military code makes provision for hanging many kinds of persons, and gentlemen are not excluded.

The preparations being complete, the two private soldiers stepped aside and each drew away the plank upon which he had been standing. The sergeant turned to the captain, saluted, and placed himself immediately behind that officer, who in turn moved apart one pace. These movements left the condemned man and the sergeant standing on the two ends of the same plank, which spanned three of the crossties of the bridge. The end upon which the civilian stood almost, but not quite, reached a fourth. This plank had been held in place by the weight of the captain; it was now held by that of the sergeant. At a signal from the former, the latter would step aside, the plank would tilt, and the condemned man go down between two ties. The arrangement commended itself to his judgment as simple and effective. His face had not been covered nor his eyes bandaged. He looked a moment at his "unsteadfast footing," then let his gaze wander to the swirling water of the stream racing madly beneath his feet. A piece of dancing driftwood caught his attention and his eyes followed it down the current. How slowly it appeared to move! What a sluggish stream!

He closed his eyes in order to fix his last thoughts upon his wife and children. The water, touched to gold by the early sun, the brooding mists under the banks at some distance down the stream, the fort, the soldiers, the piece of driftwood—all had distracted him. And now he became conscious of a new disturbance. Striking through the thought of his dear ones was a sound which he could neither ignore nor understand, a sharp, distinct, metallic percussion like the stroke of a blacksmith's hammer upon the anvil; it had the same ringing quality. He wondered what it was, and whether immeasurably distant or near by—it seemed both. Its recurrence was regular, but as slow as the tolling of a death knell. He awaited each stroke with impatience and—he knew not why—apprehension. The intervals of silence grew progressively longer; the delays became maddening. With their greater infrequency the sounds increased in strength and sharpness. They hurt his ear like the thrust of a knife; he feared he would shriek. What he heard was the ticking of his watch.

He unclosed his eyes and saw again the water below him. "If I could free my hands," he thought, "I might throw off the noose and spring into the stream. By diving I could evade the bullets and, swimming vigorously, reach the bank, take to the woods, and get away home. My home, thank God, is as yet outside their lines; my wife and little ones are still beyond the invader's farthest advance."

As these thoughts, which have here to be set down in words, were flashed into the doomed man's brain rather than evolved from it, the captain nodded to the sergeant. The sergeant stepped aside.

II

Peyton Farquhar was a well-to-do planter, of an old and highly respected Alabama family. Being a slave owner and, like other slave owners, a politician, he was naturally an original secessionist and ardently devoted to the southern cause. Circumstances of an imperious nature, which it is unnecessary to relate here, had prevented him from taking service with the gallant army which had fought the disastrous campaigns ending with the fall of Corinth, and he chafed under the inglorious restraint, longing for the release of his energies, the larger life of the soldier, the opportunity for distinction. That opportunity, he felt, would come, as it comes to all in war time. Meanwhile he did what he could. No service was too humble for him to perform in aid of the South, no adventure too perilous for him to undertake if consistent with the character of a civilian who was at heart a soldier, and who in good faith and without too much qualification assented to at least a part of the frankly villainous dictum that all is fair in love and war.

One evening while Farquhar and his wife were sitting on a rustic bench near the entrance to his grounds, a gray-clad soldier rode up to the gate and asked for a drink of water. Mrs. Farquhar was only too happy to serve him with her own white hands. While she was fetching the water her husband approached the dusty horseman and inquired eagerly for news from the front.

"The Yanks are repairing the railroads," said the man, "and are getting ready for another advance. They have reached the Owl Creek Bridge, put it in order and built a stockade on the north bank. The commandant has issued an order, which is posted everywhere, declaring that any civilian caught interfering with the railroad, its bridges, tunnels, or trains will be summarily hanged. I saw the order."

"How far is it to the Owl Creek Bridge?" Farquhar asked.

"About thirty miles."

"Is there no force on this side the creek?"

"Only a picket post half a mile out, on the railroad, and a single sentinel at this end of the bridge."

"Suppose a man—a civilian and student of hanging—should elude the picket post and perhaps get the better of the sentinel," said Farquhar, smiling, "what could he accomplish?"

The soldier reflected. "I was there a month ago," he replied. "I observed that the flood of last winter had lodged a great quantity of driftwood against the wooden pier at this end of the bridge. It is now dry and would burn like tow."

The lady had now brought the water, which the soldier drank. He thanked her ceremoniously, bowed to her husband, and rode away. An hour later, after nightfall, he repassed the plantation, going northward in the direction from which he had come. He was a Federal scout.

III

As Peyton Farquhar fell straight downward through the bridge he lost consciousness and was as one already dead. From this state he was awakened—ages later, it seemed to him—by the pain of a sharp pressure upon his throat, followed by a sense of suffocation. Keen, poignant agonies seemed to shoot from his neck downwards through every fiber of his body and limbs. These pains appeared to flash along well-defined lines of ramification and to beat with an inconceivably rapid periodicity. They seemed like streams of pulsating fire heating him to an intolerable temperature. As to his head, he was conscious of nothing but a feeling of fullness— of congestion. These sensations were unaccompanied by thought. The intellectual part of his nature was already effaced; he had power only to feel, and feeling was torment. He was conscious of motion. Encompassed in a luminous cloud, of which he was now merely the fiery heart, without material substance, he swung through unthinkable arcs of oscillation, like a vast pendulum.

Then all at once, with terrible suddenness, the light about him shot upward with the noise of a loud plash; a frightful roaring was in his ears, and all was cold and dark. The power of thought was restored; he knew that the rope had broken and he had fallen into the stream. There was no additional strangulation; the noose about his neck was already suffocating him and kept the water from his lungs. To die of hanging at the bottom of a river—the idea seemed to him ludicrous. He opened his eyes in the darkness and saw above him a gleam of light, but how distant, how inaccessible! He was still sinking, for the light became fainter and fainter until it was a mere glimmer. Then it began to grow and brighten, and he knew that he was rising toward the surface—knew it with reluctance, for he was now very comfortable. "To be hanged and drowned," he thought, "that is not so bad; but I do not wish to be shot. No; I will not be shot; that is not fair."

He was not conscious of an effort, but a sharp pain in his wrist apprised him that he was trying to free his hands. He gave the struggle his attention, as an idler might observe the feat of a juggler, without interest in the outcome. What splendid effort! What magnificent, what superhuman strength! Ah, that was a fine endeavor! Bravo! The cord fell away; his arms parted and floated upward, the hands dimly seen on each side in the growing light. He watched them with a new interest as first one and then the other pounced upon the noose at his neck. They tore it away and thrust it fiercely aside, its undulations resembling those of a water snake. "Put it back, put it back!" He thought he shouted these words to his hands, for the undoing of the noose had been succeeded by the direst pang that he had yet experienced. His neck ached horribly; his brain was on fire; his heart, which had been fluttering faintly, gave a great leap, trying to force itself out at his mouth. His whole body was racked and wrenched with an insupportable anguish! But his disobedient hands gave no heed to the command. They beat the water vigorously with quick, downward strokes, forcing him to the surface. He felt his head emerge; his eyes were blinded by the sunlight; his chest expanded convulsively, and with a supreme and crowning agony his lungs engulfed a great draught of air, which instantly he expelled in a shriek!

He was now in full possession of his physical senses. They were, indeed, preternaturally keen and alert. Something in the awful disturbance of his organic system had so exalted and refined them that they made record of things never before perceived. He felt the ripples upon his face and heard their separate sounds as they struck. He looked at the forest on the bank of the stream, saw the individual trees, the leaves and the veining of each leaf—saw the very insects upon them: the locusts, the brilliant-bodied flies, the gray spiders stretching their webs from twig to twig. He noted the prismatic colors in all the dewdrops upon a million blades of grass. The humming of the gnats that danced above the eddies of the stream, the beating of the dragonflies' wings, the strokes of the water spiders' legs, like oars which had lifted their boat—all these made audible music. A fish slid along beneath his eyes and he heard the rush of its body parting the water.

He had come to the surface facing down the stream; in a moment the visible world seemed to wheel slowly round, himself the pivotal point, and he saw the bridge, the fort, the soldiers upon the bridge, the captain, the sergeant, the two privates, his executioners. They were in silhouette against the blue sky. They shouted and gesticulated, pointing at him. The captain had drawn his pistol, but did not fire; the others were unarmed. Their movements were grotesque and horrible, their forms gigantic.

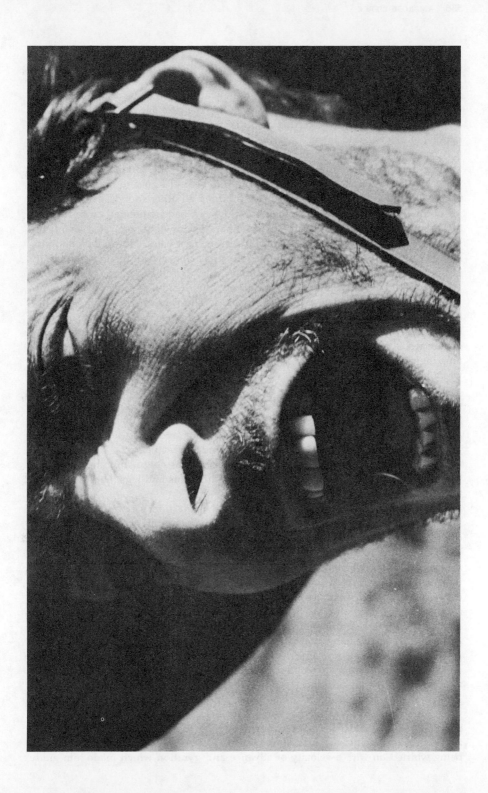

Suddenly he heard a sharp report and something struck the water smartly within a few inches of his head, spattering his face with spray. He heard a second report, and saw one of the sentinels with his rifle at his shoulder, a light cloud of blue smoke rising from the muzzle. The man in the water saw the eye of the man on the bridge gazing into his own through the sights of the rifle. He observed that it was a gray eye and remembered having read that gray eyes were keenest, and that all famous marksmen had them. Nevertheless, this one had missed.

A counterswirl had caught Farquhar and turned him half round; he was again looking into the forest on the bank opposite the fort. The sound of a clear, high voice in a monotonous singsong now rang out behind him and came across the water with a distinctness that pierced and subdued all other sounds, even the beating of the ripples in his ears. Although no soldier, he had frequented camps enough to know the dread significance of that deliberate, drawling, aspirated chant; the lieutenant on shore was taking a part in the morning's work. How coldly and pitilessly—with what an even, calm intonation, presaging and enforcing tranquillity in the men—with what accurately measured intervals fell those cruel words!

"Attention, company! . . . Shoulder arms! . . . Ready! . . . Aim! . . . Fire!"

Farquhar dived—dived as deeply as he could. The water roared in his ears like the voice of Niagara, yet he heard the dulled thunder of the volley and, rising again toward the surface, met shining bits of metal, singularly flattened, oscillating slowly downward. Some of them touched him on the face and hands, then fell away, continuing their descent. One lodged between his collar and neck; it was uncomfortably warm and he snatched it out.

As he rose to the surface, gasping for breath, he saw that he had been a long time under water; he was perceptibly farther downstream—nearer to safety. The soldiers had almost finished reloading; the metal ramrods flashed all at once in the sunshine as they were drawn from the barrels, turned in the air, and thrust into their sockets. The two sentinels fired again, independently and ineffectually.

The hunted man saw all this over his shoulder; he was now swimming vigorously with the current. His brain was as energetic as his arms and legs; he thought with the rapidity of lightning.

"The officer," he reasoned, "will not make that martinet's error a second time. It is as easy to dodge a volley as a single shot. He has probably already given the command to fire at will. God help me, I cannot dodge them all!"

An appalling plash within two yards of him was followed by a loud, rushing sound, *diminuendo*, which seemed to travel back through the air to the fort and died in an explosion which stirred the very river to its deeps! A rising sheet of water curved over him, fell down upon him, blinded him, strangled him! The cannon had taken a hand in the game. As he shook his head free from the commotion of the smitten water, he heard the deflected shot humming through the air ahead, and in an instant it was cracking and smashing the branches in the forest beyond.

"They will not do that again." he thought, "the next time they will use a charge of grape. I must keep my eye upon the gun; the smoke will apprise me—the report arrives too late; it lags behind the missile. That is a good gun."

Suddenly he felt himself whirled round and round—spinning like a top. The water, the banks, the forests, the now distant bridge, fort and men—all were commingled and blurred. Objects were represented by their colors only; circular horizontal streaks of color—that was all he saw. He had been caught in a vortex and was being whirled on with a velocity of advance and gyration which made him giddy and sick. In a few moments he was flung upon the gravel at the foot of the left bank of the stream—the southern bank—and behind a projecting point which concealed him from his enemies. The sudden arrest of his motion, the abrasion of one of his hands on the gravel, restored him, and he wept with delight. He dug his fingers into the sand, threw it over himself in handfuls, and audibly blessed it. It looked like diamonds, rubies, emeralds; he could think of nothing beautiful which it did not resemble. The trees upon the bank were giant garden plants; he noted a definite order in their arrangement, inhaled the fragrance of their blooms. A strange, roseate light shone through the spaces among their trunks and the wind made in their branches the music of aeolian harps. He had no wish to perfect his escape—was content to remain in that enchanting spot until retaken.

A whiz and rattle of grapeshot among the branches high above his head roused him from his dream. The baffled cannoneer had fired him a random farewell. He sprang to his feet, rushed up the sloping bank, and plunged into the forest.

All that day he traveled, laying his course by the rounding sun. The forest seemed interminable; nowhere did he discover a break in it, not even a woodman's road. He had not known that he lived in so wild a region. There was something uncanny in the revelation.

By nightfall he was fatigued, footsore, famishing. The thought of his wife and children urged him on. At last he found a road which led him in what he knew to be the right direction. It was as wide and straight as a city street, yet it seemed un-traveled. No fields bordered it, no dwelling anywhere. Not so much as the barking of a dog suggested human habitation. The black bodies of the trees formed a straight wall on both sides terminating on the horizon in a point, like a diagram in a lesson in perspective. Overhead, as he looked up through this rift in the wood, shone great golden stars looking unfamiliar and grouped in strange constellations. He was sure they were arranged in some order which had a secret and malign sig-nificance. The wood on either side was full of singular noises, among which—once, twice, and again—he distinctly heard whispers in an unknown tongue.

His neck was in pain and lifting his hand to it he found it horribly swollen. He knew that it had a circle of black where the rope had bruised it. His eyes felt con-gested; he could no longer close them. His tongue was swollen with thirst; he re-lieved its fever by thrusting it forward from between his teeth into the cold air. How softly the turf had carpeted the untraveled avenue—he could no longer feel the roadway beneath his feet!

Doubtless, despite his suffering, he had fallen asleep while walking, for now he sees another scene—perhaps he has merely recovered from a delirium. He stands at the gate of his own home. All is as he left it, and all bright and beautiful in the morning sunshine. He must have traveled the entire night. As he pushes open the gate and passes up the wide white walk, he sees a flutter of female garments; his wife, looking fresh and cool and sweet, steps down from the veranda to meet him. At the bottom of the steps she stands waiting, with a smile of ineffable joy, an attitude of matchless grace and dignity. Ah, how beautiful she is! He springs for-ward with extended arms. As he is about to clasp her, he feels a stunning blow upon the back of the neck; a blinding white light blazes all about him with a sound like the shock of a cannon—then all is darkness and silence!

Peyton Farquhar was dead; his body, with a broken neck, swung gently from side to side beneath the timbers of the Owl Creek Bridge.

ON OWL CREEK

Robert Enrico

Adapted from the short story "An Occurrence at Owl Creek Bridge" by Ambrose Bierce

(Shot breakdown and complete text)

The story takes place during the American Civil War, in the northern part of Alabama.

The whitewashed back of a tree rises out of the darkness, set against the "scorched earth" landscape of a war. A poster is nailed to the tree. It is a military order:

ORDER

ANY CIVILIAN CAUGHT INTERFERING WITH THE RAILROAD BRIDGES, TUNNELS OR TRAINS WILL BE SUMMARILY HANGED.

April 4th, 1862

The camera frames the sinister landscape (roll of drums).

Dollies through the dead branches of a forest which are etched against a gray dawn. In the distance a bugle sounds assembly; and then one hears the bark of shouted commands:

Fall in . . . First squad stand fast . . .
Fall out.
At-ten-tion!
Forward . . . maaarch! 1 . . . 2 . . . 3 . . . 4. 1 . . . 2 . . .

The cadenced steps of soldiers are heard.

The camera discovers very far away, at the end of a ravine, a wooden railroad bridge, the Owl Creek bridge.

Moving shot through the dead branches to frame the bridge in a closer view. Two sentinels cross paths at this instant. Their steps resound on the wood. In the distance, the cadenced marching steps approach. Dollying closer, the camera discovers a sentinel on duty at the end of the bridge.

Moving shot along the bank of the stream from behind the branches of the trees, first along the bridge, then a shot of the bridge, very close. The two sentinels have now halted at each end of the bridge. On the opposite bank stands a small shrine (or stork). To one side rises a stockade. A company of soldiers, commanded by a **Lieutenant**, crosses the bridge, halts on the flat ground at the base of the stockade, and faces the bridge.

Voice of Lieutenant: 1 . . . 2 . . . 3 . . . 4 . . . Company . . . 1 . . . 2 . . .
Halt! Left face! At ease!

Closer shot of **Lieutenant** inspecting the appearance of his soldiers, who are standing at "parade rest". . . . Noise of sharp heel clicks against ground. A **sergeant** in the Federal Army suddenly appears, walks past the company and onto the bridge, followed by a dolly shot. He is carrying a rope.

Medium shot of bridge as seen by the company of soldiers. The **sergeant** has halted at the center of the bridge. He is followed at some distance by another, dimly seen group, then by a **Captain** wearing his full-dress uniform. This group halts alongside the **sergeant**.

Close-up of· a man in civilian clothes, a silk tie around his neck. His hands are tied behind his back. He is held by two soldiers. His anxious eyes gaze upwards as he hears the hissing sound of the rope which has been flung by the sergeant.

The rope coils around a solid crossbar on the bridge, high above all their heads . . .

The camera frames the group again. The **sergeant** prepares a slip knot at the other end of the rope.

Close-up of **sergeant** testing the knot he has tied.

Medium shot of the middle of bridge: a plank laid like a seesaw over the crossties of the bridge, one end jutting out over the void. The **Captain** takes up a position on one end of the plank, the end which rests on the ties in the middle of bridge. Then the two soldiers force the condemned man to step over the bridge's parapet and place him on the other end of the plank, his back to the void.

Close-up of condemned man, **Peyton Farquhar**. Someone tears off his silk tie. Then a hemp rope is fitted around his neck. **Peyton** lowers his eyes, overcome by dizziness. He sees . . .

Camera tilts to his feet at the end of the plank which trembles above the swirling waters of the stream.

The light of the dawning day is now whiter.

Close-up of a gesture of impatience made by the hands of the **Lieutenant** on the hilt of his sword.

The impatient **Lieutenant** looks at the bridge and appears to want to stare straight into the face of the doomed man. . . .

Close-up of **Peyton** who turns his eyes away from the void, and as if he feels this menacing look weighing on him, gazes in the direction of the stockade.

Moving shot from **Peyton's** standpoint: before him the company of soldiers, all lined up and standing at parade rest, the butts of their rifles on the ground and their hands crossed on the stocks. At the end of the line stands the **Lieutenant**, the point of his sword touching the ground, his left hand covering his right on the hilt, looking fixedly at him with a certain disdain. . . . A little farther on, one end of the bridge is guarded by a "support" sentinel with his rifle in a vertical position before his left shoulder, the hammer resting on the forearm flung straight across his chest and held very stiffly. He seems unaware of what is happening in the middle of the bridge. . . . The railroad makes a curve and dives into the forest.

Close-up of **Peyton** whose anxious gaze continues its investigations . . .

He turns his eyes toward the other end of the bridge. On that side, too, no way of escape: another sentinel, his rifle at the ready, has his back to him. The railroad tracks disappear behind a slope.

Extreme close-up of **Peyton** who now feels a look on his back and his eyes swivel to find another sentinel, perched on a rock that overlooks the bridge and the bank of the stream, in the direction in which the stream flows. The hands of the two soldiers bind Peyton's legs.

Moving shot shows the final precautions: the muzzle of a cannon points from the stockade, which is built of a pile of tree trunks pierced with loopholes, no doubt intended to guard the railroad. . . . Down there, in the distance, the soldiers finish tying **Peyton's** legs.

Closer shot of the tied legs resting on the plank. A soldier finishing tying . . . in the distance the mist crowds against the bank, completely shrouding the view.

Tilt camera down over the swirling, rapid stream whose eddies are lit up by the sun's first rays (the chirping of birds in the surrounding woods grows louder) . . . a piece of dancing driftwood goes swiftly down the current. Pan shot follows it.

Peyton's Inner Voice: How slowly it goes. What a sluggish stream, seen from here.

Close-up of **Peyton's** eyes following the current of the stream. The dawning rays of the sun warm his face and, as though he feels their heat, he tries to look straight ahead but is dazzled by the sun and shuts his eyes. . . .

Long shot of ravine upstream: the sun strikes the crest of a hill, bursting like a fireworks . . .

Closer shot of the **Captain** standing opposite **Peyton** on the plank. He turns to the sun, then again to the soldiers. (Off camera: Sharp successive sounds of blows.)

Closer shot of bridge: this is the end of the preparations. The two soldiers step off and to the side, then stand rigidly at attention. The **sergeant** then turns to the **Captain**, salutes and places himself alongside the officer so as to replace him as the counter-weight. The officer steps off the plank and stands at attention. Pan shot showing opposite each other on the plank the **sergeant's** boots and the bound legs of the doomed man . . . Slow dolly shot that climbs the length of the doomed man's body, all tied up, surrounded . . . This is the end. The camera frames **Peyton's** face who, in a last, supreme effort of thought, tries to concentrate on the vision of his loved ones, his wife and children . . .

Peyton's murmuring voice, *calling to his wife*: Abby! Abby! Abby!

Long shot (at first the image is presented at normal speed and then it is seen in slow motion, slower and slower): **Peyton's** house, a rich Southern mansion. Beneath the shade of a large tree, sitting in a rocking chair, we see **Abby** dressed in an ample white gown. She is embroidering. Two children are playing on a seesaw. **Abby** stops, rises and walks straight toward the camera, smiling more and more invitingly, walking more and more slowly.

(As this image unfolds, a sharp distinct, metallic percussion sounds out at regular intervals, as slowly as the tolling of a funeral bell. The silences become shorter and shorter, the percussions become louder, sharper, and more distinct, striking the ear with a wounding sound like the stabs of a knife.) The dream image slows down to complete immobility and then is wiped out by

Captain's Voice: (*Off*) Take his watch!
Another voice: Yes, sir.

These orders bring us back to reality.

Close-up of **Peyton**, suddenly dragged back into the nightmare. **Peyton's** face is white. He is afraid, drops of sweat trickle down his face, tears well from his eyes. The light of the rising sun blinds him when he opens his eyes. His mouth moves to shout. He grows calm when he sees . . .

The hand of a soldier pulls from **Peyton's** vest pocket a gold chain at the end of which hangs a watch. . . . The hand rests on the catch of the watchcase. (A crystalline sound of music is heard, immediately interrupted by the click of the catch.) The hand extends the watch to the hand of the **sergeant**, who puts it in his cartridge pouch.

Lieutenant's Voice: (*Off*) At-ten-tion! (*Followed by the stamp of the heels of the company snapping to attention.*)

Long shot of the moment of silent meditation which precedes the execution. The bridge is lit up by the jagged, scorching rays of the sun. Everyone stands there immobile.

Identical long shot, but closer: The **Captain** keeps his eyes lowered, the **sergeant** examines **Peyton**, seen from the back. Sobs break the silence.

Extreme close-up of **Peyton**, his panic-stricken eyes. He is terribly frightened. He trembles, cries.

Peyton's Inner Voice: If I could manage to free my hands . . . I could perhaps throw off the sliding knot and jump into the stream . . . By diving, I could evade the bullets. Then I could swim to the bank and reach the woods. . . . Run away.

Medium shot of **Captain** who looks at **Peyton** and nods his head at the **sergeant**. Closer shot at level of the surface of the plank, from the bridge's side. The **sergeant's** boots clatter, then take a step to one side. The plank drops, dragging with it the doomed man.

Long shot of bridge: the body is falling.

(Sound of rope breaking.)

Point of view shot (seen by **Peyton**): his feet plunge into the void, reach the water's surface and are engulfed by the stream.

(Sound of water splashing, followed by underwater silence.)

Long shot underwater: a sheaf of bubbles forms under the water. **Peyton's** body slowly sinks toward the darkness at the bottom of the stream.

Closer shot of **Peyton** who looks as though dead, sliding sideways with the current, the rope broken.

Medium shot of **Peyton** continues to slide along.

Closer shot of **Peyton** continuing to sink but starting to move his legs.

Extreme closeup of **Peyton** still sinking. He opens his eyes, air bubbles foam out of his mouth. He looks up . . .

Long shot: a soft clarity, above him, inaccessible, distant, which seems to be going farther and farther away. . . . The panning camera swings about to show the bottom of the stream, engulfed in blackness. **Peyton** touches the bottom. A cloud of mud is stirred up. Then he begins the fight for life. He struggles, tries to free his hands. Close-up of hands. After a terrific effort the rope is torn off, his arms fall to his sides . . .

The camera frames **Peyton's** distorted, suffocating face. His hands finally manage to clutch the sliding knot. Then, furiously, they take it off, fling it aside . . .

Like a water snake, the rope flutters, sways and is carried off by the current.

Medium shot underwater: **Peyton** makes desperate efforts to reach the surface but his bound legs drag him toward the bottom.

In a final effort, he takes off his last bonds and then removes his shoes.

His face is disfigured by pain, asphyxiation.

Medium shot: his hands strike the water violently and carry him towards the surface of the water. . . . The underwater light of the sun gradually touches him with its glow . . .

On the surface of the water, his head emerges like a tangle of straw. He shuts his eyes in the blinding light. His crushed chest dilates. He swallows a great gulp of air which he immediately exhales in an inhuman cry. He strikes the water's surface with his hands . . .

(With this inhuman cry the music is released. A chant, a hymn to life, sung by the grave voice of a Black.)

Peyton's face turns to the bank. He looks at the forest.

> **Song**
> A livin' man
> A livin' man
> I want to be
> A livin' man.

Moving shot from **Peyton's** standpoint towards the forest which sparkles and gleams in the light, emerging from the mists.

> **Song**
> An' all the world
> He moves around
> He walks around
> He turns around

Moving shot through the blades of grass, right down to the tiny drops of dew, glistening like diamonds.

> **Song**
> I see rainbow
> In each dewdrop
> Upon a mil'lion
> Blades of grass

Moving shot through leaves right down to the veins of a leaf.

> **Song**
> I see each tree
> I read each vein
> I hear each bug
> Upon each leaf

Moving shot to a microscopic green-fly moving across the vein. Moving shot through the silvery threads of a spider's web . . .

> **Song**
> The buzzing flies
> The splashing fish
> They move around
> This livin' man

Moving shot through a silvery spider's web which catches a fly in the threads of its net.

> **Song**
> A livin' man
> A livin' man

Extreme close-up of the fly enveloped by the spider in its web.

> **Song**
> I wanna be
> A livin' man.

Long shot (silhouetted in black shadows): slowly (images in slow motion) the edge of the forest pivots about and **Peyton** rediscovers the other reality: the bridge. The voices and shouts of the soldiers, the commands of the officers are deformed by their slowness, and their movements are extremely slow too. On the bridge the **Captain** sends the men to get their arms, he flings an order to the Lieutenant.

> **Captain**: Catch him. He must be hanged!
> **Sergeant's Voice**: Yes, sir.
> **Captain**: Tell Lieutenant Madwell to open fire. If it is necessary, fire the cannon as well.
> **Sergeant's Voice**: Yes, sir. (*shouting*) Go get your guns.

Medium long shot: the stockade (slow motion). The soldiers and **sergeant** run for their weapons. The company is busy loading their rifles. The gun crew prepares the cannon.

> **Lieutenant's Voice:** Guards stand fast. Stead-y men, stead-y.

Long shot tilted up (as seen by **Peyton**): on the bridge the **sergeant** and soldiers reach the **Captain**, who points to **Peyton**. (The voices gradually become real, the movements gradually resume their normal cadence.)

> **Captain's Voice:** He must not escape! There he is! He's not moving!

Close up of **Peyton**, paralyzed, in the water, staring fixedly at the **Captain**.

> **Captain's Voice:** (*Off, like a sentence of doom directed straight at* **Peyton**) Peyton Farquhar, you are caught like a rat in a trap . . . in a trap . . . trap, trap!

Long shot, tilted down (as seen by **Peyton**): the soldier's face and his hand loading rifle.

> **Peyton's Inner Voice:** This eye is gray . . . All sharpshooters have gray eyes.

The sharpshooter fires but misses.
Tilted shot on **Peyton** who swims away, downstream from the bridge, in the

direction in which the current is flowing. Some other rifle shots are heard. The **sergeant** shoots twice.

All the bullets miss **Peyton** who, swept along by the current, goes farther and farther away. But on the bank, the company begins to fire.

Lieutenant's Voice: At-ten-tion!

Closer shot of **Lieutenant** bringing the sword before his face.

Lieutenant's Voice: Rifles at the ready.

All the rifles are aimed at **Peyton**.
Extreme close-up of **Lieutenant** shouting: Fire!
Tilted shot (seen by **Peyton**): the salvo of rifles. Tilted shot moving along the stream: **Peyton** swims like a madman . . . the bullets tear the bark from the trees, seen close up. But one can already hear the rifles being reloaded.

Orders: Load! Ready! Aim! Fire!

At this instant **Peyton** dives to escape the bullets.
Under the water, deafening noise of salvos. **Peyton** swims to the bottom of stream, then rises up to the surface again: some metal fragments sink through the water in slow oscillations.
Peyton emerges, out of breath, greeted by the whistle of some isolated bullets. He swims vigorously towards the lower part of the bank, while turning to keep a lookout towards the bridge. (Moving shot).
Moving shot from subjective viewpoint: behind the trees which go past: the cannon is being loaded.
Moving shot of **Peyton** swimming faster.

Officer's Voice: (*off*) Load! . . . Ready! . . . Fire!

(Moving subjective shot) behind the trees which file past: the cannon fires.
The shell hits the water and lifts a liquid mountain. It comes down with a crash on **Peyton**, blinding and strangling him. He disappears under the water but reappears and starts swimming again . . . while in the distance the noise made by the soldiers can be heard. Suddenly he stops . . . before him, sliding slowly over the water, comes a snake. **Peyton** dives again, followed by the camera, then reappears a little farther on at the moment when . . .
Tilted shot from a height, a sentinel has seen him and shoots, but with no more success than the others.
Moving shot follows **Peyton** swimming . . . swimming . . . swimming like a madman.

Distant Voice: Fire at will! Commence firing!

The order is carried out. Whistling of bullets accompany this incredible feat of swimming. And suddenly . . . the water banks, and forest all begin to whirl about. Everything gets mixed up, blurs. The rifle shots, the noises on the stream disappear and are replaced by the roar of a cataract. . . .

Caught in the swirls and currents of the stream's rapids, **Peyton** is swept along by a swift, twirling movement through a landscape of gorges.

Swept from rock to rock, **Peyton** struggles, is engulfed by waves, rises up again, still alive.

Long shot of ravine: the stream drags **Peyton** down into a narrow gorge from which the water falls in cascades. **Peyton** vanishes in the foam and reappears much farther on, where the stream is calm again and broadens out in a slowly moving current.

Peyton floats on the surface, like a drowned man. The calmer water forms small ripples which die out on a little beach, surrounded by rocks (a dolly shot runs along the beach). He is thrown up on the sand. He stays there, immobile.

Motionless, **Peyton** seems to be dreaming. In the foreground, in a close-up, his right hand is dripping with blood. Behind him his feet are still in the water.

The hand moves, scratches the sand. He opens his eyes and lifts his head.

Close-up of **Peyton** looking with astonishment at his hand, then comes to his senses and bursts out laughing.

Close-up of hand: he moves it slowly, clenches his fist, brings his fingers together tightly, caresses the sand.

Closer shot of **Peyton** laughing, caressing the sand, digging his fingers into the snad and throwing handfuls to the sky. The grains of sand glitter in the sun.

Long shot of small beach: **Peyton** laughs like a madman. He flings sand over his bruised and battered body. He shouts with joy. He hoists himself out of the water and rolls onto the dry ground. Stretched out on his back, he continues to laugh, his eyes staring up at the sky. The trees above him look like the gigantic plants of some well-kept garden. A strange light gleams between the leaves which are shaken by a light breeze. (And from this light murmur is born again the musical theme of the song . . . Just as this theme, which is still being sung, was a shout of violent life, so now it creates an atmosphere of tenderness and softness, the atmosphere of an enchanted place in which one would like to remain forever.)

Long shot of beach through the murmuring leaves. **Peyton** has turned over and hauls himself to the edge of the forest. He stops in front of some flowers and brings his face close to them to breathe in the perfume. (The music is interrupted by a whistle followed by a crashing sound among the trees: a cannon shot.)

Fear again grips **Peyton**, who leaps to his feet.

Long dolly shot of rapids crashing through the gorges: the shell has set fire to a clump of trees. **Peyton** climbs the small slope which separates him from the forest and runs deeper in among the trees.

(The flight through the forest is rhythmed by three drum solos, interrupted by the silence of the forest and but one sound: the sound of **Peyton's** running and the heavy sound of his breathing: it is the gasping of someone who is mortally frightened.)

(First drum solo) continuation of moving shot through the labyrinth of a forest of birch trees, following **Peyton** who is running like a lost dog, panic-stricken and entrapped.

(Another sound of whistling bullets, followed by the crash of broken branches.)

Peyton flings himself on the ground, then he runs again.

(Second drum solo)

Moving shot continued, preceding **Peyton** who runs deeper and deeper into the forest. He hesitates, falls, gets up, starts running. He huddles next to the trees. He changes direction, runs in a straight line, and finally, exhausted, bangs into a tree.

Close-up: his face and hands slide along the trunk, and scratch the bark until he collapses on his knees at the foot of the tree.

He gets up again and begins walking, staggering like a drunken man. A root makes him stumble into a ditch. He manages to get up and walk again.

(Third drum solo)

Long shot of rectilinear path that runs through the forest. Night falls. He searches for his path down there in the distance, then runs to reach it. He arrives, seen from close up, and the camera moves up in a quick dolly shot to get ahead of him. He runs for a long time until he collapses, at the end of his breath and strength. Night has fallen. He rises again and walks with great difficulty.

Before him in the half darkness, at the edge of the forest, a road appears, as straight as a city street. The black trunks of the large trees which border it form two rectilinear walls which meet at the horizon in a single point.

(Moving camera)

The road is traced by the tops of the trees against the dark sky: a soft light illumines the leaves.

(Moving shot)

In this soft, unreal light, **Peyton** goes forward. His neck hurts him; he brings his hand to his swollen neck, where the rope has left a mark.

(Moving shot)

He advances now like a somnambulist, his eyes shut . . . He is sleeping on his feet (Moving shot).

His feet, cut to the quick, bloody, move softly on the turf of the carriage road (Moving shot).

He walks and walks, and then gradually a soft white light invades his face—it is the day which is breaking.

He stops, opens his eyes and closes them, bedazzled, then slowly he opens them again and sees . . .

Dolly shot very slowly ahead: it is the gate to his house . . .

Everything shines beautifully beneath the morning sun.

Peyton precedes the camera, recognizes the iron gate which opens by itself, then is lost among the trees.

On the white entrance way, through the thick foliage, **Peyton** walks but seems not to move forward. He lifts his eyes, a wan sort of smile forming on his face.

Dolly shot ahead very slowly: through the foliage the house appears, then behind the columns of a porch, his wife, **Abby**, who seems to recognize him, does recognize him, smiles at him and walks toward him, her arms opened wide.

(This image is accompanied by the musical theme of the song.)

Static close-up: **Peyton** seen head on, his face swollen and sorrowful, gazing at her. He manages to produce a grimacing smile, then flings his arms out ahead of him.

(The music begins again like a funeral tolling, repeating tirelessly the same theme in a kind of refrain but never completing it.)

Medium shot: camera moves ahead toward the stairway to the porch. **Abby** advances, smiling and welcoming, her arms opened, coming down the stairs.

Peyton squeezing out a grimace of a smile, runs straight on, his arms outstretched, to **Abby**. He runs, runs, but does not move forward.

Long shot: dollying forward to flight of stairs. **Abby** advances, smiling and welcoming, repeating the same gestures, opening her arms, coming down the steps.

Peyton in same position still runs toward **Abby**.

Closer shot: dolly shot towards porch. **Abby** advances, the same as before, repeating the same gestures, opening her arms, coming down the steps.

Static close-up: **Peyton** in same posture, runs towards **Abby**. The effort is greater. He can't keep it up; he is utterly exhausted.

Extreme close-up: dolly shot toward the stairway. **Abby** advances, making the same movements, but her smile is veiled in tears. She finally halts at the foot of the stairway.

Peyton's Voice: Abby! . . . Abby! . . . Abby!

Dolly shot backwards accompanying **Peyton** who finally approaches and arrives before **Abby**. He lifts his arms tenderly to caress her . . . She extends her delicate arms to the wound on **Peyton's** neck and suddenly, like an automaton, **Peyton** rears up in a nervous spasm. His head is flung back with an inhuman cry.

(Sound of rope stretching taut)

Medium shot: Peyton is hanging, his neck broken. His dead body sways beneath the ties of the bridge over Owl Creek.

Extremely slow dolly shot backwards to discover the bridge as a whole, on which the soldiers are marching off . . .

Sergeant's Voice: Right face! Forward maaarch!

The camera leaves the bridge and goes off through the trees which border the bank.

Distant Voice of Lieutenant: At-ten-tion! Right face. Forward maaarch! 1 . . . 2 . . . 3 . . . 4. 1 . . . 2 . . . 3 . . .

The cadenced steps go off into distance.

A series of dolly shots on the sunlit trees, over which are superimposed the credits, preceded by the translation of the text of the poster seen at the beginning of the movie.

Last dolly shot frames the bridge from a distance, as at start of movie: two sentinels are on guard. **Peyton's** hanged body sways slowly beneath the bridge. (Roll of drums).

END

This book was designed by **Joan Ingoldsby Brown.**

It was set in 9 point Elegante
with Melior display type
on the Fototronic TXT
by **Applied Typographic Systems** of Mountain View, California.

Marginal notes were hand lettered by **Jane Wentzel.**

Printing and binding was done by **Kingsport Press** of Kingsport, Tennessee.

Project Editor, **Barbara Carpenter;**
Sponsoring Editor, **Frank B. Geddes.**

The cover was designed by **Joan Ingoldsby Brown.**